The
Complete
Food Catalogue

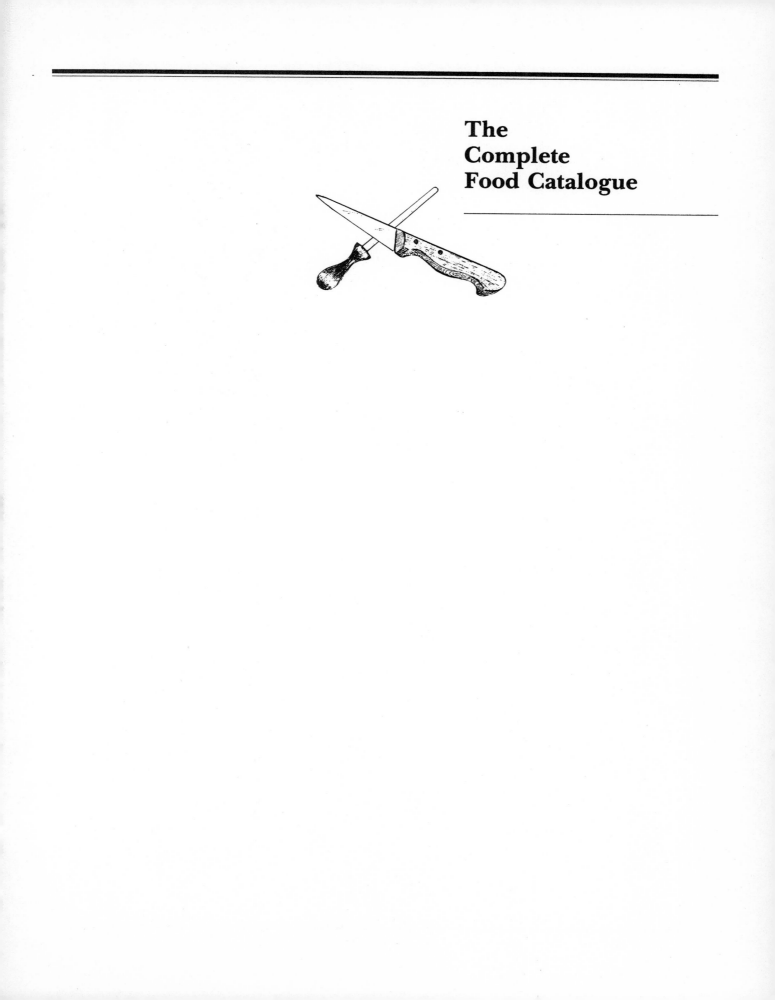

BY JOSÉ WILSON AND ARTHUR LEAMAN
The Dollar Saving Decorating Book
The First Complete Home Decorating Catalogue
Decorating American Style
Decorating with Confidence
Color in Decoration
Decorating Defined
Decoration USA

BY JOSÉ WILSON
American Cooking: The Eastern Heartland
Good Earth & Country Cooking (with Betty Groff)
Editor:
House & Garden's New Cook Book
House & Garden's Party Menu Cook Book

The Complete Food Catalogue

Hundreds of mail-order sources
from all over the world for the best of
every kind of food, with recipes, cooking tips,
and the finest in equipment and gadgets for the
kitchen—all yours without leaving your doorstep

JOSÉ WILSON and **ARTHUR LEAMAN**

Holt, Rinehart and Winston ★ New York

ACKNOWLEDGMENTS

We gratefully acknowledge the kind cooperation of the many companies who sent us their catalogues and photographs.

We particularly want to express our thanks to Helen and Roz Barrow for the planning and design of this book;
to Martin Kreiner for gathering and collating catalogues;
to Jeanette Mall and Stuart Fischer for assistance with the manuscript;
to Johnnie Dinstuhl and Marion Frost for typing the manuscript;
and to Otto Maya for special photography.

J.W. and A.L.

Copyright © 1977 by José Wilson and Arthur Leaman
All rights reserved, including the right to reproduce this book or portions thereof in any form.

Published simultaneously in Canada
by Holt, Rinehart and Winston of Canada, Limited.

Library of Congress Cataloging in Publication Data
Wilson, José.
  The complete food catalogue.
  Includes index.
  1. Food—Catalogs. I. Leaman, Arthur, joint author. II. Title.
TX354.5.W54   380.1'45'6413   77-1190
ISBN Hardbound: 0-03-017706-5
ISBN Paperback: 0-03-017701-4

First Edition
Designer: Helen Barrow
Printed in the United States of America
10 9 8 7 6 5 4 3 2 1

FOREWORD

by James A. Beard

DURING THE YEARS *I have been writing a syndicated column I have often talked about foods that can be ordered by mail. Just the other day, going over my list of sources, I was amazed at the choice and variety of foods that can be obtained simply by sending a letter and a check.*

First, flours and meals, the old-fashioned stone-ground kind that everyone wants nowadays. Hard-wheat flour, soft-wheat flour, buckwheat flour, rye and whole-wheat flour are hard to find outside of health-food stores. Yet there are places throughout this country that specialize in them. Two I can think of offhand are Great Valley Mills and Walnut Acres in Pennsylvania, which supply me with unbleached white flour and other types of flour for my baking. I am particularly happy at being able to order soft-wheat flour, which is so admirably suited to most cakes and pastries.

I am inordinately fond of fine country hams, and I have found excellent examples from Kentucky, Virginia, Missouri, Vermont, New York–practically everywhere in the country. Along with ham goes bacon, and there are also bacons and Canadian-style bacons to be had that retain the true old-time quality–not the paltry stuff sold in supermarkets. You can also order selections of sausages by mail. Some are delicious, others are less satisfactory. Many places sell top-quality meats, shipped frozen. I have had a great deal of experience with some of these meats, which I keep in my freezer for emergencies and special dishes. I have bought by mail some of the best corned beef I have ever tasted, boned saddle of veal and more unusual offerings, such as the frozen quail I use for dinner parties, and all kinds of furred game and game birds. Another great boon are the delicatessens and packing companies that will send you smoked salmon and sturgeon. These I love to serve for Sunday brunch with masses of scrambled eggs and toasted English muffins.

Good tea is something we tea-lovers yearn for, and I know at least two places in Boston (from one of which my good friend Julia Child buys her tea) that have teas you are unlikely to encounter in your local store. Some of America's best cheeses, such as Vermont cheese, the Maytag Blue from Iowa, and the delicious Rouge et Noir Camembert, Brie, breakfast, and schloss from California can all be ordered by mail–in fact, as far as I know, Maytag Blue is sold only this way. Then there are all those lovely fruits. It's getting harder and harder to buy good fruit these days when so much of it is shipped to the market underripe, but fruits ordered by mail arrive at their peak of flavor.

Shopping by mail is both a luxury and a privilege. It does tend to cost more than local shopping, but only in this way can you experience some of the best eating to be found here. If we don't want it to vanish from our lives, it behooves us all to support the people who are struggling and striving to keep the cause of good food alive and order from them regularly.

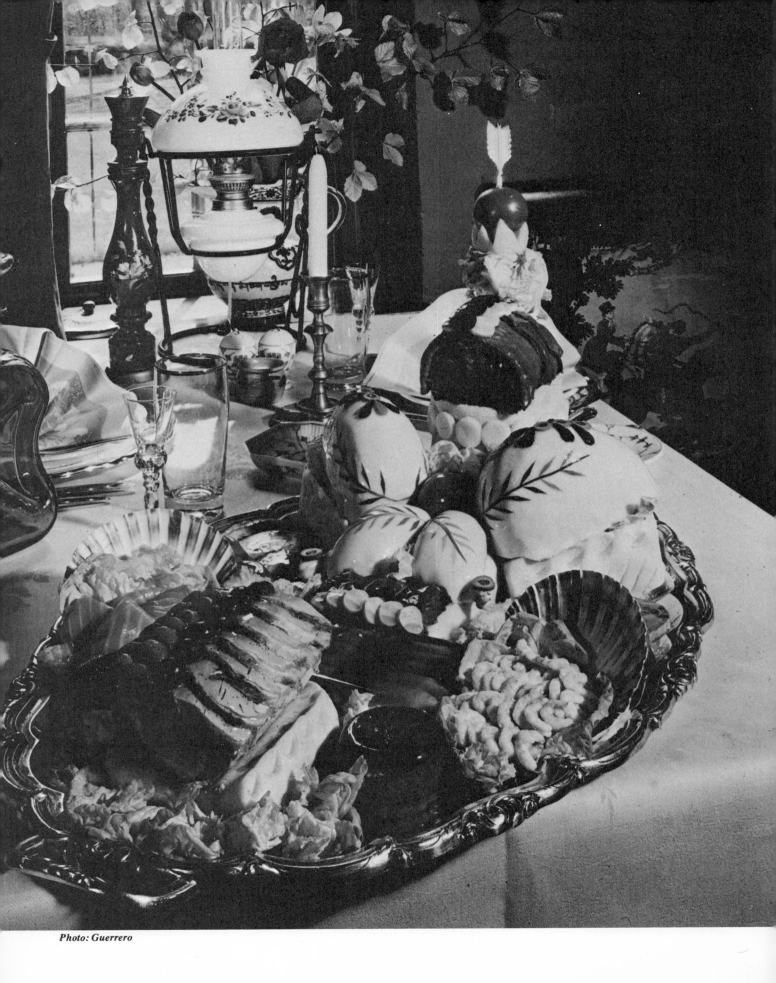

CONTENTS

INTRODUCTION

MAIL-ORDER FOODS are one of the biggest small businesses in this country. Anyone with a good product can do well, and the fact that the mail-order food business is booming shows that there are many quality products available. Many families who have owned and operated a mill, a smokehouse, or a fruit farm for generations have built up a devoted following of customers who swear by the products, order them year after year, and tell their friends about them. To that extent, mail-order food is often a word-of-mouth business because the satisfied customer is the best salesman. Some small businesses don't even advertise, finding it either too costly or unnecessary. On the other hand, large companies with a big mail-order volume do advertise and send out, yearly or seasonally, tempting full-color catalogues.

For the last eight years I have been assisting James Beard with his weekly syndicated newspaper column, which reaches 10 million readers. After the column reprinted as a foreword to this book appeared, the syndicate was so swamped with requests for the names and addresses of the places he mentioned that they begged us never to do it again! So Arthur Leaman and I, having just finished *The First Complete Home Decorating Catalogue* for Holt, Rinehart and Winston, decided that our next project should be a catalogue of mail-order foods. We already had our own favorites, we canvassed our friends for theirs, and we culled magazines, newspapers, and source lists in cookbooks for places that sold food and cooking equipment by mail.

As we had found with our previous book, although we sent repeated mailings requesting information, catalogues, or brochures, many places never replied. Others replied but did not send, or did not have, a catalogue or a price list. If some of your favorites are missing from this book, that is probably why, and we would appreciate any information you send us for our next edition. Food, we found, is one of the more volatile industries. A store or source can go out of business fast. So we have been careful to list only those that replied to our mailings or that we know, from current advertisements, are still around and will mail-order. That, alas, is no guarantee. The situation may have changed by the time this book reaches the public, so we advise you not to send money without inquiring first.

All right, you may say, with all the food that is stocked by stores and supermarkets, what can mail-order companies supply that I can't get in my own town? Homemade products, for one thing. It is not likely that you will find a Kentucky country ham in your supermarket, or freshly stone-ground flour, or preserves made in someone's kitchen from the fruits of a private orchard. Unless you are on the West Coast you may never taste San Francisco's famous sourdough bread, or the local crayfish, or Rouge et Noir Camembert, or Pacific Northwest alder-smoked salmon. We who live in New York are blessed with a cornucopia of foods, from fresh truffles to every kind of ethnic specialty you could possibly want; but if your home is a small town in the Midwest or New England, you cannot always amble down the street to a store that sells freshly roasted and ground coffee or the best China teas or green peppercorns or Beluga caviar. Yet the mailman or UPS can deliver them to your door. In the summer, outside the city, I have come to depend on mail-order catalogues for many of the foods I would buy in New York—smoked fish, prosciutto, imported Parmesan cheese, the best French virgin olive oil, tiny Niçoise olives, couscous, filo pastry, Basmati rice, moutarde de Meaux—things that I have become accustomed to having in my kitchen and that the local markets do not carry. In the winter, where can one buy citrus fruits as ripe and luscious as those shipped direct from the groves of Florida or Texas, or big black Medjool dates like those that can be ordered in season from an Arizona ranch? Buying by mail is like having the best produce of every state in your own back yard.

Mail-order catalogues are fun to get, fun to read. In compiling this book, Arthur Leaman and I became enormously intrigued by the fascinating and useful information many of them contain and also by the sense of being in touch with people who really know and care about the products they make and sell. You can learn how hams or salmon are smoked in different regions, which coffees and teas are considered the finest, the many uses of spices and seasonings. Seed catalogues are full of unusual vegetables you may never taste unless you grow them yourself—like spaghetti squash, celtuce, lemon cucumbers, scarlet runner beans, blue potatoes, sorrel, black salsify, French mâche (corn salad), Charentais melons, Hamburg parsley, and Egyptian walking onions. Or you can buy pots of old-fashioned and unfamiliar herbs like lovage and borage, hyssop and costmary. You can enlarge your food horizons every day through the services of mail-order companies—and encourage them to continue providing the unusual and desirable foods that are fast disappearing from our culinary world.

Spellings for many foreign foods tend to vary from country to country or company to company. Where such differences occur in this book, they will be listed in the index in addition to the more customary spelling.

A few words of advice. Read the catalogues and price lists carefully. Check if the cost of the item includes delivery or if this is extra and then figure out (if this is a consideration) whether you are saving or not. In some cases, we found you can actually buy a brand-name food cheaper by mail than from the gourmet department of your local store or specialty food shop. In other cases, especially if the price does not include shipping costs and the shipment is made by air, you may pay much more than you bargained for. The cost of shipping food from abroad can be extremely high. But if the rate of exchange is in your favor you may still be able to get tea or candy or smoked salmon cheaper than you can at home. Bear in mind, however, that foodstuffs coming into this country, unless they are classified as gifts with a value of under $10, are subject to duty, which varies from one food to another. The stores abroad that regularly ship food packages to the United States are *au courant* with the current rules and regulations, and you should inquire about duty when you write for catalogues. We have included a number of these foreign stores and companies not so much because we recommend ordering delicacies from abroad (there are actually very few you cannot buy, here), but because we consider this one of the simplest, nicest, and most satisfactory ways to send a gift to a friend or relative overseas. Anyone in England would love to get a side of smoked salmon, a package of Fortnum's special teas, a marvelous hamper of Christmas goodies, or the perishable foods, wines, and spirits that may only be shipped within the country—and you avoid the trouble and expense of packing and mailing.

Finally, be aware that in these inflationary times food prices are constantly subject to change. Some companies won't even quote prices, knowing they are bound to go up from one season to the next; others do so with a caution. The prices we give were current as of summer 1976, but almost certainly they will have risen by the time the 1977 catalogues and price lists are printed—and so may the shipping costs and the price of the catalogue itself.

JOSÉ WILSON

Many of the delightful sketches of food and equipment throughout this book are from the catalogues of Aphrodisia, Cake Decorators, Caravansary, Cross Imports, Hilltop Herb Farm, Johnny's Selected Seeds, Kitchen Bazaar, Nichols Garden Nursery, Northwestern Coffee Mills, Perma-Pak, Inc., Sahadi Importing Company, Sundials & More, from *Madame Chiang's Mandarin Recipe Book* and *The Zucchini Cookbook.*

CHAPTER ONE

COFFEE AND TEA

"There are few hours in life more agreeable than the hour dedicated to the ceremony known as afternoon tea."
—*Henry James*

ANZEN JAPANESE FOODS AND IMPORTS / Dept. CFC
736 N.E. Union Avenue, Portland, OR 97232

Price list, free, 20 pages.

Anzen has a good selection of Japanese and Chinese teas. There's genmai (toasted rice and green tea), $1.63 for 12 oz.; green tea, $3.60 for 14 oz.; Hatsutsumi tea, Uji Gyokuro tea, jasmine, oolong, and black tea; also jasmine, oolong, and restaurant blend in tea bags (45¢ for 16 bags). Listed (but not priced) are tea sets and individual tea pots and tea cups.

R. N. AGARWALA & SONS / Dept. CFC
Nehru Road, Darjeeling, India

Price list.

One item and one item only. Golden Glowery Orange Pekoe tea in 4½-lb. quantities for approximately $3.35, but postage from India will add nearly 150 percent to the cost.

BON APPETIT / Dept. CFC
213 South 17th Street, Philadelphia, PA 19103

Bon Appetit will mail-order coffee by request, ground to your specifications. Their selection includes Colombian, Colombian–Costa Rican, Costa Rican, Bon Appetit Blend, French Roast, Guatemala Antigua, Kenya Plantation, Mexican Altura, Mocha-Java Blend, Mocha French Blend, Viennese Blend, currently $2.15 a ½ lb., $3.90 a lb., although prices are subject to increase. There's also Brazil Santos, Italian Roast, Old New Orleans Blend with Chicory ($2.20 a ½ lb., $4 a lb. at current rate), and Jamaican High Mountain and Kona Hawaiian ($2.35 a ½ lb., $4.35 a lb. at 1976 rates). Presumably you can also buy the unground beans. Write for details and most recent quotations.

Due to the recent sharp rise in the cost of coffee, prices given in this chapter may no longer apply.

To make perfect tea

Use a china or earthenware pot. While the kettle is coming to a boil, warm the tea pot by filling it with scalding hot water. Dump out the water, add 1 teaspoon loose tea for each cup plus 1 for the pot and when the water comes to a full rolling boil, immediately pour onto the tea. Let it steep for 3 to 5 minutes, no longer, before pouring. Black teas can be served with milk (no cream) and sugar, if desired. Honey is best for sweetening green teas. Do not oversteep or the tea will develop a metallic acid taste.

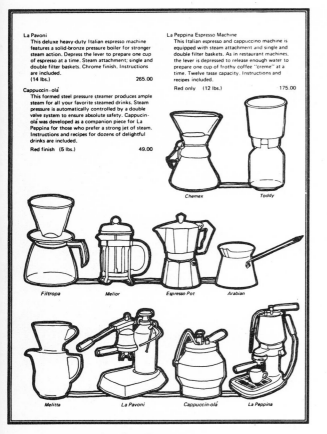

La Pavoni
This deluxe heavy-duty Italian espresso machine features a solid-bronze pressure boiler for stronger steam action. Depress the lever to prepare one cup of espresso at a time. Steam attachment; single and double filter baskets. Chrome finish. Instructions are included.
(14 lbs.) 265.00

Cappuccin-olá
This formed steel pressure steamer produces ample steam for all your favorite steamed drinks. Steam pressure is automatically controlled by a double valve system to ensure absolute safety. Cappuccin-olá was developed as a companion piece for La Peppina for those who prefer a strong jet of steam. Instructions and recipes for dozens of delightful drinks are included.
Red finish (5 lbs.) 49.00

La Peppina Espresso Machine
This Italian espresso and cappuccino machine is equipped with steam attachment and single and double filter baskets. As in restaurant machines, the lever is depressed to release enough water to prepare one cup of frothy coffee "creme" at a time. Twelve tasse capacity. Instructions and recipes included.
Red only (12 lbs.) 175.00

Chemex   Toddy

Filtropa   Melior   Espresso Pot   Arabian

Melitta   La Pavoni   Cappuccin-olá   La Peppina

Coffee makers from Caravansary

Herb teas, herbs, and spices from Celestial Seasonings

CARAVANSARY / Dept. CFC
2263 Chestnut Street, San Francisco, CA 94123

"Coffee and Teas," free, published seasonally, 6 pages.

A caravansary was the site where old-time caravan travelers through Asia and Africa could stop for rest, safety, and food. This caravansary offers four California locations for the traveler or one-stop shopping by mail for the home-bound. Coffee, shipped by UPS within 24 hours of roasting, is Caravansary's forte. While they prefer to send the coffee in whole-bean form, they will, if you wish, grind it (request your grind). Their list of coffees is impressive. Among the light-bodied are El Salvador ($2.55 a lb.) and Kona. Medium-bodied include Brazil Santos ($2.60 a lb.), Celebes Kolossa ($3.15 a lb.), and Guatemala Antigua ($2.65 a lb.). Among the heavy-bodied are Mocha Yemen, Java Arabica, and Ethiopia Harrar. They also list Viennese, Italian, and French dark roasts; decaffeinated Colombian and dark roast Colombian (both $3.20 a lb.); and chicory ($2.15 a lb.). There are 7 blends. Aram's Blend, an after-dinner coffee, is ¼ Colombian, ¼ French roast, ¼ Kenya, and ¼ Mocha ($2.85 a lb.). Armenian Blend, a strong, dark roast ground to a powdery consistency for Middle Eastern-style coffee, is 1/3 each Mocha, Colombian, and French roast ($2.95 a lb.). There's also a New Orleans French roast and chicory blend ($2.60 a lb.). These prices are current and subject to change.

While not as strong on teas, they do have 9 black teas, including an India Nilgiri Kalgar ($1.80 a ½ lb.), a pan-fired green tea, and 7 blends, such as Russian black, spicy orange, and a cluster of herbal teas, including hibiscus, lemon grass, linden flower, and mu (60¢ an oz.).

Caravansary has a good selection of coffee makers and espresso machines, as well as coffee mills made by Braun, Emide, and Salton. The Chemex toddy maker, which produces a coffee extract with cold water (you add hot water to it, just like instant coffee), is $15. They have the Melitta coffee maker, the Filtropa, the Melior, and the Arabian coffee maker, or ibric, the long-handled pot of tin-lined copper or brass ($8.50 for the 3-cup ibric, $12.95 for the 6-cup). Espresso makers are the Mini-Gaggia, a very stylish little machine that makes 1 or 2 cups at a time ($240), and La Peppina, a heavy-duty machine with steam attachment for warming milk ($175).

CASA MONEO / Dept. CFC
210 West 14th Street, New York, NY 10011

"Mexican Food—Comida Mexicana," free, published annually, 8 pages, also price lists of South American, Cuban, and Portuguese foods.

Casa Moneo carries Colombian coffees ($1.75 a lb.) and various yerba maté teas from Argentina at about $1 a lb.

CELESTIAL SEASONINGS, INC. / Dept. CFC
P.O. Box 4367, Boulder, CO 80302

Product brochure, free, published periodically, 10 pages, illustrated, color.

Celestial Seasonings are importers and growers of herbs, as well as packagers and blenders of herb teas and other related products. Most of their herbs come from Central and South America, the Middle East, Europe, and the United States, and for the most part the herbs grow wild and are hand-picked. Their herbal teas, sold in wholesale quantities, with a minimum order of $35, are divided into caffeinated blends (such as the maté teas), noncaffeinated blends, and single herbs. There is a complete description of the teas in the brochure, and new customers can order a sample pack of six different teas (four tea bags each)—Red Zinger (hibiscus flowers, rose hips, lemon grass, peppermint, orange peel, wild cherry bark), Sleepy Time (a gentle herbal blend that includes chamomile flowers and spearmint), maté orange spice, peppermint, Lemon Mist, and Roastaroma Mocha Spice (roasted barley, malt, chicory root, carob, dandelion root, plus allspice, cinnamon, ginger, and star anise). Price of the sampler was not given on our list. The blends may be purchased by the pound, at prices ranging from $1.50 for maté chicory to $3.45 for Sleepy Time, packaged in bulk by the case (12 boxes) or in case lots of 12 boxes, each containing 100 tea bags. You see this company's products in health stores all over the country, so if you drink a lot of *tisanes* you may well be better off buying direct. They also have some other products, such as bee pollen and ginseng, golden seal and gotu kola tablets, ginseng roots and powders.

CHEESE COFFEE CENTER / Dept.CFC
2110 Center Street, Berkeley, CA 94704

Mail-order catalogue, free, published semiannually, 12 pages, black and white.

A good selection of coffees is stocked by the Cheese Coffee Center, at prices ranging from $3.20 to $4.15 a lb. They have Guatemala Antigua, Haitian, Kenya, Mocha-Java, Mocha Yemen, Mysore (India), Celebes Kalossie, Turkish stone ground coffee, espresso (Italian roast), decaffeinated Colombian, French chicory ($1.95 a lb.), and sweetened espresso chocolate, too ($1.95 a lb.). Coffees are shipped in the bean or ground to order (specify grind or type of pot). They also have coffeepots of different types and manual or electric coffee grinders. Teas are sold in bulk (½ lb. or 1 lb.), in tins or tea bags of the name brands, such as Georgian Blend (Dublin), Jackson's of Piccadilly, McGrath's, Ridgways, Twinings, Troika (Russian black tea), and Typhoo. You'll find all the usual fermented black teas, semifermented oolong, unfermented green teas, and a pretty good range of herbs for *tisanes* and herbal teas, such as the Celestial Seasonings and Magic Mountain blends, the German Pompadour tea bags of herbal teas, and Korean ginseng. If you are a tea fancier, you might make the acquaintance of this store with one of their tea samplers. The India Tea Pack has Assam, Darjeeling, Kalgar, and orange pekoe; the China Pack, Lapsang souchong, jasmine, lichee, and oolong; and the San Francisco, Epicurean Spiced, Irish Breakfast, lichee, and choice oolong, all at $3.50. There are also herbal tea samplers.

O. H. CLAPP & CO. / Dept. CFC
47 Riverside Avenue, Westport, CT 06880

"What you should know about Vintage Teas" and price list, free, published periodically, 4 pages.

Clapp's six teas are Keemun, Chinese oolong, jasmine, Yunnan, Darjeeling, and Formosan oolong, $7.50 for an 8-oz. chest, except for the Chinese oolong, which is $7.50 for 6 oz. and Formosa oolong, $7.50 for 5 oz. A sampler of all six is $5. Tea diffusers are $1.50.

The information booklet is commonsensical, saying, for instance, about Chinese jasmine tea: "The second brew is often preferable to the first . . . . Make a pot of tea first, and after you have finished it, pour the same amount of boiling water onto the same leaf . . . a good flavor but lacks the astringency of the first brew."

COFFEE WHOLESALE WAREHOUSE / Dept. CFC
20622 Superior, Chatsworth, CA 91311

"Coffee Wholesale Warehouse Catalog," free, 8 pages, illustrated.

Is coffee your cup of tea? If so, this catalogue offers the nation's best-selling and top consumer-rated coffee brewers with a full one-year warranty on parts and labor.

You can fill your Bunn, Silex, Mr. Coffee or Brew-Matic brewer with coffees from around the world, such as old favorites like Colombian, Kenyan, and Costa Rican, as well as blends from New Guinea and Salvador, or house blend, either regular or decaffeinated. All are sold by the pound, unground. A warning that the volatile coffee market will increase prices is stamped on the price list. Famous brands come in hotel- and restaurant-portion packs to serve 8 to 10 people. A case of 46 packs, including filters, ranges from $9.43 for Maxwell House to $13.41 for Brim.

Useful gifts for a coffee lover from the Cheese Coffee Center

---

*

When melting chocolate, use coffee in place of water to intensify the flavor.

*

Coffee beans and ground coffee will keep their freshness longer if stored in the freezer or refrigerator.

*

Chill iced tea or coffee with frozen tea or coffee cubes to avoid diluting the flavor. When freezing the tea cubes, you might add a mint leaf or a squeeze of lemon juice.

*

Mexican Coffee

Heat 6 cups water, ½ cup dark brown sugar, a piece of cinnamon stick, and 6 cloves in a saucepan. Stir until sugar dissolves. Add 6 tablespoons regular-grind dark-roast coffee and bring to the boil. Simmer 2 to 3 minutes, stir, cover, and leave in a warm place until the grounds settle. Strain into coffee cups.

CONTE DI SAVOIA / Dept. CFC
555 W. Roosevelt Road, Chicago, IL 60607

Catalogue, 75¢ (refunded with purchase), published annually, 28 pages, black and white.

Conte di Savoia imports a great many foods, among them the Twinings teas from England, such as Darjeeling, Earl Grey, jasmine, English Breakfast, Irish Breakfast, orange pekoe, and green gunpowder, and lists a large selection of coffees in ½-lb., 1-lb., or 12-oz. cans, among them Hawaiian Kona, different brands of Italian espresso, Blue Danube Viennese coffee with fig seasoning, and Bugisu High Grown African. Prices, which range from $1.10 to $1.69 a pound for coffee, fluctuate with the market and are probably higher by now. Shipping costs are extra. They also have a small selection of coffee makers, drip and espresso types, and the tin-plated brass or copper Turkish coffeepot in various sizes.

CREOLE DELICACIES CO., INC. / Dept. CFC
533-H Saint Ann Street, New Orleans, LA 70116

"Happy Gifts of Food from Old New Orleans," free, published annually, 12 pages, illustrated, color.

"Café d'Orleans," the famous New Orleans coffee blend of Colombian coffees and imported chicory, is sold in two 1-lb. bags for $7.25 ppd.

CULPEPER LTD. / Dept. CFC
Hadstock Road, Linton, Cambridge, England

General price list and medicinal herb list, $1, published seasonally.

Among the all-natural products sold by Culpeper, the famous English herbalists, is their exclusive Indian Ocean tea, a fine broken orange pekoe, unsprayed with chemical insecticides. It comes in ¼-lb. and 1-lb. tins and in tea bags. While prices fluctuate with the rate of exchange, 1 lb. would be about $4–$4.50. Naturally, they have *tisanes* (herbal teas), too, German and Belgian chamomile, celery, cowslip flowers, lime blossom, peppermint, raspberry leaf, rose hips, and yerba maté (green maté), from about 30¢ to about 65¢ for 1¾ oz.

THE DAILY GRIND / Dept. CFC
Nashville, IN 47448

Price list, free.

The Daily Grind, a gourmet shop and coffeehouse that recently moved from Bloomington to Nashville, Indiana, sells by mail a selection of coffees (whole bean or ground) and teas. In mild roast coffees they list Venezuelan, Guatemalan Antigua, Brazilian Santos, Colombian Supremo, Salvador, Jamaican High Mountain, Mexican Altura, Costa Rican, and Sumatran; in medium roast, Hawaiian Kona, Mocha, and Kenya, at prices ranging from $3.58 to $4.48 a lb. Listed under Unique Coffees are a Vintage Colombian (10 years old), decaffeinated Colombian, and decaffeinated espresso and Espresso-Colombian; under Blended Coffees, Mocha-Java, Captain's Blend (Kenya Espresso), John's Blend (Guatemalan/Mexican/Sumatran) and Heritage Blend (Costa Rican/Vintage Colombian). You can order a Gourmet Coffee sampler for $12.95 pp. and get ¼ lb. each of 8 of the coffees. Teas, priced at 45¢ to 63¢ an oz., are Lapsang souchong, Keemun, orange pekoe, Darjeeling Supreme, orange spice, English Breakfast, Earl Grey, and Green Apple Leaf. There's a 2 lb. minimum mail-order requirement for coffees, plus $1.50 postage and handling; a 2-oz. minimum for teas, plus 50¢ postage and handling. When ordering ground coffees, specify grind—fine, drip, or perk.

D. M. ENTERPRISES / Dept. CFC
Box 2452, San Francisco, CA 94126

"Calico Kitchen's Portfolio," free, published two to three times a year, 12 sheets, illustrated, color.

Cappuccino might have been inspired by the Capuchin monks of Italy, but San Franciscans have made it their own special brew. A taste of this North Beach version is available in packets of four servings ($2.50).

Calico Kitchen also sells three exotic teas from the Orient (Lichee, Dragon, Narcissus), packaged in 2½-oz. boxes ($6), and six packets of tea (Lichee, Narcissus, Gunpowder) attached to note cards that contain tea lore and brewing instructions ($4.50).

They also have EVA coffee filters and a tea filter set (40 disposable tea filters with a plastic holder) that lets you make your own tea bag from loose tea ($2.95; 40 replacement filters, $1.49). If you love really good ground chocolate and cocoa, Calico Kitchen has the famous San Francisco Ghirardelli product (Ghirardelli Square is the old chocolate factory, now converted to shops and restaurants), 3 lbs. for $6.

EAST WIND / Dept. CFC
2801 Broadway, New York, NY 10025

Mail-order price list, free, 5 pages.

East Wind has the usual assortment of Chinese teas at prices slightly lower than the average store. Keemun black tea is 80¢ for 4 oz.; Yunnan, $1.60 for 4½ oz.; jasmine varies in price from $1.80 for 8 oz. to $1.95 for 4 oz., depending on the brand; and green tea is $1.80 for a 3½-oz. tin. There are four different oolongs, starting at 75¢ for 8 oz. There's also a ginseng leaf tea from Shantung, $1.75 for a 2½-oz. box.

EGERTONS / Dept. CFC
Lyme Street, Axminster, Devon, EX13 5DB, England

"Egertons Postal Gift & Shopping Service," $1.50 if air-mailed, free otherwise, published annually, 73 pages, color.

For over 40 years Egertons has sold Kenya coffees and teas from Nairobi Coffee & Tea Ltd. There's a mild Kenya straight, Mayfair blend (a Continental roast), and a dark Viennese blend of coffee and figs. You can order 2 lbs. for $11.25, 10 lbs. for $42, or coffee parcels of ½-lb. bags of any mixture of the three. The "Pride of Kenya" tea is sold in tea bags (5 lbs., $22.93) or loose in ½-lb. packs totaling from 2 lbs. ($10.18) to 10 lbs. ($36.53). They also carry the Ridgway teas and coffees.

EMPIRE COFFEE & TEA COMPANY / Dept. CFC
486 Ninth Avenue, New York, NY 10018

Price list and catalogue, free, published annually, 14 pages, illustrated.

Among Empire's Italian roasts (strong espressos) are Colombian, Mocha, a Neapolitan blend of African, Brazilian, and Santos, and a Roma mixture of French and Italian roasts.

French roasts, Continental demitasse style, include Kenyan, Viennese (a mild French), Colombian medellin, a Turkish-Greek blend, Mocha-Java, and Colombian Bogota.

Green unroasted beans range from aged Mocha to Costa Rican, Mexican, Bolivian, and Brazilian peaberry.

Decaffeinated beans as well as instant, canned, and individually packaged coffees are available.

Loose teas sold by the pound or in ¼-lb. tins include oolong, jasmine, Earl Grey, Darjeeling, Russian Caravan, Prince of Wales, Irish-style black, Young Hyson, yerba maté, and green Chun-mee ($1.80 to $5.98).

San Francisco specialties from "Calico Kitchen's Portfolio"

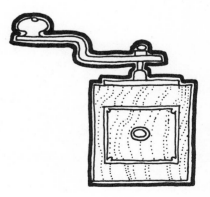

* * *

A tiny pinch of salt added to the boiling water will enhance the flavor of coffee.

* * *

Leftover coffee grounds and tea leaves are a very good mulch for plants and the garden. Azaleas benefit especially from the acidity of coffee grounds.

* * *

The inside story of a famous store, leaflet from Fortnum & Mason

FAUCHON / Dept. CFC
26 Place de la Madeleine, 75008 Paris 8e, France

Price list, free, published annually, 8 pages.

Fauchon presents Ceylon, India, and China teas packed under their own label, all 8¾ oz. From Ceylon comes Aislaby (about $5.55), flowery orange pekoe (approximately $4.60), and broken orange pekoe ($5.50). India's contributions are Darjeeling ($7.00) and Assam ($5.60). China teas are Lapsang ($5.40), Earl Grey ($5.55), and jasmine ($4.30). All prices are listed in francs, so you have to go by the current rate of exchange.

R. W. FORSYTH LTD. / Dept. CFC
30 Princes Street, Edinburgh EH2 2BZ, Scotland

"The days of Christmas at Forsyth's," free, published annually, 16 pages, black and white.

The teas sold in gift packs by Forsyth's are Melrose and Twinings, and they come in decorated caddies, tins, decorated jars, and miniature tea chests. A miniature tea chest of choice quality Ceylon tea runs from about $1.80 for 1 lb. to about $6 for 5 lbs. The decorated jars of Twinings teas are all made by the Cauldon Bristol Potteries, and one, the Old English jar, is a numbered collector's item (about $15 with ¾ lb. orange pekoe tea). An amusing idea for a small gift to go along with the tea is a muff tea cozy in modern or traditional designs, sized to fit pots of 2-, 4-, and 6-cup capacity. There's a muff coffee cozy, too.

FORTNUM & MASON / Dept CFC
181 Piccadilly, London W1A 1ER, England

"Fortnum & Mason Export Food," free, published seasonally, 15 pages, illustrated, color.

Fortnum & Mason has been the official grocer to the royal family since the early 18th century. Their special Royal Blend tea, a favorite at Buckingham Palace, is sold in handsome containers of Mason's Ironstone. A 3-lb. ironstone jar is $40.67, the ½-lb. ironstone tea caddy is $16.35, and a charming tea-filled ironstone pot is $18.04. A pound tin with clock design is just $4.13, or a gift box with six ½-lb. tins of specially selected Fortnum & Mason teas is $12.60. The teas are also included in the export gift packs. For $15.02 you can purchase one tin of Royal Blend tea, a Chinese rose-design jar filled with strawberry preserves, and an Old Foley chrysanthemum jar of vintage marmalade. Fortnum & Mason's packaging is particularly handsome, making any gift doubly pleasing.

FOX MOUNTAIN FARMS / Dept. CFC
P.O. Box 408, Taos, NM 87571

Folder, free, published annually, illustrated.

Fox Mountain Farms has something a little different in the *tisane* line: Their special blends are packaged in handmade floral pouches. Griswold Inn's Famous 1776 tea, blended for the 200-year-old Connecticut inn, contains orange flowers, lemon grass, sassafras root, rose hips, and blackberry, blueberry, raspberry, strawberry, and peppermint leaves. This and seven other special blends costs $3 for 4 oz. There are two after-dinner blends that you combine with Cognac or whiskey to taste. One combines maté, carob, cinnamon, and ginseng ($5 for 4 oz.). Or there's an herbal cappuccino (cinnamon and allspice combined with maté, chicory root, barley, malt, dandelion root, all roasted) for those who must forgo regular coffee. You can even cook with their tea blends. Fox Mountain Farms has a recipe for a basting sauce for broiled chicken that combines 1 cup of their New Mexico breakfast tea (lemon balm, comfrey, chamomile and hibiscus flowers, raspberry leaves, alfalfa, and rosemary) with ¼ cup of honey and ¼ cup soy sauce.

GILL'S FIRST COLONY COFFEE / Dept. CFC
Box 11005, Norfolk, Virginia 23517

Catalogue and price list, free, published periodically, 6 pages.

Gill's has a fine selection of unblended coffees that are not generally available. They come in 3-lb. mix-or-match assortments and include Mexican Altura Coatepec, grown at altitudes over 4,000 feet, giving it a rich, mild taste ($1.95 a lb.); the three-centuries-old "Dutch Old Government Java," with its woody taste ($2.25 a lb.); and Hodiedah short-berry Mocha, grown, the story goes, in little gardens bordering ancient Arabian trade routes ($2.35 a lb.).

You'll find coffees grown in the mountains of South America, Africa, Hawaii, and the delightful Jamaican Blue Mountain.

First Colony also presents their own blends in vacuum cans, plus gift packages of assortments of three. The gourmet selection includes a pound each of Colombian Supremo to start the day, Kilimanjaro for after dinner, and Mocha-Java blend for any time of day ($6.95 for three). The after-dinner assortment includes three 12-oz. tins of drip-ground espresso, French roast (a combination of South American and Ethiopian blends), and the New Orleans blend of coffee and chicory ($6.50 for three). For $69.50 you can give 3 lbs. of First Colony's gourmet coffee each month for a year. (Prices listed are 1976.)

Teas are available in two assortments (6¼-lb. tins for $10.95 or 25 packets of bags for $10.50) that include Earl Grey, Ching Wo, and Lady Londonderry blend, or in combination with coffees ($15.95 and $19.95).

GRACE TEA CO., LTD. / Dept. CFC
799 Broadway, New York, NY 10003

"Unsurpassed Cup Quality," $1, published annually, 4 pages, illustrated.

Grace caters to the tea connoisseur. They make no excuses for their high prices ($4 to $4.90 per ½ lb.), and their teas have been widely praised by experts.

Professional tea tasters recommended Winey Keemun, an English breakfast tea ($4) for its "fine silvery leaf . . . extra slow hand fired" to produce a "smooth winey flavor of real distinction."

They also offer the original Earl Grey mixture of superb black teas ($4.40), the "Before the Rain" Jasmine, a springtime crop that is later blended with summer flowers, and green gunpowder leaf pellets, full of body and character ($4.80).

Grace says the best tea in the world costs $20 per pound, but the second best is their Darjeeling, grown at an altitude of 6,000 feet ($4.90).

Their special connoisseur blend is available in bags (50 for $3.90), or you can try a tasting assortment of the English classics in five 2-oz. tasters for $8.50.

As they say, "cup quality" is the only criterion professional taste-testers use to judge the superiority of one tea over another, and their teas are clearly superior.

GRAYS OF WORCESTER, LTD. / Dept. CFC
Orchard Street, Worcester WR5 3DP, England

"For the pleasure of the Gourmet," free, published annually with seasonal supplements, 26 pages, black and white.

Grays list 4 teas, packaged in 5-lb. miniature tea chests, for around $15 delivered, at the present rate of exchange. There's Earl Grey, jasmine, Ceylon Celestial (a "luxury blend for the connoisseur"), and a special blend that also comes in a lovely ironstone tea jar with typical Staffordshire decoration in brown and honey tones. This Brown Ascot jar, with 1 lb. of the special tea blend, costs around $18 delivered.

Coffee Ricotta

Turn a 1-pound container of fresh ricotta cheese into a bowl. Beat with an electric hand mixer until very light and fluffy, then mix in 2 tablespoons sugar, 2 tablespoons heavy cream, 3 tablespoons coffee-flavored liqueur (Kahlua or Tia Maria), and ¼ cup pulverized dark-roast Turkish coffee. Blend thoroughly, beating until light, creamy, and well mixed. Spoon into pots de crème or small ramekins and chill for 2 hours. Serve with crisp plain wafers. Serves 6.

Café Brûlot

Put in the blazer pan of a chafing dish 6 lumps of sugar, 2 or 3 cloves, 1 piece of cinnamon stick, and the rind of 1 orange and 1 lemon, pared off in a long continuous strip. Add 1½ cups cognac and heat. Warm a silver ladle, dip up some of the warm cognac, add a lump of sugar and ignite. Lower the ladle into the bowl to ignite the rest of the cognac and immediately pour in 3 cups very strong dark-roast coffee, ladling up some of the mixture and then pouring it back to blend the liquids. When flames die, serve in demitasse cups. Makes about 12 servings.

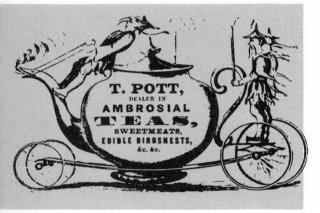

*

Soak prunes in strong tea rather than water for a delicious flavor.

*

For a bad sunburn, apply pads soaked in strong tea. The tannic acid will relieve the pain and redness.

*

GREEN MOUNTAIN HERBS / Dept. CFC
P.O. Box 2369, Boulder, CO 80302

Catalogue and price list, free, published annually, 20 pages, black and white.

Green Mountain Herbs sells not only herbs but also black and green teas such as jasmine, oolong, pan-fried green, Ceylon orange pekoe, English Breakfast, orange spice, Earl Grey, Darjeeling, Assam, and Keemun at what are, for these times, very reasonable prices, around $2 for 8 oz. of jasmine or oolong, $2.35 for Keemun, but their forte is herbal teas. They carry the Celestial Seasonings and Magic Mountain brands, a large selection of traditional Oriental teas like day lily, heavenly root, two peony, and 8 blends with delicious names—Mellow Moments (hibiscus flowers, anise seed, rose hips, chamomile, spearmint, orange blossoms, lemon verbena) and Wild West being two of them. Prices range from 85¢ to $1.80 for 2 oz.

HERTER'S INC. / Dept. CFC
RR 2, Mitchell, SD 57301

"Herter's Sportsman's Catalog," $1 (refundable with $10 purchase), published annually, 352 pages, illustrated, color and black and white.

George L. Herter has spent a good deal of time exploring in Africa, and one of his finds was the wild small-bush Kenya hill coffee, a very aromatic small bean that makes a full-tasting brew. He sells this in 14-oz. vacuum tins, either the roasted whole beans or regular grind, at $3.17. To grind the beans there's an old-fashioned hand coffee mill, the kind with a handle on top and a drawer at the bottom ($9.57). Tea bags of Herter's Serendip 100 percent Ceylon tea are $1.57 for 50 bags.

HILLTOP HERB FARM / Dept. CFC
P.O. Box 866, Cleveland, TX 77327

Catalogue, 50¢, published annually, 16 pages, illustrated, black and white.

The herbal teas made and sold by Hilltop Herb Farm for $1.45 an oz. (for 4 ozs. or more, deduct 10 percent) include apple spice, eleven herb, peppermint and chamomile, pink and lemony, and Serenitea. Tranquilitea, a blend of many herbs, designed to soothe and pacify, is sold in 3-oz. containers at $2.85 or in bulk at $13.25 a lb. They also sell other straight herbs (not blends) for *tisanes* at $1.35 an oz. If you want to make German May wine, they have the essential herbs and recipe for $3. Another neat idea of theirs is to make and sell small cotton drawstring bags for brewing tea, bouquet garni, soup seasonings, or soaking seeds for planting. You can wash and use the bags time after time (20¢ if ordered separately, 3 for 50¢, or 7 for $1 if ordered with herbs).

IRON GATE PRODUCTS COMPANY, INC. / Dept. CFC
424 West 54th Street, New York, NY 10019

Product lists (prices on request), free, 9 pages.

"21" Club coffee and cafe espresso in 1-lb. (coffee) and 12-oz. (espresso) tins, 12 tins to a case, are among the "21" specialties of Iron Gate.

ROBERT JACKSON & CO., LTD. / Dept. CFC
171 Piccadilly, London WIV OLL, England

"Robert Jackson's Food, Wine, Hamper and Gift List," published seasonally, illustrated, black and white.

Robert Jackson's tea department is a favorite haunt of tourists anxious to find a traditional English present to take home. The Oriental gift pack contains ¼-lb. boxes of Russian, Lapsang souchong, Formosa oolong, and Ching Wo China tea ($2.75), while the Regency Street Scene gift pack emphasizes new blends of African, Darjeeling with African, Ceylon with Darjeeling and Indian blends ($1.80).

Decorative caddies hold ¼ lb., ½ lb., or, in some cases, 1 lb. of different teas, among them Assam, Darjeeling, Earl Grey, Lady Londonderry, Lemon, Russian, and Ching Wo, and they are also available in tea bags. Jackson has the syrups for iced tea and coffee from Hédiard in Paris—syrups of tea, mint, coffee, and sugar in 70-centiliter (cl.) bottles, from about $2 to $3.

LE JARDIN DU GOURMET / Dept. CFC
West Danville, VT 05873

Catalogue, 50¢, published annually, 32 pages, illustrated, black and white.

The teas are Twinings from England—Earl Grey, Lapsang souchong, Keemun, Formosa oolong, jasmine, Darjeeling, English, Irish, and Ceylon Breakfast, orange pekoe, and Prince of Wales and Queen Mary's Tea, from $2.25 to $2.95 a ½-lb. tin, and the Pompadour herb teas from Germany in units of 5 tea bags for 85¢; in coffee, Motta and Medaglia d'Oro espressos, $1.75 and $1.55 a 12-oz. tin. Jardin du Gourmet has two coffee makers, the drip-type Neapolitan coffee maker and the Moka Express, as well as various sizes of the Turkish coffeepot.

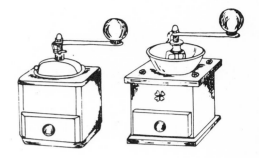

LEKVAR-BY-THE-BARREL / Dept. CFC
1577 First Avenue, New York, NY 10028

"A Continental Bazaar," free, published annually, 56 pages, illustrated, black and white.

This old-established store in Manhattan's Yorkville district sells fresh roasted coffee in whole beans or freshly ground (specify your grind). They have 100 percent Colombian, Mocha, Java, French roast, and Brazilian at $2.50 a lb., French chicory at $1.49 a lb., a green Colombian for roasting at $2.15 a lb., and they will blend the first six to order. Coffees in cans include Melitta, Turkish, Hawaiian Kona, Jamaican Blue Mountain, and French Market coffee with chicory. They also have various coffee grinders, including one for Turkish coffee, espresso machines, and other coffee makers. In teas they list Darjeeling, Earl Grey, gunpowder, jasmine, Formosa oolong, Lapsang souchong, pan-fired green and China black, a Ceylon Russian mixture, and their own "spice" blend tea, which is $2.50 a lb. Imported Kneipp herb teas are $2.69 a 3-oz. box.

Coffee Jelly
Soften 1 envelope gelatin in ¼ cup cold water, then add 3 cups very hot, strong, dark-roast coffee. Stir until gelatin is dissolved. Sweeten to taste with sugar, stirring until dissolved. Pour into a 1½-quart mold and chill until set. Unmold and serve with whipped cream flavored with Grand Marnier or coffee liqueur.

MAISON GLASS / Dept. CFC
52 East 58th Street, New York, NY 10022

"Maison Glass Delicacies," $1, published annually, 72 pages, illustrated, black and white.

In teas, Maison Glass stocks Mark Wendell's Hu-Kwa ($7.95 a lb.), Boston Harbour ($3.50 a ½ lb.), Kardomah Earl Grey and other British teas, such as the Twinings and Jackson's of Piccadilly brands. You can have a Twinings tea sampler of ¼-lb. tin each of Prince of Wales tea (Keemun), Formosa oolong, Darjeeling, and Ceylon Breakfast, or Queen Mary's Tea (Darjeeling), Earl Grey, Lapsang souchong, and English Breakfast, or buy the teas by the ½-lb. or 1-lb. tin. They have a few herb teas (linden, chamomile, mint, orange, verbena), 25 bags to a box for $1.75, and Bigelow's Constant Comment tea. Under "coffee by Maison Glass" you'll find a French roast and a regular roast, plus a selection of others, such as Jamaican Blue Mountain coffee in the instant version, regular, espresso or decaffeinated, freeze-dried coffee from Switzerland, Turkish coffee, and a ground espresso blend. No coffee beans or rare coffees here.

MANGANARO FOODS / Dept. CFC
488 Ninth Avenue, New York, NY 10018

"Manganaro's for Gourmet Foods," free, published annually, 22 pages, illustrated.

Manganaro's coffee is all of the demitasse or espresso type from their own dark-roast coffee beans, ground to your specifications ($2.50 a lb.), through a list of brands such as Medaglia d'Oro, Vivo, Motta (all $1.85 a tin), and Maimone espresso ($2.25 for a 12-oz. tin). Only one tea, an

Café Glacé

Stir ½ cup sugar into 1 quart hot, strong, dark-roast coffee until dissolved. Cool. Add ½ cup cognac and pour into tall glasses over ice cubes. Top with whipped cream flavored with sugar and cinnamon.

herbal chamomile, is 90¢ for a package of 8 tea bags. There's a wooden coffee mill from West Germany ($9.95) and three kinds of espresso maker. One is the two-part steam-process type (3-, 6-, 9- and 12-cup sizes, $7.75 to $16), another the drip type, and the third an electric espresso machine (3-cup or 6-cup capacity, $21.95 and $26.75).

NICHOLS GARDEN NURSERY / Dept. CFC
1190 North Pacific Highway, Albany, OR 97321

"Nichols Herb and Rare Seeds," free, published seasonally, 60 pages, illustrated, black and white.

The very wide-ranging Nichols catalogue has a good assortment of teas (Keemun, Lapsang souchong, English Breakfast, oolong, pan-fired green, jasmine, natural-leaf green), of which perhaps the most interesting is their small-leafed orange pekoe, taken from the first picking of the tea plant, which they import in wooden cases from Ceylon, package in airtight bags, and sell at the very reasonable price of $3 a ½ lb. There are also various herbal teas, such as Oriental Mu tea (herbs and ginseng) and Mormon or Squaw tea, from the foliage of a pinelike shrub that grows in the high deserts of Utah, Nevada, and California, used for centuries by the local Indians and the early Mormons as a medicine and tonic ($1.75 for 4 oz., $4.25 for 12 oz.).

NORTHWESTERN COFFEE MILLS / Dept. CFC
217 North Broadway, Milwaukee, WI 53202

Catalogue free (25¢ donation accepted), published annually, 27 pages, illustrated, black and white.

Northwestern began business as Milwaukee's first coffee and tea merchant in 1875, and their emphasis has always been on keeping that business personal and quality-oriented, as you will appreciate if you study their catalogue. The catalogue, incidentally, is one of the most beautifully produced and illustrated (with delightful sketches and quotations) and the most clearly, informatively, and intelligently written as we have ever seen. They tell you everything you could possibly want to know about their products, both those they manufacture and those they distribute for others (such as cheeses and dried fruits), which have to meet their own high standards. That they can run such a quality business with only eight employees bears out Mies van der Rohe's contention that less is more.

Theirs has to be one of the finest collections of coffees available, starting with their own blends, in all of which they use only the very best arabicas, none of the low-quality robusta varieties. These comprise an American breakfast blend, a fancy dinner blend (with a touch of dark roast), Hawaiian Kona blend, Kenya XX blend, Mocha-Java blend, New Orleans chicory blend, and Stapleton Restaurant blend, the favorite of Milwaukee's best restaurants for over 100 years. These are sold in ½-lb., 1-lb., and 5-lb. quantities, and prices range from $2.35 to $2.80 a lb., although they add a footnote that coffee prices have been very unstable and, if the price goes up, they ship and bill you for the difference. Shipping and handling charges ($1.50) are not included in the price.

Their straight (unblended) coffees consist of some that are readily available, others that are scarce or rare. All straights are carefully roasted freshly before sale, and they suggest you use them, if you wish, to create your own blends. Straights include Brazilian Santos or Parana, Celebes Kalossi (the rarest of their coffees), Colombian Excelso, Colombian aged (also rare), Guatemalan High Grown, Mocha Yemen, and Sumatra Mandeling. These are also sold in ½-lb., 1-lb., and 5-lb. quantities at prices ranging from $2.50 to $3.75 a lb. You may, if you wish, order the raw (green) beans and roast them yourself at 50¢ a lb. less. They even sell the coffee roaster ($15).

While most of their coffees are a rich brown American roast, they also have a French roast and an espresso roast. For those who want it there is a 100 percent Colombian decaffeinated coffee as well as a Café Salvador instant coffee, regular or dark roast. As they point out, even instant coffee can taste good if processed from good coffee, and they use fine-grade El Salvadors. They have two coffee samplers, either whole-bean

COFFEE·TEA·SPICES·NUTS·CHEESE

NORTHWESTERN COFFEE MILLS
217 N. Broadway • Milwaukee, Wis. 53202

(four ½-lb. bags of Stapleton, Colombian, French roast, and Mocha-Java in a white mailing carton for $6.25) or ground (six 2½-oz. packages of Stapleton, Mocha-Java, French roast, Mexican, Colombian, and Fancy Dinner with a 32-page coffee recipe book, packaged in a burlap bag, for $3.75), either of which would be a good way to get acquainted with their offerings. Chicory ($1.75 a lb.) when added to coffee gives you New Orleans coffee, or you can drink it alone as a coffee substitute. They have a very good selection of coffee mills and coffee makers, which you'll find described in more detail in chapter 12, and various types of coffee filters for different machines and coffee makers.

As for teas, you'll find the introductory remarks about the differences between top-quality, lower-grade, and tea-bag-grade teas extremely enlightening, as well as the explanations of the differences between black (fully fermented) and green (unfermented) teas, straight teas, and blends. If you are interested in a blend that isn't on their list, they even offer to make it up for you if you send them a sample.

In black teas they have Assam, Darjeeling Second Flush (the finest grade), orange pekoe, Lapsang souchong, Russian Pamir Tura (coppery-colored and mild), English Breakfast (Black Keemun), an Irish Blend (very strong), and Backsettler Blend (hearty and brisk). In green teas there are two, gunpowder (the leaves are rolled into tight balls, resembling buckshot) and pan-fired Formosa (the latter they recommend for first-time users of green tea, as it is light in the cup, with a mellow tart taste, the white wine of teas). Scented teas (those blended with herbs, spices, oils, and flowers) include Earl Grey, jasmine, lemon-spiced, mint herb blend (black teas and peppermint leaves), orange-spiced, and star anise blend. There are two oolong (semifermented) teas: Formosa oolong and Mainland China oolong. Teas are sold by the ¼ lb., ½ lb., and 1 lb. and range in price from $3.60 to $5 a lb. for Mainland China oolong.

Herbal teas, as they point out, are not really teas at all, as they do not originate from the tea plant, although they are brewed and enjoyed like regular tea (so why not, we feel, adopt the charming French name for them, *tisanes*?). Their herbal teas, some whole, some cut and sifted, are Hungarian chamomile, lemon balm, lemon grass, lemon verbena, mu, rose hips, peppermint, spearmint, and sassafras and range in price from $1.40 to $3.80 a ¼ lb. They also have three forms of Korean ginseng: cut and sifted root, powder, and whole root, and yerba maté, the South American herbal-type tea that contains caffeine. Carob powder (or St. John's bread), a natural substitute for chocolate, is also available at $1.25 a lb. Northwestern stocks a tea kettle, two types of teapot, and various tea infusers (spoon and ball), which are described in more detail in chapter 12.

A tea sampler, six 2-oz. packages of orange pekoe, orange spice, Earl Grey, Formosa oolong, Darjeeling, and English Breakfast, packaged in a burlap bag with a chromed brass tea ball ($5.50), is a good way to try out some of the teas, or, if you are a *tisane* lover, get the herb tea sampler of six ½-oz. packages of chamomile, sassafras, rose hips, lemon verbena, peppermint, and licorice root, with the same tea ball and packaging for $4.

OLD NORTH CHURCH GIFT SHOP / Dept. CFC
193 Salem Street, Boston, MA 02113

"The Old North Steeple," 4 pages, illustrated, black and white.

The Old North Church is where Paul Revere hung those famous lanterns, which might stand today, as far as foods are concerned, for "two if for tea." The gift shop has a good selection of teas. Twinings Earl Grey, Melrose's English Breakfast, Mark T. Wendell's Hu-Kwa, and Boston Harbour are all $3.35 for an 8-oz. tin. Boston Harbour tea is a special blend from Davison, Newman, the English firm whose shipments to the colonies were so unceremoniously dumped into Boston harbor in those long-ago tea parties, and their petition to George III for reimbursement is printed on the tin (though it takes a magnifying glass to decipher it). There's also an English copper luster teapot with the firm's insignia and founding date for brewing tea ($20).

---

*

Three ways to melt chocolate without fear of scorching: (1) on a heavy plate set over a pan of hot water; (2) in the top of a double boiler over hot water; (3) in a small heavy pan in a 300°F. oven.

*

When making Irish coffee, whip the heavy cream slightly. It will float and not disintegrate.

*

PAPRIKAS WEISS, IMPORTER / Dept. CFC
1546 Second Avenue, New York, NY 10028

"Imported Foods and Cookware Catalogue," $1 for annual subscription, published four times a year, 66 pages, illustrated, black and white.

In the Paprikas Weiss "International Roundup of Coffees and Teas" you'll find, among others, a Chinese restaurant blend tea ($2 a ¼ lb.), Russian Samovar Tea, Darjeeling Gold Tip ($2.50 a ¼ lb.), Twinings teas in tins or tea bags, herb teas from Germany, Chinese green, black, oolong, and herb teas, including one made from chrysanthemum blossoms (box of 10 packets, $4.60), and a gift basket of 8 Chinese teas for $39.95. There are a good many bulk coffees, roasted, ground and packed to order, an unroasted green coffee, a German decaffeinated coffee, and Hungarian espresso or regular blends ($2.98 a tin). They also carry coffee grinders, an electric and a German lap model ($19.98), a Turkish coffee mill, coffee makers, teapots, and ball or spoon-type tea infusers.

PEPPERIDGE FARM MAIL ORDER CO., INC. / Dept. CFC
Box 7000, Norwalk, CT 06856

"Gift Catalog," free, published periodically, 32 pages, illustrated, color.

Two coffees to accompany the cookies and breads from Pepperidge Farm. Colombian Supremo is a fine blend of Bourbon Santos beans and the finest of Colombian coffee, and the Mocha-Java combines Hodeida shortberry Mocha and Java coffee.

SAHADI IMPORTING CO., INC. / Dept. CFC
187 Atlantic Avenue, Brooklyn, NY 11201

"The Silent Salesman," free, published biannually, 24 pages, illustrated, black and white.

Sahadi has dark-roast Middle East-style coffee, the pulverized kind for making Turkish coffee ($2.10 a 1-lb. tin), coffee beans, either French roast ($2.25 a lb.) or American roast ($2.10 a lb.), Ceylon tea in a wood box ($3.50 for 1 lb.), and a trio of Twinings teas—Darjeeling, Earl Grey, and English Breakfast. Their Turkish coffee makers (like little brass pitchers, with a lip and a long handle) come in brass or enamel, different sizes and prices ranging from $4 in brass, $1.75 in enamel for the smallest size to $10 for the largest brass pot.

SCHAPIRA COFFEE CO. / Dept. CFC
117 West 10th Street, New York, NY 10011

Price list and order form, free, published periodically, 2 pages.

Three generations of Schapiras have been coffee roasting and tea blending since 1903, and their shop in Greenwich Village is always jammed with customers. Fortunately, they also sell by mail, so you don't have to stand in line. Their list of coffees and teas is well written and explanatory. For instance, one of the unblended coffees, Djimmah, is described as "a rare coffee from Ethiopia. Flavory but light. Spicy Bouquet." About Maracaibo they say, "the pride of Venezuela. We have a high regard for the aromatic and winy quality of these beans." Now that really tells you something. Other unblended coffees are Guatemalan, Java, Colombian Excellso, Mexican-French roasted, and Ethiopian Mocha. Prices vary from about $2.70 to about $3 a lb. Among the blends is their own Flavor Cup coffee, a Colombian blend, in three styles—brown roast, French roast, and Italian roast ($2.20 to $2.30 a lb.)—a Viennese blend of Maracaibo and Mexican-French for after dinner, a powder-grind Turkish blend, a New Orleans blend (French roast and chicory), and a decaffeinated coffee. You can have a coffee sampler of any five coffees, ½ lb. of each, gift-boxed. Coffee is shipped the day it is roasted, and you can specify if you want it ground.

In teas there is again the Schapira's own Flavor Cup, a private blend

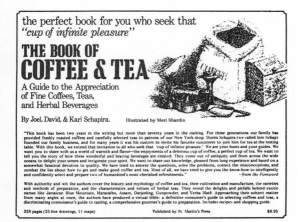

of India and China teas ($3.50 a lb.), and 11 others, including Imperial Mandarin (delicate and flowery), China green (light, slightly tart, a pale-green color), and Russian Blossom (a blend of Keemun, Assam, and green, bright, clear flavor). Prices range from $3.50 a lb. to $4.75 for Imperial Mandarin, and teas are also available in ½-lb. and ¼-lb. packs. There are tea bags ($1.35 for a box of 50, $1.60 for Imperial Mandarin), tea samplers and tea-bag samplers. The 3 herb teas (chamomile, mint, and rose hips) are $1.50 for a box of 30 tea bags. Shipping charges are extra. Schapira also carries coffee makers, such as the Melitta and espresso pots, hand grinders, and the Moulinex electric coffee mill (request the special order form for these). You can also buy "The Book of Coffee and Tea," written by brothers Joel, Karl, and David.

THE SENSUOUS BEAN / Dept. CFC
228 Columbus Avenue, New York, NY 10023

Price list, free.

This small company offers 11 different coffees, including Kenya ($3.15 per lb.), decaffeinated ($3.15 per lb.), Mocha ($2.57 per lb.), and their own Sensuous blend ($2.75 per lb.). There are 10 types of loose tea, all $1.50 per lb., such as Assam, fine oolong, Russian-style, and Sensuous breakfast blend. In tea bags they have Irish Breakfast (48 bags for $1.65), spiced tea ($1.50 for 34 bags), and Twinings Earl Grey, English Breakfast, jasmine, and lemon-scented (25 bags for $1.50). Pompadour herb teas include chamomile, linden flowers, peppermint, and rose hips, $1.90 for 25 bags, or mint-in-tea, 34 bags for $1.50.

The Sensuous Bean also has Tricolette drip coffee makers from $1.65 for the 1-cup to $5.90 for the 4–8 cup, and 1–6 cup Melitta for $7.95 or the 2–8 cup for $9.45.

SEY-CO PRODUCTS CO. / Dept. CFC
7651 Densmore Avenue, Van Nuys, CA 91406

Catalogue, free, published annually, 15 pages, illustrated, color.

The *A La Carte* food list of Sey-Co includes a small collection of teas. Keemun (4 oz. for $1.25), Rex Dynasty Lapsang souchong (4 oz. for $3.75), oolong (4 oz. for $1.25), and green tea, "real gunpowder tea, fermented to achieve a rare bouquet" (4 oz. for $1.50), are sold in individual containers and by the dozen. There are also coffees—Mocha, Java, and espresso ("a blend of the finest Colombian, Venezuelan, Bourbon and Mocha coffees").

SIMPSON & VAIL, INC. / Dept. CFC
53 Park Place, New York NY 10007

"Coffees and Teas," free, published annually, 5 pages.

Eleven coffees and 25 teas and tea blends are available from Simpson & Vail. Coffees, available in 6-oz. "sampler" tins for $1.25 or 1-lb. bags (beans or ground), run from a traditional American roast, high-grown in Central America ($1.80 a lb.), to Tanzanian peaberry, a winy-tasting fancy arabica ($2.50), the Kona blend from Hawaii ($2.95), and Supremo from Colombia ($2.95).

Kenyan Kaproret tea is just one of half a dozen black teas ranging in price from $2.70 to $4.80 per pound. Two Formosan green teas are represented: Imperial gunpowder ($3.05 a lb.) and pan-fired ($3.50). There are also mixed and blended teas. Their iced-tea blend ($3.50 a lb.) stays clear when ice is added. Aromatic tea blends include the Morgan Blend ($3.95 a lb.), a mixture of Earl Grey and Lapsang Smokey Souchong. Some of the teas are available in bags, 100 to a box ($1.95–$3.50).

Simpson & Vail also sells special gift combination boxes with assortments of teas and coffees packed in decorative canisters ($3.95–$18.95).

Herbal teas or *tisanes* do not stimulate like tea and coffee and for centuries have been used to soothe the nerves, quiet the stomach, induce sleep and relaxation, or act as restoratives. They are usually served after dinner or at bedtime, but also make a pleasant mid-afternoon drink. The general rule for amount of herb per cup of water is: for strong herbs, ½ to 1 tablespoon fresh or ¼ to ½ tablespoon dried; for mild herbs, double the amounts. Use a china, not a metal pot, steep for 3 to 10 minutes in water that has come to a rolling boil, then strain into the cup.

✳

Tea infuser

Hot Tea Toddy

Put ¼ cup dark rum and a lemon slice studded with a clove into each double old-fashioned glass. Put a silver spoon in the glass to prevent it cracking and then fill with freshly brewed hot tea. Add a cinnamon stick for stirring.

Café Royale

Pour hot, strong, dark-roast coffee into demitasse cups. Float 1 tablespoon cognac on top. Put a lump of sugar on a spoon and hold it over the surface of the coffee. Pour a little warmed cognac onto the sugar and ignite. Lower the spoon gently into the coffee, swishing it back and forth until the flames die out.

SPECIALTY SPICE SHOP / Dept. CFC
2757 152nd Avenue, N.E., Redmond, WA 98052

"Specialty Spice Shop Catalogue," free, published annually, 6 pages.

Besides a wide variety of spices, this specialty shop also has bulk teas, both regular and herbal, and coffees. There's a Black Formosa Assam, jasmine, oolong, and some unusual herbal teas, such as hibiscus (from Jamaica), lemon grass, and wood betony. In coffees you'll find Colombian, including one decaffeinated, Mexican espresso, and the Spice Shop's special blend of espresso and Colombian. No prices were quoted on our list. You'll have to request the current ones.

UWAJIMAYA / Dept. CFC
P.O. Box 3003, Seattle, WA 98114

Price list, free, published semiannually, 5 pages with order blank.

A good source for Japanese and Chinese teas. Some of the Japanese teas listed are bancha ($2.35 a 12-oz. package), genmai cha, green tea ($2.49 a 12-oz. package), mugi cha, shin cha, and kokuryu, which probably mean something to a Japanese tea fancier, though they don't to us. In Chinese, there's green, oolong, jasmine, and black tea, plus a Chinese restaurant blend (16 tea bags, 2 packages for 85¢). Some are in tea bags, some loose. Loose green tea is 98¢ for 100 grams (about 3 oz.). Uwajimaya also has tea kettles ($5.50 to $9.95 for different sizes), teapots from $4.25, teacups at 40¢ apiece, and tea sets from $9.75.

VANDER VLIET'S HOLLAND IMPORTS / Dept. CFC
3147 West 111th Street, Chicago, IL 60655

Catalogue, free, published annually, 34 pages, black and white.

Among the imported foods in this catalogue are the Twinings of London teas, in tins or tea bags, among them Ceylon Breakfast and China black ($2.85 for an 8-oz. tin), Queen Mary, Russian Caravan, and Lapsang souchong ($3.35 for an 8-oz. tin). Some of the teas are not available in tea bags, but you can get a gold, silver, or green tea bag sampler (60 assorted tea bags) for $2.75 and Twinings herbal teas in packages of 25 tea bags for $1.50. They also list Van Nelle Golden Cup tea (20 bags, 69¢), Hamstra tea bags, and various coffees, among them a 1-lb. bag of Mocha-Java beans for $2.19, Moccona freeze-dried and instant coffees, and decaffeinated instant.

THE VERMONT COUNTRY STORE / Dept. CFC
Weston, VT 05161

Catalogue, 25¢, published annually, 98 pages, illustrated, black and white.

The Vermont Country Store sells unblended coffees—Java, Santos, Colombia, Guatemala Antigua—in beans or ground to your specification, decaffeinated coffee, French or Italian roast for demitasse, and their own rich blend of 4 different coffees ($2.95 a lb.). They also have the Moulinex coffee mill and the Tricolator coffee maker. In teas, you'll find various China teas, including the rare China Pouchong, an extra-choice green tea ($2.95 a ½ lb.), a basket-fired green tea from Japan, Darjeeling, and something a bit different, a Vermont Country Mix of green and black China tea that was popular 50 years ago in rural Vermont and has been revived by the Vermont Country Store ($3.25 a ½-lb. tin). They stock good-looking tea strainers and tea infusers, a shell-shaped silverplate reproduction of the 18th-century scoop used with a tea caddy (a nifty little gift at $6), the Rockingham brown glazed English teapot in 3-, 5-, and 7-cup sizes ($6.50 to $7.50), and another good gift for tea-loving friends, an insulated calico tea cozy ($6.50).

MARK T. WENDELL, IMPORTER / Dept. CFC
51 Melcher Street, Boston, MA 02210

Information booklet and price list, free, published seasonally, line drawings.

Since 1904 Mr. Wendell has supplied his customers with his exclusive Hu-Kwa tea, a fine smoky Lapsang souchong, named after a 19th-century hong (warehouse) merchant in Canton. This rare tea is grown only in the province of Foo Kien, China, and sells for $5.50 per lb. or $6.75 in the original lithographed tin caddy. Mr. Wendell, a famous tea connoisseur, offers a variety of other fine teas, including Keemun, the Burgundy of teas ($4.75 per lb.), China Ping Suey, a mild black tea ($5.50 per lb.), and Japanese Green, a pale, flavorful, unfermented tea ($4.75 per lb.). A sampler gift set at $5.50 contains 3½ oz. of Hu-Kwa, 4 oz. of Earl Grey, and 3½ oz. of China Yunnan.

Rare Hu-Kwa tea imported by Mark T. Wendell

WHITE FLOWER FARM / Dept. CFC
Litchfield, CT 06759

"The Garden Book," published spring and fall, plus 3 issues of garden notes, $4 a year (or free to customers whose orders total $15 or more), 68 pages, illustrated, black and white.

Although White Flower Farm is mainly in the business of raising plants, they also sell whole, fresh-roasted Mocha-Java coffee beans (shipped only on Mondays, after roasting, to insure freshness). The blend of beans costs $5.50 a lb., $15 for a 4-lb. package, postpaid, although prices may have gone up by now.

WHITTARD & CO. LTD. / Dept. CFC
111 Fulham Road, London SW3 6RP, England

Price list, free.

Whittard has been in business in London since 1886, selling tea and coffee to people around the globe.
   They have 5 varieties each of Ceylon teas, Indian Darjeeling, Assam choice, and Indian fannings.
   China teas are Lapsang, Keemun, Chingwo, jasmine, and Black Dragon Formosa oolong.
   Whittard sells many coffees, including Santos, Mocha, Java, and Mysore, and they will blend to specifications. In the coffee sundries category, you'll find pure ground chicory, ground roasted figs, sugar crystals, pure cane sugar, and several mints and chocolate cremes to be enjoyed with after-dinner coffee. All prices are quoted in sterling and are subject to constant market change.

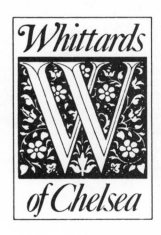

Whittards of Chelsea

THE WHOLE HERB COMPANY / Dept. CFC
P.O. Box 686, Mill Valley, CA 94941

"Star Herbs," free, published annually, 28 pages.

A wide selection of premium teas are offered here, as well as blends of herbal tea mixed from "a multitude of botanicals to create a special brew." The full-bodied black teas (Assam, Ourdale, Darjeeling) offer the largest variety of tastes, while the green teas (gunpowder, Young Hyson) are lighter and more subtle. The semifermented teas, such as oolong, are between black and green in color and flavor.
   Among their herb- and spice-blended teas are Bright Eye Tea composed of gotu kola, ginseng, damiana, eucalyptus, peppermint, spearmint, cardamom seed, eyebright, and comfrey; the Lighthouse blend of spearmint, anise seeds, yerba santa, rose hips, kava kava, and sarsaparilla; and a Fasting Tea of alfalfa leaf, raspberry leaf, nettle, sage, yarrow, and yerba maté.
   The Whole Herb Company also furnishes herbs, spices, essential oils, ginseng products, health-care items, vitamins, incense, and an interesting book list for further reading.

Café Granité
Make a syrup with 1½ cups sugar and 2 cups water. Bring it to a boil and continue boiling for 3 minutes. Combine the syrup with 6 cups freshly made, very strong dark-roast coffee. Cool. Turn the mixture into refrigerator trays, filling them about ⅔ full and freeze. Stir several times as the mixture freezes around the edges and becomes mushy. Then freeze until set. To serve, scrape the granité into chilled parfait glasses with a heavy metal spoon. It should be flaky. Serve, if you wish, with heavy cream, or whipped cream.

Venetian Coffee
Combine equal parts of hot strong coffee and hot chocolate. Pour into cups and top with lightly whipped cream. Sprinkle grated orange zest and shaved chocolate on top.

YANKEE TEA TRADER / Dept. CFC
P.O. Box 747, Escondido, CA 92025

Product price list, free, 2 pages.

Yankee Tea Trader sells regular and herbal teas, herbs, and spices. Their teas from India, Ceylon, Japan, Taiwan, and mainland China include Keemun, jasmine, gunpowder, Young Hyson, Fine Oolong (Taiwan), Darjeeling and Assam (India), Gyokura (Japan), Uva Highland (Ceylon), Pingsuey and Yunnan (mainland China). Then there are the blends, such as orange spice, Russian, English, Irish and Oriental blends, Queen Victoria and Earl Grey, fruit-flavored teas (Summer Apricot, Fresh Peach, European Black Currant, Valencia Orange Blossom, Caribbean Lime), and a variety of herbal teas and blends. As overseas prices change constantly, the price list is revised every month.

YOUNG & SAUNDERS LTD. / Dept. CFC
5 Queensferry Street, Edinburgh EH2 4PD, Scotland

"Food & Wine List," free, published seasonally, 42 pages, black and white.

Specially selected coffees and teas are part of the Young & Saunders food list. They have a matured old Java coffee, a Mountain Blend, Shandwick Blend (high-grade African, South American, and New Guinea coffees, medium roast), Ferry Blend (Kenya and Costa Rica, medium roast), and straights such as Kenya and Mysore, among others. These are sold by the pound at prices ranging (according to the current rate of exchange) from around $2 to around $3. Young & Saunders' single, garden, and blended teas include Ceylon, Darjeeling, Assam "Creamy Cup," Earl Grey, China Blend (Keemun, Ichang, Panyong, Lapsang, and Formosa oolong), Lapsang souchong, jasmine, Keemun, and green from mainland China. Prices per lb., again at current rate of exchange, range from around $1 to over $2. There are also prepacked coffees in tins, such as the Savoy Hotel blend, prepacked teas and tea bags. Prices, quoted in sterling, are subject to change and the fluctuating exchange rate and do not include overseas shipping charges.

ZABAR'S / Dept. CFC
2245 Broadway, New York, NY 10024

Price list, free, published periodically.

You can buy Jamaican Blue Mountain coffee at Zabar's, on the upper West Side of Manhattan, and if you wonder why it costs somewhere in the neighborhood of $5 per lb., *New York* magazine said: "Try a half-pound of this acidy, full-bodied coffee with its superb, savory flavor . . . ." There are other coffees at Zabar's (roasted on the premises), such as High Mountain Supreme, also from Jamaica, a Colombian blend, a Costa Rican blend, and Zabar's own blend. Two mild coffees are giant bean Maragogipe Guatemalan and Hawaiian Kona, and among the full-bodied are Kenya AA, Kenya Peaberry, and a Mocha-style blend. There is also a Mocha-Java blend, a decaffeinated blend, Viennese and French-Italian roasts, and a decaffeinated espresso. Zabar's will ship anywhere, but the order must be for at least 5 lbs.

See Appendix, page 239, for additional sources not included here.

CHAPTER TWO

CHEESE
AND BREAD

A feast of French cheese, wine, and fruit. Courtesy Food & Wines from France, Inc.

ARGONAUT VENTURES, INC. / Dept. CFC
P.O. Box 40218, San Francisco, CA 94140

"Fun Cooking & Things with Sourdough Jack," price list, free, published annually, 5 pages, illustrated, black and white.

For over a quarter century San Francisco's Sourdough Jack Mabee has been filling kitchens across the country with the heady fragrance of sourdough. His original one-page recipe folder has grown into a 112-page cook book with hundreds of recipes for sourdough bread, biscuits, pancakes, waffles, and cakes and a complete 12-page section of sprout growing ($3.80 postpaid), complete with sourdough starter stapled to the inside cover, or you can buy the starter set separately for $1.75 ppd.

The Gift Pack includes everything needed to get going: Sourdough Jack's new cook book, a ½-oz. package of authentic sourdough starter, and a fermenting storage pot, $7.50 ppd. "Ed's Grass Patch" sourdough bread recipe, so named because of the thick matting of sprouts that covers the crust after baking, can be produced with the help of the Sprouting Kit, $2.50, with choice of sprout seeds (alfalfa, mung, lentil, fenugreek, peas, wheat).

BACHMAN GIFTS / Dept. CFC
Box 898, Reading, PA 19603

"Bachman Gifts and Goodies from the Historic Land of the Pennsylvania Dutch," free, published annually, 32 pages, illustrated, color.

Pretzels galore from Bachman's, in all shapes and sizes. The Pretzel Bakery Assortment ($8.60 delivered) has cheese stix, plain stix, bite-size pretzels, Dutch-style pretzels, thin twisted pretzels, and the new petite pretzels. The Harvest Haus tin has 3 varieties: thin, Dutch, and pretzel logs. There are all kinds of other gift packs, some combined with popcorn, or Lebanon bologna and cheese spread, or bologna and smoked cheese. Or you can have any of the pretzels alone. One of the more

*

To make breadcrumbs, trim the crusts from slices of day-old bread. Break up, put in the blender or food processor, and reduce to crumbs (they may also be put through a meat grinder or a Mouli cheese grater). If not used immediately, store in the refrigerator in a plastic bag or screw-topped jar, but use before they stale. For dry crumbs, dry out in the oven at low heat. For buttered crumbs, melt butter in a skillet, add crumbs, and stir with a wooden spoon until well coated.

*

A note on breadcrumbs. They never grow stale because they're soon used up. All dried bread is to be saved. Break up, put in blender. Always available and certainly economical.
—from "Cooking with Herbs at Longpond Farm"

*

Cheese Fondue

Shred 1 pound Swiss Emmenthal, Gruyère, or a mixture of the two. Dredge cheese with 2 tablespoons flour or potato starch. Rub a cut clove of garlic around the inside of a *caquelon* (the traditional earthenware pot used in Switzerland) or a similar glazed earthenware casserole or enameled cast-iron casserole. A heavy chafing dish may also be used. Set the pan over low heat on top of the stove (or the chafing dish over a medium flame), add 2 cups dry white wine (Neuchâtel, Chablis, Riesling, California Chardonnay or Fumé Blanc) and heat until bubbles start rising to the surface. Add the cheese gradually, stirring constantly with a wooden spoon until melted. Season with a little salt, freshly ground black pepper, a few gratings of nutmeg, and 4 to 6 tablespoons kirsch or cognac. Transfer pot to a warmer at the table and keep fondue hot, but below the simmering point (or keep warm in the chafing dish over a low flame). If it gets too thick, thin out with a little more heated wine, a tablespoon at a time.

Serve with bite-size pieces of French bread with the crust on. The pieces of bread are speared on long handled fondue forks or ordinary forks, dipped into the fondue, twirled around and then removed and eaten. The knack is to keep them from dropping into the pot. With this, drink the white wine used for the fondue. Serves 6 to 8.

GIFTS OF GOOD TASTE

attractive packagings is the denim set, a trio of denim-patterned ice bucket, picnic hamper, and cooler, each with a different offering. The ice bucket is filled with large pretzel sticks ($9 delivered), the hamper with bite-size pretzels, logs, petites, plain and cheese stix ($13.50 delivered), and the cooler with cheese corn, corn chips, Taco chips, popcorn, and cheese twists ($16.80 delivered), or you can order the 3 for $35.

B&B FOOD PRODUCTS / Dept. CFC
 Route #1B, Cadiz, KY 42211

"Your Gift Catalog," free, published annually, 16 pages, illustrated, black and white.

Broadbents (B&B Food Products) sell cheese as well as ham. There is Wisconsin natural aged sharp cheddar, around $7 for a 2½-lb. wheel; an Executive Cheese Pack of four 1-lb. blocks of aged Wisconsin cheddar, Colby, mild brick, and Swiss; plus 1½ lbs. of summer sausage (around $15, available only November through April); and packs of such things as their own country hambit cheese (a blend of American and Swiss cheeses with bits of B&B country ham) in a glazed crock with or without summer sausage, or a crock of aged cheddar spread. Cheese is also included in some of their other gift packs. Country mixes are another offering. There's a 1-lb. bag each of Southern-style spoonbread mix, pancake mix, biscuit mix, and whole-wheat pancake mix (around $5). Or you can choose a gift pack of 2 lbs. country bacon, 2 lbs. pancake mix, and two "little brown jugs" of Kentucky honey and sorghum molasses for around $20. A family sample pack teams a 1-lb. bag of spoonbread mix and a 1-lb. bag of biscuit mix with 2 lbs. smoked bacon, 14 oz. summer sausage, a crock of hambit cheese, and half an uncooked Kentucky country ham (about 6 lbs.) for around $30.

BETTER FOODS FOUNDATION, INC. / Dept. CFC
 300 North Washington Street, Greencastle, PA 17225

Brochure, free, 8 pages.

Breads freshly baked on Monday, Tuesday, and Wednesday and made with whole grains, raw milk, raw sugar, soya, unsulphured molasses, and similar natural ingredients are one of the specialties. A pound loaf of crunched wheat and soya, whole-grain rye, whole-grain wheat, or unbleached white and soya is around 55¢. "Land and sea" protein bread is 75¢. Banana bread or date and nut loaf are 69¢, sticky buns 55¢.

Raw-milk cheeses from Illinois and New York include mild or sharp cheddars ($1.95 a lb.), Longhorn ($1.90 a lb.), and there's imported Swiss at around $1.90. The cost is slightly less for 2 lbs. or 5 lbs. Prices do not include postage.

BLACK DIAMOND CHEESE / Dept. CFC
 P.O. Box #1, Belleville, Ontario, Canada

"Gifts of Good Taste," free, published annually, 12 pages, illustrated, color.

Canadian Black Diamond cheddar is famous, and rightly so. You can order the cheddar and various other cheeses, such as Dutch Gouda, Colby, and Danish Havarti, in their various selections and gift packages. Black Diamond extra-old cheddar is available in sizes ranging from 2½ lbs. to 10 lbs. (the 10-lb. size has the traditional black wax coating) and prices from $7.50 to $25 delivered. The International Selection consists of 15 lbs. of cheese (Dutch Gouda, Danish Havarti, and extra-old cheddar) with a 10" x 14" hardwood slicing board ($35), while the Family Cheese gift combines 5-lb. blocks of mild, medium, and extra-old cheddar ($34). Gift packages consist of cheeses with onion soup bowls, cheese boards, a wine rack, ice bucket, nut bowl, or canister set.

BREMEN HOUSE INC. / Dept. CFC
218 East 86th Street, New York, NY 10028

"Bremen House Catalog of Gourmet Foods," free, published twice a year, 20 pages, illustrated, black and white.

This catalogue lists a few German cheeses, such as hand cheese, Limburger ($1.45 for 8 oz.), kochkaese (cooked cheese), and kraeuterkaese (herbed cheese), plus baby Gouda and French Brie and Camembert ($1.98 for 8 oz.). Imported dark breads include packaged pumpernickel, rye, and dark rye, around $1 for 8 oz.

CABOT FARMERS' COOPERATIVE CREAMERY CO., INC.
Dept. CFC
Cabot, VT 05647

Brochure and price list, free, published annually or as prices change.

The Cabot Farmers' Cooperative Creamery was formed in 1919 and is now the largest butter and cheese plant in New England, doing business under the name of Rosedale Brand. Their natural, raw-milk aged Vermont cheddar is sold by mail, but no price list or order form was included with the brochure they sent us, so you will have to request details.

CALIFORNIA SEASONS, INC. / Dept. CFC
P.O. Box 1350, 379 Cannery Row, Monterey, CA 93940

"California Seasons Gift Catalog," free, published annually, 15 pages, illustrated, color.

John Steinbeck made Cannery Row famous, but now California Seasons is the big cheese there. And it is cheese they sell in gift boxes combined with other California-originated products.
California's own Monterey Jack comes in 3-lb. wheels ($8.75) or in half-wheels with sardines ($4.95), San Francisco Italian salami ($7.45), date walnut cake ($8.75), with a "chub" of salami and two jars of artichoke hearts ($9.95), with almonds, mushrooms, candy slices, artichoke hearts ($9.85), and other combinations of those items ($11.75 to $24.50).

CARAVANSARY / Dept. CFC
2263 Chestnut Street, San Francisco, CA 94123

"Gourmet Gift Ideas from the Caravansary," free, published winter/spring, 14 pages, illustrated, black and white.

Caravansary's Gourmet Corner shows some of the gift baskets they make up at their two stores. From the cheese department you can order a natural-wood dairy bucket filled with cheeses—Danish blue, kasseri, Brie, and Reblochon—plus *The Cheese Book* by Vivienne Marquis and Patricia Haskell, cheese posters and pamphlets, all for $21, shipping extra.

CASA MONEO / Dept. CFC
210 West 14th Street, New York, NY 10011

"Mexican Food–Comida Mexicana," free, 8 pages, published annually, also price lists of South American, Cuban, and Portuguese foods.

Casa Moneo has Mexican cheese of two kinds: queso anejo (like a Mexican Jack) for $1.35 a lb. and queso blanco (white cheese) at $1.40 a lb., plus an Argentine cheese, type not specified. In breads they have, naturally, tortillas, either canned (71¢–80¢ for 18, according to brand, $1.45 for 30) or the frozen wheat tortillas used for burritos, $1.35 a dozen. A 5-oz. package of tostadas is 68¢. Also crackers and plain or flavored bread sticks from Cuba.

*

Combine breadcrumbs and grated Parmesan cheese as a topping for casseroles, stuffed vegetables.

*

A perfect team–Monterey Jack and San Francisco salami, from California Seasons

A wheel of Monterey Jack, from the Cheese Coffee Center

*

To make large croutons, slice day-old French bread about ¼-inch thick and rub on both sides with a split garlic clove. Brush each side well with olive oil, put on a baking sheet, and bake in a 400° oven until golden brown, turning once.

For small croutons, slice bread ½-inch thick, rub with garlic, brush with oil, then cut into ½-inch dice and bake in the oven until golden brown.

*

CHEESE COFFEE CENTER / Dept. CFC
2110 Center Street, Berkeley, CA 94704

Mail-order catalogue, free, published semiannually, 12 pages, black and white.

The Cheese Coffee Center has an impressive list of imported and domestic cheeses. You'll find here, in addition to all the familiar favorites, Armenian string cheese ($2.19 a lb.), strong Pyrénèes Chiberta and Morbier le Nozeroy, and the mild Tomme, Swiss raclette, and the marvelous French l'Explorateur ($2.99 a ½ lb.). There is a good selection of cheddars, including Oregon raw-milk cheddar and Tillamook, the California Rouge et Noir breakfast cheese, Brie and Camembert, different types of Monterey Jack, including a dry Jack and a hot pepper Jack, and cheese balls of varied flavors (garlic and herb, port wine, curried, and smoked oyster, or cream cheese with orange, peach, or chives). An interesting and comprehensive selection.

CHEESELOVERS INTERNATIONAL / Dept. CFC
Cheeselovers International Building, Freeport, NY 11520

"Overseas Arrivals Options List," free with $6 club membership, 6 pages, published monthly, illustrated, color.

This cheese club sends you $6 worth of imported cheeses free when you join, the $6 being the one-time registration fee, after which you receive a monthly flyer, illustrated in color, of the dozen or so cheese choices of the month, which you can order directly. In the flyer we have the cheese are various types, such as English Cheshire, Leicester, Double Gloucester, French Camembert and Port Salut, Danish Blue Castello, Norwegian Jarlsberg, Dutch cumin cheese, and some described as club exclusives. Although the membership literature stresses the savings you get by buying direct by mail for, they claim, as low as 3¢ to 7¢ above wholesale (and lists some rather unrealistic retail prices to bear this out), we can't see that they offer much more than convenience, some free gifts and booklets, and other fringe benefits. Although the cheeses pictured are in wheels, what you actually buy is a piece mostly weighing from 4 to 10 oz., and at current cheese prices the $2.49 for 6 oz. of Port Salut or $3.49 for 4 oz. of Blue Castello in the flyer we have is hardly a bargain. If you are mainly interested in buying cheese, compare prices with your local cheese store or with one of the other companies we list in this section.

THE CHEESE 'N' MORE STORE / Dept. CFC
Route 5, Merrill, WI 54452

Brochure, free, published annually, 1 page.

Cheese 'N' More is in the heart of America's cheeseland, but they don't limit themselves to American cheeses such as Colby (originally made in neighboring Colby, Wisconsin) or Brick (another Wisconsin favorite). They also have Jarlsberg from Norway; Rondele, the triple-crème spiced cheese from France; baby Swiss; and Gouda from Holland.

There are domestic versions of Port Salut and provolone and flavored types such as salami cheese and port-wine cheese.

No prices are listed in the brochure. For more information, write them directly. Or visit the store, which resembles a 50-foot cheddar with a wedge cut out for the entrance.

CHEESE OF ALL NATIONS / Dept. CFC
153 Chambers Street, New York, NY 10007

"Cheese of All Nations," $1, published periodically, 68 pages, illustrated, black and white.

Phil Alpert's cheese emporium, long a fixture in Manhattan, has a mind-boggling assortment of over 1,000 imported and domestic cheeses, ranging from Toureg from Africa, made by the Berber tribes, to 10 cheeses from Yugoslavia, most of them made from sheep's milk.

France, of course, has the biggest listing, 386 cheeses, with all the old favorites, including 5 different Bries, a good selection of chèvres (goat's-milk cheeses), among them a triple-crème chèvre, and many that are less familiar, such as Oustet from the Pyrenees and Pithiviers au Foin (ripened on fresh hay). There are cheeses from Albania, Armenia, Argentina, the Azores, Cyprus, Greece (including feta, kasseri, and kafalotyri), Iraq, Israel, Lebanon, Luxembourg, Mexico, Rumania, Turkey, Syria, and Venezuela and, of course, all the better-known cheese-producing countries. You can buy the Swiss raclette bagne, the melting cheese served scraped onto boiled potatoes, and the special raclette stove, in case you want to give a raclette party in your ski lodge. In American cheese you will find the soft creamy Teleme, the Rouge et Noir Camembert, and an aged Monterey Jack, sharp and zesty. For dieters, there's a special page of low-fat, low-salt, and part-skim-milk cheeses and spreads. There are also cheese gift packs and a Cheese-of-the-Month Club (3 months, $16; 1 year, $50). Due to market conditions, prices are subject to change (they were not given in this catalogue, but you can request a price list) and shipping and handling are extra (starting at $1.20 for 2 lbs.). There's a minimum order of 1 lb. or more of each cut cheese and $2 for each shipment, but you'll probably go well over the minimum if you are a real cheese lover.

CONTE DI SAVOIA / Dept. CFC
555 W. Roosevelt Road, Chicago, IL 60607

Catalogue, 75¢ (refundable with purchase), published annually, 28 pages.

Conte di Savoia has a good list of cheeses, with emphasis, as you might expect, on the Italian. They have the grating cheeses like Parmigiano ($2.99 a lb. for imported), Pecorino Romano, Sardo, and an aged ricotta Siciliano ($1.69 a lb.); Provolone and the creamy, blue-veined Gorgonzola ($1.89 a lb. imported, $1.39 domestic); cacciovallo, the peppery pepato, sharp incannestrata, a creamy ricotta Romano, a fresh domestic ricotta, and imported mozzarella (89¢ a lb.). There's Brie, Camembert, and Roquefort from France; Swiss Emmenthal; Dutch Edam; and some of the popular soft spreading cheeses like Boursin and Gourmandise.

CROWLEY CHEESE / Dept. CFC
Healdville, VT 05147

"Crowley Cheese," free, published annually, 5 pages, illustrated, black and white.

Crowley Cheese is Yankee "store cheese" made by hand in central Vermont's oldest cheese factory, established in 1825. For this cheese, a type of cheddar like Wisconsin Colby, the curds are broken to avoid matting together when packed into the steel hoops to make wheels. It comes, like other cheddars, mild, medium, and sharp and is sold in 3- and 5-lb. wheels ($8.50 and $12.75). Prices are higher the farther you are from Crowley's immediate shipping area. Visitors are welcome to tour the factory, where they can purchase other New England specialties not available by mail, such as maple syrup, honey, and homemade jams and jellies.

CUBA CHEESE & TRADING CO., INC. / Dept. CFC
P.O. Box 47, Cuba, NY 14727

Gift brochure, free, published periodically, 1 page, illustrated, color.

Cuba, New York, is nestled in the Enchanted Mountains region of New York State near the Pennsylvania border, and the Cuba Cheese Company has eight gift packs with New York State cheddar cheese ($4.30 to $10.75; higher west of the Mississippi River).

There's New York State cheddar (mild, medium, or sharp) in 2½-lb. loaves or 5-lb. blocks, old York cheddar spread (aged 9 months) in 22-oz. crocks, and a variety pack of sage, cheddar, caraway, and Colby in 10-oz. sticks.

Caesar Salad
Lightly brown 2 cups ½-inch cubes of white bread in olive oil with 1 clove garlic; be careful they do not burn. Remove to paper towels to drain. Rub a large pottery or glass salad bowl with 1 cut clove garlic. Break 2 heads of washed, chilled, and crisped romaine into pieces with your fingers and put in the bowl. Pour ½ cup olive oil over the romaine and toss until leaves are well coated. Break 1 coddled egg (cooked in the shell for 1 minute in boiling water) over the salad and toss again until leaves are well coated with the egg, then add 2 tablespoons lemon juice or wine vinegar, ½ teaspoon salt, ½ teaspoon freshly ground black pepper, 12 anchovy fillets, cut in small pieces and drained of oil on paper towels, the croutons, and ½ cup grated Parmesan cheese. Toss lightly together (the croutons must stay crisp, not become soggy) and taste for seasoning. Serve at once. Serves 6 as a salad course before the meat, California style, or 4 as a main luncheon course.

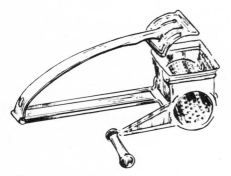

Mouli cheese grater

---

*

Thinly slice English muffins as if for Melba toast. Toast the slices, then brush with melted butter and put in a 300° oven until crisp. One side may be sprinkled with grated Parmesan cheese before they are put in the oven. Good with soups, salads, or with scrambled eggs and brunch dishes.

*

Cheese can be stored in the freezer. The cheese should be tightly wrapped in moistureproof wrap and thawed out slowly in the refrigerator before use to avoid becoming crumbly and mottled in color.
—*from "Cheese of All Nations Catalogue"*

*

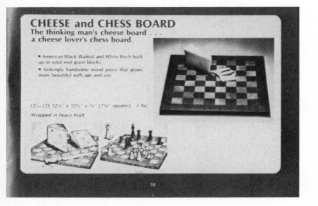

Handsome cheese boards from the J. K. Adams Company

DEER VALLEY FARM / Dept. CFC
RD 1, Guilford, NY 13780

Price list, free, published annually, 20 pages, black and white.

The folks at Deer Family Farm make in their bakery and sell by mail a selection of 100 percent organically grown whole-grain breads—whole-wheat, rye, raisin, Cornell Formula, 3-Grain (wheat, rye, and oats), French, Italian, and whole-wheat hamburger and frankfurter buns among them. The flour, raw milk, and eggs used in the bakery products come from the farm, and the breads are sweetened only with honey, maple syrup, or unsulphured molasses. Prices run about 73¢ for a loaf of whole-wheat bread, 12¢ for a hamburger bun or roll, 89¢ for a loaf of whole-grain raisin bread. They also make quick breads (whole-wheat banana bread, brown bread, and date-nut bread), bran muffins (6 for 60¢), maple nut buns (15¢ each), fruit-filled Danish buns, and fruit-filled tea ring. Cornell Formula pizza with tomatoes and cheese and old-fashioned sourdough starter in an earthenware jar ($2.90) are on the list, too.

Their whole-milk cheeses come from New York and Wisconsin. Washed-curd cheddar (which contains less salt) is $1.95 a lb., Wisconsin Muenster $1.82, Wisconsin Swiss $2.35, and Wisconsin raw-milk cheddar, with or without caraway seeds, is $1.95. Swiss cheese from Switzerland is $2.43 a lb.

DEPT. OF FOOD SCIENCE AND TECHNOLOGY / Dept. CFC
East Campus, University of Nebraska-Lincoln,
Lincoln, NB 68583

Price list and order form, free, published annually.

In case you are wondering what a university is doing in the mail-order business, be advised that the Department of Food Science and Technology sells to the public a limited amount of cheese made in the department's food pilot plant in connection with the teaching and research programs. There are usually several varieties available, including mild and sharp cheddar, smoke-flavored cheddar, caraway cheddar, New York cheddar (a washed-curd cheddar with a sharp flavor), Colby (similar to cheddar but softer, with more openings and a mild flavor), Husker (an uncolored cheese, similar to Colby, developed at the university many years ago), Iowa-style Edam and Swiss (so described because the process was developed at Iowa State University), made in loaves. Cheeses are sold in pieces or packed in gift boxes. There's also a blue cheese made by the Treasure Cave Company of Faribault, Minnesota, sold by the half lb. or in wheels of eight ½-lb. pieces or solid wheels of 5 to 6 lbs. Prices for gift boxes range from $4.70 for a 1-lb. box to $11.85 for a 6-lb. box of different cheeses. Pieces of cheese vary in price according to the type and how much is ordered.

D.M. ENTERPRISES / Dept. CFC
P.O. Box 2452, San Francisco, CA 94126

"Calico Kitchen's Portfolio," free, published two to three times a year, 12 sheets, illustrated.

If you have been yearning for real San Francisco sourdough bread, pine no longer. You can give yourself (or a friend) a subscription of 2 round or long loaves every month for a year, to be delivered on the date you specify, for $38 in the West, where shipments are by UPS, $61 by airmail to the central states, or $50 by UPS/air to the East. Or you can be more modest and order just 2, 4, 6, or 12 loaves to be shipped at one time. There are gift packages that include the bread. North Beach Picnic has 2 round loaves, a 1-lb. wheel of Monterey Jack cheese, a 1-lb. stick of Italian dry salami, a hardwood bread board and bread knife, tucked in a French string bag, for $18 West, $21 East. Or you can have the loaves, bread board, and packaged Golden Gate Seasoning for $5.50 ($7 in the East). Other possible gift combinations are: 2 loaves of bread, a wheel of Jack cheese and 1 lb. of salami; 2 loaves of bread plus bread board and knife; no bread, just 1 lb. each of Jack cheese and salami; 2 loaves of bread, 1 lb. Jack cheese, and bread board with the French string bag. For bread and cheese lovers, this would make a welcome and offbeat gift.

EARLY'S HONEY STAND / Dept. CFC
Rural Route 2, Spring Hill, TN 37174

"Old Fashioned Foods and Gifts from the Tennessee Hill Country," free, published annually, 19 pages, illustrated, color and black and white.

Cheddar doesn't come only from Vermont, New York, and Wisconsin. Early's has theirs made by a cheese maker right there in Tennessee, and it is aged from 8 to 12 months, which gives it a good sharp flavor. Nor does it come in dinky little wedges. You buy a wax-protected block that runs 5 lbs. or more ($11.50 to $12.20 ppd., according to zone). If you're in the market for stone-ground corn meal for your corn bread or hoe cakes, Early's has that, too ($2.95 to $3.70 a 5-lb. bag), and they also sell real corn grits, buttermilk biscuit mix, griddle-cake mix, and white stone-ground, self-rising cornmeal, all in 2-lb. bags at $2.45 to $2.85 a bag, according to zone.

FIGI'S INC. / Dept. CFC
Central Plaza, Marshfield, WI 54449

"Figi's Gifts in Good Taste," free, published annually, 64 pages, illustrated, color.

The cheeses featured by Figi in gift hampers and boxes are the Wisconsin versions of cheddar, Edam, Colby, brick, Jack, and so on, and they are available in all kinds of packs and combinations, with or without other foods. You can also order bulk cheese cuts of 14 different varieties, such as medium or sharp cheddar, Longhorn, Port Salut, Bleu, Swiss, Provolone in amounts of between 1 and 1¾ lbs., or small wooden crates containing 6-oz. or 3-lb. wheels of cheese. Cheeses from other countries such as Switzerland, Holland, Norway, Sweden, France, Belgium, Denmark, and Austria can be ordered from a separate folder called "Adventures in Cheese." These tend to be of the bland type such as Swedish Fontina, Swiss Belsano, Dutch Gouda, and French Doux de Pyrénées. Prices for these cheeses range from $3.50 for a small Gouda or a wedge of Jarlsberg to around $23 for a wheel of Doux de Pyrénées.

FORTNUM & MASON / Dept. CFC
181 Piccadilly, London W1A 1ER, England

"Fortnum & Mason Export Food," free, published seasonally, 15 pages, illustrated, color.

From Queen Elizabeth's official grocer and provision merchant comes a fine array of English cheeses—Cheddar, Stilton, Cheshire, Double Gloucester, Caerphilly, Wensleydale among them. A handsome teak tub containing half a Stilton cheese ($42.80), a quad pack of earthenware jars filled with assorted cheeses ($15.02), and a decorated covered casserole of Stilton ($15.02) are a few of the tempting offerings.

R.W. FORSYTH LTD. / Dept. CFC
30 Princes Street, Edinburgh EH2 2BZ, Scotland

"The days of Christmas at Forsyth's," free, published annually, 16 pages, black and white.

Although Forsyth's carries over 60 varieties of home-produced and imported cheese, Stilton is the one featured in their Christmas catalogue. Stilton is sold by the pound, with port wine in jars, in white earthenware jars with a black polished lid, or in Tuxford and Tebbutt pottery jars in assorted colors.

Croque Monsieur
For each sandwich, butter one side of a slice of bread. Arrange on it a thin slice of country ham, cut to fit; top with a thin slice of Gruyère or Emmenthal cheese, also cut to fit. Top with another buttered slice of bread and press firmly together. Brush outside of the slices with melted butter and trim off the crusts. Heat a heavy iron skillet and brush lightly with clarified butter, add the sandwich, and sauté gently on each side, turning once or twice, until nicely browned, about 3 minutes a side. Press down with a spatula as it cooks and add a little more melted butter if necessary. Serve hot.

Doux de Pyrénées cheese, from Figi's Inc.

Camembert aux Noix
Cream ¼ cup softened butter until light and fluffy. Blend in ¼ cup ground pecans, 2 tablespoons lemon juice, and a few drops of Tabasco. Cut an 8-oz. wheel of Camembert or Brie in half horizontally while still firm. Spread with the butter mixture. Chill until the filling is firm. Slice in thin wedges ½ hour before serving. Serve on toast points. Makes about 16 wedges.
—from "The Wonderful World of French Cheeses"

*

Always serve cheese at room temperature. Remove from refrigerator 1 hour before using. This is especially important for soft-ripening cheeses, such as Brie and Camembert.

*

On the Plaza in historic Sonoma

Home of

SONOMA JACK

Open Daily 9:00-6:00   Phone 996-2300
2 SPAIN STREET, SONOMA, CA. 95476

FRASER-MORRIS / Dept. CFC
872 Madison Avenue, New York, NY 10021

"Gifts for Festive Occasions from Fraser-Morris," free, published seasonally, 11 pages, illustrated, color.

Among the fresh cheeses that can be mail-ordered from Fraser-Morris are Ile de France Brie ($11.50 a kilo, just over 2 lbs.), Italian Bel Paese (approximately 5 lbs., $4.98 a lb.), French Port Salut and Beaumont, and Canadian Black Diamond Cheddar ($13.25 a 2½-lb. wheel). There's also the soft creamy French Gourmandise, either kirsch or walnut-flavored (approximately 4 lbs. 3 oz., $3.98 a lb.), and Dutch Edam. Among the processed types, there's a gift box of Swiss cheeses, the kind that come in foil-wrapped wedges, 16 to a box ($7.25), and two gift-box selections with things like Swiss Gruyère, Danish cheese spreads, and smoked cheese sticks from Austria. There's also a cheese-and-cracker snack pack with cheeses from France, Italy, Germany, and Switzerland, plus a box of Carr's English crackers.

GALAXY PRODUCTS, INC. / Dept. CFC
P.O. Box 215, Sonoma, CA 95476

"Sonoma Cheese Factory Gift Catalog," free, published annually, 16 pages, illustrated, color.

The Sonoma Cheese Factory is in the town of Sonoma, smack in the heart of the wine country, and they do a rousing business in their delicatessen selling cheese (they stock 101 different kinds), meats, breads, and the local wines to wine-imbibing visitors. Their specialty is Sonoma Jack, and their recipe for this mellow creamy cheese was brought from Italy by Celso Viviani, who founded the cheese factory in 1931. They make a caraway Jack, cheddar, and the delicious California cheese, Teleme (this is not available by mail). They will also ship dry salami, from the Bay Area's Columbus Salame Company, grapevines, jams, Mary Taylor's Mayacamas Foods dried soups and spice mixes, and some Sonoma-oriented books, including *Mangiamo*, written by Sylvia Sebastiani, wife of winery owner August Sebastiani. You can order their Sonoma Jack by the 11-lb. wheel ($17.95), 3-lb. wheel, or 2-lb. block ($3.95) and an 8-lb. wheel of dry Jack (for grating) for $19.95. There's a Jack sampler box of 1 lb. each caraway and Sonoma Jack and 1 lb. golden cheddar for $6.25 and an Adobe Petaluma gift box of those cheeses plus a ½ lb. salami. For slicing cheese they have a Swedish cheese slicer for $3.50. California residents can order gift boxes of cheese and Sonoma wines. Sonoma Jack, incidentally, is a cheese that keeps well under refrigeration.

THE GOURMET PANTRY / Dept. CFC
400 McGuinness Blvd., Brooklyn, NY 11222

"Pleasure Packed Gifts from the Gourmet Pantry," free, published annually, 72 pages, illustrated, color.

Most of the cheese gift selections are the foil-wrapped process type, but you can also find here a gaily wrapped 2-lb. Edam cheese ($7.50) and a 3- to 3¼-lb. wheel of aged sharp cheddar ($9.99). A handy little gadget is a grater with measuring-jar bottom into which you can grate cheese (or nuts and other foods) directly ($4.50).

GREAT VALLEY MILLS / Dept CFC
Quakertown, PA 18951

"Gift Suggestions from the Pennsylvania Dutch Country," free, published annually, 16 pages, illustrated, black and white.

Schmierkäse (cottage cheese) is something every good Pennsylvania Dutch child grows up knowing how to make, so it is natural that one of the items in Great Valley Mills' catalogue is a "Home Cottage Cheesery," a kit with a water-jacketed cheese vat, thermometer, instructions, and recipe booklets for making all types of cottage cheese ($11.95). Apart from this they have a small selection of cheeses such as cheddar, blue, Edam, Gouda, their own Pennsylvania Dutch cheese ($2.90 a lb.), a soft cheese suitable for snacks or toasted sandwiches, and a cheddar-cheese crock, plus various gift packages of, or including, cheese. Of these, the wheel or half wheel of upper New York State sharp cheddar would seem to be the most desirable (a 5½-lb. wheel is around $16). Pennsylvania Dutch pretzels ($7.25 for a 2-lb. tin) would go nicely with the cheese, with a drink or as a snack.

GREEN MOUNTAIN SUGAR HOUSE / Dept. CFC
RFD 1, Ludlow, VT 05149

"Sugar House and Gift House Products," free, published annually, 8 pages, illustrated, black and white.

Green Mountain Sugar House is noted for its maple-syrup products, but they also sell Vermont cheddar cheese made from whole natural milk with no added ingredients, aged for nearly a year.

They have a 5-lb. wheel (made by the Seward family in East Wallingford) at $11.80 and a 3-lb. wheel (from the Cabot Farms) at $7.55. Cabot also makes a variety pack for Green Mountain. Your choice of three 9-oz. bars of smoked, sage, cheddar, or very sharp cheddar for $7.50.

The pancake enthusiast will delight in the two "Country Store" mixes, buttermilk and buckwheat, sold in 2-lb. bags for $2.75 to states east of the Mississippi (Area 1) and $3.15 to those west (Area 2).

HARRINGTON'S IN VERMONT, INC. / Dept. CFC
Main Street, Richmond, VT 05477

Catalogue, free, published seasonally, 32 pages, illustrated, black and white.

Among the other goodies shipped by Harrington's, whose main business is smoked meats and poultry, you'll find cheese—2-, 2½-, and 5-lb. blocks of aged cheddar, smoked Vermont cheddar, cheddar spread in a crock, Alpenjoy (a mild smoked cheese from Bavaria with bits of salami buried in it), and a tripack assortment of smoked cheddar, plain cheddar, and sage cheese (12 oz., $5.45). The cheddar also comes in gift packs with all-beef salami, with bacon, with smoked pheasant and canned smoked rainbow trout, or with Vermont McIntosh apples (13 apples and 1 lb. cheddar from $10.25 to $11.60, depending on shipping zone).

HARWOOD HILL ORCHARD AND GIFT SHOP / Dept. CFC
Business Route 7, Bennington, VT 05201

Brochure, order form and price list, free, published annually, 8 pages, illustrated, black and white.

Along with fruit, jams, and jellies, Harwood Hill Orchard and Gift Shop sells Vermont cheddar in 3-, 5- and 12-lb. wheels and ½-lb. or 1-lb. bricks. There's sharp cheddar, smoked cheddar, and sharp sage cheddar, a 1-lb. trio sampler of all three, plus a mild Jack cheese in an 8-oz. brick. We can't quote prices, as we don't have their list.

HICKIN'S MOUNTAIN MOWINGS FARM / Dept. CFC
RFD 1, Black Mountain Road, Brattleboro, VT 05301

Brochure, free, published periodically, 5 pages, illustrated, black and white.

Hickin's sells aged Vermont cheddar in 5-lb. and 3-lb. wheels, a 2½-lb. block, and 1-lb. or 9-oz. sticks at prices ranging from $1.75 (for a 9-oz. stick) to $9.95 (for a 5-lb. wheel), or cuts of cheddar for $2.10 a lb. Their cheddars come regular, very sharp, natural-smoked, or flavored with sage and caraway. That's only the beginning. For $2.10 a lb. you can get Swiss cheese, Gouda, longhorn (Colby type), mozzarella, "Monty" Jack, Amish, taco cheese, a weight-watcher's cheese, some labeled peppy pepper, onion, smoked hot pepper (that's $2.20), and quite a few others. There are also gift packages of cheese (a sampler of 12 is $8.25) or cheese combined with other products, such as ham, honey, pickles, fruitcake, and apples.

French-Swiss Sandwich.
Put thick slices of Gruyère cheese between slices of white bread, dip them in beaten egg and milk, as for French toast, and sauté in butter until browned on both sides. Serve hot.

Vermont's own cheddar, chowder, and ham, from Harrington's in Vermont

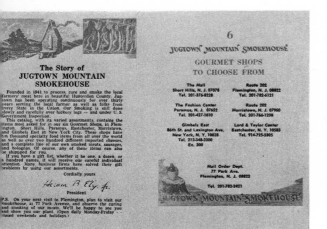

Motto of Maison Glass

★

When cooking cheese, use low heat. When cheese is melted, it is cooked. Overcooking and excessive heat makes it go stringy. Room temperature cheese takes less time to melt.

JUGTOWN MOUNTAIN SMOKEHOUSE / Dept. CFC
P.O. Box 366, Flemington, NJ 08822

"Jugtown Mountain Smokehouse," free price list and order form.

In addition to lots of smoked meat products, Jugtown Smokehouse, which maintains "gourmet shops" throughout New Jersey, has a line of smoked cheeses (cheddar, Swiss, Gruyère, Gouda, Colby longhorn) and natural spreading cheeses with different flavorings—cheddar with chutney, cheddar with jalapeños, Caerphilly with Guinness stout, Swiss with pecans and kirsch, for example. The spreading cheeses are around $3.50 a tub, the smoked cheeses $5 for 2-lb. or 1½-lb. packages. Cheese sampler gift packages can be supplemented by "breads of all nations," an assortment of breads ranging from sourdough to Swedish limpa.

KOLB-LENA CHEESE COMPANY / Dept. CFC
301 W. Railroad Street, Lena, IL 61048

Catalogue, free, published seasonally, 16 pages, illustrated, color.

One of Wisconsin's long-established and famous cheese companies, founded in 1925, Kolb-Lena has a large and excellent selection marketed under the Delico label. Among them are Colby, cheddar, Swiss, brick, blue, Brie, Camembert, Limburger, feta, schnee kaese (similar in flavor to brick but with a velvety white rind), and a soft-spreading cheese called Rexoli-Lunch. These are sold in various forms—wheels or half wheels of Swiss, blue, wheels and rounds of Brie, rounds of Camembert, loaves of cheddar, Colby, brick and schnee, wedges of feta, and in gift-box combinations of different cheeses. A "beginner's box" of hard cheeses contains about 3 lbs. of aged cheddar, Colby, Swiss, and a brick for around $8.50, a 1-lb. box of samples of blue, Rexoli, Camembert, Brie, and Heidelburg is around $4.85, and a prize assortment of nine different cheeses (about 4 lbs.) is $16. There's a 75¢ charge to cover additional postage charges for shipments beyond 1,000 miles.

MAISON GLASS / Dept. CFC
52 East 58th Street, New York, NY 10022

"Maison Glass Delicacies," $1, published annually, 72 pages, illustrated, black and white.

Maison Glass has a pretty good list of imported cheeses and a few domestic, starting with Appenzeller from Switzerland. There's the rich triple-crème Boursault (8 oz., $3.25), bleu de Bresse, Stilton, and all the other old familiar faces, and the crackers to go with them, such as Bath Olivers (8-oz. package, $1.25), water biscuits, cream crackers, Bremner wafers, flatbread, and crispbread. Under Cocktail Bits and Biscuits you'll find such things as rice crackers, twiglets, benne bits from the South, and Dutch cheese-filled crisps or cheese sticks.

MANGANARO FOODS / Dept. CFC
488 Ninth Avenue, New York, NY 10018

"Manganaro's for Gourmet Foods," free, published annually, 22 pages, illustrated.

Manganaro has, as you would expect, a pretty complete selection of Italian cheeses, plus a few of the favorites from other countries, such as Camembert, Roquefort, Swiss Gruyère, Emmenthal, Greek feta, Edam and Gouda, New York State and Canadian cheddar, and Danish blue. Among the grating cheeses you'll find the great Parmigiano Reggiano, or grana, in several famous brands, $5 a lb.; Pecorino Romano ($3.75 a lb.); a sardo from Argentina; and ricotta Siciliano, aged for grating. There's also the creamy blue-veined Gorgonzola ($4 a lb.); provolone, so good with pears, and the smaller provolette (both $4.20 a lb.); Friulana, a cheddar-type cheese from Venice; the mild Bel Paese, Fontina, Fonduta, Taleggio, the mild creamy-spreading ricotto Romano, and the mild but smoky Asiago. A quintet of strong, sharp, robust cheeses are caciocavallo (also good for grating), ragusano, incannestrato, pepato (with whole black peppercorns), and pecorino di tavola. These range from $3.60 to $4 a lb. To go with your cheeses, Manganaro has breadsticks and a fair assortment of English and French crackers.

MAPLE GROVE, INC. / Dept. CFC
167 Portland Street, St. Johnsbury, VT 05819

Catalogue, price list, free, published annually, 6 pages, illustrated, color.

Not shown in the catalogue but included on the price list are various Vermont cheeses. There's a 3-lb. or 2-lb. wheel of aged sharp cheddar ($10.75 or $7.70 ppd., slightly higher west of the Mississippi), a 12-oz. sampler of 3 cheeses—aged sharp cheddar, hickory-smoked, and butternut—8 oz. of butternut, a mellow, all-purpose cheddar, or of aged sage cheese, caraway cheese or sharp cheddar, and a 5-oz. Smoky Mountain bar, hickory-smoked cheddar with salami bits ($3.15).

MARIN FRENCH CHEESE COMPANY / Dept. CFC
P.O. Box 99, Petaluma, CA 94952

Price list, free.

Visitors to San Francisco find the famous sourdough French bread is perfectly paired with the Rouge et Noir brand cheeses made by the Marin French Cheese Company in neighboring Petaluma—Brie, Camembert, breakfast, and Schloss. This is a small family-owned cheese factory, and their cheeses are seldom found in other parts of the country because production is limited and they sell most of it locally. But they do sell mail-order, for which we can count ourselves lucky. They make excellent examples of Brie and Camembert, and their little breakfast cheese—soft, white, and buttery in flavor—is heaven on toast with jelly, like the fresh white cheeses of Europe. Schloss, a cheese that originated in Austria as Schlosskaese (castle cheese), was a favorite of the House of Bismarck. It has something in common with Limburger but with a touch of the elegance of Brie to uplift that plebeian image to something more patrician. This is a tawny tangy yet mellow little brick of golden cheese with a soft ripened texture. The brochure describes it as "a man's cheese, replete with delicate naughtiness, ideal with black pumpernickel and a stein of beer." You can order the four cheeses in various ways. Camembert comes in a pack of three 8-oz. wheels for $7.18 ppd., in twelve 1-oz. portions, or in six 4-oz. half wheels. Schloss and breakfast are sold in packs of six 3-oz. cheeses, priced at $5.99 and $5.62 ppd. respectively. Brie comes in one 24-oz. wheel ($7.09 ppd.), four 6-oz. portions, or four 3-oz. portions. Prepaid price includes shipment to any of the states, and prices are subject to change without notice. The Marin French Cheese Company has various gift assortments of the four cheeses, two of which include all-beef or Italian salami, priced from $12.98 to $15.98 ppd. If you can't get to San Francisco, you can always treat yourself to gift assortment #75, two 1-oz. portions of Camembert, one 3-oz. portion of Brie, and 3 oz. of schloss and breakfast cheese for $6.

MAYTAG DAIRY FARMS / Dept. CFC
Box 806, Newton, IA 50208

"Fine Cheese from the Maytag Dairy Farms," free, published annually, 11 pages, illustrated, color.

The famous Maytag blue, which many caseophiles swear is the finest blue cheese made in this country, is sold only by mail. A 4-lb. wheel of this creamy-textured, cave-ripened cheese is $10.70, a 2-lb. wheel $6.10, or, if you want smaller packs, it is available in 1-oz. wedges (24 wedges, $7.70; 48 wedges, $14.40), 4-oz. wedges, and 8-oz. wedges. We have found, though, that the cheese keeps so well under refrigeration that it is more practical to buy a wheel. In addition to their own cheese, Maytag sells carefully aged Swiss, cheddar, and Edam cheeses in 2-, 3- and 4-lb. combinations (1 lb. of each cheese is $8.20) and a combination package of the three augmented by four 8-oz. wedges of Maytag blue and aged cheddar and blue cheese spreads in stoneware crocks ($21.25). There are other packaged selections available, or you may buy crocks of the spreads and refills for the crocks (a 20-oz. crock of either spread is $6.30, refills $4.80). Glass refrigerator storage jars, in which the cheese rests on built-up ridges that allow water to be added to the bottom of the container to keep the cheese moist and fresh, are also available from Maytag. With the catalogue you get a little leaflet that tells you about the

Hamburger à la Francaise
Crumble ¼ pound Roquefort cheese into 3 pounds ground chuck or lean ground beef. Add ½ cup minced chives or green onions (including tops), ¼ teaspoon Tabasco, 1 teaspoon Worcestershire sauce, 1 teaspoon coarsely ground black pepper, 1½ teaspoons salt, and 1 teaspoon dry mustard. Mix together lightly. Let stand 2 hours to give flavors time to blend, then lightly press the meat into 12 patties. Broil or barbecue until browned on both sides and done the way you like them. Serve on toasted and buttered French rolls or hamburger buns.

Finger Sandwiches
Combine ¼ cup softened butter, 3 ounces crumbled Roquefort cheese, 2 tablespoons chopped chives, and ½ cup chopped watercress. Blend thoroughly. Trim crusts from 12 slices white bread. Spread cheese mixture on 6 slices; top with remaining bread slices. Cut each sandwich into thirds. Makes 1½ dozen.
—*from "Roquefort Chefmanship Recipes"*

THE STORY OF

Sesame-Cheese French Bread

Split a long loaf of French bread lengthwise and toast the cut side under the broiler. Meanwhile, lightly brown ¼ cup sesame seeds in a hot iron skillet, covering the pan and shaking them over the heat. Remove seeds and crush in a mortar. Combine the toasted seeds with 2 to 3 ounces sweet butter and ¼ cup grated Parmesan cheese. Spread thinly over the toasted surfaces of the bread. Reform the loaf, wrap in foil, and keep hot until ready to use.

Pumpernickel Cheese Balls

Mix together ¼ pound softened butter, ¼ pound grated sharp cheddar cheese, a little freshly ground black pepper or Tabasco to taste, and 1 tablespoon chopped chives. Chill until firm, then roll into small balls and chill again for 30 minutes. Toast 4 slices pumpernickel bread until crisp and then put in a blender or food processor and make into crumbs. Roll the cheese balls in the pumpernickel crumbs and serve as a cocktail hors d'oeuvre. Makes about 20 balls.

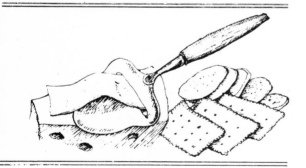

Teak-handled cheese plane from Northwestern Coffee Mills

development of Maytag blue and gives tips on care and serving. You might be interested to know that it will keep almost indefinitely if sealed in an airtight, moisture-proof bag and frozen.

NICHOLS GARDEN NURSERY / Dept. CFC
1190 North Pacific Highway, Albany, OR 97321

"Nichols Herb and Rare Seeds," free, published seasonally, 60 pages, illustrated, black and white.

Nichols doesn't sell only herbs and seeds; they also take pride in presenting Oregon "Rogue Gold" cheeses from the Rogue River Valley. Their cheddars are made from raw milk, with no color added, which is about as natural as you can get. The aged sharp cheddar is $3.95 for 1 lb., $6.25 for 2 lbs., slightly higher east of the Rockies, and there's also a smoked raw cheddar at $3.95 a lb. and a salt-free cheddar for dieters at the same price. The Oregon blue cheese (5-lb. wheel, $12.98, higher east of the Rockies) is made from a traditional Danish formula and slowly ripened to a rich creaminess. This is not shipped during the summer. There's also a yeast 'n' cheese blend of natural Italian cheese (type not specified) with nutritional yeast in 50-50 proportions that they recommend for cooking (8 oz., $1.65). Should you want to try your hand at making cheese, there's the Wagner Gourmet Home Cheesery Kit ($11.95), and, if you want to continue, extra cheese rennet tablets are available (25 for $3.95). Eight quarts of milk will make 2 pounds of cheddar. For yogurt addicts, Nichols has an electric yogurt incubator ($11.95), yogurt culture to start the first batch, and also acidophilus-yogurt culture, directions included. For bread bakers they list two sourdough starters: Oregon pioneer hop-yeast starter, the kind that was taken to the Alaska Gold Rush ($2 a jar with directions and recipes), and French lactic starter, the type used for French sourdough breads (also $2 with directions and recipes). They also have Red Star baker's yeast, fresh-dried yeast in bulk, 1 lb. for $2.35, a considerable saving over packaged yeast.

NORTHWESTERN COFFEE MILLS / Dept. CFC
217 North Broadway, Milwaukee, WI 53202

Catalogue, free ("25¢ donation accepted"), published annually, 28 pages, illustrated, black and white.

Northwestern sells cheese because of their proximity to many small Wisconsin cheese factories with a top-rate product that can only be purchased locally, and they make their selections after establishing close personal contacts at each factory. Although they do carry a few imported cheeses for those who want them, they feel, rightly, that the best Wisconsin cheese is hard to find away from rural Wisconsin and that good imported cheese can be had all around the U.S. A very enlightened attitude.

Their cheddar-type cheeses come from two different factories, and the cheesemakers use different formulas and different milk. Their Italian cheese is made in Sheboygan County by a company that carries on the tradition brought to this country by Wisconsin's Italian cheesemakers, and their Swiss-type cheese, cellar-aged for one year, comes from Ryser Bros. in Dane County, who also make an uncolored, pure rawmilk cheddar. Cheese is shipped only on Mondays, via UPS, and there are no shipments between Memorial and Labor Days. They list about 25 cheeses and 5 cheese spreads, among them Parmesan and Romano ($2.55 and $2.25 a lb. respectively, or 50¢ extra if freshly grated), a 1-year-old provolone, Limburger ($2.25 a lb.), brick, caraway Colby and plain Colby, Monterey Jack, whole-milk mozzarella ($1.90 a lb.), blue, organic goat cheese, Muenster, and various cheddars—mild, medium, aged 1 year, and extra-aged (3 years). The Swiss comes in two sizes, baby or 1-year-old wheel. Prices range from $1.90 to $3.85 (for the organic goat cheese) per lb., and on orders of 5 lbs. or more there is a 15 percent discount. They also have cheese samplers, 10" x 10" wooden crates packed with either Wisconsin or imported cheeses, or a combination of the two with 2 boxes of fancy crackers that would make a nice gift for a cheese-loving friend. The Wisconsin selection (4 lbs. of cheddar, brick, Italian, and Swiss types) is $14. They have a good assortment of crackers, such as Bremner's, Carr's, Jacob's, Finn Crisp, flatbread, rice crackers, rye wafers, wheat germ crisp, and stoned wheat thins, priced from 75¢ to $1.40 a box, and a Norwegian teak-handled cheese plane, a slicer and server in one ($3.50). This is one of the most attractively produced and written catalogues we have seen (the art is exceptionally good), and the 25¢ donation they invite to defray printing costs is well worth contributing.

J.M. NUTTALL & CO. / Dept. CFC
Dove Dairy, Hartington, Buxton, Derbyshire, England

Descriptive brochure, free.

Stilton is the famous blue-veined English cheese that takes its name from a village in Huntingdonshire where it was served at the Bell Inn in the late eighteenth century, although never made there. The preparation of Stilton is confined to three counties, Leicestershire, Derbyshire, and Nottinghamshire, where it is made in country creameries like Dove Dairy. Their Stilton, marketed under the Dairy Crest label, can be ordered for shipment by sea, airmail, or air freight in a 16-lb. wheel, 8-lb. half wheel, or popular small 5-lb. version. Write for prices and details.

PAPRIKAS WEISS IMPORTER / Dept. CFC
1546 Second Avenue, New York, NY 10028

"Imported Foods and Cookware Catalogue," $1 for annual subscription, published four times a year, 66 pages, illustrated, black and white.

Paprikas Weiss sells dairy cheeses from Britain, such as Cheshire, Leicester, Double Gloucester, Dunlop, cheddar, Caerphilly, Wensleydale, and Stilton, at prices ranging from $10 for a 5-lb. block of Caerphilly, Wensleydale, or Double Gloucester to $65 for a whole 18-lb. wheel of Cheshire (apparently these are sold only whole, not cut). Their other cheeses are a Vermont cheddar in a 2½-lb. gift box ($11.98), 27-lb. wheel or 40-lb. block, a Swiss version of Jarlsberg (11-lb. block, $30), a 6 lb. Danish blue ($21), soft white Bryndza ($4.50 a lb.), and their own Liptauer ball, which they make with American cheddar, Hungarian paprika, and caraway seeds (12-oz. gift box, $3.98). There's also Beaumont, St. Paulin, and Roquefort from France.

PEPPERIDGE FARM MAIL ORDER CO., INC. / Dept. CFC
Box 7000, Norwalk, CT 06856

"Gift Catalog," free, published periodically, 32 pages, illustrated, color.

A trio of cheddars from Vermont, New York, and Canada are gift-packaged with a cheese plane (½ lb. of each, $9.95; 1 lb. of each, $14.95). Two-lb. blocks of New York and Vermont cheddar are sold separately at $7.95, and 2 lbs. of the Canadian costs $9.95. A gift pack of sharp cheddar spread, cheddar spread laced with Cognac, and cheddar with kirsch costs $8.95.

THE PICKING BOX / Dept. CFC
Box 441, Hammondsport, NY 14840

"Wine Country Foods & Gifts," 35¢, 6 pages, illustrated, black and white.

Some of the wine-country gifts from The Picking Box are New York State cheeses. There's sharp cheddar ($1.95 a lb.), cheddar cured in port wine ($2 a lb.), and a Wine Cellar cheese spread that's whipped with sherry ($1.50 an 8-oz. tub or $5 for 2 lbs.). A gift package called Cheese Man's Delight has ½ lb. of medium-sharp cheddar, ½ lb. very sharp cheddar, ½ lb. port wine cheddar, and a tub of the cheese spread for $8.50 delivered.

Trademark of J. M. Nuttall & Co.

Dark breads to serve with cheese, from Paprikas Weiss

★

When making a cheese sauce, always stir the grated or shredded cheese in after the sauce has cooked. Let it melt into the sauce over low heat, then serve.

★

Salvage leftover pieces of hard or firm cheese that have become dry by grating them. Put in a screw-topped jar and keep in the refrigerator. Use in cheese sauce, soufflé, as a seasoning, on pasta, sprinkle on top of dishes to be gratinéed.

★

★

Four ounces of cheese, grated or shredded, will make 1 cup.

★

Cheese for cooking should be grated, shredded, or cut into small pieces so that it melts quickly.

★

Gift box from Sugarbush Farm

ROGUE RIVER VALLEY CREAMERY / Dept. CFC
311 North Front, Central Point, OR 97502

Price list, free.

From Oregon's picturesque Rogue River Valley come two distinctive regional cheeses: Oregon blue-vein cheese in 5-lb. wheels, or sharp and mild cheddar in 5-lb. bricks. Write for current prices.

SAHADI IMPORTING CO., INC. / Dept. CFC
187 Atlantic Avenue, Brooklyn, NY 11201

"The Silent Salesman," free, published biannually, 24 pages, illustrated, black and white.

In cheeses, Sahadi has imported Greek feta in jars ($2.40 for a 1-lb. jar) and a huge 35-lb. tin ($56), imported and domestic kasseri cheese, Syrian white cheese, the braided cheese called halabiyeh, mizitri (a dried ricotta, $2.50 a lb.), and kefolitiri, an imported cheese for macaroni. They advise that as cheese must be kept refrigerated it should not be ordered for shipment to distant places in warm weather. The flat, small, or large loaves of Arab bread (sometimes called pita) are available by the dozen in plastic bags. Small loaves are 95¢ a dozen; the large, $1.90.

SCHIPHOL AIRPORT / Dept. CFC
Tax-Free Shopping Center, Amsterdam, Holland

"Amsterdam Airport Mail-order Department," free, published periodically, 24 pages, illustrated, color.

Dutch Edam, Gouda, and homemade Leiden with cumin seeds come in various combinations with a cheeseboard made of the famous Delft blue tiles set in mahogany, accompanied by cheese knives. Write for the order form that lists current prices, including mailing costs.

SUGARBUSH FARM / Dept. CFC
R.F.D. 2, Woodstock, VT 05091

Mail-order folder, free, published seasonally, 4 pages.

Sugarbush Farm, run by the Ayres family, is a very personal mail-order company; the Ayreses even trade recipes with their customers. Their main stock-in-trade is their cheese, from the familiar Vermont cheddar (sharp, medium-sharp, and smoked) and sage cheese, to two specialties, a mild Green Mountain Jack, an Eastern version of California's Monterey Jack, and a rich, creamy Green Mountain bleu. The cheddar is sold in wheels, blocks, and foot-long bars, the sage and Jack cheeses in foot-long or half-size bars, and the bleu in half-size bars. Prices range from around $3.65 for a foot-long bar of hickory-and-maple smoked cheese, sharp cheddar, sage cheese, Jack cheese, or two half-size bars of bleu to $13.95 for a 6-lb. wheel of sharp cheddar. Postage and handling are extra, and only the smoked cheese is mailed year round. The other cheeses, being more perishable, are not mailed June to September.

SUNDIALS & MORE / Dept. CFC
New Ipswich, NH 03071

Catalogue, free, 48 pages, published seasonally, illustrated, color and black and white.

The "More" includes a tin of Bachman pretzels in an assortment that includes cheese stix, plain stix, bite-sized, Dutch style, thin, twisted, and new "Petite" pretzel, all individually wrapped, $10. From Kenyon's Corn Meal Company of Rhode Island there is stone-ground yellow cornmeal (1½ lbs., $1.20), corn muffin mix (1½ lbs., $2), or corn pancake mix (1½ lbs., $1.82) and buttermilk-and-honey pancake mix (1½ lbs., $2), and to go with them a quart jug of New Hampshire maple syrup ($7). A make-your-own bread and sandwich kit ($5.75) is great fun for children. Each kit comes with a bread pan, bag of flour, recipe, and jars of sandwich fillings such as peanut butter and jelly.

THE SWISS COLONY / Dept. CFC
1112 7th Avenue, Monroe, WI 53566

"Gifts of Perfect Taste," free, published annually (for Christmas), 92 pages, illustrated, color.

Another of the Wisconsin-based gift-package catalogues with emphasis on cheese but with lots of other foods, such as fresh fruit, nuts, steaks, smoked turkey, cakes, and candies. The majority of the cheeses are Wisconsin-made, such as a wheel of Swiss, in 2-lb. or 5-lb. sizes (around $6 or $14), cheddar, brick, Colby, caraway, aged American, and domestic versions of Edam, Gouda, Brie, Camembert, cheese balls, and spreads. These are available in all kinds of combinations and gift packs, all cheese or cheese and other foods. If you look hard you'll find a few imported cheeses such as Swiss Gruyère at $5.95 for 1½ lbs., but the accent is mainly American. A Cheese Gift of the Month Plan brings varying quantities of different Wisconsin cheeses for $40, $70, or $100.

TILLAMOOK COUNTY CREAMERY ASSOCIATION / Dept. CFC
P.O. Box 313, Tillamook, OR 97141

Brochure and price list, free.

Tillamook cheddar-style cheese has been made in the rich dairy county of Tillamook, Oregon, since 1894 and is now one of the most famous of American cheddars. This was the first community in the United States to brand its cheese products and advertise them under a brand name. The sailing-ship symbol commemorates the original and only means of transporting the cheese out of the county in those days.

Tillamook is made from modified raw milk, which means it is not pasteurized but heated to 148°F. for 16 seconds (pasteurization is 161°F. for 16 seconds), a compromise that retains the action of the natural enzymes on the cheese. It is aged for three months for medium cheddar, six to nine months or more for sharp. No preservatives, mold inhibitors, or other chemical additives are used, and the coloring is natural, from the seeds of the tropical anatto (or achiote) tree that yield an orange-yellow dye. The cheese is sold by mail in various ways. A 5-lb. loaf is $11.65 for medium, $11.95 for sharp if mailed to the West, slightly higher for the East. There's a 2-lb. baby loaf (also available unsalted for those on low-sodium diets) for under $6, slightly over for the East; a twin-loaf baby pack of medium and sharp; and a Bars 'n Board pack of two 10-oz. bars with a cutting board of the Pacific Northwest alderwood ($5.05 to $5.50, according to zone). Tillamook also makes a smoked cheddar, Monterey, and a caraway spiced cheese, which are available with the cheddar in other packs, such as the Party Pak, a selection of 10-oz. bars of each of the cheeses ($11.30 to $12, according to zone).

THE VERMONT COUNTRY STORE / Dept. CFC
Weston, VT 05161

Catalogue, 25¢, published annually, 98 pages, illustrated, black and white.

Freshly baked bread made from 100 percent whole-grain, stone-ground wheat flour is a specialty of the Vermont Country Store, which will also sell you the flour to make your own. Three 22-oz. loaves, packed in a carton and shipped fresh from the bakery, cost $3.15. To go with the bread, there is their private stock of natural cheddar, aged 12 months, $7.50 for a 3-lb. wheel, $12.50 for the 5-lb. size, or a 3-lb. wheel of Vermont sage cheese (cheddar flavored with fresh sage leaves), also $7.50. Or you can buy the cheddar in 1-lb. bars, sage cheese, caraway cheese, and smoked cheddar in 9-oz. bars, or a pack of 3—cheddar, sage, and smoked cheddar. You'll find in this catalogue the famous common crackers of New England, 1½ lbs. packed in a split-ash basket for $3.85, seafood crackers for chowders and soups ($1.89 the 2-lb. bag), and crunchy little wine crackers for nibbling with a cup of tea or a glass of port or sherry.

Camembert Mariné

Lightly scrape the crust from 1 whole ripe Camembert cheese, preferably imported. Put in a small round dish, pour over it enough dry white wine to cover, cover the dish, and let it stand overnight. Drain and dry the cheese. Mash and mix with ¼ pound softened sweet butter until perfectly smooth. Chill until easy to handle, then form into its original shape. Cover top, bottom, and sides with finely chopped toasted almonds or toasted bread crumbs and chill until ready to serve. Remove it from the refrigerator about half an hour before serving so it will soften up. Serve with hot toasted water biscuits, Melba toast, or thinly-sliced toasted French bread.

Alderwood cheese board plus Tillamook cheddar, a gift from Tillamook County Creamery

*

Aged cheeses have more flavor than young cheeses, so less is required in cooking. When buying cheddar or Parmesan for cooking, the older, the better.

*

Firm or semi-soft cheeses such as cheddar, Gruyère, Emmenthal (more commonly known as Swiss), Monterey Jack can be shredded or grated, using a box-type hand grater, a Mouli-type rotary grater, or a food processor with shredder attachment. Very hard dry cheeses such as Parmesan, Pecorino Romano, Sardo, Asiago, should be grated, using a hand grater, or by cutting them into small pieces and grating in the blender. Preferably, grate or shred cheeses as needed. Softer cheeses should be cut by hand into small dice, crumbled, or mashed.

*

Limburger-Onion Sandwich

Butter slices of rye or pumpernickel bread and spread with soft Limburger cheese. Top with slices of sweet onion that have been marinated for 30 minutes in a mustardy vinaigrette sauce.

★

Shredded sharp Cheddar gives special zip to scalloped potatoes, omelets, and scrambled eggs ... Green Mountain Jack makes wonderful grilled cheese sandwiches ... add thin slices of Bleu cheese on top of your hamburger while broiling ... wrap crumbs of Bleu cheese in biscuit dough and bake until brown for a perfect cocktail snack ... cube sage cheese and add to salads ... it also goes well with fruits for desserts ... and sage cheese with pumpkin pie is a Vermont Thanksgiving tradition.
—*from Sugarbush Farm, Woodstock, Vermont.*

★

After boiling or steaming vegetables such as green beans, asparagus, shredded green cabbage, broccoli, Brussels sprouts, leeks, cauliflower, carrots, drain well, put in a baking dish, pour melted butter over them, sprinkle with grated Parmesan cheese, and put in a 400° oven just until the cheese melts.

★

WALNUT ACRES / Dept. CFC
Penns Creek, PA 17862

"Walnut Acres Natural Foods," free, published 5 times a year, 24 pages, black and white.

Among other natural foods on the Walnut Acres list is cheese. They have a goat cheese made from organically produced milk, lightly salted, $2.14 for a 9-oz. block, which they caution is irregular in supply, their own smoked cheese spread made with smoked cheddar, butter, green pepper, garlic, onion, and spices ($1.55 the 8-oz. jar), and New York and Wisconsin raw-milk cheddars. The New York State cheddar, made only with rennet, is medium sharp. No rennet is used in the mild Wisconsin cheddar. Both are sold in 1-lb., 2½-lb., and 5-lb. sizes at prices ranging from under $3 to under $11. Walnut Acres carries the Crowley Colby cheese from Vermont, also made from unpasteurized raw milk with no preservatives, in 3-lb. or 5-lb. wheels. If you are interested in making your own cheese, they have Hansen's cheese rennet and vegetable rennet tablets, 12 for about $2.40.

Walnut Acres ships freshly home-baked bread twice a week, the day after it is made, except from May 1 to October 1, when it is available only at their store. The breads, all made from organically raised grains and natural ingredients, with no preservatives or additives, include whole-wheat, crushed wheat, whole-wheat raisin bread, rye bread, with or without caraway seeds, and soy-carob and are priced from 70¢ for a loaf of plain rye to 84¢ for a loaf of raisin bread.

WEAVER'S FAMOUS LEBANON BOLOGNA, INC. / Dept. CFC
P.O. Box 525, Lebanon, PA 17042

"From the smokehouses of Weaver's," free, published annually, 16 pages, illustrated, color.

Not only the famous Lebanon bologna but the equally famous Pennsylvania Dutch-style pretzels are made by Weaver. The Pennsylvania Dutch like their pretzels big and chunky, the kind known as "beer pretzels," and you can buy them either this way or in a special package (a canister with Amish horse-and-buggy motif) with two other kinds, extra-thin pretzels and little bite-size "nutzels." Or you can order a snack package of three kinds of pretzels plus smoked cheese and 1 lb. of Lebanon bologna (around $10).

WHOLE GRAIN SALES / Dept. CFC
Rte. 2, Waunakee, WI 53597

"Nature Ramblings and Organic Foods," 4 mimeographed pages, published seasonally, send self-addressed stamped envelope and 10¢.

Owner Leon Horsted lists a semisoft Colby cheese produced from the milk of a naturally run Wisconsin farm ($2.10 a lb., 2 lbs. for $4.10) among his organic foods, as well as cheddar at $2.20 a lb. or 2 lbs. for $4.30.

WIN SCHULER'S, INC. / Dept. CFC
145 South Eagle St., Marshall, MI 49068

"Win Schuler's Bar-Scheeze Gift Catalog," free, published annually, 12 pages, illustrated, color.

Win Schuler's Bar-Scheeze, the cheddar spread featured in his restaurants, is sold in 18-oz. stoneware crocks. One crock—filled with the standard spread or with smoky bacon or onion-garlic—is $5.45, six crocks for $29.95. A combination of the three is $14.95. Refills are available in all flavors ($6.95 for two).

Between May 15 and September 15, Win Schuler products are shipped only to Michigan, Indiana, Ohio, and Illinois.

THE WISCONSIN CHEESEMAN / Dept. CFC
P.O. Box 1, Madison, WI 53701

"Gift Selections," free, published annually, 96 pages, illustrated, color.

This large mail-order gift package company has an enormous variety of different combinations of Wisconsin natural and process cheeses and crocks of cheddar-cheese spreads. Packages of cheese alone range from $4.45 for a selection of cheeses (aged cheddar, mellow American, Tuscany, kümin, Amstel, Edel-Swiss) with a hardwood cutting board to a complete assortment of natural and process cheeses, cheese spreads, and cheese logs, about 10 lbs. in all, for $17.95. Monterey Jack, Colby, caraway cheddar, and brick are among some of the many different kinds of cheese in the packages. You'll find cheese packaged with canned fish, with cakes and candies, jams and jellies, nuts, sausage and ham, fresh fruit, packed in Mexican straw hampers, wicker bread baskets, salad bowls, ice buckets, casseroles, individual aluminum cook-and-serve casseroles, just about every conceivable way. There's also a ceramic fondue set with a package of heat-and-serve Swiss fondue and 4 long-handled forks for $7.95. One of the typical selections of natural cheese comprises 4-oz. wedges of Monterey Jack, American, Colby and caraway cheddar, and blocks of Edam, aged cheddar, brick, and American for $5.95. A trio of cheddar-cheese spreads is $4.50.

YOUNG & SAUNDERS LTD. / Dept. CFC
5 Queensferry Street, Edinburgh EH2 4PD, Scotland

"Food & Wine List," free, published seasonally, 42 pages, black and white.

Many of the items in Young & Saunders food catalogue are obviously impractical to order, as they are generally available here, but among their more interesting foods are the Scottish and English cheeses, which they will ship anywhere in the world. There's Scottish cheddar, Orkney Farmhouse and Orkney Farmhouse smoked cheeses, Caboc (rolled in oatmeal), Islay, and Arran Dunlop. In English cheeses, there's a matured English Farmhouse cheddar, midget cheddar, Blue Farmhouse Cheshire, Red Farmhouse Cheshire, Double Gloucester, Derbyshire Sage, Lancashire, Midget White Wensleydale, and Stilton (a whole Stilton weighs 16 lbs., but you can also get a small quantity in an earthenware jar). Prices, quoted in sterling, are subject to change and the fluctuating exchange rate and do not, of course, include shipping.

A different breakfast—fruit, cheese, and bread. Courtesy Food & Wines from France, Inc.

Everlasting Cheese Spread
This recipe is recommended for all leftover cheese. If and when cheese becomes dry and hard, you start and continue this mixture forever. To start use: 1 pound of sharp chedder, 4 ounces of cream cheese, 1 jigger (1½ ounces) of olive oil, 1 teaspoon dry mustard, 1 teaspoon caraway seeds, 1 jigger (1½ ounces) of brandy or kirsch. Grate or dice the cheddar, add the cream cheese and olive oil. Stir well. Add mustard, caraway seeds, and brandy. Mix well until smooth. Store in earthenware crock in refrigerator. Serve at room temperature. Do not finish this basic mixture but keep adding grated leftover cheeses of all kinds. Add a dash of brandy or mustard. This continuous chain mixture will help you utilize all leftover cheese.
—*from "Cheese of All Nations Catalogue"*

See Appendix, page 239, for additional sources not included here.

46

Crown roast of lamb, roast pheasant, boiled crabs.
Courtesy Food & Wines from France, Inc.

CHAPTER THREE

MEAT, FOWL, AND SEAFOOD

ALEWEL'S, INC. / Dept. CFC
    South Street / Louis Street, Concordia, MO 64020

"Alewel's Famous Old Missouri Meats," free, published annually, 8 pages, illustrated, color.

Alewel's Missouri country hams are sugar-cured and hickory-smoked, and you can buy either a whole country ham (average 12 lbs., around $35), a smoked boneless ham, smoked picnic ham, or a precut country ham, boned and sliced for frying or broiling. They also have slab and sliced bacon, smoked pork sausage, and both pork and beef summer sausage. Beef summer sausage is dry-cured rather than cooked and comes ready to eat, needing no refrigeration. A small sausage weighs about 14 oz. ($4.25), a large one 20 oz. ($5.50). Then there are various gift packs of sausage, bacon, cheese, and sliced ham.

AUNT LUCY HAMS / Dept. CFC
    3 W. Frederick Street, Box 126, Walkersville, MD 21793

"Country Foods by Aunt Lucy," 8-page leaflet with order blank, free, mailed five times a year.

Maybe when Aunt Lucy Products began, in 1929, there really *was* an Aunt Lucy. Now she appears, like Aunt Jemima, in the logo—a cameo portrait of a rather dour and prim black lady. Aunt Lucy hams are dry-sugar-cured in the old country way, hickory-smoked and aged for a year (which makes them harder and dryer) or six months (moister), and they can be ordered uncooked or fully cooked and glazed, either by the whole or half ham (half hams are smoked only six months). Aunt Lucy also has aged ham slices, sliced or whole sandwich ham, slab and sliced bacon, hickory-smoked sausage, smoked turkey, and a few extras other smokehouses don't have—canned scrapple, country puddin' (cooked and seasoned pork meat), and country-style "crumbly" sausage, which, according to the folder, is·a unique type of all-pork sausage seasoned and cooked in an iron kettle until crumbly, a recipe developed by Aunt Lucy herself at hog-butchering time and delicious with grits, pancakes, fried potatoes, or eggs. You can also get white and yellow cornmeal and old-fashioned buckwheat flour for your mush, spoon bread, and pancakes. Prices range from around $1.85 a lb. for slab bacon to about $4.70 a lb. for boneless fully cooked and sliced aged sandwich ham.

B&B FOOD PRODUCTS / Dept. CFC
Route #1B, Cadiz, KY 42211

"Your Gift Catalog," free, published annually, 16 pages, illustrated, black and white.

An excellent source for Kentucky country hams. The Broadbent family (B&B Food Products) specializes in the famous Trigg County hams, from corn-fed hogs, dry-cured, hickory-smoked, and properly aged. Each ham is carefully rubbed with salt, sugar, and their own "secret" ingredients at certain stages of the curing process. It is the dry-rub procedure, they say, that makes country hams drier in texture than ordinary hams and much more flavorful (conventional supermarket hams are cured by pumping them with salt water to add moisture and weight, whereas country hams lose about 20 to 30 percent of their weight during curing and aging). Kentucky country hams are also different from other Southern country hams in being short-trimmed so there are no long shanks with extra bone and little meat. The smallest cooked ham (7 to 8 lbs) will serve more than 20 people. Broadbents' hams come with directions for cooking, carving, and serving and are priced according to shipping zone. They have both cooked and uncooked hams (the uncooked, if properly wrapped, will keep for a year without refrigeration). Prices range from around $27 for an 11- to 12-lb. uncooked ham to between $42 and $45 for a 10- to 11-lb. cooked ham. They have smoked country bacon, also dry-cured and rindless for easy slicing (around $12 for a 4- to 5-lb. piece), country smoked pork sausage, beef and pork summer sausage in 1½- to 2-lb. rolls, smoked turkey and smoked turkey breast (a 5-lb. turkey breast is around $20), and other products, too, such as prime strip sirloin and filet mignon steaks, relishes, cheese, pancake and spoon-bread mixes, honey, sorghum molasses, and various gift packs. The Blue Grass Bounty teams a fully cooked 6- to 7-lb. country ham with a jar of pickled watermelon rind, champagne salad dressing from Kentucky chef Stanley Demos, bourbon pecan cake, and hard sauce (around $45). There's a B&B sausage assortment of summer sausage and beer sausage and something rather different—a pantry pack of relishes, plus an 8-oz. bag of baked ground country ham to use in scrambled eggs, quiche, or ham salad (around $8).

BISSINGER'S / Dept. CFC
205 West 4th Street, Cincinnati, OH 45202

"Bissinger's Guide to Gourmet Gifting," free, published for Christmas and Easter, 12 pages, illustrated, black and white.

Bissinger's has one of the widest selections of candies to be found (see chapter 6), but they also sell prime frozen steaks, smoked country ham, smoked pheasant, and fresh Beluga caviar.

They warn that prices in this category are extremely volatile. Write them directly for current quotations.

BREMEN HOUSE INC. / Dept. CFC
218 East 86th Street, New York, NY 10028

"Bremen House Catalog of Gourmet Foods," free, published twice a year, 20 pages, illustrated, black and white.

Bremen House is one of the German specialty stores in Manhattan's Yorkville district, with a big delicatessen counter where sausages, smoked and prepared meats are sold. You'll find such German favorites as Kasseler leberwurst, Thuringer blutwurst, bratwurst, teewurst, lachs-schinken, nuss-schinken, bauernschinken, and Westphalian ham at prices ranging from around $2.40 to $4.40 a lb. Imported smoked

Kentucky specialties from B&B Food Products

★

When braising or stewing meat or poultry, put a piece of waxed paper under the lid of the pan to collect the steam and prevent the moisture diluting the dish.

★

Avoid flare-ups of fat from broiled meats by putting slices of bread in the pan, under the broiler rack, to catch the dripping fat.

★

To slice meat or poultry thinly (for scaloppine, beef birds, sukiyaki, escalopes of turkey breast), freeze it slightly first and it will cut more easily.

★

*

To brown meat for stews and braised dishes without adding calories, put the meat under the broiler instead of sautéing in fat.

*

Before carving a roast, let it stand for 15 minutes in a warm place, or cover it lightly with foil, after taking it from the oven. This allows the juices to settle and the connective tissues to become firm, making it easier to carve.

*

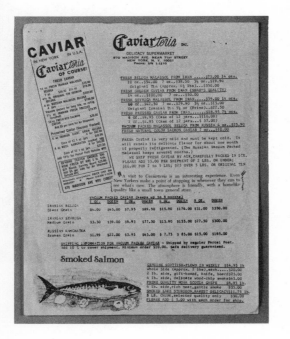

meats include Ardennes smoked ham from Belgium, Hungarian-style salami, Holstein cervelatwurst, plus headcheese and pig's knuckles in aspic. From Poland comes canned game—deer with mushrooms, roast wild boar goulash, and deer goulash—from Germany canned sausages, and from Scotland game in wine sauce. Among the seafoods are Dutch salt herrings in plastic kegs ($7.25 a 4-lb. keg), herring fillets and rollmops, herring fillets in Hungarian mustard sauce, and canned conger eel.

CASA MONEO / Dept. CFC
210 West 14th Street, New York, NY 10011

"Mexican Food–Comida Mexicana," free, 8 pages, published annually, also price lists of South American, Cuban, and Portuguese foods.

Casa Moneo specializes in Spanish and Latin American foods. They have the hot or mild Spanish sausage, chorizo, in different forms: in links, $1.50 a lb.; vacuum-packed (75¢ for 6½ oz.); and packed in 6-lb. tins at $13.95. They also have Argentine canned corned beef and Brazilian corned beef ($1.29 a 12-oz. can) and carne seca, Brazilian sundried, salted beef necessary for feijoada ($2.89 a 1-lb. package). From Portugal they import canned mackerel, small sardines, octopus, and the minute baby eels called angulas ($1.60 a lb.).

CAVIARTERIA INC. / Dept. CFC
870 Madison Avenue, New York, NY 10021

Price list, free, published twice a year or as prices change.

Beluga is sold by Caviarteria, caviar importers, wholesalers, and specialists. You can get fresh Iranian Beluga malassol ($75 for 14 oz.) and Sevruga malassol, as well as the even more expensive fresh golden caviar (Shah's quality), $100 for 14 oz., and the less expensive fresh pressed caviar ($9.95 a 4-oz. jar) or vacuum-packed caviar. Fresh caviar is very mild and must be kept cold. It keeps its delicate flavor for about a month when refrigerated, whereas vacuum-packed caviar will keep up to 6 months. Vacuum-packed Beluga malassol from Russia is around $26 for 4 oz., Iranian Beluga $16 for 4 oz. Shipments, packed in ice, are made by air. That's only a beginning, for Caviarteria, a small shop, actually stocks well over 2,000 specialty foods. Their price list also offers smoked salmon from Scotland and Nova Scotia, smoked sturgeon, and gift packages of their specialties, such as caviar, smoked salmon, smoked sturgeon, fresh duck pâté, foie gras with truffles, hand-dipped chocolates, and wheels of French Brie cheese. For $100 you can send someone a surprise package that arrives from October through May with a different food each month, or if you feel really generous there are other gift plans from $200 to $5,000 that cover the whole year.

CHEESE COFFEE CENTER / Dept. CFC
2110 Center Street, Berkeley, CA 94704

Mail-order catalogue, free, published semiannually, 12 pages, black and white.

Listed under Meats/Cold Cuts are various kinds of sausage, such as Italian-style dry salami, Lebanon bologna, mortadella, pepperoni, chorizo, cervelat, hot or sweet coppacola, and different liverwursts, one a Bavarian with pistachios ($2.89 a lb.). Prices average between $2 and $5 a lb. There's also prosciutto ($3.99 for ½ lb.), baked or boiled ham, pastrami, headcheese, smoked turkey breast, and corned beef. All orders are shipped UPS the day they are received, and prices are subject to change due to market fluctuations.

CLAIBORNE JOHNSTON / Dept. CFC
100 Johnston Bldg, 12 South 3rd Street, Richmond, VA 23205

Price list and order form, free.

Puget Sound alder smoked sturgeon, red salmon, and albacore packed in 3¾-oz. tins come in cartons of 6 tins (2 each of your choice) for $8.50 ppd. Apparently Claiborne Johnston also has cooked, ready-to-serve

Smithfield hams, Virginia country hams, bacon, and smoked turkeys, but the prices were not given on the list we received, so best inquire.

CONTE DI SAVOIA / Dept. CFC
555 W. Roosevelt Road, Chicago, IL 60607

Catalogue, 75¢ (refunded with purchase), published annually, 28 pages.

Various salamis are listed in this catalogue, such as citterio, spiced lightly with garlic and black pepper ($3.99 a lb.); the milder Genoa; casalinga, with large chunks of ground pork, garlic, pepper, cured in an age-old tradition; soppressata, with more marbling of fat, no garlic; Toscano; and a mild, delicately flavored dry-cured type. There's also imported or domestic prosciutto ($3.99 a lb. for imported, $2.99 domestic), mortadella, the mild cured ham called coppa di piacenza, and various canned or salted and dried meats and fish such as sardines and anchovies in salt, baccala (salt codfish), simmenthal (sliced cured beef in gelatin), and various other specialties. From other European countries come herring fillets in mustard, tomato or Burgundy sauce, foie gras, pâté de campagne, canned abalone, cockles, mussels, Israeli gefilte fish, and Polish canned game with chanterelles.

CROSS BROS. MEAT PURVEYORS, INC. / Dept. CFC
3550 North Front Street, Philadelphia, PA 19140

Price list and order form, free.

Quick-frozen prime steaks are shipped in dry ice by Cross. Strip loin steaks, 8, 10 and 12 oz.; 6-oz. or 8-oz. tenderloin steaks; 8-oz. and 10-oz. boneless rib steaks, any of these packed 8 to a box, or a mixed box of 3 strip loin and 3 tenderloin steaks. You will have to request current prices.

DAY & YOUNG / Dept. CFC
Orchard Lane, Santa Clara, CA 95052

"Holiday Gifts," free, published annually, 28 pages, illustrated, color.

Day & Young's extra plump (approximately 2¼ lb.) hickory-smoked pheasants were raised in California's evergreen coastal mountain range, grain-fed from birth. Available for delivery the year round, $13.95.

Another gift is a mini delicatessen, complete with hardwood parquet chopping block, 6" x 6" x 4", a miniature stainless-steel cleaver, a smoked 7-oz. beef log, 7 oz. of natural Edam cheese, and 7 oz. Italian sharp cheese for $9.95.

DELTA CRAYFISH / Dept. CFC
608 Highway 12, P.O. Box 566, Rio Vista, CA 94571

4-page leaflet with recipes, free, black and white.

Call them crayfish or crawfish, these succulent little shellfish are wonderful eating. There was a time when they were scarcer than hen's teeth. Not any more. Now they are available in good quantities from the upper reaches of the sloughs and rivers of northern California from May 15 to late November and can be shipped to you live by air. The native California species is *Pacificatus leniusculus*, not to be confused with species found in the ponds, swamps, and still waters of Louisiana and Mississippi. Hand-graded to a minimum length of 4" (head tip to tail end), they are washed, packaged in crushed ice, and shipped by air anywhere in the country (plans are afoot to ship them anywhere in the world). Apparently they are such good travelers that they will hold in a refrigerated cooler at 38 degrees for about two weeks, though we doubt anyone who received them could forbear to cook and eat them on the spot. You can use them in recipes as you would crab or lobster for dishes like crayfish cocktail, crayfish Louis, crayfish bisque, and, of course, they are traditional in jambalaya and gumbo. However, we like them best just cooked *à la nage* (swimming) in a well-seasoned court bouillon, for which you'll find a recipe in the leaflet. Price per lb. FOB San Francisco furnished on request.

Lamb Chops with Horseradish Sauce
Broil 4 sirloin lamb chops ¾ to 1 inch thick, 3 to 4 inches from the heat or on an outdoor grill over hot coals for about 6 minutes a side, or to desired degree of doneness. Meanwhile, combine in a small bowl ½ cup sour cream, 1½ tablespoons prepared horseradish, ¼ teaspoon crumbled dried rosemary, ½ teaspoon salt, ⅛ teaspoon pepper, and ¼ teaspoon paprika. Mix well and serve with the chops.
—from The American Lamb Council

Prime steaks from Cross Bros.

Ecrevisses à la Nage
Prepare a court bouillon. Combine in a large pot 1 quart fish stock (made with fish bones, vegetables, and water), 1 bottle dry white wine, 2 thinly sliced carrots, 1 thinly sliced medium onion, 2 thinly sliced celery ribs, 12 parsley stems, 2 bay leaves, 1 thinly sliced lemon, 1 smashed garlic clove, 12 whole white peppercorns, 1 dried red chili pepper, a few sprigs of fresh thyme, a few cloves, and sea salt to taste. Bring to boil and boil 10 minutes, then add 24 live crayfish. Reduce the heat, cover, and simmer 5 to 6 minutes. Serve warm in the liquid, in soup plates, or cool in the court bouillon and serve cold.
—from Delta Crayfish Brochure

Smoked meats from Early's Honey Stand

Ways to serve smoked trout
- Filleted as an hors d'oeuvre on a thin piece of buttered rye bread or on unsalted crackers—plain or with lemon juice, chopped onion, and ground pepper.
- Whole as a first course on a bed of watercress or leaf lettuce with a vinaigrette sauce.
- Filleted as a sandwich with a fresh bagel, a slice of Bermuda onion, and a light spread of pure cream cheese.
- As a main fish course, warmed quickly 5 to 10 minutes in a hot oven (do not dry out) and garnished with a tart Hollandaise sauce.
- For an elegant breakfast, filleted, thoroughly warmed in a low oven or quickly under the broiler, and placed to the side of eggs scrambled in sweet butter—with a tulip glass filled with chilled champagne and a curl of lemon peel.
—from Garrapata Trout Farm Booklet

EARLY'S HONEY STAND / Dept. CFC
Rural Route 2, Spring Hill, TN 37174

"Old Fashioned Foods and Gifts from the Tennessee Hill Country," free, published annually, 19 pages, illustrated, color, black and white.

Mr. Early says his customers "are a loyal bunch. I have hundreds and hundreds that have been ordering 20 years and a good number . . . 30 years or longer." A good part of Early's appeal is his folksiness as well as his foods. Despite the name, Early's biggest sellers are smoked sausage and bacon, country hams, and cheese. Old-time pork sausage (shipped November 1 to March 20 only) contains no fillers and is made from an old family recipe. Like all other Early meats, it is smoked over green hickory wood. Mr. Early, the proprietor, writes that this pork sausage "is common only in the middle Tennessee area . . . and our customers have led us to believe it is the best of the lot."

Hand-rubbed with honey and dry-sugar-cured, then smoked, Early's bacon bears no resemblance to the store-bought facsimile. It needs no refrigeration, so it is great for campers.

Whole smoked hams, 12 to 16 lbs., run about $31. A box of presliced ham, containing 4½ lbs., is about $17. Both come with directions for baking and frying.

Early's also sells green hickory chips for your barbecue, barbecue sauce, and smoked seasoning.

ESPECIALLY MAINE / Dept. CFC
Vinegar Hill Road, Arundel, ME 04046

"Especially Maine," free, published periodically, 23 pages, illustrated, black and white.

A wooden clam basket packed with 17 Down East seafood delicacies, including lobster, clam, crab and sardine spreads, deviled lobster, clam chowder, whole clams, crab meat, clam juice, clams in the shell, lobster and clam bisques, and lobster Newburg, is an exclusive offering from Especially Maine ($27.50).

A mini-basket with 8 cans of the Maine seafood is $10.50. Colorful lobster terry towels for the kitchen that double as lobster bibs are $2.25.

Maine sardines, packed in soybean oil and with (or without) hot green chilies, come 12 to a can (75¢).

FAUCHON / Dept. CFC
26 Place de la Madeleine, 75008 Paris 8e, France

Price list, free, published annually, 8 pages.

Fauchon has those great French specialties, foie gras and rillettes, packed under their own label. Fauchon foie gras (goose liver) is available in blocs from 4½ oz. (about $13) to 1 lb. 12¾ oz. ($73). Fauchon's French sardines come packed in olive oil, flavored with lemon, tomato, pimiento, spices, and Muscadet wine, or green pepper. Naturally, you can get here extra-large snails, from 1 doz. to 6 doz. The pâtés range in size from 4½ oz. to 14 oz. There's mousse of goose liver and the wonderfully rich rillettes d'oie (goose pâté). Prices are quoted in francs, so you have to go by the current exchange rate.

FIGI'S INC. / Dept. CFC
Central Plaza, Marshfield, WI 54449

"Figi's Gifts in Good Taste," free, published annually, 64 pages, illustrated, color.

Like most gift catalogues, Figi's includes smoked turkey, fully cooked and ready-to-eat (around $20 for the 9- to 10-lb. size, $16 for the 6½- to 7½-lb.); smoked turkey breast; ready-to-eat skinless, shankless, and defatted ham (9½ to 10½ lbs., around $30); various Wisconsin smoked sausages (summer sausage, pizza sausage, all-beef sausage, beerwurst, braunschweiger); and smoked bacon. The Smokehouse Gang package teams sausages, bacon, and sliced pastrami. Sausages also appear in many of the gift packages with cheese or other foods.

FIN 'N FEATHER FARM / Dept. CFC
RFD 2, Dundee, IL 60118

Catalog, free, published annually, 24 pages, illustrated, color.

In business for 40 years, Fin 'n Feather Farm smokes birds, hams, bacon, and summer sausage and also sells gift packs of jams and jellies, cheese, canned goods, and quick-frozen boneless strip and Delmonico (boneless rib eye) steaks. A gift-boxed smoked pheasant, 2 to 2¼ lbs., is $11.50 ($21.95 for two), smoked turkey is $21.95 for an 8-lb. bird, a brace of smoked Rock Cornish hens are $13.95, a 5-lb. smoked capon is $21.95, and a smoked duck $10.50. Or you can order unsmoked oven-ready pheasants for $21.95 a brace. The all-beef summer sausage weighs 1½ lbs. and costs $6.50, or $11.95 for two.

R. W. FORSYTH LTD. / Dept. CFC
30 Princes Street, Edinburgh EH2 2BZ, Scotland

"The days of Christmas at Forsyth's," free, published annually, 16 pages, black and white.

While the fresh game and poultry in the Christmas catalogue of this Edinburgh department store cannot, of course, be shipped, you might like to try some of the canned game they carry, such as whole grouse in wine sauce, whole pheasant in Madeira sauce, the Isle of Arran pâtés of venison or hare (5 oz. about 90¢), or perhaps smoked trout or smoked salmon.

FRASER-MORRIS / Dept. CFC
872 Madison Avenue, New York, NY 10021

"Gifts for Festive Occasions from Fraser-Morris," free, published seasonally, 11 pages, illustrated, color.

Fraser-Morris has been delivering and shipping gift packages, bon voyage baskets, and various food specialties for many years from their Madison Avenue location in New York. They have, as you might expect, most of the luxury foods, such as giant Beluga caviar ($22.50 for 3½ oz.), pâté de foie gras ($14.25 for a 5½-oz. baby bloc, $51.50 for a 10 ⅞-oz. terrine), and aged Smithfield ham, cooked in wine ($3.95 a lb. for a 9- to 13-lb. bone-in ham, $5.95 a lb. for a 7- to 10-lb. boneless ham). Whole smoked turkey cured in herbs and spices, 10 to 15 lbs., sells for $3.35 a lb. and baked country ham for $4.25 a lb. for the bone-in type, $5.25 for the boneless. There's also Scotch or Nova Scotia smoked salmon, sliced and put back on the frame, $19.95 a lb. for the Scotch, $12.95 a lb. for Nova Scotia.

GALAXY PRODUCTS, INC. / Dept. CFC
P.O. Box 215, Sonoma, CA 95476

"Sonoma Cheese Factory Gift Catalog," free, published annually, 16 pages, illustrated, color.

A natural partner to Sonoma cheese is salami from the Bay Area's famous Columbus Salame Company. The Sonoma Cheese Factory sells the Columbus dry salami (1 to 8 lbs., $3.95 to $26.95) and the dry coppa (made from the lean pork shoulder meat), 2½ lbs., $12.95. A ½-lb. dry salami is included in one of their cheese gift boxes, too.

GARRAPATA TROUT FARM / Dept CFC
Doud Arcade, P.O. Box 3178, Carmel, CA 93921

Brochure, free, published periodically, with price list, illustrated, black and white.

Native trout raised in a natural environment, in waters flavored with many wild herbs and roots, and cold-smoked by a painstaking Old World method to moist succulence. As the trout are not totally dehydrated, they are somewhat perishable, but they will keep for three weeks under 38° F. or for six months in the freezer. Complete instructions for storing and serving are included in the brochure. A "boodle"

Whole Smoked Trout

To prepare whole smoked trout, first cut through the skin the entire length of the backbone from head to tail with a sharp knife. Starting from the cut just behind the head, cut down toward the belly and diagonally back and about ⅓ inch behind gill opening and behind pectoral fin. Pinch corner of skin flap, which has just been cut behind head, and peel gently back to expose the moist succulent flesh. Lift the exposed fillet from the bone with a fork or knife and serve.
—from Garrapata Trout Farm Booklet

*

Render excess fat from duck or chicken to use for sautés or sauces. Cut fat into small pieces, put in a skillet with a little water and cook until fat is melted and water evaporates. Strain clear liquid fat into a jar.

*

Marinate thick fish steaks for 15 minutes in lemon juice before broiling. This partially "cooks" the flesh and cuts down on the broiling time, and the fish doesn't dry out.

*

of smoked trout contains 16 fish and weighs between 4 and 4½ lbs. One box or boodle costs $23 delivered in California, $25 in other states, with an additional $2 air parcel post for shipments to Hawaii, Alaska, and Canada. The price drops if you order from 2 to 5 boxes. Garrapata Trout Farm also sells for $1 a booklet of special recipes, "The Delicate Fresh & Smoked Trout."

GIFTHAMS LTD. / Dept. CFC
    The Quadrant, Hoylake, Wirral, Cheshire L47 2EE, England

Catalogue, free, published annually, 20 pages, illustrated, color.

The only food from the gift catalogue that Gifthams exports is West of Ireland smoked salmon, but if you have friends in the UK and would like to send them a ham, leg of pork, Scotch rib of beef, turkey, or one of the numerous gift hampers or wine and spirit packs, this is a good and reliable source. No prices are given in the catalogue, so you will have to request the price list too.

THE GOURMET PANTRY / Dept. CFC
    400 McGuinness Blvd., Brooklyn, NY 11222

"Pleasure Packed Gifts from the Gourmet Pantry," free, published annually, 72 pages, illustrated, color.

One of the simpler gifts in this catalogue is the whole smoked turkey (9 to 10 lbs., around $22 delivered) or, if you don't want quite as much meat, the 4- to 5-lb. turkey breast ($17.99). There's also a dry-cured, hickory-smoked, ready-to-eat ham, with shank, skin, and excess fat removed, 9 to 10 lbs., around $30, and a Cheese 'n Sausage Rack, a 10" footed slicing board and wrought-iron rack with hooks for hanging sausages and cheeses, which comes with Danish salami and smoked cheese links and a serrated-edge slicing knife (around $12).

GRAFFAM BROS. / Dept. CFC
    P.O. Box 205 (Central Street), Rockport, ME 04856

Price list, free, revised annually.

Hand-picked Maine lobsters, or lobsters and clams, packaged in a refrigerated insulated carton complete with cooking container. Lobsters are priced according to weight and are cheaper if you buy the culls (one-claw lobsters). Twelve 1-lb. lobsters are $39.75, the one-claws $33.75. At 1¼ lbs., 12 lobsters are $49.50, at 1½ lbs. $58.25. Fourteen 1-lb. lobsters and 1 peck of clams runs $49.95. That averages out about $3.30 a lb., not much more than if you buy them where they are caught; but, of course, prices of lobster do fluctuate by season and availability, and prices quoted are FOB Logan Airport in Boston. You are notified of airline, flight number, air bill, and time of arrival and pay the freight charges when picking them up at the airport at your end. Approximate air freight charges on a single airline are $15 east of Chicago, $20 east of Dallas, and $25 for the West Coast.

GRAYS OF WORCESTER, LTD. / Dept. CFC
    Orchard Street, Worcester WR5 3DP, England

"For the pleasure of the Gourmet," free, published annually with seasonal supplements, 26 pages, black and white.

This overseas gift catalogue has some interesting canned seafood and meats. From New Zealand come smoked eel fillets, packed exclusively for Grays, and scallops in mushroom sauce. Jugged hare and a game pie filling with stock and wine that needs only to be put in its pastry shell, whole quail stuffed with pâté de foie and canned in sherry sauce, haggis, Prague ham, and authentic English "bangers" (pork sausages) are a few of the things we noticed. Prices, quoted in sterling, are for UK delivery, so you should ask for a quotation on any foods you are interested in. Your orders, incidentally, can be charged to credit cards, such as Master Charge or BankAmericard, or paid for by check.

GREAT VALLEY MILLS / Dept. CFC
Quakertown, PA 18951

"Gift Suggestions from the Pennsylvania Dutch Country," free, published annually, 16 pages, illustrated, black and white.

The Pennsylvania Dutch hams sold by Great Valley Mills are cured in spiced vinegar and sugar, then smoked for two weeks over apple and hickory wood, and short-trimmed (no long shank bone). These are fully cooked, ready-to-eat hams, and they range in weight from 10 to 12 lbs. ($28) to 14 to 16 lbs. ($35), prices delivered (add 10 percent west of the Mississippi). Other Pennsylvania Dutch meat delicacies are, naturally, bologna—old-fashioned beer bologna, Lebanon bologna, and ring bologna—smoked sausage, smoked tongue, slab or sliced bacon, ready-to-eat dried beef (thinly sliced for serving, $7.25 a lb.), plus smoked turkey, and Canadian-style bacon. Pennsylvania Dutch scrapple comes in cans (three 1-lb. cans are $3.75 plus shipping). You can order anything separately or in their special gift packs. The Old Smoky pack contains a 10-lb. ham, 2 lbs. bacon, 2 lbs. sausage, a can of scrapple, and 1 lb. each of ring and Lebanon bologna and costs about $42.50 (plus 10 percent west of the Mississippi). Or you can have a package of the three bolognas—beer, Lebanon, and ring—for $8.50.

GWALTNEY, INC. / Dept. CFC
P.O. Box 489, Smithfield, VA 23430

Brochure, free, published annually, 4 pages, illustrated.

The dry-cured, aged Smithfield hams of Virginia are famous the world over. Even Queen Victoria, 100 years ago, ordered them. By law, the name Smithfield can be applied only to hams produced in Smithfield, Virginia, through a process that has changed little since the Indians taught the first settlers the secrets of dry-curing hams. Gwaltney, the oldest Smithfield ham company, has been seasoning and curing quality Virginia hams for four generations. Their rich, lean, Smithfield and Williamsburg hams (the Williamsburg has a milder cure) are hardwood-smoked, cured, and slowly aged to a robust flavor. Each ham, uncooked or fully cooked, comes in a shipping carton with preparation, serving, carving, and keeping instructions. Or you may order a 2½- to 3-lb. slab of Williamsburg dry-cured bacon. Prices, subject to change, include shipping via UPS. Inquire about current prices when you send for the brochure.

HARRINGTON'S IN VERMONT, INC. / Dept. CFC
Main Street, Richmond, VT 05477

Catalogue, free, published seasonally, 32 pages, illustrated, black and white.

This company has four stores in Vermont and Connecticut and does a big mail-order business in corn-cob-smoked country hams, uncooked and fully cooked, and other smoked meats, such as Canadian bacon, smoked bacon, smoked pork loin, smoked air-dried beef (something of a rarity), and various smoked birds—turkey, pheasant, duck. Except in the summer months they will ship bags of fresh country pork sausage made with lean meat and seasoned with their own blend of herbs and spices—no filler in this. Prices for hams range according to size and whether they are uncooked or fully cooked, whole or half, from around $23 to around $50. As shipments are prepaid, prices differ according to zone. Recipes go with every shipment. Smoked pork loin, so delicious in choucroute garni, or roasted and served cold with horseradish applesauce, runs $18 to $19 a lb., according to zone, for a 4-lb. roast of about 12 chops. The air-dried beef is $7 to $8 a lb., but being dehydrated and served in paper-thin slices, a pound goes a long way. Serve it like prosciutto, as a first course, or as a canapé, wrapped around cream cheese or bread sticks. A 3-, 6- or 12-month membership in the Harrington Food Club makes a welcome Christmas gift for a food-loving friend. The 3-month membership ($56 to $61, according to zone) brings

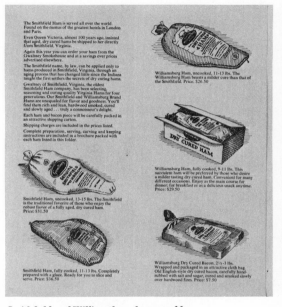

Smithfield and Williamsburg hams and bacon from Gwaltney

Hams in the smokehouse at Harrington's in Vermont

Pacific Northwest canned seafood, from Hegg & Hegg

a smoked turkey at Thanksgiving, smoked pheasant at Christmas, and smoked ham at Easter. Harrington's has some good-looking carving boards, too, and a nice folksy book of *Treasured Recipes from Early New England Kitchens* that would make a good addition to a collection of regional cookbooks. Ordering is made easy by their 24-hour phone ordering service. Just give your name, address, phone number, order, and Master Charge or BankAmericard number. Shipments are by UPS or, for distant states, by air at 10 percent over the regular prepaid price.

HARRY AND DAVID / Dept. CFC
  P.O. Box 712, Medford, OR 97501

  "Harry and David's Christmas Book of Gifts," free, published annually with supplementary brochures, 28 pages, illustrated, color.

Harry and David started Fruit-of-the Month Club in 1936, and now they have a Smokehouse Club as well. Smoked pheasant (2½ lbs., $14.95), turkey (9½ to 10½ lbs., $26.95), and sugar-cured ham (10 to 13 lbs., $37.95) can be delivered for Christmas, Thanksgiving, and Easter in the three-box plan for $76.95. The 5-box club adds to this 3¼ to 3½ lbs. of sugar-cured bacon and smoked sausage for $99.95.

HEGG & HEGG / Dept. CFC
  801 Marine Drive, Port Angeles, WA 98362

  "Gourmet Gift Harvest from the Pacific Northwest," leaflet and price list, free, published in fall for Christmas mailing, illustrated.

A variety of smoked and canned seafoods from the Pacific Northwest. A whole 4-lb. Puget Sound alder smoked salmon, vacuum-sealed in a plastic container with recipe folder included, is a very reasonable $14.25 ($15 east of the Rockies), half a smoked salmon is $8 (or $8.75). Among the canned packs, the "Pacific Harvest" has alder smoked red salmon, smoked butter clams, smoked sturgeon, tiny North Pacific shrimp, and Puget Sound steamed clams in shell for $7.75 ($8.25 east of the Rockies). Or you can buy cans of red sockeye salmon, Dungeness crab meat, shrimp, and albacore tuna by the case (12 cans) or half case (6 cans). A 6½-oz. can of Dungeness crab meat is $4.50; a 7½-oz. can of red sockeye salmon works out at just over $1.50, and it's about the same for smoked sturgeon. For a gift, there's an amusing little pack of four ¼-lb. tins of smoked fish (salmon, shad, sturgeon, albacore) in a fish-shaped reed basket tied in netting for $5.59 ($6.45 east of the Rockies). All prices include postage.

HICKIN'S MOUNTAIN MOWINGS FARM / Dept. CFC
  RFD 1, Black Mountain Road, Brattleboro, VT 05301

  Brochure, free, published periodically, 6 pages, plus price list, illustrated, black and white.

While home-grown produce and homemade goodies are the main interests of Frank and Mary Hickin, they also sell Vermont cob-smoked meats, whole or half hams, boneless or bone-in, picnic and daisy hams, buffet ham (heart of ham), slab and sliced bacon, Canadian bacon, and beef salami. Hams range in price from $2.49 a lb. for a whole 10- to 12-lb. or half 5- to 7-lb. ham, bone-in, to $3.99 for the buffet ham, which runs 4 to 5 lbs. or 2 to 3 lbs. for a half. Picnics of 3 to 6 lbs. are $1.95 a lb., daisy hams of 1 to 3 lbs. $2.99 a lb. Sliced or slab bacon is $2.59 a lb., Canadian bacon $3.99 a lb., and a 12-oz. salami $2.69 a lb.

HUDSON HAM HOUSE / Dept. CFC
  RFD 3, Box 27, Culpeper, VA 22701

  Leaflet, free.

Country-cured Lord Culpeper hams from the foothills of the Blue Ridge Mountains. The Hudson family cure their hams by hand-rubbing them with seasoned salt, ground peppercorns, and sugar (they are never smoked), according to a centuries-old Virginia recipe, then age

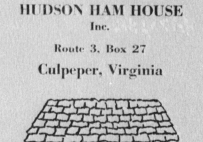

and process them. The leaflet tells you the best way to store hams for an extended period—remove the cellophane wrapper so the ham can breathe, put it in a porous fabric bag, such as an old pillow case, and hang in a cool, dry place. Never put an uncooked aged ham in the refrigerator; refrigerate only after cooking or cutting. They advise that if you are slicing a steak off the ham to fry, you cut all the way, sawing through the bone. If you cut only to the bone, you waste too much. Hudson also sells smoked picnic shoulder and bacon. No price list is included because of the fluctuations in the pork market.

IMPERIAL WILD BOAR COMPANY / Dept. CFC
Palo Corona Ranch, P.O. Box AQ, Carmel, CA 93921

"Imperial European Wild Boar," free, 1 page, published every two years.

Tired of eating the same old meats? Then how about genuine European wild boar from "the acorn-filled wilderness of the Santa Lucia Mountains in California"? A whole fresh frozen young wild boar, cleaned and dressed, weighing 120 to 200 lbs., is $2.25 a lb., a smaller 80- to 120-lb. boar $2.75 a lb., and a whole suckling pig (45 to 80 lbs. dressed) $2.95 a lb. Or you can order 15- to 20-lb. fresh wild boar hams ($3.25 a lb.) or shoulders ($2.75 a lb.) and, when available, a loin section for $4 a lb. There are also smoked hams, shoulders, and bacon ($3.50, $3, and $2.50 a lb., respectively). Prices (which have probably risen since this was written) are for meats wrapped and ready to ship FOB Monterey, and there is a minimum order of 25 lbs. or over. As 95 percent of the orders from restaurants, clubs, group banquets, and individuals are for whole boars, the company doesn't always have in inventory supplies of the fresh and smoked hams, shoulders, loin sections, and bacon, and they also ask that you give them 6 to 8 days' notice. The optimum dressed weight for a roast wild boar in terms of taste, succulence, and firmness of texture is 100 lbs., so you'll probably have to plan on barbecuing your pig or cutting him into half or quarter roasts. The leaflet gives full directions for cooking the fresh or smoked meat.

IRON GATE PRODUCTS COMPANY, INC. / Dept. CFC
424 West 54th Street, New York, NY 10019

Product lists (prices on request), free, 9 pages.

If you are interested in buying a whole wild boar (80 to 120 lbs.), the hindquarters or forequarters of a buffalo, a whole or half bear, a whole venison, venison saddle, hind leg or stew meat, a saddle or shoulder of hare, or just a whole 4- to 6-lb. rabbit, you can order them from Iron Gate Products. Game birds, some sold by the case, include bobwhite quail, chukar partridge, muscovy and mallard ducks, adult and baby broiler pheasant, snow grouse or ptarmigan, squab pigeons, and Canadian quail. Iron Gate imports fresh Beluga and Sevruga caviar directly and sells it in 2-kilo (about 4¼-lb.) tins, 1-kilo tins, 14-oz. and 7-oz. tins. There's also fresh salmon caviar in 14-oz. tins and pasteurized caviar—Beluga, Sevruga, natural-pressed, and Imperial Iranian. Under seafood you'll find imported Dover sole and New Zealand Dover sole, plaice, trout, turbot, Coho salmon, frogs' legs, bay scallops, fillets of sole, gray sole and mahi-mahi, Malpeque oysters (shipped direct from Prince Edward Island, Canada), Chesapeake lump crab meat (pasteurized), frozen Dungeness crab, and Alaskan king crab meat and claws. Many of these are sold only in case lots. Smoked fish, such as Canadian lake sturgeon, Iranian Beluga sturgeon, Scotch and Nova Scotia salmon, trout, eel, whitefish, chubs, are sold by the pound or in sides. There's also frozen turtle meat and Mediterranean red shrimp. In hams, you'll find domestic prosciutto, Westphalian, Saratoga, and Hickory Valley boneless. There are other items available in quantity, too, such as a case of 24 cans of hearts of palm, a 25-lb. drum of wild rice, snails from Strasbourg, and pâté de foie gras. Write for prices of any foods that interest you.

Smoked Salmon Pâté
Combine in a blender ⅔ cup chopped smoked salmon, 1 teaspoon grated Parmesan cheese, 2 teaspoons capers, 1 cup heavy cream, 2 teaspoons lemon juice, ¼ teaspoon dill, and ⅛ teaspoon pepper. Blend on low until smooth. Serve as an hors d'oeuvre on pumpernickel bread or Melba toast. (For this pâté, you can use the little bits of salmon the knife has passed over when slicing, and those from the hard-to-slice area around the head which otherwise would be wasted.)
—*from The House of Kilfenora*

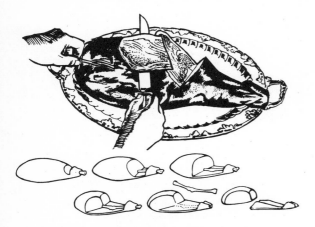

Carving technique for Joyner Smithfield ham

Good things from Scotland, Landmark catalogue

JOYNER SMITHFIELD HAMS / Dept. CFC
Box 387, Smithfield, VA 23430

"Smoked Meats, Smithfield and Country Hams," leaflet and price list, free, published annually, illustrated, color.

Old-fashioned, "long-cut," peanut-fed hams, dry-cured according to the centuries-old Smithfield process, pepper-coated, hardwood-smoked, and well aged are the specialty of Joyner of Smithfield, a company established in 1889 and now a division of Swift & Co. In addition to the Smithfield ham, they have a "red eye" ham, a dry-cured country-style ham with a milder flavor. This Southern-style ham has a short butt end and is perfect for slicing and pan-frying or broiling (the traditional "red eye" gravy is made by adding water or black coffee to the pan drippings after the ham is fried, hence the name). Prices, always subject to change without notice, are just over $2 a lb. for a 10- to 16-lb. uncooked ham and $2.90 for a 9- to 12-lb. baked, glazed, and ready-to-serve ham. Smithfield hams are, of course, more expensive—$2.75 a lb. for uncooked hams, $3.25 a lb. for an 8 to 12 lb. cooked ham, which comes skinned, fat-trimmed, baked, and glazed. All prices are parcel post prepaid. The leaflet gives very clear directions for cooking, storing, and carving, with some simple recipes—and you are gently reminded that Smithfield ham should always be sliced paper-thin.

JUGTOWN MOUNTAIN SMOKEHOUSE / Dept. CFC
P.O. Box 366, Flemington, NJ 08822

"Jugtown Mountain Smokehouse," free price list and order form.

Founded in 1941 to process, cure, and smoke the meat of the farmers in Hunterdon County, Jugtown has been operating a smokehouse ever since and has also branched out with "gourmet shops" in Flemington, Short Hills, Paramus, Eastchester, Morristown, and at Gimbels East in New York City. You can visit the Flemington plant Monday through Friday to see how they cure and smoke the meats. You'll find they have the usual range of country hams (whole country hams, 12 to 16 lbs., are $2.75 a lb.); slab, sliced, Canadian, and Irish-style bacon; beef bacon; fresh and smoked link sausage and fresh sausage meat, plus some other things like smoked pork chops and beef chips. Ready-to-eat smoked poultry includes turkey, goose (6 to 8 lbs., $22.50), duck, capon, chicken, and pheasant. In addition, they have smoked and spreading cheeses, peanut butter, honey and fruit cake, plus a very wide range of gift packages of their various products. The "Bring Home the Bacon" box ($12.50) has a pound each of sliced bacon, breakfast beef, Canadian bacon, and 12 oz. of Irish bacon.

JURGENSEN'S GROCERY COMPANY / Dept. CFC
601 South Lake Avenue, Pasadena, CA 91109

"Jurgensen's Christmas Catalogue," free, published annually, 36 pages, illustrated, color.

In the Jurgensen's Christmas catalogue you'll find Smithfield hams, either uncooked (12 to 14 lbs.), cooked and bone-in (9 to 12 lbs.), or cooked and boneless (9 to 11 lbs.); Jones Dairy Farm Old-Fashioned Dry Cure Hams and tenderized hams, canned Polish hams, and other Christmas specialties, such as whole smoked turkey and smoked turkey breasts and Jurgensen's prime-grade meats: a box of 6 New York-cut steaks, or 12 tenderloin steaks, 1¼ inches thick, or 12 loin lamb chops, 1¼ inches thick. No prices are listed for these, nor for the fresh Beluga malossol caviar.

LANDMARK / Dept. CFC
Carrbridge, Inverness-shire PH23 3AJ, Scotland

"Scottish Fare," free, published annually, 6-page brochure.

Landmark specializes in the good things of Scotland, one of which, naturally, is smoked salmon. You can order a 1½-lb., 2-lb., or 4-lb. side of smoked salmon, but as the prices quoted in the brochure are for delivery within the UK, you will have to request their overseas postage charges.

LAWRENCE'S SMOKE HOUSE / Dept. CFC
  Route 30, Newfane, VT 05345

Brochure and price list, free, published annually.

Corn-cob-smoked hams, bacon, and salami, plus a few other goodies, such as smoked rainbow trout, various cheeses, and, of course, Vermont maple syrup come from this 25-year-old family business. From the old-fashioned smokehouse in the Vermont hills you can order a whole smoked ham, 9 to 10½ lbs., for $34.95, half hams, boneless hams, smoked picnic shoulder and daisy roll (boneless pork shoulder butt), country-style slab bacon ($14.50 for a 4- to 4½-lb. piece) or sliced bacon, Canadian-style bacon, and all-beef salami. A pair of smoked rainbow trout, 8 oz. each, are $6.25. Prices include postage and handling and they'll take Master Charge and BankAmericard as well as checks or money orders.

LEKVAR-BY-THE-BARREL / Dept. CFC
  1577 First Avenue, New York, NY 10028

"A Continental Bazaar," free, published annually, 56 pages, illustrated, black and white.

Among the strictly-from-Hungary items in this catalogue you'll find Hungarian salami ($4 a lb.) and canned ham; Hungarian fish soup, fish ragout, paprika fish salad, and broiled fish with potatoes, all canned. France is represented by Strasbourg pâté de foie and foie gras au naturel (7-oz. tin, $27.95; 14-oz. tin, $49.95).

LE JARDIN DU GOURMET / Dept. CFC
  West Danville, VT 05873

Catalogue, 50¢, published annually, 32 pages, illustrated, black and white.

The meat and fish products carried by Jardin du Gourmet are imports, such as French foie gras in terrines and blocs (one novelty is a pâté-à-Gogo flavored with Scotch whisky), canned snails (tin of 12, $2.10), jars of Romanoff Iranian caviar (1 oz. of the giant grain, $5), canned shad roe, mussels, gefilte fish, mackerel in white wine, French tuna (4-oz. tin, $1.25), and pickled eels in jelly. Also canned prepared foods such as cassoulet, choucroute, and the like. On the page with the foie gras you'll find, naturally enough, canned goosefat, so good for sautéing.

FRANK LEWIS / Dept. CFC
  P.O. Box 517, Alamo, TX 78516

"Royal Gifts," free, published annually, 16 pages, illustrated, color.

Most of this catalogue is given over to ruby-red grapefruit, in different combinations and gift packs, but you can also order, October through April 15, smoked turkey (10 to 11 lbs., $24.95), Canadian bacon, smoked Rock Cornish hens ($12.95 for 2), and boneless ham, all fat removed so that it is all lean meat (6 to 7 lbs., $28.95).

MAISON GLASS / Dept. CFC
  52 East 58th Street, New York, NY 10022

"Maison Glass Delicacies," $1, published annually, 72 pages, illustrated, black and white.

The meats and fish in the Maison Glass catalogue are the deluxe kind—smoked turkeys ($45, about 12 lbs.) and turkey breast, cooked Smithfield hams, Virginia country hams, smoked salmon from Nova Scotia ($14 a lb.), smoked Beluga sturgeon ($15 a lb.), and smoked brook trout. Of course, they have fresh Beluga caviar, the less expensive pressed caviar, preserved caviar, and even the lowly salmon caviar ($5.50 a 4-oz. jar). Truffled Strasbourg foie gras comes in terrines and blocs, or as a less expensive purée or mousse, or you might like to try the new duck liver with green peppercorns ($13.95 for the 5-oz. bloc).
  Maison Glass takes orders not only for wild game (duck, partridge, pheasant, quail, wild turkey) and oven-dressed suckling pig but also for some offbeat delicacies like whale steaks, turtle steaks, reindeer, buf-

Broiled Ham Steak Grand Marnier
[*served at Dave Chasen's, Los Angeles*]
Select a center cut slice of ham 1 to 1½ inches thick. Slash the fat around the edges and arrange the ham on a shallow flameproof serving dish. Combine 2 tablespoons brown sugar with 1½ teaspoons dry mustard and enough orange juice to make a paste. Spread half of this mixture on top of the ham and broil until brown and glazed on top (about 10 minutes). Turn the steak, spread the rest of the paste on the second side, and continue broiling for 5 minutes. Arrange 3 or 4 slices of orange, lightly sprinkled with sugar, on top. Brown and glaze. Just before serving, pour 4 tablespoons warmed Grand Marnier over it and ignite. Bring to the table flaming.
—*from Grand Marnier Recipe Booklet*

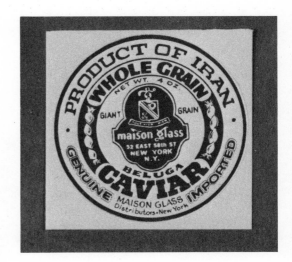

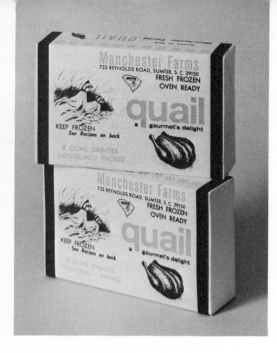

Grilled Quail

Thaw 12 quail, place on a wooden board, flatten with the broad side of a cleaver, and salt and pepper to taste. Make a marinade with 1 cup dry white wine, 4 tablespoons lemon juice, 4 tablespoons minced onion, 4 bay leaves, 8 peppercorns, and a generous pinch of allspice. Marinate the quail for 2 to 3 hours. About 20 minutes before serving time remove quail from marinade and roll in fine bread crumbs. Broil for 20 minutes, 10 minutes a side. Serve hot with melted butter, bread sauce, and red or white currant jelly. Serves 12.

—*from Manchester Farms*

falo, wild goat, mountain sheep, elephant roast, hippopotamus steaks, llama steaks and chops, wild boar, and rattlesnake meat—for which they'll quote a price. Also in the smoked-bird category are capon, duck, goose, Rock Cornish hens, and pheasant ($4.75 to $6.95 a lb., or $6.75 for a smoked Rock Cornish hen, $19.95 for a smoked pheasant). They carry freshly sliced prosciutto ($8 a lb.), Italian salami, and German cervelat and a wide variety of canned meats, seafood and prepared dishes, such as smoked kipper pâté, mackerel in white wine, smoked or pickled mussels and oysters, quenelles de veau, deer filets with chanterelles, even lion meat ($4.50 a 4½-oz. tin), in case you have a hankering to try it. There is such a long list of delicacies here that we can list only a small proportion.

MANCHESTER FARMS / Dept. CFC
  P.O. Box 97, Highway 521N., Dalzell, SC 29040

  Price list and recipes, free.

How about quail on toast for breakfast? Not just any quail but Bill Odom's Pharaoh quail, a hardy breed that matures quickly. Bill Odom was the "chicken doctor" for Campbell's Soup until he started his own business nearly five years ago. For two years he raised bobwhite quail and sold on a direct-order operation, but an outbreak of quail bronchitis interrupted his production for six months.

He decided to experiment with the Pharaoh, the species that Cleopatra allegedly served to her suitors. The birds are individually wrapped and frozen just before shipping in a dry-ice container. Their average weight is 3 to 4 oz. per bird. Each order contains 16 birds for $34.95, including shipping, and a half-dozen quail recipes.

MANGANARO'S FOODS, INC. / Dept. CFC
  488 Ninth Avenue, New York, NY 10018

  "Manganaro's for Gourmet Foods" and price list, free, published periodically, 26 pages, illustrated, black and white.

An excellent selection of meats and some canned and salted fish are listed in Manganaro's catalogue. You'll find here both imported and domestic salami: Citterio brand, spiced with garlic and black pepper; sopresetta, with more marbling, no garlic; Sicilian style; Genoa style; casalinga style; and zampino, a boiled type of sausage, mildly flavored with garlic. There's also pepperoni and cotechino, the sausage that is traditionally cooked with lentils ($3.40 a lb.). Imported prosciutto is $7.50 a lb. in bulk (5-lb. average) or sliced, domestic $5 a lb. sliced or $2.50 a lb. whole, bone-in (average weight is 18 lbs.). Pancetta, the Italian-style cooking bacon, is $4.60 a lb. Apart from the baccala (boneless dried salt cod) from Italy, at $2.85 a lb., and the salted anchovies ($3.50 a lb.), most of the fish is canned. Scungilli (conch), sliced and pickled in brine, is $1.50 an 8-oz. tin. Cuttlefish in its own ink is $1.50 a 4-oz. tin. Pickled eels in vinegar, spices, and salt are available only in season, mid-November to early March. Prices, which change with fluctuations in the food market, do not include shipping.

MARINE HARVEST, LIMITED / Dept. CFC
  124 Union Street, Aberdeen AB1 1JJ, Scotland

  "Lochinvar Smoked Salmon," 10-page color foldout, price list and order form, free.

Marine Harvest supplies Scotch smoked salmon to American Express, Neiman-Marcus, and other exacting customers, so you know it must be good. Their process involves the use of salt, Demerara sugar and dark rum from the Caribbean, and the sides of salmon are smoked over oak and juniper chips. You can buy sides weighing from 1¾ to 4 lbs., and such accessories as a smoked salmon slicing knife and board and a lemon press. Prices, which change yearly, are quoted in sterling and include airmail postage for destinations outside the UK. Marine Harvest requests that remittances for orders outside the sterling area be made in sterling, which your bank can arrange. The color foldout, which is printed in English, French, and German, gives serving suggestions, storage instructions, and shows you in a graphic diagram how to prepare and slice your side of salmon.

MCARTHUR'S SMOKEHOUSE / Dept. CFC
Millerton, NY 12546

Free price list.

McArthur's has a whole line of smoked foods—unbaked or baked and glazed hams (cured in tubs of molasses and salt water, then smoked over hickory logs), regular and Canadian-style bacon, smoked turkey, capon, game hens, beef, trout, pork loin and crown roast of pork (a delicious and different roast for a dinner party), and even a boneless smoked leg of lamb (2½ lbs., about $15). It seems they had a customer who didn't care for lamb, but this won him over. They also offer ham morsels, slices of boneless ham cut into pieces ¼" thick and 1½" across, a smart idea for people who can't use a whole or half ham but like that country smokehouse flavor in their ham casseroles and mousse. In addition there's corned beef brisket (4½ lbs., around $14), sausage meat, link sausage (also available smoked), and good old British bangers (mild-flavored pork sausages) from the original recipe, made primarily for their English customers who yearn for that taste of home.

McArthur's mustard ($2.50 in a 9-oz. canning jar) is a special sweet, hot, and saucy blend they came across in Washington and consider perfect with their hams or as a glaze. You can also order things that go naturally with their products, such as cheddar cheese, pancake mixes, and dried whole peas in case you want to make soup from that good ham bone. Shipping and handling charges must be added to the prices, which might have gone up by the time you read this.

MIDWAY GROVES / Dept. CFC
Route 3, Box 28, Sarasota, FL 33580

Catalogue, free, published annually, 16 pages, illustrated, color.

Fruit is not the only thing sold by Midway Groves. They also have such Florida specialties as stone crab claws, Florida lobster, and rock shrimp, cleaned and precooked, shipped in dry ice in a special reusable cooler with recipe and serving suggestions included. There are surf-and-turf combinations (lobster halves stuffed with crab meat and filet mignon steaks) and shore dinners with stuffed lobster, blue crab claws, and Key lime pie, or stone crab claws, shrimp ring with cocktail sauce, and Key lime pie. Or you can order the Florida combination of 2 lobsters and 3-lb. stone crab claws.

MURRAY'S STURGEON SHOP / Dept. CFC
2429 Broadway, New York, NY 10024

Price list, free.

Not just sturgeon but every kind of smoked fish, plus homemade pickled salmon, pickled herring, canned fish, and caviar, even bagels and bialys (if you don't know a bialy from a bagel, a bialy has no hole, is onion-flavored and delicious toasted). Only certain things, such as smoked butterfish, salmon trout, winter carp, and kopchunka, are seasonal. At any time you can luxuriate in fresh Iranian Beluga malassol (giant-grain) caviar, $89 a 14-oz. tin; fresh Sevruga malassol (small-grain) for $66 a 14-oz. tin; Nova Scotia smoked salmon at $13 a lb.; the less expensive lox ($8.75 a lb.); or smoked sturgeon, brook trout, whitefish, sable plate (Alaska black cod, $5.55 a lb.) and, if you are a kipper fancier, McGregor kippers, $1.99 a lb. Bagels and bialys are 15¢ apiece. In domestic and imported canned seafood, there's salmon, tuna, sardines, mackerel, brook trout, herring, anchovies, sprats, mussels, clams, shrimp, lobster, and shad roe. Some salmon, tuna, and sardines also come in dietetic packs (no salt or oil added). All orders are packed in ice to last 48 hours (charge for ice, $1) and are sent express mail or air freight for next-day delivery. Prices quoted are FOB Manhattan and subject to change.

McArthur's Smokehouse
Millerton, New York 12546
Phone 914-789-3441 or 3446

*

To determine the cooking time for fish (whole, steaks, or fillets), lay the fish on the counter and measure with a ruler or tape measure at the thickest point, from bottom side to top. Allow exactly 10 minutes cooking time per measured inch, doubling the time if fish is cooked from frozen state.

*

Steak au Poivre Flambé

For each person, thaw 1 frozen boneless strip sirloin at least 1¼" thick and score the fat. About 20 minutes before cooking, press 1 to 1½ teaspoons freshly ground coarse pepper into each side of each steak. Pan broil or oven broil to the desired doneness (pan broiling is preferable). To pan broil, melt 1 tablespoon rendered beef fat in a heated skillet and, when the pan is very hot, sear the steaks for 2 to 3 minutes on each side. Reduce the heat a little and continue cooking. Turn once or twice until the meat is done to your taste, 10 to 12 minutes for rare. Test by cutting near the center with a sharp knife. Pour ⅓ cup warm cognac over the steaks in the skillet and flame. Place steaks on a hot serving platter. Pour off any excess fat from the skillet and pour the remaining juices over the meat.
—*from "The Omaha Steaks Cookbook," recipe by James Beard*

Boneless strip steaks from Omaha Steaks International

BILL NEWSOM'S HAMS / Dept. CFC
127 North Highland Avenue, Princeton, KY 42445

"Colonel Bill Newsom's Kentucky Country Hams," free, published annually, 6-page leaflet with recipes, order form.

Kentucky is famous for its country hams, and Bill Newsom's are dry-cured, slow-smoked over green hickory, and aged many months by methods used for over 200 years in this part of the state. The leaflet informs you that after 8 to 10 months of aging, white streaks form in the meat from a concentration of salt and protein. These are in no way harmful to the meat but an indication that the ham has been properly aged in true Kentucky style. Prices on request.

OLDE PHILADELPHIA STEAK COMPANY / Dept. CFC
4021 Market Street, Philadelphia, PA 19104

Six-page color foldout with recipe sheet, $1 (refundable with purchase), published annually, also price list, order form.

Steaks (filet mignon, boneless and bone-in sirloin strip, Chateaubriand and London broil) and rock lobster tails are all pictured in glorious, mouth-watering color on heavy, glossy stock, with some rather overblown captions relating more to ancient chateaux and huntsmen in Elizabethan manors than to meat. The beef is U.S. Prime, corn-fed, aged, and tender, cut in different thicknesses and weights. A package of four 14-oz. boneless sirloin steaks, 1½" thick, is quoted at $31.90; a whole 4- to 4½-lb. Chateaubriand is $41.25; six 8-oz. filets mignons, 1¾" thick, are $32; and the 10-oz. lobster tails are $43.50 for a package of 6. You can order "surf and turf" packages of filet mignon and lobster tails if you happen to go for that currently popular steakhouse marriage. There are also combination steak packages. Prices are postpaid and include shipping charges.

OMAHA STEAKS INTERNATIONAL / Dept. CFC
4400 South 96th Street, Omaha, NB 68127

"Omaha Steaks International Catalog," free, published annually, 24 pages, illustrated, color.

Steaks galore and plenty more. Omaha Steaks International has just about any steak you might want, from porterhouse and T-bone to filet mignon, filet of prime rib, boneless strip sirloin, chopped sirloin, and even a weight-watcher's healthburger (chopped sirloin with 50 percent less fat than allowed by USDA standards). Prices range from about $18 for two 10-oz. boneless strip sirloins, 1" thick, to $67.50 for sixteen 8-oz. filets of prime rib, 1" thick, and there's plenty of choice in between. That's only the beginning of the meats. You can order roasts (prime rib, saddle of veal, boneless leg of spring lamb), veal, pork, and lamb chops, pork tenderloin filets, veal cutlets, tenderloin tips for stroganoff or kebabs, corned beef, ham, bacon, and pork sausage, and specialties like individual beef Wellingtons ($31 for four 7-oz. portions). The beef is aged prime and choice grade, and all the meats are flash-frozen. If you're not in the mood for meat, there's pheasant, stuffed Rock Cornish hens, quail, smoked turkey and chicken, chicken Kiev, chicken Wellington, chicken Cordon Bleu, stuffed crêpes—or maybe you'd rather have Florida stone crab claws, caviar, Irish smoked salmon, lobster tails, or fillets of St. Peter's fish, the species caught in the Sea of Galilee centuries ago, now being specially raised for the market ($27.50 for eight 6- to 8-oz. fillets). Ordering from this catalogue is like ordering from a restaurant menu, except that few menus could offer such a range of food. And with each order you get the 24-page, full-color *Omaha Steaks Cookbook*, with recipes by James Beard, who has written that he finds top-quality frozen meats no different from fresh and occasionally better. Special gift plans, covering four seasons, six holidays, or a year of food, range from $128 to $387. Prices include free delivery within the 48 connecting states (air charges for Hawaii, Alaska, Canada, and international destinations are extra), and orders may be charged to any of the major credit cards. There's also a toll-free number to call.

PAPRIKAS WEISS IMPORTER / Dept. CFC
1546 Second Avenue, New York, NY 10028

"Imported Foods and Cookware Catalogue," $1 for annual subscription, published four times a year, 66 pages, illustrated, black and white.

The catalogue lists Belgian Westphalian-style smoked boneless ham (3 to 4 lbs., $30); the Paprikas Weiss beef-and-pork salami and Hungarian salami and sausage (made to their own recipe, the former only in the winter and slowly cured and dried for months), $4.98 a lb.; their own bacon, double-smoked the Hungarian way ($3.50 a lb.); imported Hungarian canned ham; and other delicacies such as different forms of canned carp (soup, salad, prepared with sour cream, mushrooms, and paprika), pork goulash, and smoked sausage with sauerkraut. They also carry Polish canned game; French rendered goose fat, so good for cooking; foie gras and pâté de foie; and Iranian Beluga and Sevruga mallasol caviar, both fresh and vacuum-packed.

PEPPERIDGE FARM MAIL ORDER CO., INC. / Dept. CFC
Box 7000, Norwalk, CT 06856

"Gift Catalog," free, published periodically, 32 pages, illustrated, color.

If you thought Pepperidge Farm only made baked goods, their gift selections of pâté, ham, turkey, and steaks will surprise you. A teak server with cocktail pâté, pâté of smoked turkey, pheasant supreme, smoked rainbow trout, and old-fashioned chopped and sautéed chicken livers will be useful for many occasions (2⅛ oz. each, $13.95; the pâtés only, $6.95).

Baked, glazed hickory-smoked ham arrives in a cloth bag with serving suggestions (4 to 4½ lbs., $21.95; 8 to 9 lbs., $39.95). Or you can order moist smoked turkey breast, ready to eat and easy to slice, $19.95 for 4 to 4½ lbs.

Two of America's favorite foods—steak and cheesecake—are teamed in a gift box with four 8-oz. filets mignons and a 22-oz. cake for $39.95. Eight boneless strip sirloins (12 oz. each, $49.95) or eight 6-oz filets mignons ($39.95) are shipped in dry ice to arrive in perfect condition.

PFAELZER BROTHERS / Dept. CFC
4501 West District Boulevard, Chicago, IL 60632

"Pfaelzer Brothers Gourmet Meats," free, published annually, 20 pages, illustrated, color.

For over half a century, Pfaelzer Brothers of Chicago have been known for their quality meats, especially steaks and beef roasts, and the catalogue is filled with mouth-watering color pictures of filets mignons, strip steaks, porterhouse and chopped sirloin, Chateaubriand, English-cut heart of rib roast, and rolled sirloin tip roast. Beef isn't all they have. There are also hams, turkeys, stuffed chicken breasts, lobster tails, and, rather surprisingly, pizza (six 12" party pizzas, with both sausage and pepperoni sausage, are $22). All the products are individually wrapped, quick-frozen at 50 to 60 degrees below zero, put in cartons, and shipped in plastic foam containers with dry ice. Prices tend to rise every year, but as this was written the 12-lb. rib roast was around $60, the boneless loin strip steaks ran $34.95 for four 12-oz. steaks, 1¼" thick, and the 4-lb. Chateaubriand was $54.45. Pfaelzer also has combination meat packages at prices ranging from $38.95 for steaks and chopped sirloin patties to $209 for a full loin cut into 58 steaks and patties plus a 4-pound sirloin roast. There is the usual "surf and turf" (filet mignon and lobster tail) combination and a couple of special gift ideas: Chateaubriand packaged with a maple carving board/chopping block or 6 filet mignon steaks with an electric broiler.

RITCHIE BROS. / Dept. CFC
37 Watergate, Rothesay PA20 9AD, Scotland

Brochure, free.

Ritchie Brothers, salmon-curing specialists, will ship you by air, postpaid, a 2-lb. side of authentic bland-cured Scots smoked salmon from their Isle of Bute smoke kilns for $26 (at last report, though prices may

Spicy Hungarian-style sausage from Paprikas Weiss

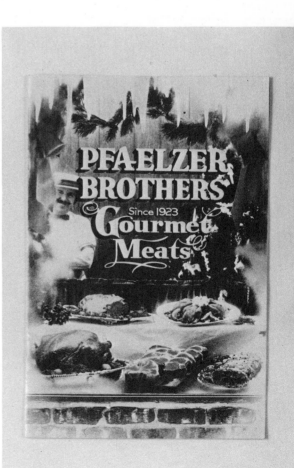

have increased since). Their salmon, taken from the pure rivers in the highlands of Scotland and smoked by their own secret formula, is guaranteed by Ritchie "to please the most fastidious gastronome."

SAHADI IMPORTING CO., INC. / Dept. CFC
187 Atlantic Avenue, Brooklyn, NY 11201

"The Silent Salesman," free, published biannually, 24 pages, illustrated, black and white.

This is the place to order basterma (dried beef with garlic and spices, $5.50 a lb.) and soujouk (dried sausage with garlic and spices, $4.50 a lb.), two Middle Eastern specialties. Among the usual roster of imported canned fish (sardines, anchovies, mackerel) you'll find tarama, the dried salted gray mullet roe used for taramasalata (80¢ a 10-oz. jar) or ready-prepared taramasalata for $1.

SALTWATER FARM, INC. / Dept. CFC
Varrell Lane, York Harbor, ME 03911

Catalogue, free, published 4 to 6 times a year, 8 pages, illustrated, color and black and white.

Now in their 28th year of business, Saltwater Farm is the place to order a lobster bake (or you can send a friend a gift certificate). Lobsters and steamer clams from those icy Maine waters come nestled in rockweed, shipped by air freight in a polystyrene container with disposable metal steamer inside, ready to boil. A feast of eight 1¼-lb. lobsters will run you around $58 (although, like everything else, prices are bound to increase before you read this) and steamers are around $10 a peck (enough to feed 16 people). Prices are FOB Boston. Air freight charges, quoted on the order form, are extra. You can stock up on the accessories for a lobster bake: disposable place settings with plate, glass, butter cup, napkin bib, flatware and picks, tablecloth, even the garbage bag to throw the disposable debris into. You have to supply your own lobster crackers. For an extra $2.95 you can get a salt-and-pepper set shaped like lobster claws. There's also the traditional clam steamer, with a spigot in the bottom for tapping the broth (4-gallon size, $21.25). Saltwater Farm has branched out into other foods, too. Irish smoked salmon sides (2 to 2¼ lbs., $23.50), Maine lobster tails, Florida lobster and stone crab claws, rock shrimp, stuffed red snapper, Florida shore dinners, strip sirloin steaks, lobster tail and filet mignon combinations are shipped deep-frozen.

They have packages of canned chowders and soups, crab meat, seafood dips, seafood spreads, lobster meat, lobster Newburg, some attractively packaged in pine kegs or baskets, and really good-looking chowder cups, wheel-thrown by the Rackliffe family of Blue Hill, Maine. Shaped like outsize coffee cups (and also good for café au lait), they have a lovely soft grayish-white glaze.

SEY-CO PRODUCTS / Dept. CFC
7651 Densmore Avenue, Van Nuys, CA 91406

Catalogue, free, published annually, 15 pages, illustrated, color.

Sey-Co's list of specialty foods includes whole grain Beluga caviar (about $30 for 4 oz.), French pâté de foie gras with truffles (about $20 for a 3¾-oz. terrine) and liver pâté, pâtés of smoked salmon, smoked turkey and smoked rainbow trout, and escargots (a 7½-oz. tin of 24 snails and shells is around $6). They also have various canned seafoods, including Iceland brook trout ($2.75 for a 10-oz. tin), smoked sturgeon, smoked oysters, and shad roe.

J&M SHEARER, LIMITED / Dept. CFC
8 Victoria Street, Aberdeen AB9 1FL, Scotland

Brochure, free, published seasonally (for Christmas).

Sides of Scotch smoked salmon, from 1¾ to 2¼ lbs., or ½-lb. and 1-lb. packets of sliced smoked salmon, smoked rainbow trout, smoked mackerel, and smoked eel are the specialties of Shearer, who also offer a

A real nice clambake—and other products—from Saltwater Farm

★

To remove liquid from the inside of a boiled lobster, pierce the shell with the point of a heavy knife where head joins body, turn upside down and let water drain out.

★

Include wine or tomatoes in list of ingredients when cooking pot roast, stew, or tough cuts of meat. The acidity helps break down the tough fibers.

★

carton of four traditional French-style pâtés—pâté de foie, country pâté, country pâté with garlic, and chicken pâté. Prices to overseas addresses will be supplied on request, and Shearer advises that shipments are dispatched by air parcel post only in the colder months—not from May through October. The brochure has some very useful information about storing smoked fish in the freezer or the refrigerator and gives a few judicious serving suggestions. The export manager mentions that this would be the ideal Christmas gift for relatives or friends in the UK—no duty, no danger of parcels getting lost.

SPORTPAGES / Dept. CFC
13719 Welch Road, Dallas, TX 75240

"Sportpages," free, published periodically, 33 pages, illustrated, color.

We all know Scotch and Nova Scotia smoked salmon. Well, the one Sportpages offers is Belgian, cold-smoked over beechwood for 4 to 5 days. It comes vacuum-packed for freshness and is $30 for a side of approximately 2 lbs.

SUNNYLAND FARMS, INC. / Dept. CFC
Box 785, Route 1, Albany, GA 31705

"Pecans Plain and Fancy," free, published annually, 32 pages, illustrated, color.

Sunnyland Farms, whose specialty is pecans, also sells Georgia country hams, specially dry-cured for them with pepper and salt. A whole ham of around 14 lbs. is $38.25. Or you can buy two slabs of country-cured bacon, weighing between 4¾ and 5¼ lb., for $13.65. Prices are approximate and subject to change.

THE SWISS COLONY / Dept. CFC
1112 7th Avenue, Monroe, WI 53566

"Gifts of Perfect Taste," free, published annually (for Christmas), 92 pages, illustrated, color.

In addition to Wisconsin cheeses, cakes and candies, nuts and fruits, this gift catalogue has a fair selection of meats, smoked poultry and ham, bacon and smoked sausage. Their boneless strip steaks are $52 delivered for eight 12-oz. steaks, and there are also 6-oz. steaks, combinations of filet and strip steaks, filet of prime rib steaks, tenderloin steaks (all flash-frozen and shipped in an insulated chest). Other meat and fish specialties are frozen breast of chicken Kiev, Regal or Cordon Bleu, King crab legs, lox, lobster tails, and Cape Cod fish fillets—lemon sole, striped bass, and scrod ($34.50 for twelve 6- to 8-oz. fillets). In smoked poultry, a whole turkey is $21.95, ringneck pheasant $10.95, and two Rock Cornish game hens $9.95. A boneless ham roll is $14.95 for 4 lbs., 2 lbs. of Canadian-style bacon $10.95, an assortment of 1-lb. bacon, braunschweiger, beerwurst, Swiss-style summer, all-beef and old-fashioned summer sausages $13.95, and a 7-lb. side of slab bacon $17.95. All prices are delivered.

TEEL MOUNTAIN FARM / Dept. CFC
Box 200, Stanardsville, VA 22973

Literature, free on request.

Ellie and Don Pruess are in the business of raising milk-fed baby beef and veal naturally and organically—no chemical fertilizers, herbicides, or pesticides are used on their 350 acres of pasture and woodland, and the animals are never given antibiotics or hormones to add weight. The cows graze at will, eating grass, wild herbs, plants, and vines, and the calves drink only their mother's milk. The baby beef is from 7 to 8 months old and weighs between 450 and 500 pounds before processing, when the animal is cut by the quarter into 56-lb. packages of steaks (sirloin, porterhouse, T-bone, and rib, 1" thick, individually wrapped) and roasts, plus ground beef and stew meat in 1-lb. packages. The smaller, younger veal is also sold by the quarter animal, in 28-lb. packages of cutlets, roasts, scaloppine, chops, ground and stewing meat. Or

Baked and Glazed Kentucky Country Ham
Soak ham overnight in cold water, if hard or over a year old. Clean ham with warm water or vinegar and a bristle brush. Place cleaned ham, skin side up, in an open pan. Bake uncovered at 300° until meat thermometer registers 170°, allowing 25 to 30 minutes a pound. When ham is done remove the skin with a sharp knife. Cover or coat with one of the following glazes: (1) a mixture of brown sugar moistened with cider vinegar, juice from pickled peaches, fruit juice, or cider; (2) a mixture of 1 cup brown sugar and 2 tablespoons flour or ¼ cup fine bread crumbs; (3) a thin layer of prepared mustard liberally coated with brown sugar. Bake in a 400° oven until golden brown and glazed.
—from "Colonel Bill Newsom's Kentucky Country Hams"

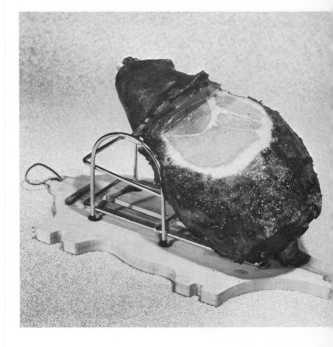

you can have a 56-lb. combination package of half veal, half baby beef, with an assortment of cuts. The meat is processed in a plant under state and USDA inspection, aged, cut, wrapped in small-family-size portions, labeled, sealed, and flash-frozen. Each 28-lb. box of meat takes freezer space of 24" x 12" x 6", and you can arrange with friends or neighbors to split a shipment with them. Shipments are made by their own freezer truck within the home delivery area, or by air, packed in dry ice, over longer distances, with a charge for each. They will send you details of their farming practices, information on how to make a reservation for an order (supplies are limited) with prices, and an invitation to visit the barn the last Sunday of each month, from 1 to 5 P.M., to see how the beef is raised. Write ahead of time for directions.

Canned herring label, from Vander Vliet's Holland Imports

VANDER VLIET'S HOLLAND IMPORTS / Dept. CFC
   3147 West 111th Street, Chicago, IL 60655

Catalogue, free, published annually, 34 pages, black and white.

Among other imports in this catalogue are canned blood, liver, breakfast and beer sausages, 98¢ a 4½-oz. tin (Stockmeyer brand), mussels in vinegar and marinated mussels, jars of herring—whole pickled, salted matjes, herring snacks, rollmops—canned fried herring, fillets of herring in sauce, fillets of mackerel in tomato sauce, smoked conger eel in oil, and, when available, fresh smoked eel at $6.50 a lb.

WEAVER'S FAMOUS LEBANON BOLOGNA, INC. / Dept. CFC
   P.O. Box 525, Lebanon, PA 17042

"From the smokehouses of Weaver's," free, published annually, 16 pages, illustrated, color.

Lebanon bologna is a Pennsylvania Dutch specialty, and practically all of it is made in the Lebanon Valley, where, in the early 1800s, the Pennsylvania Dutch settlers first began to make this very distinctive and flavorful large, smoked, spiced beef sausage. Daniel Weaver made the first commercial Lebanon bologna in 1885, and the family has been in business ever since, making bologna from their own secret recipe. They are proud of their old-fashioned smokehouses and have free plant tours for visitors Monday through Friday. Naturally, they have other smoked meats—ham, slab or sliced bacon, Canadian bacon, and that marvelous smoked dried beef that you slice paper-thin and eat like the Swiss air-dried beef, *viande de Grisons*. Then there's a sweet bologna, Pennsylvania Dutch smoked cheese and Pennsylvania Dutch pretzels of three kinds, the thin ones, the fat beer pretzels, and little bite-size "nutzels." You can order the meats separately or have different combination packs of smoked meats (a 3½-lb. Lebanon bologna, a 1-lb. package of sliced dried beef, and 1 lb. of sliced bacon, for example, bologna and pretzels, or bologna, pretzels, and cheese). Prices range from around $5 up.

THE WISCONSIN CHEESEMAN / Dept. CFC
   P.O. Box 1, Madison, WI 53701

"Gift Selections," free, published annually, 96 pages, illustrated, color.

The catalogue has a small selection of smoked meats and poultry, both alone and in gift packages with other foods. Smoked turkey ($19.50 for the 9-lb. size), smoked turkey breast (4 to 5 lbs., $13.95), and combination packages of turkey with cheese, smoked game hen with cheese and canned fish, smoked turkey roll with preserves, honey, cookies, and cheese, and a hickory-smoked 10-lb. semiboneless country ham packaged with cheese, German mustard, preserves, and stuffed olives ($29.95) are just a few. There's also a smoked pheasant package with a selection of cheeses and other foods ($18.95), or the smoked pheasant alone ($12.95). Smoked birds and ham are not available June, July, and August.

   Turning to other meats, you'll find a quartet of smoked sausages (all-beef, summer sausage, mettwurst, German-style braunschweiger) for $5.45, two types of summer sausage (regular and all-beef) packaged with smoked bacon and a 1-lb. can of Holland ham ($9.95), and various combinations of cheese and sausage or sausage with other foods. Canned fish, such as mackerel fillets, sardines, lobster and shrimp pâtés, crab meat spread, are included in many of the gift packages, as are the smoked bacon, canned ham, and sausages.

YOUNG & SAUNDERS LTD. / Dept. CFC
5 Queensferry Street, Edinburgh EH2 4PD, Scotland

"Food & Wine List," free, published seasonally, 42 pages, black and white.

In the Young & Saunders catalogue you'll find a good selection of pâtés and pastes in tins and terrines, such as smoked goose pâté, pâté maison, pâté de canard à l'orange, smoked duckling pâté and pâté de foie gras, smoked and frozen Scotch salmon and smoked trout, canned seafoods such as soft herring roes and pressed cod roes, Scottish herrings and kippers, smoked mackerel, and smoked frogs' legs. Prices, quoted in sterling, are subject to change and the fluctuating exchange rate and do not include overseas shipping charges, which you should request. If you want to send a Christmas package to friends in the UK, there are many more foods you might select from, such as the York and Belfast hams, the pâté en croute (available only during the Christmas season), and, of course, the wines, liqueurs, and liquors; especially the straight-malt whiskys. Or your friends might welcome a bottle of American bourbon or Mexican tequila.

Dried Beef and Oyster Soufflé
Shred ¼ pound air-dried beef. Melt 2 tablespoons butter in a skillet and sauté the beef briefly. Stir in 2 tablespoons flour and ½ teaspoon dry mustard and cook 2 minutes. Pour in 1 cup milk and cook, stirring, until thick and smooth. Remove from heat and stir in 4 egg yolks, one at a time. Season to taste with salt and freshly ground black pepper. Stir in 1 cup drained and chopped oysters. Beat 5 egg whites until stiff and fold in. Pour the mixture into a greased 1½-quart soufflé dish. Bake in a preheated 350° oven for 30 minutes until puffed and browned. Serve immediately. Serves 4.

—from "Treasured Recipes from Early New England Kitchens"

See Appendix, page 239, for additional sources not included here.

Poires Princesse

CHAPTER FOUR

FRUITS AND NUTS

Poires Princesse

Mix together 1 cup champagne wafer crumbs, 1 can (15½ oz.) crème de marrons or sweetened chestnut purée, and a 2-oz. package Gervais cheese. Drain and dry 12 large halves of poached pears (canned may also be used). Spread the chestnut cheese mixture on the flat side of 6 of the halves and top with the remaining halves. Stand the pears upright on a platter to resemble whole pears. Chill until ready to use. Place 2 tablespoons cornstarch in a saucepan and stir in ¼ cup sugar, 1 cup heavy cream, and ½ cup dry white wine. Stir over low heat until sauce bubbles and thickens. Cool and then stir in 1 teaspoon vanilla. Chill. Place a mint sprig on the top of each pear. Surround pears with strawberry slices. Spoon sauce over pears and serve at once with additional champagne wafers. Serves 6.

—*courtesy Food and Wines from France, Inc.*

AHLERS ORGANIC DATE AND GRAPEFRUIT GARDEN
Dept. CFC
P.O. Box 726, Mecca, CA 92254
Price list, free, published annually, 5 pages.

Ahler's dates are organically and naturally grown, sun-cured, and preserved with no commercial fertilizers, insecticides, or preservatives.

Soft dates include Khadrawy, Halawy, Deglet Noor, and Zahidi in 3½-, 5½-, 11- and 20-lb. boxes ($8.45 to $29.95). They are also sold in cases of nine 1-lb. boxes ($22.95).

Medium-soft dates in 3- to 20-lb. boxes are $6.25 to $26.95; all-purpose, small Zahidis in 10- and 20-lb. boxes are $11.95 and $22.95; and ground dates are $8.25 for 1 qt. to $13.95 for 8 lbs.

All dates, as well as coconut-date balls, are lower-priced when ordered in quantities of 120 lbs. or more. Ahlers includes a few date-filled recipes with its price list and orders.

White marsh seedless grapefruit, organically grown, unsprayed and unwaxed, are $6.50 for 34 lbs. Prices again are lower for 120 lbs. or more shipped to one address. Kinnows, tangelos, and lemons (30¢ per lb. or $8.50 for 36 lbs.) are shipped in limited quantities.

ALAMO FRUIT / Dept. CFC
Box 666, Alamo, TX 78516

"Holiday Gifts," free, published annually, 32 pages, illustrated, color.

Ruby red grapefruit and Tex-gold oranges from the historic Rio Grande Valley in Texas are the specialties of Alamo Fruit. The holiday feature is a handwoven Mexican basket filled with 24 lbs. of luscious grapefruit and oranges ($15.90), but the three-layer special is a bargain—about 38 lbs. for $15.95. Grapefruit, oranges, hard candies, fruit cakettes, and Texas pecan roll slices are the surprises tucked into the Holiday Star package ($11.75 for approximately 11 lbs.).

Two gift plans are available: three shipments at Christmas, Valentine's Day, and Easter ($32.85), or five shipments at Christmas, January, February, March, and April ($54.75)—fresh fruit when you really want and need it.

Grapefruit and pineapples ($14.95 for 26 lbs.); oranges, grapefruit, and avocados ($9.85 for 11 lbs.); smoked meats, 8 tropical jellies and marmalades ($8.90); and pecan fruitcakes ($7.25 for 1¾ lbs.) round out the product list from this award-winning business. Shipments are November to April in most cases.

AULT BEE FARMS / Dept. CFC
Rte. 2, Box 64, Weslaco, TX 78596

Price list, free.

Canned papaya, flavored with honey, lemon, and pineapple, is the product Ault Bee Farms sells year round, but they also will ship fresh ripe papayas in season. Write for details and latest prices.

BOWLBY CANDY CO. / Dept. CFC
P.O. Box 312, Waupaca, WI 54981

Brochure and price list, free.

Jumbo salted cashews at $2.98 a lb. bag or $6.50 a 2-lb. gift tin and deluxe mixed nuts at $3.35 a lb. bag or $7.25 for a 2-lb. gift tin are among the offerings of the Bowlby Candy Co., which also makes a wheat-germ pecan substitute called Bowlby's Bits.

LUCY BRALEY'S CANDY KITCHEN / Dept. CFC
Cranberry Highway, Massachusetts State Tourist Route 28, South Middleboro, MA 02346

Price lists and order forms, free, updated periodically.

In addition to candies, Lucy Braley sells jumbo salted peanuts, cooked in olive oil, light, medium, or dark, or unsalted and oven-roasted (no oil) and mixed. Prices run about $1.50 a lb., with packing and shipping extra. Or you can order salted or unsalted and oven-roasted mixed nuts (almonds, Brazils, cashews, filberts, peanuts, and pecans) for about 65¢ a lb. more.

CALIFORNIA ALMOND GROWERS EXCHANGE / Dept. CFC
P.O. Box 1768, Sacramento, CA 95808

"Almond Gifts from California," free, published annually, 20 pages, illustrated, color.

El Capitan, the most popular gift assortment from C.A.G.E., contains a 6-oz. tin each of hickory-smoked, cheese, onion-garlic, barbecue, and blanched almonds ($6.50). El Presidente triples the selection to 18 tins ($15.75). Custom orders for any combination are arranged to your special request: 4-tin packs at $5.45; 6 tins, $7; 12 tins, $11.75; and 18 tins, $16.25.
A spectacular cornucopia of almond gifts includes 32 gold-foil-wrapped pieces of almond nougat, 1 lb. of Jordan almonds, three 6-oz. tins of Fresco after-dinner almonds, a 6-oz. tin of whole natural nuts, 2 cans of roasted, salted, diced and roasted, blanched and slivered almonds in 6-oz. tins of snacking flavored almonds, a wooden nut bowl, and a stollen cake, all for $27.50.
Jumbo 4-lb. tins of the most popular flavors are an economical way to buy nuts ($9.25), and remember that nuts can be stored almost indefinitely in the refrigerator or freezer.
Almond creamix, an almond paste, is delicious for marzipan candies, tortes, and cakes ($10.50 a 7-lb. tin).
Almonds for cooking, wonderful additions to main dishes, salads, and desserts, come in many styles. A 4-lb. tin of unsalted blanched whole almonds is $9.25; a 3-lb. tin of sliced blanched, $7.50; while a 4-lb. tin of green-onion-flavor slivered is recommended on green beans, baked potatoes, in salads ($9.75).

CASA DE FRUTA / Dept. CFC
6680 Pacheco Pass Hwy., Hollister, CA 95023

"Casa de Fruta," price list and order form, free, published annually, 4 pages, illustrated, color.

Dried fruit from California at reasonable prices. Figs ($1.50 for 14 oz.), dates ($1 per lb.), apples ($1 per 8 oz.), peaches or pears (10 oz. for $1), raisins ($1 for 18 oz.), pineapple (12 oz. for $1.50), and bananas (50¢ for 3½ oz.) are available individually, as are walnuts and almonds, or in combination gift packs.
The "San Luis" pack ($14.50) has 7½ lbs. of apricots, apples, peaches, pears, and prunes; the "Monterey" ($14.25) contains 4¼ lbs. of apricots,

Gift catalogue, California Almond Growers Exchange

Sicilian Pasta Sauce
Heat ½ cup fruity olive oil in a skillet and add 2 finely chopped garlic cloves and 16 chopped anchovy fillets. Warm through in the oil. Add ½ cup raisins, ½ cup pine nuts, and ¼ cup chopped pitted Italian black olives. Season with a little freshly ground black pepper and pour over 1 pound spaghetti or fettucine, cooked and drained. Toss well together and serve.

CEW's Oranges Glacées

Select 6 medium oranges and peel two of them, removing only the colored part in wide long strips. Cut into thin julienne strips about 1" long and blanch in boiling water for 5 minutes. Drain and set aside. Peel all the oranges, removing pith and outer membrane completely. Cut crosswise into thin slices and put into a large glass bowl. Make a syrup with 1½ cups sugar and ¾ cup water. Heat slowly to the boiling point and let boil for 10 to 15 minutes, until slightly thickened. Add julienne peel and cook another 1 to 2 minutes. Stir in 1 tablespoon liquid caramel and 2 teaspoons Grand Marnier, pour over orange slices, and let stand for several hours in a cool place. Serve slightly chilled, but not ice cold, accompanied by plain cookies.

—*from Williams-Sonoma's "A Catalog for Cooks"*

Gift box of fruits, from Day & Young

Pears 'n Squares

8 of our juiciest California Crown pears are the center attraction in this lovely gift full of holiday excitement. But don't overlook the 2 jumbo apples and 4 square trays with their delightful variety of gourmet dried fruit and candies that make the setting complete. The tangy apricots, zesty prunes, rich dates, and fruit candies (rolled in coconut chips) are a special taste experience you won't want to miss! The perfect Christmas thought for loved ones who dream fondly of fresh fruit this time of year. Shipping weight about 7 lbs.

Order Gift No. 14 . . . delivered $11.95

Available for delivery between November 10 and January 5 to the connecting 48 states and Hawaii.

dates, cherries, figs, pineapples, walnuts, pears, peaches, and prunes. Fruits come combined with chocolate in the "Pajaro" ($13.50).

CHEESE COFFEE CENTER / Dept. CFC
2110 Center Street, Berkeley, CA 94704

Mail-order catalogue, free, published semiannually, 12 pages, black and white.

In addition to cheese and coffee, this store also sells miscellaneous nuts and dried fruits and shelled sunflower seeds ($1.29 a lb.). The fruits include unsulphured and Turkish apricots, dates, Calimyrna figs, prunes, pineapple rings, and Thompson raisins, ranging in price from around 95¢ to $3.69 a lb. for unsulphured apricots. Trail mixes, $1.59 a lb., keep backpackers going on different mixtures such as natural (with lots of fruit), nut and seed, carob or banana. The nuts start at $1.69 a lb. for unshelled roasted peanuts and go up to $4.79 a lb. for raw macadamias. Among the nut selections are California or Persian pistachios; raw, shelled, or unshelled pine nuts; and cashews, raw or roasted and salted.

COVALDA DATE CO. / Dept. CFC
P.O. Box 900, Coachella, CA 92236

Price list, free, published seasonally, 3 pages.

From the largest all-organic date planting in California comes a gigantic selection of dates in a myriad of shapes, sizes, and varieties. There are 17 different 5-lb. packs, from a family special for $7.25 delivered to extra-fancy Medjool, $17.20 delivered. A 12-pack sampler with two 1-lb. sacks each of choice Deglet Noor dates, datettes (chopped pieces), datelets (bite-size date-coconut confection), hydrated dates, desert brownie dates, and Zahidi dates is $21.20 delivered. Creamed dates (date butter), 2 qts., is $10.70 delivered, and 3 lbs. of stuffed dates in layered gift pack is $8.15 delivered.

Covalda also offers jumbo Mahan pecans ($39.60 for 25 lbs.), Black Mission figs (5 lbs., $7.10), Thompson seedless raisins (15 lbs., $17.55), shelled walnuts (2½ lbs., $7), and sun-dried unsulphured apricots (15 lbs., $50.45).

If you get together with your friends and neighbors you can take advantage of the 10 percent discount offered for orders of 250 lbs. or more.

CREOLE DELICACIES CO., INC. / Dept. CFC
533-H Saint Ann Street, New Orleans, LA 70116

"Happy Gifts of Food From Old New Orleans," free, published annually, 12 pages, illustrated, color.

Pecanfections, mammoth pecan halves in orange, rum, and cinnamon flavors, are the newest nut offering from Creole Delicacies ($10.95 for three 8-oz. containers). Large pecans are available in the shell in 3- and 5-lb. sacks ($5.95 and $8.95), or shelled in 2-lb. boxes for $8.95.

Ready for shipment from December 10 for deliveries through January 1 are the large Louisiana navel oranges in boxes of 12 for $8.95 or ½ bushel (approximately 30 oranges) for $18.95. No shipments to Arizona, Florida, and California.

DAY & YOUNG / Dept. CFC
Orchard Lane, Santa Clara, CA 95052

"Holiday Gifts," free, published annually, 28 pages, illustrated, color.

Santa Clara seems to be the hub of mail-order fruit companies (Mission Pak is practically next door). Day & Young are particularly proud of their Crown pears, which come in 3 box sizes from 6¾ lbs. to 13 lbs. ($7.95 to $12.95). The Crowns come in giant size ($10.95 for 8 to 10 pears) and petite ($8.95 for 24 to 30 pears).

For $15.95 you get a box each of 9 oranges, 8 Crown pears, and 9 apples, or three boxes of either apples or pears with a total weight of about 18 lbs.

Assortments of dried apricots, pears, figs, dates, prunes, cherries, and pineapples come packed on a redwood tray ($5.95 to $17.95) or in a shallow wicker basket ($5.95 to $9.95).

A Yule box of miniature fruitcakes, 4 oz. of hard candies, 4½ oz. of chocolate-covered cherries, and 4 oz. of unshelled nuts, combined with pears and apples, is $11.95. Pears, apples, nuts, cheese, and dried fruits are combined in a 13-lb. gift box ($15.95). A handsome handwoven basket holds 11 lbs. of Crown pears, apples, Day & Young fancy marmalade, dried dates, prunes, and apricots, plus fruit candies ($22.95).

Day & Young, like Mission Pak, has a fruit-for-all-seasons club for 3 months ($26.95) and 6 months ($49.95). You get pears in December, Mineola tangelos in February, grapefruit in April, Bing cherries in June, peaches in August, and Ribier grapes in October, 42¾ lbs. of fruit in all.

DEER VALLEY FARM / Dept. CFC
RD 1, Guilford, NY 13780

Price list, free, published annually, 20 pages, black and white.

Deer Valley Farm has a good list of unsulphured dried fruits, some organically grown, including 4 types of prunes from Sunray Orchards in Oregon and dried pitted black cherries ($1.69 a lb.). From November to May they have biologically grown MacIntosh, Cortland, Wealthy, Spy, and Red Delicious apples in boxes or at a lb. rate of 45¢ or 49¢ (prices vary from time to time), as well as oranges, grapefruit, and lemons. They also have the usual range of nuts, in shell or shelled, ranging in price from 74¢ a lb. for shelled raw Spanish peanuts to $3.40 a lb. for pecan halves.

FRASER-MORRIS / Dept. CFC
872 Madison Avenue, New York, NY 10021

"Gifts for Festive Occasions from Fraser-Morris," free, published seasonally, 11 pages, illustrated, color.

California sun-dried fruits, including figs, dates, apricots, pears, jumbo prunes, pineapples, and cherries (1 lb., $4.25; 3 lbs., $11.50); brandied peaches (½ gal., $12.60); deluxe mixed nuts (1 lb., $4.25); macadamia nuts (9 oz., $4.25); and pistachio nuts (4¾ lbs., $18.25) are available both individually gift-packed from Fraser-Morris, as well as in some lavish gift hampers. The Imperial hamper contains Elberta peaches, glacé fruits, holiday fruitcakes, Darjeeling tea, minted almonds, almond cookies, Swiss chocolates, stuffed olives, Raffetto canteloupe balls, and pure fruit preserves ($49.95, plus delivery charges).

FRAZIER FARMS, INC. / Dept. CFC
405 W. Grand Avenue, Escondido, CA 92025

Price list, free, updated seasonally.

Frazier Farms sells nuts (raw or roasted and salted), seeds, dried fruits, and a few miscellaneous items such as carob peanuts, carob raisins, carob chips, and banana chips. Raw nuts, which range in price from 59¢ a lb. for Spanish peanuts to $3.49 a lb. for pecan halves, include almonds, Brazil nuts, cashews, filberts, pecans, pistachios ($2.25 a lb.), Spanish and Virginia peanuts, and walnuts. In roasted and salted nuts there are almonds, cashews (whole or in pieces), mixed nuts, pepitas, and peanuts. Seeds (sesame, pumpkin, sunflower, chia, flax, and alfalfa) start at 59¢ a lb. for flax and go up to $1.95 for 12 oz. of pumpkin seeds. Dried fruits, from 79¢ to $2.59 a lb., include figs, raisins, large and pitted prunes, pineapples, and unsulphured apples, apricots, pears, and peaches. All prices are FOB Escondido.

GOLDEN ACRES ORCHARD / Dept. CFC
Rte. 2, Box 770, Front Royal, VA 22630

Price list, free, published annually.

Golden Acres Orchard apples are organically grown, their unfiltered apple juice has no chemical additives, and their "ole time" apple cider vinegar is made the natural way.

Red Delicious, Jonathan, Stark crimson, Winesap, and Prime Gold apples are shipped at harvest (September 15 to December 15), while

Pepper Pecans
In a heavy skillet, sauté 1 pound pecan halves in a little butter. Add 2 teaspoons Worcestershire sauce, a few dashes of Tabasco sauce (optional), salt and pepper to taste. Roast 20 minutes, or until brown, in a 300° oven, stirring occasionally. Serve hot.
—*from Sternberg's Collection of Pecan Recipes*

*

Put shelled nuts in plastic bags and store in the freezer. Exposure to warm temperatures turns the oil in nuts rancid.

*

When chopping sticky dried fruits, dip the knife blade in hot water to prevent them clinging to the blade.

*

Citrus fruits from Goochland Gardens

★

For a quick energy-giving snack or a cocktail nibble, combine mixed salted nuts and raisins. The contrast of salt and sweet is very pleasant.

★

To prevent cut fruits from discoloring, rub cut surfaces with lemon juice. If they are to be cooked, drop them into a bowl of water with a squeeze of lemon juice or a teaspoon of salt.

★

California Grapefruit and Papaya Salad
Peel 3 papayas and slice lengthwise. Arrange on romaine leaves alternately with the sections from 3 grapefruit. Make a vinaigrette dressing with ½ cup olive oil, 3 tablespoons lemon juice, and salt and freshly ground black pepper to taste. Chill before serving. Serves 6.

Imperial Red York and Golden Delicious are available October 1 to December 16.

If you order 10 bushels ($100), approximately 425 lbs., you'll get an eleventh bushel free. One bushel, of any variety, approximately 42 lbs., is $14.25, and a ¼ bushel is $4.95.

Apple juice is $8.75 for a case of 4 gallons, with a 3-case minimum ($23). From September 1, apple cider vinegar is available in a minimum order of 6 cases of 4 gallons each ($72). Cases of juice and vinegar can be mixed so long as minimum requirement is met.

GOOCHLAND GARDENS, INC. / Dept. CFC
P.O. Box 366, Fort Meade, FL 33841

"Goochland Gardens' Florida Citrus," free, published annually, 2 pages, illustrated, color.

Goochland Gardens can send you tangelos (December to March) and murcotts, also known as honey tangerines (February to April), as well as various oranges: hamlin (November, December), page (November to January), navel (November to January), pineapple (January, February), temple (January to March), Valencia (April to July), and, of course, tangerines (November to February).

Goochland also has grapefruit: Duncan, pink seedless, ruby red, and marsh seedless (November to June).

A ¼ bushel of either oranges or grapefruit (not mixed) is $10.35, while a bushel is $24.25.

You can also get from ¼ to a full bushel of a mixture of oranges, grapefruit, and unspecified jellies ($11.35 to $25.25).

THE GOURMET PANTRY / Dept. CFC
400 McGuinness Blvd., Brooklyn, NY 11222

"Pleasure Packed Gifts from the Gourmet Pantry," free, published annually, 72 pages, illustrated, color.

Among the gift packages are some simple boxes of fruits, dried fruits, and nuts. A package of 18 lbs. of Florida oranges and grapefruit is $10.95, or you can order 24-, 36-, and 48-lb. boxes. Medjool dates are $6.99 for a 1-lb. box, and giant dessert apricots are $7.50 for a 1-lb. tin. The Family Fruit Pack combines apples, California Crown pears, dried fruits, shelled nuts, and a baby Gouda cheese for $14.99. A buffet tray holds 2 lbs. of "moisturized" dried fruits ($4.99).

HALE INDIAN RIVER GIFTS / Dept. CFC
Indian River Plaza, Wabasso, FL 32970

"Hale Indian River Fruit Gifts," free, published annually, 16 pages, illustrated, color.

From this colorful catalogue you can select navel oranges or seedless grapefruit by themselves or mixed ($10.25 for ⅜ bushel), navels with pink grapefruit at the same price, tangerine-size "zipper skinned" page oranges ($10.75 for ⅜ bushel), ruby-red seedless grapefruit ($17.95 a bushel), or tangelos, also $17.95 a bushel.

Also available during the fruit season—mid-November to mid-June—is a Florida sampler of 8 navels, a box of coconut frosties, candied fruit, and jars of tangelo marmalade and guava jelly ($10.25). A woven basket filled with 18 navels, 3 pink grapefruit, jars of orange-pineapple-cherry marmalade and orange-blossom honey, and chocolate-dipped coconut patties is $16.25.

Or join the Tropical Fruit Club for 3 ($29.75), 6 ($59.50), 9 ($92.25), or 12 ($118.95) months. At Christmas you'll get ⅜ bushel of navels; January, ⅜ bushel of tangelos; February, ⅜ bushel of temple oranges; March, ⅜ bushel of ruby-red grapefruit; April, ⅜ bushel of honey tangerines; May, ⅜ bushel of marsh seedless grapefruits; June, ⅜ bushel of Valencia oranges; July, 12 mangoes; August, 9 avocados; September, six 1-lb. jars of jellies, marmalades, and honey; October, ⅜ bushel of tangerines; and November, ⅜ bushel of page oranges.

HARRY AND DAVID / Dept. CFC
Bear Creek Orchards, Medford, OR 97501

Catalogue, free, published annually, 28 pages, illustrated, color.

While Harry and David Holmes are famous for the Fruit-of-the-Month Club they initiated in 1937, the pride of their orchards is the huge, succulent Royal Riviera comice pear. The pears come in various gift packs, either in combination with other fresh or dried fruits or alone in boxes of from 6½ to 24 lbs., at prices from around $8.45 to $19.95. A box of miniature Royal Rivieras is around $11.45 for 9½ lbs. The Fruit-of-the-Month Club includes other fruits and is described in detail in chapter 11.

HARWOOD HILL ORCHARD AND GIFT SHOP / Dept. CFC
Business Route 7, Bennington, VT 05201

Brochure, order form and price list, free, published annually, 8 pages, illustrated, black and white.

Harwood Hill Orchard is owned and operated by the third generation of the Bohnes family, who grow 40 varieties of apples, pears, plums, and berries and market their produce and other Vermont products at their sales barn, which was built in 1785. They will ship McIntosh, Cortland, Northern Spy, Red Delicious, and mixed varieties of apples from September through January in 15-, 30-, and 45-apple packs, or gift-boxed with other products such as cheddar cheese, maple syrup, and their own unique rosy-red apple syrup. As we don't have the price list we can't quote costs.

HOUSE OF ALMONDS / Dept. CFC
P.O. Box 5125, Bakersfield, CA 93308

"Gift Selections," free, published annually, 22 pages, illustrated, color.

The catalogue is a full house of almonds—almonds roasted and salted, blanched and roasted, flavored with cheese, hickory-smoked, garlic-and-onion, barbecue-flavored, almond candies, even almonds pure and natural. Almonds predominate, but you can also get roasted salted pistachios, California colossals ($8.75 for two 11½-oz. tins or $15.95 for a 4-lb., 12-oz. tin). You can order one can of each kind of almond (except the natural) in a gift pack called The Flavor Treasure ($10.50), almonds in various combinations or separately, in case lots of twelve 14-oz. tins, twenty-four 7-oz. tins, or forty-eight 4-oz. tins. A 2-lb. carton of natural, shelled, unblanched almonds is $6.75, and a burlap bag of 5 lbs. of almonds in the shell is $7.95. House of Almonds also ships California sun-dried fruits (cherries, dates, figs, prunes, peaches, pears, and apricots), either alone or in combination packs with almonds, and the king of dates, the black Medjool ($7.50 a tin, shipped only between November 10 and March 31).

The Sun Giant harvest selection, a gift plan for 3, 5, 7, or 12 months, encompasses Red Delicious apples, navel oranges, royal mandarins, Medjool dates, ruby-red grapefruit, avocados, artichokes, early peaches, plums, nectarines, colossal raisins, Ribier grapes, and persimmons—all these only in the year's selection, of course—for a grand total of $94.95. A 5-month selection brings apples, oranges, mandarins, Medjool dates, and grapefruit, for $41.95.

JURGENSEN'S GROCERY COMPANY / Dept. CFC
601 South Lake Avenue, Pasadena, CA 91109

"Jurgensen's Christmas Catalogue," free, published annually, 36 pages, illustrated, color.

California fresh or glacé fruits in boxes and hampers are just part of the catalogue selection. There are huge Fuerte avocados from San Diego county in boxes of 8 and 16; a combination box of grapefruit, oranges, avocados, and nuts, individually foil-wrapped; a small basket of fruit packaged with boysenberry jelly, candy, and lemon puff cookies;

Toasted Pecans

For each cup of shelled pecan halves, put 1 tablespoon melted butter or margarine in a shallow pan. Put in the pecan halves and stir well. Sprinkle with salt. Brown in a 350° oven for about 20 minutes, stirring frequently. Remove from oven. Sprinkle with more salt if necessary. Spread pecans on paper towels to cool.

Variations: for a more spicy treat, pecans may be sprinkled with any of the good seasoning salts, a little curry powder, paprika, chili powder, etc., while being toasted. Be sure to stir well so the seasoning is evenly distributed.

wooden trays, boxes, and baskets of dried fruits or glacé fruits priced from around $7 for a 1-lb. tin of glacé fruits to around $18 for a 5-lb. wooden tray of dried fruits. Various selections of salted nuts are packed in acetate drum boxes, walnuts in the shell in burlap bags (5 lbs. around $7), and some packages combine canned California green olives and smoked and cheese almonds.

KAKAWATEEZ, LTD / Dept. CFC
130 Olive Street, Findlay, OH 45840

Price list, free.

Kakawateez is the Mexican-Indian name for peanuts. And except for peanuts (79¢ for 7 oz.), all nuts are sold in 6½-oz. jars, $1.29 for cashews, $1.55 for almonds, $1.29 for filberts, $2.98 for pistachios, $2.59 for macadamias, $1.29 for Brazils, and $1.39 for mixed nuts. They are available in packs of four as well as in larger quantities.

Kakawateez does both wholesale and retail business, so you'll also find pizza peanuts (99¢ for 9½ oz.), redskins (79¢ for 9½ oz.), and onion-flavored peanuts (99¢ for 9½ oz.), sold in packs of a dozen.

THE KIRK COMPANY / Dept. CFC
P.O. Box 340, Puyallup, WA 98371

Catalogue, free, published annually, 20 pages, illustrated, color.

Gift packages of Washington State Red and Golden Delicious apples, individually wrapped and boxed. Apples, graded from the top of the crop, are larger than normal. A 20-lb. gift pack is $17.45; 10 lbs. runs $10.25. A Christmas nut bowl—a 10-inch round wooden salad bowl heaped with mixed nuts in the shell—is $7.95.

LAZY J ORGANIC FARMS / Dept. CFC
1580 Rubenstein Avenue, Encinitas, CA 92024

Price list, free.

The owner of Lazy J, who signs himself Organic Charlie White, sells organically grown fruits and vegetables. In season there are Jerusalem artichokes, asparagus, kumquats, navel and Valencia oranges, Mineola tangelos, and sapotes, at prices ranging from 25¢ a lb. for oranges and tangelos to 90¢ a lb. for sapotes. Available year-round are avocados (75¢ a lb.), lemons, and honey. Packing and shipping costs are extra.

LEE'S FRUIT CO. / Dept. CFC
P.O. Box 450, Leesburg, FL 32748

Price list and informational brochures, free, published annually, 2 pages.

Lee McComb believes that grapefruit are essential to good health and that compost-grown citrus fruits are better for you than those grown with chemical fertilizer. He sells compost-grown oranges, grapefruit, or a mixture of the two by the bushel, ¾ bushel, and ½ bushel ($15.75, $13.50, $9.90) from November 15 to June 1. If you order the fruit, you can also buy orange-blossom honey ($1.25 per lb.).

LEKVAR-BY-THE-BARREL / Dept. CFC
1577 First Avenue, New York, NY 10028

"A Continental Bazaar," free, published annually, 56 pages, illustrated, black and white.

Lekvar-by-the-Barrel specializes in baking supplies, so their list of nuts and dried fruits is pretty extensive. They have whole almonds, walnuts, filberts, Brazil nuts, pecans, pine nuts, peanuts, and pistachio nuts as well as ground almonds, walnuts, hazelnuts, Brazil nuts, and pecans, at prices ranging from $2 a lb. for whole or ground Brazil nuts to $3.95 a lb. for whole or ground pecans and black walnuts. They also have bitter kernels at $3.20 a lb., natural coconut flakes, and shredded sweetened coconut. Among the dried and candied fruits are Smyrna figs, sour prunes, dark and white raisins, currants ($1.98 a lb.), candied Australian peaches, pears, apricots, candied citron, angelica, orange and lemon peel, candied cherries, and crystallized ginger.

FRANK LEWIS / Dept. CFC
P.O. Box 517, Alamo, TX 78516

"Royal Gifts," free, published annually, 16 pages, illustrated, color.

Frank Lewis' pride are his Royal ruby-red grapefruit, a variety discovered by accident in the orchard of a Texas neighbor in 1929. You can order them on their own or in gift packs with pecans and petits fours, jams, and Medjool dates from November 15 to December 30. A package of king-size ruby reds, each fruit weighing nearly 2 lbs., is $11.95 for 5 to 6 fruits, $19.95 for 18 to 23 fruits. A family pack of 18 medium-sized fruits is $11.95; a package of 6 fruits, each weighing a lb. or more, $7.95; and there are other packs with more fruits. Join the Fruit Club and you'll get a monthly shipment of 16 to 20 ruby-red grapefruit each of the winter months, December through April, when the season ends, for $12.95 a month. Early orders are advisable, as there is a limited supply of grapefruit. All prices are delivered and are subject to change each year. Frank Lewis also sells a 1½-lb. basket of sun-dried fruits for $8.95, a 2-lb. box of dry roasted and lightly salted mammoth pecan halves for $11.95, and 1-lb. or 2-lb. packages of the huge luscious Medjool dates for $7.95 and $10.95.

LOUISIANA PECAN SHELLING CO. / Dept. CFC
P.O. Box 784, Mansfield, LA 71052

Prices on request.

This company sells only shelled pecans from their own groves. An economy 5-lb. pack of the mammoth halves is $14.95, a 2-lb. gift box is $7.50, and prices include postage anywhere in the continental U.S. Send them your gift list and they'll mail direct.

MAISON GLASS / Dept. CFC
52 East 58th Street, New York, NY 10022

"Maison Glass Delicacies," $1, published annually, 72 pages, illustrated, black and white.

Maison Glass nuts are roasted and salted several times daily, so you know they are fresh when shipped. The "specialty of the house" is a 2-lb. gift tin of assorted nuts—almonds, pecans, cashews, hazelnuts, and macadamias ($17.50). You can order Italian filberts, Georgia pecans, Indian cashews, macadamia nuts, pistachios, and Spanish Jordan almonds by the pound at prices ranging from $5.50 to $8. They have gift boxes of assorted dried fruits, or you can take your choice of jumbo apricots, prunes, Calimyrna figs, dates, Turkish figs, and pitted prunes. Crystallized orange or grapefruit peel is $1.95 for an 8½-oz. box. Fruits in heavy syrup include the usual apricots, cherries, peaches, pears, and the more unusual guava shells ($1.25 a 15½-oz. tin).

MIDWAY GROVES / Dept. CFC
Rte. 3, Box 28, Sarasota, FL 33580

Catalogue, free, published annually, 16 pages, illustrated, color.

Midway Groves ships from November 20 to December 18 navel oranges, Orlando tangelos, pink grapefruit, and Midway special seedless grapefruit in cartons and gift packs (picnic basket, champagne hamper, planter, or wastebasket). From January 1 to 15 there are Mineola tangelos; from January to March, pineapple oranges; Temple oranges in February; Murcott "honey" oranges, mid-February to March; Valencia oranges March through May 15; mangoes June 15 through August 15; and avocados July 15 through October—just about a year of fruit. They have Christmas gift certificates for later shipment and monthly or 6-week-interval plans for shipping oranges and grapefruit by the bushel. The Tree-T'-You Club brings navels in November, Orlando tangelos in December, Mineola tangelos in January, Murcotts in March, Valencias in April, and Midway Special seedless grapefruit for the entire season, if specified. You can also buy mammoth pecan halves in 2-lb. or 3-lb. boxes and various selections of glacé fruits in tins and trays. Prices in our catalogue are not current, so we won't quote them.

Date Nut Bread

Beat 2 tablespoons unsalted butter with 1 cup sugar and 1 egg until light and fluffy. Reserve 2 tablespoons from 2 cups all-purpose flour. Sift the remaining flour with 1 teaspoon baking powder and 1 teaspoon baking soda. Grate the rind and squeeze the juice from 1 large orange. Put the orange juice in a cup measure and add enough boiling water to make 1 cup liquid. Alternately add the sifted flour mixture and the liquid to the creamed butter mixture. Stir in the grated orange rind. Dredge 1 cup chopped dates with the reserved flour and fold into the batter with 2 cups chopped walnuts. Spoon into a well greased 5" x 9" loaf pan. Bake in a 350° oven for 1 hour, or until the sides of the bread start to shrink from the pan. Cool on a rack.

From the Northwestern Coffee Mills catalogue

NUTS & SEEDS

In order to insure the best taste we sell only the largest available grade of each type of nut or seed we carry. We also turn our inventory rapidly to keep both our raw and roasted nuts fresh. Our dry roasted nuts, carefully roasted in our own ovens, are about 15% more expensive than the traditional wet (fried in hot vegetable oil) roasted nuts. This is due to a moisture weight loss entailed in the dry roasting process. In wet roasting weight is added to the nuts as they soak up some of the hot oil. We feel that our unsalted, dry roasted nuts are far better tasting than those roasted in oil. We advise that you store whatever nuts or seeds you purchase in a cool and dry place (such as your refrigerator) to preserve their freshness and to protect them from pest or odor contamination.

IN SHELL	1 lb.	5 lb.	10 lb.
Peanuts,			
Fresh Roasted #1 Virginia	.70	3.25	6.00
Peanuts, Raw Hand Picked #1	.60	2.75	5.00
Peanuts, Salted in the Shell	.80	3.75	7.00
Pistachios,			
Natural 8 Crown Colossal	2.95	14.25	27.50
Pistachios, Red 4 Crown Supreme	2.75	13.25	25.50
Sunflower Seeds, Salted	.80	3.75	6.50
SHELLED, DRY ROASTED			
Almonds, Nonpareil 18/20	2.25	10.75	20.50
Cashews, Jumbo 210 Count	2.60	12.50	24.00
Peanuts, Virginia/Spanish Blend	.80	3.75	7.00
SHELLED, ROASTED & SALTED			
Parched Corn	1.50	7.00	13.00
Soybeans	1.10	5.00	9.00
Sunflower Kernels	1.40	6.50	12.00
Prize Mix (Parched Corn,			
Soybeans, Sunflower Kernels,			
& unsalted, roasted Peanuts)	1.30	6.00	11.00
RAW SHELLED NUTS			
Almonds, Nonpareil 18/20	1.95	9.25	17.50
Brazils, Fancy	1.35	6.25	11.50
Cashews, Jumbo 210 Count	2.25	10.75	20.50
Cashews, Fancy Pieces	1.30	6.00	11.00
Filberts, Oregon 20/24	2.00	9.50	18.00
Wisconsin Hickory Halves	4.75	23.25	--
Peanuts, Blend Redskins	.70	3.25	6.00
Pecans, Mammoth Halves	2.65	12.75	24.50
Pepitas (Pumpkin Seeds)	2.50	12.00	23.00
Pignolias, Large Spanish	3.90	19.00	37.00
Raw Nut Mix, Fancy	2.00	9.50	18.00
Sunflower Seed Kernels #1	1.10	5.00	9.00
Walnut Kernels, Black	3.25	15.75	30.50
Walnut Halves & Pieces, English	1.60	7.00	13.00

& NUT BUTTERS

We dry roast, grind and package our own nut butters. They are 100% pure nuts; no salt, oil, sugar, preservative or other chemicals are added. If oil or salt is desired, you can add your own, thus controlling the agreeable consistency and flavor to your own taste.

ROASTED	8 oz	2 lb	7 lb
Almond Butter	1.80	5.20	15.25
Cashew Butter	1.20	3.20	9.40
Cream City Blend	1.25	3.25	9.60
Peanut Butter	.95	1.95	5.65
RAW			
Cream City Blend	1.25	3.25	9.60
Walnut Butter	1.45	3.85	11.60

The Cream City Blend includes: almonds, brazils, cashews, filberts peanuts, sunflower seeds & walnuts.

MISSION PAK / Dept. CFC
Santa Clara, CA 95050

"Bright holiday gifts from Mission Pak," free, published annually, 28 pages, illustrated, color.

Mission Pak claims their greatest success is glacé fruits, made by a process pioneered by Mission Pak's founder, George Page, which replaces the moisture inside with orange-blossom honey. Packages of assorted glacé fruits—Deglet Noor dates, pineapples, cherries, pears, prunes, apples, apricots, Calimyrna figs, and oranges—come in 1- to 5-lb. packs ($5.95 to $17.95).

Fresh fruit, of course. Mission Imperial pears are $8.95 for 9 lbs. and Imperial pears $14.95 for 13 lbs. A "Tangy Trio" of red apples from Washington State, Mission Imperial pears, and navel oranges is $14.95 for about 18 lbs. Ruby-red grapefruit is sold in 9- and 16-lb. boxes ($8.95, $11.95). Navels by themselves are $8.95 for a box of 9 to 12 oranges, and Deglet Noor dates come in 2-, 3-, and 4-lb. boxes ($6.95 to $11.95).

Assortments of 2 lbs. of dried and glacé fruits come on a 14" x 7½" redwood tray ($8.45) or in a wicker basket shaped like a bell ($8.95). A woven basket is packed with California navel oranges, home-style orange marmalade, and individually wrapped walnuts and dates ($13.95). A "Double Take" assortment combines crunchy Cascade apples and plump Imperial pears ($11.95 for 12 lbs.), and a cheese and fruit basket with cheddar, Swiss Gruyère, Napoli and Sharpy spread, dried dates, prunes, pears, cherries, and jumbo figs stuffed with almond and walnut halves is a real bargain at $7.95. Mission Pak has just initiated a "Fruit for all Seasons" plan so you can get fresh, dried, and glacé fruits all year round ($27.95 for 3 months, $49.95 for 6 months).

MOBILE PLANTATION / Dept. CFC
Rte. 2, Box 190A, Theodore, AL 36582

Price list, free.

Extra-large pecan halves in 2- or 5-lb. gift boxes ($7.50, $14.75); unshelled Stuart pecans in 5- or 10-lb. boxes ($7.50, $12.75), and broken pecan pieces excellent for cooking and baking ($10.75 for 5 lbs.) are available from Mobile Plantation only in November, December, and January.

NORTHWESTERN COFFEE MILLS / Dept. CFC
217 North Broadway, Milwaukee, WI 53202

Catalogue, free (25¢ donation accepted), published annually, 28 pages, illustrated, black and white.

In order to ensure the best taste, Northwestern carries only the largest available grade of each type of nut or seed, and their inventory has a rapid turnover to keep both raw and roasted nuts fresh. Their dry roasted nuts, roasted in their own ovens, are rather more expensive than the usual wet (fried in hot oil) roasted nuts, due to moisture loss entailed in the dry-roast process, but well worth the extra money, as the flavor is better. They sensibly advise storing nuts and seeds in the refrigerator to preserve their freshness. We'd go one step further and suggest keeping them in the freezer if you are going to have them around for any length of time.

They sell nuts in the shell in 1-lb., 5-lb., or 10-lb. quantities (fresh roasted peanuts, raw peanuts, salted peanuts, pistachios) and also sunflower seeds. Prices range from 60¢ (for raw peanuts) to $2.95 (for pistachios) per lb. There are also shelled dry-roasted peanuts, almonds, and cashews; roasted and salted parched corn ($1.50 a lb.); soybeans, sunflower kernels, and a special prize mix (these three, plus unsalted roasted peanuts). Raw shelled nuts range from almonds to black and English walnuts and include hickory nuts. Prices are from 70¢ a lb. for peanuts to $4.75 a lb. for the hickory halves. Large Spanish pignolia nuts are $3.90 a lb. They dry-roast, grind, and package their own 100 percent pure nut butters (no salt, oil, sugar, preservatives, or chemicals). Add salt or oil to taste, if you wish. The nuts for the butters are either roasted (almond, cashew, Cream City Blend, peanut) or raw (walnut, Cream City Blend) and range in price from 95¢ a ½ lb. for peanut butter to $1.80 a ½ lb. for almond butter. The Cream City Blend is a mixture of almonds, Brazil nuts, cashews, filberts, peanuts, sunflower seeds, and walnuts. Sounds delicious.

We include their Canadian/Minnesotan wild rice ($1.75 a ¼ lb., $6 a lb.), because technically it is a seed—of an aquatic grass. The rice is hand-picked, carefully parched and sorted to include only the longest (about ½ inch), tenderest kernels. Recipes are included with the orders.

Northwestern's dried fruits (other than the imported candied ginger) are organically grown and unfumigated, moist and rich in flavor. The selection covers peeled apple rings, apricots, coconut, Medjool dates, figs (Black Mission and extra-large Calimyrna), jumbo prunes, and Monukka raisins. Prices are from 70¢ to $1.70 a lb., and the candied ginger is $1.75 a lb.

NUTWORLD / Dept. CFC
  P.O. Box 1, Dundee, OR 97115

  Price list and order form, free.

The prices are good and even better if you buy by the case, which can be anything from 5 lbs. of pistachios to 35 lbs. of almonds or hazelnuts. In less than case lots, add 10¢ per lb. Walnuts, halves or pieces, are $1.39 a lb. (25 lbs. a case); whole hazelnuts, $1.89 a lb. (35 lbs. a case); black walnuts, very hard to find these days, $2.69 a lb. (25 lbs. a case); and pistachio nuts, $2.55 a lb. (5 lbs. a case). There are also pecans, Brazil nuts, cashew pieces, almonds whole or sliced, and peanuts. You can buy the hazelnuts whole, sliced, or as meal; the walnuts in halves and pieces or nuggets. Hazelnuts, walnuts, and mixed nuts in the shell are also available.

Dried fruits, also sold by the case or by the pound, include pineapple with or without sugar; large prunes (70¢ a lb., 25 lbs. to a case); peaches, pears, and apples ($1.60 a lb., 25 lbs. a case); and apricots ($1.60 a lb., 28 lbs. a case). Again add 10 percent for less than case lots. All prices are FOB Dundee and subject to change without notice. As nuts freeze well, you could split an order with friends and put the surplus in the freezer.

PAPRIKAS WEISS IMPORTER / Dept. CFC
  1546 Second Avenue, New York, NY 10028

  "Imported Foods and Cookware Catalogue," $1 for annual subscription, published four times a year, 66 pages, illustrated, black and white.

Nuts here are sold shelled and whole, ground, sliced, or slivered. Whole or ground almonds, walnuts, and hazelnuts are $3.98 a lb.; sliced, slivered, or whole blanched almonds, $1.50 a ½ lb.; pignolias, pistachios, and black walnut kernels, $2.50 a ¼ lb. They also have bitter kernels for marzipan ($1.50 a ¼ lb.).

PEPPERIDGE FARM MAIL ORDER CO., INC. / Dept. CFC
  Box 7000, Norwalk, CT 06856

  "Gift Catalog," free, published periodically, 32 pages, illustrated, color.

A gift of assorted walnuts, Brazil nuts, pecans, almonds, and filberts comes in a wooden steel-banded nut bucket with nutcracker and six picks (1½ lbs. nuts, $11.95), jumbo peanuts in a 40-oz. tin for $6.95. Or choose a combination of 8 shiny red Delicious apples packed with 12 ounces of old-fashioned chocolate fudge, $7.95 (not shipped to residents of California and Arizona).

PIONEER-SEMINOLE GROVES / Dept. CFC
  P.O. Box 2209, Cocoa, FL 32922

  "Citrus and Gift Catalog," free, published four times a year, 16 pages, illustrated, color.

Citrus fruits, mangoes, pineapples, avocados, pecans (in the shell or shelled), tropical jams and jellies, and Florida candies are the offerings from this company. A holiday season 3-box plan brings Orlando

★

Chestnuts will peel more easily if you put them in the freezer for at least 24 hours. Remove, thaw, cut a crisscross slit in the top and bring to a boil in water to cover. Leave in the water and peel while hot.

★

To prevent discoloration when cutting avocados, use a silver or stainless steel knife. Leave the pit in the avocado (or in a bowl of avocado dip) until ready to use and cover surface tightly with plastic wrap. Rubbing a cut lemon on the cut surface also helps.

★

Food gifts from the PEPPERIDGE FARM Mail Order Company

★

When making applesauce, don't add sugar until the apples have softened. Taste and add the necessary amount of sweetening.

★

When squeezing lemon juice directly into a dish, put cheesecloth over the cut lemon and squeeze the juice through it, leaving seeds and pulp behind. If you are serving a half lemon with fish, tie it in a little cheese-cloth bag.

★

Honey-dipped dried apples from Rancher Waltenspiel

Nutted Brown Rice

Chop sufficient walnuts, pecans, filberts, or almonds to make ½ cup and toss them over medium heat in ¼ cup hot butter until lightly browned. Meanwhile, cook 1 cup brown rice according to package directions. Mix the sautéed nuts with the cooked rice and serve with roast poultry or game. Serves 4 to 6.

tangelos at Thanksgiving, seedless navel oranges at Christmas, and rare red tangelos in January ($23.95). With the 6-box plan you add temple oranges in February, honey tangerines in March, and pink seedless grapefruit in April ($47.50). Or you can order a single 10-lb. box of any of the fruits at prices from $7.95 to $8.45. The Summer Cooler trio brings summer Valencias, mangoes, and Persian limes; the Autumn Joy pineapple, tropical jellies and marmalades, and avocados. You can have a 3-box plan or order a single box. Other selections include a bushel, ¾, ½, or ¼ bushel of all oranges, all grapefruit or mixed fruits, gift packages of citrus fruits with preserves, nuts, and candies, or you can have the standing-order plan, which brings you citrus fruits every week, every other week, every month, or every other month, either all oranges, all grapefruit, or a combination of the two, in sizes from ¼ bushel to a full bushel. Shipments can be in a series of 3 or 6 or 9 or 12 (or more), starting when you wish, and prices range from $27 for 3 shipments of ¼ bushel to $204 for 12 shipments of 1 bushel, delivered to one address only. Shipments may be charged to Master Charge or BankAmericard. Whole pecans in the shell are $6.95 for 2 lbs., $10.95 for 5 lbs.; shelled pecan halves come in 1¼ and 2¼ lbs. at $7.95 and $10.95.

RANCHER WALTENSPIEL
Timber Crest Farms / Dept. CFC
4791 Dry Creek Road, Healdsburg, CA 95448

Price list, free.

For 19 years Rancher Waltenspiel has grown, processed, and packaged organically grown dried fruit that is sold plain and honey-dipped. Honey is used as a preservative for the dried prunes—breakfast, large, and jumbo ($1.13 to $1.36 a lb.); Monukka or Thompson raisins ($1.50 a lb.); Calimyrna or mission figs ($1.38 a lb.; $1.23 for 12 oz.); peaches ($1.31 for ½ lb.); cherries ($1.28 for ½ lb.); or papaya slices (44¢ for 2.6 oz.). Gift boxes are available: small ($4.60), with large prunes, apricots and pears; medium ($7.28), with those three plus dates, peaches, and apples; and large ($10.78), with all the above plus Thompson raisins, almonds, and Calimyrna figs.

The plain dried fruit is sold in 5-lb. bags that include the same as above ranging in price from $4.98 for breakfast prunes to $11.62 for apricots.

RIGG'S PECANS / Dept. CFC
P.O. Box 428, Camden, AL 36726

"Rigg's Gourmet Delight Pecans," free, published seasonally, six pages, black-and-white illustrations.

For Christmas, send extra-fancy pecan halves ($7.60 for 2 lbs.), medium pecan halves ($7.65 for 2¼-lb. box), or extra-large pecan pieces, perfectly sized for cookies and cakes ($6.95 for 2¼ lbs.). Or treat yourself to pecan logs—a nougat center studded with red cherries, dipped in cream caramel, and rolled in tiny pecan halves ($4.95 for 18-oz. box).

A holiday box of 6 oz. of roasted pecan halves, 6 oz. of natural halves, and 8 oz. each of sugar, rum, and cinnamon pecans is $8.95. Pecan brittle ($5.60 per lb.), pecan pralines ($5.45), and pecan fruitcake ($6.60 for 2 lbs.) are other items available from Rigg's.

ROOS QUALITE PECAN COMPANY / Dept. CFC
P.O. Box 8023, Savannah, GA 31402

Brochure and price list, free, 8 pages, black and white.

Mammoth pecan halves are packed in transparent 1-, 2-, 3-, and 5-lb. gift boxes priced from $6.75 to $22, or in 2-, 3- and 5-lb. cartons. Or you can order pecan pieces at $4 a lb. Roos does not ship less than 2 lbs. Salted mammoth pecan halves are $7 a 1-lb. box, salted large cashews $7.50 a 1-lb. box. Write for prices of pecans in the shell. Roos also has 8½-oz. boxes of crystallized grapefruit or orange peel ($5.75) and imported crystallized ginger (10-oz. pot, $7.50).

SAHADI IMPORTING CO., INC. / Dept. CFC
187 Atlantic Avenue, Brooklyn, NY 11201

"The Silent Salesman," free, published biannually, 24 pages, illustrated, black and white.

Sahadi has a very good selection of candied and dried fruits—figs from Australia, Greece, and Smyrna, sun-dried pineapple, dried apples, nectarines, pears and peaches, prunes, white and black raisins, dates from Iraq and California, glazed Australian apricots, peaches, pears, and quince (these are $3 for an 18-oz. container). The list of nuts and seeds is even more impressive. You can get the tiny white pignolia (pine nuts) for $3.60 a lb.; pistachio nuts of different sizes, shelled or in the shell (from $2.30 to $2.60 a lb. in the shell, $5 a lb. shelled); almonds, cashews, walnuts, filberts, and various seeds (pumpkin, melon, sunflower), roasted and salted, plain roasted, or raw.

SAVAGE CITRUS BARN, INC. / Dept. CFC
Rte. 1, Box 150, Raymondville, TX 78580

"Savage Citrus Fruit," free, published annually, 1 oversized page, illustrated, color.

Sweet and juicy ruby-red grapefruit in 13- or 40-lb. cartons ($10 and $15) and tree-ripened oranges are shipped by Savage from November 15 to March 15 to all states but Alaska, Arizona, Florida, California, and Hawaii. No shipments to Canada.

SEY-CO PRODUCTS / Dept. CFC
7651 Densmore Avenue, Van Nuys, CA 91406

Catalogue, free, published annually, 15 pages, illustrated, color.

Sey-Co's nuts are the cocktail-nibble kind: extra-large pretzel-salted peanuts, cashews, almonds, cocktail pecans, mint-toasted hazelnuts ($1.50 for a 6-oz. tin), and big luscious macadamia nuts, double-roasted ($2.65 a 4½-oz. tin). They also have various cocktail crackers, including one that tastes like pecan but is made of wheat germ, and all kinds of olives, from the supercolossal Spanish green ones to the tiny green cocktail type, stuffed with onion, anchovy, almond, or pimiento, or spiced with dill, garlic, and sweet peppers ($1.75 for an 8-oz. jar).

In fruits they have a 2¼-lb. "Westerner" box of apricots, prunes, figs, dates, pears, pineapples, cherries, and walnuts (no sugar) for $7.50, plus jumbo pitted California prunes.

SPHINX DATE RANCH / Dept. CFC
5201 East Camelback Road, Phoenix, AZ 85018

"Sphinx Date Ranch Gift Offering," free, published annually, 8 pages.

Sphinx dates are a special variety of the world-famous black Medjool date, large, luscious, and flavorful. Dates are relatively expensive because, unlike most fruit, they must be pollinated by hand. (The male date tree has fragrant flowers but no dates, while the female tree bears dates but has no fragrance. Hence, bees head for the barren male tree, following the fragrance.)

Sphinx Date Ranch sells jumbo Medjools in quantities from 2 lbs. ($7) to 15-lb. trays ($31.50), as well as variations for the date lover: chocolate-dipped ($5.50 per lb.), pecan-stuffed ($4.75 per lb.), and assorted ($10 for 2 lbs.), plus brown dates for cooking and baking ($4.75 for 2 lbs.).

Other products from Sphinx include date rolls (macerated dates rolled in coconut and topped with almond, $4.75 for 2 lbs.), orange-date nut loaf, apricot-pineapple nut loaf ($5.50), date-pecan and apricot-pecan loaves ($4.75), plus pecans ($6.75 per lb.), pecan log ($4.50 per lb.), apricot-coconut roll ($7.50 for 2 lbs.), and a 2-lb. assortment of glacéed or sun-dried pears, figs, apricots, peaches, and dates ($9.95 for glacéed, $8.50 for sun-dried).

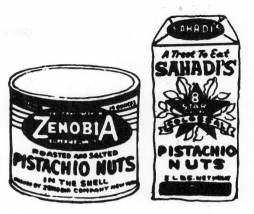

Lebanese Pine Nuts and Raisins

Soak 2 cups white raisins in warm water for an hour until plump. Drain. Combine 1 cup honey and 1 cup water in a pan, bring to a boil, and boil for 3 minutes; then add the raisins and the grated zest of 1 to 2 lemons (about 1½ tablespoons). Cook over low heat for 10 minutes. Remove from heat, pour into a bowl, and stir in 1 cup pine nuts. Chill until ready to serve. Serve with yogurt if desired.

Dates, plain and fancy, from Sphinx Date Ranch

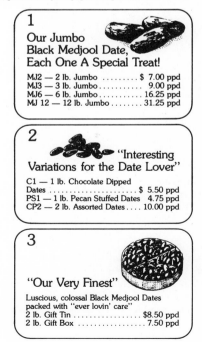

1

Our Jumbo
Black Medjool Date,
Each One A Special Treat!

MJ2 — 2 lb. Jumbo .... $ 7.00 ppd
MJ3 — 3 lb. Jumbo .... 9.00 ppd
MJ6 — 6 lb. Jumbo .... 16.25 ppd
MJ 12 — 12 lb. Jumbo .... 31.25 ppd

2

"Interesting
Variations for the Date Lover"

C1 — 1 lb. Chocolate Dipped
Dates .... $ 5.50 ppd
PS1 — 1 lb. Pecan Stuffed Dates   4.75 ppd
CP2 — 2 lb. Assorted Dates .... 10.00 ppd

3

"Our Very Finest"

Luscious, colossal Black Medjool Dates
packed with "ever lovin' care"
2 lb. Gift Tin .... $8.50 ppd
2 lb. Gift Box .... 7.50 ppd

Shelled pecans from Sunnyland Farms

Orange Sultane
[served at Restaurant Troisgros, Roanne, France]
Remove the thin colored outer peel or zest from 6
navel oranges. Cut it into fine julienne and blanch for
10 minutes by placing in a small saucepan with 2 teaspoons cold water and bringing to a boil. Add 1 cup
sugar and cook until candied. Divide the oranges into
quarters and remove the white pith. Marinate the
oranges in 1 cup Grand Marnier and 2 tablespoons
grenadine syrup. Pour the candied orange peel over
them and let stand for 24 hours. Serve cold in sherbet
glasses with chopped pistachio nuts. Serves 6.
—from Grand Marnier Recipe Booklet

STERNBERG PECAN COMPANY / Dept. CFC
P.O. Box 193, Jackson, MS 39205

Price list, free, published annually.

Sternberg sells only fancy mammoth pecan halves. Prices range from
$7.50 for a 2-lb. package to $30 for 10 lbs.

SUNNYLAND FARMS, INC. / Dept. CFC
Box 785, Rte. 1, Albany, GA 31705

*"Pecans Plain & Fancy," free, published annually, 32 pages, illustrated,
color.*

Jane and Harry Willson sell to commercial pecan users, but the top end
of the crop is regraded and hand-picked for their mail-order customers. Their catalogue is a showcase for an impressive range of nuts.
Prices listed here are approximate.

The firm-textured but small Schleys are highest in polyunsaturated
oils that give pecans their unique flavor ($9.60 for 5 lbs.). Stuarts are the
big and tasty stalwarts that can be cracked by hand ($8.75 for 5 lbs.).

Shelled pecan halves have no wasted weight, and the difference in
shipping costs makes the per-pound price of meats alone nearly the
same as unshelled pecans. There are mammoth toasted and salted
halves ($9.40 for 2 lbs., $12.30 for 3 lbs., and $67.20 for a case of six
3-lb. boxes sent to one address), a box containing 1 lb. each of mammoth pecan halves, extra-fancy pieces, English walnut pieces, and fresh
Georgia peanuts ($11.70) or slivered almonds ($6.50 for 2 lbs.).

Black walnut pieces, hickory-smoked almonds, pistachios, cashews,
hazelnuts, Brazil nuts, and almonds are other nuts available from
Sunnyland Farms.

SUNRAY ORCHARDS / Dept. CFC
Rt. 1, Box 299, Myrtle Creek, OR 97457

Free brochure.

Sunray Orchards in Oregon was founded in 1923 for the express purpose of growing and drying prunes, and the present owners, John and
Pat Herman, discovered that all prunes are not alike—different varieties are distinctively different. Furthermore, prunes left to ripen fully
on the tree are the best and tastiest. They have four varieties of
prune—the Italian prune, naturally tart with a distinctive flavor; the
slightly tart yet sweet Brooks prune; the date prune, a very sweet
French type; and the large, sweet, and meaty Perfection prune developed right there in Douglas County. The prunes are organically grown
and dried in "hot air" dehydrators at an even constant temperature, the
time varying according to size and variety, after which they are stored
and processed before being boxed and bagged. Processing consists only
of washing the prunes with mountain spring water. No additives or
preservatives are used. They also have arranged with other organic
growers to sell dried pears, peaches, cherries, walnuts, and filberts. No
price list came with the brochure, so you will have to inquire about
shipments.

THE SWISS COLONY / Dept. CFC
1112 7th Avenue, Monroe, WI 53566

*"Gifts of Perfect Taste," free, published annually (for Christmas), 92
pages, illustrated, color.*

Fresh and dried "moisturized" fruits and assortments of nuts are featured in this gift catalogue. In fruits, a combination box of oranges and
grapefruit is around $10; 12 lbs. of navel oranges, $9.75; 12 lbs. of
ruby-red grapefruit, $9.50; and 10 to 14 large Comice pears, $8.95.
There's a Fruit of all Seasons plan, a fruit Gift of the Month plan, and
various combinations of fruits in gift boxes or in baskets with other
foods. Dried fruits (dates, figs, candied pineapple, apricots, pears,
prunes) in boxes and trays are available alone or in combination with
fresh fruit and nuts. A Holiday Nut Crate has four burlap bags, each
holding 6 oz. of pistachios, almonds, cashews, pecans, or you can order

3½-lb. sacks of pecans, pistachios, and fancy mixed nuts, barrels of nuts, tins of mixed nuts, and all kinds of other combinations. A peck of peanuts in the shell in a red and green basket is $8.95, a 14-oz. tin of macadamia nuts $5.95, and a rope-handled basket of 2 lbs. of mixed nuts in the shell, with nutcracker and four picks, $9.95.

WALNUT ACRES / Dept. CFC
Penns Creek, PA 17862

"Walnut Acres Natural Foods," free, published five times a year, 24 pages, black and white.

Among the natural foods in this catalogue are organic dried fruits from Timbercrest Farms, some of them honey-dipped. These include apples, apricots, Black Mission figs, pears, pineapples, prunes, peaches, Monukka raisins, dried cherries, and mixed fruits. Other unsulphured dried fruits are bananas, banana flakes, and various forms of dates—organic Deglet Noors, datelettes (coconut and organic dates, ground together), date butter, and date sugar. The Timbercrest fruits are sold in 1-, 3-, 5-, and 25-lb. lots at prices ranging from $1.36 to $2.83 a lb. Most of the nuts are raw unblanched, with only the shell removed. These include almonds, black walnut pieces ($2.88 a lb.), whole or split cashews, Turkish filberts, pecan halves, pignolias ($2.49 a ½ lb.), and Spanish or Virginia peanuts. There are also dry-roasted almonds; pistachios roasted in the shell, natural color, no dyes, salted or unsalted ($1.86 a ½ lb.); dry-roasted, organic, unsalted peanuts; and candy-bar-type snacks, a mixture of nuts, seeds, and date pieces.

THE WISCONSIN CHEESEMAN / Dept. CFC
P.O. Box 1, Madison, WI 53701

"Gift Selections," free, published annually, 96 pages, illustrated, color.

The catalogue shows various packages of fresh fruit with cheese, nuts, candies, and jellies. One is a box of 6 ruby-red grapefruit with 7 Wisconsin cheeses, a jar of wildflower honey, and jars of wild plum jam and chokecherry jelly ($9.95). Another teams Washington State apples and Anjou pears with mixed nuts in the shell, cheeses, and imported candies ($12.95), and a third packages apples, pears, grapefruit, jams, jelly, and cheese in a handwoven basket ($17.95). In dried and glacé fruits there's a box of big luscious Australian apricots (1-lb. size, $5.95), a tree-shaped wicker basket of glacé fruits (1-lb. size, $5.95), a box of nut-topped dates (1-lb. size, $3.95), and a fruit box of various fruits (figs, dates, plums, pears, and apricots), $3.99 for the 1-lb. size, $6.95 for the 2-lb. size.

Mixed nuts (pecans, filberts, cashews, pistachios, almonds, Brazil nuts) come in combination with an assortment of cheeses ($6.95) in a triple-pack with cheese and cookies ($9.95) or alone in a "Nut Assortment" of three 6-oz. tins of mixed nuts, Virginia peanuts, and redskin peanuts ($4.25). Or you may order unshelled mixed nuts (almonds, walnuts, filberts, pecans, Brazil nuts) in a burlap bag (2½ lbs. for $4.95) or packaged in a bucket complete with nutcracker and picks ($5.99). Pecans (3 lbs.) and pistachios (2 lbs.) are also available in the burlap bag, $6.75 for the pecans, $7.95 for the pistachios.

Old-fashioned apple peeler-corers at Harrington's in Vermont

Fried Apple Rings with Sausage
With wet hands, shape 1 pound sausage meat into flat cakes. Pan broil about 15 minutes, pouring off fat as sausage fries. Core, but do not pare, firm cooking apples. Slice into rings about ½ inch thick. Dip rings in milk and then in flour. Fry on both sides in the sausage fat. When lightly browned, remove, and sprinkle with sugar.
—*from "38 Serving Ideas and Recipes for Harrington's Smoked Treats"*

See Appendix, page 239, for additional sources not included here.

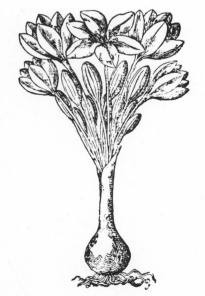

SAFFRON

CHAPTER FIVE

THINGS SWEET, SOUR, SPICY, AND SAVORY

ALAMO FRUIT / Dept. CFC
   Box 666, Alamo, TX 78516

"Holiday Gifts," free, published annually, 32 pages, illustrated, color.

Alamo Fruit has a collection of 3-oz. jars of 8 different jellies and marmalades (amber, orange, and grapefruit marmalades; red grapefruit, lime, orange, tangerine, and jalapeño-pepper jelly) for $8.90 and an earthenware jug of 2 lbs. of luscious orange-blossom honey for $7.95.

ANZEN JAPANESE FOODS AND IMPORTS / Dept. CFC
   736 N.E. Union Avenue, Portland, OR 97232

Price list, free, 20 pages.

Even if you aren't interested in Oriental cooking, there are some canned, frozen, and packaged fruits and preserves on the very complete Anzen list. Preserved ginger in a round coral jar is $6.95; in blue Hawthorne jar, $4.95; ginger in syrup, $1.77 for 4 oz.; ginger marmalade, $1.97 a lb. jar; and crystallized ginger, 83¢ for 4 oz. There's frozen passion-fruit concentrate and passion orange concentrate, 59¢ for 6 oz.; guava jelly, guava nectar, lichees in syrup, sliced canned papaya, and mandarin oranges (41¢ for 11-oz. can).

APHRODISIA PRODUCTS, INC. / Dept. CFC
   28 Carmine Street, New York, NY 10014

"Aphrodisia—an experience in herbs, spices and essential oils," $1, published periodically, 112 pages, illustrated, black and white, with seasonally adjusted price list.

Aphrodisia is a small, crammed, lively little shop in Manhattan's Greenwich Village with an amazing stock and a knowledgeable staff, and that is reflected in their catalogue, well worth $1 for the clarity of the writing, attractiveness of the format, and wealth of information.

Very intelligently, they have not attempted to classify their herbs, spices, and foreign food seasonings but have listed them all alphabetically, starting with "Absinthe (*Artemisia absinthium*). According to legend, this plant, also known as wormwood, was driven out of the Garden of Eden. Commercially, absinthe is used to flavor vermouth—and is part of many homemade 'bitters.' An infusion prepared from the herb and sprayed on the leaves of plants will repel slugs, crickets, house flies, and other tender-bodied insects."

That's the kind of information you'll find throughout the catalogue, which was prepared, according to the introduction, to represent the accumulated experiences of many people closely associated with Aphrodisia, to serve as a guide and reference book, and to answer the most frequently posed questions. In this they have certainly succeeded. The information and suggested uses for herbs and spices are fascinating, and there are recipes dropped in along the way to illustrate the use of the unfamiliar. Did you know, for instance, that berberi is a hot Ethiopian spice mixture, usually made into a paste with oils and used in stews, lentil and meat dishes, and breads? There's a recipe for kifto, an Ethiopian ground-beef dish, and lentil wat, both using berberi.

Reading this little book might start you out on a whole new adventure in spice cooking. The book details the differences between the different forms of ginger (ground Jamaican, dried ginger root, fresh ginger root, and crystallized ginger), different types of dried mushrooms (Japanese, Polish, Chilean, Chinese tree fungus), black, green, and white peppercorns and things like cayenne pepper (not a peppercorn but a capsicum pepper) and Szechuan pepper. It gives a recipe for the French *quatre épices*, or four spices, a blend of ground pepper, cloves, nutmeg, and ginger, for garam masala, the basic Indian spice mixture, Cantonese salt, Zebrovka (vodka flavored with buffalo grass) and May wine, flavored with woodruff. Aphrodisia sells their own specially blended herbal teas and many of the seasonings needed for Chinese, Indian, and Indonesian cooking, including Indian chutneys and pickles and Indonesian sambals. Incidentally, they invite wholesale inquiries from food co-ops.

ARMANINO MARKETING CORP. / Dept. CFC
1970 Carroll Avenue, San Francisco, CA 94124

"Culinary Fare of San Francisco," free, published annually, 1 page, illustrated, black and white.

Armanino is well known for their freeze-dried chives, but their offerings here are not confined to chives and make great gifts.

San Francisco seasoning is a delicate blend of freeze-dried shallots, chives, basil, leeks, and garlic, which comes in a 4-oz. Belgian glass wine carafe with glass stopper and includes a recipe booklet ($5). Also available in 1¼-oz. jar ($1.05) and a 4-oz. tin ($2.75).

A fine gift idea is a combination box of chopped shallots, chives, Italian parsley, diced green bell peppers, and San Francisco seasoning with a recipe booklet ($6.50).

Armanino offers ready-made pesto ($1 a pouch; case of 12 pouches, $9) for the most super spaghetti sauce in the world. Or try their freeze-dried flavorings in handsome tins: shallots (2 oz.), chives (9/16 oz.), green bell peppers (¾ oz.), red bell peppers (1¼ oz.), leeks (¾ oz.), Italian parsley (⅞ oz.), or mushrooms (¾ oz.), all $2.50.

AULT BEE FARMS / Dept. CFC
Rte. 2, Box 64, Weslaco, TX 78596

Price list.

E. B. Ault's bees pollinate E. B. Ault's papaya trees, which provide E. B. Ault with large (up to 9 lbs.) papayas he then flavors with honey (from his bees), pineapple, and lemon. The product contains no preservatives and comes in pint and quart cans ($2 to $3).

A pint jar of pure honey is $1.75, and a 6-oz. jar of honey with 283 milligrams royal jelly is $2.50. One ounce of pure royal jelly (the partly digested pollen and honey that is fed to the queen bees) is $25 in case you are interested. Mr. Ault will also ship fresh ripe papayas in season.

★

Paprika and cayenne pepper are affected by heat and light and have a short shelf life. Buy in small amounts, store in the refrigerator, and use quickly.

★

To make your own vanilla sugar or vanilla extract, make a lengthwise slit in vanilla beans and put two or three in a jar of sugar or a bottle of brandy. Replenish sugar or brandy as used.

★

In recipes calling for mustard, combine dry mustard with prepared Dijon mustard. It blends in better and has more flavor.

★

Quick Crêpes Dessert
Spread freshly made crêpes with raspberry or pineapple preserves, roll up, sprinkle lightly with sugar, and flame with heated cognac or rum.

CEW's Poached Pears with Tomato Preserves
To make this refreshingly different European dessert, first make a simple syrup: combine 4 cups sugar with 2 cups water in a wide shallow pan; bring to a boil and add juice of ½ lemon. Peel four firm ripe Bartlett pears, cut in half, and enlarge the central cavity with a melon baller. Add pears to simmering syrup and poach for about 20 minutes, turning frequently so they cook evenly. Remove, drain, and cool. Just before serving, fill the centers with French Tomato Preserves.
—*from Williams-Sonoma's "A Catalog for Cooks"*

★

Always grind pepper freshly in a pepper mill and use black peppercorns, which have more flavor and pungency than white.

★

Paprika and curry powder taste unpleasantly raw if not cooked. Sauté slowly in a little fat first when used in stews, sauces, and curries. They can be cooked with the vegetables or the butter and flour roux for a sauce.

★

BACCHANALIA / Dept. CFC
273 Riverside Avenue, Westport, CT 06880

"Bacchanalia—Winemaking Supplies," free, published annually, 16 pages, illustrated, black and white.

Bacchanalia sells not only winemaking supplies but also the Four Monks Brand wine vinegar from California, aged for four years and full of flavor: 12 4/5 fl. oz. of either the red wine or sherry-wine vinegar is $1.75. Or, to make your own vinegar, you can buy a California wine-vinegar culture (4-oz. bottle and instructions, $3.50).

B&B FOOD PRODUCTS / Dept. CFC
Route #1B, Cadiz, KY 42211

"Your Gift Catalog," free, published annually, 16 pages, illustrated, black and white.

Southern-style pickles and relishes are natural companions to the Kentucky country hams that are B&B's main specialty. A melon pickle pack teams sweet pickled watermelon rind, sweet pickled cantaloupe, and melon medley (a blend of watermelon rind, cantaloupe, and honeydew in heavy sugar syrup). There's also a party pack with corn relish, hot chowchow, and pepper jelly, plus 12-oz. beef summer sausage and 1 lb. each of aged Swiss and sharp cheddar cheese. The pantry pack combines pepper relish, relish supreme (less spicy than pepper relish), and melon medley with 8 ounces of ground baked ham.
B&B's "little brown jugs" each hold 24 ounces of pure Kentucky honey and that acquired taste, pure sorghum molasses (you either love it or loathe it), to pour on your hot biscuits or pancakes (around $8). With a 2-lb. cloth bag of B&B pancake mix, add another $1.

BEAVERTON FOODS / Dept. CFC
Box 104, Beaverton, OR 97005

"Flavor Adventure with Horseradish, Mustard, Sauces and Fondues," free, published annually, 4 pages, illustrated, color.

If you like your food with the zing of horseradish, the fire of taco sauce, or the zest of mustard, Beaverton condiments are for you. Try cream horseradish in sandwiches, whipped horseradish with smoked fish, and the milder English horseradish with meat. Kosher white is extra hot and sweet, while the kosher red version is somewhat tempered with the addition of beets. If you have a palate for hotter sauces, there's Beaverton's red or green taco sauce (both medium hot), jalapeño taco sauce (extra hot), or their Diablo hot sauce, a fiery blend of tomatoes, mustard, and chilies.
Perhaps Beaverton's strongest point is their collection of mustards: Hot Chinese, Extra Hot 'N' Sweet Chinese, Dusseldorf, Russian, Western Hickory Smoked, Dijon, Bavarian, Hofbrau, and Louisiana.
All these condiments are available in 4-oz. jars, 60¢, packed 12 to a case; six 4-oz. jars, any assortment, $4.40; or six 2-oz. jars for $3.25. The fondue flavors, cheese or bourguignonne, are $2.50 per 16-oz. jar.

BETTER FOODS FOUNDATION, INC. / Dept. CFC
300 North Washington Street, Greencastle, PA 17225

Brochure, free, 8 pages, black and white.

Better Foods sells their own brand of old-fashioned peanut butter, made with peanuts only and lightly salted ($1.10 a lb. jar, $2.05 a 2-lb. jar, or $5.60 a 5-lb. tin), Mennonite Country honey ($1.30 a 1-lb. jar), Kime's apple butter (natural, no sugar), Barbados and blackstrap molasses, cider vinegar, and soy-oil mayonnaise, one without salt. They stock three kinds of raw sugar—Gran-U-Raw, light, with some of the molasses removed; Yellow D, medium dark; and Kleen Raw, really dark, full of molasses. Prices range from $1.06 a 2-lb. bag of the light to $1.37 for the dark, and the sugar is also available in 5- and 10-lb. bags.

BLUFF GARDENS, INC. / Dept. CFC
    658 West Bluff Drive, Harbor Springs, MI 49740

Catalogue, 25¢, published May and October, 12 pages, illustrated, black and white.

The people at Bluff Gardens raise miniature vegetables for sale to the neighboring resort hotels, but that isn't all they do. Fresh fruits and vegetables are made into jams, jellies, and relishes in their jelly kitchens and the sugarhouse is in production every spring for maple syrup. Their syrup is sold in pint, quart, and half-gallon tins ($4.85 to $10.25 ppd., higher west of the Rockies), and you can buy pints of the syrup in gift packs with the jams, relishes, and marmalade. In jams and jellies there's a pantry pack of 12 jars, which you select from their list, including blueberry, cherry, grape, mint, peach, plum, raspberry, rhubarb-strawberry, strawberry, and rhubarb-orange marmalade ($15.50 ppd., add $1.50 west of the Rockies). Other items are curry dip, creamy French dressing, Dressing Supreme (oil and vinegar, delicately flavored), chili sauce, green tomato relish, bread-and-butter pickles, Dressing & Vegetable Dip (mild Thousand Island dressing), and chocolate topping, all in various gift-package combinations. A charming little catalogue.

BREMEN HOUSE INC., / Dept. CFC
    218 East 86th Street, New York, NY 10028

"Bremen House Catalog of Gourmet Foods," free, published twice a year, 20 pages, illustrated, black and white.

This catalogue has a good assortment of honeys from Germany, Holland, Sweden, Italy (black locust, $2.50 for 13 oz.), Denmark, and New Zealand, European preserves (sour cherry, red currant, quince, black currant, and blackberry jelly), and that Old World specialty, Basserman's plum jam ($3.90 a 31-oz. tin). As befits a German store, they stock canned red cabbage and wine sauerkraut, pickled gherkins, and various German mustards—sweet Bavarian, medium hot and extra hot, and Dusseldorf.

BUDERIM GINGER GROWERS' CO-OP ASSN. LTD. / Dept. CFC
    P.O. Box 114, Buderim, Queensland 4556, Australia

Price list, free.

The ginger growers of Buderim on Australia's "sunshine coast" operate the only ginger factory Down Under, drawing thousands of ginger fanatics each week.

    Items on sale include a 1-lb. presentation gift pack of crystallized ginger ($2 Aust.) and a large hamper with an assortment of crystallized ginger, ginger in syrup, ginger marmalade, strawberry conserve, ginger topping, rosella jelly, and ginger-date-nut spread ($6.58 Aust.).

    Each gift pack and hamper comes with a free recipe booklet, which may just open your eyes to the possibilities of this neglected delicacy. Remember, though, that shipping costs (by sea) are in most cases 100 percent or more of the item's cost.

CALIENTE CHILI, INC. / Dept. CFC
    P.O. Drawer 5340, Austin, TX 78763

"Wick Fowler's Famous 2-Alarm Chili Ingredients," folder, free, published annually, illustrated, color.

The late Wick Fowler became famous for one product—his 2-Alarm Chili—which was used in the first chili-cooking contest, between Wick Fowler and humorist H. Allen Smith, held in the ghost mining town of Terlingua, Texas. His family still participates in chili-judging and belong to the Chili Appreciation Society International in Dallas. Chiliheads take their passion seriously. This is no paltry chili mix. Nine ingredients are packaged in 7 individual packets so you may control the flavor to taste and the heat from false alarm to 4-alarm intensity. To make 1½ quarts of chili, combine the ingredients with 2 lbs. of coarsely

ginger

An I had but one penney in the world, thou shouldst have it for gingerbread. Shakespeare
           Love's Labor's Lost

Chili jellies, from Canterbury Canneries

ground or diced beef and an 8-oz. can of tomato sauce, and cook. One family-size package of 2-Alarm Chili is $1.50 postpaid. Or you can order up to 24 packages ($26).

CANTERBURY CANNERY INC. / Dept. CFC
P.O. Box 17171, San Antonio, TX 78217

Brochure, 50¢ (refundable with purchase), published annually, 2 pages, illustrated, color.

Canterbury Cannery makes two unusual hot chili relishes: jalapeño jelly and rojo picante, a spicy sauce of jalapeños, water, vinegar, tomatoes, onions, and spices. Both are excellent with meats.

You can get rojo picante and jalapeño jelly in 3-, 6-, or 12-jar packs, by themselves or mixed. Twelve jars of jalapeño jelly cost about $24.50, while twelve 8-oz. containers of rojo picante are $23.50. The Fiesta Pac—6 jars of jalapeño jelly, 6 of rojo picante—is $24. Prices do not include postage.

CARAVANSARY / Dept. CFC
2263 Chestnut Street, San Francisco, CA 94123

"Gourmet Gift Ideas from the Caravansary," free, published winter/spring, 14 pages, illustrated, black and white.

Among the gourmet gift ideas is a nifty box packed with Pommery moutarde de Meaux, herbes de Provence for meat and fish, Puget virgin olive oil, the famous California Barengo wine vinegar, and a tin oil can for dripping the oil into mayonnaise. The gift box is $20, or you can order the items separately—4/5 pt. of the Barengo wine vinegar is $1.39, for instance.

CASA MONEO / Dept. CFC
210 West 14th Street, New York, NY 10011

"Mexican Food—Comida Mexicana," free, 8 pages, published annually, also price lists of South American, Cuban, and Portuguese foods.

Spicy peppery things predominate in the catalogue listings. Lots of chilies, of course, both dried and canned, such as chilies serranos, chili piquin in vinegar (tiny, very hot), chilies jalapeños, and the green whole chilies, some hot but mostly mild, the kind used in a lot of California-Mexican cooking. There are also various blends of chili powder from Texas, California, and New Mexico and the spicy powders and pastes for mole and adobo. In relishes you'll find green or red jalapeño relish (85¢ a can) and all kinds of sauces of different degrees of hotness for enchiladas, tacos, and for eating with Mexican dishes as a condiment. The Mexican Ortega brand of green chili sauce is 45¢ for a 7-oz. can, and their mixture of canned tomatoes and chopped green chilies, very useful in cooking, is about 40¢. From Cuba comes the seasoning mixture called sofrito criollo (64¢ for 8½ oz.). Casa Moneo has a good list of herbs and spices for Latin American cooking, including achiote (the little red seed that flavors and colors), the herb epazote, cinnamon, cumin, oregano, coriander seeds, and allspice. All run about 15¢ for varying quantities. Prices are subject to change. (If you'd like to find out more about the types and uses of chilies, herbs, and spices in Mexican cooking, the best book we know is *The Complete Book of Mexican Cooking* by Elisabeth Lambert Ortiz, available in a Bantam paperback at $1.25.)

Latin Americans and Spaniards are also notoriously sweet-toothed, and the foods at Casa Moneo reflect this. You'll find many tropical specialties, such as orange paste from Colombia, mango paste, mango cream, guava marmalade (18 oz., 91¢), guava paste and guava jelly from Cuba, quince spread and quince jam ($1.35 a lb.) from Portugal. There's sweet confectionery, known as dulce, some made with sweet potatoes flavored with vanilla, chocolate, or cherries, or with various fruits, such as quince and mango. Mexican and Colombian chocolate is available in various brands ($1.50 for 8¾ oz.). You have to know something about the foods and language of the countries to buy from the Casa Moneo lists, because half the time there are no translations.

CHUTNEY KITCHEN / Dept. CFC
　　Vintage 1870, Yountville, CA 94599

　　"Chutney Kitchen Chutneys," free, 1 page.

Visitors to the Napa Valley wineries often stop for lunch at Chutney Kitchen, a delightful restaurant and store in the complex of old converted brick buildings known as "Vintage 1870." If you can't get there, you can order by mail Chutney Kitchen's unusual and absolutely delicious homemade hand-chopped chutneys, less hot and more fruity than the usual commercial blends.

　　These totally natural chutneys, which have no watermelon rind as a filler, aren't limited to the curry-condiment tray. Chutney Kitchen suggests you fold their apricot, sour cherry, and almond chutney into vanilla ice cream, with brandy poured over the top, or you may eat it with poultry. The pineapple–Pacific fruits chutney, containing 22 ingredients, makes a good marinade for shrimp. Other interesting mixtures are green tomato and sweet pepper (best with lamb or with sour cream as an omelet filling); spicy fig and walnut (good with ham); plum, green pear, and walnut (eat with turkey or add to muffin batter); and California blue prune (have this with veal, poultry, or use as a glaze for roast suckling pig).

　　The chutneys are sold in ½ pints or pints, at prices from $2 to $3.75.

Homemade chutney from Chutney Kitchen

CLAIBORNE JOHNSTON / Dept. CFC
　　100 Johnston Bldg., 12 South 3rd Street, Richmond, VA 23205

　　Price list and order form, free.

Among other products, such as Smithfield and country hams and Puget Sound smoked salmon, Claiborne Johnston sells cocktail artichokes, an artichoke relish, and pear preserves by the carton. A carton of six 8-oz. jars of cocktail artichokes is $7.95 ppd., the relish is $6.95 ppd. for a carton of six 9-oz. jars, and the pear preserves, three 20-oz. jars to a carton, cost $6.75 ppd.

CLARK HILL SUGARY / Dept. CFC
　　Canaan, NH 03741

　　Folder, free.

Clark Hill Sugary brings a touch of New England to wherever you are. The purest maple syrup, creamy maple butter, the rich essence of pure maple syrup, and the finest maple sugar candy. No additives. No preservatives. Each a special taste usually enjoyed only in New England.

　　The unique flavor results from their traditional method of gently lifting the sap from the sugar maples instead of letting it drip into a bucket. Perhaps it is the youthfulness of the New Hampshire trees or the way the syrup is coddled on its way to the jugs.

　　Pure maple syrup is sold by the half gallon, $8; quart, $5; and pint, $3. Creamy maple butter is $5 for a 1½-lb. jar, $3 for a 12-oz. jar. Pure old-fashioned maple sugar candy costs $9 for a 2-lb. tin and $5 for the 1-lb. size.

　　Postage and handling for the syrup is $1 per jug ($2 in the West) and $1 per unit of maple butter and maple candy. Additional products are offered from time to time.

Jugs of maple syrup from Clark Hill Sugary

COLONIAL GARDEN KITCHENS / Dept. CFC
　　270 W. Merrick Road, Valley Stream, NY 11582

　　Catalogue, 25¢, published monthly, 112 pages, illustrated, black and white.

A good place to track down some of the old-time preserves and relishes. There's Cape Cod beach plum jelly, New England rhubarb preserve, Pennsylvania Dutch fruit butters (apple, prune, peach), spiced watermelon rind and marble-sized beets, Vermont apple-cider jelly, quince jelly from Long Island, and, from overseas, the famous English Tiptree preserves (ginger, loganberry, wild strawberry, and lemon marmalade), Rose's lime marmalade, Dewar's Scotch whisky marmalade, a plum jam

Chutney-Stuffed Peach Halves

Blanch 4 ripe peaches, peel and halve. (Firm canned peach halves may also be used.) Remove pits and fill each cavity with mango chutney. Put in a greased baking dish. Dot the tops of the peaches with 1 tablespoon butter, cut in small pieces, and pour over them the juice of 1 lemon. Bake in a 450° oven for 20 minutes, then reduce the heat to 300° and continue baking until just soft (for canned peaches, heat through), adding lemon juice if the peaches show signs of sticking. Serve hot with baked ham or roast pork. Serves 4.

with Jamaica rum, and a peach jam with Benedictine. Prices range from just over $1 to around $3 or $4 for the rum and liqueur-flavored jams. If you are a honey-fancier, there's a Swedish wildflower honey and one from the jungles of Yucatan. All the maple sugar and syrup products are available here, too.

THE CONDIMENT SHOP / Dept. CFC
P.O. Box 666, Highlands, NC 28741

Price list, free.

The Condiment Shop deals in homemade jams and jellies made from wild fruits and berries that grow on the mountains of western North Carolina, so you'll find some really unusual ones here, such as wild muscadine, wild plum, wild coon grape, fox grape, Scuppernong grape, possum grape, wild elderberry, and huckleberry. Prices range from $1.10 to $2 for an 8-oz. jar, $1.40 to $2.40 for a 12½-oz. jar. Also listed are chutneys (apple, cranberry, ginger, Indian green tomato, pineapple), fig and rhubarb conserves, pickles, and relishes. There's an iced pumpkin pickle, iced green tomato pickle, zucchini pickle, an artichoke in mustard relish, a pear relish, and a pumpkin delight. Prices are generally around $1.10 for an 8-oz. jar. A few miscellaneous items are apple butter, chestnut-rum ice cream sauce ($1.75 an 8-oz. jar), hot pepper sauce, soup mix, and sourwood honey. A very interesting collection. The Condiment Shop packs in gift boxes of 6 or 12 jars, and postage is extra (whenever possible they ship UPS). Prices, as usual, are subject to change without notice.

CONTE DI SAVOIA / Dept. CFC
555 W. Roosevelt Road, Chicago, IL 60607

Catalogue, 75¢ (refunded with purchase), published annually, 28 pages, not illustrated, black and white.

This catalogue has a pretty wide selection of preserves and honeys from different countries. Picking at random, we found Irish Willwood brand preserves in 1-lb. stone crocks (ginger, strawberry, apricot, gooseberry, black currant) and 1-lb. stone crocks of marmalade, some of which are sugarless, for 95¢, as well as Greek Hymettus honey, a slew of Sharon Valley preserves and marmalades from Israel, lingonberries from Sweden, and coconut syrup from the Philippines.

In the spicy category, Conte di Savoie has Italian mostarda, candied fruits in mustard syrup ($1.39 for 14 oz.); English pickled walnuts, Korean pickled garlic, and a wide range of pickles from India, such as mango, lime, hot lemon, karela, chili, and Pickapeppa sauce from Jamaica (59¢ a 5-oz. jar). They have the usual list of dried herbs and spices and a few unusual ones used in Indian cooking, which seems to be one of their major areas of sale. They also have some of the seasonings for Chinese cooking, such as hoisin and plum sauces, and Mexican mole paste and serrano and jalapeño peppers.

COTTAGE HERB FARM SHOP / Dept. CFC
311 State Street, Albany, NY 12210

Catalogue, 25¢, published annually, 3 pages, drawings.

Dried herbs such as basil, chervil, lovage, and sweet marjoram are sold here at 50¢ a jar ($3 minimum order required), as well as special blends for meats, fish, tomatoes, stews and sauces, salads, omelets, and poultry. Specialties of the house include herb mustard sauce (59¢ a jar), Hades (hot) mustard (69¢), an herbal pâté mix (69¢), and, for your feline friend, catnip (75¢ a bag).

CRABTREE & EVELYN LTD. / Dept. CFC
Box 167, Woodstock, CT 06281

"Crabtree & Evelyn, Purveyors of Fine Comestibles to the Gentry," free, published periodically, illustrated, 10 pages.

"The definition of 'food' is long and complex, with a host of qualifying phrases. 'Gourmet food' adds insult to injury, with its tinge of snobbery.

"We've always loved 'comestibles,' commonly seen on the façade of grocers in France and occasionally in England. Check the largest dictionary and you'll find 'anything edible.' What could be simpler?"

With that explanation, the English company of Crabtree & Evelyn offers a literate and alluring catalogue of "rather common foods made with loving care." The U.S. distributors are located in Woodstock, CT.

Tracklements, or herbal jellies, to accompany meat and game, made of apple juice from Bramsen and other apples, plus selected whole herbs, are sold in 1-lb. jars. Currant, mint/apple, sage/apple, and thyme/apple are $2.75. The explanation of the affinity of certain tracklements for certain meats or game is fascinating.

Whole-grain English mustards, made of mustard seeds grown in Norfolk, England, and southern Scotland, are blended with Jamaican allspice, Madagascar pepper, Mexican chilies, and other ingredients (12 oz. about $3.25).

Seven kinds of homemade English marmalade and three types of chutney are sold in 1-lb. jars priced at $2.50.

Or try Crabtree & Evelyn's two types of English country honey, liqueur preserves, fruit preserves, and French flower-petal jellies.

Delightful products, charming catalogue.

CREOLE DELICACIES CO., INC. / Dept. CFC
533-H Saint Ann Street, New Orleans, LA 70116

"Happy Gifts of Food from Old New Orleans," free, published annually, 12 pages, illustrated, color.

Louisiana is both the Strawberry State (viz. "Fraises de la Louisiane") and the Creole State, and Creole Delicacies offers the state's distinctive culinary products.

Strawberry preserves are sold in white pine pails ($11.95 for 2½ lbs.), in a redwood urn ($12.95 for 2½ lbs.), or along with "Pêche de la Louisiane" (peach preserve) and "Figue de la Louisiane" (fig preserve) in a crate ($7.95 for three 10-oz. jars). Also available are orange marmalade, blackberry, watermelon rind, and kumquat preserves.

"Sirop plantage," pure Louisiana cane syrup, comes in cartons of four 12-oz. tins ($6.75), while the remoulade sauce, delightful on seafood or salads, is $8.95 for three 10-oz. jars.

A redwood tray filled with strawberry preserves, "sirop plantage," remoulade sauce, deveined Louisiana shrimp, and old-fashioned New Orleans pralinettes is $16.75.

The seasonings of Louisiana, herbs blended for Creole recipes in five combinations—gumbo filé, Creole spicy, omelet blend, Creole herb blend, and crab and seafood boil—come in their own rack with a cookbook, *A Collection of the Most Famous New Orleans Creole Recipes*, for $9.75.

CULPEPER, LTD. / Dept. CFC
Hadstock Road, Linton, Cambridge, England

General price list and medicinal herb list, $1, published seasonally.

Culpeper, the famous English herbalists, are well known for their delightful shops in London, Cambridge, and other cities, but they do a mail-order business, too. Twice a year they publish a list of their offerings, which range from medicinal herbs to herbs and spices for cooking, mustards, teas, and *tisanes*, natural-sugar products (brown sugar lumps and plantation molasses), and candies made from raw sugar. Their herb selections are whole leaves or sprigs, not dry or dusty powders, packaged in cellophane with recipe. There's a whole wild-herb collection in a box (wild bay leaves, thyme, fennel, rosemary); various herb and spice blends for meat, poultry, fish, salad, and the barbecue; a bouquet garni mixture (charmingly called a broth posy) and a fines herbes mixture; ground spices in jars and pretty little cotton bags of herbs and spices. Something rather unusual is the dried sliced garlic, 1 oz. of which equals 5 oz. of raw fresh garlic. There's also green ginger in brine from Malaysia, which should be stored in the refrigerator in sherry or vodka after opening, and from the spice island of Grenada a handmade cane or palm basket filled with ginger, mace, cloves, nutmeg, turmeric, cinnamon, and tonquin bean (used like vanilla) with an accompanying

Packages of herb blends from Culpeper, Ltd.

Canadian Bacon with Maple Glaze

Place a 2-pound piece of ready-to-eat Canadian bacon in a shallow pan and bake in a 325° oven for 30 minutes. Remove from oven and garnish with orange slices held in place with whole cloves. Mix ½ cup cider, ½ cup maple syrup, and 1 teaspoon prepared mustard and pour over the bacon. Bake 30 to 35 minutes longer, basting frequently.
—*from "38 Serving Ideas and Recipes for Harrington's Smoked Treats"*

recipe booklet. A 3-oz. jar of English mustard or a 17½-oz. stone jar of old-fashioned coarsely ground French mustard are both 100 percent natural. Prices are quoted in sterling and fluctuate according to the rate of exchange. As of now, the herb and spice blends would be about 45¢ apiece, or $3.60 for 8, the dried garlic about 50¢, the whole wild-herb collection about $1.35. The other items on the Culpeper list range from books such as the *Culpeper Herbal* to the creams, lotions, toilet waters, talcum powders, shampoos, potpourri, pomanders, sleep cushions, and herb-scented sachets for which they have long been noted. All their products are natural and superbly good and make the most enchanting gifts (if you can bear to part with them, that is). Overseas surface-mail shipments add 25 percent to the cost of the goods, with a minimum order of around $4. Airmail brings the cost up to 50 percent of the goods, with a minimum of $8.

CUMBERLAND GENERAL STORE / Dept. CFC
Route 3, Crossville, TN 38555

"The Wish & Want Book," $3, published seasonally, 272 pages, illustrated, black and white.

Food preserving is big in this catalogue, so you'll find here supplies such as noniodized pickling salt in 5-lb. bags (63¢) and Mrs. Wage's pickling lime for cucumbers, with recipes on the package (50¢ a 1¼-lb. bag). For sausage makers there is Legg's Old Plantation Pork Sausage Seasoning, a blend of salt, red and black pepper, sage, and sugar (85¢ for a ½-lb. bag that will season 25 lbs. of meat).

DEER VALLEY FARM / Dept. CFC
R.D. 1, Guilford, NY 13780

Price list, free, published annually, 20 pages, black and white.

Deer Valley Farm has a good list of honeys, some of them organically pure. Among them are tupelo honey, uncooked safflower honey, orange-blossom and clover honeys, and two comb honeys. They also have various nut butters (almond, cashew, peanut), of which the cashew nut butter is their own ($1.89 for 1 lb.), Hain's sesame butter and Sahadi sesame tahini, apple, peach, plum, raspberry, and strawberry butter, rose hips jam, papaya preserves, and the Barth line of jams and jellies. Date sugar ($2.10 for 12 oz.) is occasionally available and always the Turbinado light brown sugar ($8.55 for 10 lbs.), cane syrup at $1.49 for 12 oz., maple syrup, carob syrup, and sorghum syrup. In relishes, Deer Valley Farm lists the Walnut Acres bread and butter pickles ($1.04 a pt.), garden relish, tomato purée, tomato catsup, and sauerkraut.

MRS. DE WILDT / Dept. CFC
R.D. 3, Bangor, PA 18013

"Indonesian and Imported Foods," price list, free, 4 pages.

Clover and heather honey and apple syrup from Holland are on the sweeter side of Mrs. De Wildt's list. From Hawaii comes coconut syrup (85¢ for a 12-oz. tin) and papaya slices in syrup. Preserved stem ginger in syrup (9-oz. jar, $1.50), dried ginger slices in sugar, and mango slices in syrup from Taiwan are among the Chinese delicacies, while Java contributes pitted guava halves or lichees in syrup (each $1.15 for a 30-oz. tin) and undiluted guava juice for fruit punches and tropical cocktails.

Among the things hot and spicy on this list are Indian chutneys (Major Grey, hot mango), a green mango pickle, whole lemon pickle (18-oz. jar, $2.40), and green chili pickle. From Malaysia there's a ready-to-use curry sauce and a hot-and-sweet chili sauce. Indonesia contributes fiery hot sambals (hot chili pepper pastes), a spiced vegetable chutney ($1.50 for a 12¼-oz. jar), serundeng (fried spiced coconut and peanuts), and various spices and spice mixtures for fried rice, vegetables, and saté.

D. M. ENTERPRISES / Dept. CFC
P.O. Box 2452, San Francisco, CA 94126

"Calico Kitchen's Portfolio," free, 12 sheets, published two to three times a year.

Calico Kitchen specializes in products made in, or associated with, San Francisco. In seasonings they have a four-packet card of Golden Gate Seasoning ($1.50) for blending herbed butter, which they suggest you brush on another of their offerings, sourdough bread, and broil until bubbly. San Francisco Seasoning is a special blend of Armanino's freeze-dried herbs with spices, delicious on meats, fish, in dressings for salads, or on vegetables (1¼-oz. jar, $2.50; 4-oz. jar, $5). Then there's a trio of pepper jellys—mild green, tangy red, and hot yellow—(box of 3, $6) to use as a condiment, spread on crackers or bagels with cream cheese, add to tuna sandwiches, or turn into a tangy ham glaze by combining equal parts mustard and jelly. Hardly San Franciscan, but good to add to hot-red wine as a Christmas drink, are the hot mulled wine spices, known as "gluhfix" in Germany, from whence proudly they hail ($1.60 for the 15 individual envelopes of spices). On the sweeter side, there is iron bark tree honey (1 lb., $3.50) and macadamia nut butter (12 oz., $3.50), both of which come in a gift box for $6.50, or organic unfiltered white clover honey from New Zealand (1 lb. jar, $3.50).

EARLY'S HONEY STAND / Dept. CFC
Rural Route 2, Spring Hill, TN 37174

"Old Fashioned Foods and Gifts from the Tennessee Hill Country," free, published annually, 20 pages, illustrated, color, black and white.

Early's started selling honey in 1925 when the mother of the present proprietor, Erskine Early, nailed a tin can to a signpost. "The different sized jars of honey were priced," he wrote us, "and folks could pick out the honey they wanted, put the money in the can and go on. This method of roadside merchandising was not unusual in those days. We never lost a jar of honey. Sometimes the can would have more money than there was honey missing. . . . I was 7 years old at the time."

Except that Early's biggest sellers are now smoked sausage, smoked bacon, country hams, and cheese, Mr. Early and his store haven't lost a bit of their folksiness. "Our customers," he says, "are not just numbers or a dollar sign or a computer number."

Pure Tennessee honey from Early's (about $4 a qt.) is mostly sweet white Dutch clover, and "if the apple folks hadn't coined the term 'golden delicious,' that's what we'd call it!"

Open-pan cooked sorghum comes in unbreakable quart bottles (about $5) or little brown jugs (as does the honey), stoppered and sealed with old-fashioned sealing wax (a jug of each is about $5).

The sorghum and honey are also part and parcel of Early's gift boxes, which include smoked ham and bacon as well as Mrs. Early's three old-fashioned relishes: chowchow (in a 16-oz. reusable canning jar), watermelon-rind pickle (also 16 oz.), and a 7½-oz. jar of corncob jelly (the flavor? hard to describe; maybe a tiny bit like apple). You can order five jars of the same, or an assortment of all three for between $7 and $8 ppd., according to zone. They also ship in unbreakable pint bottles a lively (but not hot) barbecue sauce and green hickory chips (about $2 a 2-lb. bag) to throw on your barbecue for that old smoky flavor.

EGERTONS / Dept. CFC
Lyme Street, Axminster, Devon EX13 5DB, England

"Egertons Postal Gift and Shopping Service," $1.50 if airmailed, free otherwise, published annually, 74 pages, illustrated, color.

For the fancier of unusual marmalades, a speciality box contains six 12-oz. jars, one each of grapefruit, vintage orange, bitter lemon, tangerine, orange ginger, and thick-cut, $16.

Honey Butter
Combine ½ cup soft butter and ½ cup honey, beating until well blended. Serve as a spread for toast or toasted English muffins.
—*from Lang Apiaries*

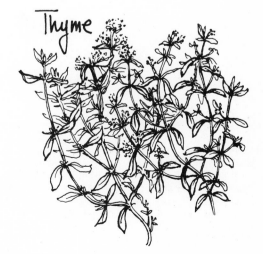

Jug of maple syrup from Especially Maine

A liqueur preserves box has six 12-oz. jars of black currant with rum, apricot with sherry, peach with brandy, marmalade with vintage brandy, Scotch whisky, or Navy rum, all six for $19.45. Another intoxicating selection includes five 12-oz. jars of cranberry with Burgundy, red currant with port, Morello cherry fresh fruit preserve, strawberry with Curaçao, Scotch whisky marmalade, and 10½ oz. of mincemeat with brandy, $19.45.

From the West Country comes pure honey from Devon and Cornwall packed in ½-, or 1-lb. pottery tea caddies, $11 and $12.63, or a twin pack containing two 8-oz. jars of honey, one clear, one set.

ESPECIALLY MAINE / Dept. CFC
Vinegar Hill Road, Arundel, ME 04046

"Especially Maine," free, published periodically, 23 pages, illustrated, black and white.

Specializing in Maine-made products, this small shop and mail-order business sells 1 lb. of pure blueberry honey for $1.80, and 100 percent pure maple syrup, in attractive 1-pt. jugs, is $3.50. There are also two very attractive glazed pottery jars for jam, topped with ceramic blueberries or strawberries, $10 each.

Shaker herbal vinegars from the Sabbathday Lake colony in 8-oz. bottles come in four flavorings: sweet cicely, tarragon, mint, and basil (each 75¢).

Handmade imitation vanilla flavoring made in the same oaken vats and bottled with replicas of the labels that the Dolan Company used at the turn of the century are offered in two sizes: 4 oz. (75¢) and 16 oz. ($2.25). Alcohol content is only 3 percent.

FAUCHON / Dept. CFC
26 Place de la Madeleine, 75008 Paris 8e, France

Price list, free, published annually, 8 pages.

Delicious, distinctive French preserves, including chestnut cream, mirabelle plum, tomato, tangerine, jasmine, and rose petal, all in 11½-oz. jars, are part and parcel of Fauchon's collection of sweet things. For sherbets, Fauchon sells mashed apricots, strawberries, raspberries, pears, or bananas (all in 8¾-oz. jars from $1.16 to $3.10).

White pears are packed in syrup, other fruits in Armagnac or fruit eau de vie. Agen prunes in Armagnac cost around $14 for 34 oz., Montmorency cherries in Armagnac around $16.50 for 35½ oz.

The Fauchon honeys and mustards are famous. In honeys, there's heath, lavender, lime tree, fir, mountain, prairie, Burgundy, and Gatinais, all in 13½-oz. jars, from just over $2 to around $3. Prices are quoted in francs, so go by the current rate of exchange.

Their list of mustards includes a 1-lb. stone jar of old-fashioned mustard (about $2) and 7½-oz. jars of more exotic and varied types, flavored with green pepper, horseradish, tarragon, lemon, orange, garlic and parsley, mint, curry, paprika, lime, shallot, and chervil. They also offer herbs of Provence, honey, black olives, pink pepper, olives and anchovies and sherry wine vinegar, in a wide range of prices. If you were having a ham and sausage party, you could have a great sampling of mustards. Interesting to use in salad dressings, too. There's a 10 percent discount for export orders, and shipping charges are extra.

R. W. FORSYTH LTD. / Dept. CFC
30 Princes Street, Edinburgh EH2 2BZ, Scotland

"The days of Christmas at Forsyth's," free, published annually, 16 pages, black and white.

Scottish heather honey and Strathmore liqueur honey in pottery jars decorated with game birds or dogs (1 lb., about $6), Dorset mincemeat with brandy, Scottish brandied peaches, and stem ginger in syrup are some of the sweet things in Forsyth's Christmas catalogue. The stem ginger comes in jars of different sizes and shapes, with decorations such as blue-and-white hawthorn, dragon, coral, flowery panel, or in plain navy blue or green.

Honeyed Figs

Dissolve ¾ cup clear honey in ¾ cup boiling water. Wash, peel, and halve 24 ripe figs and pour the dissolved honey over them. Chill for several hours. When ready to serve, pour ⅓ cup kirsch over the figs. Serve topped with vanilla ice cream. Serves 8.

FORTNUM & MASON / Dept. CFC
181 Piccadilly, London W1A 1ER, England

"Fortnum & Mason Export Food," free, published seasonally, 15 pages, illustrated, color.

Fortnum & Mason's packaging is so beautiful. Take, for instance, a white wicker oblong tray of four Lowestoft jars decorated with enameled Mandarin prints and filled with vintage marmalade, exotic honey, brown candy-crystal sugar, and young stem ginger ($39.22). The contents are delicious and the jars decoratively useful when empty.

A Crown Devon strawberry-decorated jar brims with delectable strawberry preserve ($8.97). A Crown Staffordshire "Orchard" jar contains the vintage marmalade ($8.97). A Royal Winton "Floral" jar filled with brown candy-crystal sugar is $6.55, and an Irish pottery jar of the same crystal sugar is $4.47. There are 16-oz. jars of old English mincemeat for $1.47, ribboned boxes of crystallized and glacé fruit from $6.55 to $22.28, a beehive jar of pure English honey for $6.55, and a white wicker bread tray of jars of vintage marmalade, black cherry, apricot, strawberry and peach preserves, a lovely gift for $16.84.

By Appointment
To Her Majesty Queen Elizabeth II
Grocers and Provision Merchants
Fortnum & Mason Ltd
London

FOR YOUR HEALTH / Dept. CFC
1136 Eglinton Avenue, West, Toronto, Ontario M6C2E2, Canada

Catalog, 50¢, updated periodically, 48 pages.

Although For Your Health is primarily a health-food store, their list of spices, ranging from allspice to vanilla, is well worth a look. You'll find here the hard-to-get vanilla powder ($4.95 a ¼ lb.), Hungarian paprika ($1.95 a ¼ lb.), Spanish paprika ($1.50 a ¼ lb.), whole yellow or brown mustard seeds (95¢ a ¼ lb.), annatto seed (achiote, much used in Latin American and Spanish cooking) at $1.95 a ¼ lb., both whole black and whole green cardamon ($2.95 a ¼ lb. for the black, $9.95 for the green), and crystallized ginger at $1.55 a ¼ lb. They also list Canadian wild rice ($3.95 a ¼ lb.).

THE GOURMET PANTRY / Dept. CFC
400 McGuinness Blvd., Brooklyn, NY 11222

"Pleasure Packed Gifts from the Gourmet Pantry," free, published annually, 72 pages, illustrated, color.

In this gift catalogue you'll find Trappist preserves (apricot-pineapple, strawberry, cherry, and Seville orange marmalade) packaged with a crystal jam jar, Italian cherries in cherry brandy packed in a cocktail shaker, cherries in syrup in a blue-and white jar, a gift-boxed set of the Trappist preserves, plus three different honeys ($5.99) and a 12-jar gift pack of dietetic preserves (no sugar, saccharine, or cyclamates).

GRAFTON ENTERPRISES / Dept. CFC
Box 123, Townshend Road, Grafton, VT 05146

Price list, free.

Pure Vermont maple syrup with no additives or preservatives in pints ($5), quarts, ($7.50), ½ gal. ($11), and full gal. ($20).

GREAT VALLEY MILLS / Dept. CFC
Quakertown, PA 18951

"Gift Suggestions from the Pennsylvania Dutch Country," free, published annually, 16 pages, illustrated, black and white.

Delicious preserves and relishes are a specialty of the Pennsylvania Dutch, and Great Valley Mills has them. There are Pennsylvania Dutch fruit butters: apple (with or without sugar), peach, quince ($2.50 for 2 jars), all kinds of preserves from blackberry to tomato ($1 to $1.75 a jar), honeysuckle honey, and Haycock Mountain honey (each $1.60 for a 1-lb. jar). In relishes there are the traditional corn relish and chow-chow, bread-and-butter pickles, and chili sauce. Great Valley Mills has maple syrup, maple butter, and blackstrap or Colonial molasses as well. Some of the gift packs in the catalogue feature, or include, preserves, honey, and relishes.

GREEN MOUNTAIN SUGAR HOUSE / Dept. CFC
R.F.D. 1, Ludlow, VT 05149

"Sugar House and Gift House Products," free, published annually, 8 pages, illustrated, black and white.

Green Mountain Sugar House still uses wood, oil, and steam to boil maple sap down into maple syrup. Each year they produce 2,500 to 3,500 gallons of Vermont Fancy, Grade A, Grade B, and Grade C syrups. The prices per gallon are $13.50 for Fancy, $13 for Grade A, $12.50 for Grade B, and $9 for Grade C. Pints, quarts, and half gallons are also available.

When they make maple syrup during the spring thaw (March 1 to 15), they also make maple cream, which is thicker and more textured but has that same taste of winter, snow, and fresh air ($4 per lb.).

Green Mountain has pancake mix to go with their syrups—Country Store buckwheat or buttermilk mix ($2.75 for 2 lbs.). Or try their creamed honey ($4.55 for 2½ lbs.) on toast.

HARRY AND DAVID / Dept. CFC
P.O. Box 712, Medford, OR 97501

"Harry and David's Christmas Book of Gifts," free, published annually with supplementary brochures, 28 pages, illustrated, color.

Besides the many fruits and smoked meats offered by Harry and David, there are several sauces, garnishes, and relishes to pep up your palate. For meats, there are four sauces: teriyaki of pineapple and peach, Louisiana Pepper, creamy mustard with pear vinegar, and sour-cream horseradish, case of four, $6.95, or the all-purpose meat sauce made with tomato, honey, onion, thyme, oregano, and lots more, case of six 12-oz. jars, $8.95.

To go with meat or poultry there are Cherrydills (Royal Anne cherries sweet-pickled in fruit vinegars), sweet pickled watermelon rind, or Bear Creek relish (a sweet-and-sour of pineapple, cucumbers, onions, tomato paste, and herbs), case of six tins, $7.95.

There are two kinds of vinegar—pear or four-fruits, a case of six 4/5 pt., $7.45; sweet chip or dill pickles; 15 preserves, including wild mountain blackberry and Oregold peach; three jellies and three fruit butters (apple, peach, and pear), case of six tins, $7.95; three syrups (red raspberry, blueberry, and wild mountain blackberry), six 16-oz. jugs, $10.95; and buttermilk pancake and waffle mixes.

HARWOOD HILL ORCHARD AND GIFT SHOP / Dept. CFC
Business Route 7, Bennington, VT 05201

Brochure, order form and price list, free, published annually, 8 pages, illustrated, black and white.

Harwood Hill has a nice assortment of jams and jellies, which are made especially for them, light and dark honey in ½-lb., 1-lb., and 2-lb. jars or 5-lb. pails, honey spread, and pure Vermont maple syrup in three grades, Fancy (light amber with a delicate flavor), Grade A (medium amber), and Grade B (dark amber, with a richer, more caramel flavor), sold in gallons and half gallons. The jams, in 12-oz. jars, include apple butter, black or red raspberry, seedless blackberry, wild strawberry, strawberry-rhubarb, currant and raspberry, and blueberry. In jellies they list apple, crabapple, grape, mint-apple, quince, raspberry, red currant, strawberry, and wild elderberry. Their line of relishes has corn relish, spiced apple rings, sweet or hot piccalilli, and spiced crabapples, and there's a special sweet 'n' sour salad dressing, a blend of maple syrup and maple vinegar, in an 8-oz. jar. A unique product is their rosy-red apple syrup to use on waffles, pancakes, and ice cream, available in quarts, pints, and half pints. We don't have the price list, so can't quote costs.

HERTER'S INC. / Dept. CFC
R.R. 2, Mitchell, SD 57301

"Herter's Sportsman's Catalog," $1 (refundable with $10 purchase), published annually, 352 pages, illustrated, color and black and white.

Among the unusual selection of foods in this catalogue you'll find Herter's Famous 5-Alarm Sauce, a kind of super catsup for game, hamburgers, and hot dogs made with tomatoes, vinegar, onions, lemon, caramel, carrots, celery, parsnips, turnips, parsley, salt, red pepper, and spices ($1.59 a 14-oz. bottle) and a 3-Alarm sauce, aged in oak whiskey barrels, at 10¢ less. They have pure concentrated flavors (oil of lemon, tangerine, lime, spearmint, wintergreen, Jamaica rum, black walnut, butterscotch) and fruit flavors; invert sugar, used for professional candy making, with candy recipes ($9.20 a gallon); maple syrup, wild fruit syrups (blueberry and chokecherry, $1.79 a qt.), and cream of toffee syrup, Nesselrode sauce, and freeze-dried horseradish (65¢ for an 8-oz. bottle).

HICKIN'S MOUNTAIN MOWINGS FARM / Dept. CFC
R.F.D. 1, Black Mountain Road, Brattleboro, VT 05301

Brochure, free, published periodically, 6 pages, plus price list, illustrated, black and white.

Looking at the Mountain Mowings Farm brochure makes you just itch to go there and visit the Hickins, who love growing things, at their off-the-beaten-track farm in Vermont. In an average season they have 100 different kinds of vegetables and fruits, including snow peas, lemon cucumbers, 25 varieties of lettuce, and tiny new potatoes only as big as marbles. When they are not harvesting vegetables or pampering plants, they prepare staple, year-round products of which they are proud. Maple syrup is made in the sugarhouse, jams and jellies on the kitchen stove from ripe fruit with no artificial flavorings, and the same kitchen produces pickles and a maple fruitcake. Choose from the list, and the Hickins will attractively package and mail any item or combination you choose. That's personal service.

Included in the jellies are the usual apple, red raspberry, and strawberry, but there are also crabapple, elderberry, hot pepper, lemonmint, parsley, and spearmint (prices are $1.95 for 9 oz., $3.30 a lb.). Jams range from apple butter (or a new maple-apple butter), wild blackberry, and blubarb (undoubtedly a combination of blueberry and rhubarb) to a slow-boiled beach chop, sour cherry, and cherry-berry. Two new items are tomato ketchup and maple chili sauce. Prices run the same as for the jellies.

Vermont honey comes in jars from ½ lb. (89¢) to 5 lbs., or is sold in a 1-lb. jar of cut comb, strained, or 1-lb. creamed or whipped ($1.49). Maple syrup is sold all the way from a 2-oz. jar to a gallon ($16.95).

The Hickins also make fresh fruit syrups—wild blackberry, red or black raspberry, strawberry (these come unsweetened or sweetened with sugar or maple syrup), peach, apple, spiced apple, and blueberry in sizes ranging from 4 oz. ($1.75) to 32 oz. ($9.30).

If you yearn for truly homemade pickles, this is the place to try. Frank and Mary Hickin make their own small batches of pickles, sweetened with their own maple syrup, from tried-and-true recipes. There's quite a list, starting with bread-and butter pickles and corn relish, all kinds of icicle pickles (cauliflower, crookneck, lemon cuke, pattypan, zucchini), mustard crock pickles and relish, pepper relish, piccalilli, and pickled eggplant. Dill pickles include zucchini, tomato, kohlrabi, crookzini (crookneck, pattypan, and zucchini squash), dilly beans, carrots, and lemon cukes. They also have old-fashioned sour pickles and stuffed peppers. Prices for the pickles range from 80¢ for 2 oz. of dilly beans, carrots, or lemon cukes to $16.50 a gallon. Most pickles are sold in half-gallon and gallon sizes.

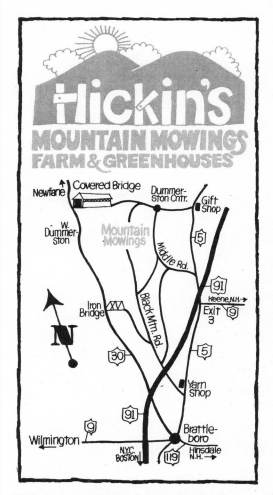

Visitor's route to Hickin's Mountain Mowings Farm

HICKORY HOLLOW / Dept. CFC
  Rte. 1, Box 52, Peterstown, WV 24963

Brochure and price list, 25 ¢, 6 pages, updated periodically, black and white.

Hickory Hollow's little brochure is packed with good things they make and sell, such as a radish relish (a semi-hot blend of organic black Spanish radishes, apple cider vinegar, and sea salt, 75¢ for 6 oz.), herb and fruit vinegars from their organic apple cider vinegar (mint, raspberry, mountain blend), an herb salad dressing and herb-soy dressing, herb jellies (garden sage, sassafras, orange-mint), and, for 75¢ each, a sufficient quantity of culinary herbs and spices to fill a 2-oz. spice jar. They also list dried orange peel from organically grown oranges, hickory bark for your barbecue, and an herb sampler of some rather offbeat, as well as customary, herbs, $6 complete with rack and the 6 apothecary jars of herbs.

HIGH BAR WHOLESALE SPICE CO., INC. / Dept. CFC
  2919 Long Beach Road, Oceanside, NY 11572

"The Whole Spice Catalog," free, updated periodically, 8 pages, black and white.

If you use spices in quantity you can save considerably by buying them wholesale. High Bar lists bay leaves at $1.80 for 1½ oz., cream of tartar at $3.75 a lb., nutmeg at $2.50 for ½ lb., black peppercorns (type not specified) at $3.25 a lb., pickling spice at $1.10 a ¼ lb., sesame at $1.95 a lb., and contrasts them with the prices you'd pay in a supermarket. They also sell packaged seasonings for poultry, hamburger, sausage, seafood, gelatin ($7.50 a lb.), dehydrated red and green pepper and mixed vegetable flakes, pure extracts of vanilla, lemon, almond, peppermint, and orange (from $3.95 for 16 oz. to $6.75 for 16 oz. of peppermint), artificial extracts, restaurant and institutional fully prepared mixes for muffins, pancakes, pastry, and hot breads, to which you only add water, and individually packaged servings of Sanka, Maxwell House coffee, ketchup, salt, pepper, and sugar that could be useful for office lunches, picnics, and camping. They also list 2-lb. jars of honeys (clover, buckwheat, orange blossom, tupelo, alfalfa, wildflower, Yucatan, sourwood) at prices ranging from $2.25 to $5.25 a jar, with a minimum order of 3 jars and $1 off if you buy 5 jars.

HILLTOP HERB FARM / Dept. CFC
  P.O. Box 866, Cleveland, TX 77327

Catalogue, 50 ¢, published annually, 16 pages, illustrated, black and white.

A delightfully written and amusingly illustrated little catalogue with a Victorian flavor. From the Hilltop Herb Farm's canning kitchen come herbal and wine jellies, jams and marmalades, Colonel Jim's pimiento or apple chutney, and "country fresh" relishes—Dixie, corn, sweet pepper, hot green tomato, and Granny's chowchow. Two fiery hot relishes (their answer to a bumper tomato and hot pepper crop) are amusingly named Hellfire and Damnation and Fire and Brimstone. Relishes are $2.35 an 8-oz. jar, plus postage. The jellies include cranberry basil, lemon verbena, tomato horseradish ($2.20 an 8-oz. jar, plus postage), and the marmalades and jams are unusual—apple devil, ruby red, 14-carat, and cucumber. They have gift boxes of different groups of relishes, jams, and jellies, from $9.45 to $12.50 ppd. There's also an herb mustard, herb wine vinegars ($1 for 4 oz.), herbal salts, and seasoning blends.

HOUSE OF SPICES (INDIA) INC. / Dept. CFC
  76-17 Broadway, Jackson Heights, NY 11373

Catalogue, free, 12 pages, black and white.

This catalogue devoted to foods for Indian and Pakistani cooking has a pretty good list of spices and spice mixtures, such as garam masala ($1.20 for 4 oz.), white, green, and black cardamom, Zanzibar cloves (50¢ an oz.), saffron ($1.25 for 4 oz., very reasonable), turmeric and

HILLTOP HERB FARM CANNING KITCHEN PRESENTS!

Herbal Jellies, Jams, Marmalades and Relishes that taste just like you remember Grandmother making..... All jars 8 oz. net weight. Please add 25% for postage on these items only! Minimum Order....3 jars .... any assortment.

Jellies: Apple Rose Geranium, Cranberry Basil, Hot Pineapple Lemon Verbena and Tomato Horseradish..... $2.20 each plus postage.

Wine Jellies: Burgundy, Sauterne or Sherry...$2.35 each plus postage.

Marmalades: Apple Devil, Strawberry-Rhubarb Jam, Ruby Red, 14 Carat and Cucumber....$2.50 each plus postage.

Chutney: Colonel Jim's, Pimiento or Apple...$2.35 each plus postage.

Country Fresh Relishes: Dixie, Corn, Sweet Pepper, Lady Ross, Green Tomato (Hot), Granny's Chow-Chow. These relishes only $2.35 each plus postage.

DON'T FORGET THE 25 % POSTAGE

We can now offer very good quality glass apothecary bottles in which to store your herbs and spices. They come with corks and will hold approx. 2 fluid ounces or 1 ounce of loose herbs.....6 bottles with corks for $1.75.... Measurements: Approximately 3 3/4" high and 1 5/8" in dia.

Hilltop's Faaantastic Cousin Marr's Jalapeno Jelly.....just the thing for a spur o' the moment snack or the most sophisticated cocktail party. It's wonderful with meats or cheeses....Just spread a bit of cream cheese on a cracker and top with a dab of Jalapeno Jelly. Be the first on your block! $2.50 each plus 25% postage.

tamarind, seedless or concentrate. You'll also find here a lot of pickles (mango, lemon, chili, ginger and lime, mango-dry-date-gunda, eggplant) in different styles—Gujarati, South Indian, Maharashtrian, Bedekar, and Punjabi—ranging in price from $1.50 to $2.50 a jar, mango pulp, slices and juice, rose syrup, rose water, and rock sugar ($1.10 a lb.).

INTERNATIONAL SPICES INC. / Dept. CFC
6687 North Sidney Place, Milwaukee, WI 53209

"Meet the Newest Twist in Spice Ideas," free, published periodically, 4 pages, illustrated, black and white.

In this age of disposable this and throw-away that, it was inevitable that someone would come up with disposable plastic mills that hold and grind whole spices (any spice, from peppercorns to cloves, releases more flavor when freshly ground), and that's the stock-in-trade of International Spices, Inc. You can buy individual mills of black or white peppercorns, sea salt, chili pepper, mustard, coriander, and so on, or combinations such as black and white peppercorns and sea-salt crystals packaged in a basket ($5.49) or on a cork tray with wooden handle. There are also packs of different herbs and spices for different styles of cooking—Greek, Mexican, Italian, French, Chinese, but these seem a little forced. A sextet of spices (black and white peppercorns, sea salt, nutmeg, cloves, fennel) in a wicker basket is around $10. The mills are sold in retail stores and also directly by mail from International Spices. If you are an ardent picnicker or a constant traveler, you'll find the pepper and salt mills especially useful to carry along.

ROBERT JACKSON & CO., LTD. / Dept. CFC
171 Piccadilly, London WIV OLL, England

"Robert Jackson's Food, Wine, Hamper and Gift List," free, published seasonally, illustrated, black and white.

Jackson's has honeys in beautiful bone-china jars, honeys in stone pots, gift packs of honeys—honeys from all over the world. Just a few of the selections they stock are French lavender, tilleul, Bourgogne and prairie, Yorkshire or Scotch heather, Oxford, Devon, and Wiltshire set or clear. Prices range from around $1.75 up. You'll also find all manner of fruit and flower purées and jellies from Paris: from Hediard, jellies of orange, jasmine, violet, or rose petals (around $1.70 a 230-gram jar); and, from Fauchon, jellies of apricot, black currant, quince, gooseberry, and raspberry.

Mustard fanciers will love the list of exotic mustards flavored with herbs, spices, and fruits, many of which come in handsome pots to add to your collection. Choosing at random, we like the sound of a gift pack of four Maille mustards (à l'Ancienne, au poivre vert, à l'estragon, à l'echalote) for around $3.60; the Bornier Fruitarde, a choice of apricots, plums, or oranges with a blend of mustard, vinegar, cognac, spices, and aromatic herbs; and The Vicar's Mustard, from a 19th-century recipe created by a country vicar's wife (around $1.80 for an 11-oz. jar). Condiments from Fauchon, to be used as an accompaniment to cold meats, as a base for a cold sauce, or mixed with cream as a dip, include green peppercorn, sorrel, saffron and béarnaise—also Des Tzars, which one can only guess at. Jackson's not only has the green peppercorns from Madagascar but pink peppercorns, too (poivre rose de l'Ile Marrice). Picked while still on the branches, they add a deliciously piquant flavor to a pâté, broiled fish, or steak.

KEMOO FARM FOODS, LTD. / Dept. CFC
Box 3002, Honolulu, Hawaii 96820

Brochure, free, 4 pages, illustrated, color.

Typical Hawaiian delicacies from Kemoo Farms include a package of two jars each of guava jam and guava jelly ($6.95). They also have a special macadamia nut, pineapple and coconut cake, and fresh fruit candies, listed in the chapter on Cakes and Candies.

Disposable grinder from International Spices Inc.

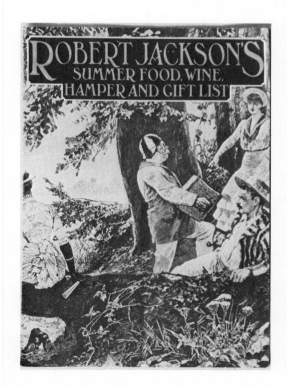

Kentucky Sauce

In a saucepan combine ½ cup dry red wine, 1 tablespoon bourbon, 1 teaspoon Worcestershire sauce, ½ cup tart black currant jelly, and ¼ teaspoon salt. Heat, stirring, until jelly melts. Blend 1 teaspoon flour with ½ cup sour cream. Add to sauce and cook, stirring, until thickened. Do not boil. Serve with roast venison or other game.

Garlic bulbs

THE KIRK COMPANY / Dept. CFC
P.O. Box 340, Puyallup, WA 98371

Catalogue, free, published annually, 20 pages, illustrated, color.

Gift packs of old-fashioned berry preserves in 6 flavors—strawberry, red raspberry, blackberry, loganberry, gooseberry, and boysenberry, put up in wire-rimmed storage jars, $17.95. These and other goodies—maple syrup and fireweed honey—are from the Snoqualmie Falls Lodge in Washington. In case you don't know what fireweed honey is (we didn't), a little note on the back of the catalogue tells you that for pure fireweed honey, the beehives have to be trucked into the mountains, where the fireweed grows, and fenced to keep the bears out. Bears, it seems, go wild over fireweed honey.

LANG APIARIES / Dept. CFC
R.D. 2, Gasport, NY 10467

Price list and recipe booklet, free with self-addressed stamped envelope, published periodically.

Lang's Apiaries will sell you their natural clover, buckwheat, and fall-flower honey, send you a small recipe booklet containing information on how to use and store honey, types of honey and nutritional values, and gently suggest membership in the Natural Food Association ($5 a year).

Prices vary with the mailing zone. To New York City it is $6.50 for a 5-lb. pail, $15.50 for three 5-lb. pails, and $30 for six 5-lb. pails.

Should you happen to be around Gasport, you can make an overnight stop at the campsites scattered around their property.

LE JARDIN DU GOURMET / Dept. CFC
West Danville, VT 05873

Catalogue, 50¢, published annually, 32 pages, illustrated, black and white.

Syrups from France (orgeat, grenadine, cassis, mint), the West Indies (Falernum), and coconut syrup from Hawaii and the Philippines are among the sweet things in this catalogue. In preserves, there's the Willwood brand from Ireland, Rose's lime marmalade (85¢ a 1-lb. jar), grapefruit marmalade from Israel, French bar-le-duc, and some German jams and jellies. In pickles, French cornichons, Indian hot mango, hot orange peel, lime, bamboo, and brinjal pickles ($2.25 a jar). Good prices on mustard—a 3¾-oz. jar of Dijon mustard, Bocquet brand, is 50¢, or you can get a 9-lb. tin of French mustard for only $9.95 that will fill several empty jars.

LEKVAR-BY-THE-BARREL / Dept. CFC
1577 First Avenue, New York, NY 10028

"A Continental Bazaar," free, published annually, 56 pages, illustrated, black and white.

You'll find a worldwide selection of honeys, jams, and preserves in this catalogue. There are honeys from Central America (coffee-blossom, $1.98 a 1-lb. jar), Holland, France, Germany, Greece, Hungary (acacia flower, $2.98 a 1-lb. jar), Israel, and packages of comb honey. Lekvar (prune butter) comes in cans, jars, or homemade, fresh from the barrel ($1.59 a lb.), and Hungarian jams are $1.25 a 1-lb. jar, $1.49 for the sour cherry. Lingonberries, stirred with sugar, are $2.49 for a 14-oz. jar. There are also imported fruit syrups, sweet-sour gherkins, chutney, poppy-seed filling for cakes and pastries, French mustards, oils and vinegars, and a long list of spices and herbs. Naturally, this Hungarian store has genuine Hungarian paprika (sweet rose paprika, medium sharp rose paprika, sharp paprika, 95¢ a ¼ lb. or $2.98 a lb.), and whole or ground poppy seed.

MAGIC GARDEN HERB CO. / Dept. CFC
P.O. Box 332, Fairfax, CA 94930

"Herbs, Nature's ancient gift to man," 25¢, 2-page brochure, published two or three times a year, illustrated, black and white.

Culinary herbs and spices as well as the usual list of botanicals for other purposes, such as herbal teas, are sold by Magic Garden Herb Company. Most of them are the kind widely distributed, but they also have fenugreek for Indian cooking, rose hips, marigold (add the dried flowers to soups, broths, salads, and yellow cakes), and juniper berries, often hard to find in stores. These are sold by the pound or in 1-oz. packages for $1.

MAISON GLASS / Dept. CFC
52 East 58th Street, New York, NY 10022

"Maison Glass Delicacies," $1, published annually, 72 pages, illustrated, black and white.

A fantastic array of jams, jellies, pickles, chutneys, dressings, spices, and savory sauces are distributed throughout the Maison Glass catalogue. We saw at least 20 mustards, including Creole (80¢ a 5½-oz. jar), German, Dijon, and mustard with green peppercorns ($2.75 a 9-oz. crock), tandoori spice blend, crab boil and shrimp boil spices, sherry peppers ($4.50 a 5-oz. bottle), English mushroom and walnut catsups, the Trader Vic dressings and sauces, the Conimex Indonesian spices and sambals, Hungarian and Spanish paprika, and all kinds of vinegars (wine, tarragon-flavored, pear, Japanese rice vinegar, French cider vinegar and champagne vinegar, Spanish sherry vinegar). There are five pages of syrups and flavorings, preserves and honeys. You'll find here French grenadine, citron and cassis (black currant) syrup, English golden syrup, French jams, sugarless jams from Ireland, Hero jams from Switzerland, English marmalades, Tiptree and Dickinson's preserves, including seedless loganberry, wild blackberry and boysenberry and tiny wild strawberry or green fig, and such other delights as English lemon curd ($1.60 a lb. jar), lingonberry preserves, quince, guava and wild beach plum jelly. In the pickle line, Maison Glass has Harry & David's cherry dills (pickled cherries, $2.25 an 11¾-oz. tin), hot or mild pickled okra, cocktail beets, carrot and celery sticks, asparagus tips, tiny tomatoes (a new idea for Martinis), and our old friend, dilly beans. "Pin Money" pickles include sweet corn and pepper relishes, sweet mixed pickles and mustard pickle, cauliflower and burr gherkins. Others list sweet pickled cantaloupe, spiced crab apples, pickled pears and peaches, and pickled watermelon rind ($1.35 a 10-oz. jar). One page offers 48 honeys from all over the world—jungle honey from South America ($2.25 a 1-lb. jar), German Black Forest honey, Italian black locust honey, Tasmanian leatherwood honey, Rumanian acacia honey, New Zealand lotus honey, and, from the USA, holly, palmetto, sourwood, sage, and tupelo honeys. There's a coffee-blossom honey from Central America ($1.95 a 1-lb. jar) and a whole slew from France—champagne, Burgundy, Jura, Provence, Roquefort, fir tree, rosemary, and lavender. You could put together a great gift selection for a sweet-toothed friend. Honey prices range from $1.75 to $6.50.

MANGANARO'S FOODS INC. / Dept. CFC
488 Ninth Avenue, New York, NY 10018

"Manganaro's For Gourmet Foods" and price list, free, published periodically, 26 pages, illustrated, black and white.

Manganaro lists two Italian honeys, mountain flora and Sicilian orange blossom ($2.80), and French Narbonne honey ($2.90). They also have candied fruits preserved in brandy, and mostarda, the candied fruits in mustard-flavored syrup that make such a heavenly sweet-and-spicy relish with bollito misto or other boiled or roasted meats and fowl. Italian fruit syrups from Motta include anise, mint, almond, raspberry, tamarind, and wild cherry ($2.25 for a ¾ qt. bottle). The French syrups, orzata, grenadine and Dijon creme de cassis, are $2.90 for the same size.

Mayacamas special seasoning blends

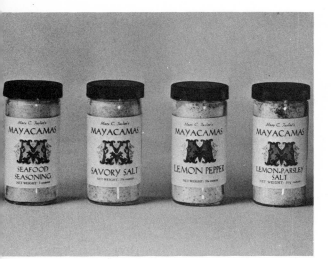

MAYACAMAS FOODS LTD. / Dept. CFC
19275 Arnold Drive, Sonoma, CA 95476

"Mary C. Taylor's Seasonings and Dry Soup Mixes," free, published annually, 4 pages, illustrated, black and white.

Mary Taylor and her husband, Jack, used to own the Mayacamas winery in the Napa Valley. Though they have since sold it and now live in the neighboring wine county of Sonoma, the name continues in Mayacamas Foods, distributors of Mary's special blends of seasonings, which she has been making for a good 25 years. There are nine different kinds (all $1.40 per jar): herb mix, savory salt, curry blend of 16 ingredients, salad delight, salad medley, chicken barbecue, lemon pepper, lemon parsley salt (great on fish or as a seafood seasoning, but "limiting this to use only on fish is shortsighted," says Mary), and "Rub A Dub" meat seasoning.

Mary's special dry soup mixes come in 4-oz. jars that make 2 quarts ($1.75 per jar or $18.50 for a case of 12) or in 7½-oz. jars that make one gallon ($2.85 per jar, $30 per case) and include such favorites as mulligatawny, cock-a-leekie, mock turtle, and avgolemono.

Soups and seasonings are available in gift packs ranging in price from $9.50 to $11.95, complete with recipes.

MIDWAY GROVES / Dept. CFC
Route 3, Box 28, Sarasota, FL 33580

Catalogue, free, published annually, 16 pages, illustrated, color.

Tropical marmalades and jellies, Florida orange blossom honey, and papaya nectar are part of the offerings in this catalogue. The marmalades are calamondin, grapefruit, grapefruit-cherry, tangerine, kumquat, Seville orange, sweet orange and Temple orange, the jellies, mint, guava, mango butter, and a tropical fruit conserve. Your choice of three 1-lb. jars is around $5, though probably higher by now. There's also a wild honey, organic and uncooked.

MORNING FRESH HERB COTTAGE / Dept. CFC
P.O. Box 403, Miller Place, NY 11764

Brochure, free.

Morning Fresh Herb Cottage grows culinary herbs and blends herbs and spices, but they package and sell by mail only one item—their blend of herbs and spices for salads and salad dressings. The ¾-oz. package of Morning Fresh Salad Herbs costs $1.25 ppd. and comes with complete directions for using in many different ways.

NICHOLS GARDEN NURSERY / Dept. CFC
1190 North Pacific Highway, Albany, OR 97321

"Nichols Herb and Rare Seeds," free, published seasonally, 60 pages, illustrated, black and white.

The Nichols catalogue has the usual spices and some that are a little different, such as a catsup spice seasoning (1 oz., 95¢), gumbo filé for Creole cooking, apple pie seasoning (a blend of spices from an old New England recipe), and a Super Salad Seasoning that comes from the kitchens of a well-known San Francisco restaurant (sesame and dried cheddar are among the ingredients and it can also be used on baked potatoes, macaroni, eggs), 95¢ for 2 oz. For sausage makers, Nichols has their country pork sausage seasoning, from another New England recipe, with 12 different spices and herbs (4 oz., $1.60, will season 6 lbs. of sausage), and an Italian pork sausage seasoning at the same price. Listed under "Specialty Oriental Gourmet Foods" you'll find teriyaki sauce mixes, various Japanese seaweeds and dried Japanese wild forest mushrooms (1½ oz., $2.35). Peppermint oil, direct from the Oregon peppermint fields, unadulterated and pure, is $2.50 for ½ oz., and one drop will flavor a large cake. Oregon dill oil will do the same for dill pickles—add 3 drops to a quart jar.

NORTHWESTERN COFFEE MILLS / Dept. CFC
217 North Broadway, Milwaukee, WI 53202

Catalogue, free (25¢ donation accepted), published annually, 28 pages, illustrated, black and white.

Coffee and tea merchants traditionally handle spices in their product line, as the problems of importing and processing are similar. Northwestern Coffee Mills follows this tradition in offering the best crop of spices and herbs for each variety, freshly ground where appropriate, for all cooking purposes. Everything is correctly listed—for instance, cayenne pepper, Hungarian and Spanish paprika, and whole or crushed Japanese chili peppers and ground Turkish chili peppers under the heading "Capsicums." Their mace is Indonesian, extra fancy (65¢ an oz.), their black peppercorns are Tellicherry and Lampong, and their white peppercorns Indonesian (all 50¢ an oz.). They also have both sweet soft-stick and sharp hard-stick cinnamon. Included in the listings are cassia buds from China, pure Spanish saffron ($5.30 for ¼ oz.), Dalmatian sage, Greek and Mexican oregano, Moroccan coriander and fenugreek (40¢ an oz.). How nice, for once, to know the origin of herbs and spices. There's also sea salt (40¢ a lb.), gumbo filé, and various dehydrated seasonings, such as dried mushrooms, lemon and orange peel. Spices, seeds, and herbs are sold whole, or ground at 5¢ per oz. extra. A well-considered and complete list.

ORIENTAL FOODS AND HANDCRAFTS / Dept. CFC
3708 N. Broadway, Chicago, IL 60613

"Pakistani-Indian Foods," price list, free, 3 pages.

Spices and condiments predominate on this list. In spices you'll find loose curry powder and loose garam masala (a mixture of hot spices), turmeric, green and white cardamom, mustard seeds, curry leaves, and all the others used in Indian cooking. Pickles include mango, mixed lemon, gunda and date, lemon and chili, tomato vegetable, brinjal, and stuffed chili pickles, ranging in price from 75¢ to $2.75.

PAPRIKAS WEISS IMPORTER / Dept. CFC
1546 Second Avenue, New York, NY 10028

"Imported Foods and Cookware Catalogue," $1 for annual subscription, published four times a year, 66 pages, illustrated, black and white.

As you'd expect, there are lots of preserves and relishes in this Hungarian store's catalogue. They carry the Robertson's of Scotland preserves and marmalades, Swiss jams, jellies, and marmalades, which include a black-currant-and-ginger jam, an elderberry jelly and juniper berry jelly ($1.98 a jar), German and Swiss fruit syrups, German honeys, Irish Willwood pickles (tomato, mustard, sweet, mixed, and piccalilli, $1.98 a 9-oz. jar), Hungarian hot peppers, French cornichons, and French and English mustards. They also have a complete line of herbs and spices, including the finest imported fresh blue poppy seed ($2.98 a lb.) and Hungarian rose paprika (the soul of Magyar cooking) from the southern town of Szeged, where the finest is grown, sweet, half sweet or hot, $3.98 a lb.

PENNER APIARIES / Dept. CFC
Rt. 3, Box 3886, Red Bluff, CA 96080

Price list, free, published seasonally.

Honey from California and from Canada is Penner's specialty.
   Produced in Saskatchewan (by California bees), a gift pack of four 1-lb. cartons is $6.75 on the West Coast and $8.75 east of the Rocky Mountains.
   The "Canadian and Thistle" pack—2 cartons of natural Canadian solid honey and one 2-lb. jar of liquid northern California "Golden Star Thistle" honey—is $6.75 in the West, $8.75 in the East.
   "Honey and nuts," 2 cartons of the Canadian honey plus ¾ lb. each of

Fennel

When from the boughs a savory odor blown,
Grateful to the appetite, more pleas'd my sense
Than the smell of sweetest fennel...
   Milton, *Paradise Lost*

Hungarian rose paprika from Paprikas Weiss

Wine jelly and sauce from The Picking Box

crisp brown natural almonds and walnuts, plus recipes, is $7.50 or $9.50 in the East.

The "Jumbo," 18 1-lb. cartons of solid Canadian honey along with the "Gems of Gold with Honey" cookbook, is available only on the West Coast. All prices include postage.

THE PICKING BOX / WINE COUNTRY FOODS AND GIFTS
Dept. CFC
Box 441, Hammondsport, NY 14840

"Wine Country Foods & Gifts," 35¢, refundable with purchase, 6 pages, illustrated, black and white.

The Picking Box sells Margaret's Gourmet Wine Goods (Margaret being Margaret Sprague), among which you'll find three wine jellies (Burgundy, rosé, and sherry) at $1.15 a jar; a Burgundy or Rhine wine salad dressing, to which you can add oil; Burgundy wine barbecue sauce; and two dessert toppings (Sangria and sherry) for fruit, ice cream, or cheesecake. The sauce and toppings are $1.35 each. Other products from The Picking Box are New York State pure maple syrup in sizes ranging from ½ pt. to 1 gal. ($2.35 to $16.30 delivered); 1-lb jars of New York State honey, $2 delivered; cheeses and a booklet of 31 recipes from cooks in Hammondsport's wine country ($1). There are various gift packs of the jellies, sauce, and toppings, some with an 8-oz. tub of Wine Cellar cheese spread (whipped with sherry), each package containing literature, a folder of wine recipes, and a decorative frill of plastic grapes, at prices from $3.20 to $11.55 delivered.

PICKLE-RITE ACRES / Dept. CFC
Pulaski, WI 54162

Price list, free, published seasonally.

Pickles, beets, and sauerkraut from America's Pickle Capital. Midget dills, sweet relish, wood-aged sauerkraut, as well as cherry peppers, crab apples, cauliflower buds, and sweet pickles are all organically grown.

And for anyone on a restricted diet, Pickle-Rite has low-calorie, naturally sweetened pickles and cucumbers, as well as sodium- and sugar-free dills and low-sodium, salt-free kraut.

There are organic vegetables and fruits available in glass jars, too: green peas, sliced carrots, sliced red beets, red cabbage, applesauce, cranberry drink, and spiced pears. Write for up-to-date prices.

PIONEER/SEMINOLE GROVES / Dept. CFC
P.O. Box 2209, Cocoa, Fl 32922

"Citrus and Gift Catalog," free, published four times a year, 16 pages, illustrated, color.

While Pioneer-Seminole Groves specializes in citrus fruits, they have other gifts from Florida, such as their line of jellies, fruit butters, marmalades, pickles and relishes, and honeys. Among the tropical jellies are guava, lemon, orange, and orange-mint; butters include guava, mango, papaya, orange, and tangerine; marmalades, too many to list, have such unusual combinations as papaya-pineapple, orange-pine-cherry, and kumquat-cherry. These come in 2½-oz., 8-oz., and 16-oz. jars in packages of 6 or 12 for small jars, 3, 6, and 12 for the larger sizes. Six of the 2½-oz. jars are $4.95, 6 of the 8-oz. $5.95, and 6 of the 16-oz. $10.95. Southern delicacies such as artichoke relish, corn chowchow, sweet hot red pepper jelly, watermelon pickle, fig preserves, or rhubarb-raspberry preserves are $8.95 for three 18-oz. jars. Muscadine jelly is $4.75 for a 1¼-lb. jar. A miniature orange crate of 3-oz. jars of orange blossom, palmetto, and wildflower honeys is $3.50, a cracker basket of three 2½-oz. jars of assorted fruit butters and marmalades is $4.50, and three 8-oz. jars of coconut toast spread cost $5.50. They also list a coco-lada coconut drink mix for rum or brandy cocktails and a piña-colada mix.

*

To get the last bit out of an almost empty jar of mustard or prepared sauce, add a little water or stock, replace cap and shake well. If you use Dijon mustard in vinaigrette dressing, add vinegar or lemon juice to the jar, shake, and use in the dressing.

*

Add honey, rather than sugar, to whipped cream. It helps to stabilize the cream and the flavor is delicious.

*

M. M. POONJIAJI & CO. / Dept. CFC
 42 A. Podar Marg (1st Marine Street), Bombay 400 002, India

Brochure, free, 4 pages, published seasonally, illustrated, color.

For $22 you will be sent by registered sea mail twelve ½-lb. bottles or tins of your choice of any of the following of Poonjiaji's products: sliced mango pickle, mango pickle in oil, lime pickle, combination pickle, sweet sliced mango chutney, Major Grey's chutney, hot mango chutney, Madras curry paste, and Madras curry powder (the Ship Brand green label).

G. B. RAFFETTO, INC. / Dept. CFC
 87-34th Street, Brooklyn, NY 11232

Color brochure and order form, free.

Raffetto dessert toppings, relishes and fruits preserved in spirits and liqueurs are famous. Now you can order them in gift assortments by direct mail. For $10 each you have a choice of six different assortments, two boxed sets of three different brandied or liqueur fruits and four boxed sets of Deluxe Toppings, Exotic Relishes, Condiment Assortment, or Polynesian Delights (these include stem ginger, preserved kumquats, duck sauce, and peach chutney). Prices are for deliveries east of the Mississippi. Add $1 for deliveries west of the Mississippi.

ROLLING LEDGE MAPLE ORCHARD / Dept. CFC
 R.F.D. 4, Enosburg Falls, VT 05450

Price list and information sheet, free, published seasonally.

The brevity of this price list belies Rolling Ledge's interest in and variety of chemical-free, pure Vermont maple syrup.

Did you know that Fancy or Grade A syrup (a light amber color with a delicate flavor) should be used with ice cream, on cereal, pancakes, and waffles, while Grade B (dark amber, strong flavor) is better used as a table syrup or in puddings, custards, cakes, toppings, cookies, or as a baked ham glaze? Or that Grade C (very dark, strong caramel flavoring) is produced during the warm weather months at the end of the season and makes a fine substitute for molasses in baked beans and dark breads?

Well, Ruth and Don and Carrol and Darlene, the proprietors, know a lot about their product, which they sell in 1-gal. (Grade A: $10.50; Grade B: $9), ½ gal. (A: $6.25; B: $5; C: $4), and pint cans. There's also maple sugar, maple cream (5 lb., $9.75), maple candy, sugar cakes, and a gift assortment of 8-oz. maple cream, ½-pt. syrup, and 1 lb. of sugar cakes ($6.50). Orders over $100 are not charged the normal 5 percent shipping charges.

SAHADI IMPORTING CO., INC. / Dept. CFC
 187 Atlantic Avenue, Brooklyn, NY 11201

"The Silent Salesman," free, published biannually, 24 pages, illustrated, black and white.

Sahadi has a good range of imported spices, with emphasis on those used in Middle Eastern and Indian cooking, such as cardamom, cumin, coriander, ginger, turmeric, saffron, fenugreek, chili pepper, and cinnamon, both stick and ground. Spices are sold by the pound or quarter pound and are very reasonably priced, ranging from 25¢ for 4 oz. of coriander seeds to $1.75 for 4 oz. of whole or ground cloves. The dried vegetable and flavoring section lists Syrian dried mint ($5 a lb.) and some unusual things like zaatar, an herb used in Moroccan cooking.

You'll find the familiar Major Grey chutney and less familiar lemon pickle, mango pickle, and hot green mango pickle from India, while the Middle East contributes pickled turnips, hot or mild pickled okra (90¢ a 14-oz. jar), pickled peppers and eggplant. Mustard oil and coconut oil, used in certain Indian recipes, are each $1.75 for a 16-oz. jar.

Some of the exotic preserves, syrups, and juices include pomegranate syrup ($3.50 a 1-lb. jar), carob syrup, tamarind syrup, fig and rose-petal jam, guava juice and guava shells, mango juice and sliced mangos in syrup, jams from Greece and Lebanon, and various honeys, such as clover, orange-blossom, and wildflower.

Sauce Diable

Chop 1 shallot or 3 green onions and sauté until limp in 2 tablespoons butter. Mix in the juice of 1 lemon, 1 teaspoon Worcestershire sauce, 1 tablespoon Dijon mustard, and a dash of Tabasco. Mix into 2 cups brown sauce and cook, stirring, until smooth. For a hotter sauce, add more Tabasco and mustard. Serve with thinly sliced broiled flank steak, grilled kidneys, or broiled chicken.

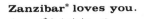

Zanzibar* loves you.

(*the herb dragon)

SAN FRANCISCO HERB & NATURAL FOOD CO.
herbs, tea blends, spices

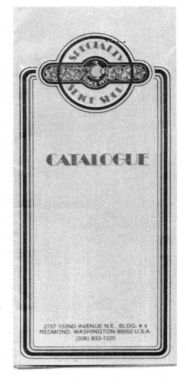

SAN FRANCISCO HERB & NATURAL FOOD CO. / Dept. CFC
P.O. Box 40604, San Francisco, CA 94140

Catalogue, free, published seasonally, 10 pages, black and white.

Spices and herbs sold in bulk lots of 1, 5, or 10 lbs. and packages by the oz. in case lots of 12 packages. Among the spices you'll find such things as both black and yellow mustard seed, black and natural sesame seed, blue poppy seed, star anise, cinnamon chips, and turmeric. Prices are better in bulk, if you wish to buy that way and split an order with friends. As an example, in bulk, star anise (for Chinese cooking) is $1.75 a lb. ($1.45 a lb. if you buy 10 lbs.), whereas packaged it costs 57¢ for 1½ oz., $4.56 for a case of 12 packages.

SAVAGE CITRUS BARN, INC. / Dept. CFC
Rte. 1, Box 150, Raymondville, TX 78580

"Savage Citrus Fruit," free, published annually, 1 oversized page, illustrated, color.

Savage preserves, unlike their citrus fruits, are available year round. They have a selection of 6 preserves, 6 jellies, and 6 relishes. Available in pint containers are watermelon rind, strawberry, fig, blueberry, apricot, and dewberry preserves; jalapeño pepper jelly, hot pepper relish, piccalilli, pickled beets, bread 'n' butter pickles, and corn relish.

In half pints you'll find ruby-red grapefruit, valley lemon, Mexican lime, wild orange, orange/jalapeño and jalapeño jellies.

Any 6 jars are $16.

SCARPA'S CIDER MILL / Dept. CFC
Box 38, Mission Home, VA 22956

Price list, free, on request.

Mario J. Scarpa makes old-fashioned cider vinegar from whole, unsprayed apples and sells it by the quart, $1.25, or gallon, $4.75.

SEY-CO PRODUCTS CO. / Dept. CFC
7651 Densmore Avenue, Van Nuys, CA 91406

Catalogue, free, published annually, 15 pages, illustrated, color.

This catalogue of fancy foods includes a large range of jams and jellies, from English gooseberry preserves and Seville orange marmalade to crab apple and mint jelly. Jams and jellies cost from $1 to $1.40 for a 10½-oz. or 1-lb. 12-oz. jar. There's also wild blackberry syrup, maple syrup, and lots of pickles and relishes—pickled watermelon rind, corn relish, pickled okra, green tomato piccalilli. Any assortment can be gift-packaged at no extra charge.

SPECIALTY SPICE SHOP / Dept. CFC
2757 152nd Avenue, N.E., Redmond, WA 98052

"Specialty Spice Shop Catalogue," free, published annually, 6 pages.

Specialty Spice Shop has a wide-ranging list of herbs, spices, mixtures like garam masala (the spice blend properly used in curry), seasonings for sausage, hamburger, vegetables and other items you might not expect to find, such as brewer's yeast (flakes or powder), alfalfa seeds, dried chestnuts, sour salt, sugar crystals in different colors (green, orange, pink, yellow), white shredded shrimp, red sago, dried European and Oriental mushrooms, mung beans, kelp powder, coconut milk powder and shredded coconut, various chili peppers and chili powders (both hot and mild), and annato seeds (achiote, used in Latin American cooking). It's a very interesting list. They sell in amounts of 2 and 4 oz., ½ lb. and 1 lb. No prices in the catalogue, so you'll have to request them. Teas, coffees, nuts, oils, sachets, and potpourri are also part of their stock in trade.

THE SPICE MARKET / Dept. CFC
94 Reade Street, New York, NY 10013

Price list.

The Spice Market sells spices at very reasonable prices, and their large list includes such things as ground turmeric ($1.15 for 8 oz.), green peppercorns packed in brine ($1.15), juniper berries ($1.60 for 4 oz.), and vanilla beans (2 for 80¢). Prices are subject to change, and there's a minimum order of $5.

R. B. SWAN & SON / Dept. CFC
25 Prospect St., Brewer, ME 04412

Price list.

The Swans sell Maine wild blueberry, wild raspberry, and wildflower honey in 6-lb. plastic containers, but you must write for the prices.

NORM THOMPSON / Dept. CFC
1805 N.W. Thurman Street, Portland, OR 97209

Catalogue, free, published seasonally, 80 pages, illustrated, color.

Primarily a clothing catalogue designed to appeal to Pacific Northwest-erners. One page is given over to a glowing account of Hubbs Farm jams and jellies, which are homemade in a tiny cannery near Mount Hood by the old-fashioned way of cooking in open copper kettles over an open fire with just fruit and sugar. One selection has six 12-oz. jars of jams (strawberry, red raspberry, wild blackberry, seedless blackcap), jellies (loganberry, wild huckleberry), and syrup (wild blackberry, wild huckleberry) for $28.50 ppd. The second has three jars of loganberry jelly, strawberry preserves, and blackberry jam ($12.50 ppd.).

THOUSAND ISLANDS APIARIES / Dept. CFC
Rte. 2, Clayton, NY 13624

Price list, free, published seasonally, 2 pages, illustrated.

Deep in upper New York State, Thousand Islands Apiaries produces liquid, creamed (finely granulated), or comb honey at reasonable prices.

A 3-lb. tin of elfin gold liquid honey is $4.80, a case of four 3-lb. tins $16.25, and a 46-lb. can $47. A 4½-lb. tin of creamed honey is $6.25, and a case of 24 individually wrapped 2½-oz. pieces of comb honey (available only after July 20) is $12.

Here is Thousand Islands Apiaries' recipe for an old-fashioned "switchell": Mix ½ cup of apple cider vinegar with ½ cup of honey. Use 3 or 4 teaspoons of this combination with ice and water and you've got a cool, refreshing summer drink.

THE VERMONT COUNTRY STORE / Dept. CFC
Weston, VT 05161

Catalogue, 25¢, published annually, 98 pages, illustrated, black and white.

The Vermont Country Store sells old-fashioned apple butter ($1.25 a 28-oz. jar), pure Grade A maple syrup, maple butter, homemade peanut butter that is nothing but peanuts, no preservatives, with or without salt ($1.39 a pint jar), New England mincemeat made from a century-old recipe ($1.89 a 1-lb., 12-oz. jar), and English ginger marmalade (grapefruit and crystallized ginger). There's a nice selection of their own jams, jellies, and relishes, among them a cranberry conserve, corn relish, red pepper relish, green tomato piccalilli, rose hips jelly, beach plum jelly, and wild blueberry jelly. These are sold in cases of 6 jars at prices from $5.95 to $7.25 for raspberry preserve. Other products they carry are the French moutarde de Meaux, made with whole mustard seeds, sea salt, Tellicherry peppercorns (95¢ a 3-oz. jar, but a bargain if you buy a lb. for $3.50), a bag of 20 nutmegs for $1, and the famous Outerbridge's sherry peppers. If you have ever been to Bermuda you'll have seen this spicy bottled potion of peppers and spice

---

*

Use Tabasco instead of black pepper as seasoning for sauces, mayonnaise and Hollandaise, egg dishes. It does not leave flecks in the sauce.

*

Use liquid from a jar of chutney to baste ham for a lovely piquant flavor.

*

Cinnamon Maple Toast

For each person, toast a thick slice of bread on one side. Spread untoasted side with soft butter, sprinkle with maple sugar, a dusting of cinnamon and chopped walnuts, butternuts, or pecans. Place slices on baking sheet and put under broiler. Broil until sugar is melted and bubbly.

—*from "Treasured Recipes from Early New England Kitchens"*

Busy bees at Thousand Islands Apiaries

Gift basket from Vermont General Store & Grist Mill

Mustard Sauce
Combine in a small bowl 1 cup mayonnaise, 1 teaspoon horseradish, 1 teaspoon dry mustard, 1 teaspoon fresh lime juice, salt and black pepper to taste.
—*from "The Omaha Steaks Cookbook"*

steeped in sherry on restaurant tables. Just a drop adds zest to soups, curries, chowders, and Bloody Marys. A folder of Bermuda recipes comes with each bottle of sherry peppers ($2.50).

VERMONT GENERAL STORE & GRIST MILL, INC. / Dept. CFC
Woodstock, VT 05091

Catalogue, 50¢, with recipe booklet, 6 pages, illustrated, black and white.

In addition to stone-ground pancake and muffin mixes, the store sells by mail 100 percent pure Grade A Vermont maple syrup, made the old-fashioned way by evaporation over maplewood fires in the sugar-house. It takes nearly 5 gallons of sap to fill just one 17.2-oz. bottle, which costs $3.95 plus 55¢ shipping east of the Mississippi or 80¢ shipping west of the Mississippi. You can also buy metal containers of quart, half-gallon and gallon sizes ($6.25, $9.95, and $17.50, plus shipping). There's a minimum order of $5 exclusive of postage and handling charges. Or order the bottle of maple syrup packaged with two of their stone-ground whole-grain pancake mixes, wheat and cornmeal and wholewheat and cornmeal buttermilk, in a basket lined with a checkered napkin for $10.50 plus $1 for shipping, or 2 baskets for $19.75, $1.75 for shipping.

WALNUT ACRES / Dept. CFC
Penns Creek, PA 17862

"Walnut Acres Natural Foods," free, published five times a year, 24 pages, black and white.

Walnut Acres prepares many of the foods they sell by mail and to health-food stores. One is peanut butter, made with freshly roasted, organically raised peanuts, with or without salt—and absolutely nothing else. It will keep up to 4 weeks without refrigeration, 8 to 10 weeks refrigerated, and may be frozen. Regular style, salted or unsalted, is $1.12 a lb. jar, crunchy $1.13. There's also coconut peanut butter (half peanuts, half coconut, no salt, no oil), a raw peanut butter, peanut butter-honey spread, and peanut butter-honey-sesame spread. Other nut and seed butters are almond, raw cashew, and sesame seed, or tahini. Walnut Acres makes pickles with their own organically grown vegetables. Medium and small dills are $1.37 and $1.47 a quart, and the garden relish, made with organic vegetables, apple cider vinegar, alfalfa honey, salt and spices, is 98¢ a pint. Their apple butter contains only unsprayed apples, vanilla extract and spices, no sugar, and their jams and jellies are made from unsprayed or wild fruit, sweetened with alfalfa honey ($1.43 a pint). Walnut Acres also sells pure flavorings and extracts, natural honeys and honey and fruit spreads, pure unsulphured molasses, maple syrup, sorghum syrup, and carob honey syrup, made with carob powder, honey, water, vanilla, arrowroot, and salt ($1.82 a lb. jar).

WELL-SWEEP HERB FARM / Dept. CFC
317 Mt. Bethel Road, Port Murray, NJ 07865

Brochure, free, published annually, 3 pages.

In addition to shipping herb plants and herb seeds, Well-Sweep Farm sells their own herb vinegars (orange mint, dill, basil and garlic, basil and tarragon, salad burnet, tarragon) for 75¢, an herb salad dressing for $1.25, and mint sauce for $1.15.

WHITE FLOWER FARM / Dept. CFC
Litchfield, CT 06759

"The Garden Book," published spring and fall, plus three issues of garden notes, $4 a year (or free to customers whose orders total $15 or more), 68 pages, illustrated, black and white.

In addition to plants, White Flower Farm sells the superb Tellicherry black peppercorns, grown in the highlands of southwest India, the kind you are unlikely to find in your local supermarket. Tellicherry pepper has a full aroma but is not harsh like Malabar or Lampong, the usual commercial peppercorns. Current price is $5.25 ppd. for the 1-lb. package, but it will probably have gone up by now. If you think a pound of pepper is a lot, you'll be surprised how quickly it gets used up—or you might arrange to split the package with a friend. This makes a great spur-of-the-moment house gift, too.

WILLIAMS-SONOMA / Dept. CFC
   576 Sutter Street, San Francisco, CA 94102

   "A Catalog for Cooks," $1, published biannually, plus "January sale/New Kitchen Ideas," both 26 pages, illustrated, color.

Every year Chuck Williams goes foraging in Europe, and every year he comes back with lots of goodies for Williams-Sonoma in equipment and food. In Paris he found in a side-street charcuterie some delicious preserves, rhubarbe, tomates rouges, and tomates vertes ($6 for the three 12-oz. jars). Rhubarb jam you may know, but if you have never tried red and green tomato jams, you'll love them. Also from France come green and black olives, which the French probably cure better than anyone. The green are pickled in a special spiced brine, the black are dried and cured in olive oil (great for salade Niçoise). A 7-oz. jar of the two is $6.25. Williams-Sonoma also carries excellent French white wine vinegars, tarragon- or garlic-flavored, and a couple of mustards from a small, exclusive mustard house, Dijon, and a Burgundy mustard with whole mustard seeds—both very attractively packed in clear glass jars ($5 the pair). Another Chuck Williams find is a French vanilla-flavored liquid caramel ($3.50 for two 4½-oz. bottles).

WINEMAKER'S SHOP / Dept. CFC
   Bully Hill Road, R.D. 2, Hammondsport, NY 14840

   "Winemaker's Shop Price Guide," free, published seasonally, 2 pages.

The Greyton H. Taylor Wine Museum and The Winemaker's Shop are in the wine region of Hammondsport, New York. Some of the items that are sold by the shop are imported vine leaves in brine (98¢ for a 1-lb. jar), Burgundy, sherry, and rosé wine grape jellies ($1.35 for 8 oz.), specialty grape juice for making jellies and wines or to drink plain, and various books on wine and wine cookery, one a vegetarian cookbook called *Wings of Life* ($5.95). Grapes and juices are available in September and October, the native variety of grapes for juices and jellies, French-American hybrid and vinifera grapes for winemaking.

THE WISCONSIN CHEESEMAN / Dept. CFC
   P.O. Box 1, Madison, WI 53701

   "Gift Selections," free, published annually, 96 pages, illustrated, color.

While jams and jellies play only a minor part in the Wisconsin cheeseman's gift packages, you'll find strawberry preserves, cranberry jelly, wild plum jam, and orange butter packaged with a porcelain Delft jam jar ($7.95); 2 lbs. of strawberry jam in a white plastic, gold-trimmed bucket ($5.99); a jam/jelly/honey assortment that contains wild chokecherry, wild blueberry and wild grape jellies, wild plum and wild cranberry jams, linden and wildflower honeys ($4.85); a Jamboree of 17 jars of jams, jellies, and honeys ($6.95); and 6 honeys, jams, and jellies packaged with a cut-glass preserve server and spoon ($5.95). These sweet things are also available in packages with fruitcake, tea, cheese, and the many assorted gift hampers and packs.

YANKEE TEA TRADER / Dept. CFC
   P.O. Box 747, Escondido, CA 92025

   Product price list, free, revised monthly, 2 pages.

Yankee Tea Trader lists 28 herbs and spices and in many cases identifies the country of origin. They have Lampong black pepper, Malabar white pepper, Ceylon cinnamon, Saigon and Batavia cassia, Grenada nutmeg, Greek oregano, African ginger root, Panang cloves, California

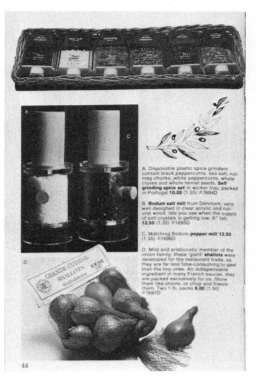

Spice grinders and shallots, from "A Catalog for Cooks"

Glaze for Open-Face Tarts
Melt a 1-pound jar of pure preserves (apricot, raspberry, red currant jelly) in a heavy saucepan over medium heat until it comes to the boiling point. Flavor with a little cognac or a fruit brandy such as kirsch. Use apricot or currant glaze as is, strain raspberry to remove seeds before using. A drop or two of crème de cassis will bring out the flavor in the raspberry preserves.

★

Freezing reduces the strength of flavors. Overseason or oversweeten foods to be frozen.

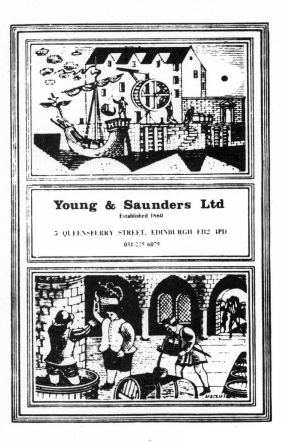

and Mediterranean basil leaves, Dalmatian sage, and Dutch poppy seed. Gumbo filé, star anise, vanilla beans, and sea salt are also on the list. Prices quoted, which are revised as necessary, are for ½ lb., ¼ lb., and 2 oz. and range from around 20¢ for 2 oz. of Mediterranean basil leaves to $3.30 for 2 oz. of cardamom. Sea salt is less expensive, 5¢ for 2 oz., and vanilla beans more expensive, $4.20 for 2 oz.

YOUNG & SAUNDERS LTD. / Dept. CFC
5 Queensferry Street, Edinburgh EH2 4PD, Scotland

"Food & Wine List," free, published seasonally, 42 pages, black and white.

The Young & Saunders catalogue has a nice assortment of honeys, such as Scottish flower, Scottish heather, Strathmore Liqueur, New Zealand clover, and Tasmanian leatherwood; the Tiptree line of preserves; Elsenham and Tiptree marmalades, among them a bitter lemon, tangerine, and dark breakfast; whiskey marmalade and Isle of Arran marmalade; various savory jellies, such as rowan and apple, port wine, aspic with Madeira and brandy, plus cloudberry preserve and lemon curd. In pickles you'll find sweet spiced walnuts and pickled walnuts, silverskin onions, mixed pickles, and various Indian mango, brinjal, and lime pickles. Prices, quoted in sterling, are subject to the fluctuating exchange rate and do not include overseas shipping costs.

See Appendix, page 239, for additional sources not included here.

CHAPTER SIX

CAKES, COOKIES, CANDIES, AND OTHER CONFECTIONS

AHLERS ORGANIC DATE AND GRAPEFRUIT GARDEN
Dept. CFC
P.O. Box 726, Mecca, CA 92254

Price list, free, published annually, 5 pages.

Ahlers makes sugar-free candies from their organically grown dates. Coconut-date balls come in boxes of three 12-oz. bags ($7.25), 1½-lb. bags ($8.25), or three 1½-lb. bags ($10.95). Coconut-date bars, 32 of them at 1½ oz. each, are $10.95, and "snowballs" made of dates, walnuts, and unsweetened coconut run $6.95 per lb. or $10.25 for 2 lbs.

ALAMO FRUIT / Dept. CFC
Box 666, Alamo, TX 78516

"Holiday Gifts," free, published annually, 32 pages, illustrated, color.

Piñatas, those colorful paper constructions filled with candies and nuts, are symbolic of parties in Mexico. For your festivities, Alamo Fruit will send a clown piñata ($9.90) or a snowman ($9.75). Other sweets available from this Texas citrus house are pecan log rolls ($5.95), pecan pralines ($6.95), and a pecan fruitcake ($13.40 for 4½ lbs.).

ANZEN JAPANESE FOODS AND IMPORTS / Dept. CFC
736 N. E. Union Avenue, Portland, OR 97232

Price list, free, 20 pages.

Anzen's list has some confectionery, Oriental-style, such as almond cookies, fortune cookies (59¢ for 3½ oz.), coconut biscuits, sesame cookies, fortune candy, sesame crunch, and sesame snaps. Hawaiian haupia pudding coconut mix is 73¢ for 3 oz.

Chocolate shells and mints, from Astor
Chocolate Corporation

Orange Nut Cake Grand Marnier
Preheat oven to 350°. Cream 1 cup butter with 1 cup
sugar until light and fluffy. Add 3 egg yolks and continue beating. Add 1 teaspoon Grand Marnier. Sift 2
cups flour with 1 teaspoon baking powder and 1 teaspoon baking soda. Add to the batter alternately with 1
cup sour cream, beginning and ending with dry ingredients. Stir in the grated rind of 1 orange and ½ cup
chopped mixed nuts. Beat 3 egg whites until stiff, fold
into batter, and pour into a greased 9-inch tube pan.
Bake for 55 minutes. Test with a cake tester in center
for firmness. For topping, mix ½ cup sugar with ¼ cup
orange juice and ⅓ cup Grand Marnier. Spoon over
the hot cake in the pan. Let cool before removing from
pan. Serves 8.
—from Grand Marnier Recipe Booklet

ASTOR CHOCOLATE CORP. / Dept. CFC
48-25 Metropolitan Avenue, Brooklyn, NY 11237

*"Chocolate Dessert Specialties," free, published annually, 1 page,
illustrated, color.*

For the insatiably sweet-toothed, Astor offers chocolate shells ($7.50–
$8.50 for 3 boxes) and suggests that these specialties (not shipped in
summer) be filled with ice cream, fruits, nuts, whipped cream, liqueurs,
or eaten by themselves. There are also individually wrapped milk-
chocolate dinner mints (three ½-lb. boxes, $7.50).

BACHMAN GIFTS / Dept. CFC
8th and Reading Avenues, Box 898, Reading, PA 19603

*"Bachman Gifts and Goodies from the Historic Land of the Pennsylvania
Dutch," free, published annually, 32 pages, illustrated, color.*

Among the gifts and goodies are tins of Dutch cookies, caramel nut
crunch (corn puffs with caramel coating, studded with roasted cashews
and pecans), a caramel-coated corn and peanut snack called "Hanky
Panky," peanut crunch ($9.35 delivered), sweet-and-sour hard candies,
chocolate-covered pretzels, and three 1-lb. canisters of different
Pennsylvania Dutch candies, frosted yum yums, hard candy, and
peanut crunch ($9.40 delivered).

B&B FOOD PRODUCTS / Dept. CFC
Route #1B, Cadiz, KY 42211

*"Your Gift Catalog," free, published annually, 16 pages, illustrated, black
and white.*

Bourbon and pecans are two of the most popular products from the
South. B&B supplements its Kentucky country hams and smoked turkeys with a vacuum-packed bourbon fruitcake, a "Plantation Pudding"
bourbon pecan cake, and a sampler pack of bourbon hard sauce, bourbon sundae sauce, and bourbon sauce supreme (use as a glaze on ham,
sweet potatoes, or pour over baked apples or plum pudding). The
sampler pack is around $7, the fruitcake about $7, and the pudding
about $6.

BETTER FOODS FOUNDATION, INC. / Dept. CFC
300 North Washington Street, Greencastle, PA 17225

Brochure, free, 8 pages, black and white.

Better Foods bakes and sells cookies as well as health foods. They have
oatmeal and raisin, old-fashioned molasses, raisin soya gems, peanut
butter, sugarless honey-date, bran-raisin, and a couple of others, ranging in price from 59¢ to 79¢ a dozen. Among the other foods they stock
are Holland honey cake (one with no salt), fruit and honey cake, sugarless honey-sweetened cookies made with wheat germ, honey drop
candy, and Ricola herb candy.

BISCUITERIE DU BASTION / Dept. CFC
44 Blvd. Jamin, 51100 Reims, France

Color brochure, free.

Confections made by Fossier, a company in the Champagne region
town of Rheims, include the little tongue-shaped biscuits de Reims,
better known here as champagne biscuits; massepains, marzipan
cookies; croquignoles, made with flour, sugar, and egg whites; and pain
d'épices, or spice cake. According to the legend on the reverse side of
the brochure, these are packaged in various combinations. No prices
are included on the brochure, so you will have to request them.

BISSINGER'S / Dept. CFC
205 West 4th Street, Cincinnati, OH 45202

"Bissinger's Guide to Gourmet Gifting," free, published for Christmas and Easter, 12 pages, illustrated, black and white.

Besides the traditional holiday candy packs (1- to 5-lb. assortments, $4.95 to $10.95), chocolate-covered nuts, taffy, cookies, nougats, mints, rum and brandy cakes, and petit babas, Bissinger's displays a fascinating knack for pleasing the sweet-toothed crowd, young or old.

For Christmas there is a Knusperhaus kit so that the kids can build a festive cookie house ($12.50); a chocolate mill to shave chocolate onto ice cream and other desserts (with 12 oz. chocolate, $7.50); 48 different gingerbread people ("using copious amounts of honey"), 8 inches tall and 4 inches wide; plus glass snifters and stackable jars filled with liquor-flavored hard candies ($2.95 to $6.50). Bissinger's has candy calendars and lollipop figures of hobby horses and drummer boys that are great as stocking stuffers or tree decorations.

For Easter an old-fashioned bonnet is filled with marshmallow eggs or assorted chocolates ($3.50 to $7.95). A pear, lemon, strawberry, or orange tree is laden with hard candies ($5.95).

Bissinger's also offers a confection-of-the-month plan for 4, 8, and 12 months ($33 to $82.50), as well as individually tailored gift baskets of candies, cookies, and hors d'oeuvre.

BLUM'S OF SAN FRANCISCO, INC. / Dept. CFC
209 Utah Avenue, South San Francisco, CA 94080

"Blum's," free, published periodically, 4 pages, illustrated, color.

Blum's candies, cookies, and cakes are sold in 50 states as well as Guam, Hong Kong, and Australia and have been a special San Francisco treat since 1890. They sell a traditional assortment of chocolate (1 to 5 lbs., $5.25 to $20.75), chocolate-covered nuts, almondettes (whole roasted almonds dipped in dark caramel), as well as mints, light and dark chocolate creams (raspberry, strawberry, orange, coffee rum, and mint), nougats, petits fours, miniature and regular fruitcakes, and party cookies (1 lb., $5.75).

BOCOCK-STROUD CO. / Dept. CFC
501 West 4th Street, Winston-Salem, NC 27102

Brochure, free, 8 pages, illustrated, black and white.

This company sells by mail the original Old Salem Moravian ginger cookies, in round or assorted shapes ($2.50 for ½-lb. tube of the round, or $5.50 for a 1-lb. tin of the assorted). These famous little cookies, which originated over a century and a half ago, are paper-thin, cut with colonial-type cutters, sweetened with molasses and tangy with spices. There are also Old Salem sugar crisps or chocolate cookies at $5 a 14-oz. tin, cheese petites, cocktail nibbles tangy with cheese and sprinkled with paprika, $5.50 a 1-lb. tin, and a sliced fruitcake. You can order combination gift packages of the cookies, or the cookies and cake, at prices from $10 to $15. All prices include postage.

BOWLBY CANDY CO. / Dept. CFC
P.O. Box 312, Waupaca, WI 54981

Brochure and price list, free.

The Bowlby Candy Company calls themselves "manufacturers of Black Ladle Butter Brittles and Chocolates." Their butter toffee (peanut) brittle is $1.89 a 1-lb. bag or $4.25 for a 1¾-lb. gift tin; the chocolate-covered toffee brittle is $5.95 a 2-lb. tin. In addition to candy they sell jumbo salted cashews, mixed nuts, and various snack products, such as Bowlby's Bits (made from vegetable oil, wheat germ, and protein), Sun Buds (a mix of Bowlby's Bits with peanuts, pepitas, soybeans, sesame sticks, and other things), Nuttyest of All (a combination of nuts, Bowlby's Bits, raisins, sunflower seeds, pepitas, soybeans, sesame sticks, garlic buds), and Lettuce Love, another mixture that presumably can also be tossed in a salad. UPS or parcel post and handling are not included in the prices.

Cooking chocolate from Bissinger's

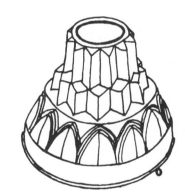

Tower cake mold

★

Don't store different cakes and cookies in the same container. They will take on the strongest flavor and become stale more quickly.

★

Ground nut brittle can be substituted in recipes calling for praline. Break into pieces, grind to a powder in the blender, and store in the freezer. It is delicious added to chocolate sauce or sprinkled over ice cream.

★

LUCY BRALEY'S CANDY KITCHEN / Dept. CFC
Cranberry Highway, Massachusetts State Tourist Route 28, South Middleboro, MA 02346

Price lists and order forms, free, updated periodically.

A great assortment of candies comes from Lucy Braley's kitchen. In fudge, there's plain chocolate, chocolate walnut, chocolate coconut walnut, chocolate marshmallow, chocolate peanut butter, chocolate raisin, plain vanilla, vanilla coconut walnut, chocolate chip divinity, walnut divinity, even a cranberry fudge. Penuche comes plain, ginger, pecan, walnut, and peanut butter. She has assorted paper-wrapped caramels and nougats, rolled butterkrunch with various nuts on the outside, nut brittles, saltwater taffy in 20 flavors, pecan logs, 14 flavors of cream rolls, 7 flavors of cream mints, assorted chocolates with soft centers, hard and chewy, chocolate-dipped fruits and nuts, and, to amuse the children, "Braley-Barley" Pops, lollipops in rocket or figure shapes. Prices run around $2 a lb. for the candies, $1.50 for the lollipops. Postage is extra, and special gift wrappings are available.

BREMEN HOUSE INC. / Dept. CFC
218 East 86th Street, New York, NY 10028

"Bremen House Catalog of Gourmet Foods," free, published twice a year, 20 pages, illustrated, black and white.

Listed in this catalogue are many of the traditional German cookies, cakes, and marzipan specialties. Dresden Christmas stollen, wrapped and boxed, is available in various sizes; the 1¼-lb. size costs $10. Iced or chocolate-covered baumkuchen is $7.50, an 11-oz. tin of lebkuchen is $5.75, and there are also almond speculaas, pfeffernüsse, zimtsterne (glazed cinnamon stars), honey cakes, and assorted Christmas cookies. In candies you'll find Lindt, Droste, Tobler, Hofbauer, and Sarotti chocolates; milk-chocolate cat's tongues; nougat caramels; rum cordials; coffee cordials; chocolate coffee beans; candy bears; and violet pastilles. Various boxed assortments of chocolate-covered and cream-filled wafers range in price from around $1.35 for 4¼ oz. to $13.95 for a 1-lb. 4¼-oz. decorated tin. You can also buy here the Carlsbad wafers oblaten ($2.50 for 8 oz.).

CASA DE FRUTA / Dept. CFC
6680 Pacheco Pass Hwy., Hollister, CA 95023

"Casa de Fruta," price list and order form, free, published annually, 4 pages, illustrated, color.

From Casa de Fruta you can get naturally delicious candies made from fruits and nuts, dried fruit and dried roasted nuts dipped in milk chocolate ($5.95 for 1 lb. 12 oz.), and "original candy creations" for the Holiday gift pack ($9.95).

Bolado, candy-coated walnuts, is $3.95 for 9 oz.; almond bark, almonds bathed in chocolate, vanilla, and cherry, $3.95 for 9 oz.

Other candies are strawberry clusters ($1.75 for 5 oz.), pineapple-coconut clusters ($1.50 for 7 oz.), a combo of orange-apricot and pineapple ($1.50 for 7 oz.), date/walnut/coffee candy ($1.50 for 7 oz.), and rocky road, walnuts and marshmallow in milk chocolate ($1.50 for 7 oz.).

Candies are also available with selected dried fruit in the Pajaro gift pack, 3 lbs. of sweet things for $13.50.

Candy shipments are made from October through April and are postpaid.

CATHERINE'S CHOCOLATE SHOP / Dept. CFC
Route 7, Great Barrington, MA 01230

"Catherine's Chocolates," free, published periodically, 6 pages, illustrated, black and white.

Bittersweet, milk, and white chocolates are available from Catherine's in 1- to 4-lb. assortments ($3.50–$15), as are French butter cookies, chocolate creams (1 to 4 lbs., $3.50–$14), fudge and peanut brittle, nuts dipped in all three kinds of chocolate, nuts and fruit in milk or bittersweet chocolate, as well as caramels and nougats.

Catherine's also has an assortment of dietetic chocolates ($4.50 a lb.) and chocolate-covered pretzels ($3.75 a lb.).

COLLIN STREET BAKERY / Dept. CFC

Box 104, Corsicana, TX 75110

"This World Renowned Gift Cake Sold Only by Mail," free, published periodically, 8 pages, illustrated, color.

Sometimes people forget where the Collin Street Bakery is located, so they send their orders addressed to Fruitcake, Texas. The letters get delivered, so you know that their fruitcakes are special. Fans include Dave Brubeck, Zubin Mehta, Mrs. Cornelius Vanderbilt, Jr., and the cast of *The Mary Tyler Moore Show.*

The subject of these raves, the original deluxe fruitcake, comes in 2-, 3-, and 5-lb. sizes ($6.45–$14.70) packed in a tin and sent anywhere in the world. Write, wire, or cable ("Fruitcakes") to order one or more cakes (prices drop as number of cakes ordered increases).

COLONIAL GARDEN KITCHENS / Dept. CFC

270 W. Merrick Road, Valley Stream, NY 11582

Catalogue, 25¢, published monthly, 112 pages, illustrated, black and white.

Among the imported English candies in the Colonial Garden Kitchens catalogue are chocolate truffles, mint creams, fruit jelly candies, and butterscotch. Then there are candy-coated chocolate sticks from the Pennsylvania Dutch, licorice twigs from Sweden, fudge, and penuche. Among other temptations for the sweet-toothed are brown rock-candy crystals (known as coffee sugar in Europe), much more attractive than plain old granulated sugar on a demitasse tray. Imported cookies include light, crisp gaufrette wafers and the tiny almond-flavored macaroons from Italy called amarettini.

CONTE DI SAVOIA / Dept. CFC

555 W. Roosevelt Road, Chicago, IL 60607

Catalogue, 75¢ (refundable with purchase), published annually, 28 pages, not illustrated.

Italian cakes and candies like panettone, panforte, and torrone are in the Conte di Savoia catalogue; also Motta and Perugina chocolates, amaretti (crisp little macaroons), confetti (sugar-coated Jordan almonds), and nutella, a nutty fudge spread. The panettone comes in 1-, 2- and 3-lb. sizes ($1.95 to $5.99) and the amaretti in a 10-oz. package ($1.49), 1-lb. tin ($2.59), or 5 lbs. ($8.50).

CREOLE DELICACIES CO. INC. / Dept. CFC

533-H Saint Ann Street, New Orleans, LA 70116

"Happy Gifts of Food from Old New Orleans," free, published annually, 12 pages, illustrated, color.

Creole Delicacies' scrumptious fruitcake is filled with three times the usual quantity of pecans, nuts, and glazed fruits—no raisins, and mellowed in brandy and sherry, 2½ lbs. for $8.95, or the Creole miniature fruitcakes packed in tins of 8 ($5.25) or 15 ($9.25).

Pralines, the creamy pecan confection that traces its ancestry back to the time of Louis XIV, made fresh to order, also available in rum and chocolate flavors, come in boxes or souvenir cotton bale of 10 large ones for $4.75 and $6.50 or a tin of 14 pralinettes for $5.25.

Continental confections, alternating layers of cake, jams, and jellies, saturated with liqueur flavors—cherry, crème de cacao, apricot, orange, brandy, and rum—are packaged 30 to the box, $7.95. The 1½-lb. fruit pecan confection, a combination of glacé whole cherries, dates, pecan halves, and pineapple chunks, is $7.75.

"From the land of dreamy dreams" come old-fashioned beignets, fried to a golden brown, dusted with sugar and served hot. Or make your own French doughnuts with an easy-to-make mix, instructions included, two 13½-oz. bags, $3.95.

Macadamia Nut Cookies

Cream ½ cup butter with 5 tablespoons confectioners' sugar and 1 teaspoon vanilla. Mix in 1¼ cups sifted flour and 1 cup grated macadamia nuts. Roll into rolls about the thickness of a pencil, 3" long, and shape each one into a crescent. Put on a greased baking sheet and bake in a 350° oven for 10 to 15 minutes until light brown. Let cool slightly, then remove. These may be sprinkled while warm with confectioners' sugar. Makes about 5 dozen cookies.

Animal candy molds

★

When lining a mold or spring-form pan with lady fingers, butter the sides of the mold well first and they will hold in place.

★

When baking pears, sprinkle them with crumbled almonds, macaroons, or amaretti. Good with baked peaches, too.

★

Symbolic design, Dauphine Chocolat catalogue

Rum Pumpkin Pie
Bake a 9-inch pie crust for 5 minutes at 400° while combining filling ingredients. Mix together 1 cup brown sugar, 2 slightly beaten eggs, 1½ teaspoons mixed pumpkin pie spice (or ½ teaspoon each ginger and cinnamon and ¼ teaspoon each nutmeg and mace), 1¾ cups canned pumpkin, ½ cup milk, ½ cup cream, and 4 tablespoons Myers's rum. Pour pumpkin mixture into partially baked pie shell, lower oven heat to 350°. Bake 1 hour or until silver knife inserted in filling comes out clean. Serves 6.
—*from Myers's Rum Recipe Booklet*

DAUPHINE CHOCOLAT B.V. / Dept. CFC
24 Prof. Oranjestraat, Amsterdam, Holland

Catalogue, $2, published annually, 16 pages, illustrated, color and black and white.

This company specializes in sending gift packages of Dutch products all over the world, not only chocolates but also Delft, pewter, and musical windmills with turning sails. Their special pride are the Ringers liqueur-filled chocolates in wooden boxes, sold in sizes from ¼ lb. to 1½ lbs., and they also have Rademaker's coffee candies (hopjes), Droste chocolates, very attractively boxed, Droste pastilles, and the famous chocolate apples (milk, semisweet, and orange) and Driessen chocolate tiles, each one wrapped to look like an antique Delft tile. There's also an assortment of chocolates for diabetics. No prices in the catalogue, so you will have to request the price list.

DAY & YOUNG / Dept. CFC
Orchard Lane, Santa Clara, CA 95052

"Holiday Gifts," free, published annually, 28 pages, illustrated, color.

The holiday gifts include marzipan candies in fruit shapes (11 oz., $5.95); chocolate-covered cherries (12 oz., $5.95); honey nut corn, a blend of almonds and pecans coated with a rich caramel honey sauce (14 oz., $5.95); petits fours (2 lbs., $6.95); an 8"-high gingerbread house; and Santa's boot filled with 5 lbs. of petits fours, butter rum cake, Dobosh and toffee tortes, chocolate Santas, walnuts, peppermint candy canes, and chocolate-covered cherries ($9.95). There is also macadamia nut cake (1¼ lbs., $5.95), chocolate-covered sugar plums ($6.95 a lb.), and apricots and pears rolled in coconut (1¼ lbs., $6.95).
   Confectionery is mixed with fresh and dried fruit in handsome gift boxes. The "Tower o' Flavors" is 5 boxes of 6 petits fours, an assortment of shelled mixed nuts, dried fruit, two apples, and 6 crown pears ($12.95).
   Brandied fruits—pears, figs, pineapples, and peaches—in 10½-oz. jars ($9.95) are another good gift.

DEER VALLEY FARM / Dept. CFC
R.D. 1, Guilford, NY 13780

Price list, free, published annually, 20 pages, black and white.

Deer Valley Farm makes cakes and cookies in their own bakery from their own organically grown grains. There's a whole-wheat pound cake made with butter, a whole-wheat sponge cake and angel cake, whole-wheat carob cake, molasses cupcakes (15¢ each), and a nut cake with no flour or baking powder, only eggs, nuts, sunflower seeds, honey, vanilla, and sea salt. The whole-wheat fruitcake, available only November and December, comes in sizes from 1 to 3 lbs. at $2.25 a lb. Other cakes run around $1.55 to $1.65 a lb. Among the cookies are butter cookies ($1.75 a lb.), molasses cookies, carob cookies, peanut-butter cookies, oatmeal or sesame cookies (99¢ a dozen), carob nut brownies, and date-nut bars ($1.10 a dozen). The whole-grain flours, raw milk, and eggs used at the bakery come from the farm, and all other ingredients are organic. They also have pies, but these are not always available.

MRS. DE WILDT / Dept. CFC
R.D. 3, Bangor, PA 18013

"Indonesian and Imported Foods," price list, free, 4 pages.

Among the other foods Mrs. De Wildt imports from Holland are the famous Verkade's cookies, in packages and tins. Speculaas (spiced almond cookies) are $3.95 for a 14-oz. tin or $1.35 a 7½-oz. package. The delicious coffee-iced café noir cookies are 95¢ a 7-oz. package, and there are also the traditional petit beurre and tongue-shaped champagne cookies. Candies range from hopjes and licorice cats to Danish marzipan and chocolate initials, in semisweet or milk chocolate (2½ oz., 65¢).

D. M. ENTERPRISES / Dept. CFC
  P.O. Box 2452, San Francisco, CA 94126

  "Calico Kitchen's Portfolio," free, published two to three times a year, 12 sheets, illustrated.

Aplets, Cotlets, and Grapelets are amusingly named fruit and nut candies made by Turkish immigrants to Washington State who based their recipe on the famous Middle Eastern rahat locoum, otherwise known as Turkish Delight. The candies are unique blends of three fruits (apples, apricots, and grapes) with walnuts, and they could be served as an after-dinner nibble, in place of dessert, on the coffee tray, or just enjoyed for their fruity flavor. A box of 5 oz. of each of the candies is $5, or you can try a 13-oz. pack of Aplets and Cotlets for $4.

DICKINSON & MORRIS LTD. / Dept. CFC
  10 Nottingham Street, Melton Mowbray, Leicestershire LE13 1NW, England

  "Ye Old Original Melton Hunt Cake," free, published periodically, 1 page, illustrated, color.

Dickinson & Morris Ltd. is sole distributor of the Melton Hunt Cake, 3 lbs. 10 oz. of fresh butter, farmhouse eggs, the "finest of fruit and peel, all blended and laced with Jamaica rum."

While cakes have been made on the site for centuries, this specific delectable—from a recipe supplied to D & M by "the nobility, clergy and Gentlemen of the Melton Hunt"—has a history of merely 120 years. Price, including postage and packing, is $13.50 US to the U.S.A., $12.50 Canadian to Canada, and 4.80 pounds sterling to any address in the United Kingdom.

EAST WIND / Dept. CFC
  2801 Broadway, New York, NY 10025

  Mail-order price list, free, 5 pages.

If you like Chinese candy, East Wind has it. There's milk candy, pearl candy, sesame candy, and kao-liang candy, ranging in price from 85¢ for 8 oz. of sesame candy to $1.95 for a 1-lb. box of milk candy. Also honey noodle cake, rice cake, fortune cookies, almond cookies, and sesame cookies.

EGERTONS / Dept. CFC
  Lyme Street, Axminster, Devon EX13 5DB, England

  "Egertons Postal Gift and Shopping Service," $1.50 if airmailed, free otherwise, published annually, 74 pages, illustrated, color.

Egertons has gathered cakes and candies from all over the United Kingdom and makes them available, by mail, to the world.

From the 100-year-old Ormeau Bakery in Northern Ireland come shortbread fingers ($9.90), liqueur Irish whiskey cake (28 oz., $12), and traditional Simnel cake, a fruitcake topped with toasted marzipan with a layer of soft marzipan in the center ($12.50 for 2 lbs. 2 oz.). Ormeau also supplies the fudge parcel: four ½-lb. blocks of butter fudge (plain, fruit, raisin, and walnut) for $10.68 and, from the hamper selection for Christmas, a 2-lb. plum cake, 1-lb. plum pudding, 21 oz. of butter shortbread, and 28 oz. of Irish fruitcake ($26.88). Other Ormeau hampers are priced from $10.68 to $43.

Purdys of Norfolk make the world-famous Mr. Guinness' cake, with Guinness stout, sultana raisins, peel, walnuts, and mixed spices, which is "like eating a dream" ($10.88 for 2 lbs.). There's also Haig whisky fruitcake (2 lbs., $11.38), Lemon Hart rum plum pudding (2 lbs., $11.13), Dry Sack sherry raisin cake (2 lbs., $10.88), and Purdy pie packs—mince pie, bakewell pie, and peggotty pie (sugar syrup filling in short pastry) for $10.38.

For the lover of traditional cookies there are assortments of West Country biscuits. The "Truro" pack has two tin drums of Cornish Fairings (crisp crunchy ginger biscuits), two of cherry choclets (a new

Old-Fashioned Popcorn Balls
In a saucepan mix 1 cup sugar, 1 cup pure Vermont maple syrup, 2 tablespoons butter, and a dash of salt. Cook to the soft-ball stage on a candy thermometer. Remove from heat. Add 1 teaspoon vinegar. Stir until foamy. Pour over 3 quarts popped corn. Shape with buttered hands into balls as soon as it can be handled.
—from "The Vermont Maple Syrup Cookbook"

Melton Hunt Cake from Dickinson & Morris

★

Crumble day-old chocolate cake, put in a dish and sprinkle well with sweet sherry. Cover with softened vanilla ice cream, add another layer of crumbs, flavored with sherry, and ice cream. Freeze until ready to serve. Top with whipped cream and shaved chocolate.

★

Top a coffee mousse or frozen dessert with little coffee bean candies.

★

Sugar Cookies

Cream together ¼ pound butter, 2 tablespoons margarine, and 1⅓ cups sugar. When light and fluffy, beat in 2 eggs, one after the other. Add ¾ cup buttermilk, 1 teaspoon baking soda dissolved in a tablespoon of boiling water, and 1 teaspoon vanilla. Sift 3 cups flour with 1 teaspoon baking powder and ¼ teaspoon salt. Combine with the egg-butter-buttermilk mixture and blend well. Refrigerate for 30 minutes. Drop the mixture by teaspoons onto a greased baking sheet, about 2" apart, as the cookies will spread during baking. Bake in a 350° oven for 15 minutes or until barely light brown. Makes about 36 cookies.

The finest in chocolate chip cookies since 1975

Gift card, The Farmhouse

biscuit-type made with cherries and chocolate), one of Cornish Shorties (shortcake), and one of Country Maide (a lemon butter biscuit), $14.38. The "Old Fashioned" pack contains a 14-oz. tin of gingerbread and a 7-oz. tin of mint humbug candy from Devon, $8.58.

Then there are tins and boxes of Clare chocolates, mints, jellies, fondants, noisettes, marzipan, and hard candies, at prices ranging from $9.13 for a 1-ft.-long box of candies, jellies, and fondants to $25.25 for a 3-lb. assortment of exquisite handmade chocolates. From Devonshire comes a 1-lb. package of clotted-cream fudge in assorted flavors for $5.13 or the "Devon treats" pack with ½-lb. boxes of butterscotch, clotted-cream toffee, and county selection, the three for $8.13.

The famous Farrah's Harrogate toffee, in tins of small wrapped pieces, is $6.50, or a "Six Drum" selection of 12-oz. tin drums of Harrogate toffee, treacle toffee, fruit drops, mint shells, butter drops, and Old Fashioned Humbugs is $13.63.

From Addisons come traditional Christmas puddings (for Christmas sale only) made with ale and spirits, from $7.25 for a 1-lb. 7-oz. pudding; Dundee fruit cakes, topped with almonds and packed in fancy tins, 2-lb. to 4-lb. sizes, $11.20 to $15.93; and other festive cakes, such as a 5-lb. dark, rich fruitcake, iced and decorated with almond marzipan, all year ($18.28).

FAMOUS AMOS CHOCOLATE CHIP COOKIES / Dept. CFC
 7181 Sunset Boulevard, Hollywood, CA 90046

Price list, free.

Says Amos in *A Brief History of the Chocolate Chip Cookie:* "1929 was a bad year for most things. But it was a good year for the chocolate chip cookie. It was then that the first chocolate chip cookie was baked in a tiny farmhouse kitchen in Lowell, Massachusetts. In fact, that day has come to be known as Brown Thursday. (Not to be confused with Black Tuesday or Blue Monday.)"

Wally Amos was determined to become famous. And he has. Besides his chocolate chips, he also makes chocolate chips with nuts and with peanut butter, plus his new butterscotch cookies with nuts (1½ lbs., $7.50; 2 lbs., $8.50, in tin).

FANTASIA CONFECTIONS / Dept. CFC
 3465 California Street, San Francisco, CA 94118

Price list, free.

Fantasia makes two items available by mail: tins filled with buttery, creamy cookies (1¼ lbs. and 2½ lbs., $10.95 and $17.95) and Dresdner stollen with glazed fruits and nuts, flavored with rum and brandy (1½ lbs., $7.45).

THE FARMHOUSE / Dept. CFC
 Belaire #8, Village Two, New Hope, PA 18938

"The Farmhouse," free, published seasonally (spring and Christmas), 1 page.

Maxine Cook bakes breads and cakes as seasonal specialties and offers them with a personal touch. From the edge of the Delaware River in historic New Hope come her Christmas delights: whiskey cakes, Dresden christollen, and fancy dill bread.

Prices for both her Christmas and spring selections are available on request, and she will gift-wrap them.

FIGI'S INC. / Dept. CFC
 Central Plaza, Marshfield, WI 54449

"Figi's Gifts in Good Taste," free, published annually, 64 pages, illustrated, color.

Cakes, cookies, candies, and confections abound in this gift catalogue, mostly the kind you find in similar catalogues, such as petits fours, mints, tortes and chocolate-roll holiday log, fruitcake, butter cookies, salt-water taffy, hard candies, and fudge, and they come alone or in the numerous gift hampers and packages.

THE FLYING BEAR CANDY STORE / Dept. CFC
356 N. Main Street, Ft. Bragg, CA 95437

Brochure and price list, free.

At the Flying Bear, a tiny candy store and factory 150 miles north of San Francisco on the Mendocino coast, they are still making candy pretty much the way it was done when the building was new, 85 years ago. Nearly all the candy is stirred, poured, rolled, cut, dipped, and packed by hand, and the ingredients used are only the purest freshest cream, butter, milk, chocolate, and other good things, no preservatives of any kind. They even make their own marshmallows for the Rocky Road, roast and crush almonds for the English toffee. It is hardly surprising that they claim people will drive 90 minutes on winding roads to buy their whipped mint truffles and that their mail-order business has grown over the last few years to the point where they send their candy to 49 states and 17 countries.

They have 9 boxed selections. No. 1 consists of hand-dipped chocolates, with a trickle of chocolate used to write the initial of the flavor on top ("S" for strawberry, for example). No. 2, the Flying Bear Sampler, includes a little of nearly everything they make in the candy line, plus a few hand-dipped chocolates. Box No. 3 is half chocolates, half sampler; No. 4 Nuts and Chews; No. 5, Soft Pack—chocolate creams, truffles, mints, etc; No. 6, Truffles, a fairly light whipped chocolate square with a touch of mint flavor. No. 7 is English toffee, also known as almond roca or Victoria brittle, squares of toffee hand-dipped in milk chocolate, then in hand-crushed roasted almonds. No. 8, their famous Rocky Road (marshmallow, chocolate, and chopped walnuts), is packed in big uncut slabs for you to cut apart because it stays fresher that way. Fudge is Box No. 9, three different kinds—chocolate, penuche, and vanilla. Prices, which include delivery, insurance, and gift card, are $4.20 a 1-lb. box, $8.40 for 2 lbs., $12.60 for 3 lbs., and $21 for 5 lbs., plus postage and handling charges varying from $1.10 to $1.80 for the pound box, more for larger sizes, according to zone.

R. W. FORSYTH LTD. / Dept. CFC
30 Princes Street, Edinburgh EH2 2BZ, Scotland

"The days of Christmas at Forsyth's," free, published annually, 16 pages, black and white.

The Christmas catalogue of Forsyth's, the famous Edinburgh department store, is loaded with delicious holiday fruitcakes, some heady with brandy or rum, Christmas puddings (the Dorset one contains brandy; Walker's export both brandy and rum), tins of Scottish shortbread, petits fours, and all sorts of chocolates and candies. With your Christmas pudding you might try Royal Ascot genuine Cumberland rum or brandy butter (like hard sauce) that comes in a 5-oz. tub or 8-oz. stone jar with lid.

FORTNUM & MASON / Dept. CFC
181 Piccadilly, London W1A 1ER, England

"Fortnum & Mason Export Food," free, published seasonally, 16 pages, illustrated, color.

Treat your friends royally with Fortnum & Mason's wonderful export gift boxes of rich fruitcakes, packed in 2-, 3-, and 4-lb. tins ($8.37 to $15.02); plum puddings, well laced with brandy, specially packed for overseas (2 lbs., $6.79; 3 lbs., $8.73; 4 lbs., $11.39); tin of petticoat tails (shortbread), $3.89; a 2-lb. Dundee cake, $3.28; or tins of chocolate almond or chocolate lemon biscuits, $2.44 each.

An attractive ribboned gift box containing a tin of assorted sweet biscuits, 1 tin of Sherribisks, 1 tin of spiced fruit biscuits, and 1 tin of "Loch Lomond" shortbread fingers is $13.81.

A Sweet Suggestion From:
The Flying Bear Candy Store
356 N. Main St.
Ft. Bragg, California 95437

A gift box of Christmas goodies from Fortnum & Mason

Export Box 'C'

Biscottini

Split 24 ladyfingers. Thoroughly combine ¼ cup Sambuca Romana, ½ cup softened butter, and ½ cup finely chopped almonds. Spread mixture on flat side of each ladyfinger half. Place on a cookie sheet and toast in a preheated 350° oven for 6 to 8 minutes until lightly brown. Cool. Store in a covered container.

—from "53 Ways to Say I Love You in Italian"

FRASER-MORRIS / Dept. CFC

872 Madison Avenue, New York, NY 10021

"Gifts for Festive Occasions from Fraser-Morris," free, published seasonally, 11 pages, illustrated, color.

Fruitcakes filled with fruits and nuts and aged in brandy (4-lb. tin, $15.95), a confection tray containing chocolate lentils and discs, French and cream mints, fruit slices and assorted hard candies ($18.50), and English plum puddings in various sizes (1-lb. crock, $4.95) are among the gift items from Fraser-Morris that will satisfy any sweet tooth.

Italian Perugina chocolates (1 lb., $8.95), Lindt chocolates from Switzerland (17½ oz., $9.50), and Lady Godiva in milk and dark assortments are all sold in handsome gift packages. Also special low-calorie hard candy (28 oz., $4.95), Moravian ginger cookies (1 lb., $7.25), and marrons glacés (8¾ oz., $7.95).

THE GOURMET PANTRY / Dept. CFC

400 McGuinness Blvd., Brooklyn, NY 11222

"Pleasure Packed Gifts from the Gourmet Pantry," free, published annually, 72 pages, illustrated, color.

Did you know that Guy Lombardo's favorite candy is cashew and rice crunch? Well, it is, and his picture appears on the 1-lb. box sold by The Gourmet Pantry (around $5 delivered). Other confections in this gift catalogue are chocolate and mint pretzels ($5.99), rum cakes, almond mints, petits fours, marzipan fruit candies, stollen, macadamia nut cake, baklava, Droste chocolates from Holland ($6.50 for a 1-lb. assortment), and a package of maple-sugar candies, maple-nut fudge, mountain mints, and maple syrup ($7.99).

MISS GRACE LEMON CAKE CO. / Dept. CFC

443 South Robertson Boulevard, Beverly Hills, CA 90211

Price list, free.

Of course, Miss Grace sells lemon cakes, made from the juice and rind of fresh lemons ($7); carrot cakes with walnuts and spices ($8); chocolate-chip cookies; cherries n' cream and mousse pies. And that's all.

GRAYS OF WORCESTER, LTD. / Dept. CFC

Orchard Street, Worcester WR5 3DP, England

"For the pleasure of the Gourmet," free, published annually with seasonal supplements, 26 pages, black and white.

This luxury food and gift catalogue lists some delicious-sounding handmade Belgian chocolates in 17½-oz. or 2-lb. 3-oz. boxes, plain and milk chocolate truffles, Old English fudge, and leaf-shaped marzipan wafers from France. Christmas specialties are Scotch black bun, like a fruitcake in a pastry crust, traditionally tartan-wrapped; Christmas puddings liberally anointed with rum and brandy; and Mr. Guinness cake, a magnificent fruitcake laced with Guinness stout. Prices, quoted in sterling, are for UK delivery. For overseas delivery, request a quotation.

GREAT VALLEY MILLS / Dept. CFC

Quakertown, PA 18951

"Gift Suggestions from the Pennsylvania Dutch Country," free, published annually, 16 pages, illustrated, black and white.

That luscious German coffee cake, stollen, is one of Great Valley Mills' Christmas suggestions. They bake it themselves from unbleached flour, raisins, and citrus fruit and seal it in foil to retain the freshness ($6.50 delivered, plus 10 percent west of the Mississippi). They have a homemade fruitcake, too, made with a minimum of flour, a maximum of fruit, rum, eggs, butter, and brown sugar; a tin of home-style cookies (2 lbs. for $6.50); and some fudge and sugar mints made by a neighbor ($6.95).

HARBOR SWEETS / Dept. CFC
  Box 150, Marblehead, MA 01945

  Price list.

This old-fashioned candy store offers homemade sailboat-shaped chocolate-covered almond buttercrunch called "Sweet Sloops," gift-boxed, 10½ oz., $4.95 ppd.

HARRY AND DAVID / Dept. CFC
  P.O. Box 712, Medford, OR 97501

  "Harry and David's Christmas Book of Gifts," free, published annually with supplementary brochures, 28 pages, illustrated, color.

Harry and David's fruitcake confections contain no rind, peels, or fillers, only whole cherries, juicy pineapple, and pecans ($7.95 for 1½ lbs., $10.95 for 2¾ lbs.).

There are dessert cakes, Hawaiian-pineapple-macadamia nut, apricot-orange, apple-date, packed 3 cans to a case, $9.95.

Petits fours will stay fresh in the refrigerator for up to six months ($7.95).

A traditional Christmas pudding rich with currants, raisins, walnuts, butter, and spices is cellophane-wrapped, then tied in gingham with a bow ($8.95).

HERTER'S INC. / Dept. CFC
  R.R. 2, Mitchell, SD 57301

  "Herter's Sportsman's Catalog," $1 (refundable with $10 purchase), published annually, 352 pages, illustrated, color and black and white.

Herter's catalogue has some rather unusual candies—buffalo chip candy (filled with lingonberries, white raisins, toffee chips), Fort St. Charles whiskey cherry candies (like a small wild cherry in shape, with a semiliquid center), cactus candy ($1.69 a lb. box), French burnt peanut candies, and more usual ones such as imported English toffee and chocolate pastel mints. In cakes, there's a Minnesota Bendictine fruitcake, made with wild-rice flour, wild honey, black walnuts, butternuts, high-ground lingonberries, currants, hops, and French bitters ($3.75 for a 2-lb. cake); and a toffee-and-fruit cake ($4.79 for a 2-lb. cake), containing tiny pieces of melted toffee, raisins, currants, cherries, and pistachio nuts, the surface glazed with angelica-flavored toffee.

HICKIN'S MOUNTAIN MOWINGS FARM / Dept. CFC
  R.F.D. 1, Black Mountain Road, Brattleboro, VT 05301

  Brochure, free, published periodically, 6 pages, plus price list, illustrated, black and white.

The Hickins make their own maple syrup in their own sugarhouse, and they use it in many of their products, such as a rich moist maple fruitcake ($3.85 a lb.) and some of their pickles. They also sell maple candies and cream, granulated maple sugar ($2.25 a jar), and fudge (homemade by Fussy Frank)—chocolate nut, peanut butter, penuche, and plain chocolate (1 lb., $3.25). For homemade flavor, this is the place.

HOME OF BRIGHAM'S CANDIES / Dept. CFC
  449 Mapleton Avenue, Suffield, CT 06078

  "Brigham's Candies—From our Home to your Home" and price list, 50¢, published annually, 6 pages, illustrated, color.

Brigham's has been a family business since 1912, making hand-dipped chocolates and candies with no artificial substitutes or preservatives. And if their candies are as rich as their photographs, say goodbye to your diet.

They present a traditional assortment of chocolates—dark and white, hard, chewy, and soft ($4 a lb.); chunk chocolate in both white and milk ($2.60 a lb.); fruit slices in cherry, orange, lemon, lime, and licorice ($1.85 a lb.); jelly beans ($1.40 a lb.); lollipops in chocolate and fruit

Holiday confections from Harry and David

★

To make plain cookies more interesting, sandwich them with butter cream in an appropriate flavor, spread frosting on the top.

★

A different way to flame Christmas pudding: make a hole in the top deep enough to hold half an eggshell. Pour heated brandy into the shell, ignite at the table.

★

Chocolate cups, sold by mail, make great individual dessert containers. Fill with coffee mousse, orange sherbet, praline ice cream, or with liqueur to serve with after-dinner coffee.

★

Traditional English cookies from Robert Jackson

flavors plus butterscotch, licorice, and root beer (5¢ each); and chocolate cigarettes (55¢ a lb.). There are mints, too, ranging in price from $1.85 to $4 per lb.

Less familiar are acorns, marzipans dipped in chocolate ($2.40 a lb.); Super Kisses of solid chocolate in 5- and 13-oz. sizes ($1.55 and $2.90); crispy straws, peppermint and peanut candy coated with chocolate ($2.90 a lb.); misty mints, teardrop peppermints sprinkled with nonpareils ($1.85 a lb.); scotties, fruit or licorice-flavored jellies ($1.40 a lb.); chocolate-covered ginger ($4.35 a lb.); and turtles, pecans smothered in dark or white chocolate ($4.35 a lb.).

Brigham's also has some dietetic candy bark-milk with cashews and peanut clusters, $3.60 a lb., as well as fudge and butterscotch toppings ($1.25 a lb.).

They prefer not to make chocolate deliveries during the summer.

HOUSE OF ALMONDS / Dept. CFC
P.O. Box 5125, Bakersfield, CA 93308

"Gift Selections," free, published annually, 21 pages, illustrated, color.

Among the gift selections of nuts and dried fruits are various cakes, such as an almond-date delight, a 2-lb. cake filled with dates, almonds and pineapple ($6.95); a holiday fruitcake; and a 1¼-lb. honey cake. All kinds of fruit and nut candies, too, such as almond munch, almond nut corn (corn, almonds, caramel, and butter), chocolate-covered almond brittle ($8.95 for 2 lbs. 5 oz.), fudgy almond logs, Medjool dates stuffed with almonds and rolled in powdered sugar ($8.65 for a 3-lb. 1-oz. tin), combinations of sugar-coated Jordan almonds, chocolate-covered almonds, and chocolate almond clusters. A Trio of Treats consists of three tins of chocolate-dipped English toffee garnished with diced almonds, almond brittle, and almond chocolate clusters ($12.95 for 3 lbs. 9 oz.).

ROBERT JACKSON & CO., LTD. / Dept. CFC
171 Piccadilly, London W1V OLL, England

"Robert Jackson's Food, Wine, Hamper and Gift List," free, published seasonally, 10 pages, illustrated, black and white.

While this famous Piccadilly food store stocks chocolates and confectionery from all over the world, the greatest demand is for their own handmade chocolates. Assorted chocolates, loose, are around $3.60 a lb., rum-and-vanilla truffles are around $3.75, and Vienna mints $3.50. The latter two come in gift boxes. Among the traditional English confectionery you'll find Harrogate toffee, Derwent toffee, and Cornish specialties such as clotted-cream butterscotch (about 90¢ for 7 oz.) or a gift box of assorted Cornish confectionery (clotted-cream fudge and toffee, buttermints, honey, and ginger). There are bonbons from Fauchon and Hediard in Paris, too.

In the cake and cookie category, Jackson's have all kinds of canned cookies (known there as biscuits), Scottish shortbread, and old-fashioned Yorkshire biscuits from the Bronte Village, Haworth (about $1.75).

JURGENSEN'S GROCERY COMPANY / Dept. CFC
601 South Lake Avenue, Pasadena, CA 91109

"Jurgensen's Christmas Catalogue," free, published annually, 36 pages, illustrated, color.

As you'd expect, there are lots of·cakes, cookies and candies in this Christmas catalogue, including Jurgensen's own fruitcakes, in sizes from 1 lb. (around $3.50) to 5 lbs. (around $17; slightly higher if gift-boxed), miniature fruitcakes in boxes of 12 or 18, Patio fruitcakes from New Orleans, and various festively decorated cakes made in Jurgensen's bakery. They make their own plum puddings, too, mellow with brandy, in 1-lb. to 5-lb. sizes, which are priced the same as the fruitcakes. Among the candy selections you'll find assorted toffees, butter mints, Jurgensen's "Unsurpassed" chocolates and miniature chocolates, chocolate-covered mints, raspberry candies, and marzipan fruits. An amusing item is Ghirardelli's "World's Biggest Chocolate Bar," which tips the scales at 5 lbs. (around $17).

KEMOO FARM FOODS, LTD. / Dept. CFC
Box 30021, Honolulu, Hawaii 96820

Brochure, free, 4 pages, illustrated, color.

The main product is "Happy Cake" made with Hawaiian macadamia nuts, glazed pineapple, and coconut, $9.50 ppd. in the U.S. (orders for mainland and foreign deliveries should be directed to Kemoo Farm's branch in Lodi, California), $8.50 each for three or more cakes, $8 each for 12 or more. The Macadamia Monarch package contains the 2-lb. Happy Cake and four tins of Royal Hawaiian macadamia nuts ($17.50 the box). The Royal Kona Coffee and Happy Cake package has the cake plus 1 lb. of Royal Kona Coffee ($13.50). Other confections from Kemoo Farm are their Fruit Thins, fresh fruit candies (Mandarin-Mint, Passion Fruit, Guava, Pineapple, Toasted Coconut) at $6.95 for a 30-oz. box, and a boxed set of two 7½-oz. jars of guava jam and two of guava jelly ($6.95).

LANDMARK / Dept. CFC
Carrbridge, Inverness-shire PH23 3AJ, Scotland

"Scottish Fare," free, published annually, 6-page brochure.

Among the gift hampers Landmark packs for Christmas are two rather special confections. One is a 1-lb. 2-oz. whisky cake made from country butter, eggs, fruit, and almonds, all plumped into rare old Scotch whisky and sealed in an airtight tin; the other a hamper of shortbread—12 oz. of Highlander shortbread, a 16-oz. box of shortbread fingers, and a 14½-oz. box of the delightfully named Petticoat Tails (wedges of shortbread), which is said to have been a corruption of the French petits gateaux. As their brochure prices are for delivery in the UK only, you will have to request overseas postage charges when writing for the brochure.

LE JARDIN DU GOURMET / Dept. CFC
West Danville, VT 05873

Catalogue, 50¢, published annually, 32 pages, illustrated, black and white.

There are a few imported confections in this catalogue, such as French and Dutch gaufrettes, or wafers, Irish Whiskey Fruit Cake (28-oz. tin, $4.60), rum, brandy, and mint cakes in tins, petit beurre and champagne biscuits, English plum pudding in 1-lb. crocks ($2.25), marzipan, sliced crystallized ginger, and the French crystallized flowers used for cake and dessert decorations—rose petals, lilac, mint leaves, whole red roses, violets, assorted flowers, at prices from $1.75 for 2½ oz. of assorted flowers to $2.75 for 4 oz. of crystallized violets.

LEKVAR-BY-THE-BARREL / Dept. CFC
1577 First Avenue, New York, NY 10028

"A Continental Bazaar," free, published annually, 56 pages, illustrated, black and white.

Among the imported candies sold by Lekvar-by-the-Barrel are rum beans ($1.59 for a 7-oz. box), apricot delight with pistachio nuts, Tobler chocolate bars, marzipan fruits and figures, chocolates in various festive shapes wrapped in colored foil to hang on the Christmas tree, La Vosgiennes fruit pastilles, and potato sugar candy. And, of course, they have pfeffernüsse (spice cookies, $1.25 for a 1-lb. bag), lebkuchen (6 pieces in a decorated tin, $6.98), and Pischinger torte (chocolate, hazelnut praline), $3.75 the ½-lb. box.

MAISON GLASS / Dept. CFC
52 East 58th Street, New York, NY 10022

"Maison Glass Delicacies," $1, published annually, 72 pages, illustrated, black and white.

Maison Glass has a big assortment of imported and domestic cookies, such as pfeffernüsse, gaufrettes, lebkuchen, Scotch shortbread, petits

Luscious fruit cake from Kemoo Farm Foods

Original Creamy Pecan Pralines
In a heavy saucepan combine 1 pound light brown sugar, 1 cup cream, 2 cups pecan halves, and a pinch of salt. Cook over medium heat, stirring constantly, to soft-ball stage on a candy thermometer. Do not undercook. Remove from heat and add 1 teaspoon vanilla. Cool 5 minutes. Stir rapidly until mixture begins to thicken and coats pecans lightly. Drop from tablespoon onto lightly greased aluminum foil to form patties. If candy becomes too stiff, stir in a few drops of hot water. Let patties stand until cool and set. Remove from foil, wrap individually in plastic wrap, and store in covered tin. This is the praline enjoyed by those who live in the pecan-growing region. Try crumbling a few over ice cream.
—from Sternberg's Collection of Pecan Recipes

Blueberry Gingerbread

Cream ½ cup butter and 1 cup sugar. Add 1 egg and mix well. Sift together 2 cups flour, ½ teaspoon ginger, 1 teaspoon cinnamon, and ½ teaspoon salt. Dissolve 1 teaspoon baking soda in 1 cup buttermilk. Add flour and buttermilk mixtures alternately to creamed mixture. Mix in 3 tablespoons molasses and 1 cup blueberries. Pour into a greased 9-inch square pan. Sprinkle top with 3 tablespoons sugar. Bake in a 350° oven for 50 to 60 minutes.

—*from "Blueberry Recipes"*

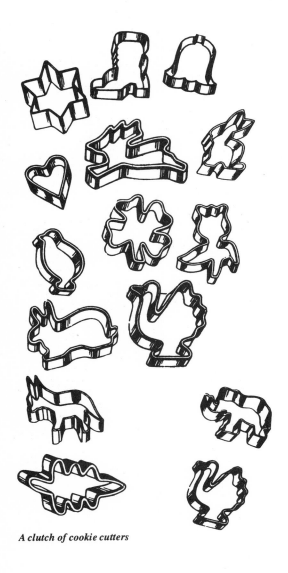

A clutch of cookie cutters

fours, but perhaps the most interesting are the Moravian cookies from Old Salem, North Carolina—sugar crisps, ginger cookies, chocolate wafers, and cheese petits, from $7.95 a 14-oz. tin. In cakes, they are strong on fruitcakes of different types, such as the Charlotte Charles and Grace A. Rush brands, but it is the Purdy cakes from England that have the most catchy names—peggoty pie, Dry Sack raisin cake ($9.75 a 2-lb. tin), and rich Dundee cake. You can find here English plum puddings in bowls ($5.50 for the 1-lb. size), white or brown rock candy crystals for coffee sugar, maple-sugar candies, and an impressive list of chocolates and candies, from their own Maison Glass chocolates deluxe (French cream caramels, silky truffles, chocolate-covered marzipan, maple walnut creams, caramel surprise, and others, $6.50 for a 1-lb. box) to chocolates from Holland and Switzerland, coffee-flavored chocolate beans, wild strawberry and raspberry candies, chocolate-covered orange peel, and tiny mint lentils from Denmark ($3.50 a 14-oz. box).

MANGANARO FOODS / Dept. CFC
488 Ninth Avenue, New York, NY 10018

"Manganaro's for Gourmet Foods," free, published annually, 22 pages, illustrated.

Manganaro has the traditional Italian cakes, such as panettone ($4.25 for the 1-lb. size), panforte de Siena ($4.40 for the 1-lb. size), pandoro, a specialty of Verona, and Colomba, a dove-shaped Easter cake, available only in the spring. There's also torrone, or nougat ($3.40 a lb.), amaretti, the crisp little Italian macaroons ($5.50 a lb.), and various assortments of Motta and Perugina chocolates. French almond paste is $2.25 a lb.

MAPLE GROVE, INC. / Dept. CFC
167 Portland Street, St. Johnsbury, VT 05819

Catalogue, free, price list, published annually, 6 pages, illustrated, color.

Vermont maple-sugar candies, some 100 percent pure maple sugar, others a blend of cane and maple sugars, maple nut and chocolate nut fudge, taffy candy, and crystallized mint creams in attractive gift boxes are the specialties of Maple Grove. The Cabin Candies (cane and maple sugar), maple-sugar candies, and the mints come in various fancy shapes and are priced from around $2.80 ppd. for 8 oz. of mountain mints ($2.85 west of the Mississippi) to $11.40 for 3 lbs. of Cabin Fancies. The fudge is around $2.30 for 8 oz. There are also gift assortments of candies packaged with other products, such as maple syrup and maple cream.

MARY OF PUDDIN HILL / Dept. CFC
P.O. Box 241, Greenville, TX 75401

"Gifts of Good Taste for Holiday Giving," free, published annually, 10 pages, illustrated, color.

Mary of Puddin Hill is Mary Jane Lauderdale, and her rags-to-riches saga is the result of her delicious fruitcakes and a belief in the advice of a friend: "Do lazy people's work for them."

Mary's pecan fruitcake, a blend of pecans, cherries, pineapple chunks, comes in 1¾- to 4½-lb. sizes ($7.45 to $14.50), as well as in miniature "Little Puds" (18 or 28 "Little Puds" for $7.15 and $9.25). The Little Puds can be ordered in a gift box with roasted pecan halves ($11.45) or with "sugared and spiced" pecans ($11.75). Mary also makes a walnut fruitcake ($8.40 for 1¾ lb.).

She's expanded her line to dessert bread—Polynesian treat, strawberry surprise, orange jubilee, banana-nut bananza, apple yummy, and egg nog (all 6 for $18.10)—and breakfast breads, whole wheat, prune, pineapple bran, and walnut honey (3 for $10.60).

Mary makes candies, too: pecan pralines ($9.80 for 2 lbs.); miniature fruitcakes dipped in chocolate ($9.85 for 21 oz.); "whatchamacallits," clusters of butterscotch, peanuts, raisins, and "something secret" ($7.70

for 18 oz.); "thingamajigs," caramel and pecan centers covered in white chocolate ($7.65 for 13 oz.); and the Executive Bean Bag, 2 lbs. of jelly beans in a cotton duck bag ($11.80). Nut candies are almond mari, an almond brittle; coffa walnuts, coffee-flavored walnuts; spice pecans; and rum walnuts ($8.20 for four 4-oz. cans). A "VIP" assortment of a 2¾-lb. fruitcake, 26½ oz. of Little Puds, whatchamacallits and pecan halves, 21 oz. of chocolate-coated fruitcakes, and 12 oz. of orange jubilee dessert bread is $31.70.

Fondue au chocolat is delicious and fun for a party. Break Toblerone bars into pieces. Melt in a heavy pan with Grand Marnier and heavy cream, stirring until smooth. Keep warm over a candle warmer. Dunk fingers of sponge cake, angel food cake, lady fingers, tiny cream puffs, orange sections or other fruit into the chocolate.

⋆

MIDWAY GROVES / Dept. CFC
Route 3, Box 28, Sarasota, FL 33580

Catalogue, free, published annually, 16 pages, illustrated, color.

Sweets from the South occupy one spread of this gift catalogue. There's saltwater taffy, chocolate-dipped coconut patties, Creole pralines, pecan roll with a nougat center, pecan and chocolate bark with rum flavoring, orange brittle with bits of real orange peel, orange candy (jellied squares of orange juice, with or without pecans), mint pecans, a box of pecan-stuffed dates, pecan puffs, pecan log roll, and chocolate pecan brittle. Various gift packs combine natural citrus and pecan candies, and one combines candies with Florida jellies and marmalade. Prices in our catalogue are not current.

MISSION PAK / Dept. CFC
Santa Clara, CA 95050

"Bright holiday gifts from Mission Pak," free, published annually, 28 pages, illustrated, color.

Macadamia nuts grown in Hawaii's fertile volcanic soil go into Mission Pak's macadamia nut cake ($5.95 for 1¼ lbs.). There is also a rich glacé fruitcake in 1-, 2-, 3-, and 5-lb. sizes ($6.95 to $16.95), or in miniatures for fruitcake flambé, for which they supply a brandy flambé sauce ($7.95).

If visions of sugarplums dance in your head, Mission Pak has chocolate-covered sugarplums in 1- and 2-lb. boxes ($6.95 to $9.95).

Some of their other delightful confection ideas are marzipan candies in fruit-shaped pieces ($5.95 for 11 oz.); the Snowman Piñata, a candy-filled figure that the children try to break open while blindfolded; and a sturdy Santa's boot filled with butter rum cake, a 9-layer Viennese Dobos torte, a toffeetorte, petits fours, and four chocolate Santas ($9.95).

Children will love aplets and cotlets, apricot and apple candies rolled in chopped nuts ($8.45 for 3 lbs.), or chocolate-covered cherries ($5.95 for 12 oz.) wrapped in gold and red foil in a make-believe champagne bottle.

NEW HAMPTON GENERAL STORE / Dept. CFC
R.F.D., Hampton, NJ 08827

"General Catalogue," free, five editions yearly, 80 pages, illustrated, color.

The New Hampton Bazaar & Emporium catalogue has an old-fashioned flavor. And they offer many flavors of penny candies—no longer just a childhood memory—liberty streamers, satin balls, bananas, rock candies, licorice cigars, jawbreakers, and more. All are available boxed ($1.95; three boxes, $5.65). Or a bag stuffed with one pound of lemon and lime lumps ($2.45). Licorice pillows, molasses peppermint drops, butterscotch, horehound candy, and watermelon slices can be bought by the pound ($1.50 to $2.50). Saltwater taffy is $2.95 for 2 lbs.

There are old-fashioned candy sticks, too, in licorice, cinnamon, peppermint, lemon, sassafras, and butterscotch (any three bundles of six, $1.95), as well as peanut or cashew crunch.

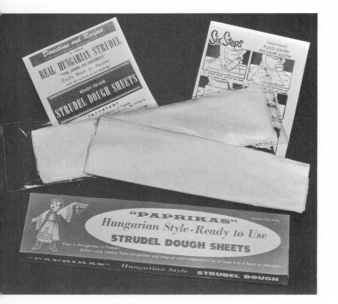

Strudel sheets and instructions, from Paprikas Weiss

NUTWORLD / Dept. CFC
P.O. Box 1, Dundee, OR 97115

Price list and order form, free.

Candies from Nutworld, in the hub of Oregon's nut and fruit industry, include carob hazelnut (or walnut) clusters, carob-covered prunes, carob or almond bark pixies, mint or cinnamon hazelnuts, or hazel brittle (all $2.50 per lb.). There are also honey or glacéed peaches, pears, and apricots for $3.10 per lb.

Gift boxes weighing from 1 to 5 lbs. made from your choice of fruit, nuts, and candies are $3.50 to $11.50.

PAPRIKAS WEISS IMPORTER / Dept. CFC
1546 Second Avenue, New York, NY 10028

"Imported Foods and Cookware Catalogue," $1 for annual subscription, published four times a year, 66 pages, illustrated, black and white.

You'll find lots of sweet things here, such as various imported candies (honey candy, Jamaica rum beans, chocolate almonds, burnt almonds, fruit-flavored cream-filled chocolates shaped like miniature liqueur bottles, green mint cordials, wild raspberry drops, non-alcoholic cordial chocolates and marzipan fruits) and some of the famous European cakes and cookies, such as Dobos torte, Viennese hazelnut wafers, their own freshly baked Hungarian confections, walnut or poppyseed roulade ($5.98 each), Linzer tarts, and baked golden horseshoes filled with walnuts or poppyseeds ($9.90 a dozen).

PEPPERIDGE FARM MAIL ORDER CO., INC. / Dept. CFC
Box 7000, Norwalk, CT 06856

"Gift Catalog," free, published periodically, 32 pages, illustrated, color.

The cookies and breads that made Pepperidge Farm famous are not sold mail order, but there is an interesting range of Godiva chocolates, fudge, fruitcakes, and yuletime cookies in their catalogue.

Rich creamy fudge (12 oz. each of plain and walnut) is made of pure natural ingredients ($6.95).

Ten oz. of the traditional pfeffernüsse, a crisp round spice cookie covered with smooth white frosting, is teamed with 16 oz. of holiday nut rolls made of cream cheese, apricots, and nuts (both tins $9.95).

Delicious toppings for ice cream or cake come in everybody's favorite flavors—dark chocolate, milk chocolate, butterscotch, and strawberry—all made without artificial preservatives, colors, or flavors. A box of four 11-oz. jars plus four ice-cream dishes is $14.95.

A brandy-laced fruitcake with pineapple, pecans, and raisins (1½ lbs., $6.95) or four holiday cake rings are delicious samples of the baker's art. Each cake ring is packed in a reusable tin: applesauce date nut (1½ lbs., $6.95), old-fashioned almond (1 lb., $5.95), Swiss chocolate almond (1 lb., $5.95), and pineapple macadamia (1¾ lbs., $6.95).

French-type cakes and babas, soaked with rum or brandy, are delicious hot or cold, plain or garnished with whipped cream or fruits. Four rum cakes, four brandy cakes, and 16 petits rum babas are easy emergency desserts ($7.95).

For someone who appreciates truly fine chocolates, the Belgian chocolatier Godiva makes light and dark chocolates filled with mousse, mocha, and praline (1 lb. Golden Ballotin, $8.95). Or there's the Pepperidge Farm assortment of dark and milk chocolates filled with creams, caramels, nuts, crunches, and clusters, 1½ lbs., $6.95.

PHANNY'S PHUDGE PARLOR / Dept. CFC
P.O. Box 101, Whittier, CA 90608

"Phanny's Phudge Parlor," free, published periodically, 16 pages, illustrated, color.

Phudge phans and phanatics: keep the phaith! Phabulous Phanny's phantastic phudge comes in 14 phlavors phrom natural chocolate to Phertility phudge, chock-phull of Vitamin E, and Skinny phudge, phatless and 90 percent butterphat phree. And as Phanny admits, phairly expensive (1 lb., $5).

A ceramic "phanny kiss" (a design phrom Phanny's biggest competitor), a phar-out ceramic peanut, a phabulous ceramic egg, or a phony ceramic walnut, all stuphed phull of candy and/or nuts, each $17.50.

Two lbs. of chocolate, vanilla, peanut butter, and chocolate mint phudge in phreight crate are $10.00.

Phudges are also phurnished in one- and two-phoot bars (1 and 1½ lbs., $5 and $7.50), made with whiskey (1 lb., $15 with ceramic Phanny jug or $6.50 with phreight crate).

Aphicionados say: phine and candy!

PIONEER-SEMINOLE GROVES / Dept. CFC
P.O. Box 2209, Cocoa, FL 32922

"Citrus and Gift Catalog," free, published four times a year, 16 pages, illustrated, color.

The sweet-toothed will find some unusual candies in this catalogue. Orange fruit crisps are around $4 for a ½ lb.; coconut patties, over-layered with chocolate, are $2.75 a ½ lb.; and tropical slo-pokes (pecan halves and caramel dipped in chocolate) are $3.75 for 7 oz. There's a fat pecan roll of caramel topped with pecans; sugared jellied squares made from fruit juices; chopped pecans in such tropical flavors as papaya, guava, mango, and orange ($3.75 for 12 oz.); crystallized orange and grapefruit strips; citrus candies; and orange candy with pecans. The children would be enraptured by the chocolate fudge alligators—Pappy Alligator, over one foot from head to tail, is $4.75, and 10 baby alligators are the same price. Saltwater taffy in tropical flavors is another temptation from this catalogue.

ROOS QUALITE PECAN COMPANY / Dept. CFC
P.O. Box 8023, Savannah, GA 31401

Brochure and price list, free, 8 pages, black and white.

Pecan confections from this company include 8-oz. boxes of pecan brittle, chocolate pecan fudge, and sugar 'n spice pecans, your choice of any two combinations, $7.75. They also have benne candy (benne is the Southern name for sesame seed), benne bits for cocktails, and benne wafers, a sweet cookie, bite-size cocktail crackers that taste like pecans or pizza, and wild-rice tea cakes, a semisweet cookie with a wild-rice flavor, all of which sell for the same price, $5.50.

A.L. ROTH CANDY KITCHEN & MACAROON BAKE SHOP
Dept. CFC
2627 Boardwalk, Atlantic City, NJ 08401

Brochure, free, published annually, 2 pages, illustrated, color.

Almond macaroons, Macarums (coconut macaroons blended with rum), candies and such confections as sugared dates, glacé fruits, and crystallized ginger come from Roth's candy kitchen and bake shop. The Macarums are $3.20 a lb. tin, $5.95 for a 2-lb. gift tin, the almond macaroons $4.85 for a gift box of 24, or $8.25 for a party pack of 48. You'd expect an Atlantic City candy store to have salt-water taffy and they do, plain and fruit or nut filled, but that is just the beginning of the candy list. From here you go on to a nut candy selection, pecan nougat roll, pecan and nut candies, black walnut chews, chocolate barks, chocolate-coated marshmallows, creamy fudge in various flavors, coated satin straws (mint and peanut butter), rum truffles, marzipan, chocolate-coated nuts and fruits, chocolates, a health candy of fruits, nuts, and honey, and a nice assortment of dietetic candies with no cyclamates, no salt, and no sugar ranging from mint soufflé ($4.60 a lb.) to Figaro, a blend of chocolate and hazel-nut butter ($4.95 a lb.). There are also various gift packages such as the Seashore Surprise, 2 lbs. salt-water taffy, 1 lb. fudge, and 1 lb. Macarums for $10.95. All prices are delivered. If you are a candy fancier, this is an interesting brochure.

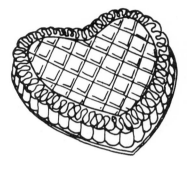

Decorative cake molds

Honey Taffy
Put 2 cups sugar, 2 cups honey, and ⅔ cup cold water in a heavy saucepan and boil until it reaches 288° on a candy thermometer. Add ⅛ teaspoon salt. Pour into a buttered dish to cool, then pull taffy until white.
—from Lang Apiaries

SAHADI IMPORTING CO., INC. / Dept. CFC
187 Atlantic Avenue, Brooklyn, NY 11201

"The Silent Salesman," free, published biannually, 24 pages, illustrated, black and white.

The most insatiable sweet tooth could be placated with Middle Eastern candies and pastries. Sahadi has rahat locoum, better known as Turkish Delight, either plain, pistachio-filled ($2.20 a lb. box) or almond, filbert and cashew filled halva, apricot candy squares, sesame candy squares, sugar-coated almonds in white or assorted colors, sugar-coated chick peas, coriander and aniseed and those incredibly sweet Middle East delicacies, baklava and katayif. The baklava comes either pistachio-filled ($6.50 for 2 lbs.) or walnut-filled ($6.25 for 2 lbs.).

SALTWATER FARM, INC. / Dept. CFC
Varrell Lane, York Harbor, ME 03911

Catalogue, free, published 4 to 5 times a year, 8 pages, illustrated, color and black and white.

What makes a better ending to a clambake than Indian pudding? Saltwater Farm, better known for their lobsters, clams, and other seafoods, will supply a canned Indian pudding, that delectable New England blend of corn meal, spices, and molasses, to round out the feast (4 1-lb. cans are $4.75 ppd.). Or, if you prefer a blueberry pie, they have blueberry pie filling. There's also a Captain's Candy sampler of saltwater taffy, blueberry, chocolate nut and peanut butter fudge and Maine Railroad candy ($9.95), or a Thoroughly Sweet sampler of candy, preserves, syrups, Indian pudding, and rum-flavored mincemeat.

SEY-CO PRODUCTS CO. / Dept. CFC
7651 Densmore Avenue, Van Nuys, CA 91406

Catalogue, free published annually, 16 pages, illustrated, color.

This thin catalogue packs a lot of calories.

Vienettes, fancy party cookies decorated with chocolate, cherries, and nuts come 40 to a box ($3.85). Twelve miniature fruitcakes ($3.85), French marrons (11 oz., $5), Hawaiian royal macadamia pineapple cake ($6.75), and brandied plum pudding ($1.50) are a few of the temptations for the person with a sweet tooth. Seasonally available (October to March) in a gift box is the famous Viennese 8-layer Dobos torte ($4.75). Lots of candies and other sweet things, like chocolate-coated Australian jumbo apricots ($5.95 a 16-oz. tin), marzipan and coffee-flavored candies.

A gift of cake and coffee from Sey-Co Products

SPHINX DATE RANCH / Dept. CFC
5201 East Camelback Road, Phoenix, AZ 85018

"Sphinx Date Ranch Gift Offerings," free, published annually, 8 pages.

Prickly-pear cactus candy made from the juice of cactus fruit ($3.95 per pound) is one of Sphinx Date Ranch's more unusual products. There are also date rolls made of macerated dates rolled in coconut and topped with almonds ($4.75 for 2 lbs.), orange-date nut loaf, apricot-pineapple nut loaf ($5.50), date-pecan and apricot-pecan loaves ($4.75), plus a pecan log ($4.50 per lb.), apricot-coconut roll ($7.50 for 2 lbs.), and an assortment of glacéed fruits (2 lbs., $9.95).

SUGARBUSH FARM / Dept. CFC
R.F.D. 2, Woodstock, VT 05091

Brochure, free, 4 pages, published seasonally.

Old-fashioned soft pure maple sugar ($5.20 for a 1-lb. 4-oz. tin) is available from Sugarbush Farm, as well as pure maple-sugar bonbons in fancy shapes ($4.50 for 12 oz.), pure maple-sugar hearts, and brick sugar for cooking (½ lb., $1.75). Postage and handling are extra.

SUNNYLAND FARMS, INC. / Dept. CFC
Box 785, Route 1, Albany, GA 31705

"Pecans Plain and Fancy," free, published annually, 32 pages, illustrated, color.

Sunnyland Farms' candy items include choco-nuts, fancy pecan halves dipped in creamy milk chocolate; pecan logs, a nougat filling coated with caramel, then rolled in crunchy pecans; pecan pralines; pecan brittle, and pecan bark.

A pecan fruitcake that is 75% fruit and nuts will stay fresh for months in its reusable tin ($9.15 for 2¼ lbs.). Another version uses only pecans, cherries and pineapples ($7.60 for 2 lbs.). There is also a 2-lb. pecan-date cake at $7.45.

Pecan clusters, big pecan pieces smothered with creamy caramel then covered with rich milk chocolate, come packed in a 1-lb. gift tin for $6.55. Pecan brittle, home-made in Sunnyland Farms' kitchen, is $10.45 for a 3-lb. box. Pralines, large cartwheels loaded with pecans, made fresh to order, are packed 8, 12 or 20 to the box ($5.85, $6.95 and $9.45). Eight flavors of pecan bark including white chocolate, butterscotch, peppermint, and carob are $8.80 for a 1-lb. 11-oz. tin, plus a vanilla and chocolate dietetic bark for those who can't use sugar. Deglet Noor dates stuffed with pecans are $7.75 for 1¼ lbs. and date-nut balls, $7.15 for a 1-lb. 6-oz. gift box. Prices are subject to change, so write for current listings.

THE SWISS COLONY / Dept. CFC
1112 7th Avenue, Monroe, WI 53566

"Gifts of Perfect Taste," free, published annually (for Christmas), 92 pages, illustrated, color.

There's a vast array of confections in this gift catalogue, from Dobos torte, cheese cake and petits fours to a real gingerbread house with stick candy trim ($8.95 or $12.95 for the extra-large house) and a Christmas cookie house. You'll find tins of Christmas mints, macadamia chocolates, cookies, sugarplums, Hawaiian macadamia nut cakes, butter-rum fruit cake and a Christmas fruit cake with glazed nuts and glacé fruit on top ($7.95 for a 2-lb. size), fudge brownie cream cakes, a chocolate yule wreath, stollen, old-fashioned fudge, peanutty butter crunchy (peanuts and popcorn in a honey and butter glaze), mambos (coconut and rum balls), butter toffees, coconut patties, and heavenly hash—a chocolate-coated mixture of pecans, cashews, and marshmallows ($4.35 for 1¼ lbs.). Liqueur chocolates from Holland are $4.45 the ½ lb., a lb. box of assorted chocolates, $3.50 and marzipan fruits $4.25 for a box of 24. Forget the calories when you look through these pages.

VANDER VLIET'S HOLLAND IMPORTS / Dept. CFC
3147 West 111th Street, Chicago, IL 60655

Catalogue, free, published annually, 34 pages, black and white.

There's a preponderance of sweet things in this little catalogue. Lots of Dutch cookies like speculaas, butter cookies, gingerbread men, spritz cookies, St. Claus windmill cookies, and specialty breads, cakes, and pastries such as honey cake, ginger cake, Frisian coffee cake, Hofstra whole rye bread, currant bread, currant-raisin bread, and fruit buns. In candies, things like fruit drops, chewy mints, Tobler Swiss chocolate, Van Dungen chocolate shoes, animals and windmills (98¢ to $1.98 a package), wooden shoes filled with chocolates (small pair, $4.95), hopjes, filled coffee, honey or fruit bonbons and a large assortment of Droste chocolates. They also list the Estee dietetic and sugarless sweets.

THE VERMONT COUNTRY STORE / Dept. CFC
Weston, VT 05161

Catalogue, 25¢, published annually, 98 pages, illustrated, black and white.

Jumbo wholemeal cookies baked with stone-ground meal come fresh from the bakery of the Vermont Country Store. The cookies are 4" in

Apricot Balls

Mix 1 pound dried apricots, chopped, and ½ cup white seedless raisins in a bowl. Sprinkle ½ cup cream and ½ cup Amaretto di Saronno over them and let stand overnight. Add 2 cups shredded coconut, ½ cup finely slivered almonds, and ½ cup gingersnap crumbs. Blend well and roll into small balls. Roll balls in confectioners' sugar. Makes about 3 dozen.
—*from "Your Amaretto di Saronno Gourmet Secrets"*

a catalog for cooks
fall/winter
from WILLIAMS-SONOMA

diameter, packed 15 to a box for $4. Fruit cake, full of walnuts, candied cherries, almonds, pineapple, raisins, rum, whiskey, and brandy, in a round tin, is $10.95 for a 3-lb. cake. Naturally, they sell maple candy in fancy shapes, maple-nut fudge ($2.50 for a 1-lb. slab), and cakes of hard maple sugar, lots of old-time hard candies, and two old-fashioned confections, crystallized candied ginger and candied orange peel, $3.25 for 1 lb. of ginger, $2.75 for 1 lb. of orange peel.

WALNUT ACRES / Dept. CFC
Penns Creek, PA 17862

"Walnut Acres Natural Foods," free, published 5 times a year, 24 pages, black and white.

Walnut Acres processes or bakes many of their products, among them ginger, oatmeal and peanut butter cookies, made with organic whole-wheat flour and other natural ingredients like unsulphured molasses, date powder, untreated well water, cold pressed safflower oil, and always fresh butter and whole eggs. A 12-oz. plastic pack of cookies costs from $1.12 for ginger cookies to $1.25 for peanut butter cookies. Plum pudding, made with all natural and organic ingredients and steamed, is another of their products, $1.12 for an 11-oz. tin. Not their own but, we presume, equally good are the wheat-germ cookies and Holland honey plain cake, made with rye flour, honey, and buttermilk. Candies here are the natural kind, too, mainly made with things like toasted sesame seeds, honey, coconut, carob powder, and non-fat dry milk.

WHITTARD & CO. LTD. / Dept. CFC
111 Fulham Road, London SW3 6RP, England

Price list, free.

Although coffees and teas are the specialties here, Whittard sells after-dinner candies as well. Bendicks bittermints, chocolate crème de menthe, mint crisps, and Turkish delight are available in quantities ranging from 200 to 1,000 grams (from just under ½ lb. to about 2¼ lbs.) and prices of $1.50 to $10. A minimum order of nearly $13 is required.

WILLIAMS-SONOMA / Dept. CFC
576 Sutter Street, San Francisco, CA 94102

"A Catalog for Cooks," $1, published biannually, plus "January sale/New Kitchen Ideas," both 26 pages, illustrated, color.

The most amusing candies we've come across in a long time are the caviar candy mints sold by Williams-Sonoma (a brainwave of art director Milton Glaser, they come in a tin labeled "Pushpinoff Caviar Candy Mints," Pushpin being the name of his design studio). They look exactly like whole-grain black caviar—imagine what a sensation they'd make on the coffee table. Another delicious confection are the crêpes dentelles, thin crispy rolled wafer cookies from Brittany, marvelous with ice cream (2 cans of cookies, $6).

THE WISCONSIN CHEESEMAN / Dept. CFC
P.O. Box 1, Madison, WI 53701

"Gift Selections," free, published annually, 96 pages, illustrated, color.

Many of the candies and cakes in this catalogue come in combination with cheeses and other foods, but some can be ordered on their own. Petits fours, butter cookies, assorted chocolates and imported candies, mints, butter rum cakes, gingerbread boys, and pecan logs can be bought in separate boxes in a wide range of prices. A shiny red apple cookie canister comes packed with holiday cookies and Tobler Swiss chocolate Napolitains for $8.50, a trio of apothecary jars hold mint, orangeade, and lemonade hard candies shaped like peas, carrots, and corn ($3.95), an international candy assortment contains chocolates and hard candies from England, Ireland, Switzerland, Colombia, Holland, Argentina, and the U.S. ($6.95), a box of holiday petits fours with Christmas wreath and candle decorations is $5.75 and 9 miniature fruit

Cookies and candies from The Wisconsin Cheeseman

cakes come packaged with brandy hard sauce ($3.95). Crystallized ginger in a blue-and-white porcelain ginger jar costs $5.95 and 11½-oz. tins of creme de menthe cookies and rum cookies are $3.95 each. And that's only a sampling of the offerings.

MILTON YORK CANDY CO. / Dept. CFC
P.O. Box 416, Long Beach, WA 98631

"Milton York Fine Candies," free, published periodically, 4 pages, illustrated, black and white.

An old-established (since 1894) candy manufacturer whose specialties are "energy chews," roasted salted peanuts dipped in light or dark chocolate ($3 a lb.); chocolate, rum, and peanut butter "velvet," which as they say, is "difficult to describe," and cranberry jells dipped in chocolate (both $3 a lb.).

Butter toffee, pecan log roll and sweet prunes dipped in chocolate ($3.40 a lb.) come separately or in assorted gift boxes ($3.45 - $9.95, 1 - 3 lbs.).

Taffies, fudge, peanut brittle, raisin and nut clusters (all $3 a lb.), and the "Milton York Special", a sandwich of light chocolate "bread" filled with dark chocolate and almonds ($3 a lb.) are all home-made, using rich dairy butter, thick rich whipping cream, top-quality dipping chocolate, and fresh roasted nuts.

The York Candy Company is closed January through March and makes no summer shipments of chocolates.

Decorative candy molds

See Appendix, page 239, for additional sources not included here.

CHAPTER SEVEN

GROWING THINGS

Casserole aux Tomates

In a small skillet heat ¼ cup olive oil and sauté 6 chopped shallots until golden brown, about 5 minutes. Place shallots and pan drippings, 6 firm sliced tomatoes (these may be peeled first), ½ cup chopped Provençal olives, 1 teaspoon crumbled dried tarragon and chervil, and 2 cans (14-oz.) celery hearts, drained and sliced, in a greased 2-quart casserole. Season to taste with salt and freshly ground pepper and mix gently. Sprinkle with 6 French biscottes, coarsely crumbled (or use similar cracker crumbs) and ¼ cup melted butter. Bake in a preheated 350° oven for 35 to 40 minutes or until brown and bubbly. Serve hot with roast meat. Serves 6.

—*courtesy Food & Wines from France, Inc.*

Kit for sun-drying fruits and vegetables from Ambit Enterprises

ALEXANDER'S BLUEBERRY NURSERIES / Dept. CFC
R.F.D. 4, Box 299, Middleboro, MA 02346

For price list and two pages of blueberry recipes, send 13¢ stamp.

Nine varieties of one- and two-year-old plants are available (Berkeley, Bluecrop, Bluehaven, Blueray, Colville, Earliblue, Herbert, Northland, Walcott), some early-fruiting, others midseason and late. Prices for the two-year-old plants range from $3.50 each ($3.25 if 5 of one variety are ordered) to $3.75 ($3.50 if 5 are ordered). The one-year-old plants are sold only in wholesale lots, 25 lots of one variety, at $1 to $1.25 each. Delivery is at recommended planting time, either spring or fall. Orders should be placed well in advance of delivery, and the two-year-old plants are in short supply. In addition to blueberries, Alexander's has a new ever-bearing raspberry variety, August Red (for spring planting only), 24 plants for $15; Canada Red rhubarb roots (3 for $7); grapes for spring planting (Catawba, Concord, Fredonia, Himrod-White); and some edible plants, such as horseradish root, Egyptian or top onions that can be harvested all year round (use shoots as chives, top bulbs as shallots), comfrey and tansy for teas.

AMBIT ENTERPRISES, INC. / Dept. CFC
P.O. Box 1790, Chula Vista, CA 92012

"How to Sun Dry Fruits and Vegetables and Save Them for a Rainy Day," $1, published annually, 34 pages, illustrated, black and white, order form and price list included.

A marvelously clear and detailed booklet that describes and sketches the 4-step procedure for preserving the fully ripe flavors of fruits, vegetables, and berries by sun drying or using artificial heat. Conditioning, sterilization, and packaging are covered with specific recipes for 39 fruits and vegetables, even lettuce. To facilitate preserving nature's way, Ambit Enterprises offers "Sun Pantry" trays, screens, and 12- or 21-oz. bottles of sodium metabisulfite (a water-soluble crystalline salt), recommended for pretreatment to preserve color and Vitamins A and C. A kit at $9.95 that includes one drying tray and some of the crystals will start you off with the help of the accompanying booklet. Additional supplies can be purchased separately.

ARGONAUT VENTURES, INC. / Dept. CFC
P.O. Box 40218, San Francisco, CA 94140

"Fun Cooking & Things with Sourdough Jack," price list, free, published annually, 5 pages, illustrated, black and white.

Sourdough Jack Mabee of San Francisco supplies a sprouting kit for quick, home-grown sprouts. The kit contains a 5½" x 8" terrarium, choice of sprout seeds (alfalfa, fenugreek, lentils, mung bean, peas, wheat), seed bed, sprouting chart, serving suggestions, and recipes for $2.50 ppd.

BORCHELT HERB GARDENS / Dept. CFC
474 Carriage Shop Rd., East Falmouth, MA 02536

Price list, published annually, 3 mimeographed pages, for cost of stamp plus 10¢.

Borchelt Herb Gardens grows more than 185 species of herbs and the potted plants are sold only on the premises, but seeds and dried herbs are available by mail. Their herbs are dried and pacaged in plastic bags holding ¼ cup (enough to fill your own 2-oz.-capacity herb jar) at 55¢, or if you want to have the herbs sent in glass jars, add 30¢ each. The herbs and spices include basil, lovage, juniper berries, dill seed, oregano, rosemary, summer savory, tarragon, and thyme. Also available are whole nutmegs (2 for 45¢), vanilla bean (49¢ a bean); and arrowroot (8 oz., $1.05). Seeds (50¢ a packet) range from agrimony to yarrow and include 5 different basils, fennel, hyssop, summer and winter savory, and French sorrel. There's even woad, which yields a blue dye, much used in Saxon England in ancient times.

W. ATLEE BURPEE CO. / Dept. CFC
Warminster, PA 18974
(also: Clinton, IA 52732
Riverside, CA 92502)

Catalogue, free, published annually, 172 pages, illustrated, color.

Burpee, one of our oldest established seed growers, celebrated their 100th anniversary in 1976 by introducing a brand-new hybrid VG (verticillim-fusarium-resistant) tomato called Big Girl, sister to 1949's Big Boy, a pair of whopping great tomatoes that can weigh a pound or more apiece. This is a catalogue to curl up with on a cold winter's night when summer and a garden bursting with produce seems far away. Dream of having your own asparagus bed, of growing golden beets (so much better in flavor than the red), celtuce, pattypan squash, lemon cucumbers, rhubarb chard, and all those other good vegetables you never seem to find in the market. Burpee has a really great selection, and they give you chatty little bits of information about cooking and eating what you produce. In addition to vegetables, fruits, and herbs, they have fruit trees, shrubs, flowering and ornamental shade trees. They even provide compost bins, cold frames, greenhouses, starter kits, trellis, fruit pickers, preserving and canning equipment, and their own spice and herb blends.

CALIFORNIA NURSERY COMPANY / Dept. CFC
Fremont, CA 94536

Price list, free, 8 pages, published annually.

The nursery stock includes fruit and nut trees (some are dwarf fruit trees), strawberry plants and grapevines, shipped bare root. The selection is wide and interesting—almonds, apricots, figs, nectarines, peaches, plums, prunes, apples, pears, crab apples, pomegranates, quince, cherries, persimmons, olives, avocados and citrus fruits, walnuts (including black walnuts), pecans, and filberts. Grapevines include table

★

Before washing head lettuce, such as Boston, cut out the core. Hold the head upside down under cold running water and the leaves will separate easily.

★

Young vegetables with thin tender skins, like carrots and new potatoes, do not need scraping or peeling. To clean, simply rub well with a plastic scouring pad.

★

Green Bean Salad

Cook 1 pound trimmed whole young green beans in plenty of rapidly boiling salted water until tender but still crisp to the bite. Do not overcook. Drain and rinse immediately in cold water to stop them cooking further. Put in a bowl and add ¼ cup finely chopped scallion or white onion and ¼ cup tiny black Niçoise olives. Toss with a vinaigrette sauce strongly flavored with Dijon mustard. Chill for 15 minutes. Serve as an hors d'oeuvre or with broiled meat or chicken.

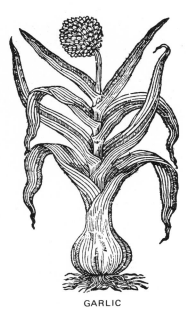

GARLIC

*

Grate potatoes for potato pancakes directly into a bowl of ice water to avoid discoloration.

*

To remove skins from garlic before chopping, whack each clove with the side of a heavy knife or a meat pounder. The skin will split and can be removed easily.

*

If you chop garlic with a little salt it will not stick to the knife.

*

varieties such as Black Monucca, Flame Tokay, Muscat, Ribier, and Thompson seedless and both American varieties of wine grapes, such as Niagara and Golden Muscat and vinifera varieties—Cabernet Sauvignon, Pinot Chardonnay, Emerald Riesling, Pinot Noir, Carignane, and Grenache among them. Grapevines run from $1.75 each for 1 to 9 vines to 85¢ each if you buy 300 or more. Fruit trees vary in price. Persimmons are $7.50 each for 1 to 9, pomegranates and quince $5.75 each for 1 to 9. Of course, you should make sure before ordering that the vines or trees you are interested in will survive in your climate. Stock is postage paid within California. In all other areas add 25% to cover packing and transportation. The minimum order is $15.

CAPRILAND'S HERB FARM / Dept. CFC
Silver Street, Coventry, CT 06238

Brochure, free, published annually.

Capriland's Herb Farm will ship herb plants in season. Prices are from $1 to $2 for herbs in 2" pots, from $2 for herbs in 4" pots. Included in their list of culinary herbs are chives, garlic chives, various basils, sorrel, burnet, lemon balm, various mints, winter and summer savory, sage, tarragon, thyme, curled and Italian parsley, Egyptian onions, lovage, angelica, dill, chervil, runnerless strawberry, rue, many oreganos, and rosemary. They also have scented geraniums ($1 to $1.50). Herb seeds are shipped from February 15 to December 15 (35¢ a package). You can order from the Seasoning Shop Capriland's mixed herb blend, an all-purpose mixture for soups and salads, for $1 a jar or 85¢ a package, poultry seasoning, Spanish saffron ($1), vanilla beans (2 for $1), cardamom, and 4 nutmegs, $1.75 with grater, 50¢ without. Herb teas are another of their specialties. An attractive Christmas gift might be their herb and spice kitchen wreath (in 6", 8", 10", 12", and 14" sizes at prices from $8.95 to $16.95), or an herb and flower wreath. These can be ordered after August 1. Other delightful ideas are herb-and-spice-scented hot pads ($2.50 each), a catnip cat or mouse, doorway basket fans with herb and spice decorations, herb and spice necklaces, and "peace pillows," inspired by 18th-century fragrant pillows tied to wing chairs to give off a soothing essence, in rose, spice, or lavender fragrance, $1.75. This sounds like a nice place to visit if you are in Connecticut. The shop is open all day April through December; from 1:00 P.M. or by appointment January through March, and there are various Herbal Luncheon programs throughout the year presented by owner Adelma Simmons or her assistants.

CARROLL GARDENS / Dept. CFC
P.O. Box 310, Westminster, MD 21157

"Your Garden Planting Guide," free, published annually, 68 pages, black and white.

While this catalogue lists mostly flowers and flowering shrubs, they have a good selection of hardy perennial herbs, 3 of any one kind for $3.85, 6 for $7.50, 12 for $14, or $1.35 each. A few of the more unusual herbs available are alecost or costmary, angelica, salad burnet, cardamom (grown for the seeds), comfrey, hyssop, lovage, skirret, and sorrel. They have the usual ones, too, such as thyme, tarragon (the desirable French strain), winter savory, sage, rosemary, parsley, mint, marjoram, chives, and basil—classed as a perennial although it is too tender to survive a winter outdoors and must be brought inside. Also cultivated blueberry plants (Bluecrop, Coville, Jersey, Rancocas, and Rubel), 3 years old and 18" to 24" high, at $3.65 each, 3 for $10.50, 6 for $19.50, or 12 for $37.50.

COMMON FIELDS NURSERY / Dept. CFC
17 Spring St., Ipswich, MA 01938

Price list, free, published annually, 3 pages.

Giant cultivated blueberries are the specialty here. Varieties offered are Weymouth (earliest), Concord (early midseason), Dixie (midseason),

Rancocas (midseason beauty), Pemberton (new late), Jersey (ideal late), Rubel (late), Atlantic (late), GN87 (midseason), 1316A (late). Prices range from $1.45 for a 2-year-old plant to $3.50 for a 5-year-old. The 3-year-old plants (bearing age) are $1.75 or 25 for $41.25. There are also leading new varieties such as Earliblue and Blue Ray (early), Blue Crop and Collins (early midseason), Berkeley (midseason), Coville (mid to late), Herbert and Blue Late (late).

COTTAGE HERB FARM SHOP / Dept. CFC
311 State Street, Albany, NY 12210

Catalogue, 25¢, published annually, 3 pages, drawings.

Cottage Herb Farms sells herb seeds (and the so-called nose herb seeds emphasizing aroma, not taste) in packets (35¢) with a $3 minimum order required. With your order you get culture directions.

The seed list is a good one. Five kinds of basil—green bush (plain, curly-leafed, Oriental, sweet) and purple sweet—plus salad burnet, woolly betony (and green betony), horehound, French sorrel, clary, green or gray (cotton lavender) santolina, lovage, and perilla. Fifty kinds of seeds in all.

D. M. ENTERPRISES / Dept. CFC
P.O. Box 2452, San Francisco, CA 94126

"Calico Kitchen's Portfolio," free, 12 sheets, published two to three times a year.

Calico Kitchen's San Francisco-oriented offerings include California-grown seeds for various Chinese vegetables. For mild weather there's an indoor or outdoor crop of Chinese chives, Chinese celery, and Chinese parsley (coriander). A cool-weather outdoor crop for spring or fall planting consists of bok choy (Chinese white cabbage), gai choy (Chinese mustard greens), and snow peas. Hot-weather crop for spring planting has cee gwa (okra), dow yuak (yard-long bean), and hin choy (Chinese spinach). Any one of these three selections of seeds is $2.25.

Zucchini Meat Loaf
Put 2 small zucchini and 2 medium onions through a meat grinder. Heat 1 tablespoon vegetable oil in a skillet. Sauté the ground vegetables lightly. Add 2 medium tomatoes, peeled, seeded, and chopped. Simmer until tender. Meanwhile, soak 1 slice day-old bread, cubed, in ¼ cup lukewarm milk for 5 minutes. Stir into the milk mixture 1 slightly beaten egg, 1 teaspoon Worcestershire sauce, 1 small garlic clove, minced, 1 teaspoon salt, and ½ teaspoon pepper. Add the sautéed vegetables and blend well. Add 1 pound ground beef and ¼ pound ground pork. Blend all together thoroughly. Pack into a 9" x 5" loaf pan and refrigerate for 1 hour before baking to blend the flavors. Bake in a 325° oven for 1½ hours. Let stand 10 minutes after taking from the oven before serving. Serves 8.
—*from "Zucchini Cookbook," courtesy Planned Parenthood of Santa Cruz County*

HENRY FIELD SEED & NURSERY CO. / Dept. CFC
407 Sycamore Street, Shenandoah, IA 51602

Catalogues, free, published spring (January), 132 pages, and fall (August), 46 pages, illustrated, color.

One of the most interesting and helpful features of the Henry Field spring catalogue is the center section on planning and planting different types of beds and gardens, including fruit, vegetable, and herb gardens. Among the sketches is one for a raised "salad bar" made with railroad ties, another for a pyramidal herb garden that can be made with a kit, and a third for a kitchen garden. They have, of course, all the necessary seeds and equipment for planting and maintaining your garden. Among the vegetables are some unusual ones, such as a purple head cauliflower with a mild broccoli flavor (59¢ a packet), a giant Japanese white globe radish, celtuce (a cross between lettuce and celery), and the vine peach or mango melon (really a cucumber) with large white-fleshed, yellow-skinned fruit that makes good preserves and pickles (57¢ a packet). Midget vegetables, including a baby head cabbage, many varieties of hybrid sweet corn, purple pod beans, shallots at $3.49 a qt. (about 200 sets), and a rich purplish-red Salad Trim lettuce (55¢ a packet) are other things we noticed. The catalogue also shows a good selection of berries, fruit trees, and nut trees, including black walnut, butternut, shellbark hickory, and Chinese chestnut, the edible kind. The fall catalogue is mostly devoted to bulbs, flowers, and trees, with a few vegetable seeds that can be planted in August for fall harvesting, such as black-seeded Simpson lettuce, kale, collards, cabbage, cauliflower, white bunching onions, and Brussels sprouts.

★

Never peel mushrooms. If they are slightly grimy, rub with a damp towel or rinse briefly under cold water. Dry well.

★

Parsley and feathery herbs such as dill lose texture and flavor when washed. Chop, put in a twist of paper towel, and squeeze under running water. Then spread out on paper towels to dry and fluff up.

★

GLN SHALLOT DISTRIBUTORS / Dept. CFC
51 DeShibe Terrace, Vineland, NJ 08360

Price list.

GLN Shallot Distributors will supply you with fresh shallots year round. For $3.95, ¼ lb. shallots will be shipped monthly for 6 months. A full year's shipment costs $7.25. For a monthly ½-lb. shipment, send $5.50 for 6 months' supply or $9.95 for ½ lb. every month for a year. Payment must be included with order. A ¼-lb. sample is available for 75¢.

THE GOURMET PANTRY / Dept. CFC
400 McGuinness Blvd., Brooklyn, NY 11222

"Pleasure Packed Gifts from the Gourmet Pantry," free, published annually, 72 pages, illustrated, color.

One of the gift ideas in this catalogue is a "Gourmet Mushroom Farm" for $10, a 10" x 14" planter with soil and mushroom spores. Add water and in 30 days you should have your mushroom crop.

GURNEY SEED & NURSERY CO. / Dept. CFC
2nd and Capitol Streets, Yankton, SD 57078

"Gurney Garden Seed and Nursery Catalog," free, published annually, 76 pages, color.

In business for more than a century, Gurney Nurseries has built a reputation as a dependable source for familiar and not-so-familiar fruits and vegetables. The comprehensive and bulky catalogue may not look as alluring as some, but it is packed from cover to cover with an enormous selection of vegetables, fruits, nut trees, flowers, gardening aids, and affiliated items such as cookbooks and canning aids. One spread, pages 42–43 in our catalogue, is devoted to very useful basic information: a planting chart for vegetables, a chart on how to change your soil pH, another on when to start seeds indoors, a fruit-planting guide, tips on planting nursery stock, pruning and planting for pollination—the kind of information you seek in a garden book is all free here. If you want to attract birds to your garden, there's a list of plants they like: blueberry, dogwood, honeysuckle, chokecherry, mountain ash, and flowering crab trees. Picking at random from the fascinating selection of offbeat fruits and vegetables, we noticed the torpedo onion, long and spindle-shaped, with red skin and sweet, mild flesh (59¢ packet); lady-finger potatoes, a small, yellow-fleshed variety an inch in diameter and several inches long that Gurney recommends for potato salad ($1.95 for ½ lb. tubers); a yellow radish and the delicious little round lemon cucumbers (both 59¢ a packet); an early yellow pepper that matures in 55 days; the only early honeydew melon (70 days) to mature in the north (63¢ a packet); a "naked" squash, one that has seeds with no hulls that may be dried and eaten like sunflower seeds (59¢ a packet); and, believe it or not, a blue-skinned, blue-fleshed potato ($2.49 for 25 sets). In fruits there's a seedless Concord grape (2-year vines are $2.45 each), Champion or Pineapple quince trees ($6.98 each), a mulberry tree ($1.99), and some native fruit trees and bushes: native plum, wild black cherry, chokecherry, sand cherry, compass cherry, buffalo berry, for unusual jams, jellies, and fruit sauces. Also persimmon trees, the kind that grow wild in the country, hardy as far north as the Great Lakes (1 to 1½ feet, $2.98 each), and that strange American fruit tree, the pawpaw (not to be confused with the pawpaw of the West Indies, or papaya), which tastes rather like a banana. If you've always wanted a black walnut or hickory-nut tree, Gurney's has them, as well as Chinese chestnut (the variety you roast or use in stuffings), pecan and butternut trees.

JOSEPH HARRIS CO., INC. / Dept. CFC
Moreton Farm, Rochester, NY 14624

"Harris Seeds," free, published annually, 26 pages, illustrated, color and black and white.

Harris is a well-known and reliable seed company, and their catalogue is a professional production, well written, with excellent color and black-

and-white photographs of vegetables and flowers. The vegetables are arranged by type, starting with asparagus, and there's an introductory section on vegetables of special merit and a good index. One of the interesting vegetables is the Presto patio hybrid red tomato that can be grown in a pot and starts to bear in July. The fruits are about 1½ inches in diameter and grow on 2-foot vines (70¢ a packet). Among the beans we noticed scarlet runners, grown mainly as an ornamental vine for the lovely scarlet flowers but a heavy producer of flat green beans that the English like. They say the vines grow over 6 feet tall; ours grow over the house! They also have a special strain of French horticultural bean, edible both green and dried, and the fava (broad or Italian) bean. Their bean seeds are treated with Captan, a harmless organic fungicide. Other vegetables you may be interested in are the Self-Blanche cauliflower, developed by Dr. Shigemi Honma of Michigan State, which does not have to have the leaves tied over the head because they curl over of their own accord (50¢ a packet); the round lemon cucumber and the long skinny Chinese or Kyoto cucumber (Harris has a Japanese strain) that is crisp-fleshed and mild and a dependable producer (50¢ a packet); and a good many varieties of lettuce—Bibb, Buttercrunch, summer Bibb (slow bolting), Boston, black-seeded Simpson, and five other loose-leaf types, including oak leaf and ruby, cos or romaine. Prices range from 35¢ to 45¢ a packet. In two varieties (Buttercrunch and Salad Bowl) you can get pelleted seed, which is much easier to plant without crowding (95¢ for a package of about 450 seeds). We've also had good luck with their Mammoth Melting sugar peas, usually known as snow peas, (45¢ a packet). Harris has a large selection of corn, both white and yellow, and lists one of the salad greens we love to grow, corn salad, known as *mâche* in France (35¢ a packet).

HICKIN'S MOUNTAIN MOWINGS FARM / Dept. CFC
RFD 1, Black Mountain Road, Brattleboro, VT 05301

Brochure, free, published periodically, 5 pages, illustrated, black and white.

Shallots may be hard to find in many parts of the country, but you can always order them from Mountain Mowings Farm. Large shallots are $1.19 for 5 oz., $3.25 a lb. They will also sell and ship summer-bearing and ever-bearing varieties of strawberry plants; red, black, and purple raspberry plants (summer and ever-bearing); blueberries; asparagus; rhubarb; leek plants; onion sets and plants; and two varieties of potato, Green Mountain and Early Rose. Inquire about current prices of these and their many other plants.

HICKORY HOLLOW / Dept. CFC
Rte. 1, Box 52, Peterstown, WV 24963

Brochure and price list, 25¢, 6 pages, updated periodically, black and white.

Hickory Hollow sells herb plants, such as chives, mint, comfrey (8 root cuttings, $2.50), horseradish roots (5 for $2) and Jerusalem artichoke tubers (12 for $3), and for 90¢ they'll send a good-size bunch of fresh dill, sage, and chives. You can also get for $1 complete plans and instructions for building a stove-top food dryer for herbs, fruits, and vegetables.

HILLTOP HERB FARM / Dept. CFC
P.O. Box 866, Cleveland, TX 77327

Catalogue, 50¢, published annually, 16 pages, illustrated, black and white.

The herb plants that Hilltop Herb Farm grows and sells for $1.75 each (shipping cost included) are divided into categories. Under "For Teas and *Tisanes*" you'll find agrimony, lemon balm, speedwell, various mints, thymes, and sages, about 35 plants in all. "For Use at the Table—Olfactory, Palate and Conversation" covers the usual herbs and a few unusual ones like lovage, fennel (bronze and green), burnet, and sorrel. Other groupings are: For Dyeing and Coloring, For a Bee Garden, For a Fragrant Garden, For Crevices and Little Pokey Places, For

A page of produce from the Joseph Harris catalogue

Leeks and Rice

Slice the roots from 5 to 6 medium sized leeks, remove upper third of green stalk. Under water, wash out sand or dirt from between leaves. Slice diagonally into 1" lengths. Place ¾ cup water, 2 tablespoons oil, ½ teaspoon salt, and 1 heaping tablespoon white rice in a large skillet. Add leeks and bring to a boil. Reduce heat and simmer for 20 to 25 minutes, depending on the kind of rice used. All the water should be absorbed. Place in a serving dish and chill several hours.
—from "Cooking with Herbs at Longpond Farm"

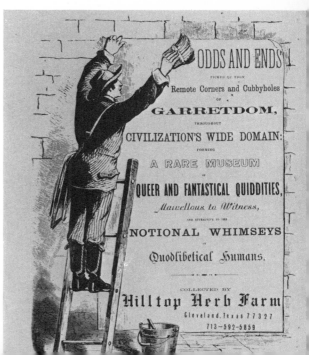

Corn with Basil Butter
Blend 2 tablespoons finely chopped fresh basil leaves with ¼ pound butter. Add salt and freshly ground black pepper to taste. Chill and serve with hot cooked ears of corn.

Oregano

★

Use leftover mashed potatoes to thicken a puréed or cream soup.

★

Save parsley stems to flavor soups and stocks.

★

Ground Covers and Weed Chokers, For Flower Arranging, For Delight to the Eye as Well as the Nose, For a Grey Garden, Scented Geraniums—Mimics of the Plant World, For Shady Acres, Including Dells and Glens, For Dry Places—and Too Far to Drag the Hose, and For Garden Borders—Both Straighteners and Curves. The quality of the writing makes this catalogue an enchantment. They also sell herb seeds at 60¢ a package.

HOWE HILL HERBS / Dept. CFC
Howe Hill Rd., Camden, ME 04843

Brochure, 35¢, published annually, 12 pages, black and white.

Howe Hill has a list of some 90 culinary, decorative, and fragrant herbs potted in 2" to 3" containers, both perennials and annuals, ranging in price from 85¢ to $3 for lemon grass. There are 9 mints, 11 thymes, 5 sages, and both the bush and the dwarf bush basil (the latter is not always easy to find). If you love geraniums, they have loads of those, too, many with lemon, peppermint, pine, and rose-scented leaves. A collection of 5 scented-leaf varieties is $3. There is also an herb collection of 5 plants of their choice (specify cooking, fragrant, or decorative) for $3.50. Herb seeds are available at 35¢ a package. While their business is mail-order, you can visit Howe Hill Herbs from June through September.

J. L. HUDSON'S WORLD SEED SERVICE / Dept. CFC
P.O. Box 1058, Redwood City, CA 94064

"A World Seed Service Complete Catalogue of Seeds," 50¢, published annually, 109 pages, black and white.

J. L. Hudson will ship seeds all over the world, in case you have friends in other countries who'd like to try some of the typically American vegetables, such as squash. Although only the last 20 pages are devoted to edible plants (including a very informative list of some of the more unusual ones and how they are used), there is plenty here to interest the gardener in search of something different. They have seeds for the Chinese yard-long bean, for burdock, the edible root used in Japanese cooking, for a Portuguese variety of cabbage, and various types of Chinese and Japanese cabbage such as pak choi and taisai, the hard-to-find cardoon and black salsify or scorzonera, and Japanese vegetables such as pot-herb mustard, smallage (the wild ancestor of celery), and shungiku (edible-leaved chrysanthemum). In the chards you'll find sea kale, the delicate variety grown in England but seldom seen here. Radish varieties include the round black and long black Spanish radishes and two Japanese types, akahime and sakurajima giant (a very large round radish, 13" in diameter, rather sweet and usually boiled or pickled). Prices range from 15¢ to 40¢ a packet. The general section of the catalogue includes herbs and some fruits that can be grown from seed, such as a strawberry that when sown in fall will germinate in spring and produce fruit the first year. The fruit is smaller than the common strawberry but has a delicious flavor.

LE JARDIN DU GOURMET / Dept. CFC
West Danville, VT 05873

Catalogue, 50¢, published annually, 32 pages, illustrated, black and white.

This mail-order company offers shallots and leeks for planting ($2.50 ppd. for 12 oz. shallots, 50 leeks, $2 ppd.), onion sets, white or yellow ($1.50 for 12 oz.), the Italian cippolini ($2 for 12 oz.), and red or white Jerusalem artichokes ($2 for 12 oz.—the more unfamiliar red type is elongated and more evenly formed than the white; indicate which type you want). Jardin du Gourmet sells live herb plants in 2" plastic pots, ranging from angelica to sweet woodruff, with laurus Nobilis (for bay leaves), 8 kinds of mint, two basils, 6 thymes, plain and curly parsley, French sorrel, tansy, hyssop, costmary, and bergamot among the choices, priced from 50¢ to $1.25. Small plant orders cannot be profitably filled, so they ask that you make your order total a couple of dollars or more and add 80¢ per order for packing and postage. They have a pretty good list of herb and vegetable seeds, including some unusual ones such as Japanese hybrid eggplant, Portuguese cabbage (with thick, fleshy, light-green leaves), and a perennial species of onion that can be planted in August to produce green onions in early spring; but most interesting of all to the vegetable gardener are the seeds they import from the famous French house, Vilmorin. Although Vilmorin sells by mail through their overseas seed catalogue, they won't send small orders, and seed orders often take up to two months to arrive. Jardin du Gourmet offers to order anything you see and want from the catalogue, in addition to the seeds they carry regularly. In the Vilmorin seeds, all of which are 90¢ a packet, you'll find long purple eggplant, 4 varieties of carrot, wild chicory, both white and red, *cornichons* (tiny gherkins), a white *courgette* (zucchini), lettuce, *mâche* or corn salad, Charentais melon, the large sorrel de Belleville, *pissenlits* (dandelions), purslane, *roquette* (arugala), black salsify, and *fraises des bois*, or wild strawberries. Beans of various kinds (including the flageolet varieties of bush bean), peas, and fava or broad beans are $1 a 3-oz. packet. A wonderful source for these French seeds, which we have found do very well here.

JOHNNY'S SELECTED SEEDS / Dept. CFC
Albion, ME 04910

"Johnny's Selected Seeds–Organic Seed and Crop Research," 50¢, published annually, 36 pages, illustrated, black and white.

A small but enthusiastic grower who conducts extensive trials of vegetable varieties from all over the world, Johnny believes that strong well-balanced soil has the highest potential for quality seeds, and his acres are fertilized with animal and green manures, seaweed, rock powders, and mineral supplements. He and his associates test hundreds of vegetable varieties each season, the best of which are listed in the catalogue. Some of the interesting varieties we noted are a small fruited early-maturing Japanese eggplant called Early Black Egg that they consider the only dependable variety they have grown; other Japanese vegetables, such as taisai (mustard greens) and shungiku (edible chrysanthemum); a variety of Bibb lettuce (resistant) from Holland; Hamburg parsley (grown for its edible root); Green Arrow peas, an English variety with very long pods; 6 Japanese winter squash; a new race of tomatoes called the Sub-Arctics, which set blossoms and ripen much earlier—the earliest and smallest is about twice the size of a cherry tomato, the others larger (90¢ a packet); and Alpine strawberries, which can be raised from seed ($1 a packet). They have a good selection of usual and unusual herb seeds, including angelica, hyssop, lovage, tansy, and woodruff. Herb seeds are 60¢ a packet for annuals and biennials, 70¢ for perennials. The catalogue is attractive, detailed, interestingly and clearly written, with a lot of useful information, including how to harvest and dry shell beans. While this is our first encounter with this catalogue, we notice that the edible-pod pea variety recommended is Mammoth Melting Sugar, which we have found to be an excellent yielder.

Oyster and field mushrooms, from the Kinoko Co.

THE KINOKO CO. / Dept. CFC
P.O. Box 6425, Oakland, CA 94621

Brochure on mushroom kits, free.

This company offers four different mushroom-growing kits for the agaricus (common field mushroom), oyster mushroom, wood ear (the kind used dried in Chinese cooking), and the Japanese enokitake mushroom. Each kit costs $6.98 ppd. and contains one specific mushroom spawn culture, nutrient medium, instructions for growing and cooking, and a mushroom incubator. If you like the flavor of wild mushrooms, this would be an amusing and rewarding hobby. According to the back of the brochure, they also have fresh shiitake mushrooms (the Japanese black forest mushroom), but no details are given as to availability.

Corn Fritters

Put in the blender 2 cups corn kernels, cut off the cob, 1 teaspoon salt, ½ teaspoon sugar, 2 tablespoons all-purpose flour, ⅛ teaspoon freshly ground black pepper, and 2 lightly beaten eggs. Whirl until mixed. Heat 2 tablespoons butter in a heavy iron skillet and drop the mixture into the pan by tablespoons. Fry on each side until golden brown. May be served with syrup or plain, as an accompaniment to fried chicken. Serves 4 to 6.

MEADOWBROOK HERB GARDEN
WYOMING, RHODE ISLAND 02898

LONE PINE FARM / Dept. CFC
Inglefield, IN 47618

Details on request.

Owner W. Marvin Lundy, who has been practicing organic farming for 33 years, specializes in the variety of Bibb lettuce called Buttercrunch. He will ship this via parcel post or UPS any time of year. In the growing season he can supply fresh corn, beans, onions, beets, carrots, okra, cabbage, and broccoli, and he has a limited amount of pecans and English walnuts. Write for details and prices.

EARL MAY SEED & NURSERY CO. / Dept. CFC
Shenandoah, IA 51603

"Earl May Planting Guide," free, published annually, 86 pages, illustrated, black and white and color.

In the Earl May catalogue, you'll find fruit trees (apple, plum, pear, apricot, peach, cherry), some of which are dwarf varieties, dwarf pears (Bartlett, Max-Red Bartlett, Kieffer, Seckel), 3½ to 5 feet high, $7.25 each or $6.85 each if you order three or more. A dwarf pear special for $20.50 includes Bartlett, Kieffer, and Seckel. Dwarf apple varieties are yellow and red Delicious, Jonathan, and Yellow Transparent, and there is, believe it or not, a 4-in-1 dwarf apple tree that grows the four varieties on one 8- to 10-foot tree ($9.95 a tree). These dwarf trees (cherry, peach, pear, and apple) produce regular-size fruit and start bearing earlier. Another asset for the gardener with limited space is that they take up much less room. Other fruits available include grape plants (Fredonia, Concord, Moore's Early, Niagara, Himrod Seedless, Caco) for juice, jelly, and wine. The Himrod Seedless, incidentally, is an extremely hardy variety developed at the New York State Experimental Station, similar to that great table grape, Thompson Seedless, but larger ($3.45 for a 2-year-old plant). In the berry category there are strawberry plants (a new ever-bearing variety is called Ozark Beauty and a new hybrid June bearer, Stoplight), blueberries, blackberries, boysenberries, the jet-black dewberries that ripen earlier than blackberries, currants, gooseberries (these may not be shipped to Washington, Idaho, New Jersey, and most of the New England states), and purple, red, black, and yellow raspberries. There are nine varieties of watermelon, one yellow-fleshed, and five types of muskmelon, including an extraordinary banana muskmelon, like a banana in both shape and flavor (50¢ a package of seeds). Nothing unusual in herbs, but you will probably be interested in the midget sweet corn, lettuce, Tiny Tim tomato, and watermelon (a midget collection of seeds for all four is $1.75), and a dwarf cucumber developed for patios and small gardens that produces all female blooms (every bloom, naturally, sets a fruit) at 60¢ a packet. A new hybrid Bermuda onion, Miss Society, is extremely mild and sweet (two bunches, 80 to 100 plants a bunch, $3.95). For those who love to cook Mexican dishes, there are seeds for the hot jalapeño peppers (50¢ a packet). If you are having difficulty finding dry beans for cooking, (red kidney, cranberry, navy, Great Northern, black-eyed peas), May has them for $1.25 a ½ lb. Loads of gadgets and equipment for preparing fruits and vegetables, too, like pitters, slicers (even an electric pea and bean sheller for $14.95). Well worth sending for this one.

MEADOWBROOK HERB GARDEN / Dept. CFC
Route 138, Wyoming, RI 02898

Catalogue, 50 cents, published annually, 28 pages, illustrated.

While Meadowbrook Herb Garden does not ship their plants, they will mail all their other herb and spice products, such as herb teas of different blends ($1.45 a box), tea herbs, herb tea bags, dried herbs and herb seasoning blends (70¢ a jar), herb seeds, and various gift-pack combinations. Their selection of dried herbs is a little bit different from the usual. They have things like salad burnet (cucumber and nut flavor), lovage (the great European soup and bouquet garni herb, with an intense wild celery flavor), calendula petals (use like saffron, but generously), iron-rich nettle and old-fashioned rue, the fish and chowder herb. Their own herb seasoning mixtures are equally interesting (for fish—basil, lemon balm, dill leaves, fennel leaves, rue and rosemary), and they have very thoughtfully provided a seasoning called Heart's Delight to relieve the blandness of a salt-free diet. The list of herb seeds is long and comprehensive, from agrimony to yarrow, and the names ring sweetly on the ear: cinquefoil, cottage pink, elecampane, evening primrose, love-in-a-mist, pussytoe, snow-in-summer. For your plants they sell liquefied seaweed and fish emulsion plant food, for your library a good selection of books on herbs (craft, culture, and cooking) and organic gardening, and for your tea-drinking, all shapes and sorts of tea infusers and strainers. Prices in the catalogue are subject to change and do not include shipping costs. The Meadowbrook Herb Garden herb and gift shop and greenhouses are open daily 10:00 to noon and 1:00 to 5:00 P.M., Sundays 1:00 to 4:00 P.M., closed holidays, in case you'd like to visit them in Rhode Island.

NICHOLS GARDEN NURSERY / Dept. CFC
1190 North Pacific Highway, Albany, OR 97321

"Nichols Herb and Rare Seeds," free, published seasonally, 60 pages, illustrated, black and white.

Nichols' catalogue is more than a seed catalogue. It's a textbook for simple self-sufficient living, full of hints, recipes, advice, and products ranging from Oregon raw-milk cheddar and wine-making supplies to Mormon or squaw tea (from a small, pinelike shrub that grows in the high deserts of Utah, Nevada, and California), elephant garlic, and a wide selection of plants and seeds, many for vegetables you aren't likely to find in other catalogues. Picking a few at random, there's a Belgian white carrot, a white bush zucchini from France, a baby beet from Holland that grows just 1 inch in diameter, asparagus chicory, yard-long Armenian cucumbers, a hybrid squash that produces mainly female flowers, giving fruit at practically every leaf, the red-skinned, white-fleshed Brunswick onion sold in French vegetable markets, Egyptian walking onions (so called because the bulb remains in the ground and the top produces annual crops of onions on the stalks), golden self-blanching celery, an early black winter squash from China, a French golden radish, and a 3,000-year-old strain of Montezuma red beans. If that isn't enough, you can get seeds for the glorious French Charentais melon and other French hybrid melons of the Charentais type, a Japanese cantaloupe, and a yellow watermelon hybrid from China. Nichols has a great variety of herb seeds at 45¢ a packet and 53 herb plants, culinary, medicinal, and aromatic (minimum order is three plants, which may be assorted, for $6.15, $1.75 for each additional plant). The prices are postpaid, and shipping starts April 15 (mostly by airmail) and continues until June 15. All the plants are organically grown and have spent at least one winter outdoors—they are not tender, greenhouse rooted cuttings. Among the plants you'll find hyssop, costmary, wild ginger, and sweet woodruff (used in May wine), as well as the more familiar kind. Dried herbs and spices include black mustard seed, often needed for Indian dishes, whole mace, and Hungarian paprika. Use unadulterated peppermint oil ($2.50 a ½ oz.) for flavoring cakes or candies, dill oil ($1.98 a ½ oz.) for dill pickles. It's the unusual vegetables here, though, that are intriguing for the inquisitive gardener.

NOURSE FARMS, INC. / Dept. CFC
R.F.D. Box 485, South Deerfield, MA 01373

Catalogue, free, published annually, 18 pages.

Nourse offers 23 varieties of strawberry plants, asparagus roots, and, for the first time, rhubarb. All are available only in April and May.

Nourse strawberries, all originating from virus-free stock, come in five categories: *early:* Darrow, Gala, and Midland; *early midseason:* Raritan, Pocahontas; *midseason:* Catskill, their best seller, and Sequoia; *late:* Sparkle and Jerseybelle; *very late:* their new Marlate variety.

All are priced at $4.25 for 25 plants, except Darrow and Marlate at $5 for 25. Some are available in garden collections to provide a longer

Mandarin Asparagus
Snap off the tender ends of ½ pound asparagus. Cut ends diagonally into 2½-inch slices. Drop into rapidly boiling water for 2 to 3 minutes. Rinse immediately with cold water. Drain. Sprinkle with a pinch of salt, a smaller pinch of sugar, and a few drops of soy sauce. Serve cold. Serves 2.
—from "Madame Chiang's Mandarin Recipe Book"

Strawberry plants from Nourse Farms

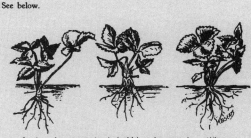

MANAGEMENT OF GROWING PLANTS

It is extremely important to set plants as early as the ground can be prepared in the spring. Timely irrigation may offset the disadvantage of late planting.

PLANTING

Set plants with roots straight down. Be sure planter shoes or hand tool penetrates deep enough to facilitate proper planting. CARE SHOULD BE TAKEN THAT PLANTS ARE SET WITH CROWNS LEVEL WITH TOP OF THE GROUND. Throughout the growing season avoid covering either old or new crowns with soil while hoeing, weeding or cultivating. Failure to observe these simple precautions accounts for a large per cent of the strawberry plant failures.

See below.

Strawberry plants set at various depths; left-hand plant set too deep; middle one too shallow; right hand just right.

PLANTING SYSTEMS

A standard system is to plant in rows 4 feet apart with 18 inches between plants. Variations include rows ranging from 3 - 5 feet apart with 18 to 24 inches between plants, depending on variety and conditions. Some commercial growers use a narrow matted row system with bed width 12 to 18 inches. By narrowing rows runners can be trained with cultivation equipment, replacing hand labor. Growers find this system lends itself to easy picking and good yields. Any system should (1) be uniform for ease of management, (2) prevent rows from growing together, and (3) prevent runner plants from setting too thickly, which results in smaller berries and lower yields.

To promote early runners and establishment of a vigorous and prolific bed, it is highly recommended that blossoms be pinched the first year.

A chatty page from the Rocky Hollow Herb Farm booklet

Cucumber and Yogurt Salad
Peel, seed, and thinly slice 1 large cucumber. Put in a colander, sprinkle with salt and leave for 1 hour to draw out the bitter juices. Rinse with cold water. Drain and pat dry on paper towels. Crush 2 garlic cloves to a paste with ½ teaspoon salt and mix into 1 cup yogurt with ¼ cup finely cut scallions and 2 tablespoons chopped fresh mint (or 1 tablespoon dried crushed mint). Season with ¼ teaspoon freshly ground black pepper. Add the cucumber and ½ teaspoon lemon juice. Serve immediately on lettuce leaves. Serves 4.

Duxelles
Chop 1 pound firm mushrooms by hand or in a food processor. Melt ¼ pound butter in a large heavy skillet. Add the mushrooms and 2 chopped shallots or scallions and cook down very slowly until all the liquid has evaporated from the mushrooms and they are a thick dark paste. Stir occasionally during the cooking time so the mushrooms cook evenly and do not stick. Add salt to taste. When cool, store in a small jar or plastic container in the refrigerator. Use this mushroom paste in scrambled eggs, omelets, stuffings, sauces, or to flavor a stew or soup. This also freezes well.

growing season and in quantities up to 5,000 plants. Moreover, Nourse supplies needed information on soil types, preparation, management, and fertility, as well as planting, irrigation, mulching, and chemical control of pests and diseases.

Mary Washington one-year asparagus roots, jumbo graded, are 25 for $4.25 up to $44 per thousand. Rhubarb is a MacDonald strain, popular throughout the Northeast (three plants for $2.75, six for $5, and twelve for $9.60).

ROCKY HOLLOW HERB FARM, INC. / Dept. CFC
Box 354, Sussex, NJ 07461

"The Folks at Rocky Hollow Invite You into Their Fantasy," 25¢, published annually, 16 pages, illustrated, two-color.

A charming booklet from the folks at Rocky Hollow Herb Farm, who grow herbs and import spices. From their aromatic harvest they create potpourri mixtures, herbal baths, and oils for the body and for cooking. One bottle of an edible essential oil, such as basil, cinnamon, fennel, parsley, peppermint or thyme, contains many times the equivalent of a fresh herb. Suggestions for using include jellies, sauces, pickles, salad dressings, vinegar, stews and chowders, fruit compotes. Most cost $3 for ⅛ fl. oz., but some are more expensive, $5.60 to $7.60. Rocky Hollow Herb Farm has special blends of herbal teas with enchanting names like Sweet Bettina (spearmint, alfalfa, chamomile, rosebuds) and Kittatinny (lemon verbena, rosebuds, chamomile, rosemary); culinary blends of bouquet garni, fines herbes, herb salad dressing (only oil and vinegar needed), steak, seafood, and poultry seasonings, Oriental seasoning (parsley, ginger, coriander, garlic, sea salt, celery seed, star anise, Szechuan pepper), Italian herb seasoning, Middle Eastern spice, and pickling spice. Other items include vanilla beans from Madagascar (one bean, 65¢), cinnamon sticks, and tarragon. They also offer some well-chosen books on herbs, such as the famous *Herbal* of John Gerard, an unabridged reproduction of the 1633 edition with 2,705 illustrations ($50) and two little books from the Brooklyn Botanical Gardens on natural dyeing with plants. A footnote to the current catalogue says that they will soon be able to send herb plants by mail.

SAHADI IMPORTING CO., INC. / Dept. CFC
187 Atlantic Avenue, Brooklyn, NY 11201

"The Silent Salesman," free, published biannually, 24 pages, illustrated, black and white.

If you are looking for something new to grow in the garden, consider seeds from Syria imported by Sahadi. Among the okra, cucumber, eggplant, and squash, you'll see strange names such as zather, mikty, mloukhiyeh, kareh, rashaad, and habak. Frankly, we have no idea what these are (though going by the illustration, one might be a white Syrian squash), but an Arabic-speaking friend or shopkeeper could probably tell you.

SANTA ROSA CHAMBER OF COMMERCE / Dept. CFC
637 First Street and Santa Rosa Avenue, Santa Rosa, CA 95404

"Sonoma County Farm Trails," free, published annually.

A map to send for and study if you are planning a trip to San Francisco for some food and wine prospecting in the Sonoma Valley, "Sonoma County Farm Trails" lists and locates on a large map of the county 168 farms, ranches, wineries, restaurants, and shops, with details about what they sell and when they are open. Among the things you can buy are fresh and dried fruits, eggs, herbs, fresh vegetables, smoked turkey, ham, bacon, fresh oysters, fresh poultry and rabbits, cider, apple juice, jams, honey, elephant and red garlic, nuts, meats, and pheasants (including pheasant eggs and chicks). You can purchase Sonoma Jack cheese at the Sonoma Cheese Factory, sourdough bread and French pastries at the Sonoma French Bakery, and taste your way through such wineries as Sebastiani, Hacienda, Valley of the Moon, Kenwood, Chateau St. Jean, Korbel, Pedroncelli, Souverain, Nervo, Alexander Valley, Simi, Trentadue, Dry Creek, and Geyser Peak. Many of the fruit farms have pick-your-own plans. The countryside is peaceful and beautiful, the county historic and great fun to explore, and there are lots of places to picnic.

S&H ORGANIC ACRES / Dept. CFC
   P.O. Box 27, Montgomery Creek, CA 96065

   Price list and order blank, free, published annually, 3 pages.

An excellent source for garlic, if you are bugged by the fact that all you can find in the supermarket are those moldy little heads in a sealed package. Owner F. F. Slewing emphasizes that his garlic is organically grown in the mountains and irrigated with spring water—or, if he buys a strain from another grower, he knows it is certified organic. His main crop is the giant elephant garlic, which averages ½ lb. or more for each head. While elephant garlic has the same flavor as regular garlic, the huge cloves can be used in the normal way or cooked as a vegetable. Elephant garlic is sold by the ½ lb. ($2.50) or 2 lbs. for $6, 5 lbs. for $11. Or you can buy the seed to start in flats and transplant to the garden in September, and they will produce the next year (50 seeds, $2). Mr. Slewing also sells the standard kind of California white garlic, good for planting or everyday use although it does not store well (½ lb. $2, 2 lbs. $5) and the Italian purple, found in Italian vegetable markets with a purply-red skin, at the same price. This has always been one of our favorites in garlics, for the flavor is true and intense. His German red garlic seeds (50 seeds for $1.50) should be grown for one year in flats before transplanting. Other members of the invaluable allium (or onion) family are shallots from French stock (one bulb will multiply and produce up to 30 bulbs; 30 bulbs are $2.25), and Egyptian onions, a perennial that grows small onions at the top of the plant rather than under the soil. Starter bulbs ($2 for 10 or $3.59 for 20) are shipped in a moist growing medium beginning the second week in June. If you want to grow your own horseradish, 10 root cuttings of the Maliner Kren variety, which produces large, hearty root crops, cost $3.25. Six root cuttings of comfrey, which can be used raw in salads, cooked like spinach or greens, or dried for herb teas, cost $2.50. Planting instructions are included with all orders.

SUNNYBROOK FARMS NURSERY / Dept. CFC
   9448 Mayfield Rd., Chesterland, OH 44026

   "Catalog of Herbs, Exotic House Plants, Geraniums, Cacti and Succulents, and Other Specialty Plants," 50¢ (refundable with purchase), published annually, 42 pages, black and white.

The first six pages of the catalogue are devoted to sweet herbs, culinary, medicinal, and fragrant, listed by their common and Latin names. There are 25 thymes, 13 mints, 10 oreganos, 12 alliums (onion family), and many unusual herbs such as bergamot and samphire. All of these are potted plants and range in price from 50¢ to $2.50 (most are 75¢ or $1, a very reasonable price). Minimum order is $7.50 and shipping charges are extra (wherever possible, they use UPS). For $1 you can get a plan for a Colonial Herb Garden and for $27.50 the plan plus plants and planting instructions. The Colonial Herb Garden, a selection of herbs of olden days for both novice and expert gardener, is guaranteed to supply years of enjoyment. Sunnybrook Nursery is open to visitors Tuesday through Saturday from 8:30 A.M. to 5:00 P.M., Sundays from 1:00 to 5 P.M., and conducted tours of the greenhouses are welcomed. Annuals and vegetable plants are available at the nursery after May 10.

TAYLOR'S HERB GARDEN INC. / Dept. CFC
   1535 Lone Oak Road, Vista, CA 92083

   "Herbs for Your Garden," 25¢, published annually, 6 pages.

An excellent source for annual, biennial, and perennial herb plants of all types, with a big selection of over 180 herbs and scented geraniums to choose from. The herbs are shipped in 2¾" plastic pots with well-established plants ready to be put into the garden or larger pots, each labeled with the common and botanical name, plant care, and brief description of their uses. Annuals are available from April through

★

Onions will peel more easily if dropped into boiling water for 3 or 4 minutes.

★

Save skins from baked potatoes, cut into strips, season, and bake in a hot oven until crispy. Serve as a cocktail snack.

★

Blueberry Griddle Cakes
Sift together 2 cups all-purpose flour, 1 tablespoon baking powder, 1 tablespoon sugar, and a pinch of salt. Cut in 2 tablespoons butter until pieces are the size of a pea. Mix in 1⅔ cups milk and 1 egg. Blend. The mixture should be lumpy. Add 1 cup blueberries and stir lightly. Drop by tablespoons on a hot greased griddle and cook as for any pancakes.
—*from "Blueberry Recipes"*

Gourds–all shapes and sizes

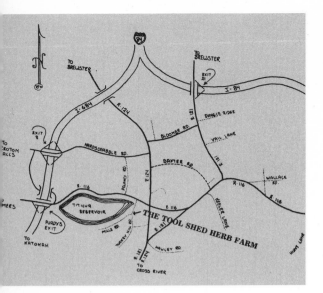

Chinese vegetable names, Tsang & Ma leaflet

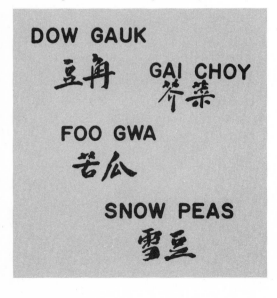

---

*

You can cook more than one vegetable in a single pot. Wrap each one in an individual aluminum foil package. Vegetables that need different cooking times are easily removed and drained.

*

October. There's a minimum order of 4 herbs for $5, 4 to 9 herbs are $1.25 each, and the price decreases to $1 each for 36 or more herbs, which includes tax, packing, and shipping. There's also a wholesale price list for case quantities of 36 plants at 40¢ each ($15.50 per case, which includes box and packing), sent FOB Vista by UPS or air, that would represent a considerable saving if you wanted a lot of plants. The catalogue is informative, listing and describing the plants and their uses. Some of the more interesting we noted are bee balm, burnet, cardoon, fenugreek, lemon grass, elephant and oriental garlic, poke (a wild plant with shoots that can be cooked and eaten like asparagus), French sorrel, and perilla, used in Japanese cooking. There are 14 different mints, 6 culinary sages, various rosemarys, and 18 scented geraniums.

THE TOOL SHED HERB FARM / Dept. CFC
Salem Center, Purdys Station, NY 10578

Catalogue, 25¢, updated as needed, 10 pages, black and white.

The nursery at the herb farm grows over 300 varieties of herb plants, but many of them are too limited in quantity to list in the catalogue, or too fragile to ship. Although they prefer a personal visit to the nursery to make your selection (a map is provided on the inside front cover of the catalogue), they do ship plants. Their catalogue lists more than 40 perennial "epicurean" herbs, from angelica to winter savory, plus many of the fragrant and decorative type. Among some of the more unusual culinary herbs you'll find lovage, which resembles celery in flavor and appearance although it is much stronger (a great herb for flavoring soups, stocks, or a bouquet garni), burnet, with its cucumber-flavored leaves that taste so good in salads, and "copper" fennel (foeniculum vulgare), the kind whose foliage and dried stalks add so much to fish cookery. Prices range from 85¢ to $1.50. There are also seeds for annual herbs such as basil, borage, coriander, and dill (35¢ a package). Orders, which must total $5 or more, are shipped April 25 through July 1, and you must add 25 percent for packaging and postage. On the back cover are directions for making herb vinegars and butters, drying and freezing herbs.

TSANG & MA INTERNATIONAL / Dept. CFC
P.O. Box 294, Belmont, CA 94002

"Chinese Vegetable Seeds," free, published seasonally, 5 pages and order form.

If you are into Chinese cooking and have a garden, this little brochure can save constant trips to the Chinese markets, for here you can obtain seeds for 16 different Chinese vegetables, with information on planting and harvesting and how to use them in Chinese cooking. Cultivation is very much the same as for other vegetables—grow leafy vegetables in cool weather, fruit-bearing types in hot weather. Seeds are available for bok choy (white cabbage), choy sum (flowering white cabbage), doan gwa (Chinese winter melon), foo gwa (bitter melon), gai lohn (Chinese kale), heung kunn (Chinese celery), mao gwa (a summer squash with a fuzzy light green skin), snow peas, cee gwa (a type of okra), dow gauk (asparagus bean, which grows two feet long), gai choy and dai gai choy (two types of mustard green), gow choy (Chinese chives, with awl-shaped leaves), hin choy (Chinese spinach), siew choy (Chinese or Napa cabbage), and, of course, coriander or Chinese parsley, called yuen sai. On each seed packet there is information on how to plant, grow and harvest, a description of the vegetable and its taste, how to prepare and cook it, and menu suggestions. Prices range from 65¢ each for three to five packets to 55¢ for 10 or more packets. Minimum order is $1.95 and prices include postage.

VITA GREEN FARMS / Dept. CFC
P.O. Box 878, Vista, CA 92083

Brochure and price lists, $1, published seasonally, 9 pages, black and white.

Vita Green Farms sells herb and vegetable seeds, herb plants, nuts and dried fruits, seeds, beans, and rice, and a wide range of fresh fruits and vegetables. The latter are shipped in various ways, parcel post for dried fruits and beans, by truck if the gross weight approximates 500 lbs., by UPS if the shipment is under 100 lbs. and the distance not too great, or by air freight if the produce is highly perishable. The rate is based on distance as well as weight, and they will furnish costs on request. The customer pays the freight on all orders. We can't list all their fruits and vegetables. Some are apples, globe artichokes, avocados, green and red cabbage, carrots, cherimoyas, dates, garlic, grapefruit, lemons, lettuce, mangoes, cantaloupe, casaba, Cranshaw and honeydew melons, nectarines, oranges, papaya, peaches, green peas, green peppers, potatoes, winter squash, zucchini, sunchokes (Jerusalem artichokes), sweet potatoes, Swiss chard, tangerines, tomatoes, and yams. Taking some prices at random, globe artichokes are 55¢ each or $6 a dozen, cherimoyas $1.50 a lb. or higher, Jerusalem artichokes 49¢ a lb. or $4.50 a 12-lb. flat, oranges (small, juicing type) 32¢ a lb. or $3.50 a 20-lb. flat, mangoes 98¢ a lb. or $7.95 a 12-lb. flat. The case price makes a considerable difference. The list of herbs, annual, biennial, and perennial (annuals are available April through October), is quite extensive, covering all the usual and many unusual kinds. There's a minimum order of 4 herbs for $5, 4 to 9 herbs $1.25 each, dropping to $1 each for 36 or more, with a special offer of 36 assorted herbs in 2" pots for $36 plus $2 postage. Vegetables, not seeded but sold by the pound for garden sowing, include Jerusalem artichokes, Spanish peanuts, shallots ($2.50 a lb.), red and white Irish and Idaho Russet potatoes, Jersey yellow sweet potatoes, and red yams—potatoes and yams 50¢ a lb. Vegetable and herb seeds are 50¢ a packet, or five packets for $2.

WELL-SWEEP HERB FARM / Dept. CFC
317 Mt. Bethel Rd., Port Murray, NJ 07865

Brochure, free, published annually, 3 pages.

A good and comprehensive selection of herb plants—221 varieties, perennial and annual, decorative, culinary and fragrant, plus 64 types of scented geraniums. The brochure lists 8 kinds of basil, 24 varieties of thyme, and such unusual things as the saffron crocus (95¢, August only) and buffalo grass (for 95¢ you can make your flavored vodka with this). There are a few vegetables such as Jerusalem artichokes (spring only, white or red root, $1) and leeks, plus strawberry plants (95¢). Prices range from 55¢ to $3 (for lemon grass), and the minimum plant order is $5. Among the additional plants listed is a caper bush ($1). Herb seeds are 50¢ a packet. Well-Sweep has some herb vinegars, and they sell dried flowers by the individual bunch (80¢) or in mixtures of bunches (small, $5.75; large, $8.25). These are not only strawflowers but things like tansy, teasel, coxcomb, fern fronds, artemisia, and pot marjoram. The largest selection of plants is available from May 10, and shipping of herbs extends from May 1 through October 1. You can visit Well-Sweep Herb Farm Monday through Saturday from 9:30 A.M. to 5:00 P.M., on Sunday by appointment only from 1:00 to 5:00 P.M. (call owners Louise and Cyrus Hyde at 201 852-5390 to arrange it). Follow the useful map on the brochure cover.

WHITE FLOWER FARM / Dept. CFC
Litchfield, CT 06759

"The Garden Book," published spring and fall, plus three issues of garden notes, $4 a year (or free to customers whose orders total $15 or more), 68 pages, illustrated, black and white.

An enchantingly written and illustrated catalogue, much more informative than most. Although flowers and flowering plants are the main business of White Flower Farm, they also sell herb plants and two varieties of *fraises des bois* (the French wood strawberries eaten with *crème fraîche* but seldom found on the market here). Fraises des Bois Charles V, planted in early spring, will produce its first berries in late June (the name commemorates King Charles V of France, who in 1360 was the first Frenchman to bring wild strawberries from the woods to the garden). Catherine the Great, a variety brought from Russia, has larger, softer, juicier fruit, a pointed berry, and a delicious flavor (stocks are limited). Plants are shipped in peat pots. Charles V costs $12 a dozen (or

Herb Butter
Have sweet (unsalted) butter at room temperature. Finely chop fresh herbs and blend with butter, in proportions of 2 tablespoons chopped herb to 6 tablespoons butter. Add a touch of salt. Freeze in a roll or long block, then cut into approximately 1 tablespoon pieces. Store in the freezer, individually wrapped in foil or plastic wrap (be sure to label different types of butter). Good butters to have on hand: parsley, dill, tarragon, basil, chive, rosemary, mint, marjoram, savory, parsley-garlic for snails. Use flavored butters on broiled steak, broiled fish, chops, vegetables.

The Garden Book
White Flower Farm
FALL 1976

$22.50 for two dozen); Catherine the Great, $18 a dozen. The herbs are perennials, and, except for bay and rosemary, all are hardy. There are chives, costmary, lemon balm, lovage, peppermint, oregano, pennyroyal, rosemary, sage, winter savory, spearmint, sweet cicely, French tarragon (the best kind), common thyme, and bay, the last-named a subtropical tree that, in cold climates, must be grown indoors in large tubs or pots. The plant, which costs $17.50, is 15 to 18 inches tall when shipped, with several stems, and can be trained into a ball or pyramid shape. Pick the leaves by cutting the stems, dry and stuff whole into a wide-mouthed jar to use for cooking. The herb plants vary in price but are mostly $2 each (chives are three for $3). An old-fashioned kitchen herb garden of three each of chives, costmary, marjoram, sage, sweet cicely, tarragon, and thyme, one each of spearmint, lovage, and winter savory (24 plants in all) costs $37.50. You can also order *The White-Flower-Farm Garden Book*, published by Alfred A. Knopf in 1971 and no longer to be found in bookstores. The book is $7.50 plus postage, and it will be autographed and inscribed (if you can think of a suitable inscription) by the author, Amos Pettingill, who also writes the notes. It's well worth spending $15 a year to get on White Flower Farm's list, for these catalogues make some of the best reading we have encountered in this field.

WILLIAMS-SONOMA / Dept. CFC
576 Sutter Street, San Francisco, CA 94102

"A Catalog for Cooks," $1, published biannually, plus "January Sale/New Kitchen Ideas," both 26 pages, illustrated, color.

If you don't live in shallot country and are ordering kitchen equipment from Williams-Sonoma, make a note that they also sell shallots (two 1-lb. sacks for $5). Shallots keep well in the refrigerator, lightly wrapped, or you can chop and freeze them.

YANKEE PEDDLER HERB FARM / Dept. CFC
Rt. 4, Box 76, Highway 36N, Brenham, TX 77833

"Catalog of Herbs with Old-Timey Uses," $1, published annually, 16 pages, black and white, no illustrations, with variety price lists of plants and seeds (variety list alone, 25 cents) and supplementary pages as new plants or seeds are available.

Despite its name, the Yankee Peddler Herb Farm (which operates both a nursery and an antique shop) is in Texas, on Highway 36, north of Brenham. Should you happen to be in the vicinity you can drop in any day, except holidays, for herbs that are in short supply and so not included in the catalogue. Yankee Peddler also offers a seed search service for unusual or hard-to-find herbs, provided a stamped, self-addressed envelope is included with the request.

Their catalogue is a fascinating and well-written little manual that gives the common and botanical names of everything from agrimony to yarrow, with information about height, whether they are annual, biennial, or perennial, and bits of lore about their "old-timey" and medicinal uses. You can acquire all kinds of interesting bits of knowledge. Did you know that watercress, an aquatic herb, doesn't need a flowing stream to grow? You can plant it in pots set in trays of water or outdoors in a sunken tub. There are hints in the booklet on growing herbs indoors and in the garden and on drying them. Among the comprehensive collection you'll find such unusual things as radichetta (asparagus or Italian chicory), lovage, garlic chives, and hyssop, also seeds of midget fruits and vegetables (4-inch ears of corn, 4-inch cantaloupes, 4-inch heads of cabbage), horseradish roots, elephant garlic, and things to give your everyday salads a special savor—sorrel, nasturtium leaves, burnet, Good King Henry. Forthcoming from Yankee Peddler is a book supplement offering a line of books on herbs and herb cookery and vegetable gardening.

Growing herbs
Herbs demand little from their gardener—a well-drained location, average garden soil, and sun. In extremely hot climates, semi-shade will do. Once established, herbs can usually fend for themselves, needing only to be cut back occasionally to induce new growth and form. Virtually disease- and insect-free themselves, herbs are famous for repelling insects from other plants in the garden.

Preserving herbs
A thorough washing with the garden hose the day before harvesting will eliminate wetting the foliage after it is cut. Herbs may be frozen, or dried in the oven or by hanging in loose bunches in a dry, shaded, airy place. Seed crops are encased in large paper bags before hanging to avoid seed being lost. When thoroughly dry, strip leaves (or seeds) from stems and store in tightly closed containers. Be sure to label.
—from "Catalog of Herbs with Old-Timey Uses" from the Yankee Peddler

See Appendix, page 239, for additional sources not included here.

CHAPTER EIGHT

FRUITS OF THE VINE

Cover illustration, Arbolyn catalogue

ARBOLYN WINEMAKING SUPPLIES / Dept. CFC
   P.O. Box 663, West Columbia, SC 29169

"Arbolyn Winemaking Supplies," free, published annually, 16 pages, illustrated, black and white.

Arbolyn sells most of the usual winemaking equipment, such as wine yeast, yeast nutrients and chemicals, measuring instruments like hydrometers and vinometers, acid test kit, glass jugs and carboys, fermentation locks, barrels and kegs, spigots, corks, crushers and presses, and all the bottling materials. They also have the Sun-Cal California wine grape concentrates—the generic red, white, and rosé types and varietal concentrates (Barbera, Chenin Blanc, French Colombard, Ruby Cabernet) that have no less than 80 percent and usually 100 percent of the grape variety. A quart of concentrate, which will make a gallon of wine, costs from $3.60 for the Chablis or white type to $5.50 for Ruby Cabernet and Barbera, both red varietals. Arbolyn has fruit wine concentrates (elderberry, black cherry, strawberry, blackberry, apple), dried elderberries and elderflowers, soft-drink extracts (root beer), and liqueur and cordial extracts, too. Their list of books includes *Home Winemaker's Handbook* by Walter Taylor and Richard Vine and *Technology of Winemaking* by Amerine, Berg, and Creuss, plus books on making your own winemaking equipment, brewing beer (they also sell brewing supplies), cheesemaking, sourdough cooking and baking, and a Moonshiner's Manual (don't take this one seriously).

BACCHANALIA / Dept. CFC
   273 Riverside Avenue, Westport, CT 06880

"Bacchanalia Wine Making Supplies," free, published annually, 16 pages, illustrated, black and white.

Whether you are a serious winemaker or just want to flirt with a few "weed wines" (the country name for the simple fruit, root, and flower

Pears Poached in Red Wine
Bring 2 cups red wine and 1 cup sugar to a boil in a saucepan. Reduce heat and simmer 10 minutes. Add 6 whole peeled and cored firm pears, 1 slice lemon rind, and 1 inch cinnamon stick. Poach fruit gently at a simmer, turning in liquid two or three times, until just pierceable with the point of a knife, but not mushy. Remove fruit to a bowl to cool. Cook the syrup down a little to concentrate it, remove lemon rind and cinnamon stick, and pour over pears. Chill until ready to serve. Serves 6.

Cover motif, Bacchanalia catalogue

★

Beer added to the batter for deep-fried foods or crêpes will make it lighter.

★

Never add wine to a dish at the last minute. It needs to cook in order to volatilize the alcohol.

★

Keep a bottle with red or white wine vinegar and add ends of bottles of red or white wine to it. Leave uncorked and the wine will turn to vinegar.

★

Shrimp in Beer

Combine in a saucepan 4 cups beer, 1 teaspoon salt, ½ teaspoon fennel seeds, 1 bay leaf, 4 allspice berries, and 1 thinly sliced onion. Bring to a boil, then reduce heat, and simmer 5 minutes. Add 2 pounds shrimp in the shell, bring liquid back to the boil and simmer for 3 to 5 minutes, according to size of the shrimp. Do not overcook. Remove from heat and cool shrimp in liquid. When cool enough to handle, shell shrimp, leaving on tail shell. Chill in liquid until ready to serve. Drain and serve as a cocktail appetizer, speared on toothpicks.

Old winery, The Compleat Winemaker catalogue

wines), Bacchanalia has most of the supplies you'll need. They have a fruit crusher ($57.50), racking tubes of plastic and glass, plastic tubing and valves, fermentation locks and corks, a 5-gallon glass carboy and plastic containers for fermentation, and the necessary yeasts, nutrients, fining agents and filters, testing equipment, and bottling supplies. The Brewer's Corner has malt, yeast, hops, chemicals, equipment, and the Bacchanalia brewer's kit for making your own ale ($11.50). Or you can start in a more modest way with grape concentrates, dried fruits and flowers, flavorings and extracts for making all kinds of things like ginger beer, root beer, liqueurs, and cordials. There's also a winemaker's sampler kit for beginners ($7.50).

The catalogue has a page of books for wine and beer makers, starting with beginner's books such as *Guidelines to Practical Winemaking* by J. H. Fessler ($4.50) and going on to books with wine recipes, on brewing, cider making, liqueurs, aperitifs, fortified wines—even the lore of still-building! They list two English magazines, *Home Beer and Winemaking* and *The Amateur Winemaker*. On orders of $15 and up you get a discount, starting at 5 percent and going up to 10 percent for orders over $25.

BROWNE VINTERS / Dept. CFC
375 Park Avenue, New York, NY 10022

"How to Fall in Love with French Wines," free, 22 pages, illustrated, color.

French wines, wine regions, and wine labels explained, simply, briefly, and carefully for those of us who enjoy wines but don't consider ourselves serious oenophiles.

This intelligently written little booklet explains how weather and soil conditions in the major wine-growing regions affect each wine's distinctive bouquet and taste; the meaning of certain words on the label; and how to pronounce the names of your favorite wines.

THE COMPLEAT WINEMAKER / Dept. CFC
1201 Main Street, St. Helena, CA 94674

"Winemaking Equipment and Supplies," free, published annually, 4 pages.

The Compleat Winemaker, located in the heart of California's Napa Valley, has had plenty of experience selling equipment and materials to local grape growers and to those really serious about home winemaking, so theirs is one of the most professional and ungimmicky of wine-supply catalogues.

They list basket presses with a capacity of 120 to 2,000 lbs. ($180 to $650), made by the Italian company Sipi, and the Sipi stemmer-crusher, hand-operated but easily converted to motor drive ($515), which crushes about 1.5 tons an hour. They have every type of necessary equipment such as filling machines (from $110 for a two-spout filler to $250 for a six-spout filler), corking machines and labeling machines, even coopering tools for those who want to attempt making their own barrels.

Vitis vinifera grapes, including two leading varieties, Chardonnay and Cabernet Sauvignon, and Zinfandel can be ordered flown from Napa to you—prices on request. Should any of your wine be less than successful, Compleat Winemaker sells unpasteurized wine vinegars, which can be used as starters to convert it into your own house brand of vinegar.

Their selection of books on wines and winemaking is above average. For the beginner, there is a paperback, *Winemaking at Home*, by Amerine and Marsh ($2) and for the professional, *Technology of Winemaking*, by Amerine, Berg, and Cruess, the most complete textbook available ($29). You know it is good, because the authors taught at the University of California's Department of Viticulture and Enology at Davis, California's prestigious wine school. There is also Hugh Johnson's complete and detailed *World Atlas of Wines*.

CUMBERLAND GENERAL STORE / Dept. CFC
Rte. 3, Crossville, TN 38555

"The Wish & Want Book," $3, published seasonally, 272 pages, illustrated, black and white.

Wine and beer making is part of country living, so naturally this general-store catalogue has some of the basic equipment, such as cider or wine presses, one a combination press and grinder ($183.95), a fruit crusher ($47.95), oak kegs for wine or beer, corks, caps and a bottle-capping machine, 5-gallon glass carboys for wine fermenting, and beer hydrometer for testing temperatures.

FOOD AND WINES FROM FRANCE, INC. / Dept. CFC
P.O. Box 940, Radio City Station, New York, NY 10019

"French Wines Correspondence Course," free, 48 pages, illustrated, black and white.

A well-written lucid booklet that serves as an introduction to the wines of France, with general information and rules about how wine is made and how to buy, store, serve, and taste it. Part 1 describes the different wine areas of France (the Loire, Bordeaux, the Rhône, Burgundy, Alsace and Champagne, with maps) and the characteristics of the wines of each region, with a brief mention of the rosé wines of France and those that are labeled V.D.Q.S. rather than *appellation contrôlée*. Part 2 covers the role of shippers and importers, explains the terms on wine labels, goes into the different shapes of wineglasses and bottles, and discusses storage, serving, vintages, and tasting, ending with a glossary of common wine terms such as *cru* (a vineyard or growth), *négociant* (a wine shipper), and *propriétaire* (a vineyard owner).

GALAXY PRODUCTS, INC. / Dept. CFC
P.O. Box 215, Sonoma, CA 95476

"Sonoma Cheese Factory Gift Catalog," free, published annually, 16 pages, illustrated, color.

The Sonoma Cheese Factory is located in Sonoma Valley wine country, and in addition to cheese they will ship grape vines by mail between January 15 and March 1 (shipments cannot be made to Arizona or New Mexico). The varieties they offer are Zinfandel, which produces a beautifully fruity wine, Cabernet Sauvignon and Pinot Chardonnay, the top red Bordeaux and white Burgundy varieties, and Thompson seedless (although this is used for wine in certain regions of California, it's frankly better grown for eating or to be dried as a raisin). A word of caution, though: These vines cannot take cold-climate winter temperatures, so be sure your state has the proper climatic conditions. For California residents only, the Sonoma Cheese Factory has gift boxes of cheese, salami, crackers, and wines from Sebastiani and Buena Vista ($12.95 to $25.95) and of Sebastiani wines, and they are preparing a series of wine supplements to their catalogue, which will have special case offerings and good buys in wine accessories. This will be sent with California orders, or you may request it. They also sell a California Wineries Calendar, with line drawings and text that highlight a different winery each month ($3.95).

GARDEN WAY / Dept. CFC
47 Maple Street, P.O. Box 944, Burlington, VT 05401

"Garden Way Country Kitchen Catalog," free, published seasonally, 16 pages, illustrated, color.

While Garden Way isn't really in the winemaking equipment business, they do have a fruit press grinder system that will press 3 gallons of cider in 25 minutes, or press grapes for wine, available either complete or in an easy-to-build kit. Also, for cider or root beer a cast-iron bottle capper that fits on the crown caps, $14.50 for the capper, $1.25 for a box of 144 caps.

Equipment from "The Wish & Want Book"

White Wine Court Bouillon

Combine in a large pot 4 cups dry white wine, 8 cups water, 2 medium onions, 2 sliced carrots, a rib of celery, 3 or 4 parsley sprigs, 1 teaspoon dried thyme, 1 bay leaf, 1 crushed garlic clove, 12 peppercorns, 2 tablespoons salt, and 2 slices lemon. For a more flavorful court bouillon, add 1½ pounds fish heads and bones, if available. Bring to a full rolling boil, skim off the scum, reduce heat, and simmer 45 minutes. Remove fish heads and bones, if used, and use court bouillon to poach whole fish. Liquid may be strained after use, frozen and reused.

Sangria

Put in a large glass pitcher the peeled rind of 1 lemon and 1 orange, 1 orange, sliced, 1 tablespoon lemon juice, and ¼ cup simple syrup (sugar and water boiled together until just dissolved, in the proportions of 3 parts sugar to 1 part water; this can be made in quantity, bottled, and used to sweeten drinks). Add 1 bottle chilled dry red wine and enough ice cubes to keep the mixture chilled. Add chilled club soda to taste, depending on how diluted you wish the wine to be.

May Wine

Mix ¼ cup woodruff, ¼ cup brandy, and ¼ cup confectioners' sugar. Cover and let stand overnight. Strain, pressing out all liquid. Discard herb. Add extract to 1 bottle chilled white wine. Serve chilled with fresh strawberries.

—*from Aphrodisia Catalogue*

Beer Batter for Deep-Fried Foods

Mix together in a bowl ¾ cup sifted flour, 2 egg yolks, 1 teaspoon salt, and 2 tablespoons vegetable oil; then gradually stir in ¾ cup room-temperature beer. Stir well with a whisk or beat with a hand mixer or rotary beater until smooth and free of lumps. (Or whirl all the ingredients in a blender.) Cover bowl with plastic wrap and leave 1 hour before using. When ready to use, stir the batter and gently fold in 2 stiffly beaten egg whites. Dip fish filets, shrimp, or vegetables into batter and deep-fry.

Apples for the cider press, Hunger Mountain Crafts brochure

GURNEY SEED AND NURSERY CO. / Dept. CFC
2nd and Capitol Streets, Yankton, SD 57078

"Gurney Garden Seed and Nursery Catalog," free, published annually, 76 pages, color.

A limited amount of winemaking and brewing supplies is included in the Gurney catalogue. There's the very simple kit for making 2 gallons of fruit, berry, or vegetable wines, $5.98; hydrometer, bottle cappers and corkers, caps and corks, wine and beer yeasts, an air lock and rubber adapter ($1.59) that fits onto the 6-gallon collapsible plastic fermenting vessel ($3.95) and, to start you off, *First Steps in Winemaking* ($1.95).

HAMMACHER SCHLEMMER / Dept. CFC
147 East 57th Street, New York, NY 10022

Catalogue, free, published seasonally, 64 pages, illustrated, black and white.

Whether you make or buy your wine, Hammacher's has all the paraphernalia for storing and serving. Simple arched black-iron wine racks, 16" wide, 12" deep and 3 or 6 feet high (the smaller takes 39 bottles; the larger, 67) cost about $100. The "wine jail house" keeps up to 300 bottles visible but safely under lock and key. The ultimate in wine storage is a super-duper temperature-controlled wine vault that plugs into a 110-volt outlet and takes from 50 to 300 bottles, with prices starting at $1,500, according to size and capacity. To look like a pro, you can buy a silver-plate replica of the traditional wine taster's cup on a 20" neck chain, the kind sommeliers sport, or recork your champagne with the useful little gadget you see in French bars where bubbly is sold by the glass (around $10). A neat little set called "uncorkers three" has an automatic corkscrew, a cork easer, the kind used by winery owners that grips the sides of the cork and is good for old crumbly corks and for recorking, and a cork retriever for getting out corks that slide down into the bottles.

HERTER'S, INC. / Dept. CFC
R.R. 2, Mitchell, SD 57301

"Herter's Sportsman's Catalog," $1 (refundable with $10 purchase), published annually, 352 pages, illustrated, color and black and white.

This catalogue has some supplies for making beer and wine, such as an all-steel hand bar-type fruit press (around $33), Minnesota white oak barrels (5-gallon size, around $19), bottle corks and bottle cappers, metal-foil capsules for covering bottle necks, compressed dried hops, malt and beer yeast, wine yeast, chemicals, saccharometers, and George Herter's own book, *How to Make the Finest Wines at Home* (mostly folk wines), 272 pages, $1.47 in paper, $2.49 in cloth.

HUNGER MOUNTAIN CRAFTS / Dept. CFC
R.F.D. 2 A, Worcester, VT 05682

Brochure and mail-order envelope, free, 1 page, illustrated.

Hunger Mountain Crafts is a workshop of three builders who design fruit presses that they produce by hand. The standard press measures 2' x 4' and weighs 145 lbs. Made of solid Vermont hardwood, it has a self-feeding grinder with a full bushel capacity ($185).

The portable press has a 1/3 bushel capacity, is 16" x 32", and weighs 50 lbs. ($112.50). Hunger Mountain Crafts will also build to order an inexpensive motor-operated commercial press.

The demand outstrips their present production capacity, so they urge you to order early. *The American Cider Book* is included with the press.

ITALIAN TRADE COMMISSIONER/ WINE DEPARTMENT
Dept. CFC
1 World Trade Center, Suite 2057, New York, NY 10048

Literature on Italian wines, free.

Because Italian wines are usually less well publicized and written about than, say, French or American, they are also more unfamiliar to most people who seldom venture beyond the names they know—Chianti, Verdicchio, Soave. This is a pity, for there are many extremely fine wines made in Italy today, which you can learn about by reading the free booklets issued by the Italian Trade Commission. The *Italian Wine Guide* gives the background of and facts about the wines of Italy, goes into the importance of the DOC, or *Denominazione de Origine Controllata*, the Italian equivalent of France's *appellation contrôlée*, which is reserved for wines of "particular reputation and worth," and then describes each of the regions and the wines made there, giving both the grape and the wine names and a little map of the area. There is a chart with a breakdown of the different types of white, red, rosé, dessert, and sparkling wines, with suggested varieties, then a pronunciation guide and quiz. Another booklet, *Denominazione*, has a region-by-region listing of all officially recognized DOC wines. A third booklet is devoted to the wines of one region, Sicily. Called *Wines of Sicily*, it has quite a bit of history, a review of the types of wine made there, some information about Marsala, and a wine taster's vocabulary. A separate map of the island indicates where the wine areas are. You can absorb a great deal of useful information from these clearly written booklets.

LEKVAR-BY-THE-BARREL / Dept. CFC
1577 First Avenue, New York, NY 10028

"A Continental Bazaar," free, published annually, 56 pages, illustrated, black and white.

A few of the items you need for making wine and beer are included in this catalogue, such as an alcohol thermometer, fermentation lock, sulphur strips for cleaning wood barrels (39¢ each), wooden bungs with taps, and for beer, hop-flavored malt extract ($2.75 a can), bottle caps, and a capping machine.

Strawberries in Red Wine
Put whole fresh strawberries in a bowl, sugar lightly, and add dry red wine to cover. Marinate for 1 hour before serving chilled as a dessert.

LOUISIANA-PACIFIC CORP. / Dept. CFC
1300 S.W. Fifth Avenue, Portland, OR 97201

"Redwood Wine Rack Construction Plans," 50¢, 11 pages, line drawings.

This instruction booklet is for the oenophile who is handy with a hammer and has the patience to build a wine storage compartment.

Louisiana-Pacific, a lumber company, suggests redwood because of its traditional role in winemaking, its attractiveness, and the ease with which it can be worked. They offer tips on placement of the rack: in a cool spot (50°–70°F), away from strong light, especially sunlight, and vibrations.

The rack plans run from simple to complicated, small to large, and range in styles from plain to chic. L-P outlines what materials to use, how much wood and hardware you'll need, and how to finish (or leave unfinished) your redwood rack: lacquer, varnish, clear wax, paint, or stain. The instructions are simple to follow and clearly written. L-P will gladly give you an idea of cost if you write.

MONTGOMERY WARD / Dept. CFC
Montgomery Ward Plaza, Chicago, IL 60681

General catalogues, Spring/Summer and Fall/Winter, plus special catalogues throughout the year. To get on the catalogue list you must make a purchase either at the catalogue counter of a Ward store or from a borrowed catalogue. To stay on the list you have to make at least two sizable purchases every six months.

You know home winemaking has arrived when you see a wine press in Ward's catalogue. Their fruit (or wine or cider) press is made of red

Do-it-yourself wine rack, from Louisiana-Pacific

Lowther fruit press, from Natural Technology Design

★

Deglaze a hot cooking pan with wine to lift the brown particles and make a quick sauce. Wine will evaporate fast and become thick. If desired, stir a little heavy cream, sour cream, or yogurt into the pan juices (if adding sour cream or yogurt, remove pan from heat to prevent curdling).

★

Corkscrews from Presque Isle Wine Cellars

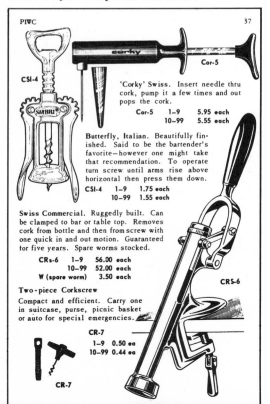

oak, with cast-iron screw and handle, and it has a crushing capacity of 60 lbs., all for a very reasonable $39.95. A companion piece, a Michigan grape crusher ($74.95), is also made of red oak with an 18½" x 18" hopper and double cast-aluminum rollers. It has a 30-lb. capacity and is for grapes only.

NATURAL TECHNOLOGY DESIGN / Dept. CFC
Wolcott, VT 05680

"Natural Technology Design," free, 1 page, illustrated, black and white.

The Lowther fruit press, a complete home fruit grinder and wine or cider press in one unit, comes to you direct from the original designer and manufacturer at the lowest possible price. The press is made of solid Vermont maple with stainless-steel grinder teeth. There are two models. The smaller, measuring approximately 16" x 32", is $88; the larger, over 2' x 4', is $160, and they are shipped FOB by truck freight or UPS, according to size. Mr. Lowther states that he'll soon have a catalogue ready listing additional products.

NICHOLS GARDEN NURSERY / Dept. CFC
1190 North Pacific Highway, Albany, OR 97321

"Nichols Herb and Rare Seeds," free, published seasonally, 60 pages, illustrated, black and white.

Home-brewing and winemaking aids are on the last two pages of the Nichols catalogue. You won't find fruit presses or stemmers and crushers, but you can get wine yeast, yeast nutrient, clarifiers and stabilizers, a three-scale hydrometer, corks, labels, fermentation locks and plastic cubitainers with fermentation lock that may be used like glass carboys for secondary fermentation of wine (2½-gallon size, $2.95). For beermaking there's a beer tester (for alcoholic content), Oregon dried hops, beer yeast, brewing salts, dried malt syrup, and all the other necessities. If you want to start out in a modest way, an elderberry wine kit contains dried elderberries from Portugal, wine yeast, winemaking additives, and instructions for making 1 gallon of wine ($2.25). The list of books is small but selective, including the very simple popular little books by Bravery: *Successful Winemaking* (95¢), *Home Brewing without Failures* (95¢), and *First Steps in Winemaking* by J. Berry ($1.35).

PRESQUE ISLE WINE CELLARS / Dept. CFC
9440 Buffalo Road, North East, PA 16428

"Everything for the Home Winemaker," free, published biennially, 48 pages, illustrated, black and white.

The title is justified by this very professional catalogue. Presque Isle Wine Cellars makes wine as well as selling supplies, and the owners have included everything the experienced winemaker needs but no gadgetry or frills. The copy is clear, detailed, and explanatory. If you are within driving distance of the winery, you can buy vinifera and French-American hybrid grapes or the pressed grape juice (a list is mailed in late August giving varieties, prices, and dates available), but as they don't ship grapes and cannot ship grape juice by common carrier, mail order is confined to Vitis vinifera concentrates from California, a white or Chablis-type (primarily Sultanina), Chenin Blanc, French Colombard, a red or Burgundy type (primarily Carignane), Barbera, Ruby Cabernet, and a pink, or vin rosé, which is a blend of the red and white concentrates. You can buy from this catalogue all the requisite chemicals, yeasts, carboys and bottles, corks and closures, lead or aluminum capsules to put over the corks, fermentation locks, funnels, hose and tubing, siphons and bottle fillers, barrels, various instruments such as hydrometers and vinometers, filters, labels, presses and crushers, including a big Milano crusher-stemmer for around $670 that would be able to handle the crush of a small winery or a group of amateur winemakers (advance orders are required) and professional laboratory apparatus, such as kits for testing for residual sugar and for acid levels. The catalogue has a very good list of books on winemaking and viticulture, such as Philip M. Wagner's *American Wines and Winemaking* and *Winegrower's Guide, Technology of Winemaking*, the definitive text on winemaking by Amerine, Berg, and Cruess, Jagendorf's *Folk Wines, Cordials and Brandies*, Hugh Johnson's *World Atlas of Wines*, and *The Wines of America* by Leon Adams, plus the full line of Sunset Magazine cookbooks and some on herbs, organic gardening, vegetable gardening. An added bonus is a selection of reasonably priced wineglasses and corkscrews, including the easy-to-use two-prong type preferred by many winemakers ($1 each). If you can get to Presque Isle Wine Cellars, you can meet owners Doug and Marlene Moorhead and buy wine from the bonded winery (they make a Chardonnay, Riesling, Cabernet Sauvignon, and Gamay, among others). A new service allows you to taste wines in spring and buy them in bulk, by the cask, or have them bottled, with special labels.

PUBLIVIN PUBLISHING CO. / Dept. CFC
P.O. Box 6063, Dallas, TX 75222

No price list information supplied.

Publivin offers books on the wines of Europe (Germany, Burgundy, Bordeaux) and *Initiation into the Art of Wine Tasting* at prices ranging from $5.95 for soft-cover books to $24.95 for *The Great Wine Chateaux of Bordeaux* by Philip Seldon, which has over 400 color plates. Add $1.50 per book for handling. They also sell a collection of 8 wine prints from the 15th, 16th, and 17th centuries, printed on parchment, at $4.95 each or $25 the set, that would make an attractive decoration for a cellar or kitchen.

SEMPLEX OF U.S.A. / Dept. CFC
P.O. Box 12276, Minneapolis, MN 55412

"A Catalog of Supplies for the Amateur Winemaker," free, published bimonthly, 21 pages, illustrated, black and white.

Semplex sells grape and fruit juice concentrates and a winemaking kit for making two gallons of wine from the concentrates ($11.95 ppd.). They also have different wine yeasts (including one for sherry yeast), nutrient tablets, clarifiers and filters, fermentation locks, wine corks, hand-corking machines, labels, hydrometers, vinometers, siphons, sulphur strips to sterilize the casks, fruit crushers and presses, a Mustix acid test strip for acidity, and wine bottles in classic shapes. Should you be interested in wine drinking more than winemaking, you might look at their stained wood bottle racks for your cellar (48-bottle size, $29.95 ppd.) or the cork-extracting claws for fishing out corks that drop inside the bottle ($1 ppd.). Semplex has a list of American and British books on amateur winemaking, and they even give you a couple of recipes for rhubarb or flower wine, gratis.

VINTAGE HOUSE, INC. / Dept. CFC
1254 Montgomery Avenue, San Bruno, CA 94066

"Vintage House Wine Cellars," free, published annually, 5 pages, illustrated, color.

The "Wine Time Machine" means you can have a wine cellar even if you live in an apartment. Housed in a handsome, predominantly teak cabinet, this Wine Time Machine provides wine storage at a consistent 55°F. 24 hours a day. Automatic controls give your wines the cool, dark, and quiet environment they require to "grow old gracefully." The cost is $1,000 (plus tax for California residents) and shipping.

See Appendix, page 239, for additional sources not included here.

Welsh Rarebit or Rabbit

Make this in the top of a double boiler with water underneath or in the top of a chafing dish over water. Bring the water to a boil, then reduce heat until water is just bubbling. Melt 2 tablespoons butter in the pan over the water and gradually add 1 pound (4 cups) shredded sharp cheddar cheese, stirring continually with a wooden spoon until melted. Mix in ½ teaspoon dry mustard, ½ teaspoon salt, a dash or two of Tabasco, and 1 teaspoon Worcestershire sauce. Beat 2 egg yolks with ½ cup ale or beer and gradually mix into the cheese, stirring all the while. Don't let it get too hot or boil, or the eggs will curdle and the cheese will become stringy. Stir until thickened, creamy, and smooth. Taste for seasoning. Serve on toast or toasted English muffins. Serves 4 to 6.

Winemaking kit and books from Semplex of U.S.A.

Wine Time Machine storage cabinet, from Vintage House, Inc.

Barths
BETTER NUTRITION IN ALL NATURAL FOODS

Long Island has more 18th century windmills than any other section of America. This one was built in 1800 and is located in the village of Water Mill, Long Island.

CHAPTER NINE

NATURAL FOODS AND GRAINS

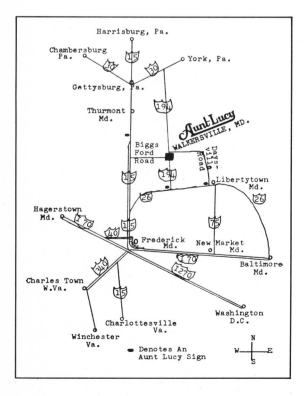

AUNT LUCY HAMS / Dept. CFC
3 W. Frederick Street, Box 126, Walkersville, MD 21793

"Country Foods by Aunt Lucy," 8-page leaflet, with order blank, free, mailed five times a year.

Aunt Lucy wants you to relish her hams, sausages, bacon, and country puddin' with the right things—buckwheat cakes, corn meal pancakes, corn meal mush, and spoon bread. Aunt Lucy yellow or white corn meal comes in 2-lb. or 5-lb. bags for 90¢ and $2, with recipes for griddle cakes and mush. Old-fashioned buckwheat flour (not a mix) in 2-lb. or 5-lb. bags, with recipes for old-fashioned and quick buckwheat cakes, costs $1.25 and $2.75.

BARTH'S OF LONG ISLAND / Dept. CFC
Valley Stream, NY 11582

Catalogue, free, published seasonally, 112 pages, with supplements, illustrated, black and white.

Barth's sells a variety of natural foods in addition to their big list of vitamins and food supplements. Among them are nuts, dried fruits, seeds, honey, unsweetened coconut meal ($1.50 a 10-oz. can), English Maldon unrefined sea salt, Irish oatmeal, Pennsylvania Dutch apple butter, and various preserves—raspberry, strawberry, black cherry, wild blueberry, red and black currant, and rose hips (around $1.35 a 12-oz. jar). For those looking for chocolate substitutes there are chocolates and bars of carob (or St. John's bread), rich in protein and natural sugar with a delicious chocolate-like flavor. The old-fashioned, all-natural peanut butter they sell comes in four styles, creamy-smooth, crunchy-nugget, with sea salt or with wheat germ (any one, $1.29 a 12-oz. can), and in case you would rather make your own, there's a peanut mix (two grades of specially selected varieties) and the Salton Peanut Butter Machine.

BETTER FOODS FOUNDATION, INC. / Dept. CFC
300 North Washington Street, Greencastle, PA 17225

Brochure, free, 8 pages, black and white.

Better Foods is in the Mennonite country of Pennsylvania, long a stronghold of the natural-foods movement (which is, after all, the way most country people are accustomed to eating), and their flour mill is in Reid, Maryland. They have an unbleached white pastry and cake flour made from soft wheat, milled with the germ in (65¢ for 2 lbs.), an all-purpose blend of soft and hard wheat, also unbleached, a 100 percent hard wheat whole-wheat flour, 100 percent rye flour (fine), pure buckwheat flour, a self-rising buckwheat flour that is good for buckwheat cakes, stone-ground yellow cornmeal, a self-rising pancake flour, and various others, such as gluten flour and soy flour. Also raw and toasted wheat germ, raw wheat bran, rolled and steel-cut oats and other cereals, a wide variety of grains and seeds, and some unsulphured dried fruits and raw nuts. Naturally, they stock herb teas, raw sugar, organically grown canned vegetables, cold-pressed oils, natural peanut butter, and some juicers, blenders, and mills, chiefly the Miracle Exclusives line. You'll find here the Cellu Dietetic water-packed canned fruits and vegetables, no salt added, instant coffee substitutes, and salt-free mayonnaise.

THE BIRKETT MILLS / Dept. CFC
P.O. Box 440-A, Penn Yan, NY 14527

Price list and order form, free.

The Birkett Mills sells various stone-ground flours, such as unbleached pastry flour (85¢ for a 5-lb. sack), 100 percent whole wheat or rye flour, wheat germ (45¢ for a 1-lb. bag, freshly milled as ordered), whole-wheat cereal, and various forms of buckwheat—flour (90¢ for a 2½-lb. sack), instant buckwheat for pancakes, brown buckwheat groats (or kasha), whole white buckwheat groats, and creamy kernels. The prices are certainly reasonable, and absolutely nothing is added to the flour or groat products in the milling, which is reassuring. The mill, incidentally, was established at Penn Yan, in New York's Finger Lakes, in 1797.

CASA MONEO / Dept. CFC
210 West 14th Street, New York, NY 10011

"Mexican Food–Comida Mexicana," free, 8 pages, published annually, also price lists of South American, Cuban, and Portuguese foods.

A good source for flours and grains used in Latin American cooking. Corn hominy, El Popular brand, is 42¢ for 29 oz.; masa de harina, the corn meal used for tortillas, $1.30 a 5-lb. package; and you can also buy the dried corn husks for tamales ($1.85 a lb.). There's a tapioca starch from Colombia and the Brazilian farinha de mandioca (manioc flour) at 50¢ a lb.

CHICO-SAN, INC. / Dept. CFC
1144 West 1st Street, Chico, CA 95926

"Chico-San, Inc. Products–a catalog of unique foods," free, published annually, 26 pages, black and white.

Since 1960, Chico-San has been selling natural foods with an Oriental flavor. Their main products are made from rice organically grown in the Sacramento Valley (and if you don't think that is unusual, read their account of the pesticides used in water and on crops by commercial growers), and those that are imported are all made without chemical additives or preservatives. They sell natural short-grain brown rice and sweet glutinous brown rice (67¢ a lb.); brown rice flour, and rice cream (a finely ground cereal or starch, $1.27 a lb.); and various other rice products such as rice cakes made with brown rice and brown sesame seed, salted or unsalted; Yinnie's grain syrup, a natural sweetener made from rice and barley, rich in maltose, with no added sugar ($11.56 a gallon or $1.27 for the smallest size); Yinnie's grain candy, made from rice and barley (no sugar) and a rice cake san-wich (rice cakes sandwiched with sesame seeds and the rice syrup (35¢ each or 24 to a case). Among their other offerings are millet cakes and buckwheat cakes, tamari soy sauce, which is aged naturally for two years ($1.38 for the 12-oz. size), sesame butter, cold-pressed sesame oil and a dark sesame oil pressed from roasted seeds, sesame salt and unrefined sea salt, tekka (a condiment for use on rice made from burdock root, lotus root, carrot, ginger, iriko, miso and sesame oil), miso (soybean paste),

Stone-ground flours and grains do not keep as well as commercial flours. Store in a cool place or the refrigerator and use quickly.

★

When cooking cornmeal, mix with cold water before adding boiling water and it will not lump. To prevent sticking, cook in the top of a double boiler over hot water.

★

Kasha-Apple Stuffing
Combine 1 egg, beaten, 1 cup medium kasha (buckwheat groats), and 1½ teaspoons salt. In a medium size skillet sauté 1 large onion, chopped, in ¼ cup butter for 2 minutes. Stir in the groats mixture and 2 cups water and bring to a boil. Cook covered over low heat for 5 minutes. Mix in 3 cups peeled, cored, and chopped tart apple, 1 cup chopped celery, and a few grinds of pepper. Toss lightly to mix well. Use as stuffing for duck, turkey, or chicken.
—from "Wolff's Kasha Cookbook"

and a pure, naturally produced malt vinegar made by a small producer in Japan ($1.30 for 5 oz.). There are some of the natural foods used in Japanese cooking, such as the dried sea plants (kombu, wakame, nori), kuzu (a wild arrowroot starch), salt plums, black soybeans, and azuki beans. The explanations of what the foods are and how to use them are very helpful.

CULPEPER LTD. / Dept. CFC
Hadstock Road, Linton, Cambridge, England

General price list and medicinal herb list, $1, published seasonally.

Culpeper, the famous English herbalists, were among the earliest to get onto the health-food kick. Their products have always been natural; that is their pride. They have a wide selection of herbs and spices for cooking, ranging in price from around 20¢ to 90¢ for a ½ gram of saffron, dried garlic slices, green ginger canned in brine, *tisanes*, an exclusive broken orange pekoe tea (Indian Ocean, a Culpeper exclusive) that is unsprayed with chemical pesticides, natural brown sugar lumps (about 59¢ a lb.), and candies made from raw sugar and natural ingredients. Their list of medicinal herbs and herbal remedies is extensive, and they also have a very complete line of their own creams and ointments, a herbal gargle, and all kinds of natural cosmetics, hair and bath preparations, potpourris, pomanders, and herb-scented sachets. There's even a natural fabric cleanser, dried saponaria, which was used in Roman times. The names of some of these preparations are enchantment enough: herb-gold pine needle milk for the bath, green lettuce-scented soap, elderflower cleansing cream, milk of lilies or mountain water lotion, miel of mignonette hand lotion—they sound almost edible! If you don't know the Culpeper products, it is time you made their acquaintance. For overseas surface mail shipments, add 25 percent of the value of the goods, with a minimum of around $4. Airmail brings the cost up to 50 percent of the goods, with an $8 minimum.

DEER VALLEY FARM / Dept. CFC
R.D. 1, Guilford, NY 13780

Price list, free, published annually, 20 pages, black and white.

Deer Valley Farm has been devoted to organic farming since 1947, and they produce and process many of the foods they sell, including the breads, cookies, and cakes made in their bakery. They have a big list of whole-grain breads, which sell from 73¢ a loaf, cakes (from $1.45 to $2.25), cookies and buns, also whole-grain, with no salt. They also sell the Red Star dry yeast and Rumford baking powder used in their own bakery, cheddar, Swiss, and Muenster cheese from New York State and Wisconsin, some made with raw milk, unsulphured dried fruits (and, from November to May, fresh apples, lemons, oranges and grapefruit), honeys, nut butters, jams and spreads. Deer Valley Farm carries many of the pickles and organically grown canned vegetables and fruits made by Walnut Acres, the Walnut Acres' soups and main dishes, the Hain's line of cold-pressed oils, French dressing and mayonnaise, blackstrap and unsulphured molasses, malt syrup (excellent for baking), whole-wheat and artichoke pasta, all kinds of herbs and spices, herb teas, grains and seeds, and various cereals and meals. You'll find quite a lot of flours, including whole-wheat bread flour and pastry flour (38¢ a lb.) and triticale flour, a cross of wheat and rye, high in protein (35¢ a lb.). A separate list of poultry, beef, and pork products is available on request.

DUTCH SCHOOL / Dept. CFC
22 North 7th Street, Akron, PA 17501

Price list, free, mailed on request, updated constantly.

The natural foods on the price list are flours from organically raised grain, stone-ground fresh for each order, raw nuts, seeds and beans, and a few miscellaneous items such as tapioca pearls, coconut shreds (unsweetened), and fresh ground sunflower meal. The flours, whole-wheat, whole-rye, and whole-rice, range in price from 42¢ to 61¢ a lb., 69¢ for 2 lbs. of yellow cornmeal (also available in a 5-lb. size). Flours

---

★

When tossing or stirring cooked rice, use forks rather than a spoon to avoid crushing the grains.

★

When cooking pasta, put a tablespoon of oil in the water to prevent the pieces sticking together.

★

Sift dry ingredients which tend to lump (cornstarch, potato starch, baking powder, confectioners' sugar) before measuring for cakes.

★

are also sold in 2-lb. and 5-lb. quantities. Tapioca pearls are 87¢ a lb.; coconut shreds, 99¢ a lb.; and sunflower meal, $1.25 a lb. The raw nuts (almonds, pecans, blanched peanuts, Brazil nuts, cashews, English walnuts, and black walnuts in season) start at $1.20 a lb. for peanuts and rise to $2.75 a lb. for black walnuts. The seeds and beans include long- and short-grain brown rice, pinto beans, soy beans, popcorn (all of these guaranteed organically grown), black-eyed peas, black turtle beans, chick-peas, flaxseed, green split peas, lentils, mung beans, navy beans, peach kernels, red kidney beans, red lentils, sesame and sunflower seeds. These are priced by the pound from 39¢ (for black-eyed peas) to $3.17 (for peach kernels). Write for prices in larger quantities.

FEARN SOYA FOODS / Dept. CFC
    4520 James Place, Melrose Park, IL 60160

"Soy-O Mixes, Protein Foods, Natural Foods," catalogue and price list, free.

Fearn Soya Foods is in the business of making products that contain soya powder, a source of protein. They have a low-sodium pancake mix, bran muffin and cornbread mixes, a rice baking mix of rice flour and soya powder (no gluten), and flavored shake mixes. Since prices fluctuate, they prefer to have you write for their catalogue and current prices.

E. L. FLOURA / Dept. CFC
    Blackduck, MN 56630

Price list, free.

Mr. Floura sells wild rice by mail and ships orders the day they are received. Minimum quantity shipped is 5 lbs. at $4 a lb., packaged in white canvas, plastic-lined bags labeled in black with a free recipe booklet if requested. You can arrange to have a shipment made to a friend with your gift card enclosed, or you can have the rice sent to you in 1-lb., 2-lb., and 3-lb. canvas gift bags at the same price, plus a charge of 30¢ a bag. The price drops on shipments of 10 lbs., 25 lbs., 50 lbs., and 100 lbs., bulk packaged or in 1-lb. sealed plastic bags. Samples will be sent on request. Prices are subject to change, depending on each year's crop.

GENERAL NUTRITION CORPORATION / Dept. CFC
    921 Penn Avenue, Pittsburgh, PA 15222

Catalogue, free, published seasonally, 66 pages, illustrated, black and white.

Primarily vitamins and food supplements, plus natural foods such as herbal teas, nut butters, honeys, dried fruits, carob bars, brown rice, sea salt, granola and other cereals, various seeds (sunflower, sesame, flax, pumpkin, chia, alfalfa), sesame tahini ($1.39 for 15 oz.), coconut, flaxseed and pumpkin seed meals, and 100 percent whole-grain flours. Listed under flours you'll find rye flour, oat flour, graham flour, gluten flour, buckwheat flour, unbleached flour, whole-wheat flour, alfalfa-leaf flour, barley flour, soy flour, and tapioca flour, also white and yellow corn meal, soy grits and wheat grits, whole hulled barley, and bran muffin mix. Prices for unbleached and whole-wheat flours are $1.19 for 2 lbs., gluten flour is $1.95 for 2 lbs., and the rice flour, often used in wheat-free diets, is $1.69 for 2 lbs.

GREAT VALLEY MILLS / Dept. CFC
    Quakertown, PA 18951

"Gift Suggestions from the Pennsylvania Dutch Country," free, published annually, 16 pages, illustrated, black and white.

While Great Valley Mills has gift packages, smoked meats, and all kinds of other products, flours, meals, and cereals are what they are best known for in the baking community. Here you can get the difficult-to-find unbleached hard bread flour and unbleached soft pastry flour (either one, $1.40 for 3 lbs., $2.70 for 6 lbs.), dark rye flour, hard or soft whole-wheat flour, soy bean flour, buckwheat flour and buckwheat

A line-up of products from Fearn Soya Foods

Wild Rice and Chestnut Stuffing
Wash 1 cup wild rice thoroughly. Put in a pan with 3 cups water and 1 teaspoon salt, bring to a boil. Then lower heat and simmer, covered, for about 40 minutes or until tender. Drain. Add ½ pound blanched cooked chestnuts (or canned chestnuts), 2 tablespoons finely chopped onion, ½ cup melted butter, salt, and pepper to taste. Toss lightly. Makes enough stuffing for a 4-pound bird.
—from "Recipes with Wild Rice" by E. L. Floura

Decorative cover design, Green Mountain Herbs catalogue

Granola

Mix together in a large pan 4 cups oatmeal, 2½ cups wheat germ, 1 cup sunflower seeds, 1 cup sesame seeds, 1 cup unsweetened coconut, 1 cup raw peanuts, and 2 teaspoons cinnamon. Heat together ¾ cup honey and ½ cup oil. Pour slowly over the dry ingredients, mixing thoroughly. Bake in shallow pans in a 325° oven for 30 minutes, stirring every 10 minutes. Remove from oven. Add 1 cup raisins and mix well.
—*from Lang Apiaries*

groats, coarse or fine yellow corn meal, coarse or fine oatmeal, raw wheat germ, and the Cornell triple-rich bread mix, white or whole wheat ($1.80 for 3 lbs., $3.50 for 6 lbs.). They have griddle cake, waffle and muffin mixes of buckwheat, whole-wheat, and unbleached flour, and some relatively new products, added within the last two or three years, such as rye meal, oatmeal flour, brown rice flour, long-grain brown rice, dried corn ($3 a lb.), rolled oats, bran flakes, cracked wheat and wheat kernel. There's also a Pennsylvania Dutch recipe book with a complete section on bread baking ($1.25). Add a 50¢ handling charge for orders under $5. These are all on their regular price list, included with the gift catalogue. The catalogue suggests as a gift for a novice baker a $6 package of 6 lbs. of unbleached hard bread flour, plus a bread-baking recipe book and baker's yeast.

GREEN MOUNTAIN HERBS / Dept. CFC
P.O. Box 2369, Boulder, CO 80302

Catalogue and price list, free, published annually, 20 pages, black and white.

Culinary and medicinal herbs and spices and essential oils are part of Green Mountains' stock in trade, and the prices seem reasonable—30¢ for a vanilla bean, 95¢ for a gram of Spanish saffron. Herbs and spices are sold in quantities of 2, 4, 8, and 16 oz., with the price decreasing for larger quantities. As prices are subject to change, orders are sent COD. There is a minimum order of $3 and a service charge of $1 for orders under $10, 50¢ for orders over $10 and under $25, and no service charge on orders over $25. You can also buy in wholesale quantities of 1, 5, 10, and 25 lbs., with a minimum order of 25 lbs.

HARVEST HEALTH, INC. / Dept. CFC
1944 Eastern Avenue, S.E., Grand Rapids, MI 49507

Catalogue and price lists, free, published annually, 16 pages, black and white, also 8-page catalogue of herbs and spices.

Harvest Health sells vitamins, food supplements, and various health foods, such as stone-ground cereals, brown rice, seeds, nuts and dried fruits, sesame chips and sesame buds for snacks, Fearn's soy products, pastas made from soy, vegetable or whole-wheat flours and eggs, herbal teas and botanicals, and culinary herbs and spices, the latter sold in small jars holding 1 oz., minimum order 6 jars for $4.95. There are also some herbs and spices in the list of botanicals, such as rosemary, American saffron, thyme, mustard seed, basil, cayenne pepper, etc. These are sold by the lb., ½ lb., and ¼ lb. Rosemary leaves are 65¢ for ¼ lb., $1 for ½ lb., and $1.50 for 1 lb., a very reasonable price. Prices are, of course, subject to change, and none are given in the general catalogue but come on separate price sheets.

HERTER'S INC. / Dept. CFC
R.R. 2, Mitchell, SD 57301

"Herter's Sportsman's Catalog," $1 (refundable with $10 purchase), published annually, 352 pages, illustrated, color and black and white.

Unexpectedly, this mail-order sporting catalogue offers high-gluten flour for making French bread ($2.35 a 5-lb. bag), a French bread mix, high-gluten sourdough bread mix, Herter's Meet Bread Mix containing 25 percent pure vegetable protein, rice flour, a sourdough pancake mix, and a wild-rice pancake mix. They also sell the long double pans for French loaves, 18" long and 5" wide, for $1.59.

HICKORY HOLLOW / Dept. CFC
Rte. 1, Box 52, Peterstown, WV 24963

Brochure and price list, 25¢, 6 pages, updated periodically, black and white.

Hickory Hollow makes fresh granola every week with oatmeal, their organically grown dried apples, fresh ground corn meal, whole sunflower seeds, honey, pressed soy oil, and pure mountain spring water, with or without organic Thompson raisins (75¢ a lb. with raisins, 70¢

without), and also a special herb-honey bread in 1 lb. loaves at $1.15. Other organic products are their herb teas, salad dressings, vinegars, herb jellies, and relish.

JAFFE BROS. / Dept. CFC
P.O. Box 636, Valley Center, CA 92082

Price list, free, published annually, 2 pages.

Jaffe Bros. are distributors of natural foods, so their produce is sold in minimum quantities of 6 pounds for such things as organic brown rice and soy beans, raw or toasted carob powder, tins of honey, dried coconut, raw and unbleached nuts, and unsulphured dried fruits, although they do have a gift mailer containing 1 lb. each of Black Mission figs, mammoth prunes, seedless raisins, almonds, and 12 oz. unsulphured apricots, all organically grown, for $8.95 ($9.50 for Alaska and Hawaii). If you are interested in large quantities, they sell organically grown, unfumigated dried fruits, with no added chemicals or preservatives, ranging in price from $3.50 for 5 lbs. of Thompson seedless raisins to $10.50 for 5 lbs. of apricots. Other fruits available are apples, pears, jumbo prunes, Black Mission figs, and a mixed pack of apples, figs, peaches, and pears. They also have whole dried bananas (a scarce red variety), with no added sugar or preservatives, and four varieties of organic unfumigated dates: Khadrawi (soft), Halawi (semimoist), Zahidi (semidry, not too sweet), and Deglet Noor. Their raw unbleached nuts are shelled almonds, cashews, walnuts, macadamias, walnuts and filberts in the shell, all sold in lots of 5 lbs., 10 lbs., or 25 lbs. Other products are unfumigated seeds (sunflower, sesame, alfalfa, chia, and golden flaxseed), organic yellow cornmeal, millet and wheat germ ($1.50, $1.95, and $1.75 for 5 lbs., respectively), rolled oats, whole kernel wheat berries, whole-wheat flour, rye flour, buckwheat flour, whole kernel buckwheat, and hulled barley. Crude sesame oil and olive oil made from organic olives are unprocessed and cold-pressed, sold by the gallon ($8.65 for sesame oil, $13.25 for olive oil). Organically grown fresh fruits (oranges, lemons, avocados) are sold in season in case lots of 10 lbs. of lemons or avocados, 35 lbs. of oranges.

LEKVAR-BY-THE-BARREL / Dept. CFC
1577 First Avenue, New York, NY 10028

"A Continental Bazaar," free, published annually, 56 pages, illustrated, black and white.

This catalogue has lots of supplies for baking, including natural and dark rye flour (59¢ a lb.), low-gluten pastry flour (65¢ a lb.), and the high-gluten winter-wheat flour required for strudel (59¢ a lb.), pumpernickel flour, whole-wheat flour, soy bean flour, buckwheat, rice, chestnut and chick-pea flours, potato starch and other grains such as fine or coarse barley, coarse or fine corn meal, farina (semolina) and farinha de mandioca (manioc meal for Brazilian cooking), even hominy grits (89¢ a lb.). There are also ground nuts for baking, sweetened shredded coconut or natural coconut flakes, almond paste ($1.75 a ½-lb. can), baking chocolate, lebkuchen and honey-cake spice, liquid food colors, edible rice paper in sheets or round pieces, non-alcoholic extracts and essences, and all kinds of cake and cookie decorations, such as colored crystal sugar, crystallized seeds, flower petals and leaves, silver shot, chocolate shot, and nonpareils. Anything you need for European-style baking you can find here, including ready-to-use sheets of strudel dough (package of 4 sheets, 98¢), thick jams and fruit butters, lekvar (prune butter) naturally being one. There's also a good selection of dried beans, peas and lentils, rice, and such things as sago, tapioca, dried chestnuts, and millet seed.

MINNEHAHA WILD RICE / Dept. CFC
420 WCCO Radio Building, Minneapolis, MN 55402

Recipe leaflet and order blank, free, printed seasonally.

That specialty grain from the lakes of the northern states, wild rice (not a real rice but the seed of an aquatic grass), is sold in 1-lb. boxes at $6.85 or 5-lb. boxes at $29.50 (five 1-lb. bags to a box). Those are today's

---

★

To cut calories, use yogurt in soups, sauces, desserts instead of cream or sour cream. Put yogurt on baked potatoes in place of sour cream, top with chives or freshly ground black pepper.

★

Use oatmeal or cornmeal to thicken stews, soups, casseroles.

★

Minnehaha wild rice

Tabbouleh

Soak ½ cup fine bulgur (cracked wheat) in cold water to cover for 30 minutes. Drain in a fine sieve, then squeeze out as much remaining moisture as possible. Pat out flat on a dish towel and leave to dry. Meanwhile peel, seed, and chop 3 medium ripe tomatoes, put in a colander to drain. Put the bulgur in a large bowl and mix in, with the hands, the tomatoes, 1 cup finely chopped green onions, 1 cup chopped parsley, ¼ cup lemon juice, and salt to taste. Then mix in ⅓ cup olive oil and ¼ cup finely chopped fresh mint. Taste and correct seasoning. Serve as a salad with Middle Eastern food or with broiled chicken. Serves 6.

Lemon Pilaf

Sauté 1 cup sliced celery and 1 cup chopped green onions, with tops, in 2 tablespoons butter until tender. Add 3 cups cooked rice, 1 tablespoon grated lemon rind, 1 teaspoon salt, and ¼ teaspoon pepper; toss lightly. Continue cooking over low heat about 2 minutes or until thoroughly heated, stirring occasionally. Serve with broiled chicken, breast of veal, baked or broiled fish. Makes 6 servings.

—from "Man-Pleasing Recipes"

prices, but they may change according to crop conditions. Wild rice, the recipe booklet emphasizes, is a 100 percent natural grain, one of the basic foods of the Sioux and Chippewa Indians. The recipe leaflet is included with each order.

NATURAL FOOD DISTRIBUTORS / Dept. CFC
519 Monroe Street, Toledo, OH 43604

Price list, free, updated monthly, 4 pages.

Dried fruits, grains, beans, nuts, and seeds sold in 1-lb., 3-lb., and 10-lb. quantities. Near each entry is an abbreviation that indicates whether it is organically grown, pesticide-free, imported, sproutable. Dried fruits include apples, unsulphured apricots, whole bananas, four varieties of dates, two of figs, papaya, peach halves, pears, pineapple, jumbo prunes, Monukka and Thompson raisins at prices from $1.15 to $3.40 a lb. Grains include hard and soft wheat, old-fashioned corn meal, wild rice ($5.75 a lb.), and hulled or unhulled buckwheat. All the usual nuts, from unblanched almonds to black or English walnuts. Imported pine nuts here are $4.45 a lb., organically grown macadamias, $6.15 a lb. Natural Food Distributors also have a 23 Herb Tea ($1.85 for 4 oz. or a large sample for $1) and a 3-V Cereal containing barley, buckwheat, sesame, flax, millet, oats, rye, wheat, alfalfa, and dried fruits, which is sold with the grains whole or ground ($5.85 for 6¼ lbs.).

NATURAL LIFE DISTRIBUTORS CORP. / Dept. CFC
86 Thomas Street, New York, NY 10013

Wholesale catalogue, free, published quarterly, 4 pages, black and white.

Natural Life is a bulk distributor of a wide range of natural foods. If you are interested in buying wholesale, this is a good source. Their dried fruits, seeds, and nuts are sold in case lots, starting at 10 lbs. for such things as alfalfa, pumpkin, sesame and sunflower seeds, sweet rice, hulled millet, and brown or white buckwheat groats and going up to 100 lbs. for long-grain rice (the price drops to 28¢ a lb. for 100 lbs.), medium-grain rice, pearl barley, and some of the seeds. Cereals such as bulgur (cracked wheat), couscous, and rolled oats are sold by 25-lb. or 50-lb. lots, bulgur at 30¢ a lb. for 25 lbs., couscous 66¢. In beans, 25 lbs. of black turtle beans would be $7.25; 25 lbs. of pinto beans, $7. Organic whole-wheat flour from Minnesota is $10.75 a 50-lb. bag; unbleached organic white flour, $12.50. There's also bulk whole-wheat pasta, peanut butter, granola, oils (sold in 5 gallons), honey (sold mostly in 1-lb. jars, by the dozen, but also in larger sizes), Hawaiian papaya, guava and passion-fruit juices, herbal teas, herbs, spices and condiments, and both raw and pasteurized cheese, mostly packed in 10-lb. cases. In raw-milk cheese there's blue, mild and sharp cheddar, Colby and Longhorn; in pasteurized, Jack, caraway Jack, Muenster, mozzarella, provolone, and Swiss. They also offer for sale certain cooking and food preparation equipment, such as the Miracle Exclusives line, spun-steel woks in 12", 14", and 16" diameters with covers and stove rings. The woks range in price from around $4 to $5.49; the rings are 98¢. Terms are net cash, with a minimum order of $50 for delivery within New York City, $75 outside, or $25, with a 2 percent discount, if the order is picked up at their warehouse.

NATURE FOOD CENTRES / Dept. CFC
292 Main Street, Cambridge, MA 02142

Catalogue, free, published seasonally, 32 pages, black and white, plus flyers and retail circulars throughout the year.

This is a countrywide chain of more than 50 retail stores and a mail-order division selling natural vitamins, food supplements, and many health foods, such as dried fruits, cereals, beans, seeds, cider vinegar, herb teas, cookies and a few pieces of cooking equipment and appliances such as yogurt makers, a mill for grinding nuts, seeds, and grains, and an automatic juice extractor. A special feature of the catalogue is the inclusion of coupons that can be turned in at some of the retail stores for free gifts, such as a jar of peanut butter or a bag of bran flakes, with a $5 or $10 purchase, just like your local supermarket. Customers also get free a small monthly magazine, *Nature's Way*, with articles, menus, and recipes. The sale prices are pretty good—cider vinegar for 29¢ a pint, with coupon; various honeys (alfalfa, avocado, sage, safflower, etc.) 99¢ a lb. jar, with coupon; grade A maple syrup, $1.74 for 12 oz.; dried fruits for 20¢ to 30¢ less than the regular price.

NATURE'S HARVEST, INC. / Dept. CFC
Box 1208, 12014-12th Avenue, Burnsville, MN 55337

Order form and recipes, free.

Nature's Harvest regular granola contains coconut, sunflower seeds, honey, almonds, sesame seeds, and sunflower oil. For $3.95 you can get a case of three 1-lb. bags of plain, raisin, or fruit granola or a variety pack containing one of each. They also sell 12-pack cases of regular, fruit, raisin, or mixed granola ($12.75 to $14.75). Their products have no salt, no preservatives, and their prices are reasonable. The free booklet has recipes for granola bread, muffins, apple crisp, and crunchy granola bars, perfect for snacking or to take backpacking where light, nutritious foods are needed for quick energy.

NICHOLS GARDEN NURSERY / Dept. CFC
1190 North Pacific Highway, Albany, OR 97321

"Nichols Herb and Rare Seeds," free, published seasonally, 60 pages, illustrated, black and white.

Nichols Nursery believes in the natural life. Their herb plants (see chapter on "Growing Things") are organically grown. They sell yogurt culture and acidophilus culture, uncolored raw-milk cheddar cheese made in Oregon's Rogue River Valley, and sprouting screens and seeds. Sprout-Ease, which fits over the top of an empty jar, has three screens: fine for tiny seeds like alfala, medium for seeds like mung beans, and coarse to wash out seed hulls for sprouts in jar. This handy little device, which costs only $2, saves buying a special seed sprouter at four or five times the price. The untreated organically grown seeds available for sprouting are alfalfa, red clover, peppergrass, black radish, mung bean, and lentil, each 50¢ a packet, though you can buy them in larger quantities. A paperback by Esther Munroe, *Sprouts to Grow and Eat*, explains all about growing and using sprouts.

NORTHWESTERN COFFEE MILLS / Dept. CFC
217 North Broadway, Milwaukee, WI 53202

Catalogue, free (25¢ donation accepted), published annually, 27 pages, illustrated, black and white.

Some of the products Northwestern Coffee Mills sells come under the heading of natural foods. Their dried fruits (peeled apple rings, apricots, Medjool dates, figs, prunes, and raisins) are organically grown and unfumigated; the coconut has no bleaches or preservatives. Prices range from 70¢ a lb. for jumbo prunes and Monukka raisins to $1.70 for Golden Royal apricots. Treated with equal care are the nuts, which are dry roasted in Northwestern's own ovens (these include peanuts, almonds, and cashews), and the nut butters they dry roast, grind, and package—these are 100 percent pure nuts, no salt, oil, sugar, preservatives, or other chemicals added. They suggest that if you desire oil or salt, add your own. There are also raw shelled nuts, ranging from almonds to black and English walnuts. Prices for the unroasted shelled nuts range from 70¢ a lb. (for peanuts) to $4.75 (for Wisconsin hickory halves). Nut butters start at 95¢ for ½ lb. of peanut butter to $1.80 for ½ lb. of almond butter. Northwestern also has a good selection of herbal teas, more correctly known as *tisanes*, as they are not really teas at all, either whole or cut and sifted. Among them are the Oriental mu tea ($1.05 an oz.) and lemon grass (whole, 50¢ an oz.). Twenty-four botanicals (herbs, roots, bark) are additional offerings, ranging from alfalfa to wormwood and in price from 45¢ to $1 an oz. Another of their natural foods, very hard to find these days, is an uncolored pure raw milk cheddar made in Dane County, Wisconsin ($2.20 a lb.) and an organic

Mung Bean Salad

Combine 1 cup mung bean sprouts, 1 cup finely chopped celery, 1 cup grated carrots, ½ cup pine nuts or chopped cashews, and 1 tablespoon sesame seeds. Add vinaigrette sauce to taste and toss lightly. Serve on a bed of watercress or lettuce. Serves 4.
—*from "Sourdough Jack's Cookery & Other Things . . . & More"*

Bio-Snacky bean sprouter from Miracle Exclusives, Inc.

Grits Pudding

In the top of a double boiler, stir 1 cup hominy grits into 2 cups boiling water seasoned with 1 teaspoon salt. Cover and cook over simmering water for 20 to 30 minutes, stirring occasionally. Mix in 2 tablespoons butter, 1 cup milk, 1 slightly beaten egg, and ¼ teaspoon Tabasco. Turn into greased 1-quart baking dish and bake in a 375° oven for 25 to 30 minutes or until set and lightly browned. Serves 6 to 8.

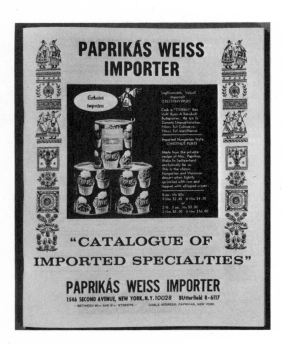

goat cheese, $3.85 a lb. There's a 15 percent discount for 5 lbs. or more. And if you have been looking for a natural substitute for chocolate, they sell powdered carob (also known as St. John's bread) for $1.25 a lb.

OLD TOWN MILL STORE / Dept. CFC
   4315 Main Street, Union Gap, WA 98903

Price list, free, updated periodically, 1 page.

Cereals and flours are the main products here, although the store also sells oils (soy, sunflower, sesame, safflower, peanut, olive, and corn germ) by the pint, quart, and 5-gallon size, no prices given, and raisins at 30¢ a lb. They have wheat germ and wheat bran; steel-cut groats; rolled barley, oats, rye, and wheat; cracked wheat, rye, and barley; bulgur wheat (another type of cracked wheat); and a fine wheat cereal. Prices run about 20¢ a lb. in 5- or 10-lb. bags. except for the rolled oats, rye, and wheat, which are 15¢ a lb. in 4- or 8-lb. bags. Wheat germ is 20¢ a lb., wheat bran 10¢, in 2- or 4-lb bags. There's a very wide range of flours: barley, buckwheat, graham, millet, oat, rye, soy, triticale, unbleached white, wheat gluten, whole-wheat and whole-wheat pastry flour, and both yellow and white corn meal. All are 20¢ a lb. and come in 5-lb. or 10-lb. bags. Prices are subject to change without notice. A good source, if you like to bake bread.

ORIENTAL FOODS AND HANDCRAFTS / Dept. CFC
   3708 N. Broadway, Chicago. IL 60613

"Pakistani-Indian Foods," price list, free, 3 pages.

Many flours are listed, some familiar, such as whole-wheat flour ($1.75 for 10 lbs.), rice flour and gram, or chick-pea flour, others with baffling names like moth, dokhra, jawar, and bajri. There's also the superb Basmati rice (75¢ a lb.) and many types of grains and dals (dried pulse vegetables).

PAPRIKAS WEISS IMPORTER / Dept. CFC
   1546 Second Avenue, New York, NY 10028

"Imported Foods and Cookware Catalogue," $1 for annual subscription, published four times a year, 66 pages, illustrated, black and white.

Paprikas Weiss can claim that they have always been in the business of selling natural foods. For fifty years they have stocked only dried beans, peas, and seeds grown naturally and processed without additives, and stone-ground whole-grain flours and cereals. Their flours and cereals include whole-wheat flour and pastry flour, whole rye flour, unbleached wheat germ, cracked wheat, oatmeal, semolina, kasha, strudel flour, and lots more. Among the dried beans, grains, and seeds you'll find fine, medium, and coarse barley, black-eyed peas, pigeon peas, pinto beans, black turtle beans, red and green lentils, and brown long-grain rice, all $1.59 a lb. or 5 lbs. for $7.

PAVO'S HEALTH FOODS / Dept. CFC
   57 South Ninth Street, Minneapolis, MN 55402

"Consumer Catalog," free, published annually, 103 pages plus index, black and white.

An unusual catalogue in that it consists of a listing of all the vitamins and minerals, natural, health, and dietetic foods and equipment carried by Pavo's, arranged by manufacturer. They start with their own Pavo line of vitamins and minerals, cereals and grains, flours, snacks, sun-dried fruits, pasta, honey, nuts, oils, salt, sugar, seasonings, and herb teas, then those of Alvita Products, ending with Zion Baking Industry with one product only—whole-wheat fig bars. Each item is numbered and listed by pack size and retail price. It would be impossible to mention the thousands of items packed into this little catalogue, which is the equivalent of listing the stock of a health-foods store, but chances are if you are looking for a particular brand of health food, such as the Hain's line, Chico-San macrobiotic foods, El Molino Mills flours and grains, the Western Commerce Corporation's special honeys, or the Cellu and

Estee dietetic foods, you'll find it in here. They also have a big list of books related to diet and health. A useful catalogue to have around.

PENN HERB COMPANY, LTD. / Dept. CFC
603 North 2nd Street, Philadelphia, PA 19123

"Dried Herbs from Nature's Wonderland," free, published semiannually, 58 pages, one-color.

Since 1924 Penn Herb Company has been in the business of selling medicinal herbs and botanicals, which are listed and priced by the pound but can be bought in smaller quantities, down to an ounce, and herbal tea blends, sold in packages (around $3). In addition, they have a fair list of health-food products—herb and honey candy, dried fruit, honeys, jams and jellies, vegetable and fruit juices, oils, molasses, raw sugar, sea salt and Herba-Mare (the Swiss herbal seasoning salt), rice, soy beans, seeds and nuts, and cider vinegar. Apple juice from organically grown apples, no sugar or preservatives, is $3 a gallon; the Biotta beet, carrot, celery, tomato, and vegetable cocktail juices from Switzerland are $1.60 for 17 oz.; the aged-in-wood cider vinegar, 70¢ a pint. There is also a large selection of books on herbs, health, and nutrition, gardening, plant identification, with a few cookbooks in the same vein.

SAHADI IMPORTING CO., INC. / Dept. CFC
187 Atlantic Avenue, Brooklyn, NY 11201

"The Silent Salesman," free, published biannually, 24 pages, illustrated, black and white.

Sahadi is the place to look for some of the unusual cereals, flours, dried pulses and seeds needed for Middle East and Indian cooking. They have bulgur (cracked wheat) in three grades: fine or medium for kibbeh and tabbouleh, coarse for pilaf, at 80¢ for a 2-lb. bag or $1.95 for 5 lbs.; semolina; chick-pea and rice flour; Basmati rice ($1.50 for 2 lbs.); couscous; small and large fava beans and fava beans shelled for falafel; red lentils; sesame seeds (white shelled, brown in shell, or toasted); and some ready-prepared products, such as a falafel dry mix (ground fava beans and spices, $1.60 a 1-lb. box); or spiced pilaf mixes—wheat, rice, and lentil.

SALTMARSH CIDER MILL / Dept. CFC
P.O. Box 132, New Boston, NH 03070

Leaflet and price list, free.

The Saltmarsh product is old-fashioned pure organic cider vinegar from whole New England apples untouched by chemical sprays, raised without chemical fertilizers, hand-sorted and pressed into sweet cider by the mill's original apple press, then fermented from two to four years in charcoaled oak barrels. The story behind the cider mill is fascinating. Constructed in 1908 by J. R. Whipple as an addition to his farm, the mill produced sweet and dry cider, cider champagne, and cider vinegar, which were served in Boston at Mr. Whipple's hotels—the Parker House, the Touraine, and Young's Hotel. The name of the mill came from Paul Saltmarsh, who bought the place in 1944 and established a reputation for fine products from organically raised fruit. Now Bob Belanger is carrying on the business and the tradition. Direct from the mill, he will ship apple cider vinegar in ½ pint, pint and quart bottles, or gallon glass jugs. Prices run from $1.25 for a 1-quart bottle to $12 for four 1-gallon jugs. Twelve ½-pint bottles are $6. Plus express charges collect.

SCARPA'S CIDER MILL / Dept. CFC
Box 38, Mission Home, VA 22956

Price list, free, on request.

Only one product here, old-fashioned cider vinegar pressed from whole unsprayed apples, made in the hills of Virginia by Mario J. Scarpa. You will have to write him for the price.

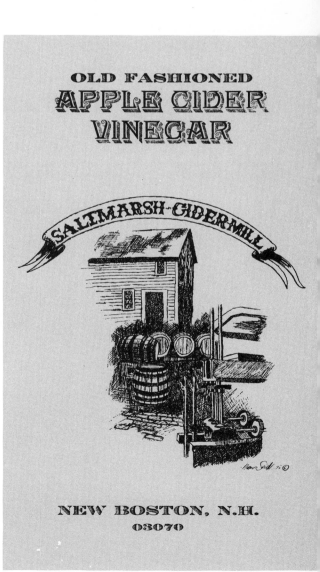

OLD FASHIONED
APPLE CIDER VINEGAR

SALTMARSH·CIDER·MILL

NEW BOSTON, N.H.
03070

---

*

An easy foolproof way to cook rice: drop rice by handfuls into a large pot of boiling salted water so water continues to boil. Boil rapidly, uncovered, for 15 minutes, drain in a sieve. Grains will be separate, fluffy, and a trifle firm to the bite.

*

Heat a whole coconut in a hot oven for a few minutes before breaking the shell open with a hammer. The meat will be easier to remove.

*

STA-WEL NUTRITION CENTERS, INC. / Dept. CFC
16 West 40th Street, New York, NY 10018

"Food for Better Living," 50¢, no regular publication date, 40 pages, black and white.

Health foods such as cereals and whole-grain products of different companies (Nu-Vita, Vigerola, Elam, El Molino, Fearn, Cellu), San Martin artichoke pasta, meat substitutes, nut butters, various domestic and imported honeys and preserves, molasses and syrups, dried fruits, fruit juices, nuts and nut products, herbal teas, oils, seasonings, dressings, herbs, apple cider vinegar, appliances, and books are featured in this catalogue, which has not been updated since 1973, so prices are no longer valid. You must request prices of any items you require. Sta-Wel has a large selection of dietetic foods (salt- and sugar-free, low-calorie, low-sodium, low-cholesterol or gluten and wheat-free for those with allergies) ranging from candies, jams and jellies, crackers, cookies and wafers to canned soups, water-packed salt-free vegetables, low-sodium cheese, baking powder, mustard, pickles, and sauces.

TEEL MOUNTAIN FARM / Dept. CFC
Box 200, Stanardsville, VA 22973

Literature, free on request.

Milk-fed baby beef and veal raised naturally and organically on 350 acres of pasture and woodland where no chemical fertilizers, herbicides, or pesticides are used. Both the baby beef (7 to 8 months old) and the younger veal drink only mother's milk; they are not grass-fed. The owners of Teel Farm, Ellie and Don Pruess, say they use only natural rock fertilizers such as ground limestone, rock phosphate, and granite dust, with manure for nitrogen and Erthrite as a soil conditioner, and spray liquid kelp on the fields to improve the availability of trace minerals. The cows are also fed Norwegian kelp, bone meal, and multivitamin supplements to supplement their grass diet, and the two bulls, Humfrey and Humperdink, get a special grain ration. None of the animals is ever given antibiotics or hormones. The baby beef and veal is processed in a plant under state and USDA inspection, aged, cut, wrapped into small-family-size portions of steaks, chops, roasts, cutlets, ground and stewing meat, and sold by the quarter animal in 56-lb. (for baby beef) or 28-lb. (for veal) packages. The meat is flash-frozen and shipped either by freezer truck in the home delivery area or by air, packed in dry ice, over longer distances. Write to Teel Farm for details of their farming practices and information on how to reserve and pay for an order (supplies are limited, orders filled on a first-in, first-out basis). If you are in Virginia and would like to see how the beef is raised, you can write ahead for directions. Visiting hours are 1:00 to 5:00 P.M. on the last Sunday of each month.

THE VERMONT COUNTRY STORE / Dept. CFC
Weston, VT 05161

Catalogue, 25¢, published annually, 98 pages, illustrated, black and white.

A very interesting little catalogue of various Vermont products, including foods. This is a family business, run by Vrest, Ellen, and Lyman Orton, and the store is open year round, Monday through Saturday, 9:00 A.M. to 5:00 P.M. They are well-known in the vicinity for their stone-ground whole-grain cereals, meals and flours, and the bread made in their bakery, all of which are available by mail. The nine breakfast cereals of stone-ground grains include samp (coarse cracked corn and wheat), Vermont lumberman's mush (medium-ground cereal of corn, wheat, and oatmeal, also good fried), cracked rye cereal, and white or yellow corn grits, which they emphasize are natural stone-ground grits, not the hominy grits of the South, which have the germ removed. They also make their own granola, flavored with pure maple syrup ($1.35 a 1-lb. box), and a high-nutrition breakfast cereal that contains wheat germ, cracked sunflower and pumpkin seeds, raisins, skim milk powder, chopped nuts, date sugar, sesame seeds, apple and banana flakes ($1.95 a lb.). There are nine different stone-ground flours or meals—bread flour, pastry flour, rye flour, oat flour, buckwheat flour, soy flour, yellow and white cornmeal, and muffin or pancake meal (whole-grain corn, wheat, and rye). Prices of flours and cereals are $1.40 a 2-lb. bag, $2.50 a 5-lb. bag, and there's a minimum order of $3 with shipping costs extra. Mrs. Orton has written a book, *Cooking with Wholegrains*, 72 pages, $1.95 in paper cover, $4.50 in cloth cover, and Vrest Orton has books on cider and homemade beer. There's a lot of interesting information here, well worth the 25¢.

VERMONT GENERAL STORE & GRIST MILL, INC. / Dept. CFC
Woodstock, VT 05091

Catalogue, 50¢, with recipe booklet, 6 pages, illustrated, black and white.

Stone-ground whole-grain pancake, bread, and muffin mixes are the specialty of the Vermont General Store & Grist Mill. Among these natural stone-ground products are whole-grain buckwheat pancake mix, whole-wheat cornmeal pancake mix, whole-wheat and cornmeal buttermilk pancake mix, whole-grain bran muffin mix, and cornmeal and rye muffin mix, each $1.69 for a 24-oz. package or in money-saving combination packages of $5 for all three pancake mixes, $3.35 for both muffin mixes, or $7.95 for all five mixes, plus shipping costs. The three stone-ground whole-grain bread mixes are Country Graham Quick Bread Mix, Honey Oatmeal Bread Mix, and 3-Grain Bread Mix (wheat, corn, rye), each $1.49 a 24-oz. package plus 25¢ for shipping. A package makes two large or three medium-sized loaves. They also sell a 10-qt. dough mixer if you don't like to knead ($22.95 plus $1.50 shipping). You can buy gift packages of the bread, muffin, or pancake mixes, the muffin mixes with a jar of Vermont clover honey, or two of the pancake mixes with Vermont maple syrup.

VITA GREEN FARMS / Dept. CFC
P.O. Box 878, Vista, CA 92803

Brochure and price lists, $1, published seasonally, 9 pages, black and white.

Under the list of Dry Items you'll find dried fruits, shelled and unshelled nuts, seeds, beans (mung, large and small limas, pinto, red kidney, soy, small white, garbanzos, lentils, and black-eyed peas). Prices for beans are 85¢ a lb., 10 lbs. for $6.80, except for mung beans, $1.20 a lb. or 10 lbs. for $10. Other items are hard red wheat (39¢ a lb., 10 lbs. for $3.50), rolled oats, and long-grain brown rice (85¢ a lb., 10 lbs. for $6.80).

VITALITY HEALTH FOOD SHOPS, INC. / Dept. CFC
51 The Old Arcade, Cleveland, OH 44114

"Vitality's Better Nutrition Quality Kitchen Catalog," free, published seasonally, 80 pages, black and white.

This company sells only wholesale and refers consumer requests to the nearest retail dealer, but you may find their catalogue helpful in identifying and locating products put out by different manufacturers and distributors of health foods, vitamins, and related equipment and appliances. It consists of an alphabetical listing of companies and their products, with suggested retail price. Some of the sources listed do sell direct, among them Chico-San, Sahadi, Fearn Soya Foods, and Miracle Exclusives.

WALNUT ACRES / Dept. CFC
Penns Creek, PA 17862

"Walnut Acres Natural Foods," free, published five times a year, 24 pages, black and white.

Walnut Acres, a large organic farm set in the rolling Pennsylvania countryside, is one of the oldest and best-known growers and producers of natural organic foods in the country, and they are very careful that all their produce is fresh as fresh when it gets to you. That is why they

Bread, muffin, and biscuit mixes from the Vermont General Store

Yogurt Honey Bread

Combine 2 cups whole milk yogurt, the juice of 1 lemon, 3 eggs, and ½ cup honey just enough to mix. Add 2½ cups whole-wheat flour, ½ teaspoon salt, and 2½ teaspoons baking powder. Do not overmix. Pour into a "brownie" pan greased with butter. Bake in a preheated 350° oven for 1 hour. Cool and slice thinly. Serve with your favorite jelly, jam, or preserves.
—from "Cooking with Yogurt Naturally, Colombo, Inc."

Sourdough Jack's Easy-to-Make Sourdough Bread
Always use unbleached hard-wheat white flour (also
known as bread flour), available in some supermarkets
and health food stores or by mail.

Prepare starter. Empty package of Sourdough Jack's
starter into a 2-cup bowl. (Never use metal bowl,
spoons, etc.) Add ¾ cup of flour. Stir in ½ cup warm
water. Cover and let ferment in a warm spot (about
85°) for 48 hours. If you do not plan to use immediately, starter can be refrigerated indefinitely. Make
ready for use by stirring well and warming to room
temperature.

Make primary batter. Empty 1 cupful of starter into
large 4-quart bowl. Add 2½ cups warm water and stir
well. Slowly add 2½ cups flour—blending well. Stir
until batter is free of lumps. Cover bowl with plastic or
wax wrap and place in warm spot (85°) for about 12
hours. After 12 hours, stir batter thoroughly, then
pour 1 cupful back into starter crock or jar. Leave 3
cups only in bowl.

Making the bread. Add to bowl containing batter 2
tablespoons melted butter, ¼ cup sugar, 2 teaspoons
salt, and mix well. Add 2 cups of flour—½ cup at a
time—and stir well. Empty dough onto a floured
board (use ½ cup of flour or more) and knead until
smooth and satiny. Grease hands well and shape
dough into two loaves. Place loaves in well-greased
pans. Place in warm dry spot (85°) and let rise about 2
hours or until doubled in bulk. Then press two fingers
lightly into dough. If impression remains, dough is
ready. Place in preheated 350° oven and bake 1 hour.
When bread is golden brown and has shrunk from
sides of pan, remove from oven. Well baked bread
sounds hollow when the bottom of the loaf is tapped
with the fingers. Remove bread from pans, brush tops
with butter, and let cool on wire rack.

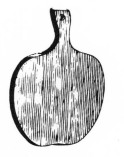

One teaspoon of potato starch or arrowroot or 2 teaspoons of cornstarch or rice flour have the thickening
power of 1 tablespoon of flour and do not require
pre-cooking. Mix with cold water and stir into a soup,
stew, or sauce at the last minute; cook only until thickened and clear.

★

prefer to sell by mail, knowing their products won't languish on the
shelves, rather than to stores, where they can't control the shelf life.
They have raised organic foods on the farm for 30 years, and they also
store and prepare them there, in spanking clean kitchens and store-
houses that would put many a factory to shame (all grains and flours are
in refrigerated storage). They use no synthetics or preservatives and
prepare foods by hand in small batches, like an overgrown farm
kitchen. They bake and ship breads and cookies, make their own peanut butter, pickles, salad dressings, sauces, and ketchup (the creamy
chive dressing, made with their own mayonnaise, apple cider vinegar,
fresh chives, untreated well water and seasonings is delicious and just
85¢ for an 8-oz. bottle), can a wide variety of vegetables and fruits
produced on the farm, make and can 26 soups and all kinds of beef and
poultry dishes (beef and chicken are also raised at the farm) from
ground beef ($2.42 a tin) to chicken stew, fruit juices, and vegetable
juices, and pack their own oils, some of which, like the peanut oil recommended for cooking, are organic and unrefined. You'll find in this
catalogue a very big list of cereals, both the ready-to-eat kind such as
granola and the Swiss familia birchermuseli, and hot cereals that need
cooking, such as grits (barley, buckwheat, corn, rice, soy), their own
organic oatmeal, and coarse or fine bulgur. The list of flours, meals,
and pancake and bread mixes is even lengthier—everything from bread
flour made of Montana organic spring wheat (43¢ a lb.; 5 lbs., $1.80)
and Deaf Smith County 100 percent whole-wheat flour ground from
hard winter wheat to a 12-grain flour they make from organic whole
wheat, rye, corn, and buckwheat flours, plus rice, soy, oats, barley
flours; millet, sunflower seed, sesame seed, and flaxseed meals. Under
baking aids you'll find a single-acting baking powder made from cornstarch, soda, and sodium acid pyrophosphate only—no aluminum
compounds (35¢ a ½ lb.), double-acting baking powder made from the
same ingredients plus mono-calcium phosphate and calcium lactate, dry
baking yeast, and sourdough starter. Naturally, they have all kinds of
grains, beans, and seeds, nuts and nut products, Erewhon organic
whole-wheat pasta, yogurt and kefir culture, unsulphured dried fruits,
some of them organic, herbal teas, chocolate and coffee substitutes,
herbs and spices, old-fashioned cider vinegar, vitamins, and food supplements. There are some "helpful household things" in the catalogue,
such as dietary gram scales, bread pans, hand grinding mill, Moulinex
grinder, seed sprouter, and yogurt makers, including a yogurt in-
cubator from California that is thermostatically controlled and makes 4
quarts in your own containers (around $23), and a selected list of books
on natural foods, cooking, raising livestock. This is a catalogue you'll
find invaluable as a source for all natural foods and grains. Incidentally,
owners Paul and Betty Keene like to have people visit (Mondays
through Fridays, 8:00 A.M. to 4:30 P.M.) for a tour of the place. See
where the foods come from and buy them at the store.

WHEATEX MILLING CO., INC. / Dept. CFC
1508 First Street, Marysville, WA 98270

"Wheatex Catalog of Natural Foods," free with stamped, self-addressed
envelope, revised periodically, 4 pages plus 4 pages of bread recipes.

When Gail and Keith Worstman answered a classified ad and bought a
mill that had been in operation since 1909, they found themselves first
in the flour business and, by extension, in the natural-foods business.
Their price list mainly consists of whole-grain cereals, flours and bulk
grains, and it is a pretty interesting one. Among the cereals are seven-
grain (wheat, oats, millet, corn, rice, flax, sesame), almond-rice, and
their own special granola blend (oats, sunflower seeds, sesame seeds,
wheat germ, soy oil, raw honey, cinnamon). The flours range from
whole-wheat flour and pastry flour and fine or coarse whole cornmeal
to rice, soy, potato, tapioca, and carob flour. There's also unbleached
flour and Do-pep, which is 80 percent gluten. These are sold in bags of
varying sizes, up to 50 lbs. Bulk grains, sold in 10-, 25- and 50-lb. bags,
include hard red wheat, soft white wheat, buckwheat groats, oat groats,
barley, corn, brown and white rice, millet, and rye. Also on the Wheatex
list are dried beans and brown or polished short-grain rice, pearl barley,

beans and seeds for sprouting, dried fruits and nuts, fruit juices and canned fruits in natural juices and "et ceteras," such as brown sugar, sea salt, Wheatex pellet baking yeast, pure apple pectin, raw honey, pure cold-pressed oils, pure apple cider vinegar, soy mayonnaise, and whole-wheat pancake mixes. Under "Pasta" you'll find whole-wheat spaghetti, lasagne and macaroni, vegetable macaroni, artichoke-flour noodles, spinach noodles, whole-wheat corn ribbons, egg noodles, brown-rice-soy shells, and soy carob macaroni. There are some gadgets like yogurt makers, vegetable steamers, and plastic sprouting lids; also a few herbs and teas, types not specified. The price list was not included with our catalogue and is revised as prices change, so best request it.

WHOLE GRAIN SALES / Dept. CFC
Rte. 2, Waunakee, WI 53597

"Nature Ramblings and Organic Foods," published seasonally, 4 pages, send self-addressed stamped envelope and 10¢.

The four mimeographed sheets have two pages of chat, little poems and quotes, after which come shipping instructions and a list of the products sold by owner Leon Horsted. Flours from organically grown grains include unbleached hard-wheat, pastry, buckwheat, corn, millet, rice, rye, and soybean, priced from 28¢ to 75¢ a lb., and there are also such things as cornmeal, wheat germ, brown rice, oatmeal, sunflower kernels, alfalfa seed, hulled barley, whole soy beans, and their own white popcorn (40¢ a lb. bag). In addition you'll find pure unpasteurized honey (2-lb. jar, $1.70), buckwheat honey, pure unfiltered maple syrup, dates, figs, prunes and raisins, sauerkraut (89¢ a qt.), unpeeled tomatoes (59¢ a lb. can), Colby cheese from the milk of a naturally run Wisconsin farm ($2.10 a lb.), Cheddar, cold-pressed safflower oil, and herbal tea bags.

THE WHOLE HERB COMPANY / Dept. CFC
P.O. Box 686, Mill Valley, CA 94941

"Star Herbs," free, published annually, 28 pages.

Introduced by a short poem of Kipling's, bolstered with snippets from Shakespeare and Longfellow, and sprinkled with bits of herb lore (placing delicious-smelling mugwort in shoes refreshes weary feet), "Star Herbs" bears out the proverb: "How can a man die who has sage in his garden?" Elegantly straightforward, it offers everything from agar-agar and psyllium seeds to yohimbe bark, Nicaraguan sarsaparilla, dragon's blood root powder, tonka beans, and frankincense tears, all reasonably priced. "Star Herbs" also has a fine list of culinary herbs and spices and a wide selection of premium teas. There are black teas, green teas, semifermented teas (between black and green tea in both color and flavor), plus herbs to make into your own teas. Or try Dr. John's blend of alfalfa leaf, orange flower petals, red clover blossoms, dandelion leaf, rose hips, and passion flower ($7.38 a lb.), or Love Potion Number Nine, containing damiana, ginseng, echinacea root, celery seed, juniper berries, angelica root, and ginger root ($5.04 per lb.). The catalogue lists ginseng products of all kinds, bath and cosmetic items made from natural ingredients, and several types of incense. For additional reading, "Star Herbs" has a complete bibliography of herb-related books.

Apple Granola Crisp

Combine 6 cups peeled, cored, and sliced apples and 1 tablespoon lemon juice in an 8 or 9-inch square pan. Combine ⅓ cup unsifted flour and ½ cup firmly packed brown sugar in a bowl, cut in ¼ cup butter until crumbly. Stir in ½ teaspoon cinnamon and 1 cup granola. Sprinkle over apples, spreading to cover. Bake in a 350° oven for 25 to 30 minutes or until apples are tender. Makes 5 or 6 servings. For Rhubarb Crisp, omit lemon juice and add ½ cup sugar and 1½ tablespoons flour with rhubarb.
—from "Nature's Harvest"

See Appendix, page 239, for additional sources not included here.

CHAPTER TEN

FOREIGN AND REGIONAL SPECIALTIES

Sake Beef with Cellophane Noodles

Have 1½ to 2 pounds flank steak sliced across the grain, ½" thick. Cut beef into ½" strips. Marinate beef in 2 tablespoons sake, 2 tablespoons soy sauce, 2 pieces finely chopped ginger root, and 1 crushed garlic clove. Heat 2 cups oil in a large saucepan. Drop an 8-ounce package of cellophane noodles (harusame) into the hot oil and cook for a few seconds until they "pop" up and expand. Remove, drain, and place on a serving platter. Heat 2 tablespoons oil in a wok, add the beef and stir fry quickly until cooked. Add a little salt and 2 tablespoons cornstarch to the marinade. Mix to a smooth paste and stir into the beef mixture, cooking just until thickened. Add 2 chopped green onions and pour beef and onion mixture over noodles. To serve, wrap in lettuce leaves and eat like a sandwich. Serves 6 to 8.
—*courtesy Tele-Press Associates*

ANZEN JAPANESE FOODS AND IMPORTS / Dept. CFC
736 N. E. Union Avenue, Portland, OR 97232
Price list, free, 20 pages.

Anzen Imports was started about 75 years ago as the Teikoku Company, selling foods and products to Japanese workers in Oregon and Washington cities, logging camps, canneries, and on railroad gangs, but in the mid-Forties it was reorganized and the name changed. They now carry not just Japanese foods but fresh, frozen, dried, and canned products used in other types of Far Eastern cooking—Chinese, Korean, Thai, Vietnamese, Philippine, and Hawaiian. It's hard to pick out items from among so many, but we noticed frozen coconut milk from Thailand, Hawaii, and the Philippines; mochi ko (Japanese sweet rice flour, 59¢ a lb.); frozen natto (fermented soy beans); poi, if you like that strange Hawaiian paste; frozen egg roll skins ($1.57 for 32 oz.); fresh Hawaiian ginger ($1.40 a lb.); and the fiery Korean pickled cabbage, kim chee ($1.46 a pt.). There's a large assortment of rice (California, Chinese, and Japanese), noodles, and all the usual things like Japanese rice vinegar, so delicious in salads (71¢ for 12.8 oz.), sesame oil, dashi (the dried kelp and bonito stock base), soy bean paste, pickles, and Japanese and Chinese soy sauce. Under the Thai listing you'll find lime leaf, fish sauce ($5.75 a gal.), salted lettuce, shrimp paste, rice sticks, dried solid fish ($1.55 for 6 oz.), and rice paper ($5.95 for 2.2 lbs.), the edible kind that is hard to find these days on which you bake macaroons and lebkuchen. A very good source for offbeat foods, according to a friend who has spent many years in the Far East.

APHRODISIA PRODUCTS, INC. / Dept. CFC
28 Carmine Street, New York, NY 10014

"Aphrodisia—an experience in herbs, spices and essential oils," $1, published periodically, 112 pages, illustrated, black and white, with seasonally adjusted price list.

A fascinating catalogue (described in more detail in chapter 5) from a fascinating little shop in Manhattan's Greenwich Village that is reminiscent of an old-fashioned herbalist. As their herbs, spices, and essential oils come from all over the world, they certainly represent the world of food, but in terms of foreign cuisine they concentrate on China, India, and Indonesia, with sections on seasonings and spices used in these three types of cooking. In Chinese foods you'll find the salted black beans to make black bean sauce ($1.45 a lb.), five spices powder, lily buds, dried lotus root, tree fungus or cloud ears ($4.30 for 4 oz.), Szechuan pepper, pickled vegetables and hot paste, Cantonese plum sauce, Hoisin sauce, ground bean paste, sesame oil, star anise and light and dark soy sauce, and the light, delicate rice wine vinegar. As Indian spices are mostly those scattered throughout the book, such as mustard seeds, coriander, cumin, turmeric, tamarind concentrate, the list of Indian specialties mainly consists of mango chutneys of different degrees of spiciness, relishes and pickles, curry paste, and the very hot vindaloo paste ($1.85 a 7-oz. jar). The list of Indonesian seasonings, spices, and hot pepper sauces and pastes, or sambala, is very helpful, for each one is explained and in some cases an indication of the use is given. There's a recipe for shrimp sambal goreng to get you started. One other handy little reference in this catalogue (more a book on the uses of herbs and spices than a catalogue) is a list of herb and spice names in other languages—French, Spanish, German, and Arabic. From this we learned that the Spanish name for chamomile is manzanilla, meaning "little apple."

BEZJIAN'S GROCERY INC. / Dept. CFC
4725 Santa Monica Blvd., Hollywood, CA 90029

"Indian Food Products–Middle Eastern Food Products," free, 12 pages, black and white.

Bezjian is an importer and wholesale distributor, so send for their list only if you are interested in large quantities—25 lbs. of lentils, 50 lbs. of Basmati rice, or a case or two of canned goods. If you should wish to buy in bulk, Bezjian carries the Sahadi Middle Eastern products, all kinds of dried beans, peas and lentils, rice, flour, cracked wheat, spices and herbs, cheeses, olives, meat products such as salami and Black Forest ham, Greek, Italian, and Spanish olive oils, pickles and chutneys, grape leaves, dried fruits, nuts and seeds, canned seafood, coffee and tea, French and English cookies, Knorr, Maggi, and Progresso soups, jams, syrups and flower waters, and such things as the Middle East lavosh, or cracker bread.

BREMEN HOUSE, INC. / Dept. CFC
218 East 86th Street, New York, NY 10028

"Bremen House Catalog of Gourmet Foods," free, published twice a year, 20 pages, illustrated, black and white.

Bremen House, in Manhattan's Yorkville area, imports a great many foods from Europe—smoked meats, cheese, cakes, candies and cookies, canned vegetables, game and seafood, tea and coffee, just about everything to eat. Among the more interesting and unusual products they carry are ground almonds and hazelnuts ($3.50 a lb.), Dutch salt herring (4-lb. plastic keg, $7.25), an assortment of honeys from Germany, Holland, Sweden, Italy, Denmark, and New Zealand, Ardennes smoked ham from Belgium, Hungarian rose paprika, backoblaten (the thin wafer papers in different diameters that go on the bottom of lebkuchen, 100 sheets to a pack), and their European-style meats, such as Westphalian ham ($4.40 a lb.), lachs-schinken ($5 a lb.), and many different wursts (sausages). If you have friends or relatives in East or West Germany, they have a large selection of duty-free gift packages (all listed in German, so you have to know what you are ordering).

BUDERIM GINGER GROWERS' CO-OP ASSN. LTD. / Dept. CFC
P.O. Box 114, Buderim, Queensland 4556, Australia

Price list, free.

Ginger in all shapes, forms, and sizes is available from the only ginger factory in Australia.

When working with filo dough, keep the sheets covered with a damp towel to prevent them drying out and becoming brittle.

Always grind whole spices freshly for Indian cooking. A small electric coffee mill (kept for this purpose alone) is a labor-savor.

Chestnuts Lyonnaise
Drain two 10-ounce cans whole chestnuts (*marrons naturels*). Dry chestnuts on paper towels. Heat ¼ cup butter in a skillet and sauté 1 chopped onion, 1 cup chopped celery, with leaves, and 1 chopped garlic clove until golden, about 5 minutes. Carefully mix in the chestnuts and heat gently, stirring occasionally, for 10 minutes, or until hot. Season to taste with salt and pepper. Serve as a vegetable dish. Serves 6.
—*courtesy Food & Wines from France, Inc.*

Elizabeth David's Green Peppercorn Butter
Using a mortar and pestle, crush 1 tablespoon canned, drained, green peppercorns with 3 slivers of garlic and ¾ teaspoon ground cinnamon. When thoroughly blended, work in 3 ounces butter, salted or unsalted. Add salt to taste (less if butter is salted). Place this flavored butter under the skin of a chicken before roasting, or in the interior of a boned loin of pork, or stir a tablespoon of the mixture into cooked rice or risotto for an unusual flavor. This keeps well in a jar in the refrigerator. It may be frozen for longer storage.

Pick a sampler hamper ($6.58 Aust.) of ginger marmalade, ginger in syrup, ginger topping, and strawberry preserves. A smaller hamper is $4.26 Aust.

While the prices are good, bear in mind that postage runs to approximately 100 percent of the cost of the package.

CASA MONEO / Dept. CFC
210 West 14th Street, New York, NY 10011

"Mexican Food–Comida Mexicana," free, 8 pages, published annually, also price lists of Latin America, Portuguese, and Cuban foods.

Casa Moneo on 14th Street has been in business for years supplying the Spanish-speaking community and anyone looking for the necessary foodstuffs for Mexican, Cuban, Spanish, South American, and Puerto Rican cooking. Unfortunately, the only printed booklet is the one on Mexican foods; so you will have to make a request (and possibly insist) to get the other lists. The Mexican catalogue has every type of canned and dried chili (ancho, mulatto, pasilla, jalapeño, serrano, to name a few), mole powder, canned nopalitos (cactus), spices like achiote (annatto), the little canned green husk tomatoes called tomatillos, masa harina for tortillas, canned corn tortillas and frozen wheat tortillas (burritos), and packages of tostadas (12 to a package, 68¢). There are many canned sauces and relishes, in varying degrees of spiciness, for tacos, enchiladas and huevos rancheros, plain and refried canned beans, Mexican chocolate, piloncillo (brown cane sugar, 70¢ a lb.) and dried corn husks for tamales ($1.75 a lb.). You can get many different kinds of dried beans here, including the black beans so widely used in Cuban cooking (69¢ for 15 oz.), guava shells and guava paste (75¢ for 10 oz. of guava paste, $1.05 for 18 oz. of the shells) and also mango paste and quince paste. Chorizos, the hot or mild Spanish sausages, are $1.50 a lb. The Brazilian foods include things you need for feijoada, such as carne seca (sun-cured salted beef, $2.85 a lb.) and farinha de mandioca (manioc flour, 50¢ a lb.), and they also list aceite de dende (palm oil). Lots of Spanish olive oils, too. While most of the lists are in Spanish and English, the Brazilian list is only in Portuguese. Prices are subject to change without notice.

CHICO-SAN, INC. / Dept. CFC
1144 West 1st Street, Chico, CA 95926

"Chico-San, Inc. Products–a catalog of unique foods," free, published annually, 26 pages, black and white.

While Chico-San is primarily in the business of selling health foods, both their own rice and rice products and imports from Japan, many of the natural products they carry are those used in Japanese cooking. There's tamari soy sauce, rich in vegetable proteins, aged for two years with no chemical additives or preservatives ($1.38 for the 12-oz. size), miso (soybean paste), cold-pressed sesame oil and the dark sesame oil pressed from roasted sesame seeds, barley koji used to make miso, bainiku ekisu (plum concentrate), salt plums ($1.65 for ½ lb.), kuzu, the wild arrowroot starch, black soybeans and azuki beans from Japan ($1.40 a ½ lb. for the soybeans, 99¢ a ½ lb. for azuki beans), sea vegetables used for stock like kombu and wakame, nori, the thin sheets of sea laver used for sushi (10 sheets, 99¢), and kanten, a sea vegetable gelatin, also known as agar-agar (½ oz. for 90¢). They have three Japanese herbal teas (mu, lotus root, ohsawa twig, a green tea) and some cooking utensils, such as vegetable knives, rice paddles, mortars and pestles. Unlike many catalogues, this one is very informative and explains exactly what each item is made from or used for.

CONTE DI SAVOIA / Dept. CFC
555 W. Roosevelt Rd., Chicago, IL 60607

Catalogue, 75¢, refunded with purchase, published annually, 28 pages, black and white.

Conte di Savoia sells imported and domestic foods, with the emphasis on Italian items. They have the Italian cheeses like Parmigiano Reggiano, Provolone, Gorgonzola, Pecorino Romano; French Brie, Roquefort, Camembert, and various other popular imports from the cheese-producing countries, such as Greek feta and Swiss Gruyère. Italian salamis and prosciutto, both imported and domestic, salt codfish or baccala, anchovies in salt, the holiday cakes and confections such as panettone, amaretti, torrone and panforte, canned whole white and black truffles and red and white wine vinegars round out their Italian specialties. Listed under the names of different countries you'll find such things as canned pfefferlinge (wild mushrooms) and preserves from Germany, French foie gras, canned soups, crystallized flowers (violets and rose petals), dried flageolet beans and the Dessaux Fils wine vinegar and tarragon leaves in vinegar, walnut oil, and cornichons. England is represented by Twinings teas, Escoffier Brand sauces (Diable, Robert, Cumberland, Melba), pickled walnuts, chutneys and jars of cockles, the tiny mollusks. From Ireland come ginger, strawberry, gooseberry, apricot, and black currant preserves in stone crocks, sugarless preserves, marmalades, Irish oatmeal and oat cakes; from Greece, Hymettus honey and stuffed vine leaves; and from New Zealand, smoked eel in natural juice and Chinese gooseberries. Other countries listed are Switzerland, Israel, Spain, Portugal, Korea (with one food, pickled garlic), Hawaii, the Philippines, Japan, Sweden, China, Australia, Holland, Puerto Rico, Mexico, Denmark, Poland, Jamaica, and India (with a pretty big listing of pickles, dals, rice, flours, coconut and mustard oil, vegetable and butter ghee, nuts and supari, or betel nut). Prices on request.

Escargots Bourguignonne
Drain 1 can (4⅔-oz.) escargots and place the snails in the shells. Spoon into each shell ½ teaspoon red wine. Mix in a bowl 1 crushed garlic clove, ¼ teaspoon coarsely ground black pepper, ½ cup unsalted butter, 2 tablespoons minced parsley, 1 teaspoon crumbled tarragon, and 2 tablespoons chopped chives. When well blended, press 1 heaping teaspoon of the mixture over the opening of each shell to seal in the snail. Place snails in a baking pan. Bake in a 425° oven for 10 to 15 minutes or until bubbly. Serves 4.
—*courtesy Food & Wines from France, Inc.*

JOHN F. COPE CO. / Dept. CFC
P.O. Box 56, Rheems, PA 17570

"John Cope's Finest Quality Pennsylvania Dutch Foods," free, one page.

Dried sweet corn is a Pennsylvania Dutch specialty, and John Cope offers both extra-fancy, special-grade dried sweet corn and fancy, regular-grade dried and evaporated corn.

Two 14-oz. canisters of special-grade dried sweet corn are $5.75 east of the Mississippi, $6.60 west of the river. The same in regular-grade is $4.60, again higher west of the Mississippi. Twenty-four cans of wet-pack dried corn are $15.50.

All prices include postage.

CREOLE DELICACIES CO., INC. / Dept. CFC
533-H Saint Ann Street, New Orleans, LA 70116

"Happy Gifts of Food from Old New Orleans," free, published annually, 21 pages, illustrated, color.

This collection of foods with a Creole flavor includes home-cooked strawberry preserves or marmalade (case of 24 10-oz. jars, $42), fig, peach, kumquat, blackberry, and watermelon rind preserves.

A 2½-lb. fruitcake mellowed in brandy and sherry ($8.95) is also available in miniatures ($9.25 for 15). A 5-lb sack of U.S. Grade 1 soft-shell pecans ($8.95), a 12- to 14-lb. Southern-style ham ($38.95), Louisiana navel oranges ($18.95 for ½ bushel), and a spice rack of Creole herbs—gumbo filé, spicy blend, omelet blend, herb blend, and crab and seafood boil ($9.75 with cookbook) are some of the other items available.

There are also New Orleans soups (crayfish bisque, turtle, shrimp creole, seafood gumbo) combined with two tins of deveined Louisiana shrimp and an 8-oz. bottle of remoulade sauce for $14.95 or in a case of 12 10-oz. tins ($18.50).

For dessert try pralines d'Orleans, a creamy pecan confection, also available in rum and chocolate flavors ($4.75), La Cuite, a taffylike syrup perfect on nut meats, biscuits or cakes, or "sirop plantage," pure Louisiana cane syrup ($8.75 for three 28-oz. tins).

★

To get juice from fresh ginger, cut the peeled root in small pieces and squeeze in a garlic press.

To make your own quatre épices (the popular French spice blend traditionally used in pâtés), mix together 3 tablespoons ground white pepper, 5 tablespoons ground cloves, 3 teaspoons ground nutmeg, and 3 teaspoons ground ginger. Store in a jar.

★

Sukiyaki

Heat a large electric skillet to 400°. Grease with 4 ounces beef suet, then discard suet. Add 1 pound beef tenderloin, in paper-thin slices, and sear on both sides. Sprinkle with ⅓ cup sugar and add ½ cup soy sauce and ¼ cup sake. Push meat to one side, add 1 bunch green onions, cut in 2-inch lengths, ½ head Chinese cabbage, sliced 1 inch thick, and 1 pound fresh spinach. Let cook for a few moments, then move to one side. Add eight 1-inch cubes of tofu (bean curd cake), 1 can shiritaki noodles, and 1 dozen large mushrooms, thinly sliced. Cook until just warmed through. Add 1 can bamboo shoots, thinly sliced, and heat through. Let guests help themselves to the ingredients as they are cooked—the meat should not be overcooked, and should be served first; vegetables can cook in the sauce throughout the meal. Add more meat as required and renew the sauce by adding more soy sauce, sake, and sugar to pan. If sauce gets too thick, add a little water. Serves 4.
—*courtesy Tele-Press Associates.*

★

Clean fresh ginger root with a brush or plastic scouring pad (it need not be peeled), slice or chop, put in a screw-topped jar, and cover with dry sherry or vodka. It will keep for months in the refrigerator.

★

Substitute pale dry cocktail sherry for the rice wine in Chinese recipes. Or use the Japanese rice wine, sake.

★

DELI-DELITES / Dept. CFC
58-65 52 Road, Woodside, NY 11377

"Deli-Delites Fine Gift Assortments," free, 1 page, illustrated, black and white.

Kosher vacuum-sealed or canned delicatessen items are mailed by Deli-Delites. They range in price from $5.95 for a 2-lb. salami to $26.95 for "The Supreme," 17 kosher items including salami, bologna, corned beef, pastrami, knockwurst, derma, canned rice and braised beef, spaghetti and meat balls, stuffed cabbage, and potato pancakes.

The "Student Survival Kit" ($18.95) is filled with salami, franks, derma, bologna, corned beef, pastrami, knockwurst, canned meat balls, stuffed cabbage, beef stew, potato pancakes.

All meat products are U.S. Government-inspected and, if necessary, Deli-Delites reserves the right to make substitutions.

MRS. DE WILDT / Dept. CFC
R.D. 3, Bangor, PA 18013

"Indonesian and Imported Foods," price list, free, 4 pages.

Mrs. De Wildt imports foods from all over the world, and sells them by mail. In the listing of Indonesian specialties you'll find all the Conimex brand sambals (hot chili pepper pastes) used as condiments with a rijstaffel or as ingredients in cooking and krupuk udang, those shrimp wafers that puff up when deep-fried ($1 for 4 oz. of the small cocktail size, $1.35 for a 3½-oz. box of the large size). In the category of prepared foods, sauces, and side dishes are bahmi (fried noodles, pork, vegetables) and nasi goreng (fried rice, pork, spices), gado gado, or spiced peanut sauce ($1.25 for 5 oz.), ikan terie (dried small fish) and atjar tjampur (spiced vegetable chutney). There are special Indonesian spices and spice mixtures, such as bumbu sesaté for satés of meat (small jar, 60¢), and a special sticky white rice (beras ketan, 65¢ an 8-oz. bag). That's only the beginning. Turn the page and you will spot lemon grass, wild lime leaves (small bag, 35¢), black shrimp jelly, dried shrimp, very hot dried small chilies (lombok rawit), rice and egg noodles, Java brown sugar, and taotjo, a special bean paste. The other imports are mainly from Holland—cheese, cookies, chocolate, honey, and canned vegetables (one very unusual, canned purslaine, 95¢ for a 14½-oz. can)—and a limited amount of things from India—chutneys, lemon and mango pickles, pappadums, Bombay duck; a few Chinese ingredients; canned tofu (bean curd) from Japan; papaya slices in syrup, coconut syrup, and toasted salted coconut chips (delicious with cocktails) from Hawaii, $1.50 for a 4-oz. tin. If you like Indonesian food, or want to try it, there's also the Conimex recipe booklet (75¢) and *The Art of Indonesian Cooking*, $6.

EAST WIND / Dept. CFC
2801 Broadway, New York, NY 10025

Mail order list, free, 5 pages.

Packaged Chinese foods are the specialty of East Wind, and the list is about as complete as you could get. In the canned and bottled products you'll find bitter melon, lotus root, bamboo shoots, water chestnuts, straw mushrooms, bean sauce both hot and sweet, duck sauce, hoisin sauce, oyster sauce, plum sauce, and in the packaged foods salted black beans (25¢ a 2-oz. bag), tree ears ($2.10 a 4-oz. bag), tiger lily, dried mushrooms, dried anchovies, and mung and soy beans. Star anise is 40¢ for 2 oz., dried bean curd $1.50 for an 8-oz. bag, and Chinese sausage $3.25 for a 1-lb. bag. There are various pickles—pickled cabbage, pickled lettuce, and the special Szechuan preserved vegetable used in that style of cooking ($1 for a 12-oz. can). Various canned and preserved fruits range from canned white peaches, kumquats, lichees, and longans to lemon prunes (35¢ a 2-oz. box), preserved plum and olive, red dates, and Tientsin dates. The teas are the usual—green, black jasmine, oolong—and there are also various candies, cookies, herbs and tonics, and kitchen utensils. For shipping and handling, 10 percent should be added to the total amount of the order, and all prices are subject to change without notice.

FAUCHON / Dept. CFC
26 Place de la Madeleine, 75008 Paris 8e, France

Price list, free, published annually, 8 pages.

Browsing through this list, it becomes clear why France is considered the culinary capital of the world. Fauchon is distinctly a specialty store, but the items here are part of what make French cuisine special.

The flavored mustards, for example: garlic and parsley mustard, mint mustard, lime mustard, shallot and chervil mustard, sherry vinegar mustard, and herbs of Provence mustard. Except for old-fashioned mustard, which comes in the red wax-sealed 1-lb. crock (about $2), all the others are in 7½-oz. jars ranging in price from about $1 for traditional mustard to $2 for horseradish mustard.

Herbs of Provence, basil, thyme, tarragon, rosemary, savory, sage, and herbs for fish are among the Fauchon herbs packed in the familiar little earthenware jars, all 1 oz. net weight, about $1.90.

Also packed under the Fauchon label are canned asparagus, green beans, artichoke bottoms, miniature mushrooms, flageolets (green kidney beans), and early June peas; dried morels and cèpes; white peaches in syrup; fruits in spirits (Agen prunes, greengages, kumquats or pineapple in Armagnac, pears in pear brandy and mirabelle plums in mirabelle brandy); mashed fruits for sherbet; jams and honeys; teas, truffles, and, of course, pâtés, foie gras, and snails. Canned cheeses (baby Brie and Camembert, goat and Muenster), too, but these are forgettable. All prices are quoted in francs, so go by the current rate of exchange. There's a 10 percent discount on exported items, and shipping is extra.

THE HELEN GALLAGHER COLLECTION / Dept. CFC
6523 N. Galena Rd., Peoria, IL 61632

"The Helen Gallagher Collection," free, published seasonally, 48 pages, illustrated, color.

One very unlikely offering from this Peoria gift house is a 2-qt. enamel gumbo pot that contains everything you need for Creole gumbo—Cajun seasoning, roux, rice, wooden spoons, filé, a bandana (to wear on your head?), a potholder, and recipes—for $18.95.

Other international cooking utensils include a wok set ($23.95), an unglazed clay cooker from West Germany large enough to hold a 15-lb. turkey ($24.95), and an 8-qt. aluminum spaghetti cooker ($18.95).

HARRINGTON'S IN VERMONT, INC. / Dept. CFC
Main Street, Richmond, VT 05477

Catalogue, free, published seasonally, 32 pages, illustrated, black and white.

New England favorites from a New England company. The New England supper provides a can each of clam chowder, baked beans, brown bread, corn chowder, Indian pudding, and Welsh rarebit, plus 1 lb. of Canadian bacon. The Green Mountain breakfast has a pound of smoked bacon, a quart of Grade A Vermont maple syrup, and a 2-lb. bag of water-ground whole-grain griddle cake mix ($12.35 to $13.95, according to shipping zone). Or you can buy cans of maple syrup and honey, chowders, steamed or minced clams, and baked beans separately.

HOUSE OF SPICES (INDIA) INC. / Dept. CFC
76-17 Broadway, Jackson Heights, NY 11373

Catalogue, free, 12 pages, black and white.

This small catalogue is a very good source for Indian and Pakistani foods—different kinds of pickles, spices, dals, flours, dried fruits and nuts, cooking oils and utensils, syrups and juices, even offbeat canned fruits and vegetables. The pickles are listed by brand and style (Gujarati style, Punjabi style, South Indian style). In cooking oils, you'll find coconut, mustard, sesame, peanut and almond, and in dals (dried pulse vegetables) chana, moong, urid, toor, vall, and masoor. There are also the waferlike breads called papad and pappadum, pan (betel nut), and

Beurek

Combine in a large bowl 1 pound grated Swiss cheese, 4 pounds fresh or frozen spinach, steamed, drained, and finely chopped, 2 cups cooked tiny shrimp (if large, cut coarsely), 1 bunch finely chopped green onions, 1 bunch parsley, finely chopped, and ½ teaspoon freshly ground black pepper. Set aside.

Remove 1 pound filo pastry sheets from the package and place 2 sheets at a time on a flat surface (keep other sheets under a slightly damp cloth or in a plastic bag to prevent them drying out). At the narrow end, spread some of the spinach-cheese filling to measure about 2 inches across and 1 inch high. Drizzle melted butter (you will need ½ pound melted butter for the recipe) over entire surface. Roll loosely in a jelly-roll shape. Place in a baking pan. Repeat filling and rolling until all pastry and filling are used. Set rolls close together in pan and brush with melted butter. Refrigerate 15 minutes before baking. Bake in a 350° oven for about 20 minutes or until golden brown. When baked, cut into bite-size hors d'oeuvre or into larger servings for a luncheon entrée. Makes 10 to 20 servings.
—from "The Caravansary–Gourmet Gallery"

A New England supper, from Harrington's in Vermont

Chicken Mandarin

Sprinkle ½ pound white meat of chicken, diced, with cornstarch and a few drops of cottonseed oil. Add 1 egg. Marinate for at least 1 hour. Cut 1 green pepper and ½ white onion into 1-inch triangles, about the same size as diced chicken. Slice ½ cup bamboo shoots into triangles and simmer in water 4 to 5 minutes. Drain and reserve. Heat wok over high temperature. Thoroughly coat inside surface with oil, then remove most of the oil. Add chicken. Toss and stir for 1 to 2 minutes. Add a splash of dry sherry, bamboo shoots, green pepper, and onion, continuing to toss and stir. Add 2 tablespoons hoisin sauce, ¼ cup chicken stock, and 2 tablespoons dried red chili peppers. Toss and stir for another 1 to 2 minutes before serving.
—*from "Madame Chiang's Mandarin Recipe Book".*

Guacamole del Norte

Peel and mash 2 ripe avocados. Mix in ½ small white onion, finely chopped, 2 or more chopped serrano chilies (according to how hot you want the guacamole), 6 Mexican tomatillos (canned green husk tomatoes), drained and chopped, salt, and pepper to taste. If available, add a little chopped fresh cilantro (Chinese parsley or fresh coriander). Combine well and put in a serving dish. Serve immediately to prevent the avocado discoloring. Serve on lettuce leaves as a salad with Mexican foods, or as a sauce or dip with fried tortilla triangles.

other after-dinner delicacies. Prices seem extremely reasonable. Basmati rice here is $3.50 for 5 lb. of Indian rice, $4.50 for 5 lb. of Pakistani rice, and the spices start at 30¢ for ¼ lb. of dill seeds or 1 oz. of mint leaves.

LE JARDIN DU GOURMET / Dept. CFC
West Danville, VT 05873

Catalogue, 50¢, published annually, 32 pages, illustrated, black and white.

This small mail-order catalogue is packed with foods from all over the world. You'll find here Urbani canned black and white truffles from Italy, French dried flageolets ($1.65 a 17-oz. box), canned flageolets and various other canned vegetables, canned and packaged soups from France, Germany, England, and Australia (kangaroo-tail soup concentrate, $1 for 10 oz.), quail eggs from Japan (6 to a tin, 55¢), and calf's-foot jelly from England. They have a very good price on the superb Plagniol virgin olive oil ($2.15 a pt.) and other notable French products such as the Dessaux Fils wine vinegars, pure walnut and peanut oils and cornichons ($1.95 an 8¼-oz. jar). You'll find here canned and dried wild mushrooms—morels, chanterelles, and cèpes—and a good selection of chestnut products, such as marrons glacés, crème de marrons, marrons, whole or in pieces, in syrup for putting on ice cream, purée of natural chestnuts, and whole chestnuts in brine for stuffings. Other imported foods include teas, preserves, foie gras, caviar, snails, canned goose fat, the Conimex Indonesian spices and sauces, and, perhaps most interesting of all, a big selection of vegetable and herb seeds from the famous French firm Vilmorin (see chapter on "Growing Things").

LEKVAR-BY-THE-BARREL / Dept. CFC
1577 First Avenue, New York, NY 10028

"A Continental Bazaar," free, published annually, 56 pages, illustrated, black and white.

This store has been a fixture in Manhattan's Yorkville district for many years, ever since Great-grandmama Roth opened her little shop to supply local residents yearning for a taste of their homeland. For over fifty years the store flourished as H. Roth & Son. Now known as Lekvar-by-the Barrel (lekvar is Hungarian prune butter, which is made freshly here), the business is still family-run and highly personal and caters primarily to European tastes and baking practices. You'll find here all the good old-fashioned cooking equipment, Hungarian specialties such as poppy-seed filling, strudel leaves, sweet and hot paprika, a very complete list of herbs and spices, and all the essentials for baking, from different flours (see chapter on "Natural Foods and Grains") through essences and extracts, cake and cookie decorations, ground nuts, dried and candied fruits to things like rose water, potash, beeswax, baking chocolate, piping gel, cream stabilizer, and edible cake decorating flowers.

The catalogue lists various egg noodles and egg drops, or tarhonya ($1.29 a lb.), various kinds of dried beans, peas and rice, including black turtle beans, French flageolets, Basmati and Arborio rice, and dried chestnuts, sago, tapioca, and millet seed. You'll also find some Chinese seasonings and ingredients, such as hot bean sauce for Szechuan cooking (79¢ a 6-oz. tin), hot chili oil and sesame oil, the line of Indonesian spices and sambals, and a few things for Brazilian cooking, such as carne seca and farinha de mandioca (salted dried beef and manioc flour) for feijoada, canned hearts of palm, and bottled palm oil, cashew juice, and coconut milk. From France come snails, foie gras, truffles, chestnut purée, mustards, the Dessaux Fils wine vinegar, Plagniol virgin olive oil, walnut and peanut oil. One of the nicest things about this catalogue is the clear organization, everything under appropriate headings, keyed to the separate price list.

MAISON GLASS / Dept. CFC
52 East 58th Street, New York, NY 10022

"Maison Glass Delicacies," $1, published annually, 72 pages, illustrated, black and white.

This leading New York specialty store has a staggering list of foods: foie gras, fresh caviar, truffles, country and Smithfield hams, smoked birds, game birds, teas and coffees, canned products from Europe, imported cheeses, cakes, candies and cookies, special oils and vinegars—you name it, they have it. Picking a few things at random, there's canned *foie gras de canard au poivre vert* (duck liver with green peppercorns, 5-oz. bloc, about $16), little brown pottery crocks of Provençal herbs, their own glace de viande ($6.25 a 12-oz. jar), praline paste ($3.95 a 14-oz. jar), that traditional English spicy spread known as Patum Peperium or Gentleman's Relish ($2.50 a 2½-oz. jar), tiny black Niçoise olives ($6.25 a 12-oz. jar), the sherry wine vinegar Craig Claiborne wrote about in *The New York Times* ($3.50 for a 1½-pt. bottle), dried and canned cèpes, morels, chanterelles, and other European wild mushrooms, and the famous Plagniol olive oil from France ($3.75 a pt.). You can get the Conimex Indonesian spices here and quite a few types of chutney, hot mango and orange pickle and tandoori spice blend, if you like Indian food. Maison Glass is always on the lookout for new items, and now they have the American-made crème fraîche (for local delivery only, $4.95 for a 16-oz. container). Rather amusingly, they have got on the ginseng bandwagon, too, and are offering Korean ginseng powder for tea and ginseng tea bags. A Maison Glass newsletter tells you about their new acquisitions (such as monkey bread), gives a menu, a bit of chat about the food products, and some recipe suggestions.

MANGANARO FOODS / Dept. CFC
488 Ninth Avenue, New York, NY 10018

"Manganaro's for Gourmet Foods," free, published annually, 22 pages, illustrated.

Manganaro's on Ninth Avenue is a New York City landmark, a fixture since 1893. It's a typical Italian grocery, with salami and cheese hanging from the rafters and every kind of Italian food you can think of, including their own fresh pasta, made on the premises with semolina, eggs and water, and cut to order (not sent by mail). Pasta is king here. They stock more than 500 different sizes, shapes, and brands, imported and domestic. There's the Russo brand from Naples, the Fara San Martino from Abruzzi, and Pasta Barilla, another best seller. All brands are 85¢ a lb. Egg noodles and green noodles are $1.35 for the imported, $1 for the domestic.

Among other specialties you'll find baccala (boneless dried salt cod) from Italy, white and black truffles (1 oz. whole white truffles, $12; black, $10, and you can write for prices of fresh truffles, which they have in season), dried mushrooms from northern Italy, pine nuts from Tuscany ($5 a lb.), 6-oz. tins of pesto from Genoa (65¢) and various kinds of antipasti ingredients such as roasted peppers, caponatina (eggplant appetizer), pickled mushrooms, artichoke hearts packed in oil and lemon juice, Italian ripe olives. There's a good selection of meats—prosciutto, salami, pancetta, and cotechino, and loads of cheeses, from the grating cheeses, Parmigiano Reggiano, Sardo, Pecorino Romano to Provolone, Gorgonzola, Fontina, Fonduta, Taleggio, plus the usual cheeses from France and other countries, for Manganaro Foods is not chauvinistic.

ORIENTAL FOODS AND HANDCRAFTS / Dept. CFC
3708 N. Broadway, Chicago, IL 60613

"Pakistani-Indian Foods," price list, free, 3 pages.

Despite the company name, the products and foods are Indian and Pakistani. You'll find here just about anything you need for Indian cooking, from spices to make your own garam masala (spice mixture) or their garam masala (55¢ for 2 oz.) to chutneys and pickles, flours, dal

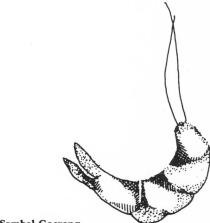

Shrimp Sambal Goereng

Heat 3 tablespoons vegetable oil in a pan. Add 2 medium onions, peeled and sliced, and sauté until golden brown. Add ½ to 1 teaspoon sambal oelek (Indonesian hot red pepper sauce), 1 teaspoon minced garlic, and 1 teaspoon laos (Indonesian ginger-like spice). Cook for 5 minutes. Stir in ½ cup shredded coconut, soaked in 1½ cups water (add water, too), ¼ teaspoon powdered bay leaves or 2 whole bay leaves, and salt to taste. Simmer for 10 minutes. Add 1 cup green beans, cut into 1-inch pieces, and cook 5 minutes. Add 1 pound shelled shrimp and cook until tender, about 5 minutes. Stir in 1 teaspoon tamarind concentrate and serve hot. Note: To make this a vegetarian dish, leave out the shrimp and substitute a pound of your favorite vegetable.

—from Aphrodisia Catalogue

(beans and lentils), rice, coconut, and mustard oils and pappadums, either plain or spiced with garlic, chili pepper ($1.30 for 14 oz.). Picking out a few items at random, we noticed Basmati rice (1 lb., 75¢), rice flour and chick-pea flour, black cumin seed, tamarind concentrate, curry leaves (1 oz., 40¢), silver leaf for garnishing food ($1 for a packet of 10 leaves), Bombay duck, raw and salted almonds, and pistachios ($1.50 for 4 oz. raw pistachios, 70¢ for those salted and in the shell). For those who like it, there are various forms of supari (betel nut).

PAPRIKAS WEISS IMPORTER / Dept. CFC
1546 Second Avenue, New York, NY 10028

"Imported Foods and Cookware Catalogue," $1 for annual subscription, published four times a year, 66 pages, illustrated, black and white.

Paprikas Weiss is an old-established store in Manhattan's German and Hungarian section, and so much is packed into their small catalogue that it is hard to know where to look. Products of different types, from different countries, are scattered throughout the pages. Listed under Hungarian specialties are the finest rose paprika, Paprikas Weiss' own salami, sausage, double-smoked bacon, lekvar (prune) and apricot butter, strudel sheets, and various forms of pasta, including egg noodle squares, egg barley or tarhonya, medium, broad, and extra-fine soup noodles. Other things we noticed were crystallized flowers from France, baking parchment, Holland-style honey cake which is grated into sauerbraten ($1.25 a package), oblaten, or unfilled cake layers, for making Dobos torte ($3.98 a tin), canned wild mushrooms from Germany and Poland and dried cèpes in bulk ($2.50 an oz.), French black truffles ($24.95 a 1¾-oz. tin), the edible rice-paper rounds for baking lebkuchen (100 of the ½-inch size, 98¢), fruit pastry fillings, concentrated nonalcoholic flavorings, bulgur and couscous, imported dried and canned soups, drums of sea salt ($2.98), tiny black Niçoise olives, and little egg spaetzle from Germany. If you ate your way through this catalogue, it would be like a gastronomic tour of the world.

WILLIAM POLL'S GOURMET SHOP / Dept. CFC
1051 Lexington Avenue, New York, NY 10021

Brochure, free, published semiannually.

Poll's is one of New York's more elegant and expensive caterers and specialty food shops, cleaving to the motto "Quality is not a compromise" and doing very nicely, too. Apart from certain items such as sandwiches, obviously only for local consumption, most of their prepared dishes can be ordered frozen. Their *papillons*, for instance, little bite-size appetizers of strudel dough filled with cheese, meat, mushroom and bacon, spinach or shrimp come 14 to the tray (12 for the spinach triangles) at prices of from $4 to $5. International specialties from their kitchen include such things as moussaka, coq au vin, and stuffed cabbage. There's a wide choice of soups and sauces, desserts and cookies, croissants and brioches. Poll's also has fresh Iranian Beluga caviar, fresh black and white truffles in season, baked Smithfield and country hams, smoked turkey, freshly roasted nuts, imported cheeses, foie gras in terrines and blocs, smoked sturgeon and smoked Scotch or Nova Scotia salmon. The brochure does not specify methods of shipping or charges, and prices for some of the foods are not listed, so you will have to request information.

RAY'S BRAND PRODUCTS, INC. / Dept. CFC
P.O. Box 154, Springfield, IL 62705

Brochure.

No catalogue or price list, as they have only three items, Ray's chili with beans, chili without beans, and Chilli-Mac (chili with macaroni), all canned. They will ship by UPS six 20-oz. cans of chili with beans for $6.50. Without the beans, it is about $2.50 more. Prices quoted are subject to change.

Hungarian salami from Paprikas Weiss

★

When making chili, substitute Mexican mole powder for part of the chili powder in the recipe. It adds flavor, richness, and thickness.

RIO GRANDE FOODS / Dept. CFC
Route 4, Tilden, TX 78072

Order blank and one page of serving suggestions, free.

The product sold by Rio Grande is what they describe as authentic Tex-Mex Style Chili made from choice beef and their secret combination of 12 piquant spices, herbs and aromatics, with no cereal fillers, additives, or preservatives. You can order chili with beans (case of six 15-oz. cans, $12; chili without beans, $16) or their special canned Tex-Mex cheese dip with jalapeño peppers ($6 for a case of six 8-oz. cans). A $6 sampler brings you two cans of chili with beans and one of the cheese dip. Add $1.75 per item for UPS shipping. They suggest using the chili to fill enchiladas, top them with the cheese dip, and bake until bubbling in a 375° oven.

ROMBIN'S NEST FARM / Dept. CFC
Fairfield, PA 17320

Catalogue, 25¢, published annually, 40 pages, illustrated, black and white.

Among the typically Pennsylvania Dutch foods in this gift catalogue are John Cope's dried sweet corn, with recipes on the box (around $1.50), apple schnitz (sliced dried apples), around $1.75 a ½-lb. package, Lebanon bologna, assorted pretzels, typical relishes, and fruit butters.

SAHADI IMPORTING CO., INC. / Dept. CFC
187 Atlantic Avenue, Brooklyn, NY 11201

"The Silent Salesman," free, published biannually, 24 pages, illustrated, black and white.

Sahadi is a big importer, wholesaler, and retailer of Middle Eastern foods, and chances are that you can find in this catalogue anything you might need, from harissa (fiery hot sauce for couscous, 60¢ for a 140-gram can) to the filo dough ($1.35 a lb. box) for baklava, bstilla, brik, or the Green spanakopita (spinach pie). Sahadi has a large range of cereals, dried legumes, nut and seeds, among them bulgur (cracked wheat) for tabbouleh and kibbeh, chick-peas and chick-pea flour, Basmati rice, couscous, red lentils and mung dal (much used in Indian cooking), pistachio and pignolia nuts. You'll find a big range of olives, black and green, oils of olive, sesame, mustard, coconut. Tahini, the sesame seed paste used for making baba ghannouj and hummus bi tahini (eggplant and chick-pea dips), is $1.10 for a 15-oz. can, or $2 for the imported Lebanese tahini. There are lots of candies, pastries, preserves, syrups, honey, and juices for the sweet-toothed Middle Easterners, including exotica such as carob syrup, pomegranate syrup, tamarind syrup, and rose-petal jam. Other specialties include tarama (fish roe) for taramasalata, stuffed vine leaves, peppers, eggplant, and cabbage, grape vine leaves for stuffing ($2 a qt. jar), dried fruits that are used so much in Middle Eastern meat dishes, the fragrant rose and orange blossom waters, and rose and orange essence. Spices, sold by the pound and quarter pound, are very reasonably priced—50¢ for 4 oz. of ground turmeric, cumin, or fennel, 40¢ for 4 oz. of fenugreek, and many herbs and flavorings you might not be able to find elsewhere, such as ground sumac, mastic (gum arabic, for flavoring rice pudding) and special herbs used in Middle Eastern cooking such as zaatar and mloukhiyeh. Sahadi also has a few pieces of cooking and serving equipment, cookbooks, backgammon tables and sets, belly-dancing costumes, musical instruments, camel-saddle seats, hassocks, low tables, spice racks, amidst other odds and ends. Prices are FOB the store and are subject to change without notice. Orders under $15 are not accepted, but there are so many things to buy here your order should easily make the minimum. Compare their prices, for instance, with those in your local specialty food shop and you'll usually come out ahead.

Dried chilies should be kept in a plastic bag in the refrigerator. To prepare them for cooking, remove stems, break in half, and take out small seeds and any veins. Tear into small pieces and soak in hot water for 30 minutes to 1 hour until softened. Rinse canned chilies in cold water before using to remove the hot liquid. Always wash your hands well with soap and hot water after handling fresh, canned, or dried chilies. They contain an oil that is very irritating to eyes and skin.

*

Cover design, Rombin's Nest Farm catalogue

*

Soak dried corn in milk overnight before cooking. It will be creamier and more flavorful.

*

Transfer the unused portion of an opened can of truffles to a screw-topped jar and cover with cognac, Madeira, or olive oil. Refrigerate and use as needed. The truffles add great flavor to the liquid, which can be used in cooking.
—from Paul Urbani

*

NATURAL BLACK TRUFFLES
EXQUISITE

URBANI CARLO

ESPOSIZIONE TRENTO 1924 - MEDAGLIA D'ORO
SCHEGGINO DI SPOLETO - Umbria (Italia)

Bagna Cauda
In the top of a double boiler, heat 1 cup butter and 4 tablespoons olive oil with 4 minced garlic cloves until butter is melted and oil hot. Turn off heat and hold over hot water. Add 4 chopped anchovy fillets, ⅛ teaspoon salt, and a 2-ounce can white truffles, thinly sliced. Let stand over hot water for 20 minutes. Prepare a dish of fresh vegetable sticks (celery, cucumber, green pepper, fennel, small sliced artichokes, etc.) for dipping into the hot sauce.
—from Paul Urbani

Taramasalata
Remove the crusts from 2 slices of day-old white bread and moisten the bread with water. Press out excess moisture. Place bread, a 4-ounce jar tarama (fish roe), ⅓ cup lemon juice, and 2 tablespoons chopped onion in a blender or food processor. Blend or process until smooth. Gradually add 1 cup olive oil or mixed olive and salad oil, blending until thick, like mayonnaise. Transfer to a bowl or covered jar and chill. When ready to serve, sprinkle with mixed parsley. Serve with toasted pita (flat Arab bread) or broken-up lavosh (cracker bread).

PAUL A. URBANI TRUFFLES / Dept. CFC
P.O. Box 2054, Trenton, NJ 08607

Recipe leaflet, free.

The Urbani family is in the truffle business in Italy, and so is Paul Urbani here in the United States. He imports Italian canned truffles— black, whole, unpeeled brushed truffles, whole peeled truffles, truffle pieces and peelings, white truffles, truffle purée, and, in season, the incredibly expensive, incredibly wonderful fresh truffles. Fresh white truffles usually arrive the second or third week in November, the black the week before Christmas. Orders, which should be sent no later than the last week in October and the last week in November, are immediately shipped by air as soon as the truffles arrive and sent special delivery from the airport, as befits such rare and perishable things. Write to Mr. Urbani for prices, which change each year, according to supply and demand, and are always astronomical. Many fine stores and mail-order companies (Le Jardin du Gourmet, for one) sell Urbani truffles. Retail price of a 1-oz. tin of whole black unpeeled brushed truffles is around $6, a 1-oz. tin of white truffles about $11.25. The pieces are $4.75 for a 1-oz. tin and the peelings $13.50 for a 4-oz. tin.

UWAJIMAYA / Dept. CFC
P.O. Box 3003, Seattle, WA 98114

Price list, free, published semiannually, 5 pages with order blank.

Uwajimaya (named for the birthplace of Fujimatsu Moriguchi, whose widow and children run the store) has grown over the years from a tiny fish market to a spacious supermarket in Seattle's Chinatown with a suburban branch and an import wholesale operation—a real family success story. The mail-order list is for all kinds of Oriental products, mostly packaged but some fresh. For Japanese cooking you'll find abura age (deep-fried bean curd) at $1.25 a can, dried daikon (the giant white radish) and shiitake (black mushroom), all the dried seaweeds and fish, noodles and rice, flours, condiments and various sauces, from shoyu (soy) to sukiyaki, teriyaki and tempura sauces, Japanese teas and fresh ginger and taro root. They also have miscellaneous cooking and serving equipment, such as rice cookers, rice bowls, tempura sets, and woks for Chinese cooking. A friend who knows a lot about Japanese cooking says it is a pretty complete list. Chinese products are the usual canned goods and sauces: canned bamboo shoots (59¢ a 19-oz. can), water chestnuts, red bean curd, bean sprouts, soy sauce, bean sauce, plum sauce, hoisin sauce, oyster sauce, and sesame oil. Chinese noodles are $1.99 for 5 lbs., the thin bean threads 87¢ for 7.75 oz., salted black beans 83¢ a lb. In teas you'll find green tea, black tea, jasmine, oolong, and a Chinese restaurant blend, mostly in tea bags but some loose (loose green tea is 98¢ for 100 grams, just under ¼ lb.). Listed under "miscellaneous" are candied ginger, almond cookies, 5-spice powder, and Thai fish sauce ($1.19 for 24½ oz.).

VANDER VLIET'S HOLLAND IMPORTS / Dept. CFC
3147 West 111th Street, Chicago, IL 60655

Catalogue, free, published annually, 34 pages, black and white.

Imports from Holland and other European countries. You'll find all the Conimex spices and sambals for rijstaffel and nasi goreng; soups and soup mixes; Dutch cheeses such as Gouda, Edam, Leyden; chocolates by Droste, Bensdorp, Van Dungen, Tobler; Callard & Bowser toffees; honey and ginger cakes; cookies and crackers; canned herring, eel, and mackerel; fresh smoked eel (when available); sausages; and even cigars in this solidly packed little catalogue. There are some rather unusual dried vegetables, such as dried kale (69¢ a package), brown beans, gray peas ($1.09 a package), canned kale, chicory (endive to us), broad beans, three Dutch mustards (Koop's regular, extra-strong, and salad mustard, 39¢ a jar), and some pickles. Sweet-sour or sour onions and gherkins are all $1.09 a jar.

THE VERMONT COUNTRY STORE / Dept. CFC
Weston, VT 05161

Catalogue, 25¢, published annually, 98 pages, illustrated, black and white.

The Vermont Country Store lists some typical New England foods, maple syrup, sugar, candy, cream and fudge, jams, jellies, relishes, and various canned products, such as oven-baked beans (yellow-eye beans with pork, soldier beans with pork, Jacob's Cattle beans with pork, so-called because they are spotted and speckled like the cattle in the Bible), brown bread, Indian pudding, corn, clam and fish chowders, fiddlehead fern greens and dandelion greens. The baked beans are around $2.25 for two 28-oz. cans, the fiddlehead ferns $1.25 a 15-oz. can. They also have the three types of dry beans in 2-lb. bags for cooking or sprouting at $1.95 a bag. Other typical Vermont products are cheddar, common crackers, and seafood or chowder crackers, stone-ground whole-grain cereals, meals and flours (including white or yellow corn grits). There are a couple of gift package samplers: a Saturday Night Supper with canned clam chowder, oven-baked beans and pork, brown bread, and Indian pudding with a jar of relish ($5.50) and a Sunday Morning Breakfast of maple syrup, stone-ground whole-grain pancake meal, with recipe, and a jar of jam ($5.95).

Creamed Dried Corn
Soak 1 cup dried corn in 2 cups milk overnight. Next day, put in a pan with 2 teaspoons sugar, 1½ teaspoons salt, 2 tablespoons unsalted butter, and 1 cup heavy cream. Bring to a boil, then reduce the heat and simmer for ½ hour, stirring frequently so it does not stick. Serve immediately with ham or roast pork. Serves 4 to 6.

See Appendix, page 239, for additional sources not included here.

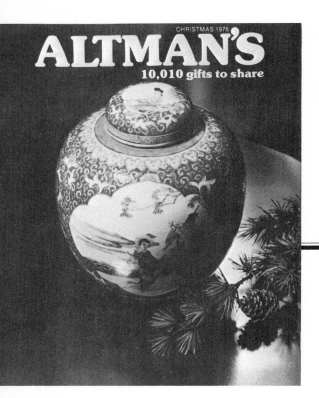

CHRISTMAS 1976
ALTMAN'S
10,010 gifts to share

CHAPTER ELEVEN

GENERAL
AND
GIFT CATALOGUES

Artichokes with Caviar
Trim medium artichokes and cook uncovered in boiling salted water until bottom leaves pull out easily, about 30 to 40 minutes. Remove from pan and drain upside down on paper towels. When cool enough to handle, remove the hairy choke from the center and chill until ready to serve. For each 2 artichokes, mix 1 ounce caviar into ¼ cup sour cream. Spoon into center of artichokes and serve.

B. ALTMAN & CO. / Dept. CFC
P.O. Box 470, Murray Hill Station, New York, NY 10016
Christmas catalogue, free, 116 pages, illustrated, color.

Recently many department stores have started putting foods in their Christmas catalogue, and Altman's is one. They have half a dozen edibles from Fortnum & Mason of London, such as a pyramid of marmalade, plum pudding, Dundee cake and tea bags, a teatime treat of marmalade and teas, and a host of their own gift hampers and boxes filled with things like Perugina chocolates, lebkuchen, fruit cakes, stollen, Bigelow teas, and mixed nuts. A box of lebkuchen, or spice cookies glazed with sugar and sweet and bittersweet chocolate, is $6.35 for 21 oz., or there's a gingerbread rocking horse for $4. An acetate box of 2 lbs. of Altman's own hard candies is $4, a 1-lb. box of Blum's light and dark chocolates, $3.75. Altman's always has plenty of interesting kitchen gifts, too.

JOHNNY APPLESEED'S / Dept. CFC
Beverly, MA 01915
"Johnny Appleseed's," free, published seasonally, 44 pages, illustrated, color.

Typical mail-order offerings but a few items of interest to the cook. From Vermont's Green Mountains, pure grade-A maple syrup in pt. ($3.50), qt. ($6.50), and ½-gal. ($10.95) tins are shown with an Armetale pewterlike pitcher and plate for $17.95. Johnny Appleseed's woven wicker pie basket with hinged lid and swivel handles holds two pies in perfect safety or one pie and a picnic lunch by using the footed tray that fits into the basket ($9.95). A sampling of syrups in five 6-oz. tins, $4.95, include Vermont maple, maple-butternut, blueberry, apple, and blackberry for pancakes, waffles, or ice cream.

BLOOMINGDALE'S / Dept. CFC
P.O. Box 2058, F.D.R. Station, New York, NY 10022

Christmas catalogue, free, published annually, 100 pages, illustrated, color.

In the current edition of Bloomingdale's Christmas catalogue there are all kinds of yummy things from their delicacies department, such as Godiva and Belgian Corne de la Toison d'Or chocolates, the latter flown in for Bloomie's alone ($9.50 for a 1-lb. ballotin, or $20 for a 1-lb. red velvet casque), a chocolate seashell filled with marzipan fruits, a 4-lb. tin of hearth-baked cookies, an imported plum pudding in its own white pottery pudding basin, a box of four jams, a crock of Northwestern strawberry preserves, glacé apricots from Australia, gift packs of ham and cheese, three bags full of coffee (Colombian Armenia Supremo, French roast, Viennese with cinnamon, available regular or decaffeinated), a box of little Italian amaretti, and a crate of imported lebkuchen, those most delicious of spicy Christmas cookies, coated with chocolate or sugar glaze ($10). Or you can order a wheel of aged New York State cheddar, a terrine of Strasbourg truffled foie gras, the Famous Amos chocolate chip cookies, Bloomie's burlap bag of 5 lbs. of peanuts ($8.50), or fruits and nuts layered in a cork-topped jar. Kitchen gifts are here in abundance, all the electric miracle workers that everyone yearns for—the Cuisinart food processor, Prestoburger hamburger cooker grill, crock pot, crêpe maker, Salton peanut butter and ice-cream machines, and Presto's Fry Baby, the deep fryer that uses only 2 cups of oil. For the cook who isn't switched on, there's a cappuccino machine that works on an electric or gas range ($100), a wok set (wok, ring, cover, cleaver, and tools) handsomely packaged in a wicker picnic basket ($37.50), or a 12-piece quiche set of 11" black steel French quiche pan, measure, cheese grater, wooden spoons, tester and whisk, 4 individual pans, and recipe book ($10).

LA BOUTTICA / Dept. CFC
164 Mason Street, Greenwich, CT 06830

Catalogue, free, published seasonally, 32 pages, illustrated, color.

A gift catalogue with a few handsome things for the kitchen and the table, among them a Lucite salt and pepper mill ($13), a silver-plated holder for a soufflé dish or round casserole ($25), a copper colander, a set of 4 copper measuring cups, a brass-strapped copper ice bucket, and an oval, tin-lined copper pan with a long brass handle, incorrectly described as an omelet pan, classically used to flambé fish at tableside or for fish sauced and glazed under the broiler ($22).

HARRIET CARTER / Dept. CFC 62
Plymouth Meeting, PA 19462

Catalogue, free, published seasonally, 112 pages, illustrated, color and black and white.

A general gift catalogue with some interesting or useful things for the kitchen or outdoors. One is a giant skillet of heavy aluminum, 27½" overall, that will fry 14 hamburgers or scramble 36 eggs, impractical for the burners on a stove but okay for a large barbecue grill or campfire ($11.98). There's an ice-cream scoop with a built-in defrosting element to keep the dipper from freezing ($2.98), spatter-blue enameled ware and a set of English tins with hinged lids for keeping tea, candies, or cookies airtight ($4.98). For indoor fireplace cooking, a revolving 12" grill, adjustable from 25" to 31" in height, rotates over logs or charcoal for even cooking, swings out for turning or seasoning ($7.98).

CASUAL LIVING / Dept. CFC
Stony Hill, Bethel, CT 06081

"Casual Living," free, published annually, 48 pages, illustrated, black and white.

An interesting catalogue with quite a few good kitchen things, such as the beechwood lemon reamer (recently rediscovered and revived by the Cordon Bleu Cookery School in London), a ridged, cone-shaped wood-

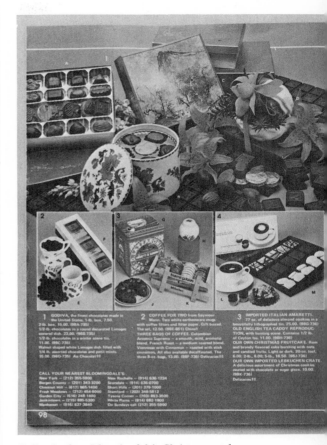

Delicacies from Bloomingdale's Christmas catalogue

Quail on Toast
Thaw 12 frozen quail, split lengthwise, and rub with salt, freshly ground pepper, Dijon mustard, and ½ teaspoon crushed rosemary. Wrap half a slice of medium thick bacon around each bird. Place in a baking dish and roast at 400° for 20 minutes, then finish under the broiler for 5 to 6 minutes, about 4 inches from the heat. Generously butter one side of 12 slices lightly toasted bread and spread with Dijon mustard. Serve the quail on the toast, with a thin slice of lemon. Serves 6.
—from "The Omaha Steaks Cookbook," recipe by James Beard

en gadget that you insert into the lemon and turn so the juice runs down the furrows but no seeds escape, one of the greatest stocking-stuffer ideas we've found ($6.50). For chocolate lovers, chocolate mixes and bases come in a wood crate (dipping chocolate, hot fudge, chocolate syrup, hot chocolate drink base, cocoa mix, confectionery sticks, and candy papers) with a recipe booklet ($15). There's also a pasta maker ($13), a wall knife rack of Vermont maple wood with slots for 6 knives, cleaver, and sharpening steel ($11), a basketful of 20 ears of corn on the cob for popcorn and, for luscious desserts, tall apothecary jars from France, each one containing cherries, raspberries, or chestnuts in Hennessy Cognac, to combine in a fruit compote, put over ice cream or in crêpes ($15 a jar), the jars, of course, reusable. From Vermont comes a breakfast of blueberries canned in syrup, stone-ground griddle-cake mix, and maple syrup packaged with an earthenware syrup pitcher ($11.50).

CLYMER'S OF BUCKS COUNTY / Dept. CFC
Chestnut Street, Nashua, NH 03061

Catalogue, free, published annually, 64 pages, illustrated, color.

There are quite a few good kitchen things tucked away in this gift catalogue, but you have to hunt to find them, as they aren't grouped by category but are dotted through the pages. If you have been looking for the Mexican molcajete, the lava-stone mortar and pestle that was traditionally used to grind chilies and spices before Mexican cooks discovered the blender, they are here in large, medium, and small sizes, ranging in price from around $4 to around $7. They have the Sabatier line of chef's knives and some good-looking handcrafted walnut or cherry free-standing knife racks, single, double, and triple rows, to hold 5, 10, or 15 knives ($15 to $25), the Pennsylvania Dutch draal-huls or rolling pin with a long handle between two side supports (around $13) and, for appearances only, a simple and attractive 4-bottle teak wine rack that can be used singly or stacked in tiers (each rack, $6), and the spice knobs (spice seeds imbedded in resin) that look so pretty on kitchen cabinet doors, 2 for $3.95, 6 for $10.95 or 12 (the full line of a dozen different spices) for $20.95. There are also miniature versions as magnets and thumbtacks, $3.50 for a set of 8 magnets or $2.95 for thumbtacks.

COLONIAL GARDEN KITCHENS / Dept. CFC
270 W. Merrick Road, Valley Stream, NY 11582

Catalogue, 25¢, published monthly, 112 pages, illustrated, black and white.

While this comprehensive catalogue has a little bit of everything for the home and is loaded with gadgets, the quality is excellent. You'll find there a lot of the well-designed cookware carried by the better kitchen shops, such as the Italian stainless-steel strainer and the spaghetti scoop, the Cuisinart food processor, Corning's ovenproof glass soufflé dishes, and the Taylor instant meat thermometer that registers from 0° to 220°F, used by James Beard and other exacting cooks. If you haven't been able to locate baking parchment, it's here, too. There are also some things you won't find everywhere, such as a hardwood cutting board with a chart of U.S. weights and measures and their metric equivalents branded on the reverse side, a Pennsylvania Dutch rolling pin (quite different from the standard one), and a machine that separates fruit and vegetable pulps from the seeds and skin. If you recognize some of the foods as being the same as those in Barth's natural-foods catalogue, it's because they are the same company. Here again the selection has been made with care and knowledge. You can order the incomparable French moutarde de Meaux (the kind with cracked mustard seeds), shallots, Maldon sea salt from England, Pennsylvania Dutch dried corn, Chinese seasonings, couscous, and fresh green peppercorns from Madagascar. Prices, which range from just over $1 for some of the gadgets to over $200 for the food processor, are what you would pay in a store, but here you have the convenience of not having to scurry around to find what you want. There's also a number you can call collect for orders of $20 and over, which can be charged to a credit card. Definitely worth a quarter.

La Salade Folle
In a large salad bowl, mix 1 head Boston lettuce, trimmed and broken into leaves, 2 cups small pieces chicory, and 2 endive, broken into leaves. Add 3 hard-cooked eggs, chopped, 2 cups French pâté de foie gras (goose liver pâté), and 2 tablespoons minced black truffles. Chill. When ready to serve, make a vinaigrette dressing with ⅓ cup olive oil, ¼ cup red wine vinegar (reduce the amount of vinegar if you wish), ½ teaspoon salt, a few grinds of pepper, and 2 tablespoons minced parsley. Pour over salad and toss gently to coat all ingredients. Serve at once. Serves 6.
—*courtesy Food & Wines from France, Inc.*

JOAN COOK / Dept. CFC

851 Eller Drive, Ft. Lauderdale, FL 33316

Catalogue, free, published seasonally, 96 pages, illustrated, color.

In the Joan Cook gift catalogue you'll find such things as the Toastmaster restaurant-type food warmer that keeps foods at an ideal 150°F. temperature ($29.95); the Vita Mix food processor that kneads, cooks, freezes, mixes, blends, pulverizes, juices, chops, grinds, and purées ($189.95); the Sunbeam Hot Shot that heats water for soups, coffee, and cocoa in 90 seconds ($22.95); and Chilton's 2-qt. mini slow cooker. For cooking in the microwave oven there's a set of four 6-oz. "petit pots" ($8.95).

The grease mop ($6.50) will pick up the grease from bacon, hamburgers, stews, and roasts. There's a sun drier ($9.95), a 17" x 17" frame for natural dehydration of foods, or the faster electric dehydrator ($49.95).

The Danish lettuce spinner both dries lettuce, spinach, and herbs and rubs off the skins of potatoes, carrots, onions, beets, and tomatoes.

CUMBERLAND GENERAL STORE / Dept. CFC

Rte. 3, Crossville, TN 38555

"The Wish & Want Book," $3, published seasonally, 272 pages, illustrated, black and white.

"The Wish & Want Book," subtitled "over 2000 items for man and beast," is in appearance just like the old-fashioned general-store catalogues or the original Sears, Roebuck. Dedicated to self-sufficient country living, it is full of things like oak kegs and wash pots, apple-butter kettles and grist mills, and tools for the farmer, farrier, and blacksmith. Some of the items are just like those in the Mother's General Store catalogue, which has been taken over by Cumberland General Store.

You'll find here old-fashioned preserving kettles in aluminum or blue-speckled enamel, 14-qt. and 16-qt. capacity; pressure canners and cold-pack canners, canning jars and the extra caps and rings; the tin cans for canning fruits and vegetables and a can-sealing machine ($136.54); and all the food-preparation tools and gadgets like cutters, pitters, and parers. Other good things we noticed in the packed pages of this catalogue include a dough tray, handcrafted of buckeye wood, just like the Early American ones, 24" long, 13" wide, and 3½" deep ($14.98); an electric stone grinding mill ($218) that will do anything from cracked wheat to fine flour; blue-speckled graniteware; the old-fashioned and very efficient lemon and lime squeezer that works like a press ($4.62); a good selection of hand-operated coffee mills, the kind with a handle on top or wheels at the sides and a drawer in the bottom; Early American stoneware bowls and pitchers in natural finish with pink and blue stripes; handwoven hardwood pie, cake and market baskets ($11 for the pie basket), and various huge cast-iron pots and kettles, such as a sugar kettle, a 52-gallon caldron, and a pot with legs and lid that can stand in the fireplace. They also have big stoneware crocks and churns and everything you need for making butter, such as hand and electric churns, a butter paddle, and butter molds.

EGERTONS / Dept. CFC

Lyme Street, Axminster, Devon EX13 5DB, England

"Egertons Postal Gift and Shopping Service," $1.50 if airmailed, free otherwise, published annually, 74 pages, illustrated, color.

A gift catalogue of distinctively English delicacies. Soups, supplied to Egertons by Turner and Price, Ltd., include real turtle, bisque de homard, clear oxtail made with wine, consommé, and venison (four 15-oz. cans, $14.63; eight cans, $25).

Other Turner and Price gift packs sold by Egertons include marrons glacés and honey ($19.33), Provençal glacé fruits, Cumberland brandy butter and Danish butter cookies ($21.43), and Belgian chocolates ($17.25 for a 1½-lb. tin).

Elsewhere in this catalogue you'll find listings for their cakes, cookies, puddings, coffee and tea, honey and preserves, and candies.

Unusual gifts from the Joan Cook catalogue

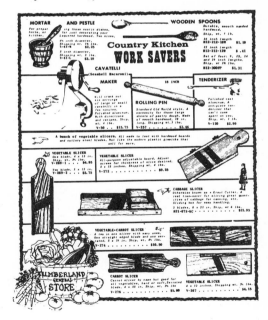

Tools for the cook, from "The Wish & Want Book"

Potted Shrimp or Salmon

Drain small canned Pacific shrimp or canned salmon. If using salmon, remove bones and skin, and flake. Combine shrimp or salmon with melted butter and cayenne pepper, grated nutmeg, or ground mace to taste. The flavor should be piquant, but not hot. Toss shrimp with butter and seasonings or mash salmon to a paste with butter and seasonings. Put in a small bowl and serve chilled with crackers or toast fingers as a cocktail appetizer. Potted salmon also makes a good sandwich filling.

Gift boxes of cheese, from Figi's Inc.

THE EPICURES' CLUB / Dept. CFC
939 Lehigh Avenue, Union, NJ 07083

"The Epicures' Club," free, published annually, 32 pages, illustrated, color.

Gift assortments of cheeses, sausages, preserves, candy, snacks, nuts, and cakes, packaged for Christmas giving.

Some of the less expensive gifts include a 1½-lb. pineapple-apricot cake ($7); a mint assortment of chocolate-covered peppermint patties and 10 oz. of pastel butter mints ($6.75); a 1-lb. or 2-lb. English plum pudding in an earthenware bowl ($5 and $6.85); three 10-oz. tins of eggnog-nut, banana-nut, and Swiss chocolate dessert cakes ($8.75); 2 lbs. of 6-oz. pieces of cheddar, Bella Alpina, Stilton, Port du Salut, Shepherd Girl, Gouda, Edam, and Muenster ($11.45); eight 7-oz. jars of assorted jellies and preserves ($9.35); and an assortment of petits fours, strawberry preserves, grape jelly, honey, and mixed nuts ($10).

A loaf pan is packed with cheeses, pickles, preserves, and olives ($13.75). A whole smoked ringneck pheasant ($14) is also sold packaged with mixed nuts, olives, smoked rainbow trout pâté, sardines, plum pudding, and orange slices for $20.95.

ESPECIALLY MAINE / Dept. CFC
Vinegar Hill Road, Arundel, ME 04046

"Especially Maine," free, published periodically, 23 pages, illustrated, black and white.

An enchanting little catalogue from a small shop and mail-order business that, with a few exceptions, sells only Maine-grown, processed, manufactured, and handcrafted products, many made exclusively for the store. From the Sabbathday Lake colony come Shaker herbs, herbal teas, and herbal vinegars. Among the herbs are some unusual ones, such as borage ($1.25), marigold ($1.65), and sassafras ($2.75). The teas, packed in tins with pretty, old-fashioned labels, include comfrey, elder flower, lemon verbena, and wild cherry bark (each $1.25). The herbal vinegars are sweet cicely, tarragon, mint, and basil (75¢ for an 8-oz. bottle). Pure Maine blueberry honey is $1.80 a 1-lb. jar, Maine maple syrup $3.50 for a 1-pt. jug, and maple candy $1.25 for a 4-oz. box. Quite unusual are the canned dandelion and fiddlehead greens, historically Maine's first vegetable crop each spring, $1.25 each for a 15-oz. can. There are gift packs of Maine canned seafoods, lobster picks and crackers, canned wild blueberries with Sarah Wyman's pie and muffin recipes on the label (85¢ for a 15-oz. can in syrup pack, 75¢ for the water pack), and some beautiful solid rock maple salad bowls ($3 for 7" diameter up to $20 for 15" diameter). Well worth sending for.

FIGI'S INC. / Dept. CFC
Central Plaza, Marshfield, WI 54449

"Figi's Gifts in Good Taste," free, published annually, 64 pages, illustrated, color.

An array of gift boxes, hampers, and packages containing everything from apples, pears, and grapefruit to cheeses, candies, and nuts. Strawberry Patch is a splint bucket of individually wrapped strawberry candy (around $4); a wooden crate holds Wisconsin cheddar cheeses; the Macadamia Trio has 3 packs of salted nuts, chocolate nut clusters, and nut brittle (around $9). There's also a Cheese of the Month Club available for 3, 5, 7, or 12 months that brings a different type of Wisconsin cheese each month, at prices from around $17 to $60.

FIN 'N FEATHER FARM / Dept. CFC
R.F.D. 2, Dundee, IL 60118

Catalogue, free, published annually, 24 pages, illustrated, color.

Primarily a smokehouse, specializing in smoked meats and birds, Fin 'n Feather also has all kinds of other gift-packed goods, such as a brunch/breakfast box of clover honey, maple syrup, hickory-smoked bacon, preserves, and pancake and waffle flour ($17.95), or a smoked pheasant buffet, the bird ringed by stuffed olives, mixed nuts, pickled cantaloupe, and different party spreads ($20.95). A do-it-yourself gift club plan allows you to select items from the catalogue to be shipped during the year, or you can choose one of their own four club plans, such as #2, which ships a smoked turkey at Christmas, smoked ham at Easter, and oven-ready turkey at Thanksgiving for $75, prepaid.

R. W. FORSYTH LTD. / Dept. CFC
30 Princes Street, Edinburgh EH2 2BZ, Scotland

"The days of Christmas at Forsyth's," free, published annually, 16 pages, black and white.

This Christmas catalogue from the Food Hall of Forsyth's, the Edinburgh department store, has a great many hampers and boxes filled with Scottish specialties, whisky and European wines, priced from around $4 to $50, that would make good gifts for friends or relatives in the UK, but probably the straightforward "provisions" that can easily be shipped overseas would be the most interesting to you. There are sides of Scotch smoked salmon, cheeses such as Stilton, in traditional jars, tins of Scotch shortbread, Scottish heather honey and liqueur honey in a pottery jar decorated with game dogs or birds (16 oz., about $6), gift packs of Melrose and Twinings teas in tins or decorated caddies, miniature tea chests of Ceylon tea or Melrose's Queen's tea, tea in decorative jars made by the Cauldon Bristol potteries (one, an Old English Jar, is a numbered collector's item), even muff tea cosies and coffee cosies to keep your pots hot! Or you can order rich Christmas cakes, such as Mackie's Scotch whisky cake, Scotch bun (a kind of currant cake) or currant loaf, Christmas puddings soaked with brandy and rum, Royal Ascot genuine Cumberland rum or brandy butter, which resembles hard sauce (about $2 for an 8-oz. stone jar), plus lots and lots of candies, chocolates, and confections, such as Ferguson's Edinburgh rock in a picture box (around $2.25), Sharwood's chocolate ginger pieces or chocolate-covered dates, Fjord chocolate truffles, or Bendick's bitter mocha chocolates. You could select a delicious confectionery sampler from this catalogue.

FORTNUM & MASON / Dept. CFC
181 Piccadilly, London W1A 1ER, England

"Fortnum & Mason Export Food," free, published seasonally, 15 pages, illustrated, color.

Fortnum & Mason is a London institution. To walk down its hushed and decorous aisles, flanked by displays of the world's luxury foods, is to be transported back to an age of civilized good taste. The small Christmas gift catalogue of export food exudes the very spirit of Fortnum's. Boxed and packaged the foods might be, but the packaging is both understated and attractive, for though this famous store adapts to the times, it does so with grace. One remembers how when a shocked customer caviled at tea bags he was reassured, smoothly and soothingly, "We only advise them for *picnics*, sir." Honeys come in flowered or plain pottery jars (one by Crown Devon looks like a beehive with bees prowling on top and sides), stem ginger in elegant Chinese miniature jars, vintage marmalade in a Royal Winton "cottage" design jar, Fortnum's Royal Blend tea in a Masons ironstone jar, tea caddy, or teapot (the latter is around $18). A gift box of six ¼-lb. tins of specially selected F&M teas is a very reasonable $9, a boxed set of 4 earthenware jars of Stilton cheese is under $7, a Christmas Gift Box of a 2-lb. Christmas pudding, 2-lb. Dundee Christmas cake, and a jar of Old English mincemeat under $16. There are also gift packages of Fortnum & Mason preserves and teatime delicacies, such as shortbread, "sherribisks," sweet biscuits, and fruit biscuits. Postage, packing, and insurance are extra.

FRASER-MORRIS / Dept. CFC
872 Madison Avenue, New York, NY 10021

"Gifts for Festive Occasions from Fraser-Morris," free, published seasonally, 11 pages, illustrated, color.

"The perfection of the viands is rivalled only by the opulence reflected in their packaging" is how Fraser-Morris introduces its catalogue.

★

Stuff dates or prunes with nuts or cheese, wrap in half-cooked strips of bacon, broil until bacon is crisp. Serve as an appetizer.

★

For a quick dessert, peel, section, and lightly sugar grapefruit. Arrange in sherbet dishes and pour a little dry sherry over fruit.

★

Teatime in India, sketch from the Fortnum & Mason catalogue

A variety of gifts from the Helen Gallagher Collection

A sampling from the Greyhound Gift House catalogue

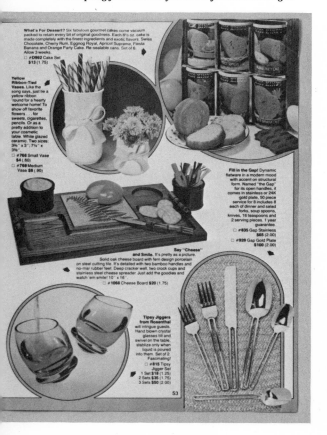

Scotch smoked salmon ($19.95 per lb.) or Nova Scotia smoked salmon ($12.95 per lb.) is sliced and put back on its own frame.

Iranian Beluga caviar comes in 4- and 8-oz. jars ($14.95 to $29.95) or in tins of 7 and 14 oz. ($45 to $90). French pâté de foie gras comes in 5½-, 7¼- or 10⅞-oz. baby blocks ($14.25 to $24.95) or in terrines.

English plum puddings are packed in 1-, 2- and 3-lb. crocks ($4.95 to $9.50), Dobos torte is $3.50 for 20 oz., Perugina chocolates from Italy, $8.95 per lb., and Lindt chocolates, 17½ oz. for $9.50. Lady Godiva chocolates are $7.50 per lb.

Cheeses, nuts, candies, teas, and preserves are combined in hampers ranging in price from $49.95 to $79.95.

THE HELEN GALLAGHER COLLECTION / Dept. CFC
6523 N. Galena Road, Peoria, IL 61632

"The Helen Gallagher Collection," free, published seasonally, 48 pages, illustrated, color.

The Helen Gallagher Collection includes a variety of kitchen utensils and serving items in aluminum, hand-blown glass, blue enamelware, ceramic, wood, and tin.

A Mexican tin wire chicken, perfect for fresh fruits or vegetables, is a reasonable $6.95; a wok set with pan, cover, and burner ring is $23.95; and a glazed Schlemmertof clay pot with its own cookbook, $19.95.

A small (18" x 18" x 30" high) butcher-block table designed for the cramped kitchen is $63.95.

GRAYS OF WORCESTER, LTD. / Dept. CFC
Orchard Street, Worcester WR5 3DP, England

"For the pleasure of the Gourmet," free, published annually with seasonal supplements, 26 pages, black and white.

Grays has an excellent selection of Christmas gift hampers, some for UK delivery only, others they will send overseas. Among the latter we noticed the Connoisseur's Game Pack, various canned game such as grouse, guinea fowl, quail, pheasant, pigeon, venison, jugged hare, and game soup (under $40 delivered), and the Pâté Perfection, with a wide range of pâtés, including hare and wild boar (under $30). Other things of interest in their general catalogue are quail eggs in jars, pickled figs from Spain, Christmas puddings liberally laced with rum and brandy, traditional English mince pies (canned), a rich fruit cake laced with Guinness stout known as Mr. Guinness Cake, some excellent handmade chocolates, pottery jars of Stilton cheese, and the Brown Ascot tea jar, a decorative ironstone jar by Mason with a pound of a luxury tea blend, a collector's item at around $18 delivered. There are many excellent but more perishable food gifts that would make marvelous presents for friends in the UK. Your orders can be charged to Master Charge or BankAmericard as well as paid by check.

GREYHOUND GIFT HOUSE / Dept. CFC
7178 N.W. 12th Street, Miami, FL 33126

"The Greyhound Gift House Wish Book," free, published annually, 68 pages, illustrated, color.

Another of those impossibly tempting gift catalogues full of things everyone loves and no one really needs. Most of the gifts are of the general type, but there is, of course, that most happy extravagance, the Cuisinart Food Processor (what status-seeking cook could be without one?) which now comes redesigned with a handle on the bowl and a recipe book by James Beard ($225), an electric pizzelle iron that makes Italian waffles or toasts sandwiches (the grids are reversible) for $35, a set of six Miss King's cakes (Swiss chocolate, cherry rum, eggnog royal, apricot supreme, fiesta banana, orange party), 8½-oz. each, vacuum-packed in resealable cans ($13), a butcher-block table and server made of red alder hardwood, with 24" square cutting surface and a rack with hooks mounted at one end ($275), a set of four amusing felt vegetable-shaped pot holders (mushroom, apple, carrots, artichoke) for $8 and some reproductions of old Italian grocery tins, canister sized with clear acrylic windows, that would look pretty on a kitchen shelf holding rice or pasta, $25 a set of four.

THE GOURMET PANTRY / Dept. CFC
400 McGuinness Blvd., Brooklyn, NY 11222

"Pleasure Packed Gifts from the Gourmet Pantry," free, published annually, 72 pages, illustrated, color.

All kinds of gift packages, many (although not all) including food. You'll find the usual smoked turkey and ham, honeys and preserves, cookies and cakes, fresh and dried fruits, nuts, cheeses, and a few rather more offbeat things, such as a rum pot containing plums, apricots, peaches, pears, and grapes steeped in Jamaica rum ($10.99) or an "Irish Blessing" plate packaged with Willwood strawberry preserves, Irish cheeses, and Irish breakfast tea ($9.99). Some pieces of cooking equipment, too, such as an electric ice-cream maker, the Salton yogurt maker and electric coffee mill, an electric hamburger broiler, electric hot-dog cooker, and the Römertopf clay cook pot with recipe booklet ($13.50).

HAMMACHER SCHLEMMER / Dept. CFC
147 East 57th Street, New York, NY 10022

Catalogue, free, published five times a year, 64 pages, illustrated, black and white.

New Yorkers couldn't get along without Hammacher's, a fixture on 57th Street for lo, these many years. This is a store that has everything conceivable for the home—and some things you would never have dreamed of. Do other stores have the electric pasta machine? Hammacher's has that plus an electric cheese grater, an electric food hydrator, an electric crêpe maker (for $600, you could start your own crêperie), and an incredible machine called the Vita Mix that does everything from making hot soup to freezing ice cream. One wonders how much stock they have in Con Edison. There's lots of cookware, such as the elegant porcelaine de Paris (around $345 for a five-piece set of covered saucepans), a clay pot for crocked chicken, a battery-operated self-stirring saucepan, and a battery-operated flour sifter (just watch the kiddies play with that one). A new twist for a weekend hostess gift would be a set of six disposable plastic spice and salt mills, ready filled with black peppercorns, sea salt crystals, nutmeg chunks, cloves, and fennel seeds packaged in a basket for around $12 or, if you like to take your own condiments on your trips, the two peppers and salt in a basket for $6.95. In the food line there are flash-frozen steaks and Frenched double lamb chops, suckling pig (an Easter order), Smithfield ham and prosciutto, stuffed Rock Cornish game hens, smoked pheasant and turkey, oven-ready goose and game (including grouse from Scotland), Florida seafood, Scotch smoked salmon, the standard caviar and pâté de foie gras, and, for Christmas, lots of gift hampers and boxes—cookies, cakes, sugar plums—the works. If you can't visit the store, the next best thing is to get the catalogue.

HARRY AND DAVID / Dept. CFC
P.O. Box 712, Medford, OR 97501

"Harry and David's Christmas Book of Gifts," free, published annually with supplementary brochures, 28 pages, illustrated, color.

Brothers Harry and David Holmes placed an advertisement in *Fortune* magazine in 1936. The copywriting was corny, but it brought spectacular results, and now thousands do their gift shopping at Bear Creek Orchards. Fruit-of-the-month began (and continues) here. With this plan, you get for Christmas, Royal Riviera pears; January, apples; February, grapefruit; March, oranges; April, pineapples; May, preserves; June, home-canned fruit; July, Kiwi berries; August, nectarines; September, peaches; October, Alphonse Lavalle grapes; and November, Spanish melons. The Royal 12-box plan is $95.95; 8 months for $66.95; 5 months, $39.95; and 3 months, $24.95.

Grapefruit and avocado combinations ($13.95), dried fruits (French plums, Australian apricots, and Medjool dates $12.95), and a basket of

*

Another easy dessert: remove rind and pith from navel oranges with a sharp knife. Slice thinly crosswise and put in a glass bowl. Sprinkle with Irish Mist and marinate for 30 minutes.

*

Ham and Cheese Squares
Combine in a bowl ¼ cup soft butter, ¼ cup cracker crumbs, 1 cup sour cream, ¼ cup grated Parmesan cheese, 1½ cups cooked minced ham, 2 teaspoons caraway seeds, and 6 eggs, beaten until light and thick. Combine well and pour onto a greased jelly roll pan. Bake in a 375° oven until browned, about 15 minutes. Cut in squares and serve as a cocktail appetizer while hot. Makes about 2 dozen squares.

mixed nuts ($9.85) make unusual and worthwhile gifts.

The Tower of Treats, five separately wrapped presents in one, has one layer of French plums, a second of English toffee, a third of creamy chocolates, a fourth of apples, and a fifth of Harry and David's trademarked Royal Riviera pears ($13.95).

HERTER'S INC. / Dept. CFC
RR 2, Mitchell, SD 57301

"Herter's Sportsman's Catalog," $1 (refundable with $10 purchase), published annually, 352 pages, illustrated, color and black and white.

An absolutely fascinating catalogue full of gifts, guns, hunting and fishing equipment, telescopes and binoculars, taxidermy supplies, canoes and rubber boats, clothing, books on cooking and living off the land, offbeat foods such as cactus and buffalo-chip candies (not made from buffalo meat but so named because it was originated by Chief White Buffalo, a Sioux Indian), cooking equipment, and a great assortment of professional knives that could be very useful in the kitchen, all reasonably priced. There's an 8" fillet knife ($2.47), a commercial fisherman's fillet knife with a spoon-shaped end for gutting fish ($5.70), Swedish steel camping and fillet knives in leather sheaths, a panfish and trout knife for cutting and scaling ($1.97), six slaughterhouse knives, a large chef's knife (just $4.37), a pocket sharpening steel ($1.67), and an unusual ceramic sharpener, two angled ceramic rods set in a walnut block ($6.40). They also have steel kitchen and game shears for $3.17, cast-iron cookware, including a three-legged kettle (about $12), and good-looking, no-frills, unbreakable vacuum bottles with plain stainless-steel exterior and interior in pint, quart, and 2-quart sizes, as well as a wide-mouthed quart size, priced from $17.47 to $23.97.

THE HORCHOW COLLECTION / Dept. CFC
P.O. Box 34257, Dallas, TX 75234

"The Horchow Collection Catalogue," $1 for six issues a year, illustrated, color.

Both the Horchow catalogue and the Horchow Collection Book for Cooks, one of the special-interest mailings, tempt you with the kind of things you may not really need but can't resist, such as an electric pasta machine at $130 (would Sophia Loren buy one?). You'll find here all those special electric gadgets that make the gift-of-the-year list—the peanut butter machine, the food processor, and a constantly changing parade of indulgences like monogrammed glass cookware for the microwave oven, an instant cream whipper (a metal can that works on a CO_2 cartridge) with decorating nozzle, and a new variation on the mandoline vegetable slicer—this one lies flat, on a plastic base into which the slices fall. The Christmas catalogue has all those food gifts such as peaches in brandy, Irish smoked salmon, candies and cakes, glacé fruits, French jams and vinegars, and more unusual items crop up in the collection's Book for Cooks—barbecue sauce from Savannah, Mexican cocktail snacks.

ROBERT JACKSON & CO., LTD. / Dept. CFC
171 Piccadilly, London WIV OLL, England

"Robert Jackson's Food, Wine, Hamper and Gift List," free, published seasonally, illustrated, black and white.

Anyone who walks down Piccadilly is irresistibly drawn by the windows of Robert Jackson's marvelous food-and-wine store, and the catalogue is almost as alluring. Jackson imports delicacies and specialties from around the world, and a random sampling is enough to make the mouth water. From the Isle of Arran come pâtés of venison and hare; from Perigord terrines of duck, venison, wild boar, turkey with Armagnac. New Zealand supplies tua-tua soup (a kind of clam) and an impressive list of tropical canned fruits—passion fruit, goldenberry, guava, cloudberries (Arctic raspberries). There is an unusual selection of condiments and mustards, including 300-gram jars of Bornier Fruitarde (a blend of mustard, vinegar, cognac, spices with either apricots, plums, or

---

Tempting foods from the Horchow Collection catalogue

Mr. Jackson's Tea Ice
Beat 5 eggs and ½ cup sugar until thick and creamy white. Slowly heat together ½ cup strong tea (Jackson's Jasmine Blossom tea), 1¼ cups milk, and 1 cup light cream to boiling point. Add to the egg mixture carefully and slowly, taking care not to curdle the eggs. Leave to cool, stirring every now and again to prevent a skin forming. When cold, pour into freezer tray or mold that has been lightly brushed with flavorless oil to prevent sticking. Freeze for several hours. Be sure to beat the ice cream vigorously with whisk or fork once or twice during the freezing process to ensure even texture. Remove from freezer to refrigerator at least 1 hour before serving so the ice cream softens slightly.
—*from Robert Jackson's Food, Wine, Hamper and Gift List*

oranges), Maille green herb mustard and tomato mustard, and something called "The Vicar's Mustard," from a recipe created by a country vicar's wife in the 19th century (about $1.80 for an 11-oz. jar). Other stores may have poivre vert (fresh green peppercorns), but Jackson also has poivre rose de l'Ile Maurice (pink peppercorns), about $2.70. Sherry vinegars, both red and white, come from Spain, and there are some unusual oils from France (one, called fondue oil, is for fondue Bourguignonne) and the vine twigs, or *sarments*, over which steaks and sausages are grilled in the French wine regions (these are dried and mixed with Provençal herbs and cost about $1.50 a sack). You'll find fruit and flower purées and gelées from Hediard and Fauchon, honeys, confectionery, and a host of other delectables too numerous to list. You just have to get the catalogue and drool your way through it.

JURGENSEN'S GROCERY COMPANY / Dept. CFC
601 South Lake Avenue, Pasadena, CA 91109

"Jurgensen's Christmas Catalogue," free, published annually, 36 pages, illustrated, color.

Jurgensen's is a household name in California, where they have 19 stores. Their Christmas catalogue consists mainly of gift hampers and packages, many containing wine or spirits (these can be delivered only within California), but others that feature cheese and pâté, cakes and cookies, dried and glacé fruits, fresh fruits, cocktail foods, olives, ice-cream toppings, and candies. An old-fashioned coffee mill is packaged with two 6-oz. burlap bags of Brazilian coffee (around $26), "Santa's Salad Makings" teams bottles of walnut oil, sherry vinegar, champagne mustard with mills of salt crystals and peppercorns in a Wedgwood salad bowl (around $32), a Banana Split set has four ceramic banana dishes, three ice-cream toppings, and a scoop (around $20). They also show some cooking utensils, such as French white cooking porcelain, hammered aluminum pots and pans, a Swedish fish smoker, and French terrines in the traditional crust finish with hare or game-bird heads.

THE KIRK COMPANY / Dept. CFC
P.O. Box 340, Puyallup, WA 98371

Catalogue, free, published annually, 20 pages, illustrated, color.

Gifts from the Northwest from a company that started by shipping evergreen wreaths and garlands and has added gift packages of regional specialties such as Washington Delicious apples, canned Dungeness crab meat, kippered salmon and tiny Pacific shrimp, seasonings from a Puget Sound restaurant called Johnny's Dock, and berry preserves and honey from the Snoqualmie Falls Lodge. Prices of the seafood packages range from $5.45 to $16.95, and 10 lbs. of boxed, foil-wrapped apples are $10.25 delivered. There's an endearingly simple homey air to this catalogue, and the packaging is both restrained and attractive. Nuts are packed in a wooden salad bowl, canned seafoods in a tray basket. The preserves are in jars with wire clamp tops, reusable for storing grains and spices.

LANDMARK / Dept. CFC
Carrbridge, Inverness-shire PH23 3AJ, Scotland

"Scottish Fare," free, published annually, 6-page brochure.

If you want to give a Christmas gift to a friend or relative in the UK, Landmark has a fine array of gift hampers filled with Scottish specialties, such as whisky cake, shortbread, oatcakes and Strathmore liqueur honey, marmalades, preserves, Scottish cheeses, and some more esoteric things. The "Brodick Box," for example, is a food hamper from the Isle of Arran containing traditional fare made to the recipes of Mary, late Duchess of Montrose—1 lb. each of Arran marmalade and marmalade with whisky, venison broth, venison pâté, venison haggis, venison haggis with whisky, and hare, pork, and liver pâté—that costs 4 pounds sixty-eight in sterling (under $10). Some of the hampers contain 10-year-old Glen Grant·whisky or Speyside malt whisky, and you

Curried Consommé
Put in the blender 1 can jellied consommé, 3 ounces cream cheese, ½ teaspoon sea salt, ¼ teaspoon curry powder, and 1 teaspoon drained green peppercorns. Blend for 30 seconds. Place in individual dishes, such as ramekins, and chill in the refrigerator for 2 hours. Serve garnished with a twist of lemon.
—*from Robert Jackson's Food, Wine, Hamper and Gift List*

Gifts of truffles and foie gras, Roquefort cheese—luxurious fillings for a simple omelet. Courtesy Food & Wines from France, Inc.

*

Save leftover orange shells, remove all remaining pulp from the inside and keep in the freezer to use as individual serving dishes for sherbet or ice cream.

*

Stir cut-up cooked prunes and apples into cooked cous-cous and serve with roast pork or spareribs.

*

Top jellied consommé with a dab of caviar for a very elegant first course.

*

Connoisseur's comestibles from the Neiman-Marcus Christmas catalogue

can also send rare Highland malt whisky by the bottle or a malt whisky hamper with a selection of the finest of Scotland's single malts, the whisky preference of connoisseurs. Liquor, naturally, can be shipped only in the UK, but if you want to order any of the special gift packs, ask for overseas postal charges when writing for the brochure.

MAISON GLASS / Dept. CFC
52 East 58th Street, New York, NY 10021

"Maison Glass Delicacies," $1, published annually, 72 pages, illustrated, black and white.

Some of the Maison Glass gift packages are a little bit out of the ordinary, if you are looking for interesting Christmas presents. For instance, a 5-pound aged Stilton cheese with a silver cheese scoop (traditionally, port is poured into the center of the cheese and the softened part scooped out, although some purists frown on this practice) and Carr's English crackers, around $39. A pretty little silvery metal basket holds a complement of imported raspberry candies and makes a nice flower or plant holder later ($32). "Connoisseur" pairs aged wine vinegar in a ceramic table jug with a stone crock of moutarde de Meaux ($17.50). Or, if you know someone who is really mad for mustard, how about seven pots of imported mustards, all different, for around $25?

MYSTIC SEAPORT STORES, INC / Dept. CFC
Mystic, CT 06355

Catalogue, 50¢, published annually, 22 pages, illustrated, color and black and white.

Mystic Seaport Stores draws on the rich history of eastern seaboard shipping to offer a range of gift ideas with a nautical or colonial theme.

There are penny candies stuffed in a basket ($3.75), a package of four fish chowders ($5.50), a collection of miniature copper pots, pans, and accessories (each $2.50), or a pretty porcelain ginger jar packed with candied ginger ($5.75). Assorted imported teas in gaily colored tins packed in a blue calico-printed tin chest are $7.50.

Add flavor to your breakfast by dusting pecan meal on top of pancakes or mix it into the batter for texture. A package of maple syrup, meal, and four wooden batter spoons is $5.25.

NEIMAN-MARCUS / Dept. CFC
Main and Ervay Streets, Dallas, TX 75201

"Neiman-Marcus Christmas Catalogue," $1, published annually, 108 pages, illustrated, color.

The ultimate "wow" catalogue of luxury gifts that may start at a Texas-scale $19,500, but then descend to the more modest under-$10 category most of us can afford. If you want a cookie jar for a pampered poodle, Neiman's has it. Or how about a Gravy Train? That was a N-M inspiration for Christmas 1975, an automatically controlled oval wood track with silver locomotive and cars holding condiments, olives, lemon, sauces and what have you—something to stimulate flagging table talk (for $8,000). The Creative Cookery section is always filled with yummy things: marrons glacés from Italy, Godiva chocolates, wheels of cheddar, steaks, smoked salmon from Scotland, tiny quail (12 to a box, $32.50 air special delivery) and all the usual Christmas gift foods such as brandied peaches, dried fruits, pralines, jellies and honey, chocolate-covered pretzels, packaged with the typical N-M pizazz. The N-M By the Month gift brings a year of succulent surprises culled from the collection. Get this one and eat your heart out.

NEW HAMPTON GENERAL STORE / Dept. CFC
R.F.D., Hampton, NJ 08827

"General Catalogue," free, five editions yearly, 80 pages, illustrated, color.

Among the gifts and novelties are, as you might expect, quite a few things for the kitchen, from gadgets like the "Gilhoolie" jar and bottle

Nature-motif towels from the New York Botanical Garden gift catalogue

opener ($4.50) and a honey dipper that serves honey without drips and drops (75¢) to such useful pieces of basic equipment as a soapstone griddle from Vermont, 10" in diameter ($26.95), a Pennsylvania Dutch deep-dish glazed earthenware pie plate ($2.95) and a cast-iron sectioned cornbread skillet that bakes the bread in wedges ($5.50). There's also a potato ricer, rather hard to find these days, for $3.75, a pie bird (shaped like a blackbird, he goes under the crust and his open beak lets the steam out) for $2.50, and a handy little stainless-steel bowl with a lip and a handle that is designed for use with an electric beater, enabling you to beat, mix, and pour (even heat, as the bowl can go on a range top quite safely). Measurements are marked on the side for 1, 2, and 3 qts. Another thing to catch our eye was a quite lovely English ironstone pitcher with equivalent measures marked on the side (3 teaspoons = 1 tablespoon, and so on) that would also be an ideal holder for kitchen spoons and tools or flowers ($8.50). There are a lot of really good things tucked away in this little catalogue.

THE NEW YORK BOTANICAL GARDEN / Dept. CFC
Bronx, NY 10458

Gift catalogue, free, published seasonally, 20 pages, color and black and white.

This charming catalogue, in addition to plants, bulbs, and things for the garden, offers a small crate of three 1-lb. jars of Crabtree and Evelyn of London's raspberry, strawberry, and apricot preserves for $9.75, a heavily padded Irish linen tea cosy, $8, or horticulturally inspired Irish linen tea towels, 19" x 30", two for $5.95. To please a chef, there is a three-piece Irish linen set of apron, towel, and oven mitt with an orange and lemon design for $14, made especially for the New York Botanical Garden.

THE ORVIS COMPANY / Dept. CFC
Manchester, VT 05254

Catalogue, free, published annually, 122 pages, illustrated, color.

A Christmas catalogue directed to sportsmen and their families, with a few interesting things for the kitchen, such as the Cuisinart stainless-steel cookware, Vermont soapstone griddles (the 12" round size is $39.50, the 8" x 16" oval, $37.50), a ceramic knife sharpener 8" long ($17.50), and a diamond knife sharpener (the grinding surface is impregnated with tiny particles of diamond dust that grind off metal at every stroke, rather than merely aligning the blade) in either pocket size (around $20) or butcher size ($48). Knives are from Russell Harrington, American cutlery makers since 1818. The 6-piece set is around $70, or you can buy the pieces (paring knife, boning knife, 8" cook's knife, 9" carving knife, carving fork, and ceramic knife sharpener) separately, and if you need a rack for your knives, there's a modular polished bird's-eye maple block that mounts on the wall and holds 12 knives and a sharpener. There's also a lettuce dryer/potato scraper, an imported gadget that works by centrifugal force ($25), single and double egg coddlers by Royal Worcester, and a new switch on the coddler—a meal-in-a-cup coddler, 4½" high and 4" in diameter in which you can coddle foods such as fish in a matter of minutes. It comes complete with recipe book for around $18. Another offbeat item is a book of game cookery based on internal temperature that you can buy with an electric heat sensing probe (not a thermometer). That will set you back about $120, though the book itself is a mere $2.50. But perhaps the ultimate gift for the sportsman who has everything is the Orvis electric duck plucker, with revolving rubber fingers that will pluck any game bird from quail to goose in no time at all. It can pluck 53 ducks in 60 minutes, and anyone who has ever had to perform that tedious chore would no doubt find it a bargain at $199, plus shipping cost of $4.75. Only two food items in this catalogue, wild rice ($6.50 a 1-lb. sack) and Grade Fancy Vermont maple syrup ($6.95 a qt.).

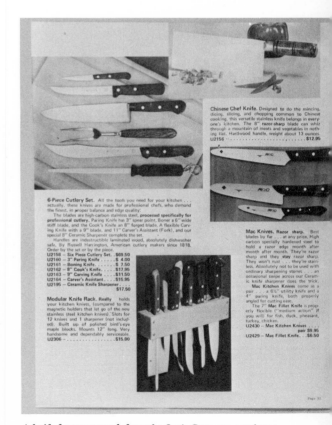

A knife for every need, from the Orvis Company catalogue

Smoked ham and turkey breast, from the Pepperidge Farm Mail Order Company

Broiled Steaks with Green Peppercorn Mustard

For each shell steak, make a paste with 1 teaspoon drained, canned, green peppercorns and 2 tablespoons Moutarde de Meaux. Spread half the paste on the top of the steak and broil until mustard paste is browned; then turn, spread remaining paste on second side, and broil until done to your taste.

PEPPERIDGE FARM MAIL ORDER CO., INC. / Dept. CFC
Box 7000, Norwalk, CT 06856

"Gift Catalog," free, published periodically, 32 pages, illustrated, color.

Recipe for a party: unwrap a Pepperidge Farm cocktail assortment, add friends, fill the glasses and relax. Assortment #1 contains 12 oz. of jumbo peanuts, 2⅛-oz. cocktail pâté, 8½-oz. cheddar cheese spread, and an 8-oz. block of New York cheddar ($8.95). The addition of Vermont cheddar, cocktail wafers, and pâté of smoked rainbow trout to the preceding makes assortment #2 ($14.95). The deluxe assortment contains those seven items as well as pretzel twigs, pâté of smoked turkey, cheddar cheese spread with kirsch, pâté of pheasant supreme, and a teak cracker server ($29.95).

Breakfast gift assortments reminiscent of those hearty leisurely meals of the old days are packaged in the four breakfast selections. The deluxe box contains smoked bacon, maple syrup, four bags of old-fashioned regular, whole-wheat, corn, and buttermilk pancake mixes, strawberry fruit spread, Dutch cocoa, honey, sugarcane syrup, Colombian Supremo coffee, and a charming Bennington pottery pitcher ($29.95).

The savory and the sweet meet in the soup gift package, which contains chicken with wild rice, chicken curry, New England clam chowder, gazpacho, hunter's borscht, shiitake mushroom, French onion, black bean with sherry, vichyssoise, Bing cherry with burgundy, strawberry with sauterne, prune soup with orange, orange with apricot, and peach apple soups (15 cans, $14.95).

Pepperidge Farm offers a choice of three- ($24.95), five- ($39.95), or seven- ($59.95) month gift plans. The last features the cocktail assortment in December, the breakfast assortment in January, Godiva chocolates in February, fruit spreads in April, ice-cream toppings in June, 10 Pepperidge Farm soups in September, and a chocolate surprise in October.

PORTER'S FOODS UNLIMITED / Dept. CFC
125 West 11th Street, Eugene, OR 97401

Specific information on request.

Porter's of Oregon has undergone such rapid growth in the past years that its old catalogue is outdated and its new one has yet to come off the presses. Specific inquiries can be directed to Porter's, and they will provide a "personalized listing" of whatever items are requested.

What Porter's lacks in depth it makes up for in variety. There are camping foods and accessories, winemaking supplies, coffee beans and teas, natural foods, kitchen gadgets, and, most importantly, products from within Oregon's boundaries—fresh and smoked fish, jams (including Oregon's incomparable strawberry, raspberry, and boysenberry), cheeses, and candies.

ROMBINS' NEST FARM / Dept. CFC
Fairfield, PA 17320

Catalogue, 25¢, published annually, 40 pages, illustrated, black and white.

In this gift catalogue filled with Pennsylvania Dutch folksiness you'll find an old-fashioned pie basket (around $10), a round, cast-iron bread pan, the deep Pennsylvania Dutch pie plate with glazed interior, old-fashioned deep custard cups (set of 6, each a different color on the outside, oatmeal glaze inside, around $5), cookie cutters, and some typical foods, such as John Cope's dried corn, apple schnitz (sliced dried apples), prune butter, sweet and sour relishes such as chowchow, peach butter, red tomato relish, pretzels (around $11 for an 8-lb. can of different types), old-fashioned horehound, sassafras and wild cherry hard candies, and Pennsylvania Dutch butter mints.

SEY-CO PRODUCTS CO. / Dept. CFC
7651 Densmore Avenue, Van Nuys, CA 91406

Catalogue, free, published annually, 15 pages, illustrated, color.

An exclusive West Coast mail-order gift shop, Sey-Co offers gift packages that combine fancy gifts for the home with Sey-Co's own food delicacies.

The "Coral Sea" package ($110) is two boxes of Sey-Co's chocolate paired with a solid bronze shark on "a sea of natural coral," a limited edition by sculptor John Perry.

Or consider an entertainment set of a large porcelain serving plate, four matching individual plates, and a gift pack of smoked rainbow trout, Gouda cheese, French mustard, fillets of mackerel, and cocktail cheddars ($18.75).

Sey-Co also includes gift packages of brunch delicacies, relishes, and cocktail nibbles ($10.95 to $14.50).

Additionally, Sey-Co has an à la carte food list of meats and pâtés, teas and coffees, olives and pickles, seafoods, seasonings, sauces, dressings, soups, nuts, crackers, desserts, fruits and sweets, all of which can be bought individually or by the dozen. Any assortment of food items will be gift-packaged on request at no extra charge.

S.F.A. FOLIO COLLECTIONS, INC. / Dept. CFC
449 West 14th Street, New York, NY 10014

"Folio," free, published quarterly, 68 pages, illustrated, color.

The Folio catalogue put out by Saks Fifth Avenue occasionally has a few pages of culinary temptations, such as a wok set in a handsome wood box (stainless-steel wok with lid and cooking ring, utensils, bamboo scrubber, chopsticks, cookbook), around $38 at last season's prices, or a hanging set of Danish beechwood kitchen tools (spoons, whisk, knife, meat mallet, rolling pin). They usually show a selection of the Fauchon specialties from Paris, such as Bordeaux wine vinegar, French olive oil, and flavored mustards. All very haute cuisine and expensive.

SHANNON FREE AIRPORT / Dept. CFC
590 Fifth Avenue, New York, NY 10036

Catalogue, $1, published annually, 67 pages, illustrated, color and black and white.

The duty-free goods at Shannon Free Airport have always been popular with travelers, but now you don't have to make a trip; you can order them from home. The catalogue naturally stresses the things for which Ireland is noted, such as sweaters and linens, glass and china, but there's also a limited selection of foods, such as Thompson's Irish-whiskey-flavored fruitcake (1¾ lbs., $4.30), tea cookies, teas by McGrath, Irish-coffee-flavored milk chocolate, and that marvelous Irish smoked salmon from Thomas Murphy, the oldest curing house in Dublin (2½ lbs., $20.95).

SLEEPY HOLLOW GIFTS / Dept. CFC
6651 Arlington Blvd., Falls Church, VA 22042

Catalogue, free, 96 pages, published seasonally, illustrated, black and white, some color.

Gadgets and gifts from all over, with a smattering of items for the cook and kitchen such as the 9¾" all-in-one knife that handles any cutting job from meat, bread, cheese to vegetables and fruits, $5, or a wooden barrel full of kitchen tools, including a slotted spoon, stirring/mixer spoon, masher/tenderizer, spatula, spoon, whip mixer, 2 skewers, and a whisk, all for $10.

The "desert pack" is a light (¾-lb.) but small (12" x 9" x 9") carrier for a six-pack of drinks. Because of the six insulated coasters, no ice is necessary and cans will stay chilled for 12 hours. Great for camping.

Sleepy Hollow offers several interesting cookbooks. *Kitchen Cheesemaking* lists more than 50 varieties from gorgonzola to blue and Cam-

Culinary collection from S. F. A. "Folio"

★

Three quick appetizers: wrap prosciutto around breadsticks; very thin slices of Virginia ham around melon fingers (skewer with toothpick); thin slices of smoked salmon or lox around cucumber sticks.

★

For a delicious sauce to serve with fish or beef, drain bottled horseradish or grate fresh horseradish, blend into sour cream or whipped cream to taste. For roast pork, stir horseradish into applesauce.

★

Turkey and Ham Divan

Cook 1 bunch broccoli in salted water until tender crisp. Slice lengthwise and arrange on an ovenproof platter or in a shallow baking dish. Cover with 6 slices smoked turkey or pheasant and 6 slices cooked ham. Melt 1 cup grated Parmesan cheese in 2 cups medium cream sauce and pour over the meat. Heat in a 400° oven or under the broiler until bubbling hot. Serves 6.
—*from "38 Serving Ideas for Harrington's Smoked Treats"*

embert with recipes and instructions on how to make your own cheese, $4.95. *Of Pots and Pipkins*, $4.95, is a collection of recipes contributed by the women of Roanoke, Virginia, for beverages, breads, desserts, meat, poultry, pickles and jams, salads and soups, seafoods and vegetables. Proceeds for the book go to the Junior League of that city. *Vegetarian Gothic*, $5.95, gives ways to serve seeds, nuts, and vegetables in salads, soups, entrées without the use of meats but maintaining a lot of flavor.

SPIEGEL / Dept. CFC
1061 West 35th Street, Chicago, IL 60609

"Get Acquainted Catalog," free, published annually, 56 pages, illustrated, color.

Spiegel, the catalogue you've heard about on TV game shows, promises to save you money, so compare. A 5-qt. Rival crockpot, the time-and-money saver, is $24.88, the Rival electric food slicer $44.88.

The original Mr. Coffee, which brews 10 5-oz. cups, is $26.88, the "All American" canner-cooker with a zero to 20-lb. pressure gauge, 2 tray racks, pan and recipes in 15-qt. (with only one tray rack), 21½-qt., and 25-qt. capacities costs from $29.88 to $49.88.

Other items are the KitchenAid heavy-duty mixer ($119.88), the Hamilton Beach Little Mac Grill ($14.88), and the General Electric Jet 84 microwave oven ($299).

SPORTPAGES / Dept. CFC
13719 Welch Road, Dallas, TX 75240

"Sportpages," free, published periodically, 34 pages, illustrated, color.

This is a new company and a new catalogue, and the theme is sports, with the majority of items strictly athletic.

Ice cream on a backpacking trip? You can have it with Natural High's Neopolitan-flavored ice cream, which requires neither water nor refrigeration ($7.50 for 12 1-oz. pouches).

For barbecues, there's a home meat smoker and roaster that will smoke meat, venison, poultry, pork, or whatever you like with wood chips, charcoal, or electricity ($100).

A natural maple butcher-block storage rack to keep knives conveniently and safely in place comes alone ($20) or with 5 German stainless-steel knives with rosewood handles ($75).

Give a tennis buff 12 oz. of tennis-racket-embossed Godiva chocolates with Grand Marnier-laced centers ($7). There's also cold-smoked North Sea salmon from Belgium, vacuum-packed ($30 for 2 lbs.).

SUBURBIA, INC. / Dept. CFC
366 Wacouta, St. Paul, MN 55101

"Suburbia Mail Shopping Service," 25¢, published seasonally, 96 pages, illustrated, color and black and white.

Most of the merchandise is in the novelty and gadget category, but some comes within the purlieus of the cook. There's an electric hibachi for $23.95; the French canning jars with snap wire closures (handy for storing sugar, flour, coffee, and rice because you can see at a glance how much is left), $8.50 for a set of 4; a revolving recipe file, like the office Wheeldex, with clear plastic pockets into which you slip index cards of recipes ($7.95 for a 500-recipe file); and Minnesota wild rice, that very expensive grain from an aquatic grass, $3.95 for a ½ lb., with instructions and recipes.

THE SWISS COLONY / Dept. CFC
1112 7th Avenue, Monroe, WI 53566

"Gifts of Perfect Taste," free, published annually (for Christmas), 92 pages, illustrated, color.

A Christmas food gift catalogue with an array of Wisconsin cheeses (and a few imports), sold alone or in gift packages with other foods, such as smoked sausage, fruitcake, smoked chicken or bacon. There are also pages and pages of other foods—petits fours, candies, preserves, teas,

nuts, fresh and dried fruits, frozen steaks and seafood, pizza, ham, smoked turkey, and, for a comment causer, a 10-foot all-beef smoked sausage ($9.25). Taking a random selection, a package of two smoked Rock Cornish game hens is around $10; a 12-oz. tin of Hawaiian macadamia nut chocolates $4.50; a burlap sack of pecans, almonds, walnuts, brazils, filberts, 3½ lbs. in all, around $6; a triple tower of oranges, pears, and apples, $14.50. A 2-lb. piece of Canadian-style bacon is $10.95, 3 lbs. of sliced Nova Scotia lox $38, and a combination package of boneless ham and a 3-lb. wheel of Swiss cheese around $26. Gift plans are also available. The Fruit of all Seasons plan brings navel oranges, apples, tangelos, pink grapefruit, apricots, Bing cherries, nectarines, peaches, pears, preserves, and "moisturized" dried fruits. There is also a 4- or 6-month fruit plan as well as a cheese Gift of the Month plan. This catalogue offers a discount on certain foods ordered before December 5 and price-off coupons for others.

TAYLOR GIFTS / Dept. CFC
355 East Conestoga Road, Wayne, PA 19087

"Taylor Gifts," free, published periodically, 112 pages, illustrated, color.

From old-fashioned Vermont comes the natural soapstone griddle with all the convenient nonstick properties of modern-day synthetics but with none of the worry about damaging the surface. It needs no greasing, doesn't burn or smoke, and rinses clean in hot water. The 10" griddle should last a lifetime ($24.98).

A little strawberry pot herb garden for that sunny kitchen window will produce basil, chives, savory, thyme, and parsley ($4.98).

The flavor and texture of cheese is protected in a 3-qt. glass container ($14.98), while any spice shelf will be improved with the addition of whole spices in their own convenient grinder-containers that stay fresh inside until the top is twisted. Black pepper, sea salt crystals, whole white pepper, whole cloves, nutmeg chunks, and fennel seeds are packed in an attractive Madeira basket ($9.98).

VERMONT FAIR / Dept. CFC
P.O. Box 338, Brattleboro, VT 05301

"Vermont Fair Catalog," free, published seasonally, 32 pages, color and black and white.

The Dunham Brothers Company was founded in 1885, and Vermont Fair is the catalogue-order offshoot of Dunham's Family Shoe Stores, so shoes, slippers, and boots are the main part of their business. There are also handcrafted steak planks, a sturdy sugar maple chopping block measuring 11" x 8" x 1¾" for around $9, and a good-looking wall knife rack, also of maple, the hard-to-find type that holds the knives' blades down so the edges don't bang together and blunt—$8.50 for a 9" single-row rack, $12 for a 12" double-row rack that holds 11 knives. In the food line, you'll find maple and other syrups (a set of 5 flavors is $5), maple cream, maple nut fudge ($3 for a 1-lb. box), Vermont cheddar, corncob smoked ham and bacon, plus food gift packages ranging from $12 for a snack package of corncob smoked salami and 2 lbs. of cheddar to $17 for salami, cheddar, maple syrup, and bacon.

VERMONT VILLAGE SHOPS / Dept. CFC
Bennington, VT 05201

"Vermont Village Shops," free, published annually, 48 pages, illustrated, color.

Tucked away among the candles and calicos, quilts, pillows, and dollhouse furniture are some attractive and useful things for the kitchen. A Vermont lady makes amusing calico potholders with chicken heads ($1.60). There's an old-fashioned, long-handled popcorn popper to hold over the fireplace ($3.50) with a package of five ears of popcorn to take off the cob ($2.75) and some handy gadgets for slicing, pitting, and squeezing fruits, including a marvelously designed cone-shaped wooden juicer that digs into and draws juice from a lemon. Should you be searching for the good old jelly strainer with stand, they have it.

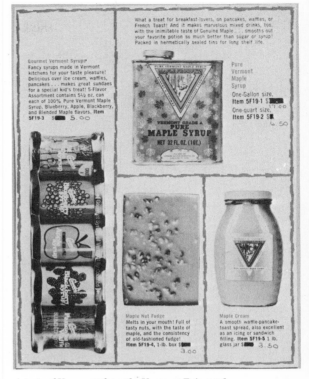

A taste of Vermont, from the Vermont Fair catalogue

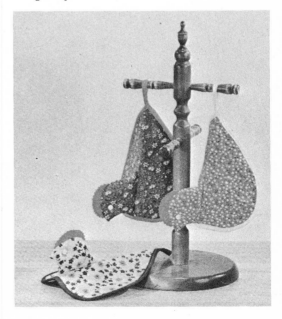

Handmade calico potholders, from Vermont Village Shops

Gift hamper from the Wisconsin Cheesemakers Guild

Smoked Salmon Balls

Chop 1 pound smoked salmon finely in a food processor or by putting it through a meat grinder. Combine with ½ pound cream cheese, 1 to 2 tablespoons sour cream, freshly ground black pepper, a squeeze of lemon juice. Roll into small balls and roll in dark pumpernickel crumbs. Chill until ready to serve. Spear on cocktail picks as an appetizer.

Especially charming (and a great Christmas gift for your favorite cook's kitchen door) are lacquered bread dough wreaths (inedible, of course), round and heart-shaped, made by Casey Junker, owner of "The Petrified Cookie" shop, $4.50 each.

WISCONSIN CHEESE MAKERS GUILD / Dept. CFC
6048 West Beloit Road, Milwaukee, WI 53219

"Christmas Cheer Round the Year," free, published annually, 47 pages, illustrated, color.

Gift packs of cheeses such as Edam, Muenster, Gouda, cheddar, kummel, Tilsit, brick, Colby, Port Salut range from $4.65 for 2 lbs. of 9 cheeses to $16.95 for 7 lbs. of 28 cheeses.

Cheeses come packed in an Oster crêperie ($24.95), a Presto electric deep fryer ($24.95), with a family songbook from *Better Homes & Gardens* ($18.95), in a hamper with sausage, ham, sardines, pâtés, caviar, and antipasto ($28.50), even in a Londoner attaché case ($17.50).

As well as cheese, the Guild sells frozen steaks such as filet mignon ($38 for 3 lbs.), New York strip ($53 for 6 lbs.), sausages ($12.95 for 4 lbs.), smoked turkey ($6.95 for 6 to 7 lbs.), frozen breast of chicken Kiev ($29 for six 7-oz. servings), breast of chicken Cordon Bleu ($29 for six 7-oz. servings), and breast of chicken with wild rice and mushroom stuffing ($29 for six 7-oz. servings).

Honey is packed in replicas of 1876 Muth handblown jars ($7.50 for 1 lb. each of clover and wildflower honeys). There's also honey candy ($5 a lb.); petits fours ($4.95 for 2 lbs.); a collection of 10 jams, jellies, preserves, and marmalades, including blackberry, grapefruit, plum, tangerine-lime, and spiced pear ($4.95); cherry pecan cake ($8.50); cookies; Dobos and crème de menthe tortes; nuts; toffee; fruitcake; and maple syrup.

THE WISCONSIN CHEESEMAN / Dept. CFC
P.O. Box 1, Madison, WI 53701

"Gift Selections," free, published annually, 96 pages, illustrated, color.

Gift packages galore are the forte of the Wisconsin Cheeseman. Starting with boxes of Wisconsin cheese alone, the catalogue goes on to show a staggering array of all kinds of combinations of cheese with smoked meats and birds, jams and jellies, cakes, cookies and candies, nuts, fresh or dried fruits, canned seafood, some sedately packaged in boxes, others in everything from an ice bucket to stoneware soup mugs. There are also gift packages of foods other than cheese, such as smoked turkey and smoked turkey breast, nuts, fruits, cakes and candies, but the emphasis is mainly on cheese. Taking a few selections at random, there's a Party Pak of 7 types of cheese plus assorted delicacies such as smoked oysters, Italian antipasto, mushroom and anchovy pâté, and Dutch cocktail onions ($9.95), a Surprise Tower of 5 gaily wrapped boxes of cheese, nuts, candies, jams and jellies, and petits fours ($13.95), an electric fondue pot that comes with four wood-handled fondue forks and a 12-oz. package of heat-and-serve fondue ($12.95), a Northwoods Breakfast package of smoked bacon, buttermilk, wild rice and Swedish pancake mixes, two syrups and four jams ($7.85), a Holiday Dinner of hickory-smoked boneless pork loin, canned onion soup, cheese dressing, Mandarin oranges, brown and wild rice, cranberry jelly, aged cheddar and Edam cheeses, mixed nuts, chocolate torte, and glazed fruits ($19.95), or the ultimate, a Luxury Hamper of cheeses and about 17 other foods ($31.95).

WOODWARD'S DEPARTMENT STORE, Specialty Food Floor
Dept. CFC
3850 98 Street, Edmonton, Alberta T6E 3L2, Canada

"Woodward's," free, published seasonally, 64 pages, illustrated, color.

From one of Canada's oldest and finest department stores come gifts containing canned sockeye salmon, shrimp and solid white tuna, Canadian Shoal Lake wild rice, Golden Valley Canadian jam in blackberry, black-currant, strawberry, and raspberry flavors, or a gourmet basket of savory appetizers and cocktail snacks that includes fish, cheese, biscuits, chutney, and cocktail sausages.

Eleven cheese assortments include a party cheese board with inlaid cutting tile and cheese knife packaged with an 8-oz. wedge of both aged and medium cheddar, a Gouda and three Danish cream cheeses, or another Woodward's gift pack contains their own premium fruitcake, all-butter shortbread, and their traditional plum pudding.

Chocolates are offered in three attractive gift packs: a 1¼-lb. assortment from Ireland, another from England, or Danish creams, nuts, and liquid-filled sweets.

ADAM YORK'S CATALOG, UNIQUE PRODUCTS COMPANY
Dept. CFC
340 Poplar Street, Hanover, PA 17331

"Adam York's Catalog of Unique Gift Ideas," free, published seasonally, 64 pages, illustrated, color.

Adam York has hundreds of gimmicks and gadgets for the kitchen: a fruit and vegetable drying kit with recipe book ($20), an electric crêpe maker ($29.95), Johnny Apple Peeler ($12.95), a crackerjack that applies controlled pressure to anything crackable ($12), a canning dipper with a contoured pouring lip ($3.25), and a reproduction of an old-fashioned coffee mill ($20). In the food line, there's a fruitcake from Butterfield Farms containing sweet French cherries, Spanish almonds, French Charbert walnuts, and Caribbean pineapple packed in a handsome reusable tin (3 lbs., $12.95), and a gift pack of Danish salami, Spanish ham, French pâté, and nine other delicacies, $24.50.

★

For a brunch dish, sauté thinly sliced smoked salmon in butter until lightly crisped, put on a toasted buttered English muffin, top with a poached egg and Hollandaise sauce.
—*from The House of Kilfenora*

★

Serve smoked salmon with scrambled eggs. As an hors d'oeuvre roll around asparagus or cream cheese.

★

See Appendix, page 239, for additional sources not included here.

Kitchen by Cardan Interiors, photographer Max Eckert

CHAPTER TWELVE

THE COOK'S EQUIPMENT

Things for the Kitchen

J.K. ADAMS CO. / Dept. CFC
Dorset, VT 05251

Catalogue, free, published every two years, 24 pages, illustrated, black and white.

Beautifully designed and crafted wood pieces are the stock-in-trade of this Vermont company. They have sturdy kitchen tables of kiln-dried Vermont hard maple, with optional accessories such as drawers, knife rack, tool tray, and wine-rack shelf (a table 36" x 24" x 32" high, without accessories, is around $200), a butcher block with knife rack on ball casters (24" x 24" x 31" high, $350), baby butcher blocks on nonskid feet, like the Jim Dandy, 10" x 10", with a chef's knife magnetically held at the side ($26.50), and end-grain maple cutting blocks and boards. (There are sketches and explanations of terms such as end grain and edge grain in the catalogue that are very useful for nonprofessionals.) Knife racks are one of their specialties, styled to give plenty of storage space in a small area. Wood racks with slots that hold knives point down are the safest, both for you and your knife blades. The slots are designed to take knives of different sizes plus a sharpening steel. A 15" triple row holds 16 knives and a steel and costs $17, but there are single and double-row racks and smaller sizes for fewer knives. The largest, a 24" double row, holds 17 knives and a steel. A modular spice rack, almost Scandinavian in its purity and simplicity of design, comes in three sizes, 14" wide with two, three, or four shelves (4-shelf size, $24), and there's a revival of that old kitchen favorite, the roller-towel rack, with its own unbleached linen towel ($16 in maple, $8 in walnut; towel, $3). Adams has lots of cutting, carving, serving, sandwich, and cheese boards, some of treenware (which means they are shaped from a solid piece of sugar maple selected for grain), and we are delighted to see that they have reproduced the English paddle-shaped block used by Smithfield butchers to pound meat (Julia Child calls it her "British basher") as a small chopping block. It has a brass ring for hanging up

Cook's work table with wine and knife racks, from J. K. Adams Company

and comes in two sizes, 15" x 5½" x 1¾" ($13) or 17" x 7½" x 1¾". Adams' catalogue has some good advice on care of culinary woodware, and they sell "Wood Care," a linseed-oil-base liquid for treating and preserving the wood (or you may use mineral oil). Should you happen to be in Vermont, their sales and display rooms are open to the public all year, weekdays 8:00 A.M. to 5:30 P.M., Saturdays 9:30 A.M. to 5:30 P.M., Sundays 11:00 A.M. to 5:30 P.M., and you'll often find sales of factory rejects and closeouts.

ANZEN JAPANESE FOODS AND IMPORTS / Dept. CFC
736 N.E. Union Avenue, Portland, OR 97232

Price list, free, 20 pages, plus list of cooking and serving equipment.

Anzen lists but does not price various pieces of cooking equipment, such as woks in different sizes and shapes made from spun steel or stainless steel with copper bottoms, wok accessories (spatula, ladle, steaming plates), bamboo and alimite steamers in different shapes and sizes, electric rice cookers (and replacement parts), chopping and slicing knives from Japan, Germany, and Portland in different sizes, either carbon steel or stainless steel, chopsticks, vegetable slicers, and various serving pieces and tea sets. If you are interested in any particular objects, request the prices and more information.

BARTH'S OF LONG ISLAND / Dept. CFC
Valley Stream, NY 11582

Catalogue, free, published seasonally, 112 pages, with supplements, illustrated, black and white.

Barth's, primarily a source for vitamins, food supplements, and natural foods, has a good assortment of food preparation and cooking equipment, such as an electric grinder for nuts and seeds, a seed sprouter (around $16) that you can order with 15 different seeds for sprouting (around $5), *The Complete Sprouting Cookbook* (120 pages, around $3), an electric yogurt maker, a juicer and pulp ejector, a water purifier, a hand-operated home flour mill that grinds any type of grain (around $20), a stainless-steel steaming basket that fits into any size pot (around $4), the old-fashioned iron Dutch oven with glass lid and bail handle, a 5-qt. stoneware slow cooker, a stainless-steel rotary food mill, and a ceramic knife sharpener. There are some handy gadgets here. One is the Flame Tamer that fits over a burner, giving you double-boiler safety for ordinary pots (around $4). Another is a crisper rack of perforated white vinyl for refrigerator vegetable bin that lets air flow around the food to retard spoilage (around $1.60), and yet another item is a natural-wood oven spade, a small version of the baker's peel that slides hot pans in and out of the oven without burning your fingers (around $1.50). Barth's also sells rolls of cooking parchment; a 20 sq.-ft. roll in cutter box is around $1.30.

BAZAAR DE LA CUISINE INTERNATIONAL, INC. / Dept. CFC
1003 Second Avenue, New York, NY 10022

Catalogue, 82 pages, published periodically, illustrated, black and white.

As of now, Bazaar de la Cuisine has established no price for the updated catalogue to be published in summer 1977, but it will probably be 50¢ to 75¢. This kitchen equipment store has one of the most complete selections of wares in New York City, everything from the French imported copper *batterie de cuisine* to more offbeat things such as a chestnut roaster, shaped like a fry pan with a perforated bottom (around $4); a café diable set; a turbotière, the diamond-shaped poacher for whole turbot that can also be used for roasting game hens and small chickens; a copper pommes Anna pan, to bake that very special cake of sliced potatoes laved in butter (around $65); and the baking dish and glass bell for *champignons sous cloche*. You'll find the Cuisinart stainless-steel cookware, different types of salt and pepper mills and nutmeg shavers, the extra-large and heavy rolling pin for pasta, larding needles, a French butter crock-cooler for keeping butter firm at the table on the hottest day, molds for *oeufs en gelée*, stainless-steel whisks, baking equipment of

★

After using a cutting board or wood counter for preparing fish, rub it with a cut lemon to remove the fishy odor.

★

If you don't have copper cleaner handy, use salt and lemon juice or vinegar. It works like a dream.

★

BAZAAR

DE LA

CUISINE

LARGEST SELECTION OF INTERNATIONAL COOKWARE

*

To remove stains from blades of carbon-steel knives, rub with a Scotch Brite scouring pad.

*

To keep a mixing bowl from moving around while you beat or stir, stand it on a folded damp cloth.

*

Line cookie sheets and baking pans with kitchen cooking parchment rather than wax paper. It does not need greasing and even sticky doughs will not adhere.

*

all types, two types of meat pounder for flattening scaloppine, a double rack that holds a 30-lb. turkey and enables you to turn it with ease (around $7), a 16" diameter iron paella pan and a 15" heavy aluminum one with lid, a French decilitre measuring glass for metric recipes (around $2), and heavy aluminum and iron omelet pans in sizes from 7½" to 12½" top diameter. There's very little you can think of that isn't here and some things you might never think of—such as a "Piccadilli" home pickling kit complete with two-gallon stoneware crock, dairy salt, pickling spices, wooden spoon, cloth spice bags, and a 48-page illustrated recipe booklet (around $18). The prices we quote are from an old catalogue and will undoubtedly be higher by now.

L.L. BEAN, INC. / Dept. CFC
Main Street, Freeport, ME 04033

"L.L. Bean Catalogue," free, published seasonally, 120 pages, illustrated, color and black and white.

Although the L.L. Bean catalogue is principally for the outdoor types—camper, hunter, fisherman—you'll find all kinds of good general-purpose cooking equipment here that isn't always easy to come by. There are old-fashioned hand-operated ice-cream freezers ($21.50 ppd. for a 6-qt. size) and an ice-cream mix, without preservatives; cast-iron cookware; lobster and clam steamers; a barbecue-smoke-cooker ($50); the old-style agateware coffee percolator; kitchen knives, including a beautifully designed, thin-bladed flexible fish filleting knife ($6.25 ppd. for the 6"-blade size) that any cook would itch to get his or her hands on—they also suggest it be used as a kitchen knife. You'll find here the Little Chief Electric Smoker made in Hood River, Oregon, that was highly praised by James Beard ($30 ppd. with 1½ lbs. of hickory chips). It cures up to 20 lbs. of meat or fish in 10 to 12 hours on regular household current and is perfect for smoking turkey breast, trout, pork loin, and other meats.

BLOOMINGDALE'S COOKS' KITCHEN / Dept. CFC
P.O. Box 2058, F.D.R. Station, New York, NY 10022

"Bloomingdale's Cooks' Kitchen," catalogue, $2.50, 80 pages, illustrated, black and white.

The Cooks' Catalogue, a massive compendium of kitchen equipment and utensils that sells for around $16, was the gift of the year for cooking friends a couple of years back. Bloomingdale's, the legendary New York department store that carries a lot of the equipment in the catalogue, has cleverly boiled down the 565 pages to a compact 80, featuring, naturally, those items that they sell, from pots and pans to flan rings and whisks. The copy and illustrations are taken straight from *The Cooks' Catalogue*, but now you know where to buy what you see, which wasn't the case before. Bloomingdale's will take orders for anything shown, although they warn that the prices quoted were based on market conditions and currency exchange rates as of November 1975 and are therefore subject to change without notice. If you have an account with Bloomingdale's, charge your purchases; otherwise they will take a check or money order.

BON APPETIT PUBLISHING CORP. / Dept. CFC
5900 Wilshire Blvd., Los Angeles, CA 90036

No catalogue. Mail-order through the magazine.

Bon Appetit, the Los Angeles-based monthly food and wine magazine, sells by mail selected pieces of cooking and serving equipment that are shown in color in each issue. A recent selection featured a Chinese cleaver with cutting board ($21), the Ah-So cork puller used by the California winemakers ($6), the Taylor Bi-therm meat and testing thermometer that starts at 0° and goes up to 220° (the one you *don't* leave in the roast while it is in the oven), and a very attractive brown ceramic tea pot that brews on the filter system ($19). We'll pass over the brandy warmer, which their wine editor can hardly have approved.

CAKE DECORATORS / Dept. CFC
P.O. Box 97, Blacklick, OH 43004

Catalogue, 75¢, 144 pages, illustrated, black and white.

Cake decorating and parties at which cakes are featured must be one of America's primary interests if this catalogue is any indication of its popularity. There are all the things you would expect to find: molds and baking pans in every size and shape (heart-shaped, guitar-shaped, horseshoe-shaped, lamb-shaped, bunny-shaped, Santa Claus shaped), from the tiniest fluted patty pans and miniature angel-food pans up. Just to show how elaborate they can get, there's a 15-piece piano pan set, two pans, piano base, bench and all the accessories, including keyboard, candelabra, and gold filigree decoration to make the birthday cake for your budding Liberace. There are pages and pages of things to top and decorate cakes with: satin bells, wedding couples, gazebos, angels, nuns, graduation hats, birds, flowers, leaves—you name it. On the more practical side, there's a very complete selection of pastry bags and decorating tubes, flower nails, spatulas, stands, cookie and other types of cutters, cream horn forms, cannoli tubes, irons for krumkake, gaufrettes, Italian pizzali, the KitchenAid electric mixer, and a battery-powered flour sifter. Also decorator's parchment (very strong to make piping cones) and supplies and molds for making candy and candles (which, though not edible, are another party essential). You'll find a whole page of flavoring extracts, from almond to vanilla, sesame seeds and poppy seeds, the minute little balls and sprinkles for scattering over cakes, cookies, and candies, concentrated gelatin in 1-lb. cans, citric acid, glycerine, egg-white powder, almond paste, fruit and nut pastry fillings, gum arabic, prepared fondant, and more. Lots of books on cake decorating, candy making, and baking, too. The catalogue, which has not been reprinted since 1973/4, does not give present prices, but these will be inserted on a separate price list. Cake Decorator's showroom has over 7,000 items, and they also give cake decorating and candy-making classes.

Kitchen scales, to stand on counter and hang on wall

CARAVANSARY / Dept. CFC
2263 Chestnut Street, San Francisco, CA 94123

"Gourmet Gift Ideas from the Caravansary," free, published winter/spring, 14 pages, illustrated, black and white.

Caravansary is known for its coffees, so it's only natural that they specialize in coffee-making equipment, from mills to espresso machines (see chapter 1). They also have a couple of very attractive teapots—the Jena glass pot found in the Museum of Modern Art as an example of good design ($25) and a charming white French porcelain teapot with the word "thé" on the outside (6-cup capacity, $18.50). You'll find Le Creuset pots, the Cuisinart food processor, Sabatier knives, the Römertopf clay pot cooker (4- to 6-lb. size, $18) and some nifty gadgets, such as a 7-in-1 dry measure, a measuring spoon that adjusts to anything from ⅛ teaspoon to 1 tablespoon ($1.50). Caravansary periodically sends out a leaflet of cooking and eating ideas called "Gourmet Gallery," which shows other cookware, such as a line of hand-crafted glazed clay cookware by a San Francisco firm called Amnion, and gives details of cooking demonstrations in the area.

CASA MONEO / Dept. CFC
210 West 14th Street, New York, NY 10011

"Mexican Food—Comida Mexicana," free, 8 pages, published annually, also price lists of South American, Cuban, and Portuguese foods.

Casa Moneo lists a very limited amount of cooking equipment, such as aluminum cooking pots or calderos from Portugal and Cuba ($2.70 to $11.60, according to size), and a plantain slicer, but we know after visiting the store that they have a very wide selection of paella pans of all sizes from Spain and a Mexican tortilla press, so if you are interested in these, request information.

W/S Apple Tart
Make pâte brisée in the food processor as follows: Using the steel blade, process 2 cups flour, 5 ounces butter, and 2 tablespoons sugar until mixture resembles coarse bread crumbs. With the motor running, add 1 egg yolk through the feed tube and only *just* enough cold water to bind the mixture into a ball. Roll out between sheets of plastic wrap and fit into a 10-inch black steel tart pan. (Save any balance for small pastries.) Bake at 400° for about 20 minutes until golden brown. Peel, core, and slice 6 to 8 pippin apples or tart cooking apples and simmer for 10 to 15 minutes in ½ cup orange juice. Paint the inside of the pastry case with sieved apricot jam. Arrange the drained apple slices inside and glaze with more apricot jam. Just before serving, paint with liquid caramel, which adds a delicious flavor.
—*from Williams-Sonoma's "A Catalog for Cooks"*

*

To weight down a cooked pâté in a rectangular mold or terrine, use a brick covered with aluminum foil.

*

Crêpes and omelets will never stick if you cook them in a Teflon-coated skillet.

*

Ethnic cookware from the China Closet catalogue

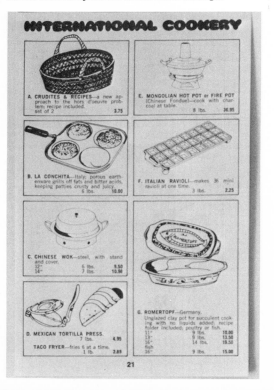

CHEESE COFFEE CENTER / Dept. CFC
2110 Center Street, Berkeley, CA 94704

Mail-order catalogue, free, published semiannually, 12 pages, black and white.

The Cheese Coffee Center sells coffee-grinding and coffee-making equipment, as you might expect. In coffee makers they stock Melitta, Chemex, Melior (the French plunger-type pot), and various espresso makers, such as the Bialetti (1- to 18-cup sizes), Gemellina (1- to 9-cup sizes), and the Neapolitan drip-type pot. In coffee grinders, they have various manual types. One is a small German lap grinder, another a large old-fashioned precision model with fly wheel from Italy. Unfortunately, as there are no illustrations, it is hard to visualize what they are like. In electric mills, there's the Emide and the Braun (in colors or black and chrome) from Germany, the Farberware, and the Ecuador from Spain. Prices range from $13.95 for the lap grinder to $125 for a replica of an American antique model. The only other piece of equipment is a Swedish cheese slicer.

CHEMEX CORPORATION / Dept. CFC
P.O. Box 897, Pittsfield, MA 01201

"Welcome Booklet" and price list, 25¢, published periodically, 19 pages, illustrated, black and white.

The Chemex coffee people are coffee purists: "instant coffee hardly qualifies to bear the label 'coffee' . . . the worst perpetrator of bad coffee is the percolator . . . making coffee taste more like reheated sludge than freshly brewed coffee."

The Chemex secret is filtration—the undesirable elements of oils, fats, acids, and sediment remain trapped in their special bonded paper filter so only pure, clear coffee comes through.

The Chemex booklet offers a range of their products: handblown glass coffeemakers in the distinctive hourglass shape (1- to 14-cup sizes, $10.95 to $18.50); filters; electric coffee warmers ($6.95 to $17.95); accessories for the coffeemakers and an assortment of cocktail, highball, and beer glasses in the same hourglass shape ($3.50 to $3.95 each); and the carafe kettle, the ultimate vessel for boiling water ($25 with grid).

CHICO-SAN, INC. / Dept. CFC
1144 West 1st Street, Chico, CA 95926

"Chico-San, Inc., Products—a catalog of unique foods," free, published annually, 26 pages, black and white.

Chico-San sells a few Japanese cooking tools, such as the extremely sharp, straight-bladed vegetable-cutting knife ($7.33), a suribachi, or mortar with pestle ($3.69 for a 6½-inch suribachi, 84¢ for the 7-inch pestle), lacquered chopsticks, and a rice paddle (63¢). They also have three books on macrobiotic and natural Oriental cooking, tofu, and traditional Japanese cuisine based on the principle of yin and yang.

CHINA CLOSET / Dept. CFC
6807 Wisconsin Avenue, Bethesda, MD 20015

"China Closet—the wishbook for everyone," 25¢, 34 pages, illustrated, black on colored paper, plus "The China Closet's Buyer Be-Aware Guide," by Edith Schubert, 26 pages.

The catalogue has a small but quite interesting selection of cooking and serving things, plus odds and ends like lucite cookbook holders, baskets, and gifts for men and women (he gets an omelet pan and a German beer warmer, she an adjustable bed tray and a Handy Hannah fix-it kit). There are some offbeat gadgets such as a croissant cutter ($9.95), a zucchini stuffer ($1.35), a taco fryer (it holds 6 tacos at a time and costs around $2.89), and an electric caramelizer ($34.95), which seems to be an updated form of the old salamander, for glazing the surface of gratins or crème brûlée, although the catalogue indicates it is for tarts and croquembouche (hardly likely, as the cream puffs would be dipped in liquid caramel). There are all kinds of molds for baking and desserts, wrought-iron hanging or standing racks for pots and pans, knives (mostly French Sabatier), ethnic cooking equipment such as a tortilla press ($4.95) and Mongolian fire-pot charcoal table cooker, and pots and pans of copper, aluminum, and enameled cast iron. While the enameled iron is identified as Le Creuset, Copco, and Waterford, there is no identification of the brand of copper or aluminum, which is a pity, because these vary so much in weight and quality. With the catalogue comes "The China Closet's Buyer Be-Aware Guide" by owner Edith Schubert, a 26-page booklet that contains some useful information on the different materials used in tableware and cookware and how best to care for them.

CHRIS-CRAFT / Dept. CFC
Algonac, MI 48001

"Chris-Craft Gifts and Gear," free, published annually, 64 pages, illustrated, color.

Though the largest part of this catalogue is given over to boating supplies and stylish clothing, there are some ingenious things for the kitchen. Much of the equipment, after all, would work just as well in a land-based galley-type kitchen where space is equally limited. There's a small Teflon-coated pan with a hinged lid and egg-poacher insert that can be used for sautéing, scrambling eggs, warming up leftovers ($10.50), a top-of-the-stove Belgian waffle iron, and a couple of useful things designed for boats, such as a nesting set of stainless-steel cookware (around $60), a sectioned fry pan of Teflon-coated aluminum that will cook three foods at once (around $13), and a two-slice toaster that fits over a burner ($2.50).

CONTE DI SAVOIA / Dept. CFC
555 W. Roosevelt Road, Chicago, IL 60607

Catalogue, 75¢ (refundable with purchase), published annually, 28 pages.

The catalogue lists certain pieces of equipment for Italian cooking, such as a pasta machine, ravioli maker, electric and hand cheese graters, slicers and meat grinders, and, of course, espresso coffee makers. They have many other utensils, not listed, so if you have anything specific in mind, ask about it. You also have to inquire about prices on equipment, as these are not given.

COUNTRY HOUSEWARES / Dept. CFC
Box 626, Wading River, NY 11792

"Country Housewares of Long Island," free, published seasonally, 6 pages, illustrated, black and white.

This small brochure shows a few housewares sold by mail, such as an aluminum dough mixer ($25), copper bowl for beating egg whites (2½-qt. size, $22), a wok set ($9), and Primavera porcelain cookware. All prices are postpaid.

CROSS IMPORTS, INC. / Dept. CFC
210 Hanover Street, Boston, MA 02113

"Cross Shop by Mail and Recipe Book," 50¢, published annually, 156 pages, illustrated, black and white.

A good basic reference book for anyone serious about cooking who doesn't want to spend time hunting through stores for something like a spaetzle machine or an outsize stock pot. Pictured and described are over 1,000 cooking and baking utensils and gadgets from France, Italy, Germany, and America—heavy aluminum pots and pans (a 12" Teflon-lined frying pan is around $18, a 40-qt. stock pot about $40); Le Creuset enameled cast-iron cookware; the Sabatier and Wusthof Trident knives (the first French, the latter from Solingen, Germany); a positive forest of roasting and baking pans, molds of all shapes and sizes, flan rings, strainers, scales, meat grinders and choppers, cutters, graters; a huge selection of pastry tubes. Prices are standard, and there

Galley-kitchen gear from the Chris-Craft catalogue

Wooden spoons from the Cross Imports catalogue

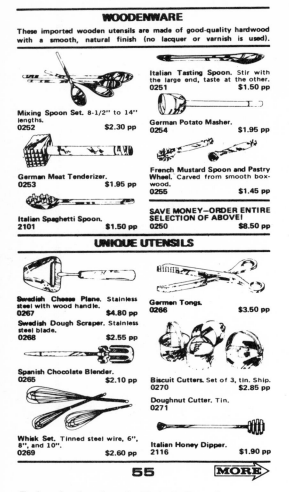

WOODENWARE

These imported wooden utensils are made of good-quality hardwood with a smooth, natural finish (no lacquer or varnish is used).

Italian Tasting Spoon. Stir with the large end, taste at the other.
0251 $1.50 pp

Mixing Spoon Set. 8-1/2'' to 14'' lengths.
0252 $2.30 pp

German Potato Masher.
0254 $1.95 pp

German Meat Tenderizer.
0253 $1.95 pp

French Mustard Spoon and Pastry Wheel. Carved from smooth boxwood.
0255 $1.45 pp

Italian Spaghetti Spoon.
2101 $1.50 pp

SAVE MONEY—ORDER ENTIRE SELECTION OF ABOVE!
0250 $8.50 pp

UNIQUE UTENSILS

Swedish Cheese Plane. Stainless steel with wood handle.
0267 $4.80 pp

German Tongs.
0266 $3.50 pp

Swedish Dough Scraper. Stainless steel blade.
0268 $2.55 pp

Spanish Chocolate Blender.
0265 $2.10 pp

Biscuit Cutters. Set of 3, tin. Ship.
0270 $2.85 pp

Doughnut Cutter. Tin.
0271

Whisk Set. Tinned steel wire, 6'', 8'', and 10''.
0269 $2.60 pp

Italian Honey Dipper.
2116 $1.90 pp

55   MORE →

Tools and gadgets from the Mother's General Store catalogue

★

Rinse the inside of a copper bowl with vinegar to remove any lingering trace of grease that might prevent egg whites mounting when beaten. Dry after rinsing.

★

When using a tart pan with a removable bottom, stand the pan on a large can after the tart is baked and the ring will slip off. The tart can then be sliced easily.

★

is a handy index of all the equipment in the back. The 85 recipes dotted throughout the book are less comprehensive and rather oddly selected. Some are reprinted from cookbooks Cross Imports carries, such as *Betty Crocker, Leone's Italian Cookbook,* Paula Peck's *The Art of Fine Baking,* and *Better Homes and Gardens New Cook Book.* Others are provided by Barbara, Rochelle, Marge, Janet, Elaine, and Judy (or Judi) and tend to be on the simplistic side, leaning heavily on cake and pudding mixes—rather odd bedfellows with Paula Peck.

CUMBERLAND GENERAL STORE / Dept. CFC
Rte. 3, Box 479, Crossville, TN 38555

"Mother's General Store—tools for living the satisfying life," 50¢, published seasonally, 130 pages, illustrated, black and white.

Turning the pages of this small paperback catalogue is like turning back the calendar to the way we were. It's full of those old-time things you may have thought had vanished forever: wood-burning cook stoves (and iron lid lifters), washboards, cuspidors, graniteware, hand-turned butter churns, the wooden front porch swing—even the good old ice pick. You'll find the 100-years-young apple parer, corer, and slicer, a product of Yankee ingenuity that does the job in five seconds flat ($12.95 plus shipping and handling), a pea sheller, corn sheller, kraut cutter, hanging scale, a reproduction of the grocer's coffee mill made of solid cast iron with a little drawer at the base and a wheel on each side, soapstone griddles (the 10" diameter size is $24.75 plus shipping and handling), hand grain mills and a formidable-looking object that is a sausage stuffer, lard and fruit press in one. Mother's (which is now operated by the Cumberland General Store) also sells herbs and spices, yogurt culture, stone-ground flours, pasta, nuts, beans and grains, fruit and nut butters and honey, a cheese-making kit, but it is the equipment that really fascinates.

"The Wish & Want Book," $3, published seasonally, 272 pages, illustrated, black and white.

Did you ever wonder what happened to the old-fashioned pyramid-shaped toaster that existed long before the days of electrical appliances? Well, the Cumberland General Store has two models that can be used on a stove or over a campfire—one is a tin plate with side supports for four pieces of toast that folds flat when not in use ($1.48), the other a steel or stainless-steel plate with sides that holds two slices ($1.70 in steel, $3.98 in stainless). There's a blue-speckled enamel coffee pot with bail handle, too, and a nice big slatted wood picnic hamper, 18" x 9" x 12" high, with hinged lid for $13.55.

DEER VALLEY FARM / Dept. CFC
R.D. 1, Guilford, NY 13780

Price list, free, published annually, 20 pages, black and white.

On the Deer Valley Farm list you'll find the Atlas, Acme, Champion, and Miracle juicers, ranging in price from around $190 for the stainless Miracle model to around $110 for a small 1-qt.-capacity Acme model, the Bio-Snacky seed sprouter and the less expensive red clay dish Beales sprouter (around $7.25), a hand mill and electric flour mill, three yogurt makers, the Moulinex salad basket, and an electric coffee grinder, which is also capable of grinding one cup of wheat or nuts (around $13).

E. DEHILLERIN / Dept. CFC
18-20 rue Coquillière, Paris 1er, France

Catalogue, free, 24 pages, illustrated, black and white.

Dehillerin, founded in 1820, is probably the most famous of all the fine old professional kitchen equipment stores selling copper cooking pans and molds, cocottes, beating bowls, knives, baking pans and cutters, ornamental *hatelets* or skewers with ends fashioned into a lobster, ram's head, fish, or swan to put the finishing touch to a noble pâté or saddle of veal Prince Orloff. (On what, though, could you possibly put a *tête de mort*, or death's head, a pâté of *amanita phalloides*?) They never update their catalogue, which hasn't changed since we first saw it some 12 or 15 years ago (they haven't even added the current Paris zip code), and they quite intransigently refuse to translate it. Everything is in French, and there isn't a price anywhere. You have to find the item you want and then write them, giving dimensions and all pertinent details, whereupon they'll let you know how much that is in dollars, depending on the rate of exchange. In our most recent copy, there was a French price list for certain copper serving pieces, which might give you some idea. Their copper is superb but, like all good copper, weighty. Shipping charges would undoubtedly be high. Our advice is to browse through the catalogue and put Dehillerin on your list of places to visit when you are next in Paris. It is a most fascinating shop, and the catalogue gives only a faint indication of the thousands of things you'll find there, stacked floor to ceiling.

Ornamental skewers from the Dehillerin catalogue

D. M. ENTERPRISES / Dept. CFC
P.O. Box 2452, San Francisco, CA 94126

"Calico Kitchen's Portfolio," free, 12 sheets, published two to three times a year.

In kitchen equipment, Calico Kitchen chooses the EVA products from Scandinavia. They have the wall scale with pendulum mechanism ($17.95), the heavy cast-aluminum waffle iron with nonstick coating ($18.95), the all-purpose slicing machine ($40), and a box-type parsley chopper that comes in white, colors, or clear, attractive enough to put on the table ($5). The chopper will also mince and grate other herbs, cheese, nuts, lemon, or orange peel. For the sourdough bread they sell by mail there's a serrated stainless-steel bread knife from England ($5.25) and a pretty handwoven bread basket ($2.50, or $1.50 if included with an order of bread).

DRANNAN'S / Dept. CFC
1103 Aledo Drive, Dayton, OH 45430

"The Secret of Smokeless and Effortless Broiling," free, 6 pages, illustrated, black and white.

The secret of smokeless and effortless broiling consists of using the Drannan WaterBroiler™ Pan and Grill, a shallow polished stainless-steel pan, 12" diameter, with handles at the sides and a grill that fits over the top. You put some cold water in the pan and the grease drips into the water, eliminating smoke, spatters, and grease from the broiling meat. Sounds simple, doesn't it? Well, Lee Drannan Smithson dreamed up this better mousetrap after experimenting with a paella pan (which this pan resembles) and a grill. He had it made and patented and now sells the stainless-steel pan and grill with another of his inventions, Forkula™ tongs, for $24.95 delivered. The tongs are an improvement on the solid metal type that often don't grip tightly when turning foods on a grill. These are made from open-ended pieces of stainless-steel wire, like the grill itself, so they slide between the bars and underneath the meat. They are double-sided and open to about 4", or close completely to pick up thin foods like bacon. A pamphlet of recipes, cooking tips, and directions comes with the set, which can be returned within one year for a full refund if you are not completely satisfied.

WaterBroiler and tongs, from Drannan's

EAST WIND / Dept. CFC
2801 Broadway, New York, NY 10025

Mail-order price list, free, 5 pages.

Chinese cooking utensils are the major part of East Wind's list. A stainless-steel cleaver is $6.50, a 14" wok, $7.95 (plus $3.95 for the cover), a wok stand $1.80, and bamboo steamers are $5.95 for the 12" layer plus $5.95 for the steamer cover. There are also 12" woks and 10" steamers. A spatula and ladle to go with the wok are $3.55 and $3.95

Papaya Sherbet

Boil ⅔ cup sugar and ½ cup water in a small saucepan until sugar dissolves, stirring. Then boil without stirring for 5 minutes. Cool syrup. Combine cool syrup and 2 cups puréed papaya (purée fresh papaya in a blender or food processor; you will need 2 ripe papayas to make 2 cups purée) and stir in fresh lime juice to taste. Mix well and pour into ice cube trays. Freeze until mushy in the center and firm around the edges. Remove to a bowl and beat until smooth. Return to trays and freeze to same state as before. Again remove and beat. Finally, return to trays and freeze until solid. Remove to refrigerator 30 minutes before serving to soften slightly.

Aids for home canning from the Garden Way catalogue

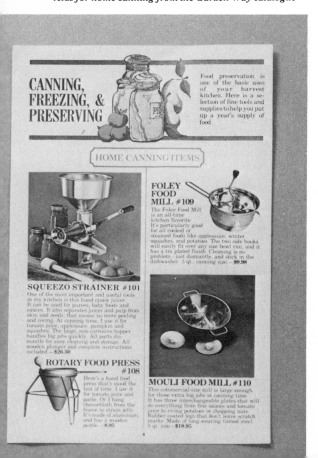

respectively, ivory chopsticks 90¢ a pair, 10¢ for bamboo. Prices are subject to change without notice, and 10 percent of the total is added for shipping and handling charges.

ESPECIALLY MAINE / Dept. CFC
   Vinegar Hill Road, Arundel, ME 04046

"Especially Maine," free, published periodically, 23 pages, illustrated, black and white.

Especially Maine has a foolproof clam opener with stainless-steel blade and lock, $3.50, heavy-duty lobster crackers, $3.50, and a set of six stainless-steel lobster scoop forks, 7¾" long, $6. To serve honey without losing a drop, there's a specially designed server, $1.80. A hinged fish grill with folding legs is ideal for charcoal cooking, $9.

HENRY FIELD SEED & NURSERY CO. / Dept. CFC
   407 Sycamore Street, Shenandoah, IA 51602

Catalogues, free, published spring (January), 132 pages, and fall (August), 46 pages, illustrated, color.

The spring catalogue has a few vegetable-preparation tools, such as a cherry pitter and a corn cutter, but there are many more in the fall catalogue to coincide with preserving time. You'll find here gadgets for canning, a food dehydrator ($54.95), bread maker, electric flour mills, and an automatic juice extractor with pushbutton controls for three different speeds to match the type of fruit or vegetable you are using ($69.99). There's also a set of stainless-steel kitchen canisters shaped like dairy cans ($16.95 the set of 4).

GARDEN WAY / Dept. CFC
   47 Maple Street, P.O. Box 944, Burlington, VT 05401

"Garden Way Country Kitchen Catalog," free, published seasonally, 16 pages, illustrated, color.

There must be something about Vermont. This state produces more good products and good ideas for living than almost anywhere we know. The Garden Way Living Center in Burlington, which is Vermont's largest food-preserving supply center, has come up with a marvelous little catalogue that assembles all those hard-to-find things for preserving food, an activity more people seem to be attempting in these inflationary times. For canning and freezing, they have food presses and mills; a hand-cranked juicer called the Squeezo Strainer that separates pulp from skin and seeds ($26.50); three sizes of pressure canner (the largest, which will hold 24 pts., 16 qts., or 6 half-gal. jars, is $119); a preserving set with hot-water-bath canner, 7-qt. blancher, colander, ladle, and canning funnel in blue speckled enamel ($24.50); and all those other things you need, such as jar lifters, canning tongs and dipper, jar wrench and pressure-sensitive canning labels (60 labels for $1.50, 120 for $2.75, 216 for $3.95). For freezing vegetables, there's a blancher, freezer boxes of rigid plastic, and two sealing kits—Dazey and Scotchpak. We noticed an electric dehydrator for drying fruits and vegetables (5-tray unit is around $100) that comes with a booklet on home-drying vegetables, fruits, and herbs; and such gadgets as cherry stoners and pitters, an apple picker (a padded basket that collects the fruit from the trees), several apple corers-and-peelers, a fruit press for juice, cider, or wine grapes, French bean slicer, corn cutter, corn sheller for dried ears, and lots of other useful things. Do you like to make your own bread and butter from scratch? There's one electric grain mill and two hand-operated ones, with stone or metal burrs; electric or manual dough mixers ($49.95 electric, $26.50 manual); and two sizes of electric butter churn. Garden Way sells the versatile old cast-iron machine that stuffs sausage casings, juices fruits and vegetables, or presses lard or cheese (the catalogue also supplies the rennet tablets and cheesecloth). There's a list of books on all kinds of food preserving, including one on homemade cheese and butter and another on butchering, processing, and preserving meat. An amazing amount of information is packed into this tight little catalogue, including canning timetables and a garden-yield guide that tells how much seed (or how many plants) is needed for a 100-foot row, what the yield will be, and how to convert bushels of fresh produce into canned quarts and frozen pints.

GURNEY SEED & NURSERY CO. / Dept. CFC
2nd and Capitol Streets, Yankton, SD 57078

"Gurney Garden Seed and Nursery Catalog," free, published annually, 76 pages, color.

The Gurney catalogue has quite a few pieces of equipment useful for preparing and putting up fruits and vegetables. One is a kitchen scale that weighs up to 10 lbs. with a removable pan on the top that is graduated by cup markings up to 1 qt. ($8.98). There are corn cutters, a food mill, canning rack and tongs, jelly strainer, cherry pitter, bean stringer and slicer, slaw cutter, apple parer, and the handy Feemster vegetable slicer with a blade that adjusts to 9 different thicknesses, from thick to paper-thin ($1.49). A rather unusual aid is the Buzy-Liz kitchen tool, a 6-piece combination aluminum funnel for filling bottles, fruit jars, and dispensers that also strains. It has a large funnel, bottle funnel, three strainers, and a retaining ring, quite a bargain at $1.59.

HARVEST HEALTH, INC. / Dept. CFC
1944 Eastern Avenue, S.E., Grand Rapids, MI 49507

Catalogue and price lists, free, published annually, 16 pages, black and white, also 8-page catalogue of herbs and spices.

Harvest Health sells some pieces of equipment such as the Corona stone hand mill, Bio-Snacky and Sprout-Ease seed sprouters, yogurt makers (with dry Bulgarian yogurt culture to use as a starter), a water filter, and two food grinders. Prices are not given in the catalogue but will be included on separate sheets, which are revised as prices change.

J. A. HENCKELS / Dept. CFC
1 Westchester Plaza, Box 127, Elmsford, NY 10523

Catalogue, free, 20 pages, illustrated, color.

Henckels is the company in Solingen, Germany, that makes the famous Twinworks knives of all types—chef's, paring, boning, slicing, carving, butcher's, serrated and scalloped edged, cleavers, as well as sharpening steels, carving forks, and stainless-steel spatulas. The knives are superbly made, with blades of Friodur steel, a high carbon alloy that resists stains and rust and sharpens beautifully. Henckels does not sell knives by mail but will supply a list of dealers who do, such as Delbon & Co., 121 West 30th Street, New York, NY 10001; Kirkham's, 71 Bay Street, Glens Falls, NY 12801 (Master Charge or BankAmericard accepted); and presumably others in various parts of the country. The catalogue, which gives no prices, shows the full range of cutlery and the proper way to sharpen a knife, so it is well worth sending for. There's also a booklet called "What Everybody Who Cooks Should Know about Knives" that has a lot of useful information about what to look for in a good knife, how to sharpen and clean it, how to hold a chef's knife, background material on the Henckels company and their knives, and photographs of the five professional knives they recommend as a basic set—chef's knife, paring knife, slicing knife, carving knife, and utility knife.

HOFFRITZ FOR CUTLERY / Dept. CFC
20 Cooper Square, New York, NY 10003

Catalogue, $2, published every two years, 48 pages, illustrated, black and white.

This large cutlery, gadget, housewares, and gift chain has everything from Sabatier knives, espresso pots, scales, poultry shears, and clam openers to things like the all-in-one knife ($5) or an English muffin breaker ($3.50). For knives and scissors, Hoffritz is the place.

Foamy Rum Pudding Sauce

Beat 2 egg yolks until thick; then beat in ½ cup sifted confectioners' sugar and ¼ cup light cream. Place in top of a double boiler over hot water and beat almost constantly over low heat until mixture thickens—about 5 minutes. Stir in 1 tablespoon Myers's rum slowly, beating until smooth. Makes 1½ cups sauce. For a foamier sauce, fold in 2 stiffly beaten egg whites.
—from "Myers's Rum Food and Drink Recipes"

Booklet from J. A. Henckels

Springerle molds, from The-House-on-the-Hill

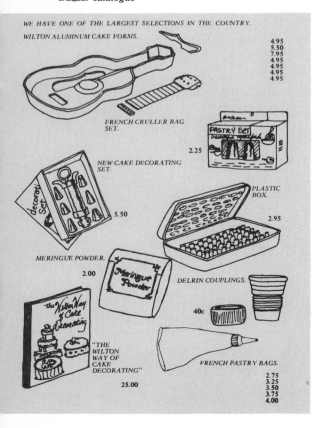

Cake-decorating equipment from the Kitchen Bazaar catalogue

WE HAVE ONE OF THE LARGEST SELECTIONS IN THE COUNTRY.

WILTON ALUMINUM CAKE FORMS.

4.95
5.50
7.95
4.95
4.95
4.95
4.95

FRENCH CRULLER BAG SET.

NEW CAKE DECORATING SET.

2.25

PASTRY SET

PLASTIC BOX.

2.95

Decorati Set.

5.50

MERINGUE POWDER.

2.00

Meringue Powder

DELRIN COUPLINGS.

40c

The Wilton Way of Cake Decorating

"THE WILTON WAY OF CAKE DECORATING"

25.00

FRENCH PASTRY BAGS.

2.75
3.25
3.50
3.75
4.00

HOUSE OF SPICES (INDIA) INC. / Dept. CFC
76-17 Broadway, Jackson Heights, NY 11375

Catalogue, free, 12 pages, black and white.

House of Spices has some Indian cooking utensils, but the only one we recognize by name is the iron kava, a griddle for baking Indian flat breads ($2.95). Others listed are an iron kadai, a brass sev machine, chakla, sansi, velan, khamani, and a 4-piece set of sieves for $1.50. Also available are assorted stainless-steel utensils, not itemized on the price list.

THE-HOUSE-ON-THE-HILL / Dept. CFC
South Strafford, VT 05070

Brochure, free, 4 pages.

If you are a cookie baker, the one offering from House-on-the-Hill might interest you. These are beautiful springerle molds of heavy metal mounted on hand-finished cherrywood that are exact reproductions of 18th-century German antiques. There are five different molds: three with 12 patterns, one with 6 patterns, and one with 4 patterns. Some depict craftsmen; others have figures and flower, bird or musical motifs. Prices range from $17.50 for the largest molds to $9 for the one with 4 patterns (ppd.), and a springerle recipe is included with each mold.

JURGENSEN'S PACIFIC EPICURE / Dept. CFC
474 S. Raymond Avenue, Pasadena, CA 91105

Wholesale division catalogue, free, 11 pages, illustrated, black and white.

Pacific Epicure is the wholesale division of Jurgensen's, the California specialty food and grocery store, and the catalogue deals with cooking equipment. There's a minimum order requirement of $50 (orders of less than $50 are subject to a service charge of $3), but the prices are pretty good and the selection comprehensive. You'll find here white ovenproof pottery au gratin dishes, ramekins, covered casseroles and soufflé dishes of various sizes, copper saucepans and sauté pans ($17.50 for a 2-pt. sauté pan), whisks, Sabatier knives; heavy tinned charlotte molds, with or without lids, removable-bottom quiche pans, heavy steel crêpe pans (the 7" diameter size is $3.25), the Vallauris French earthenware cooking pots with glazed interior and unglazed exterior (a 5½-qt. low marmite is $22.50), and lots of other good, sound, basic cooking pieces. Prices are subject to change without notice.

KITCHEN BAZAAR / Dept. CFC
4455 Connecticut Avenue N.W., Washington, DC 20008

Catalogue, free, published annually, 32 pages, illustrated, black and white.

Most of the things you find in the better kitchen shops are in this attractively presented catalogue, though there are some you may not see everywhere, such as aluminum cake forms in the shape of a guitar, panda, rag doll, Yogi Bear or Winnie the Pooh, for children's birthday cakes, from $4.95 to $7.95. They have heavyweight French copper pans with brass handles; Portuguese copper molds ($8 to $12); Le Creuset cookware in both traditional and contemporary shapes and colors; five different kitchen scales, including one from England that weighs in ounces and grams and has a plastic measuring-mixing bowl; Sabatier and Henckels knives and the Zip-Zap ceramic knife sharpener ($2.50); and the heavy black sheet-steel bread and baking pans. Nothing earth-shaking but a good selection. In addition to the Washington, D.C., shop there's a Kitchen Bazaar at 6548 Reisterstown Road Plaza in Baltimore, Maryland, too. The catalogue, of course, is only a sampling of what the shops sell, and they suggest that you call or write if you don't see a particular item. If it is not in stock they will try to locate it. (Telephone number for the Washington store is 202-244-1550; in Baltimore, 301-358-0400). They accept Master Charge, Central Charge, and Bank-Americard and will send packages anywhere in the world, gift-wrapped, with a baby whisk on the bow.

KITCHEN GLAMOR, INC. / Dept. CFC
26770 Grand River, Detroit, MI 48240

"Kitchen Glamor—tools for the fine arts of cooking, baking and decorating," free, with periodically updated price list, 28 pages, illustrated, black and white.

Since 1940 Kitchen Glamor has been outfitting kitchens and expanding culinary repertoires (cooking demonstrations by food experts and cookbook authors are given throughout the year in their specially equipped kitchen). The catalogue is broken down into sections for the different kinds of cooking equipment, starting with pots and pans (Le Creuset, Magnalite, Griswold cast iron, heavy French copper) and pieces of ethnic cooking equipment such as woks and their accouterments, a couscous pot (6-qt. size, $30), a tempura set ($25.95), a German spaetzle machine ($9.99). In knives, they carry the Trident line from Germany, ranging in price from $2.10 for the tomato slicer to $87.50 for a set of paring knife, sandwich knife, carving knife, 9" French cook's knife, 10" slicing knife with magnetic board. They sell the KitchenAid electric mixers and attachments, all kinds of slicing and cutting machines and gadgets, molds and forms for baking (a cone-shaped croquembouche form, 15½" high, is $6.95), basic tools like spatulas, measures, scales, sieves and strainers, whisks, mixing bowls, and more off-beat things such as a chestnut roasting pan ($3.69) and zabaglione bowl ($24.95). Michigan is cake-decorating country, and Kitchen Glamor fills the baker's needs with different shapes and sizes of cake pans, cooky cutters, pastry bags and decorating tubes, cake decorating sets and decorations. A useful gadget is the special brush for cleaning tubes (19¢). On the back page of the catalogue is a list of baking supplies such as silver and gold dragees, candy-making chocolate (sweet milk, sweet dark, $2.10 a lb., or colored, $1.49 a lb.), almond paste, prepared fondant icing, powdered egg whites and egg-white stabilizer, dark bitter chocolate for baking ($2.20 a lb.), extracts and oils for flavoring, imported glazed candied fruits, fruit pastry fillings, whole or ground spices and various flours—potato, rice, arrowroot, almond meal, and ground tapioca.

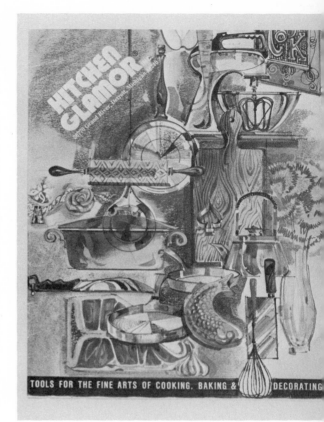

LA COCINA / Dept. CFC
5808 Kennett Pike, Wilmington, DE 19807

"La Cocina—everything for the kitchen," free, published periodically, about 12 sheets, illustrated, black and white.

La Cocina has no formal catalogue but sends out illustrated sheets to its customers of new and standard items the shop carries. Owner Monty Budd spends a lot of time in Mexico and has many items specially made there, so there is a very individual feeling to his mailings. Handcrafts are mixed in among Copco cookware and the Cuisinart food processor. A recent mailing had some beautifully designed, simple, and functional T. G. Green cookware from England at reasonable prices. A fluted oven-to-table 2½-qt. earthenware casserole was $24, a lovely white fluted 12" fish dish was $10. An improvement on the usual butcher's steel for sharpening knives is the Eze-Lap Butcher Knife Sharpener with millions of microscopic duPont Diamond cutting edges that never wear out ($48 for the large size, 10½" long, $19.95 for the pocket size). From Santa Clara de Cobre in Mexico come handcrafted copper utensils—beating bowl ($22.50), baking dish, colander, ladle, and butter melter.

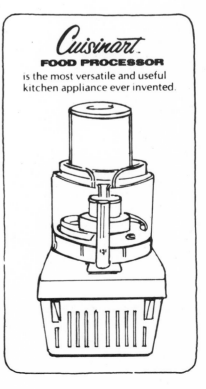

Cuisinart FOOD PROCESSOR is the most versatile and useful kitchen appliance ever invented.

Country Bean Pot (the modern way)
Place 1 pound dried beans in a large saucepan; cover generously with water. Bring to a boil. Reduce heat, cover, and simmer 1 hour or until tender. Fry ½ pound bacon until lightly browned. Remove from pan. Sauté 1 large chopped onion in bacon drippings until transparent. Crumble bacon. Place beans, 1 cup water, bacon, bacon drippings, onion, 1½ tablespoons molasses, ¼ cup ketchup, 2 teaspoons salt, ¼ cup packed brown sugar, 1 teaspoon chili powder, 1 teaspoon lemon juice, ½ teaspoon instant coffee, ½ teaspoon dry mustard, ½ teaspoon Tabasco, and 1 teaspoon Worcestershire sauce in an electric slow cooker. Mix well. Cover and cook on low 10 to 12 hours, or on high 4 to 5 hours. Serves 8.
—*from "Back to Homemade Cooking," Tabasco Booklet*

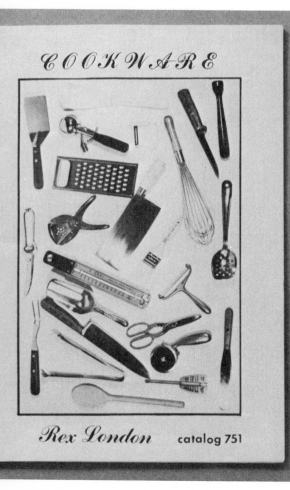

LEKVAR-BY-THE-BARREL / Dept. CFC
1577 First Avenue, New York, NY 10028

"A Continental Bazaar," free, published annually, 56 pages, illustrated, black and white.

About 36 pages of this catalogue are devoted to cooking equipment, all neatly organized under separate headings such as "Useful Gadgets," "Myriads of Molds," and "This is the Way We Bake Our Cakes." Each item is described and shown in a photograph. All the usual utensils are here, with a good selection of grinders, graters, slicers, and cutters, including the machines for making spaetzle and noodles (different models of spaetzle machines cost from $5.98 to $16.98), and a hand sausage stuffer. There are lots of scales, cake-decorating sets and tubes, cookie and biscuit cutters, aluminum stencils for making chocolate leaves (one large or two small leaves, $1.45), baking pans and molds, and odds and ends such as the spinning salad dryer, springerle boards, butter molds, little pig-shaped cutting boards (fun for serving smoked sausage and cheese), the French gadget called "support à bain-Marie," which stands in a pot so you can use it like a double boiler ($2.25), and another gadget that bores the center from cabbage ($9.95).

REX LONDON / Dept. CFC
232 Whitclem Drive, Palo Alto, CA 94306

"Cookware," free, published annually, 32 pages, black and white.

A rather unusual catalogue because most of the cookware is American and proves that made-in America can stand up to the best European products. Rex London says, "We favor American-made products, when in our opinion the quality is the best. Many of our lines are made by America's oldest companies. When the best of an item is imported, we have identified the country of origin." The selection is not large but obviously chosen with care, and much of the cookware is the kind used by chefs. The knives are from the Dexter line by Russell Harrington, cutlery manufacturers since 1818. They are made of high-carbon stainless steel with laminated wood handles, and are properly riveted. There's everything you could need: cook's knives (some with hand-forged blades, in 8", 9", 10", and 12" blade sizes), boning knives, slicers, paring knives, cleavers, and sharpening steel. They also have a Dexter ceramic sharpener, considered by professionals to be better than steel, and oilstones from Arkansas. Prices range from around $2.20 for a 3" paring knife to $21.50 for a 10" forged cook's knife. With the price of imported knives constantly soaring, these are good buys. A Chinese knife is available in stainless steel ($10.95) or carbon steel ($6.95). The catalogue has all kinds of stainless-steel spatulas and turners, measuring cups, scales, spoons, ladles, skimmers, and gadgets. The poultry shears chosen by Rex London are from the German company Henckels; thermometers are by Taylor (including the very sensitive meat thermometer that registers from 0° to 220° F.); stainless-steel bowls, stock pots, and bakeware are from Vollrath; pastry equipment from Foley. Pots and pans are heavy-gauge aluminum by Leyse (a 5-qt., 12" sauté pan is $23, a very good price), and there is also a line of cookware by Atlas Spinning Company, who have been turning out woks for San Francisco's Chinese chefs for over 40 years. Some of the Atlas items are woks and accessories, heavy cold-rolled steel frying pans, omelet and crêpe pans, the Mongolian "hot pot" cooker, unlined copper beating bowls for egg whites and zabaglione (a 10" copper bowl is $28.20). The electric mixer in the catalogue is KitchenAid by Hobart, the choice of all good cooks. To encourage you to invest in one of these expensive but fabulous machines, Rex London will knock $20 (for the $135 model) or $30 (for the $190 K5A model) off the price of such mixer accessory attachments as the grain mill, food grinder, or juice extractor. They don't show other attachments, such as the ice-cream freezer, but you can request a list of the full dozen available. While prices we quote (all ppd.) will obviously have risen by the time you read this, as with all manufactured products, at this point they are pretty good.

MAID OF SCANDINAVIA CO. / Dept. CFC
3244 Raleigh Avenue, Minneapolis, MN 55416

General catalogue, $1, plus spring and winter supplements, 25¢ each, published annually; catalogue, 192 pages, supplements 70 to 80 pages, illustrated, black and white.

If you order from the general catalogue, you receive the spring and winter supplements free. If your order was over $5, you get the catalogue sampler (containing highlights of the general catalogue), and if your order is over $15 you will automatically get the general catalogue free the following year. While Maid of Scandinavia has much the same baking and decorating supplies and equipment as Cake Decorators, including pans, molds, pastry bags, and decorating tubes, their decorations are more sportive and contemporary—tennis and baseball players, skiers, a rock-'n'-roll couple, and a lunar landing module. These catalogues also have a great deal of general cooking equipment— cooking-and-serving pieces, omelet pans, sausage and ice-cream makers, stainless-steel mixing bowls, and plenty of gadgets. They also have some useful pans for baking that are super deep (3½" sides), square pans in odd sizes, a square angel-food pan, and a high-sided sheet cake pan large enough (18" x 12" x 2") to make fifty 2" squares ($8.50). Looking through at random, our eye was caught by a corn bread skillet with a nonstick coating that bakes the bread in eight wedges ($5.98), a Danish ebelskiver pan for making those puffy little apple-filled pancakes ($4.98 or $5.98 with nonstick coating), a European basketweave rolling pin (used in Holland for marzipan), English muffin rings (they can also be used in a skillet to form perfect round fried eggs), some interesting cutters, such as a Vienna roll stamp, a fattigmand cookie cutter, a bear-claw cutter (it slits dough for bear-claw pastries), and a 4-in-1 tool that is fat separator, scoop, measure, and funnel ($1.10). Other gadgets are a citrus peeler and halver, a baked potato puffer and a butter baster, a little box that holds a stick of butter or margarine and presses it out at one end so you can hold it and butter away (corn, baking pan) without getting your fingers messy ($1.49). We liked the look of the oven peel, a flat wooden spade, like a miniature baker's peel, for sliding under hot pans to remove them from the oven ($1.49), the 11-piece measuring set (6 spoon sizes, 5 cup sizes in one), and the special rolling pins for lefse, hardtack, and flatbread (they imprint designs as they roll). Maid of Scandinavia is into crafts as well as cooking. The back pages of the general catalogue show weaving looms, bottle-cutting kits, découpage supplies, and books on bread-dough art, crewel, tole painting, and batik. All in all, an interesting catalogue and well worth getting.

MAISON GLASS / Dept. CFC
52 East 58th Street, New York, NY 10022

"Maison Glass Delicacies," $1, published annually, 72 pages, illustrated, black and white.

While Maison Glass doesn't stock much cooking equipment, they do have a large selection of plain or decorated soufflé dishes, some with covers that double as casseroles; decorative baking dishes; coeur à la crème molds, either individual ($2.25) or large ($11); Royal Worcester egg coddlers; ramekins in small, medium, and large sizes; onion soup bowls; Chemex coffee makers; a cheese slicer; mortar and pestle; Edam cheese scoop; garlic press; mills for grinding salt and pepper; chop frills ($1.50 a box of 50); and something listed as "New! Green peppercorn grinder" ($16.95), which is stretching things because green unripe peppercorns are so soft you can crush them in your hand or with a mortar and pestle.

MANGANARO FOODS / Dept. CFC
488 Ninth Avenue, New York, NY 10018

"Manganaro's for Gourmet Foods," free, published annually, 22 pages, illustrated.

Manganaro's food catalogue has a few pieces of equipment and gadgets for Italian cooking. There's a hand-operated pasta machine that rolls

Cookware from the Maid of Scandinavia catalogue

Omelet

For each omelet, beat 2 eggs, 1 tablespoon water, and ¼ teaspoon salt in a bowl with a fork until well blended. Heat a well-seasoned omelet pan or Teflon skillet, 9 inches in diameter, until very hot. Add 1 tablespoon butter and swirl it around in the pan until it sizzles. Quickly pour in the egg mixture and shake the pan around on the burner with one hand while lightly stirring the eggs with the back of a fork. Use wooden spatula with Teflon. When set but still creamy, tip up pan and, with the aid of a fork, roll the omelet out onto a plate. The omelet may be filled before rolling with sautéed mushrooms, sautéed onions, chopped ham, or any other desired filling. If using chopped fresh herbs, stir them into the egg mixture before making the omelet. Serve immediately.

*

If you don't have a double boiler, a heatproof glass bowl that fits snugly into the top of a saucepan, resting on the rim, is a perfect substitute.

*

Whip heavy cream in a chilled bowl with chilled beaters and it will mount faster. If you haven't time to chill the bowl, place it in a bowl of ice cubes.

*

and cuts noodles ⅛" and ¼" thick, a ravioli maker that cuts and seals 12 at a time ($7.75), the two-handled chopper called a mezzaluna ($3.50), cannoli tubes (set of 3, $1.50), a gnocchi and cavatelle machine ($21.95), and several kinds of cheese graters, including a heavy-duty clamp-on type ($11.95). If you've been looking for a sausage funnel for stuffing casings, theirs is just 95¢.

EARL MAY SEED & NURSERY COMPANY / Dept. CFC
Shenandoah, IA 51603

"Earl May Planting Guide," free, published annually, 86 pages, illustrated, black and white and color.

Seed catalogues are good places to look for the special equipment needed for preparing fruits and vegetables for the table, for pickling or preserving, and Earl May's is no exception. You'll find different types of apple slicers and corers, a heavy-duty strainer for juicing, straining, and puréeing ($26.95 ppd.), strawberry huller, cherry pitter, corn cutter, slaw cutter, vegetable slicer (the mandoline type), French bean slicer ($23.95 ppd.), and two kinds of pea and bean sheller, one hand-operated, the other electric (both, oddly enough, are the same price, $14.49 ppd.). What will they think of next? There's a stand-up asparagus steamer (also good for broccoli) and two powerful nutcrackers. One is a "Texas Native" nutcracker, a special design that yields unbroken pecan halves at the rate of 30 nuts a minute ($12.98 ppd.), the other a piston-power nutcracker, completely adjustable (like the Texas Native) and recommended for everything but black walnuts.

MIRACLE EXCLUSIVES, INC. / Dept. CFC
16 West 40th Street, New York, NY 10018

Price list and brochure sheets, free.

A good selection of equipment for grinding, juicing, mixing, and blending is sold directly by this company, exclusive agents for imported and domestic health-related appliances and food products. They have, among other items, a stainless-steel vegetable and fruit juicer and pulp ejector that makes a gallon of juice without stopping ($225); another type made of nickel and plastic (around $90) with an optional blender attachment (around $9); another that comes with a 6-speed blender (around $130); various electric or hand-operated mills for grinding seeds, grains, and nuts that range in price from around $15 for a compact electric seed and coffee mill to under $400 for a professional-looking electric stone mill for flour that can be adjusted to grind from fairly coarse to very fine; a combination blender-grinder-mixer; a water filter; a stainless-steel pressure cooker; electric salad maker and the three-tier Bio-Snacky sprouter, about $15. They also have a yogurt maker and electric espresso machines in 3-, 6- and 9-cup sizes ($17.95 to $26.95).

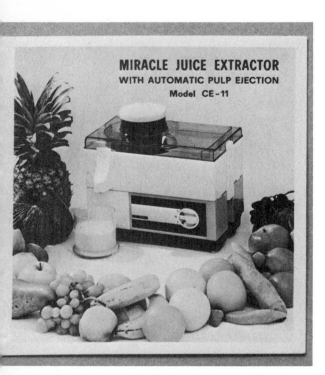

Juice extractor from Miracle Exclusives

MONTGOMERY WARD / Dept. CFC
Montgomery Ward Plaza, Chicago, IL 60681

General catalogues, Spring/Summer and Fall/Winter, Anniversary catalogue, Lawn and Garden catalogue, and Sale catalogues throughout the year. To get on the catalogue list you must make a purchase, either at the catalogue counter of a Ward store or from a borrowed catalogue, and to stay on the list you have to make at least two sizable purchases every six months.

Although better known for clothing, tools, furniture, and various other home and personal products, Montgomery Ward has a good range of sturdy and reasonably priced kitchen appliances—blenders, mixers, electric can openers, the Moulinex meat grinder and salad maker ($29.88 here), electric and manual slicers (including a commercial model at $249.95), a hand-operated noodle machine for just $34.95, and a food press for squeezing and preparing fresh fruit juices or making purées ($39.95).

NATURAL FOOD DISTRIBUTORS / Dept. CFC
519 Monroe Street, Toledo, OH 43604

Price list, free, updated monthly, 4 pages.

A limited amount of equipment for preparing natural foods such as a
grain and seed grinder, stone flour mill ($149.95), Vita Mix blender,
various juicers, sprouter lids ($1.39 or $1.98 with seeds) are included in
this list.

NICHOLS GARDEN NURSERY / Dept. CFC
1190 North Pacific Highway, Albany, OR 97321

*"Nichols Herb and Rare Seeds," free, published seasonally, 60 pages,
illustrated, black and white.*

The Nichols catalogue has a good assortment of cooking equipment,
ranging from an electric yogurt maker ($11.95 ppd.) to one of the nice
old-fashioned hand coffee mills with a handle on the top and a drawer
in the bottom (good for grinding peppercorns and spices), if you aren't
a coffee drinker), $13.95. They have the Mouli products, such as the
triple drum grater, rotating cutter with six stainless-steel blades ($5.25)
and a radiant heat plate with handle for using between pans and heat
(8" diameter fits all burners, $2.50). There's a nylon whisk, guaranteed
not to scratch Teflon, boilproof and dishwasher safe ($1.75); a heavy-
duty clamp-on wheat mill for grinding your own flour, coarse or fine
($20.95, $21.95 east of the Rockies); and a fruit and vegetable juice
extractor called the Saftborn, which extracts the juice through a steam
process and sterilizes it at the same time ($43.50 ppd., $3 more east of
the Rockies). In case you are wondering how it works, the fruit goes in a
perforated basket on top, the water in the bottom of the pan. The pot is
covered and put over heat. As the steam rises it makes the fruit release
juice into a center reservoir from which it can be drained. You can
extract juice from soft fruits in 20 minutes, harder fruits like apples in
50 minutes. Nichols also sells canning and preserving aids such as a
canning rack, dipper, funnel and tongs, jelly strainer, and jelly bags.

NORDISKA / Dept. CFC
299 Westport Avenue, Norwalk, CT 06851

*Catalogue, free, published annually, 24 pages, illustrated, black and
white.*

Nordiska is a direct importer of Scandinavian and international gifts
and gourmetware, and their prices for various housewares seem quite
reasonable. They sell such things as the classic white soufflé dishes,
singly or in a set of 1-qt., 1½-qt., and 2-qt. sizes (around $13 for the set),
white pottery ring molds and the French Pillivuyt white porcelain baking dishes and fluted round dishes, attractive decorated white porcelain
onion soup bowls, lots of teak boards and trays, Scandinavian
beechwood tools, and plastic mixing bowls and colander, canisters, and
pitchers. Everything is well designed and workmanlike. Gadgets such as
a Swedish cookie press (around $6), a tin measuring cup with metric
markings, and a heavy-duty combination meat hatchet and tenderizer
are also available.

NORTHWESTERN COFFEE MILLS / Dept. CFC
217 North Broadway, Milwaukee, WI 53202

*Catalogue, free (25¢ donation accepted), published annually, 27 pages,
illustrated, black and white.*

This coffee-and-tea house has a very good careful selection of coffee
mills and makers, teapots, tea infusers (balls and spoons), and a few
other kitchen items, such as a cheese plane (slicer and server in one)
with a teak handle ($3.50), and a simple mortar and pestle, large
enough to use for all kinds of kitchen jobs. The inside measurement is
3" x 4½" and the cost $14.

You'll find here two hand-operated coffee mills: one that attaches to
the wall, the other made of heavy cast iron with a wooden box that will

Fresh Pasta

To make enough pasta for 2 servings, mix ⅔ cup plus 1 heaped tablespoon flour, 1 large egg, and ½ teaspoon salt in the food processor, using the plastic blade, until ball of dough forms. Or mix by hand. Remove and knead a couple of times. Then flatten the dough into an elongated shape and pass it through the kneading setting of the roller on an electric pasta machine several times, folding it over each time it has been rolled, until smooth and very satiny. Adjust settings and each time roll dough thinner, until you reach setting number 2. Then change to cutting attachment for fettuccine or tagliatelle and cut pasta into strips. Immediately dust with flour to stop them sticking together and drop into a large pot of rapidly boiling salted water. Cook until tender but al dente, about 1 minute (fresh pasta cooks much faster than commercial dried pasta). Serve with desired sauce, or toss with oil and garlic, or with butter and grated Parmesan cheese.

pulverize as well as grind coffee ($12). Their three electric coffee mills are the Braun Mini Grinder ($22, bean-storage capacity, 2 oz.), the KitchenAid model that grinds a pound of coffee in under 4 minutes and can be set for different grinds from coarse to fine ($42), and another larger heavier Braun coffee mill with multiple grind settings (bean storage capacity, 3 oz., $40). Coffee makers range from the Melitta filter pot to European drip and espresso coffee makers and a Turkish brass ibrik for powdered coffee (3-cup size, $8.25). There's also the Chemex Toddy coffee maker for making coffee extract with cold water, the Cory stainless-steel vacuum coffee maker, and the Aromaster, an electric drip coffee maker by Braun. They advise you to leave coffee roasting to experts, as it is a smoky smelly business, but if you want to have a go, they sell a coffee roaster for $15 and their coffee straights (not blends) in green (raw) beans at 50¢ a lb. less than the roasted coffee. For tea, they have a stainless-steel tea kettle ($14.75), the Jena glass teapot with center tea-infusing cylinder, and a regular potbellied stoneware teapot, 40-oz. capacity, for $12. There are 9 tea infusers, in ball or spoon shape, ranging in price from 50¢ to $6, and a Tybregg tea filter, a two-part plastic handle with disposable paper filter that lets you make your own tea bags with loose tea (holder, $1; 40 filter bags, $1).

PORCELAIN

Stylish serving pieces from the Pampered Kitchens catalogue

PAMPERED KITCHENS

PAMPERED KITCHENS / Dept. CFC
110 Yorkville Avenue, Toronto, Ontario M5R 1B9, Canada

"Pampered Kitchens Catalogue of Specialty Equipment for the Serious Cook," free, published every two to three years, 60 pages, illustrated, black and white.

When Camilla Daglish started Pampered Kitchens on Bloor Street in Toronto about ten years ago, it was the first kitchen store in Canada— and a very good one, with an unerring personal selection of top-quality equipment and some unusual bits and bobs from England. Pampered Kitchens has grown and prospered, moving to a new location, with two other stores in Oakville and Ottawa, but a glance at the catalogue shows that the personal touch and selectivity are still there. Yes, there is well-made and well-designed equipment for the serious cook, as you'd expect, but it is the bonuses you don't expect that make this catalogue different. We loved the glazed dark-blue pottery spoon rest in the shape of a nesting bird; the unglazed clay baker from France, gracefully sculptural in shape, with a stylized design; the oyster knife with hand-carved birdseye maple board to hold the oyster safely. If you like to keep your salt where you can reach for a pinch or a handful, there's a pretty Delft blue china salt box with a wooden lid, or a Cumberland canister, a reproduction of an old English salt bin, shaped a bit like a right-angled section of stove pipe (the shape keeps the salt dry). Other good things from England include a mustard-and-cress farm with seed packs and special soil for growing those delicious peppery little green sprouts, a bread bin (a tall glazed stoneware pot for loaves of bread, or flour, marinating or pickling), a brown earthenware oven casserole for Lancashire hot pot (or baked beans), and some good-looking chrome-plated corn holders (do the English eat corn on the cob now?). If you've been searching for a chestnut knife with a tiny curved blade for paring the outer shell, Pampered Kitchens has it. They also have a slew of gadgets for southpaws (plus *The Left-handed Book*) and some short-handled French cherrywood salad servers of a most unusual design. Serving pieces are simple, sleek, and stylish. We liked the white porcelain oyster plate and the porcelain artichoke plate with a dark-green glaze. At the end of the catalogue there's an invaluable section on seasoning and caring for cookware (most people tell you to clean carbon-steel knives with cleanser, Pampered Kitchens says Scotchbrite pads, and they are *rite*), including how to get the protective lacquer coating off copper before you use it. Sorry we can't give you an indication of prices. No price list came with our catalogue but surely will with yours.

PAPRIKAS WEISS IMPORTER / Dept. CFC
1546 Second Avenue, New York, New York 10028

"Imported Foods and Cookware Catalogue," $1 for annual subscription, published four times a year, 66 pages, illustrated, black and white.

A good selection of cooking equipment is packed into this catalogue. You'll find copper cookware and Sabatier knives from France, old-fashioned cast-iron cookware, sturdy aluminum stock pots in sizes ranging from 8½ qt. to 60 qt. ($15.98 to $52.90, covers extra), all kinds of gadgets including a solid brass scaloppine pounder ($8.98), cutters and baking pans, whisks and molds, specialized equipment such as the cous-cousière, duck press ($375), croquembouche mold, spaetzle machines, and even a chestnut ricer for Mont Blanc ($4.98, and it rices potatoes too, of course). We also noticed a sauerkraut fork ($1.98), goosefeather pastry brush ($5 for a set of 6), a handy stainless-steel apple corer ($2.98), a machine that cuts extra-fine noodles (about $60), fluted flan rings in 6", 7", and 8" diameters ($1.19 to $1.59), two poppy-seed grinders ($18.98 and $24.98), a machine that rolls and fills ravioli (about $60), and both the Cuisinart and the Moulinex food processors (about $40 for the Moulinex).

PERMA-PAK, INC. / Dept. CFC
P.O. Box 15695, Salt Lake City, UT 84115

"Perma-Pak brochure and price list," free, published three to four times a year, 16 pages.

This packager of low-moisture dehydrated foods also sells a hand grinder for wheat, corn, nuts, and seeds, a hand-operated stone mill for flour, two electric flour mills with special grinding stones, and 10-qt. and 12-qt. bread dough mixers. The bread mixers are under $30, the electric flour grinders around $190.

SAHADI IMPORTING CO., INC. / Dept. CFC
187 Atlantic Avenue, Brooklyn, NY 11201

"The Silent Salesman," free, published biannually, 24 pages, illustrated, black and white.

Sahadi supplements their food catalogue with a few pieces of Middle East cooking equipment. You can buy the brass coffee pots for Turkish coffee in six sizes and prices from $4 to $10 (an enamel version is about half the price), an aluminum couscous pot in medium or large sizes ($15 or $17.50), bread stamps and date cookie molds, the Syrian round copper fryer for individual omelets ($9), and more ordinary things such as coffee mills and mortar-and-pestle sets.

STA-WEL NUTRITION CENTERS, INC. / Dept. CFC
16 West 40th Street, New York, NY 10018

"Food for Better Living," 50¢, no regular publication date, 40 pages, black and white.

Sta-Wel has a good assortment of appliances related to the health foods they sell, such as yogurt makers, juicers, water filters, seed sprouters, grinders and mills, and stainless-steel pressure cooker. They carry Miracle Exclusives, Acme, Salton, and Moulinex products, but the catalogue has not been reprinted since 1973, so prices no longer apply and you will have to request quotations on whatever interests you.

SUNDIALS & MORE / Dept. CFC
New Ipswich, NH 03071

Catalogue, free, 48 pages, published seasonally, illustrated, color and black and white.

While the catalogue consists mostly of sundials in all sizes and shapes, "More" has many practical things for the kitchen such as a parsley chopper ($5.75) that also grinds almonds and shaves chocolate for desserts, a line of heavy-duty commercial aluminum cookware that in-

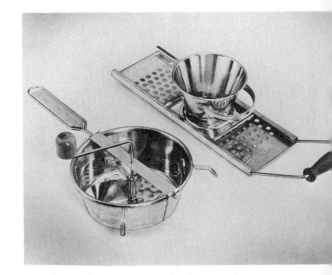

Spaetzle machines from the Paprikas Weiss catalogue

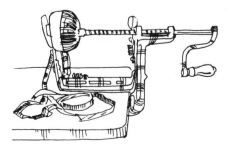

Old-fashioned apple parer, corer, and slicer from the Sundials & More catalogue

Cheese Pudding

With the metal blade in place, add ¾ pound sharp cheddar cheese, cut in pieces, to the beaker of the food processor. Process, turning on and off rapidly, until evenly chopped. Spread 6 slices white bread with butter and cut in pieces. Add the buttered bread, 1½ cups milk, 4 eggs, 1 teaspoon paprika, ½ teaspoon salt, and ¼ teaspoon or more prepared mustard to the cheese in the beaker. Process until thoroughly blended, about 30 seconds. Pour mixture into a buttered 2-quart casserole. Bake in a preheated 325° oven for 45 minutes or until pudding is set. Serve warm as a light entrée. Makes 4 servings.

—*from "New Recipes for the Cuisinart Food Processor," by James Beard & Carl Jerome.*

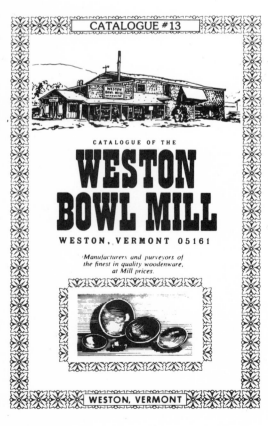

cludes a 1½-qt. saucepan ($10.25), a 2¾-qt. ($12.50), a 6-qt. stewpot ($18), all with covers, an 8" fry or omelet pan ($9), and a 3-qt. fry pan ($15). The complete set is $60. There is a 12" soapstone griddle that never needs greasing ($38), a cast-iron cornstick pan ($5), a muffin pan ($6.50), and an old-fashioned hand-cranked ice-cream freezer, 4-qt. size, ($45).

UWAJIMAYA / Dept. CFC
  P.O. Box 3003, Seattle, WA 98114

  Price list, free, published semiannually, 5 pages with order blank.

For Japanese cooking, Uwajimaya has the special electric rice cooker that makes the sticky-textured rice the Japanese prefer (from $26 for the 3-cup size to $39.50 for the 10-cup), a tempura set ($9.75), chopping knives, bamboo skewers (35¢ for a package of 100, 6" long), and chopsticks. A wok set is $10.95, but material and size are not specified. For serving, there are donburi covered bowls (from $2.75), rice bowls, teapots, and tea cups.

THE VERMONT COUNTRY STORE / Dept. CFC
  Weston, VT 05161

  Catalogue, 25¢, published annually, 98 pages, illustrated, black and white.

You'll find some interesting and unusual pieces of cooking equipment in this nifty catalogue. One that caught our eye is a combination of andirons, adjustable grill, and spit for fireplace cooking, hand-forged by a Vermont blacksmith. The grill is 16" wide and 14½" deep, the andirons 16" high and 15" deep, and the grill can be removed when you want to use the fireplace just for heating. The whole shebang is $82.50. Another nice idea from Vermont: hot food racks, handcrafted of birch, sanded, and oiled, that can be used as trivets or to cool off a freshly baked cake or loaf. They come in small, medium, and large sizes at $4, $6, and $8 and make excellent gifts. There's also the Tart Master, a little gadget that shapes, crimps, and seals in one operation ($2.95), the Vermont soapstone griddle, stainless-steel kitchen spoons (plain, slotted, and perforated), and a top-of-the-stove chrome metal "tater baker" that not only bakes potatoes but pies and other things, warms rolls, or crisps soggy crackers ($7.50). A good invention is a reversible chopping board, one side solid, the other hollowed out into a shallow bowl shape so you can chop or mince in it, 11" or 14" square, $12.95 or $17.50. Something we instantly coveted is a good-looking hand-hammered solid copper pan with block tin lining and brass handles, 12¾" diameter and 2¼" deep, a great cooking and serving piece at $29. For people who like Chinese cooking, Boston's restaurateur Joyce Chen has designed a stainless-steel, flat-bottomed wok that needs no ring. It has a handle, a copper bottom for even heat distribution and comes with a cover and an insert ring to put a plate on for steaming. The wok is 12" in diameter, and the set of wok, cover, and insert ring, with full directions and some easy recipes, is $40.

WESTON BOWL MILL / Dept. CFC
  Main Street, Weston, VT 05161

  "Catalogue of the Weston Bowl Mill," 25¢, published annually, 56 pages, illustrated, black and white.

Weston Bowl Mill is a manufacturer and purveyor of quality woodenware at mill prices, and they are so proud of their products that they guarantee cheerful repair, replacement, or refund should a customer be displeased with their products. Most of the woodenware is made in the mill or in Vermont, and the selection is wide-ranging. There are nice shallow Vermont hardwood (maple or birch) bowls, which they recommend you hand-rub with mineral oil if you are going to use them for salads or chopping. A bowl exposed to moisture can crack if not oiled. Choppers or salad servers come in different sizes and prices. Weston has boards for chopping, carving, sandwich-making, or serving, some shaped like a mouse, whale, fish, owl, lobster, pig, or apple. The

French loaf board, 22½" long by 6" wide, can be used to serve a French *bûche de Noël* or a jelly roll ($3.85). A good-looking maple end-grain chopping and slicing board with grooves for juice, ¾" thick x 15" x 10", is $14.25. Vermont pine sugar buckets with handle and wooden top make attractive storage containers for dry foods like beans and lentils or for magazines. The largest size, 13½" high and 13¼" inside top diameter, is around $19 unfinished. Weston stocks high carbon-steel kitchen knives with walnut handles, hand-forged in New Hampshire, that are very reasonably priced—a 12" chef's knife is only $9, the 7½" flexible slicing knife just $3.25. They have a "granny" fork, the old-fashioned 3-tine kitchen fork that has almost disappeared, 8½" overall, with stainless-steel tines and a wood handle, $2.50. They also make knife holders of different sizes, which can be bought with or without the knives. A 12" x 6" x 3½" holder to stand on the counter or hang on the wall, with 5 knives (parer, steak, utility, 8" slicer, and butcher knife) is $13.50. Small wooden kitchen utensils like spoons, tongs, butter molds, rolling pins are imported from France, Italy, Sweden, and West Germany. You'll find a traditional heavy potato masher ($1.75), white birch wooden scoops for flour, salt, or sugar from Sweden (set of 3, $2.50), a long-handled wood fork ($1.15), a pie crimper, butter paddles, a springerle rolling pin, and a couple of holders for wooden spoons, one a box to stand or hang, the other a wall holder with 5 holes, ½" diameter, for the spoon handles. An amusing Weston idea that would make good stocking stuffers are clothespin recipe holders on blocks of wood, one topped with a whale ($1.20 and $1.40). We also liked a wall towel rack to hold a kitchen roller towel (24" x 3¼" with 1" towel rod, $5). This is a great browsing catalogue with lots of good things to buy—and the prices are right.

WILLIAMS-SONOMA / Dept. CFC
576 Sutter Street, San Francisco, CA 94102

"A Catalog for Cooks," $1, published biannually, plus "January sale/New Kitchen Ideas," both 26 pages, illustrated, color.

Williams-Sonoma is undisputably the best kitchen shop in America. The charge of $1 is for the fall-winter catalogue; the others come free of charge when you are on the mailing list. The things in the catalogue are beautiful, stylish, and chosen with great knowledge and perception. Most of the equipment shown has been tested in Chuck Williams' own kitchen and it really works. Even if you feel your kitchen is completely equipped, look at the Williams-Sonoma catalogue and you'll find it full of irresistible temptations. The photographs are excellent and explanatory, and the text, written by Creative Director Jackie Mallorca, manages to be sparkling and informative at the same time.

Skimming over the 1976 summer issue (every new catalogue is different), we noticed the marvelous electric pasta machine that turns pasta making into play (around $130), an iron tortilla press and a tortilla griddle (this one has a wooden handle that won't heat up), rolls of kitchen parchment (two 20-sq.-ft. rolls, 15" wide, $3), the heavy-gauge sheet-steel *pain de mie* pan with sliding cover that bakes a flat-topped sandwich loaf ($9.50), a set of five heavenly stoneware bowls from France that are glazed inside, unglazed outside ($17.50 the set), James Beard's favorite wood-handled French boning knife paired with the Zip-Zap ceramic knife sharpener for $6.50 (once you have one of these knives, you'll wonder how you ever got along without it), and a very simple undecorated version of the unglazed terra-cotta Etruscan cooker that bakes a chicken or meats without liquid, here called a "chicken brick." Some of the more unusual (and useful) gadgets are a zucchini corer and melon vee that makes zigzag edges on halved melons or grapefruit ($4 the pair), an asparagus peeler from Germany, and a punch-type cherry and olive pitter that has a cup big enough to handle giant olives or even small plums ($4). Old-fashioned flour-sack dish towels that polish glasses so beautifully can be found here (set of 3, $6.50). Williams-Sonoma always has a good selection of cookbooks, a few of which are usually dotted throughout the catalogue. One is for the Cuisinart Food Processor, advertised as "not just an appliance, a new way of life." The food processor has become the great American

When baking a custard or soufflé in a pan of hot water, pour the water into the pan when it is in the oven. There's less danger of spilling.

Use a pastry blender to chop hard-cooked eggs in a small bowl.
—*from "Cooking at Longpond Farm"*

dream machine of every serious cook. It is a fabulous helper that can do anything from puréeing fish for quenelles to making pastry or a single loaf of bread dough. It chops, pulverizes, grinds, emulsifies (mayonnaise is a cinch), and has a range of attachments for shredding, grating, and slicing. If you have put off making duxelles because of the tedious chore of chopping 2 pounds of mushrooms, be advised that the processor does it in seconds. Although this machine has been on the market for quite a few years, a lot of people who buy one don't know half of the ways it can be used. Importer Carl Sondheimer very wisely asked James Beard, one of the food processor's greatest advocates, to prepare a use-and-recipe book. The result, a spiral-bound paperback called *New Recipes for the Cuisinart Food Processor*, has 130 recipes for everything from kibbeh to quenelles, some contributed by famous cooks like Jacques Pepin, Simone Beck, Craig Claiborne, Helen McCully, and Julie Dannenbaum. It's a great introduction to this miracle machine, and it comes free with the food processor or separately from cookware shops like Williams-Sonoma for $3.95 plus postage. Prices quoted do not include shipping charges and will probably have risen by the time this year's winter/fall catalogue is printed. You'll find Williams-Sonoma a great source for Christmas gifts, and they do some of the most attractive, simple gift wrapping we've seen—plain shiny white boxes tied with red ribbon, and a white W-S gift card.

THE WOODEN SPOON, INC. / Dept. CFC
   Route 6, Mahopack, NY 10541

   Leaflets, free, published periodically.

The Wooden Spoon is a company that sells various pieces of special cookware by mail, among them the Chemex carafe kettle, a pasta machine (manual, not electric), the automatic electric crêpe maker that is dipped in batter upside down (a light goes on when the crêpe is baked), a more conventional but equally expensive ($25) crêpe pan made of sandcast aluminum with a walnut handle, and an 11" tin-lined copper flambé pan for crêpes suzette ($35) with the rechaud, or alcohol-burner brazier to complete the ensemble at $28. There are other things such as the two-pronged cork puller (rather expensive at $6), the Bio-Therm meat thermometer ($12), a stainless-steel wok with chrome-plated cover and ring, and a few Oriental foods—straw mushrooms, hoisin sauce, oyster sauce, and sesame oil. Recipes are included in the product leaflets that come with the various items. The selection is small, selective, and interesting; but some of the prices seem high—$2 for 6 oz. of sesame-seed oil and that $6 cork puller, with postage and handling extra. They do, however, sell *The Cooks' Catalogue* for $11.95, a $4 discount.

Pasta machine and rotary grater-shredder from The Wooden Spoon

Slow-cooking smoker, from J. Robert Allen

Outdoor Cooking

J. ROBERT ALLEN / Dept. CFC
   9717 East 42 St., #134, Tulsa, OK 74145

   "Smoke 'N Pit," free, published annually, 6 pages, illustrated, color.

Smoke 'N Pit is an original patented slow-cooking smoker that self-bastes food with water, wine, beer, or marinade, using charcoal or electricity. Here's how it works: The meat is separated from the charcoal (or electric coil) by a pan of water. "As the slowly simmering water evaporates it combines with the smoke to do the cooking. The moisture condenses on the meat and drips back into the water where the whole process is repeated."

   It can be used to smoke, roast, steam, or barbecue. With the addition of the Smoke 'N Stack section, up to 45 pounds of meat can be cooked simultaneously. The shrinkage of meats is reduced by keeping them moist. The electric unit can also be used indoors. Both the electric and charcoal models have a colorful enamel finish, are easy to clean, and can be combined with these accessories: work table, ash guard, rib rack, hardwood chips (hickory or mesquite), and the Smoke 'N Stack (which functions as a hibachi when used alone).

EDDIE BAUER / Dept. CFC
P.O. Box 3700, Seattle, WA 98124

Catalogue, free, published seasonally, illustrated, color.

Primarily rugged outdoor clothing for men and women, but some cooking equipment is sold, too. There's the compact Sierra pocket stove for backpackers (around $16 ppd.) that weighs only 7½ oz. and, in its nylon tote bag, measures 4½" diameter and 1½" high. It can be assembled for cooking in 30 seconds and works on a lightweight butane cartridge. A larger Optimus portable stove from Sweden weighs 20 oz. and comes in a metal carrying case. It will burn 90 minutes on 8 oz. of white gas and is self-pressurized (around $15 ppd.). The catalogue has a good selection of knives for hunters and fishermen, Henckels' stainless-steel chef's, boning, and slicing knives, cutting boards handcrafted from tough red alder (a mahoganylike hardwood that grows only in Oregon), ranging in price from around $10 to around $42, and heavy-gauge aluminum Dutch ovens for camp cooking, 12" and 10" sizes, tongs for handling the Dutch oven, and a Dutch oven cookbook. There's also a sourdough set with starter, crock, directions, and recipes ($3.50 ppd.) and a *Sourdough Cookbook* ($3.95 ppd.).

L. L. BEAN INC. / Dept. CFC
Main Street, Freeport, ME 04033

"L. L. Bean Catalogue," free, published seasonally, 120 pages, illustrated, color and black and white, plus freeze-dried food list.

New Englanders and outdoor addicts swear by this famous catalogue, and well they might. It has just about everything needed for hiking, hunting, camping, and snug country living, including all kinds of cooking equipment and a long list of freeze-dried foods for backpackers—main courses of beef Stroganoff, pork chops, chicken and beef stew, scrambled-egg mix with ham for breakfast, various vegetables and fruits, and quick trail snacks like beef jerky and fruit-and-nut energy bars. There's even ice cream. On the back of the list are suggested menus for two for a week. Among the more useful pieces of outdoor cooking equipment is the Kangaroo Kitchen, a compact multipurpose propane gas camp cooker that can boil, broil, bake, smoke, steam, toast, and fry without the aid of any other utensils (around $40 ppd.). Even if you're not wild about the wilds, this is still a great catalogue to browse through. It has cast-iron cooking equipment, fish cleaning and filleting knives, as well as a board that clamps the fish in place, a few cookbooks, and a deck of edible and poisonous plant identification cards in color for around $5 (specify Eastern or Western plants). They also sell Vermont maple syrup ($2.75 a pint, plus postage). A lot of the things in L. L. Bean's catalogue aren't likely to be found other places, because they sell only by direct mail or at their salesroom in Freeport Village, so it's a good source for offbeat gifts.

CASUAL LIVING / Dept. CFC
Stony Hill, Bethel, CT 06081

"Casual Living," free, published annually, 48 pages, illustrated, black and white.

This gift catalogue has some useful things for outdoor cooking and picnicking. A six-pack insulated bucket, 8" high, in a zippered blue carrying case has a center core that you put in the freezer overnight to keep drinks cold all day ($12.95). For wine, there's a wine holder, again with removable freezing unit, that keeps white wine or champagne chilled for over 6 hours ($11). For cooking, there's a combination broiler and smoker for $60, or a compact, good-looking table grill that works on alcohol and can be used on a deck or patio. The grill has a brown ceramic base and Teflon grill plate, is 11½" in diameter, and costs $31.50.

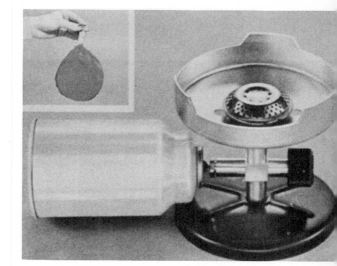

Sierra pocket stove from the Eddie Bauer catalogue

Foods and gear for the camper, from the L. L. Bean catalogue

Good ideas for the galley kitchen from the Chris-Craft catalogue

Chuck Wagon Potatoes

Heat a good amount of bacon fat in a heavy iron skillet. Half fill skillet with diced raw potatoes and some chopped onion and season with salt and pepper. Add just enough boiling water to cover the potatoes, cover with lid, and simmer over camp fire until water is absorbed and potatoes tender. For even browning, turn potatoes a few times with a spatula. Allow 1 potato and 1 tablespoon chopped onion per serving.

CHRIS-CRAFT / Dept. CFC
Algonac, MI 48001

"Chris-Craft Gifts and Gear," free, published annually, 64 pages, illustrated, color.

Though the largest part of this catalogue is devoted to nautical gear, there is some good equipment for galley or outdoor cooking and entertaining. There's a top-of-the-stove toaster (around $2.50), a two-faced grill with a smooth side for pancakes, a ridged side for cooking steaks and hamburgers ($8.95), a nesting set of stainless-steel cookware (Teflon-coated skillet, two saucepans, Dutch oven) with carrying handle that would also be good for a limited-space kitchen, and a barbecue grill that fits onto the stern flagstaff socket of a boat and swings overboard for safe cooking (around $56, bracket extra). Other handy items are the Hot Shot Beverage Maker that operates on 120 volts and heats 10 ounces of water in 90 seconds; a good-looking 25-piece set of melamine stacking dinnerware designed in Italy that was chosen for the permanent collection of New York's Museum of Modern Art, in yellow or white, around $55; a vacuum jug with air-pump action that releases its load of hot or cold drinks when a lever is pressed ($35); and the Igloo "Cool Seat," a sturdy cooler with spigot and a seat-top lid that keeps 3 gallons of ice or iced drinks cold for 48 hours and is strong enough to hold the weight of a 300-pound sailor or picnicker (around $20). Another good boat item is the basket of spices (white and black peppercorns, sea salt crystals, nutmeg, cloves, fennel seeds) in their own plastic mills (around $10). For picnics, there's the "Two Temp" insulated picnic bag with two smaller bags nested inside so you can carry hot and cold foods separately, and an outside zippered pocket for napkins and flatware ($24), and the Lucifer Char-Broil Grill that folds up like a small attaché case and opens into a grill that will cook two steaks or six hamburgers (there's an optional flashlight-battery-powered rotisserie attachment for around $8; the grill itself is around $37). And for the ultimate luxury in boat or tailgate picnics, there's the Norcold Olympia portable refrigerator/freezer that holds 50 pounds of food and comes with two cords, one for 110-volt AC current, the other with cigarette-lighter plug for use on 12-volt boat or car current (around $370).

CHUCK WAGON FOODS / Dept. CFC
Micro Drive, Woburn, MA 01801

"Lightweight Food for Everyone," free, published annually, 4 pages.

Chuck Wagon's dehydrated foods make an instant meal—just add water, heat, and eat. They need no refrigeration and are guaranteed to last a year. Less than 20 oz. per day will provide three balanced meals and a whole day's food for four takes up only 1/3 cubic foot of space. The range of foods, listed in categories with weights and cooking times, covers such items as French toast, oatmeal, scrambled eggs, mixed fruits, applesauce, vegetables, soups, 22 main dishes like chicken stew, rice and beef, chili-flavored beans, gelatin desserts and puddings (the gelatins set in 10 minutes without refrigeration), baking mixes and beverages. Each unit yields 2, 4, or 6 servings. Prices range from around 43¢ for oatmeal for two to around $3 for beef stew for two. As well as individual dishes, there are meal packs, also in 2, 4, and 6 servings, for a complete breakfast, lunch, or supper. Chuck Wagon sells "plus" items such as packets of salt, sugar, pepper, mustard and ketchup, Parmesan cheese, broth, trail snacks like beef jerky and apricot or strawberry "tear sheet" (pure fruit, unroll and eat), and plastic pouches of vegetable shortening, peanut butter, or sourdough starter mix. Shipping is prepaid within the continental U.S. and there are discounts of 10 percent on orders over $100, 20 percent on orders over $250.

HAMMACHER SCHLEMMER / Dept. CFC
147 East 57th Street, New York, NY 10022

Catalogue, free, published seasonally, 64 pages, illustrated, black and white.

Ardent picnickers will appreciate the English picnic kit sold by Hammacher's, a sturdy wicker basket fully equipped with a 6-piece service of plates, cups and saucers, stainless-steel flatware, 2 large vacuum jugs, 2 sandwich boxes, and 5 condiment jars, around $120. Team it with some of their food selections, perhaps smoked salmon and Smithfield ham, a little caviar, cheese, pâté de foie gras, smoked capon or pheasant, and you'll feel positively Edwardian. To keep drinks cold, there's an insulated blue-denim sack with center chilling unit that keeps a six-pack of beer, soda, or cocktail mixes icy all day (around $13), or a wine frigidarium, cold-energy liners to freeze and fit around wine or champagne bottles (around $10). Hammacher's has a good selection of hibachis, charcoal and electric barbecue grills and smokers, plus the accessories. Perhaps the ultimate outdoor cooker is their "hot dog cart," a rolling food and drink server with a striped umbrella over a hibachi to cook humble weiners, steaks, or hamburgers, a keep-warm compartment, cold salad tray, ice compartment, and 12-bottle wine rack. This simple little number will set you back around $1,700.

HERTER'S INC. / Dept. CFC
R.R. 2, Mitchell, SD 57301

"Herter's Sportsman's Catalog," $1 (refundable with $10 purchase), published annually, 352 pages, illustrated, color and black and white.

There's some useful outdoor cooking equipment here. A compact backpacker's stove weighs 1½ lbs., measures just 5" x 5" x 3" when folded, and works on white gas or lead-free gasoline (around $28). Another type comes with a saucepan and frying pan and weighs 21 oz. ($32.97). Or there's a 2-burner propane stove that folds like an attaché case, a portable upright combination heater and cooker with propane gas tank that costs less than 3¢ an hour to operate (around $30), and a charcoal camp stove-heater you can light with folded newspaper for just $4.75. Herter's Hudson's Bay meat, fish, and fowl smoker works on 110-volt AC current and will smoke up to 25 lbs. of meat at a time (around $26 with 5 lbs. of wood chips included), and the larger model can smoke up to 40 lbs. of meat or two 12-lb. turkeys (around $40). In cookware, Herter's has a cast-iron Dutch oven, 3-legged kettle, fish frying and baking pan, potato fryer and combination fry pan and 3" deep saucepan (the fry pan becomes the lid). Other good pieces of camping equipment are the huge skillet, 20" in diameter with a 25"-long handle (around $27), a 4-slice campfire toaster, aluminum cooking kits, and a covered round grill with long handles called a "pie and sandwich iron" that is just right for toasting sandwiches, little pies, bread, or for making hamburgers ($3.77). The catalogue has reasonably priced professional filleting and butchering knives, steak knives with carbon-steel blades ($1.67 each or $18.72 a dozen), a deep pot with perforated insert for cooking corn, spaghetti, or steaming clams, a wok set, and a big nonstick griddle, 21½" long and 10¾" wide ($10.97). Foods for backpackers and outdoors people include Herter's Hudson Bay freeze-dried foods, ranging from beef stew and chili/beans to cottage cheese and ice cream, energy fruit bars and mint bars, beef jerky ($5.37 a lb.), freeze-dried horseradish to spice up camp food, Bacon Plus (bite-size pieces of bacon-flavored protein), cans of 90 percent vegetable protein to mix into stews, eggs, breads, and cookies to increase the protein value ($3.19 for a 2-lb. can), wild rice ($2.79 for 8 oz.), sourdough pancake mix, and a wild rice pancake or crêpe mix.

MAID OF SCANDINAVIA CO. / Dept. CFC
3244 Raleigh Avenue, Minneapolis, MN 55416

General catalog, $1, plus spring and winter supplements (25¢ each or free with an order from the catalogue), published annually, 192 pages, illustrated, black and white, supplements 70 to 80 pages.

The supplements to the general baking and cake decorating catalogue have a few good things for picnicking. One is an all-purpose plastic food carrier in sections with a snap-on handle for toting pie, cake, sandwiches, or salads ($8.75), another is a collapsible net food umbrella to keep bugs away from the food ($2.35). Another picnic carrier in brushed aluminum comes in two sections. The lower unit is 4" deep for sandwiches, plates, or utensils; the upper part has a tray with a 4"-deep cover with carrying handle. The two clamp together to carry as a unit ($9.45).

Charcoal-Broiled Shrimp
Wash 2 pounds raw jumbo shrimp, leaving shells on. Marinate for 3 hours in a mixture of ½ cup oil, ½ cup soy sauce, ¼ cup dry sherry or sake, 2 finely chopped garlic cloves, and 1 tablespoon grated ginger root. Drain, put in a hinged wire broiler, or string on long shish kebab skewers and cook over charcoal for 4 to 5 minutes a side, basting with the marinade. Serve in the shells. Serves. 4.

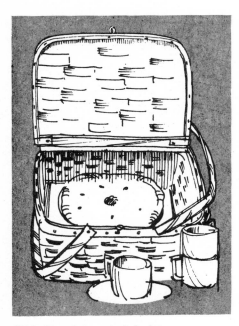

Old-fashioned pie or picnic basket

NATIONAL PACKAGED TRAIL FOODS / Dept. CFC
18607 St. Clair Ave., Cleveland, OH 44110

Price list, free, published annually.

Dehydrated foods and mixes for campers and backpackers. "Trail Packets" contain such dishes as beef hash, beef stew, beef Stroganoff, chicken à la king, macaroni and cheese, various vegetables, fruits, soups, desserts like cherry cobbler and chocolate pudding, breakfast foods, including scrambled eggs and Western omelet, and beverages. Prices range from around 42¢ for an instant fruit spread to around $7.27 for chicken stew, but most of the main dishes are in the $3 range. Each one contains 4 servings. Freeze-dried meats in a tin are also part of the product list—beef steaks, hamburger, beef and pork patties, and diced ham range in price from $2.38 for freeze-dried meatballs (about 24 to 28) to $3.18 for pork chops. The price list gives the dried weight and the yield weight. Minimum orders of $10, shipped on day of receipt.

THE ORVIS COMPANY / Dept. CFC
Manchester, VT 05254

Catalogue, free, published annually, 122 pages, illustrated, color.

This Christmas catalogue for the sportsman and outdoorsman has attractive English wicker picnic hampers fitted with a flowered china service for 4, 6, or 8, stainless-steel flatware, two sandwich boxes, and two thermos bottles. Prices range from $105 to $150. To complement the hamper, there's a 6-pack insulated bag in heavy-duty blue duck with a sealed refrigerant capsule in the center. Freeze it overnight and it will keep canned drinks cold for 10 to 12 hours (around $14).

PEPPERIDGE FARM MAIL ORDER CO., INC. / Dept. CFC
Box 7000, Norwalk, CT 06856

"Gift Catalog," free, published periodically, 32 pages, illustrated, color.

One of the gifts is a wicker picnic basket packed with an elegant lunch for two, starting with cocktail pâté and wafers, hickory-smoked Rock Cornish game hen, tinned in aspic, ½ lb. of cheddar cheese, two red Delicious apples (California and Arizona residents get a substitute tin of rum cakes), red and white checkered napkins, and wine glasses (you supply your own wine), all for $29.95.

PERMA-PAK, INC. / Dept. CFC
P.O. Box 15695, Salt Lake City, UT 84115

"Perma-Pak brochure and price list," free, published three to four times a year, 16 pages.

Perma-Pak sells dehydrated low-moisture foods packaged in poly-cello bags under their Pantri-Pak, Hostess-Pak, and Camplite labels, and in #2½, #3, and #10 cans for storage. They have fruits, vegetables such as different kinds of precooked beans, uncooked or freeze-dried corn, chopped, granulated, minced, or sliced onions, diced, flaked, shredded, or sliced potatoes, tomato crystals and tomato flakes, grains, flours, rice, pasta, vegetable-protein foods, mixes, gelatin desserts, and supplementary foods such as powdered butter and shortening. They recommend their foods for everyday use, but we see them having most possibilities for camping or emergency supplies. Frankly, we prefer our food fresh. For $19.95 you can try out a Perma-Pak Pantri-Kit that contains 9 kinds of vegetables, 8 forms of fruit, 4 spreads and mixes, and various textured soy protein products—beef, sausage, chicken or tuna extender, and bacon-flavored bits, plus their cookbook, *Culinary Capers*. There's a separate brochure and order blank for the Camplite Foods line, available on request.

RAINY DAY FOODS, INC. / Dept. CFC
P.O. Box 71, Provo, UT 84601

Catalogue, free, published quarterly, 8-page brochure and 8-page price list, brochure in color, price list, black and white.

Rainy Day Foods sells, both direct and through the mail, over 150 varieties of dehydrated foods packaged in #10 and #2½ cans for long-term storage. While their main appeal seems to be to people who are stockpiling food against some future shortage or emergency, these are obviously good for campers, too. The food list includes dehydrated eggs, fruits, vegetables, dairy products such as butter, cheese, milk, and ice cream, textured vegetable protein in the form of bacon-flavored bits, hamburger-flavored granules, seasonings, grains, beans, seeds and cereals, drinks such as lemonade and hot chocolate, gelatin, margarine, shortening powder, and baking soda. The foods are sold singly or in units of the various types, at prices ranging from around $490 for the deluxe unit to $31.95 for the Variety Pak. They list nonfood items, too: manual or electric grain mills, blenders, mixers, dehydrators, a Franklin stove, water purifiers, and a sprout pack.

SLEEPY HOLLOW GIFTS / Dept. CFC
6651 Arlington Blvd., Falls Church, VA 22042

Catalogue, free, published seasonally, 96 pages, illustrated, color and black and white.

Two six-pack carriers in this catalogue would be handy for camping, hiking, boating, or picnicking. The "Desert Pac" weighs only ¾ lb. and measures a compact 12" x 9" x 9", requires no ice, and keeps bottles or cans of drinks chilled for 12 hours in six insulated coasters ($6.95). The other six-pack carrier is a canvas-covered styrofoam case with a refrigerant container that can be removed and frozen to keep cans cold for hours (around $15).

SPORTPAGES / Dept. CFC
13719 Welch Road, Dallas, TX 75240

"Sportpages," free, published periodically, 34 pages, illustrated, color.

This new company tailors its offerings to the sports-minded or outdoorsman. For the backpacker, there's instant ice cream in individual servings of freeze-dried Neapolitan flavors, needing neither water nor refrigeration (12 1-oz. pouches, $7.50). A portable water purifier eliminates undesirable colors, odors, tastes, chemical residues, pollutants, and industrial wastes and sediments for up to 1,000 gallons of water. Lightweight (just 20 oz.) and easy to carry, it filters water through a silver-ion impregnated active charcoal system ($20). If you want to smoke, roast, steam, or barbecue up to 59 lbs. of ham, venison, pheasant, or any meat or fowl in your backyard, there's a home meat smoker with a temperature gauge, two roasting racks, charcoal, water pans, and a starter set of Arkansas hickory chips and a jar of special seasoning for $100. For filleting fish, a 6" x 24" hardwood board with a ribbed cleaning surface, steel clasp, and nonskid rubber legs is packaged with a filleting knife of fine carbon steel with rosewood handle in a leather sheath, $22.

STOW-A-WAY SPORTS INDUSTRIES, INC. / Dept. CFC
166 Cushing Highway, Cohasset, MA 02025

"Freeze-Dried Food, Dehydrated Food and Lighweight Equipment Guide," free, published annually, 46 pages, black and white.

An excellent catalogue with one of the best and most complete lists of foods, cookware, and equipment for the boater, camper, or backpacker that we have seen. Taking one instance, two hikers could eat heartily for a day from a freeze-dried sample pack weighing 2½ lbs. and costing $13.80. It contains beef stew, beans and franks, chili mac with beef, sausage patties, peas, green beans, eggs with butter, and apples. There are four complete prepackaged breakfasts, lunches, and dinners, with

Pan-Fried Fish

Choose fish that will fit into a large skillet, such as small trout, catfish, etc. Clean and remove head, if desired. Season with salt and pepper and roll in cornmeal. Heat 1 inch bacon fat in a heavy iron skillet over an outdoor fire, add fish and cook until browned on both sides. Do not overcook. Serve with wedges of lemon and tartar sauce.

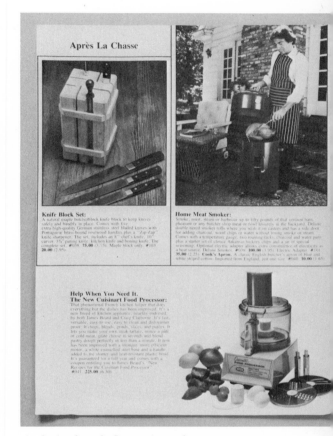

A selection from the Sportpages catalogue

their calorie counts, weights, and the amount of water needed to reconstitute them. There are many pages listing foods such as cereals and pancake mixes, egg dishes, soups, salads of chicken and tuna, stews and chop suey, freeze-dried compressed diced beef and chicken, desserts, fruits, vegetables, beverages, cakes and crackers, bread and cake mixes, condiments, shortening, seasonings, and trail snacks. Freeze-dried foods also come in #10 (gallon size) and #2½ cans; grains, cereals and flours and dehydrated fruits, vegetables, egg and dairy products and puddings in #10 cans. Stow-A-Way has a service for hikers making extended backpacking trips that enables them to collect foods at certain U.S. Post Office pick-up points along the Appalachian Trail, or other post offices to fit different areas and schedules. Cook kits in stainless steel and aluminum, a frying pan with a folding handle, cutlery sets, a G.I. can opener, pack stoves, pocket stoves, camp stoves, a solar stove, knives, water carriers and canteens, and some useful books on surviving and cooking in the outdoors are available here, too. This is a very informative and helpful guide.

NORM THOMPSON / Dept. CFC
1805 N.W. Thurman Street, Portland, OR 97209

Catalogue, free, published seasonally, 80 pages, illustrated, color.

This is primarily a clothing catalogue for men and women, designed to appeal to the tastes of Pacific Northwesterners. They have one good picnic or outdoor cooking item—the Safari grill, so named because it was adapted from the cooking stoves of natives in Kenya. They use rolled-up balls of grass for fuel; we Westerners burn the more readily available crumpled newspaper. This inexpensive ($15) grill telescopes to fit into a 12" x 12" x 8" carrying case of sturdy cardboard, so it is easy to tote to shore, mountains, or lakeside. You don't need extra equipment because the double-hinged grid top has long handles. You just turn over whatever is cooking in it, and the fat dripping from the meat onto the charred paper in the bottom keeps the fire going.

WESTLAND FOODS CORP. / Dept. CFC
1381 Franquette Ave., Concord, CA 94520

Brochure, free.

Precooked hickory-smoked bacon in a can (a 1-lb. can is the equivalent of 3 lbs. of raw bacon) that needs no refrigeration until opened. It can be heated and served in 2 minutes and was designed for cabins, camps, and boats. Three 4-oz. cans (approximately 30 slices) are $6.50, a 1-lb. can (about 40 slices) $7.50 ppd., add 50¢ east of the Rockies.

WILLIAMS-SONOMA / Dept. CFC
576 Sutter Street, San Francisco, CA 94102

"A Catalog for Cooks," $1, published biannually, plus "January Sale/New Kitchen Ideas," both 26 pages, illustrated, color.

From the French, inventors of the great fish-shaped wire grill for barbecuing, comes another good idea: a wire potato grill. Instead of baking potatoes in the coals, you put them in the long-handled grill and bake them over the coals. They would make good hamburger grills for individual hamburgers ($6 for 2 grills). Williams-Sonoma also has a stainless-steel rotisserie thermometer and the Smoke 'N Pit, an electric smoker of heavy rolled steel that holds up to 20 lbs. of meat.

See Appendix, page 239, for additional sources not included here.

CHAPTER THIRTEEN

THE COOK'S BOOKSHELF: BOOKS AND BOOKLETS

Kitchen by Cardan Interiors, photographer Max Eckert

APHRODISIA PRODUCTS, INC. / Dept. CFC
28 Carmine Street, New York, NY 10014

"Aphrodisia—an experience in herbs, spices and essential oils," $1, published periodically, 112 pages, illustrated, black and white, with seasonally adjusted price list.

Aphrodisia has a very interesting hand-picked list of books relating to herbs and spices but also has some rather unexpected choices, such as *The Alice B. Toklas Cookbook* ($1.95), *Flavors of India, Flower Cookery, Japanese Country Cookbook*. Judging by the prices, most of these seem to be in soft cover, though this is not indicated, and one wishes they had given the full names of the authors, not just the surnames, but these are minor quibbles, for this is a nice selection. We noticed a U.S. Department of Agriculture book on *Common Weeds of the U.S.* ($4.50), with illustrations, botanical information, locations maps, and plant lore we didn't even know existed.

ARGONAUT VENTURES INC. / Dept. CFC
P.O. Box 40218, San Francisco, CA 94140

"Sourdough Jack's Cookery & Things . . . & More," $3.80 ppd., 112 pages, illustrated, color and black and white.

This chatty agreeable little paperback book is written by a salty (or doughy) character, "Sourdough Jack" Mabee, a former Alaskan (hence the sourdough lore) stevedore, taxi-owner, deck hand, trader, and now the proprietor of a San Francisco restaurant and sourdough factory who ships his starter all over the world. There are many recipes for sourdough breads, rolls, pancakes, waffles, biscuits, doughnuts, cakes, and cookies, of which the most interesting is the San Francisco-style sourdough French bread recipe painstakingly worked out over many years by an enthusiast named Joe Flaherty. Time-Life picked this up for *The Great West* volume of their Foods of the World series. It's a 4-page recipe and very detailed, so if you like this bread and are a good baker, you might give it a whirl. The cookbook comes with a package of starter stapled inside the cover, with printed directions for making everyday

★

To make your own Zebrovka, put 1 or 2 blades of buffalo grass in a bottle of vodka.
—*from Aphrodisia Catalogue*

★

★
The fastest and safest way to separate eggs is to break them into the palm of your hand and let the white slip through your fingers. You never break a yolk this way.

sourdough bread. You can also buy sourdough starter in a separate crock (see chapter 2). The last third of the book has old-time Western recipes like baked buffalo stew (chuckwagon style), beans with venison, grilled cornmush, Hangtown fry, trapper's pudding, more urban fare, and many recipes with seed sprouts, for Sourdough Jack also sells sprouting kits (see chapter 7). Sourdough Jack insists that only hard-wheat bread flour makes decent sourdough bread, not the bleached or unbleached all-purpose kind, and says it is absolutely essential if you are making the French sourdough. Mills where you can buy this type of flour are listed in chapter 9.

BACCHANALIA / Dept. CFC
273 Riverside Avenue, Westport, CT 06880

"Bacchanalia Wine Making Supplies," free, published annually, 16 pages, illustrated, black and white.

Bacchanalia has two books on subjects other than wine and beer. One is *Homemade Cheese & Butter* that explains cheesemaking the simple way ($2.95). You can order a package of six rennet tablets for 95¢ to start you off. The other is *Adventures in Sourdough Cooking & Baking* by C. D. Wilford ($3.95). For $1.50 you get the sourdough starter, with instructions and recipes and for $5.95 the sourdough starter and a little crock to keep it in.

BALL BLUE BOOK / Dept. CFC
P.O. Box 2005, Muncie, IN 47302

"Blue Book of Home Canning & Freezing," paperback, 35¢.

An informative, well-written 100-page booklet with over 450 recipes and instructions on home canning and freezing of foods.

THE BIRKETT MILLS / Dept. CFC
P.O. Box 440-A, Penn Yan, NY 14527

"Wolff's Kasha Recipes" compiled by Phyllis Wolff, $1, 16 pages, illustrated, color.

Birkett Mills sells stone-ground flours and cereals, including kasha or brown buckwheat groats, a staple in Russia and Eastern Europe that is gradually becoming more popular in this country. Like the Middle East bulgur (cracked wheat), kasha has a pleasant nutty taste and texture. It makes a good alternative to rice and is delicious with kebabs and chicken, in stuffings, meat loaf, and meat balls. Birkett Mills has different grades of kasha—whole, fine, coarse, and assorted. The little booklet of about 18 recipes advises that while the medium grade is acceptable for cooking, the fine grade is better. The Birkett Mills price list and order form come with the booklet.

BOCOCK-STROUD CO. / Dept. CFC
501 West 4th Street, Winston-Salem, NC 27102

Brochure, free, 8 pages, illustrated, black and white.

This company sells Old Salem cookies and fruit cake and *Old Salem Cookery* by Beth Tartan, detailing the distinctive cooking of this early Moravian settlement, with a chapter on the Moravians and Old Salem ($5 ppd.).

BON APPETIT PUBLISHING CORP. / Dept. CFC
5900 Wilshire Blvd., Los Angeles, CA 90036

Bon Appetit, the Los Angeles-based monthly food and wine magazine, offers one-year subscriptions (12 issues, $7.95) and *The Best of Bon Appetit*, a slipcased edition of three soft-cover cookbooks containing the best recipes from *Bon Appetit*, illustrated with color photographs ($7.95 a set ppd.). It is a good way to get acquainted with the publication. There's also the Bon Appetit Book Shelf, a page in the magazine that shows current cookbooks and reference books, and Epicurean Corner, selected cooking equipment and serving pieces, all of which may be ordered by mail.

CAKE DECORATORS / Dept. CFC
P.O. Box 97, Blacklick, OH 43004

Catalogue, 75 cents, 144 pages, illustrated, black and white.

This catalogue has two pages of books, mostly on baking, cake decorating, and candy making (with titles like *Decorating Cakes for Fun and Profit*, $6), and some of the Sunset books—*Dinner Party, Entertaining, Appetizers,* and *Favorite Recipes*. The catalogue has not been reprinted since 1973/74, so you should consult the accompanying price list for current costs and for items that have been discontinued or added.

CAPRILAND'S HERB FARM / Dept. CFC
Silver Street, Coventry, CT 06238

Brochure, free, published annually.

From the Book Nook at Capriland's Herb Farm you can order books on herb culture written by owner Adelma Grenier Simmons, some of which include recipes, and *The Strawberry Book*, her history of the strawberry with legends, lore, and recipes (price on request). They also sell a chart on household herbs, a companion planting chart, medieval garden chart, and charts of a bee garden, fragrant garden, and seasoning garden.

CARILLON IMPORTERS, LTD. / Dept. CFC
745 Fifth Avenue, New York, NY 10022

"Grand Marnier Liqueur," free, published annually, 32 pages, illustrated.

Grand Marnier, distilled from the peel of bitter oranges and blended with Fine Champagne Cognac, is one of the world's most popular liqueurs for cocktails and cooking as well as after-dinner drinking. It now has a sister liqueur, Cherry Marnier, and this little booklet gives recipes for both. Grand Marnier has always been accepted in the best kitchens, so it is hardly surprising to find a lot of the recipes hail from restaurants and hotels here and in France. From the Hotel Beau Rivage in Condrieu comes Charlotte au Grand Marnier; La Grenouille in New York contributes a Garden of Eden au Grand Marnier (hot fruits with cold Grand Marnier mousse as a sauce); and the famous Restaurant Troisgros in Roanne weighs in with Oranges Sultane, a simple dessert that sounds utterly delicious. Chilled Pumpkin Soup flavored with Grand Marnier is the creation of Eugene Scanlan of our own Waldorf-Astoria, and a very interesting Mousse de Lievre a l'Imperiale, from the Relais de l'Empereur in Montelimar marinates hare in Grand Marnier. Altogether a cut above the average booklet and worth sending for.

CASUAL LIVING / Dept. CFC
Bethel, CT 06081

"Casual Living," free, published annually, 48 pages, illustrated, black and white.

There are a couple of interesting cookbooks in this gift catalogue. *The Country Art of Blueberry Cookery* by the Blueberry Lady (Mrs. Clifford Morrison) has 185 recipes for that delightful berry, from soup to dessert, with kitchen tips for preparing and cooking fresh or frozen berries ($2). *The Woman's Guide to Boating & Cooking* by Lael Morgan, who spent two years learning how (and how not) to cook on a boat has 250 pages of recipes for seaworthy fare ($3.95).

CHICO-SAN, INC. / Dept. CFC
1144 West 1st Street, Chico, CA 95926

"Chico-San, Inc. Products—a catalog of unique foods," free, published annually, 26 pages, black and white.

Chico-San has some rather unusual cookbooks for those interested in natural foods and macrobiotic cooking. The *Chico-San Cookbook*, by cooking teacher Cornellia Aihara, is a guide to traditional Oriental cooking methods, using a wide variety of natural and macrobiotic food

Soufflé Grand Marnier
[*served at Fouquet's, Paris*]
This is an entirely different type of soufflé and one which is light and exciting and a triumph for the cook. Beat 8 egg yolks with ⅔ cup of sugar over hot water in the upper part of a double boiler until the mixture makes a ribbon when held up and allowed to fall back into the pan. It should have the consistency of a zabaglione. Add approximately ½ cup Grand Marnier. Transfer the mixture to a bowl and continue beating over cracked ice until cooled. Beat 10 egg whites until firm but not dry, adding a pinch of cream of tartar. Fold into the yolk-sugar mixture and blend thoroughly but lightly. Pour into a buttered and sugared soufflé dish and bake in a 400° oven until it rises and becomes delicately brown, about 20 minutes. Serve at once.
—*from Grand Marnier Recipe Booklet*

★

To determine how fresh an egg is, place it in a bowl of water. A fresh egg sinks, a medium fresh egg sticks up, and a bad egg floats.
—*from "The Omaha Steaks Cookbook"*

*

Blueberries are easy to freeze. Do not wash; just put in one layer on a cookie sheet and put in the freezer. When frozen, remove to plastic bags and store in the freezer.

*

When sautéing vegetables for cold soups, use oil rather than butter. It will not solidify when chilled.

*

Creamy Russian Borscht
Place in a blender a 16-oz. can of sliced beets, with liquid, 1 teaspoon sugar, ¼ cup lemon juice, 4 tablespoons minced onion, ½ teaspoon salt, ¼ teaspoon pepper, ¼ teaspoon fresh or dry dill weed, and blend until smooth. Stir in 1 cup natural whole-milk yogurt until well mixed and chill thoroughly. Serve cold. Garnish each portion with a dollop of yogurt. Makes about 6 cups, or 6 servings.
—*from "Cooking with Yogurt Naturally, Colombo, Inc."*

products. Recipes range from soups and sauces to tempura, vegetables, and sea plants, snacks and desserts, even wild plants, with special sections on making pickles, miso, tamari soy sauce, and other forgotten specialties, It costs $3.95. *The Book of Tofu* by William Shertleff and Akiko Aoyagi ($6.95) is a current West Coast bestseller, which tells every last thing about tofu (soybean curd). *The Art of Just Cooking* by Lima Ohsawa, an expert in the preparation of traditional Japanese cuisine, explains the principles and techniques of natural cookery based on yin and yang.

COLOMBO, INC. / Dept. CFC
Danton Drive, Methuen, MA 01844

"Cooking with Yogurt Naturally," free, 28 pages.

Yogurt is eaten by Americans at the rate of 166,000 tons each year, according to Colombo, the first yogurt dairy in this country. More people eat yogurt than cook with it, but you might bear in mind that yogurt has far fewer calories than heavy, light, or sour cream or mayonnaise and can replace them in many recipes. It blends beautifully and gives a subtle, slightly tart Middle Eastern flavor (one caution: don't let it come to a boil or it will separate). The recipes in the Colombo booklet use yogurt in dips, hors d'oeuvre, soups, salad dressings, egg, meat, poultry, seafood and vegetable dishes, cakes, breads, and desserts—the gamut of cooking. For a low-calorie hors d'oeuvre, Colombo suggests filling scooped-out cherry tomatoes with minced onion, dill and yogurt and putting a tiny shrimp on top.

CONSUMER INFORMATION CENTER / Dept. CFC
Pueblo, CO 81009

"An Index of Selected Federal Publications of Consumer Interest," free, updated periodically, 16 pages, black and white.

Some of the consumer booklets or leaflets are free (one is a layman's guide to product terms used in grocery stores and food ads), but larger booklets, such as a 26-page budgeting, menu planning, and shopping guide, may cost about 50¢. If you are an alert consumer, the booklets on purchasing, preparing, and storing food and on diet and nutrition are quite helpful. For gardeners, there are publications on landscaping, gardening, and pest control. One called "Dishing Up the Dog and Cat Food" might help to brighten your pet's daily diet.

COUNTRY HOUSEWARES / Dept. CFC
Box 626, Wading River, NY 11792

"Country Housewares of Long Island," free, published seasonally, 6 pages, illustrated, black and white.

Along with the kitchen utensils and gifts in this little brochure is a list of the Potpourri cookbooks, on such subjects as wok and tempura cookery, crêpes and flaming desserts, crockpot cookery, and wine cookery. Country Housewares sells them at $2 each, $5 for 3, $9 for 6, and $1.50 for each additional book over 6.

CREOLE DELICACIES CO., INC. / Dept. CFC
533-H Saint Ann Street, New Orleans, LA 70116

"Happy Gifts of Food from Old New Orleans," free, published annually, 12 pages, illustrated, color.

Creole cooking is a subtle combination of the French and Spanish influences that came together in the city of New Orleans in the 18th century. *The Plantation Cookbook* ($8.95), 300 recipes gathered by the New Orleans Junior League, is illustrated with line drawings of historic plantation homes; *Brennan's New Orleans Cookbook* ($7.95) features favorite dishes from this famous restaurant; and *The New Orleans Restaurant Cookbook* ($8.95) gives the best of several restaurants in one volume. The prices include postage and handling.

CROWN PUBLISHERS / Dept. CFC
One Park Avenue, New York, NY 10016

"Making Cheese at Home" by Susan Ogilvy, $5.59 ppd.

How to make cheeses and other dairy products with simple inexpensive equipment, and readily available ingredients.

CULINARY ARTS CATALOGUE / Dept. CFC
310 Duke Street, Box 369, Tappahannock, VA 22560

"America's Church & Community Cookbook Catalogue," $1 (refundable with purchase), published annually.

Jeffrey and Jane Camp are currently working on their catalogue, which will contain titles and descriptions of about 200 American regional cookbooks prepared by groups and individuals, so we can't give you any details as to pages or format. It should be ready by the time you read this. If their old list of 80 books is anything to go by, this should be a gold mine for students of culinary Americana. To name just a few: *300 Years of Carolina Cooking* (the Junior League of Greensville, South Carolina); *Church Mouse Cook Book* (the women of St. Paul's Episcopal Church, Ivy, Virginia); *Royal Recipes from the Cajun Country; River Road Recipes* (Junior League of Baton Rouge, Louisiana); *Mennonite Maid Cookbook* (Dayton, Virginia); *Little Rock Cooks* (Junior League of Little Rock, Arkansas).

Regional cookbooks, from the Culinary Arts catalogue

CUMBERLAND GENERAL STORE / Dept. CFC
Rte. 3, Crossville, TN 38555

"The Wish & Want Book," $3, published seasonally, 272 pages, illustrated, black and white.

This general-store catalogue has a few books that pertain to country cooking and preserving. There's *Stocking Up—How to Preserve the Food You Grow Naturally*, from the Rodale Press ($8.85), a book on home freezing, another on innards, the *More with Less Cookbook* by Doris Long-acre, 500 recipes from Mennonite kitchens (soft cover, $4.95), a small book on bread making, and one on winemaking.

DANNON / Dept. CFC
22-11 38th Avenue, Long Island City, NY 11101

Recipe booklet; free (available east of the Mississippi only), 12 pages, illustrated, black and white.

Dannon made yogurt popular in the United States, selling more of it than anybody else, and their yogurts have no artificial additives or sweeteners, so they can be forgiven their fond recital of the benefits of Dannon's prune-whip yogurt to senior citizens with irregularity. The suggestions for use are mostly in the dessert and snack category, with a curious and regrettable absence of any of the Middle Eastern, Indian, and Bulgarian dishes for which yogurt is essential.

EAST WIND / Dept. CFC
2801 Broadway, New York, NY 10025

Mail order price list, free, 5 pages.

One page of the mail-order list is devoted to cookbooks, all in soft cover and all reasonably priced. *The Pleasures of Chinese Cooking* by Grace Chu is $1.50, and so is *The Easy Way to Chinese Cooking* by Beverley Lee. Kenneth Lo's *Chinese Vegetarian Cooking* and *Chinese Food* are $3.95. *Wokcraft* by Charles and Violet Schafer and Gary Lee's two books, *The Wok* and *Vegetarian*, are also $3.95. Two useful books by Buwei Chou are *How to Cook and Eat in Chinese* ($1.95) and *How to Order and Eat in Chinese* ($1.65). Add 10 percent of the total amount for shipping and handling charges.

*

Make a marinade with 2 cups yogurt, lemon juice and salt, marinate chicken parts or meat in this overnight before broiling.
—*from Dannon Yogurt Recipe Booklet*

*

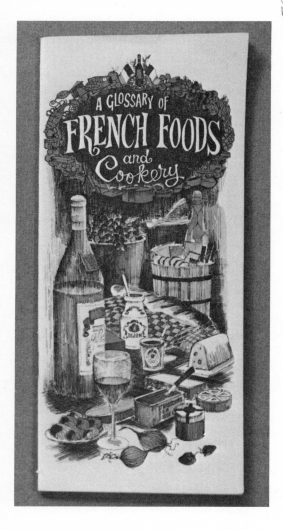

Peaches a l'Amaretto

Halve 6 ripe peaches. Remove skin, pits, and a little of the pulp. Reserve pulp. Put peaches in a greased baking dish. Mix the peach pulp, 4 ground macaroons, 1 tablespoon ground almonds, 4 tablespoons crumbled sponge cake, 2 tablespoons sugar, 1 egg yolk, and 1 ounce Amaretto di Saronno liqueur in a bowl. Beat 1 egg white until stiff and fold into the mixture. Put a small amount of the mixture in the hollow of each peach and dot with butter. Bake in a 350° oven until slightly glazed. Serve cold. Serves 6.

—from "Amaretto di Saronno Gourmet Secrets"

FOOD AND WINES FROM FRANCE, INC. / Dept. CFC
1350 Avenue of the Americas, New York, NY 10019

"A Glossary of French Foods and Cookery," free, 26 pages, line drawings. "The Wonderful World of French Cheeses," free, 15 pages, illustrated, color.

The glossary was designed to help you to read and understand the labels on French products sold in the United States, but it would be a great help with menu-reading, too. It not only gives definitions of words such as *bien cuit* (say this and you get a well-done steak), *oeufs d'alose* (shad roe), or *amuse gueule* (cocktail tidbits), but pronunciations as well. The list of French culinary words and phrases is very complete and there are many helpful bits of information about things like French mustards (those of Dijon, Orleans, and Bordeaux are the best known), wild mushrooms, different kinds of pâtés, and honeys. There's also a good glossary of French cheeses, divided into the double and triple crèmes, soft-ripened types, semisoft cheese, goat's-milk cheese, or chèvres, Roquefort and other blue cheeses, firm cheeses, hard cheese, and process cheeses—yes, France does have some of those, such as Gourmandise, La Grappe (also known as Fondu au Raisin or Tomme au Marc), Beau Pasteur, and La Vache qui Rit. For this alone the booklet would be well worth sending for.

The Wonderful World of French Cheeses is a companion book that goes a little more deeply into the background, buying, storing, and serving of French cheese. It tells you how much to buy for a cheese and wine tasting, how to present the cheeses and wines, what to serve with them and how to set the table (no flowers, please; they take on the aroma of the cheeses). At the back of the booklet are about ten recipes and ideas for using cheese, from Camembert aux noix for hors d'oeuvre to hamburgers à la Française (basically, a French cheeseburger).

FOREIGN VINTAGES, INC. / Dept. CFC
98 Cutter Mill Road, Great Neck, NY 11021

"Amaretto di Saronno Gourmet Secrets," $1.25, published periodically, 24 pages, black and white.

Amaretto di Saronno is the Italian almond-flavored liqueur, which has a long and colorful history, given on the back page of the recipe booklet. There are about 70 recipes in the booklet, from appetizers of the fruit type through relishes, vegetables, main dishes to desserts, and they are intelligently conceived. There is no attempt to drag the liqueur into everything but mainly to use it where it belongs, in a pumpkin pie or mousse, as a poultry glaze, in a peach conserve, or almond applesauce. Definitely a cut above most recipe booklets of this type.

FRUIT-FRESH / Dept. CFC
Box 1467, Pittsburgh, PA 15230

"Fruit-Fresh Recipes," free with stamped self-addressed envelope, 24 pages, illustrated, color.

Fruit-Fresh is a trade-marked color and flavor preservative made from sugar and ascorbic acid used on fruit, either fresh fruits or those you can or freeze yourself. The booklet describes how to use the product, interspersed with a few recipes and hints.

GALAXY PRODUCTS, INC. / Dept. CFC
P.O. Box 215, Sonoma, CA 95476

"Sonoma Cheese Factory Gift Catalog," free, published annually, 16 pages, illustrated, color.

In addition to cheeses and gift boxes, the catalogue has a small but interesting selection of gift items relating to Sonoma Valley history and wineries. One is *Mangiamo* ($3.95), the favorite recipes of Sylvia Sebastiani, a noted cook and hostess who is the wife of August Sebastiani (one of Sonoma County's best-known winery owners). It's a delightful little book, with a real wine-country flavor (in more ways than one because wines are used extensively in the recipes).

GARDEN WAY / Dept. CFC
   47 Maple Street, P.O. Box 944, Burlington, VT 05401

"Garden Way Country Kitchen Catalog," free, published seasonally, 17 pages, illustrated, color.

Garden Way Living Center, Vermont's largest food preserving supply center, has all the equipment, a good library of books on the subject, plus plans for building your own fruit and cider press or honey extractor beehive. There is the *Ball Blue Book*, on canning and freezing, for $1, the *Ball Freezer Book* for 50¢, the USDA *Complete Guide to Home Canning, Preserving and Freezing*, $2.50, plus manufacturers' books on pressure canning and cooking. Two of the more unusual books are *Making Homemade Cheese & Butter* by P. Hobson and *The Canning, Freezing, Curing and Smoking of Meat, Fish & Game* by W. Eastman ($4.95).

GOLD RUSH SOURDOUGH COMPANY, INC. / Dept. CFC
   65 Paul Drive, San Rafael, CA 94903

Adventures in San Francisco Sourdough Cooking and Baking ($4) is available from the Gold Rush Sourdough Company, whose only business is selling the starter for San Francisco's favorite bread. The sourdough starter with recipe folder is $1.50.

GREEN MOUNTAIN SUGAR HOUSE / Dept. CFC
   RFD #1, Ludlow, VT 05149

"The Vermont Maple Syrup Cookbook," 192 pages, illustrated, $7.35 ppd.

If your use of maple syrup is limited to pancakes, you will be pleased with the 200 recipes "carrying the special flavor of Vermont" into main dishes, breads, cakes, cookies, puddings, beverages, desserts, and sauces.

GROLIER ENTERPRISES, INC. / Dept. CFC
   Sherman Parkway, Danbury, CT 06816

"Grand Diplome Cooking Course," 20 volumes, each 144 pages, $5.98 plus shipping and handling per volume. (First volume can be received free with no obligation.) Illustrated, color.

This cooking course in book form, available only by mail, is based on the techniques of the renowned Cordon Bleu Cookery School of London and is designed to teach one month of the course per volume. Each volume has more than 60 full color photos, over 100 recipes, and instructions (how to cut up raw chicken, prepare pastry, make omelets, etc.). Also included are timetables for making an attractive full-course meal efficiently and quickly and a 144-page wine guide.

GURNEY SEED & NURSERY CO. / Dept. CFC
   2nd and Capitol Streets, Yankton, SD 57078

"Gurney Garden Seed and Nursery Catalog," free, published annually, 76 pages, color.

Half a page of the Gurney catalogue is devoted to their "Library of Good Reading," which has a few cookbooks that might interest you. There's *The Oats, Peas, Beans & Barley Cookbook* (450 recipes, $4.50); *Natural Grains*, on using natural whole grains and flours in baking (32 pages, $1.39). The *Kerr Home Canning Book*, which also tells how to freeze foods (72 pages, $1), the *Wise Encyclopedia of Cookery* (1,344 pages, $9.95) and a little book on candy making (49¢, or 19¢ with an order of $2.50 or more).

HARRINGTON'S IN VERMONT, INC. / Dept. CFC
   Main Street, Richmond, VT 05477

Catalogue, free, published seasonally, 32 pages, illustrated, black and white.

In among Harrington's smoked hams and poultry, cheese and maple syrup, you'll find *Treasured Recipes from Early New England Kitchens*, a

Cornets au Roquefort

Remove the casing from 15 paper thin slices of fine-grained salami. Cut the slices in halves. Twist slices into cones. Secure shape by pressing edges together. Chill 30 minutes. In a mixing bowl, thoroughly combine 4 ounces Roquefort cheese and 4 ounces Gervais or Petit-Suisse cheese. Blend in 1 teaspoon finely chopped fresh dill and 1 tablespoon Armagnac. Fill salami cones with cheese mixture, using a pastry bag fitted with a star tube. Chill for 1 hour or more before using.
—*from "The Wonderful World of French Cheeses"*

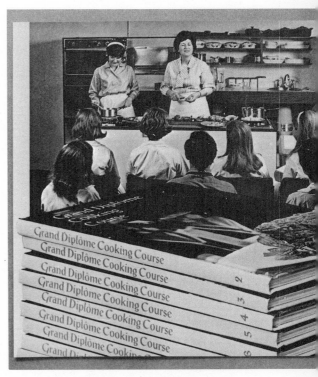

Cooking course by mail, from Grolier Enterprises

collection of recipes from the six New England states, compiled for Harrington's by Marjorie Blanchard, a native New Englander and food writer. As delightful to read as it is to cook from, this soft-cover cookbook is $4.95 plus 50¢ for postage and handling. Under the different states are Connecticut recipes for pumpkin bread and pudding, clam fritters and pie, hedgehog pudding, and buckwheat cakes; Rhode Island crab cakes, panned oysters, and barrel bake (a clambake in a barrel); Massachusetts salmon with egg sauce (the traditional Fourth of July dinner), Indian pudding, apple toot, brown bread, and fish chowder; New Hampshire oatmeal scones, black walnut cake, corn pudding; Vermont maple custard pie, baked bean soup, fried apple pies, red flannel hash, and, believe it or not, eggs poached in maple syrup. Maine contributes rhubarb pie, blueberry pancakes, blueberry slump, spiced beef, baked bluefish, and corn chowder. The final section of the book contains recipes from Harrington's own kitchen, made with their products, such as dried beef chowder, ham and asparagus casserole, and Canadian bacon and mushroom pie.

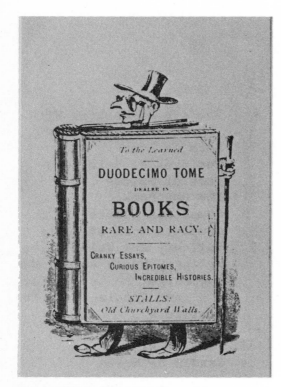

Old print from the Hilltop Herb Farm catalogue

HARVEST HEALTH, INC. / Dept. CFC
1944 Eastern Avenue, S.E., Grand Rapids, MI 49507

Catalogue and price lists, free, published annually, 16 pages, black and white, also 8-page catalogue of herbs and spices.

Harvest Health lists some herb reference books, such as *Culpeper's Complete Herbal* by the "grandaddy" of all herbalists, Nicholas Culpeper (hard cover, $7.95), *Stalking the Healthful Herb* by Euell Gibbons (soft cover, $2.95), *Herbal Tea Book* by Adrian & Dennis (soft cover, 59¢), and *Magic in Herbs* by Leonie de Sounin, herb cookery and lore (soft cover, 95¢).

HILLTOP HERB FARM / Dept. CFC
P.O. Box 866, Cleveland, TX 77327

Catalogue, 50¢, published annually, 16 pages, illustrated, black and white.

You'll find a very good book list in this catalogue, covering growing and cooking with herbs, rose recipes, cooking with spices, companion plants, natural dyes and related subjects. They also have a little book of their own, *From Our Side of the Hill*, a guide to using Hilltop Herb Farm products like herb blends, vinegars and jellies in other than the obvious ways, with lots of quick hints and recipes ($2.25), recipe sheets of popular dishes served at the farm, and some of their favorite canning recipes, 15¢ a sheet.

HOLLAND AMERICAN IMPORTING CO. / Dept. CFC
P.O. Box 266, 10343 Artesia Blvd., Bellflower, CA 90706

"Conimex: Your Guide to Delicious Chinese/Indonesian Cuisine," $1, published periodically, 38 pages, illustrated, color.

This colorful recipe booklet of Indonesian and Chinese cooking also gives pointers on Oriental dining—table settings, presentation, and the correct drink (beer, water, cold tea, mineral water or, if wine is preferred, a chilled rosé). Divided into categories, the guide has step-by-step instructions with preparation and cooking times for such basics as nasi goreng (fried rice), Indonesian curry soup, and ku lo yuk (Chinese sweet-and-sour pork), and more uncommon dishes like sambal goreng-gati (Indonesian liver), boemboe balikan (spiced fish), and ajam opor (Indonesian chicken). The recipes are precise and simple, accompanied by full-color photographs. There is both a glossary and an index.

Conimex is a supplier of the sauces, spices, condiments, vegetables, and noodles essential to these dishes, and you can buy their products by mail from companies such as Maison Glass and Le Jardin du Gourmet, both listed in chapter 10.

HOLT, RINEHART AND WINSTON / Dept. CFC
383 Madison Avenue, New York, NY 10017

"The Chinese Menu Cookbook" by Joanne Hush and Peter Wong, hard-cover, $9.95 plus 70¢ postage, 288 pages, sketches.

A step-by-step introduction to the principles and techniques of Chinese cooking with a very helpful section on planning menus. Each recipe has a timetable for preparation, cooking, marinating, and chilling, so you know exactly how long everything will take. Acceptable substitutes are suggested for hard-to-find ingredients. Written by an American woman who teaches Chinese cooking and a Chinese restaurateur and cooking demonstrator, this takes the mystique out of Chinese cooking for the novice.

H.P. BOOKS / Dept. CFC
P.O. Box 5367, Tucson, AZ 85703

"Crêpe Cookery" and "Crockery Cookery" by Mable Hoffman, each $4.95; "Richard Deacon's Microwave Oven Cookbook," $5.

H.P. Books publishes and sells by mail the above three paperback books, with a 30 percent discount for one to four single-copy orders. Postage and handling is 20¢ a book, and there are no returns. *Crockery Cookery* was a runaway best seller, with 2½ million copies sold in 1975, and *Crêpe Cookery* is Mable Hoffman's follow-up. She also tested the recipes for *Richard Deacon's Microwave Oven Cookbook.* (Mable Hoffman, incidentally, is food stylist and editorial consultant for *Better Homes & Gardens.*)

INSIDE OUT PUBLISHING COMPANY / Dept. CFC
3466 Summer Avenue, Memphis, TN 38122

"Your First Loaf" by Carole Walter, paperback, $2, 42 pages, sketches.

A basic little book for the beginner, which carefully explains the flours, leaveners, mixing methods, kneading, pan sizes, and so on. While there are many more comprehensive bread books on the market, this one is very simple and clear with step-by-step directions and sketches by the author that show what breads look like at different stages of shaping or filling and how things are done. There are recipes for more than a baker's dozen of breads, from an American-style white bread to coffee cake and Danish—but why call a recipe that includes sugar and salad oil French bread, when the classic French bread is just flour, water, yeast, and salt? In the standard mail-order manner, the publishers say the purchase price will be refunded should you be dissatisfied with the book. They also sell, for $1.25, an 8-page booklet called "The Magic Plastic Garden," about using black plastic as a vegetable garden mulch.

KITCHEN BAZAAR / Dept. CFC
4455 Connecticut Avenue NW, Washington, DC 20008

Catalogue, free, published annually, 32 pages, illustrated, black and white.

Kitchen Bazaar carries the excellent little soft-cover cookbooks produced by 101 Productions and Nitty Gritty Productions on the West Coast. Some of our favorites are *Regional Cooking of China* by Margaret Gin, *Greek Cooking for the Gods* by Eva Zane, and *Pots & Pans Etc.* by Gertrude Harris. The latter is not a cookbook but the best book we know on the subject of cookware.

★

Keep a jar of clarified butter in the refrigerator for sautéing, to serve with boiled lobster, asparagus, artichokes. To clarify, melt butter very slowly over low heat or in the top of a double boiler to prevent burning. Skim foam from top. Carefully pour clear liquid butter into jar, leaving the whitish sediment or whey behind.

★

Apple Toot
Break 2 eggs into a large bowl. Beat in ½ cup maple syrup. Sift together 1½ tablespoons flour, 2 teaspoons baking powder, and ½ teaspoon salt. Beat into the egg syrup mixture. Stir in 1 large apple, peeled and diced, ¼ cup raisins, and ¼ cup dried currants. Pour into a buttered 1½-quart baking dish. Bake in a preheated 350° oven for 35 to 40 minutes until puffed and golden. Serve with a custard sauce. Makes 4 to 5 servings.
—*from "Treasured Recipes from Early New England Kitchens"*

From Carole's Capers...

a Scenario on Baking Bread...

★

To get the most flavor from dried herbs, crush in a mortar before using or steep for 5 minutes in a little lukewarm water or wine (1 tablespoon for 1 teaspoon herb), or warm gently in a 200°F. oven for 5 minutes.

★

To prevent skin forming on a sauce that is left to stand, butter waxed paper and lay the buttered side on the surface of the sauce.

★

Georgia Peach
Place ¼ fresh peeled peach and 1 ounce Liquore Galliano with 4 or 5 cubes of ice in a blender. Liquefy at high speed. Serve in a frosted glass. Makes 1 serving.
—*from "The Gold Standard"*

KITCHEN GLAMOR, INC. / Dept. CFC
26770 Grand River, Detroit, MI 48240

"Kitchen Glamor—tools for the fine arts of cooking, baking and decorating," free, with periodically updated price lists, 28 pages, illustrated, black and white.

Kitchen Glamor stocks over 1,200 cookbooks, a selection of which is listed and shown on the center spread of the catalogue. These are divided into categories such as The Classic Cuisine, Ethnic Cooking, Candy, Decorating, Health, Specialty Baking, and the Sunset, Betty Crocker, and Time-Life Foods of the World books. You'll find here all the top names—Beard, Child, Claiborne—and all the old favorites. Should you not see what you want on the list, let them know the title and they'll send complete information.

LAMB EDUCATION CENTER
AMERICAN LAMB COUNCIL / Dept. CFC—B-148
200 Clayton Street, Denver, CO 80206

Free recipe booklets.

It's a well-known fact that many Americans regard lamb as a meat that isn't fit to eat (ever try serving it to a Texan?), hence the need for a Lamb Education Center. Educational material consists of a constantly changing supply of leaflets with half a dozen recipes. If you write, you get whatever is current. Caution: If you like your lamb rare or pink, you should adjust their roasting times and internal temperatures.

LE JARDIN DU GOURMET / Dept. CFC
West Danville, VT 05873

Catalogue, 50¢, published annually, 32 pages, illustrated, black and white.

This mail-order company has a small but rather different list of cookbooks, some on cooking with herbs and vegetables, natural grains, bread (from stuffings to croutons), others on preserving foods. They have paperback books by Beatrice Vaughan: *Citrus Cooking, Store-Cheese Cooking, Real Old-Time Yankee Apple Cooking, Real Old-Time Yankee Maple Cooking* plus one on jams and jellies and one for preserves and relishes ($1.25 each), and the hard-cover *Putting Food By* on which she collaborated with two other authors. We were pleased to see that they also list Jane Grigson's excellent *The Art of Charcuterie* (hard cover, $7.95).

LEKVAR-BY-THE-BARREL / Dept. CFC
1577 First Avenue, New York, NY 10028

"A Continental Bazaar," free, published annually, 56 pages, illustrated, black and white.

The catalogue has a well-selected and lengthy list of cookbooks, including James Beard's *Treasury of Outdoor Cooking* ($6.95), now hard to find; Paula Wolfert's *Couscous and other Good Food from Morocco* ($10.95), another rarity; books on Indian, Greek, Italian, Chinese, Hungarian, Brazilian, French, German, Viennese, and Turkish cooking and all the Dr. Oetker German cookbooks. If you are interested in foreign cookery, this is about as complete a selection as you could find.

LEROUX RECIPE OFFER / Dept. CFC
P.O. Box 956, Madison Square Station, New York, NY 10010

"Leroux Cocktail and Cooking Recipes," 50¢, published periodically, 20 pages, illustrated, color.

Leroux imports 44 different liqueurs, "from the people who brought you art, history, culture and sex"—Austria, Denmark, Italy, and France. This little booklet not only mixes Leroux liqueurs in cocktails but also with vegetables, fruits, desserts, cheese, meat, and bread—for example, green crème de menthe on peas, squash, and carrots; cherry liqueur with champagne; anisette in cheese sauce; absinthe with cooked beets, carrots, or celery. While the cocktail recipes are quite standard, the cooking suggestions are sufficiently different to appeal to inquisitive palates.

LONG-BELL DIVISION, INTERNATIONAL PAPER COMPANY
Dept. CFC
P.O. Box 8411, Portland, OR 97207

"Madame Chiang's Mandarin Recipe Book," free, 24 pages, black and white, sketch illustrations.

Hurrah for Long-Bell! They had the good sense to have a recipe booklet prepared for them by Cecilia Chiang, who runs one of San Francisco's best Chinese restaurants, The Mandarin in Ghirardelli Square, and has published a cookbook called *The Mandarin Way.* The connection between Chinese cooking and a paper company? The Long-Bell Division makes kitchen cabinets, but there is absolutely no huckstering for the product, so maybe this is just an image-building gesture. If so, it's a smart one. The booklet tells you how Mandarin or Northern Chinese cooking differs from the others, lists the few pieces of equipment you need and then goes straight into the recipes—three appetizers (including popular mu shui pork with pancakes), two soups, four vegetable dishes, and 17 seafood, poultry, and meat dishes. The sketches, uncredited, are elegant stylized pen-and-ink drawings of food and serving elements.

LONGPOND FARM, INC. / Dept. CFC
Box 58, Harvard, IL 60033

"Cooking with Herbs at Longpond Farm," $3.50, 96 pages.

A paperback cookbook by the owners of Longpond Farm, Eugene Dana and Glenn Allen, who say that despite a heavy work schedule they believe in making everything from scratch—though an occasional chicken or beef bouillon cube is considered permissible. The recipes, which range from a Turkish leek-and-rice appetizer which the authors suggest serving with quartered lemons on a bed of tarragon branches (provided you grow your own) to leg of lamb in an herbal marinade, are appetizing and not difficult. There are some interesting flavor combinations, such as pork tenderloin with rhubarb sauce, sweet potato salad with fresh sage, winter squash and oyster soup. The little tips scattered throughout the book are sensible and helpful. For instance, if you don't have a crock big enough to marinate the leg of lamb, put the lamb in a large plastic bag set in a bowl, pour in the marinade ingredients, fold over the end and secure with rubber bands, turn to mix contents, then marinate in a cool place or the refrigerator.

MAID OF SCANDINAVIA CO. / Dept. CFC
3244 Raleigh Avenue, Minneapolis, MN 55416

General catalog, $1, plus spring and winter supplements (25¢ each or free with an order from the catalog), published annually, 192 pages, illustrated, black and white, supplements 70 to 80 pages.

Ten pages of the catalogue are given over to a selection of books on various kinds of cooking, cake decorating, catering, and foreign cuisines. There are 10 diet cookbooks, including Carol Cutler's excellent *Haute Cuisine for Your Heart's Delight,* which takes the cholesterol out of classic recipes, and 7 books on bread making (a notable omission is *Beard on Bread*), but the majority are designed to appeal to the sweet-toothed.

McILHENNY COMPANY / Dept. CFC
Avery Island, LA 70513

"Back to Homemade Cooking," free, 14 pages, illustrated, black and white.

From the people who gave you Tabasco sauce comes this little booklet of recipes for soups, chili, bean, meat, and poultry dishes given in two

Lichee Chicken
Heat a wok over high temperature. When very hot, add 2 tablespoons sesame oil, 1 cup raw chicken, cut into bite-size pieces, and salt to taste. Toss and stir rapidly for 2 to 3 minutes, until chicken starts to brown. Add ¼ cup dry white wine and ¼ cup chicken stock. Toss and stir about 1 minute more. Then add 1 cup canned drained lichees and ⅓ cup chopped or finely sliced green pepper. Continue to toss and stir until heated through. Serve immediately.
—from "Madame Chiang's Mandarin Recipe Book"

Sketch from ''Madame Chiang's Mandarin Recipe Book''

Pork Tenderloin with Rhubarb Stuffing
Put 8 thin slices pork tenderloin between sheets of waxed paper and pound with a mallet until each slice measures 4" x 5" x ¼" or ½" thick. Mix together 2 cups fresh bread crumbs, 1 teaspoon powdered rosemary, 1 teaspoon powdered thyme, 1½ cups drained cooked rhubarb (reserve 1 cup juice for cooking), and salt and pepper to taste. Cover pork slices with this stuffing, roll up carefully, tucking in sides where necessary, and tie with string. Melt 2 tablespoons butter or margarine in a skillet and brown the rolls. Remove to a 6-to-8 cup casserole and preheat the oven to 350°. Deglaze the skillet with a little water, then add the rhubarb juice, ¼ cup water, and ½ cup sugar. Mix. Pour over rolls in casserole, cover, and bake 45 to 60 minutes or until tender. Serve sauce separately. Serves 4.
—from "Cooking with Herbs at Longpond Farm"

Glazed Ham au Rhum
Prepare a half ham of the ready-to-eat type for baking, by cutting off the rind and excess fat. Make a paste of 1 teaspoon dry mustard, 3 tablespoons orange marmalade, and about 2 tablespoons Myers's rum. Using shaker bottle, moisten ham all over with rum; then spread marmalade paste over fat side of ham. Slash the fat in diamonds or squares and stick a whole clove in each square. Bake ham in a 325° oven for about 1 hour or 10 minutes per pound.
—from Myers's Rum Recipe Booklet

ways—the traditional and the updated electric slow-cooker method. There's far too much use of canned soups, and beef Stroganoff hardly qualifies for the name, being cooked for 1 to 1½ hours the old way, 8 to 10 hours in the slow cooker (this, too, has a can of condensed soup) when the very essence of this famous recipe is that the beef is cut in thin strips, sautéed briefly until rare inside, and put in the sauce just long enough to reheat. Still, you may get some new ideas about how to use a slow cooker.

McKESSON WINES & LIQUORS / Dept. CFC
155 East 44th Street, New York, NY 10017

"Discover Gold," free, published periodically, 24 pages, illustrated, color.

This is a booklet on the uses of the Italian herb-flavored liqueur, Galliano. Mostly drinks but five desserts, including a very rich creamy Golden Dream pie in a graham-cracker crust and a fried shrimp recipe with Galliano in the batter, served with a sour cream and Galliano sauce.

THE MOTHER EARTH NEWS / Dept. CFC
P.O. Box 70, Hendersonville, NC 28739

"Mother's Bookshelf," free, published semiannually, 50 pages, illustrated, black and white.

"Mother's Bookshelf" lists books on gardening, do-it-yourself projects, camping, wild foods, and, of course, cooking and preserving. There are books on vegetarian cooking, on natural foods, including *Alice's Kitchen Country Cookbook* ($4.50) by Alice Okorn and *The Deaf Smith Country Cookbook* ($4.95), both soft cover, books on bread making, tofu, the cooking of the American Indians, grain cookery, sprout cookery, ice cream, honey and yogurt cookery, and lots of books on canning, freezing, preserving, and dehydrating vegetables, fruits, and herbs. You can also order the very useful handbook *Cheeses of the World* from the U.S. Department of Agriculture, a dictionary listing, analyzing, and describing over 400 cheeses (soft cover, $1.50).

MYERS'S RUM
SEAGRAM DISTILLERS COMPANY / Dept. CFC
375 Park Avenue, New York, NY 10022

"Myers's Rum Food and Drink Recipes," free, 34 pages, illustrated, color.

For once, there's no need to strain the culinary imagination, because Myers's—a dark, flavorful, full-bodied Jamaica rum—is excellent for cooking. The booklet is evenly divided between drinks and food, and the recipes are logical—rum omelet, rum in black bean soup, rum candied yams, rum pumpkin pie, cherries Jubilee.

NICHOLS GARDEN NURSERY / Dept. CFC
1190 North Pacific Highway, Albany, OR 97321

"Nichols Herb and Rare Seeds," free, published seasonally, 60 pages, illustrated, black and white.

Nichols has been in the seed and nursery business in Oregon's Willamette Valley for over 25 years. Their aim has always been to bring people closer to nature through gardening, so they have expanded their catalogue to include natural-food products and books on herbs, canning and preserving, and vegetarian cooking. The selection is wide-ranging, from Sturtevant's encyclopedic *Edible Plants of the World* (686 pages, soft cover, $5) to Anna Thomas' delightful paperback, *The Vegetarian Epicure* ($4.95) and Grace Chu's *The Pleasures of Chinese Cooking* (soft cover, $1.95). There's *The Soup Book* by Louis P. DeGouy, books on jams and jellies, dehydrating foods, a wild food cookbook and field guide, a soy bean cookbook, whole grains and honey cookbook, and lots more. If you are a believer in the natural way of life, there's a lot here to study.

NORTHWESTERN COFFEE MILLS / Dept. CFC
217 North Broadway, Milwaukee, WI 53202

Catalogue, free (25¢ donation accepted), published annually, 28 pages, illustrated, black and white.

A small but selective list of books from Northwestern Coffee Mills covers most of the foods they carry—tea, coffee, spices, nuts, cheese, and herbs. Some of the titles are *Coffee Cuisine* by Diane De Lorme, described as "a nice gift item to include with coffee products—many recipes for main dishes and desserts as well as beverages" ($3.50); a *Cheese Guide and Cookbook* by Chandonnet, covering all uses from appetizers to desserts ($3.95); *The Art of Cooking with Herbs and Spices* by Milo Miloradovich (Doubleday, hard cover, $6.95); Violet Schafer's *Teacraft* and *Herbcraft*, both soft cover ($3.95); and *Culpeper's Complete Herbal*, a large collection of herbal descriptions and remedies compiled by Nicholas Culpeper over 300 years ago, described as essential for the beginning herb library (hard cover, 430 pp., 398 herb illustrations, $8.95). There are two other recommended herb books: Joseph Meyer's *The Herbalist* and *A Modern Herbal* by M. Grieve. Various booklets are listed from the USDA, Brooklyn Botanical Gardens, the Pan American Coffee Bureau, the American Spice Trade Association, and others, priced from 50¢ to $2.25.

101 PRODUCTIONS / Dept. CFC
834 Mission Street, San Francisco, CA 94103

"101 Productions—Books/Kits Catalogue," 25¢, published seasonally, 24 pages, illustrated, color and black and white.

Some of the most intelligently conceived and attractively produced paperback cookbooks come from 101 Productions in San Francisco. They are easy to find on the West Coast, but not as well distributed in other parts of the country, so armed with their catalogue and order form you can spare yourself the search. There are about 30 cookbooks on their list (some also available in hard cover), so it isn't possible to list them all here. Some of the titles that may interest you are *One-Pot Meals, Complete Dinners from a Dutch Oven, Crock Pot, Pressure Cooker, Wok*, etc. by Margaret Gin, who also wrote their excellent *Regional Cooking of China* and, with Jana Allen, *Innards & Other Variety Meats*; Eva Zane's *Greek Cooking for the Gods* and *Middle Eastern Cookery*; *101 Secrets of Gourmet Chefs, Unusual Recipes from Famed California Restaurants* by Jacqueline Killeen; and *Fabulous Fiber Cookbook* by Jeanne Jones. Two offbeat titles are *Bread Sculpture: The Edible Art* by Ann Wiseman and *The Edible, Ornamental Garden* by John E. Bryan and Coralie Castle. *Pots & Pans Etc.* by Gertrude Harris is not a recipe book but invaluable if you are stocking a kitchen and want to know about the properties of different materials like enameled cast iron, copper, and stainless steel. The cookbooks are $4.95 in paperback, plus 75¢ for postage and handling; *Bread Sculpture* and *Pots & Pans Etc.* are $2.95, plus 75¢ for postage and handling. In the 101 Dining Out series there are guides to the best restaurants of San Francisco and northern California, the Pacific Northwest, Los Angeles and southern California, and Texas ($2.95 each). These make excellent small gifts for food-loving friends.

PALMER & LORD, LTD. / Dept. CFC
345 Underhill Blvd., Syosset, NY 11791

"53 ways to say I love you in Italian," free, 10 pages, illustrated, color.

More correctly, 53 ways to use Sambuca Romana Liqueur in cocktails, hors d'oeuvre, main and vegetable dishes, desserts, with coffee, in punches, even with tea. Sambuca, a popular Italian licorice liqueur that makes a tasty and potent after-dinner drink when chilled, is particularly suited to desserts and confections like chocolate mousse Romana or lady fingers spread with Sambuca, butter, and finely chopped almonds.

Paperback cookbooks from 101 Productions

Hasenpfeffer

Combine 1½ cups cold water, 1½ cups cider vinegar, 1 teaspoon whole cloves, 3 bay leaves, 2 teaspoons salt, ¼ teaspoon pepper, 2 teaspoons sugar, ⅛ teaspoon allspice, and 1 medium onion, sliced, in a large china bowl or crock. Add 2 to 3 pounds tender young rabbit, cut in pieces, and marinate for at least 12 hours, preferably 1 to 2 days. Remove rabbit and drain well. Coat rabbit pieces in flour and brown well in ¼ inch of hot butter or shortening in a heavy skillet. Remove excess fat and add strained marinating liquid. Cover and simmer 1 hour or until tender. Remove rabbit to a hot platter. Thicken the liquid for gravy with finely crushed ginger snaps. Serves 4 to 6.

—from Pel-Freez Rabbit Recipe Booklet

From "The Zucchini Cookbook"

MINUS MEAT

Quick and energy saving, stove-top cooking is gaining popularity. Versatile zucchini joins well with other vegetables and sauces in these meatless dishes.

ZUCCHINI STROGANOFF   serves 2

    1 large or 2 small zucchini
    1 bunch fresh spinach
    2 tomatoes
    2 tbsp. sour cream (more or less)
      Parmesan cheese
      olive oil
      garlic

Cut zucchini once lengthwise and slice thin. Dice tomatoes. Lightly saute zucchini and tomatoes in olive oil flavored with garlic. Add spinach and continue cooking, turning spinach constantly until it is reduced to manageable proportions. Lift spinach from pan with large serving spoons, leaving juice and as much of the tomato and squash as you can in skillet. Put spinach on plates. Stir sour cream into skillet mixture and when completely mixed pour over spinach. Sprinkle with Parmesan cheese.

PAPRIKAS WEISS IMPORTER / Dept. CFC
 1546 Second Avenue, New York, NY 10028

"Imported Foods and Cookware Catalogue," $1 for annual subscription, published four times a year, 66 pages, illustrated, black and white.

Paprikas Weiss's list of cookbooks is concentrated chiefly on foreign cooking. They list books on Polish, Viennese, Czechoslovak, German, Belgian, Israeli, Spanish, Mexican, Armenian, Greek, and Bohemian-American cooking, their own *Hungarian Cookery*, with more than 1,000 recipes ($6.95), and old favorites like *The New York Times Cook Book*.

PEL-FREEZ RABBIT MEAT, INC. / Dept. CFC
 P.O. Box 68, Rogers, AR 72756

"Pel-Freez Rabbit Recipes," free booklet.

More and more people are discovering how delicious domestic farm-raised rabbit meat is—plus it is high in protein and low in fat, cholesterol, and calories. Pel-Freez markets frozen rabbits, either whole or cut into serving pieces. You can buy a young rabbit, cut into 8 serving pieces, or half a mature rabbit, cut into 7 serving pieces. Young rabbit is tender enough to be treated like chicken and fried, sautéed, baked, or barbecued. Mature rabbit should be made into a stew or fricassee. Supermarket chains that carry Pel-Freez rabbits are A&P, First National, Star, Stop & Shop, and Food Marts, and some stores have frozen young rabbits that have not been cut up. The recipe booklet consists of 20 recipes, printed on the back and front of file-size cards, so you can slip them in your recipe box, all tested by *Good Housekeeping*. They range from recipes for fried rabbit to foreign dishes such as the German Hasenpfeffer (cooked with vinegar and spices and served with a sauce thickened with crushed gingersnaps) or a Hungarian rabbit with sour cream and mushrooms. Start with these, then look in French cookbooks and you'll find many more interesting ways to cook this delicate flavorful little animal.

PEPPERIDGE FARM MAIL ORDER CO., INC. / Dept. CFC
 Box 7000, Norwalk, CT 06856

"Gift Catalog," free, published periodically, 32 pages, illustrated, color.

Among the selected books is the original *Pepperidge Farm Cookbook* by Margaret Rudkin, the founder of Pepperidge Farm, with 500 recipes, many from antique volumes that were part of her private collection (440 pages, $9.95). *The Pepperidge Farm Baking Book* has specially selected recipes by Margaret Rudkin from breads to pies, cakes and cookies (150 pages, $7.95). *Ena Baxter's Scottish Cookbook* is a gastronomic travelogue with recipes for Scottish foods with names like Tattie Drottle, Tipsy Laird, and Auld Man's Milk, (96 pages, soft cover, $3.95). Two other books of interest are *The "Compleat" Blueberry Cookbook* by Elizabeth Barton, with 130 easy-to-follow, explicit recipes (156 pages, $7.95), and *The Vermont Maple Sugar Cookbook*, edited by Reginald L. Muir (192 pages, $6.95).

PLANNED PARENTHOOD OF SANTA CRUZ COUNTY
 Dept. CFC
 421 Ocean Street, Santa Cruz, CA 95060

"The Zucchini Cookbook," $2.25, 44 pages, illustrated.

Everything you might want to know about zucchini (the name means "little squash" in Italian), one of the most bountiful of the garden vegetables. Two plants produce enough for an average family. With four plants you give a lot away, unless you work your way through the recipes in this charming little cookbook. There's Greek tourlou, Italian frittata, French ratatouille, and all kinds of appetizers, breads, dips, pickles, relishes, salads, and soups. The big yellow blossoms taste delicious dipped in batter and deep-fried or made into a soup, but pick only the long-stemmed male blossoms (the females produce the zucchini) and leave a few around for pollination. One of the more unusual recipes is for a moist zucchini cake (as in carrot cake, the flavor of the vegetable is almost undetectable). At only 25 calories a cup, zucchini is excellent for low-calorie meatless and inexpensive main dishes. The fact that this book, which began as a money-raising project in 1973, is now in its third printing proves there's a vogue for zucchini cookery these days. Nice illustrations, too.

POLISH HAM QUICK 'N EASY RECIPES / Dept. CFC
Box 1004, Fleetwood, Mount Vernon, NY 10552

"Polish Ham Quick 'N Easy Recipes," free, 36 pages, illustrated, color.

The title of the booklet tells the story. The 80 recipes, which are credited on the cover as having been personally selected by Peg Bracken, author of the *I Hate to Cook Book*, are mostly the kind you can throw together without undue effort if you happen to have a canned ham on hand, such as ham with macaroni and cheese, ham loaf, ham casseroles, ham salads, and baked ham slices.

RICE COUNCIL OF AMERICA / Dept. CFC
P.O. Box 22802, Houston, TX 77027

"Man-pleasing Recipes," 25¢, 16 pages, illustrated, color.

Don't take the title too seriously—the premise is that no man likes to eat the same thing every night, so you should add zest to your menus by cooking up some rice dishes for him. The color pictures and recipes are on the home-economist level. One wishes that some effort had been made to present just one or two of the marvelous rice dishes from other countries, such as an Indonesian nasi goreng, or a Persian chello, or even a less well-known version of paella. Still, you may get an idea or two about using rice that may not have occurred to you.

RODALE PRESS BOOK DIVISION / Dept. CFC
Emmaus, PA 18049

Catalog information not supplied.

Rodale Press publishes *Organic Gardening and Farming*, and the editors have prepared a book called *Stocking Up—How to Preserve the Foods You Grow Naturally*, $8.95 plus postage and handling, which they will send on a free 15-day trial offer. Subjects covered are canning, freezing, drying, brining, jellying, juicing, cheesing, and storing, and there are more than 200 old-time natural recipes for vinegar, scrapple, sausage and head cheese, fruit leather, chutneys and relishes, liverwurst, syrups, all kinds of preserves, cheese, soups, sauces, and stuffings. One chapter is on home butchering and dressing meats and poultry.

Another useful book is *The Organic Directory* by the editors of *Organic Gardening and Farming* and *Prevention* magazines ($2.95). Basically, it is an excellent idea to list natural food, organic food co-ops and gardening clubs and distributors of natural vitamins and packaged foods, all organized by state, but there is a problem. You'll find if you write to them, as we did, that many have gone out of business since the directory came out. Still, there are so many hundreds of sources here that if you are mainly interested in who grows vegetables and fruits organically, or where to find a co-op in your area, this is a good place to look. They also list cities with farmers' markets (this, too, is a bit dated, being based on a 1972 survey of Chambers of Commerce) and have chapters on how to start a food co-op, what you should know about buying eggs, vegetable oils (with an explanation of terms such as hydrogenated, cold-pressed, solvent extracted), beef, and cereals.

ROQUEFORT ASSOCIATION, INC. / Dept. CFC
41 East 42nd Street, New York, NY 10017

"Roquefort Chefmanship Recipes," free, 40 pages, illustrated, color.

The Roquefort Association is ever-anxious to make you aware of the fact that true Roquefort can come only from France and must bear the red sheep seal. Who can blame them? The number of "roquefort" salad dressings made with any old blue must be legion. With the recipes are bits of background information about what makes Roquefort unique,

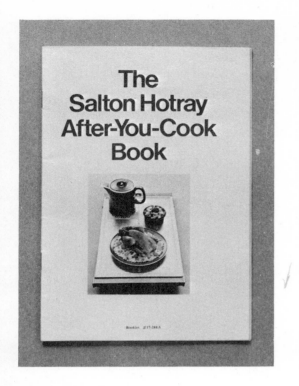

how to buy, store, and serve it, and so on. The recipes themselves are above average for an industry booklet (not a drop of canned soup, but there is one heretical recipe using garlic salt). Most recipes come from *Gourmet* magazine or chefs in well-known hotels and country clubs, who obviously entered a Roquefort competition. Worth sending for.

SAHADI IMPORTING CO., INC. / Dept. CFC
    187 Atlantic Avenue, Brooklyn, NY 11201

"The Silent Salesman," free, published biannually, 24 pages, illustrated, black and white.

Sahadi is a leading importer, wholesaler, and retailer of Middle East foods, and, as you might expect, they have cookbooks, too. There's *The Art of Syrian Cookery* and four other Arts (Greek, Armenian, Turkish, and Indian), *Lebanese Cuisine* and one of our favorites, *Food from the Arab World*, published in Beirut in English in hard cover ($6.50) or paper ($2.50). The only omission, and it is a regrettable one, is Claudia Roden's excellent book on Middle East food.

SALTON, INC. / Dept. CFC
    1260 Zerega Avenue, Bronx, NY 10462

"The Salton Hotray After-you-Cook Book," 25¢, 32 pages, illustrated, color.

Most of the booklet (some 21 pages) is devoted to color pictures and chatty descriptions of the Salton products—hotray, bun warmer, egg cooker, ice-cream machine, coffee grinder and coffee extractor, yogurt maker, and hot party server (plate-size hot tray). One wonders why the peanut-butter machine didn't make it. The final pages (22 through 31) have a selection of good if fairly standard recipes, some compiled by *Gourmet* magazine; others from industry sources such as the Poultry & Egg National Board and the Pan-American Coffee Bureau; others from cookbooks on ice cream, yogurt, and pizza. Not all of them require you to keep the food hot after you've cooked it, so the title of the booklet is a wee bit misleading. However, the recipes are well chosen, as you might expect from Salton, whose products are always reliable and well designed.

SCHAPIRA COFFEE CO. / Dept. CFC
    117 West 10th Street, New York, NY 10011

"The Book of Coffee and Tea," 328 pages with 25 line drawings, 11 maps, $8.95, plus $1 for postage and handling.

Three generations of Schapiras have run a coffee and tea business in New York since 1903, and the family experience and expertise have brewed *The Book of Coffee and Tea*, by Joel, David, and Karl Schapira, who will autograph request copies ordered from them. The book covers the history and mythology of coffee and tea, their cultivation and manufacture, the varieties and methods of preparation, the characteristics and virtues of herbal teas, plus recipes and a shopping guide. This is a consumer's bible, a full treatment of a much misunderstood subject. If you love good coffee and tea, you'll like this book.

SLEEPY HOLLOW GIFTS / Dept. CFC
    6651 Arlington Blvd., Falls Church, VA 22042

Catalogue, free, 96 pages, published seasonally, illustrated, black and white, some color.

For the cook or cookbook collector, this catalogue has some unusual books. *Breads of Many Lands*, by Florence Laffal (soft cover, $4.95), has recipes for American Indian bread, Swedish vetebrod, breads from Armenia and Tibet. *The Bourbon Cookbook*, by Tom Hoge (hardbound, $6.95), has over 400 recipes for using our native American whiskey to prepare such dishes as Bourbonburgers with confetti rice, Lobster au Whiskey, all-purpose barbecue sauce, and Yuletide cookies. *The Deep South Natural Foods Cookbook* (hard cover, $6.95), draws on traditional recipes of the South taken from old diaries, newspapers, recollections of

*

When flaming foods with spirits, warm the liquor first or it will not ignite (it's the fumes, rather than the alcohol, that light). Heat slightly in a small metal pan or pour into the hot cooking pan, ignite with a long kitchen match.

*

women of an earlier era. All types of dishes are included: breads, main dishes, stews, soups, desserts, drinks, and punches. There is also a menu guide and a chapter of Christmas and holiday meals.

STA-WEL NUTRITION CENTERS, INC. / Dept. CFC
16 West 40th Street, New York, NY 10018

"Food for Better Living," 50¢, no regular publication date, 40 pages, black and white.

Sta-Wel has a big list of diet cookbooks on such subjects as cooking for ulcer diets, salt-free diets, low-calorie diets, diabetics, allergies—even one called *How to Eat Your Way Back to a Healthy Head of Hair*. There's also *The Yogurt Cookbook* by Olga Smetinoff and *The New York Times Natural Foods Cookbook* by Jean Hewitt. As the catalogue has not been reprinted since 1973, you should request current prices on anything that interests you.

STOW-A-WAY INDUSTRIES, INC. / Dept. CFC
166 Cushing Highway, Cohasset, MA 02025

"Freeze-dried Food, Dehydrated Food and Lightweight Equipment Guide," free, published annually, 46 pages, black and white.

The guide has a list of books on the outdoor life and some cookbooks. There's *Living Off the Country, Wilderness Cookery*, and *Feasting Free on Wild Edibles* by B. Angier; *Food for Knapsackers* by H. Bunnelle; *Cooking for Camp & Trail* by H. Bunnelle and Shirley Sarvis; and a couple of others that would probably prove helpful: *How to Survive with Sprouting* and *Just Add Water*. The weight of each book is included with the price, in case you plan on packing it in a knapsack.

SWITZERLAND CHEESE ASSOCIATION / Dept. CFC
444 Madison Avenue, New York, NY 10022

"La Fondue—authentic cheese fondue recipes from Switzerland," free, 8 pages, illustrated, color and black and white.

A neat and to-the-point booklet that tells you everything you need to know about making fondue—the type of cheese to select, the necessary equipment (as they point out, the caquelon, or earthenware fondue pot, is not the same as the metal pots sold for fondue bourguignonne or beef fondue, which is cooked in oil and butter), how to remedy a fondue that curdles, and so on. Naturally, you get a spelled-out recipe, plus variations using different cheeses, also a wineless fondue, a combination of tomato purée and cheese with a touch of heavy cream (the tomatoes supply the acidity needed for the smooth consistency), and a selection of optional seasonings and flavorings and appropriate wines to drink with the fondue.

TAYLOR & NG / Dept. CFC
P.O. Box 200, Brisbane, CA 95005

Taylor & Ng is a San Francisco design and merchandising business which manufactures, wholesales, and retails housewares and publishes books designed to relate to and complement their cookware and table accessories. Their well-produced, soft-cover Yerba Buena Press cookbooks (many of them delightfully illustrated by Win Ng) are sold directly from Taylor & Ng for $3.95 each plus 75¢ for postage and handling. The self-explanatory titles are *Wokcraft, Ricecraft, Teacraft, Breadcraft, Eggcraft, Herbcraft, Chinese Village Cookbook*, and *Coffee*.

VERMONT GENERAL STORE & GRIST MILL, INC. / Dept. CFC
Woodstock, VT 05091

Catalogue, 50¢, with recipe booklet, 6 pages, illustrated, black and white.

The catalogue lists five quality paperbacks chosen by the owners of the Vermont General Store & Grist Mill because they explore subjects dear to their hearts. One is *Out of Vermont Kitchens*, compiled by the ladies of St. Paul's Church in Burlington, facsimiles of handwritten Vermont

3. RICECRAFT: Authoress Margaret Gin delves into the fact, fiction, and fancy of rice. A collection of inventive recipes takes full advantage of the international versatility of rice. Illustrated by Win Ng. 120 pages. (3/4 lb.)

4. TEACRAFT: New, from Yerba Buena, another craft compendium. This time tea, its multiplicity of uses and varieties, how to test and taste, beautifully illustrated by Win Ng. Written by Charles & Violet Schafer. (3/4 lb.)

Yerba Buena Press cookbooks, from Taylor & Ng

recipes ($4.95); the others are *The Sprouter's Cookbook* and *The Home Gardener's Cookbook* by Marjorie Page Blanchard and two by Phyllis Hobson: *Making Homemade Cheeses and Butter* and *Home Drying Vegetables, Fruits and Herbs* ($2.95 each for these). For shipping and handling, there's a charge of 75¢ with the total book order.

WESTON BOWL MILL / Dept. CFC
Main Street, Weston, VT 05161

"Catalogue of the Weston Bowl Mill," 25¢, published annually, 56 pages, illustrated, black and white.

Tucked away among the forest of woodenware made, sold, and imported by Weston Bowl Mill are a few cookbooks, some of which you are not likely to find in the stores. One is the 48-page soft-cover *Vermont Cookbook*, now in its 12th edition, with hundreds of authentic tried-and-true recipes from Vermont cooks, just $1 ppd. Then there's *The Old Cook's Almanac* of recipes, rules, and methods compiled by Beatrice Vaughan from her collection of antique handwritten cookbooks ($4.50 ppd.). *The Venison Book* by Audrey Alley Gorton has 78 pages on dressing, cutting up, and cooking deer ($3.35 ppd.). *A Garden of Herbs* by Eleanor Sinclair Rohde is about making teas, syrups, conserves, pies, wines, perfumes, candied flowers and leaves, using wild and garden herbs. Most of the recipes are from old English herbals, plus others from the herbalist author (paperbound, 300 pages, $3.15 ppd.).

JULIUS WILE SONS & CO., INC. / Dept. CFC
320 Park Avenue, New York, NY 10022

"Pernod: a new taste for a new life style" and "Finish dinner with a Flourish," both free, 12 pages, illustrated, the latter with color.

Two modest little booklets on popular French drinks—anise-flavor Pernod, Benedictine, and B and B (brandy and Benedictine). The Benedictine booklet has nothing much in the way of recipes, but there are about a dozen for Pernod, which is more suitable for cooking, though to use it in salad dressing is questionable.

WILLIAMS-SONOMA / Dept. CFC
576 Sutter Street, San Francisco, CA 94102

"A Catalog for Cooks," $1, published summer and fall, plus "January Sale/New Kitchen Ideas," both 26 pages, illustrated, color.

a catalog for cooks
summer 1976

You'll always find in the Williams-Sonoma catalogues a sampling of the very complete selection of cookbooks they sell in their three California stores (San Francisco, Palo Alto, and Beverly Hills). The catalogue we have lists Elizabeth David's delightful *Summer Cooking* (paperback, $2.95; she is England's foremost cookery writer and a pleasure to read); Helen Corbitt *Cooks for Looks*, one of the most imaginative and least boring of all diet cookbooks from recipes the author devised for The Greenhouse, the famous and expensive Neiman-Marcus beauty spa ($5.95); Anna Thomas' *The Vegetarian Epicure*, a most agreeable little paperback ($4.95); and another excellent book on vegetable cookery, now in paperback, *Cooking with Vegetables* by botanist-cook Alex Hawkes ($4.95). This one includes a lot of offbeat vegetables you aren't likely to encounter in other books.

See Appendix, page 239, for additional sources not included here.

APPENDIX

The companies listed here are additional mail-order sources we were unable to include in the main sections of the book. If no catalogue or price list is mentioned, it is because the companies mainly advertise in magazines and sell direct. Write to them for information and latest prices.

COFFEE AND TEA

American Tea, Coffee & Spice Co.,
Dept. CFC
1511 Champa Street
Denver, CO 80202
Price list.

Early Seasons Teas, Dept. CFC
1090 Sansome Street
San Francisco, CA 94111
Japanese green tea (Ohashiri Shincha) in 4-oz. gift box.

East India Tea & Coffee, Ltd. (S. Poteet),
Dept. CFC
1483 Third Street
San Francisco, CA 94107
Catalogue, free.

House of Yemen, Dept. CFC
370 Third Avenue
New York, NY 10016
Price list. Coffee, tea, dried fruit.

La Norma Coffee Mills, Inc., Dept. CFC
4416 N. Hubert Avenue
Tampa, FL 33614
Brochure, free. Coffees, coffee makers, and grinders.

Herbal Teas

Borchelt Herb Gardens, Dept. CFC
474 Carriage Shop Road
East Falmouth, MA 02536
Price list, cost of stamp plus 10¢ for handling.

Cottage Herb Farm Shop, Dept. CFC
311 State Street
Albany, NY 12210
Catalogue, 25¢.

For Your Health, Dept. CFC
1136 Eglinton Avenue West
Toronto, Ontario
Canada M6C2E2
Catalogue, 50¢.

Licata's California Nutrition Centers,
Dept. CFC
129 N. Anaheim Blvd.
Anaheim, CA 92805
Catalogue, 25¢.

Magic Garden Herb Co., Dept. CFC
P.O. Box 332
Fairfax, CA 94930
Brochure, 25¢.

Wide World of Herbs, Ltd., Dept. CFC
11 St. Catherine Street East
Montreal, PQ
Canada H2X 1K3
Price list, $1, refundable with purchase.

CHEESE AND BREAD

The Bennburry Shop, Dept. CFC
Rte. 7
Shaftesbury, VT 05262
Vermont cheddar cheese and other cheeses, canned New England foods, smoked hams and bacon, honey, pickles, maple syrup, sugar, and candies.

Cheesers Palace, Dept. CFC
1405 Maple Avenue
Zanesville, OH 43701
Cheddar, Colby, Swiss, and other cheeses.

The Cheese Shop, Dept. CFC
147 Main Street
Waterville, ME 04901
Catalogue, free. Individually designed cheese boxes, coffee, and other foods.

Diamond Dairy Goat Farm, Dept. CFC
Route 2
Portage, WI 53901
Price list. Goat cheese.

Sherry Dairy, Ltd., Dept. CFC
Milladore, WI 54454
Wisconsin Colby, Monterey Jack, mild cheddar.

Star Valley, Dept. CFC
Thayne, WY 83127
Free brochure, recipes. Swiss cheese.

Swiss Cheese Shops, Inc., Dept. CFC
Box 429
Monroe, WI 53566
Catalogue, free. Wisconsin cheese and sausage. Gift packs.

MEAT, FOWL, AND SEAFOOD

Amana Society Meat Shop, Dept. CFC
Amana, IA 52203
Catalogue, free. Smoked meats, cheddar cheese. Gift packages.

The Bruss Co., Dept. CFC
3548 North Kostner Avenue
Chicago, IL 60641
Color catalogue, free. Prime steaks.

Clambake International, Inc., Dept. CFC
678 Massachusetts Avenue, Suite 704
Cambridge, MA 02139
Brochure, free. Lobsters, steamer clams, chowders, and bisques.

Cotuit Oyster Co., Dept. CFC
P.O. Box 563
Little River Road
Cotuit, MA 02635
Cape Cod Cotuit oysters shipped fresh in shell.

Euro-Veal Farms, Inc., Dept. CFC
P.O. Box 156
Provimi Road
Watertown, WI 53094
Color brochure, free. Milk-fed veal.

The Forsts, Dept. CFC
Kingston, NY 12401
Price list, free. Smoked meats and birds, smoked sausage, steaks, McIntosh apples. Gift packages.

Gaspar's Linguica Co., Inc., Dept. CFC
540 Dartmouth Street
So. Dartmouth, MA 02748
Portuguese-style linguica (smoked spiced pork sausage).

Habberset, Dept. CFC
Media, PA 19063
Sausage and scrapple.

The House of Kilfenora, Dept. CFC
East Kingston, NH 03827
Brochure, free. Irish smoked salmon.

Imex Caviar, Ltd., Dept. CFC
855 Sixth Avenue
New York, NY 10001
Fresh Iranian Beluga caviar.

Nodine's Smokehouse, Dept. CFC
Goshen, CT 06756
Price list, free. Smoked ham, fowl, eel, cheese, beef jerky, corned, roast, and chipped beef, some bacon and hot dogs with no preservatives.

Ozark Mountain Smokehouse, Inc.,
Dept. CFC
P.O. Box 37
Farmington, AR 72730
Catalogue, free. Ham, bacon, smoked sausage, smoked turkey.

Schaller & Weber, Inc., Dept. CFC
1654 Second Avenue
New York, NY 10028
Brochure, free. Smoked bacon, Westphalian and Black Forest style hams, German sausages.

The Smithfield Ham and Products Co.,
Inc., Dept. CFC
Smithfield, VA 23430
Brochures and price list, free. Smithfield hams, bacon, and packaged meat products. Gift packages.

Snowhill Farm, Dept. CFC
R.D. 4
Coatesville, PA 19320
Price list, free. Frozen Black Angus beef and veal. Direct sales.

Stock Yards Packing Co., Dept. CFC
340 N. Oakley Blvd.
Chicago, IL 60612
Prime steaks, chopped beef, chicken Kiev.

Thalhimers Fine Food Shop, Dept. CFC
Richmond, VA 23219
Virginia hams.

United American Food Processors
Gourmet Food Division, Suite 118,
Dept. CFC
15 Spinning Wheel Road
Hinsdale, IL 60521
Catalogue, free. Prime steaks.

Voecks Brothers Finer Foods, Dept. CFC
103 E. Kimberly Avenue
Kimberly, WI 54136
Wisconsin hams, slab bacon, sausage, cheese.

Wickford Shellfish Company, Dept. CFC
67 Esmond Avenue
Wickford, RI 02852
*Brochure, free. Rhode Island-style clambake,
lobster, clams, fish.*

Wolf's Neck Farm, Inc., Dept. CFC
R.R. 1, Box 71
Freeport, ME 04032
Organic beef.

FRUITS AND NUTS

All Organics, Inc., Dept. CFC
15870 S.W. 216th Street
Miami, FL 33170
*Brochure, free. Organically grown mangoes
and avocados.*

Apricot Farm, Dept. CFC
2620 Buena Vista Road
Hollister, CA 95023
Dried fruits and almonds.

Blue Anchor, Inc., Dept. CFC
P.O. Box 15498
Sacramento, CA 95813
*Gift fruit catalogue, free. Fresh fruits (citrus,
pears, grapes, apples, kiwi, papayas,
avocados).*

Tom Byrd Gift Apples, Dept. CFC
P.O. Box 339
Timberville, VA 22853
*Color pamphlet, free. Royal Red Delicious
apples from the Shenandoah Valley,
gift-boxed.*

Citrus Corral Corporation, Dept. CFC
1175 First Street South
P.O. Drawer 1939
Winter Haven, FL 33880
Brochure, free. Indian River citrus fruits.

Comparte's of California, Dept. CFC
Brentwood County Mart
225 26th Street
Santa Monica, CA 90402
*Price list, free. Dried and stuffed fruits, no
preservatives.*

T.M. Duché Nut Co., Dept. CFC
P.O. Box 845
Orland, CA 95963
*California almonds, smoked, barbecued,
blanched, natural.*

Forty Acres Ranch, Dept. CFC
P.O. Box Y
Lakeland, FL 33602
Brochure, free. Oranges and grapefruit.

Gift Foods of California, Dept. CFC
1011 Buenos Avenue, Suite D
San Diego, CA 92110
Avocados.

Harvey's Groves, Dept. CFC
Box 430
Cocoa, FL 32922
*Catalogue, free. Citrus fruits, jellies, candy.
Gift packages.*

Laura Howard, Dept. CFC
Greensboro, VT 05841
*Vermont butternuts, burlap-bagged, with
recipes.*

King Groves Ltd., Gift Center, Dept. CFC
P.O. Box 2025
Sandusky, OH 44870
California navel oranges.

Koinonia Partners, Inc., Dept. CFC
Rt. 1
Americus, GA 31709
*Catalogue, free. Pecans and peanut products,
fruitcake, candy.*

Henry Macomb's Gift Fruit Inc., Dept.
CFC
Box 248
Los Fresnos, TX 78566
*Brochure, free. Ruby red grapefruit, citrus
jellies, orange blossom honey.*

The Packing Shed, Dept. CFC
P.O. Box 11
Weyers Cave, VA 24486
*Brochure, free. Home-cooked salted peanuts,
country hams.*

Pinnacle Orchards, Dept. CFC
416 Fir Street
Medford, OR 97501
*Comice pears from the Rogue River Valley,
individually wrapped.*

Pittman & Davis, Inc., Dept. CFC
823 N. Exp.
Harlingen, TX 78550
*Illustrated folder, free. Texas red grapefruit,
other citrus fruits, pecans, honey,
fruitcake, cheese.*

Plantation Acres, Dept. CFC
515 Plantation Road
Merritt Island, FL 32952
Lichee nuts.

Poinsettia Groves, Dept. CFC
Box 1388D
Vero Beach, FL 32960
*Illustrated color brochure, free. Navel oranges
and grapefruit.*

Priester's Pecans, Dept. CFC
227 Old Fort Drive
Fort Deposit, AL 36032
*Catalogue, free. Pecans, pecan candies,
fruitcake, ham, bacon, sausage, smoked
turkey.*

Sunnyland Farms, Inc., Dept. CFC
Route 1, Box 785
Albany, GA 31705
Catalogue, free. Gift tins and boxes of nuts.

Sunshine Groves, Dept. CFC
Box 119
Miami, FL 33139
*Mangoes shipped during the season
(spring/early summer).*

H. M. Thames Pecan Co., Inc., Dept. CFC
P.O. Box 2206
Mobile, AL 36601
Shelled pecans.

Timbercrest Farms, Dept. CFC
4791 Dry Creek Road
Healdsburg, CA 95448
*Price list, free. Sixteen varieties of dried fruit,
in bulk, consumer and gift packages.*

Village Orange Crate, Dept. CFC
121 Harrison Street
Cocoa Village, FL 32922
*Catalogue, 25¢. Tropical and citrus fruits,
frozen Florida seafood, tropical
preserves, candies.*

Young Pecan Sales Corp., Dept. CFC
P.O. Box 5779
Florence, SC 29501
Price list, free. Pecans, fruitcake.

THINGS SWEET, SOUR, SPICY, AND SAVORY

The Appleyard Corporation, Dept. CFC
Maple Corner
Calais, VT 05648
*Catalogue, free. Handmade chutney,
conserves, jellies, apple cider, maple
syrup, Vermont cheese, cereals.*

Alaskan Gourmet, Dept. CFC
P.O. Box 6733
Anchorage, AK 99502
*Brochure and price list, free. Alaskan wild
berry jellies. Smoked salmon.*

Arnaud's Restaurant—Attention Mrs.
Pauline Larré, Dept. CFC
811 Bienville Street
New Orleans, LA 70112
*Creole-style remoulade sauce from this famous
New Orleans restaurant.*

Berliner's Farm Stand, Dept. CFC
18741 Considine Drive
Brookeville, MD 20729
Bouquets garnis in muslin bags.

Big Red Barn, Dept. CFC
Rte. 5
Bellows Falls, VT 05101
*Booklet. Send stamped, self-addressed
envelope. Vermont maple and apple
syrups, honey, cheese, and other products.*

L.A. Champon & Co., Dept. CFC
70 Hudson Street
Hoboken, NJ 07652
Vanilla beans from Madagascar.

Del Norte Enterprises, Dept. CFC
P.O. Box 706
Salinas, CA 93901
Marinated artichokes in jars.

The Dickinson Family, Dept. CFC
7325 S.W. Bonita Road
Tigard, OR 97223
*Pacific Northwest jams, jellies, and syrups,
made in small batches.*

Estus, Dept. CFC
2186 San Pasqual Street
Pasadena, CA 91107
*Freeze-dried green peppercorns, chives,
tarragon. Flavored Dijon mustard.*

Franjoh Cellars, Dept. CFC
P.O. Box 7462
Stockton, CA 95207
*Brochure, free. The Working Vinegar Barrel,
oak cask with vinegar mother and starter
supply to convert wine into vinegar.*

John Harman's Country Store, Dept. CFC
Sugar Hill, NH 03585
Maple syrup, honey, preserves, aged cheddar.

Morning Fresh Herb Cottage, Dept. CFC
Miller Place, NY 11764
Blends of salad herbs and spices.

Naples Imports, Dept. CFC
P.O. Box 7533
Naples, FL 33940
*Bouquets garnis in individual muslin bags, 2 4
to a package. Modular wine racks of steel
and stained wood.*
Ocean Spray Cranberry House, Dept. CFC
R.F.D 3
Buzzards Bay, MA 02532
*Catalogue, free. Blends of cranberry jams and
jellies, cranberry fruit nut bread.*
Shoffeitt Products Corp., Dept. CFC
420 Hudson Street
Healdsburg, CA 95448
*Brochure, free. Seasonings, salad dressings,
dip mixes. Gift packages.*
Sunshine Groves, Inc., Dept. CFC
Box 119
Miami, FL 33139
Orange blossom honey.
R.B. Swan & Son, Dept. CFC
25 Prospect Street
Brewer, ME 04412
*Wild blueberry, wild raspberry, and
wildflower honeys in 6-lb. plastic
containers.*
Wray & Turnbull, Ltd., Dept. CFC
232 Madison Avenue
New York, NY 10016
*Outerbridge's Original Sherry Peppers Sauce
in 5-oz. shaker bottle or classic cruet.*

CAKES, COOKIES, CANDIES

Bailey's of Boston, Inc., Dept. CFC
26 Temple Place
Boston, MA 02111
*Brochure and price list, free. Handmade
candies.*
Butterfield Farms, Inc., Dept. CFC
330 Washington St., Suite 308
Marina del Rey, CA 90291
*Brochure and price list, free. Fruitcake,
cookies, cheeses, nuts.*
Byrd Cookie Company, Dept. CFC
P.O. Box 13086
Savannah, GA 31406
*Price list, free. Benne candy, wafers, cookies,
cocktail snacks.*
Colonial Candy, Dept. CFC
Building 18, Bomarc Road
Bangor, ME 04401
*Old-fashioned molasses kisses, Bangor taffy,
peanut-butter fudge.*
Community Bakeries, Dept. CFC
4501 W. Fullerton Avenue
Chicago, IL 60639
Homemade fruitcakes, 2 lbs. and 4 lbs.
Estee Candy Co., Inc., Dept. CFC
169 Lackawanna Avenue
Parsippany, NJ 07054
Catalogue, free. Dietetic candies and cookies.
Findley's Fabulous Fudge, Dept. CFC
1035 Geary Street
San Francisco, CA 94109
Homemade chocolate fudge.
Flowers Baking Company, Dept. CFC
P.O. Box 4395
Spartanburg, SC 29303
*Merrily Plantation fruitcake, 3-lb. ring or
1 ¾-lb. bar.*

Haven's Candy Kitchen, Dept. CFC
542 Forest Avenue
Portland, ME 04101
*Brochure, free. Candies (creams, caramels,
chocolate-covered nougat).*
Kron Chocolatier, Dept. CFC
764 Madison Avenue
New York, NY 10021
*Dark, semisweet 2-lb. chocolate brick for
cooking or eating.*
Leckerli-Huus, Dept. CFC
Gerbergasse 57
CH-4001 Basel, Switzerland
*Leaflet, free. Basler Leckerli honey cookies in
gift boxes.*
The Little Candy House, Dept. CFC
Gumdrop Square
Stockbridge, MA 01262
*Edible Hansel and Gretel candy cottage kit
with 3 pounds of candies, house form,
and directions.*
Mountain Dew Sassafras Products,
Dept. CFC
Cotter, AR 72626
*Price list, free. Old-fashioned candies,
sorghum molasses, and other syrups.*
Scottie's, Dept. CFC
20 Main Street
Granville, NY 12832
Southern-style fruitcake.

GROWING THINGS

Mr. Artichoke, Dept. CFC
11000 Blackie Road, Dept. OP
Castroville, CA 95012
*Brochure, free. Fresh and marinated
artichokes.*
Off The Beaten Path, Dept. CFC
P.O. Box 324
Southport, CT 06490
*Garden-by-Number herb kit with pattern,
seeds, stakes, booklet.*
The Wollersheim Winery, Dept. CFC
Highway 188
Prairie du Sac, WI 53578
Catalogue, 25¢. Winemaking supplies, cheese.

**Seed companies offering annual
catalogues, free.**

D.V. Burrell Seed Growers Co., Dept. CFC
P.O. Box 150
Rocky Ford, CO 81067
DeGiorgi Company, Inc., Dept. CFC
P.O. Box 413
Council Bluffs, IA 51501
Farmer Seed & Nursery Co., Dept. CFC
Faribault, MN 55021
The Charles C. Hart Seed Company,
Dept. CFC
Main and Hart Streets
Wethersfield, CT 06109
J.W. Jung Seed Co., Dept. CFC
Randolph, WI 53956
Mellinger's, Inc., Dept. CFC
2310 W. South Range Road
North Lima, OH 44452
L.L. Olds Seed Co., Dept. CFC
Box 7790
Madison, WI 53707

Seedway, Inc., Dept. CFC
Hall, NY 14463
R.H. Shumway Seedsman, Dept. CFC
628 Cedar Street
Rockford, IL 61101
Stern's Nurseries, Inc., Dept. CFC
Geneva, NY 14456
Stokes Seeds, Inc., Dept. CFC
737 Main Street, Box 548
Buffalo, NY 14240
Thompson & Morgan, Inc., Dept. CFC
401 Kennedy Blvd.
Somerdale, NJ 08083
Van Bourgondien Bros., Dept. CFC
245 Farmingdale Road, Box A
Babylon, NY 11702

NATURAL FOODS AND GRAINS

Belmont Products, Inc., Dept. CFC
105 First Avenue South
Aitkin, MN 56431
Wild rice, free recipe booklet.
Black Duck Company, Dept. CFC
2453 University Avenue
St. Paul, MN 55114
*Wild rice by the pound or case (24 ½-lb. bags),
recipes.*
Conrad Rice Mill, Dept. CFC
P.O. Box 296A
New Iberia, LA 70560
*Wild-pecan long-grain rice by the pound,
recipes.*
L & L Health Foods Co., Dept. CFC
Rt. 1, Box 197
Fairview, OK 73737
*Price list, free. Natural foods—flours, grains,
nuts, dried fruits, seeds.*
Moose Lake Wild Rice Distributing Co.,
Dept. CFC
Box 325
Deer River, MN 56636
Large-grain wild rice, recipes.

FOREIGN AND REGIONAL
SPECIALTIES

Bando Trading Company, Dept. CFC
2126 Murray Avenue
Pittsburgh, PA 15217
*Catalogue, free. Oriental foods—Chinese,
Japanese, Korean, Vietnamese, Thai,
Philippine.*
Harold's Cabin, Dept. CFC
P.O. Box 2365
Charleston, SC 29403
*Charleston specialties—benne cookies, she crab
soup, artichoke relish, apricot and peach
leather.*
The Hollinda Company, Dept. CFC
9544 Las Tunas Drive
Temple City, CA 91780
Price list, free. Dutch and Indonesian foods.
M.V. Wine Company, Dept. CFC
576 Folsom Street
San Francisco, CA 94105
*Fresh black truffles for the Christmas season,
flown from Paris, sold in ½-oz. units
with 1 ½-oz. minimum, recipes.*

THE COOK'S EQUIPMENT

Things for the Kitchen

Aristera, Dept. CFC
  9 Rice's Lane
  Westport, CT 06880
  Brochures, free. Kitchen tools for the
    left-handed.
The Blue Owl, Dept. CFC
  262 East Commercial Street
  Willits, CA 95490
  Illustrated brochure, free. Cooking equipment.
Thomas Cara, Ltd., Dept. CFC
  517 Pacific Street
  San Francisco, CA 94133
  Catalogue, 75¢. Cooking equipment, espresso,
    cappuccino machines.
Joyce Chen Gourmet Products, Dept. CFC
  390 Rindge Avenue
  Cambridge, MA 02140
  The Joyce Chen cutting board, a special
    composition material that will not dull
    knives, warp, chip, crack,
    dishwasher-safe.
FashionABLE, Dept. CFC
  Rocky Hill, NJ 08553
  Catalogue, 25¢. Equipment for the physically
    handicapped, including many cooking
    tools.

Kitchen Stuff, Dept. CFC
  P.O. Box 4333A
  Birmingham, AL 35243
  Catalogue, $1. Kitchen equipment.
The Left Hand, Dept. CFC
  140 West 22nd Street
  New York, NY 10016
  Illustrated catalogue, $1, refundable with
    purchase. Products for left-handed
    people, kitchen and other items.
Lodge Manufacturing Company,
  Dept. CFC, P.O. Box 380
  South Pittsburg, TN 37380
  Brochure and price list, send stamped
    self-addressed envelope. Cast-iron
    cooking equipment.
Pfeil & Holing Inc., Dept. CFC
  5 White Street
  New York, NY 10013
  Set of catalogues, $1.50. Cooking equipment,
    principally for baking and cake
    decorating.
R & R Mill Co., Dept. CFC
  45 West First North
  Smithfield, UT 84335
  Catalogue, free. Grinders, mills, can sealers,
    bottle cappers, and vegetable slicers.
Vermont Soapstone Co., Inc., Dept. CFC
  Perkinsville, VT 05151
  Brochure free. Soapstone products, including
    griddles and warmers.

Wilton Enterprises, Inc., Dept. CFC
  833 West 115th Street
  Chicago, IL 60643
  Illustrated color catalogue, $2. Everything for
    the cake decorator.

Outdoor Cooking

Bernard Food Industries, Inc., Dept. CFC
  222 S. 24th Street
  San Jose, CA 95103
  Brochure and price list, free. Camping foods.
Camplite, Dept. CFC
  P.O. Box 15695
  Salt Lake City, UT 84115
  Brochure and order form, free. Freeze-dried
    foods.

THE COOK'S BOOKSHELF

Legacy Publishing Company, Dept. CFC
  5616 Corporate Blvd.
  Baton Rouge, LA 70808
  Creole ethnic recipes, cookbooks in English
    and French.
Jay Nell Company, Dept. CFC
  5534 36th Avenue SE
  Salem, OR 97302
  Instructions for making fruit leather, $1.50.

STATE ABBREVIATIONS AND ZIP CODE PREFIXES

Throughout the book the official U.S. Postal Service abbreviations for each state have been used. Call your local post office for the complete, correct zip code.

AL	350-369	Alabama	NB	680-693	Nebraska
AK	995-999	Alaska	NV	890-898	Nevada
AZ	850-899	Arizona	NH	030-038	New Hampshire
AR	716-729	Arkansas	NJ	070-089	New Jersey
CA	900-969	California	NM	870-884	New Mexico
CO	800-816	Colorado	NY	100-149	New York
CT	060-069	Connecticut	NC	270-289	North Carolina
DE	197-199	Delaware	ND	580-588	North Dakota
DC	200-205	District of Columbia	OH	430-458	Ohio
FL	320-339	Florida	OK	730-749	Oklahoma
GA	300-319	Georgia	OR	970-979	Oregon
HI	967-968	Hawaii	PA	150-196	Pennsylvania
ID	832-838	Idaho	PR	006-009	Puerto Rico
IL	600-629	Illinois	RI	028-029	Rhode Island
IN	460-479	Indiana	SC	290-299	South Carolina
IA	500-528	Iowa	SD	570-577	South Dakota
KS	660-679	Kansas	TN	370-385	Tennessee
KY	400-427	Kentucky	TX	750-799	Texas
LA	700-714	Louisiana	UT	840-847	Utah
ME	039-049	Maine	VA	220-246	Virginia
MD	206-219	Maryland	VT	050-059	Vermont
MA	010-027	Massachusetts	WA	980-994	Washington
MI	480-499	Michigan	WV	247-268	West Virginia
MN	550-567	Minnesota	WI	530-549	Wisconsin
MS	386-397	Mississippi	WY	820-831	Wyoming
MO	630-658	Missouri	VI	008	Virgin Islands
MT	590-599	Montana			

INDEX OF RECIPES, SERVING SUGGESTIONS, AND TIPS

In the following list, recipes are capitalized.

INDEX OF MAIL-ORDER SUPPLIERS

A RANDOM SAMPLING:

Some of the more unusual, exotic and intriguing foods and equipment to be found in the catalogue, other than the basics. We start you off with a single page reference, but when you look through the book you may find many more sources for the same item.